Why Do You Need This New Edition?

If you're wondering why you should buy this new edition of *Exploring Biological Anthropology*, here are 10 good reasons!

1. In this new edition we have moved to the **molecular classification system** and call humans and our exclusive ancestors **hominins**, because this is the way that most of the recent literature is constructed.

2. New **illustration program** that includes more than 50 new anatomically correct bone drawings.

3. New **Insights and Advances** boxes: Chapter 3, Cloning Controversies, explores the use of cloning for conservation of endangered species or the resurrection of extinct species (the mammoth, for example); Chapter 9, Dating Controversies, now considers applications of new methods to Zhoukoudian *H. erectus* site; Chapter 12, The Denisovans, details a new fossil find in Siberia that is neither Human nor Neandertal; Chapter 14, Peopling of the New World, includes the Buttermilk Creek site; Chapter 15, If You Have DNA, Why Bother with Bones, explains the difficulty of using DNA in forensic science.

4. New or revised **Innovations** boxes: Chapter 4, A New Genetic Era, which focuses on genetic counseling and clinical application of genetic knowledge; Chapter 12, Neandertal Genes; and Chapter 13, Symbolism and Human Evolution examines when in human evolution symbolism started to be important for survival.

5. New **Visual Summaries** of each chapter.

6. Chapter 4 has updated information on the **human genome** and the application of DNA sequence information in a wide range of areas, such as obesity and the treatment of genetic disease.

7. Chapter 9 includes information on *Darwinius masillae*, a new, nearly complete primate from Messel, Germany (nicknamed "Ida"); contains new coverage of **cosmogenic radionuclide dating techniques** such as $^{26}Al/$ ^{10}Be; and the earth in the Cenozoic section includes updates to the coverage of stable carbon isotope ratios.

8. Chapter 10 discusses the implications of more recently published finds of *Ardipithecus* and the much younger Burtele foot; covers the recent finds of *Australopithecus sediba*.

9. Chapter 11 has new coverage of the recently discovered **Gona Pelvis** and information on the partial mandible from **Sima de Elefante**; updates on the age of the last surviving *H. erectus*; and inclusion of a discussion of the Flores hominin.

10. Chapter 14 includes new research on the **evolution of hominin brain size and shape.**

PEARSON

Exploring Biological Anthropology

THE ESSENTIALS

THIRD EDITION

Craig Stanford
University of Southern California

John S. Allen
University of Southern California

Susan C. Antón
New York University

PEARSON

Boston   Columbus   Indianapolis   New York   San Francisco   Upper Saddle River   Amsterdam
Cape Town   Dubai   London   Madrid   Milan   Munich   Paris   Montreal   Toronto   Delhi
Mexico City   São Paulo   Sydney   Hong Kong   Seoul   Singapore   Taipei   Tokyo

Planet Friendly Publishing
✔ Made in the United States
✔ Printed on Recycled Paper
Text: 10%   Cover: 10%
Learn more: www.greenedition.org

GREEN EDITION ®

At Pearson Education we're committed to producing books in an earth-friendly manner and to helping our customers make greener choices.

Manufacturing books in the United States ensures compliance with strict environmental laws and eliminates the need for international freight shipping, a major contributor to global air pollution.

And printing on recycled paper helps minimize our consumption of trees, water and fossil fuels. The text of *Exploring Biological Anthropology, Third Edition*, was printed on paper made with 10% post-consumer waste, and the cover was printed on paper made with 10% post-consumer waste. According to the Environmental Paper Network's Paper Calculator, by using this innovative paper instead of conventional papers, we achieved the following environmental benefits:

Trees Saved: 26   •   Air Emissions Eliminated: 2,607 pounds
Water Saved: 11,755 gallons   •   Solid Waste Eliminated: 745 pounds

For more information on our environmental practices, please visit us online at www.pearsonhighered.com/difference

Editorial Director: Craig Campanella
Publisher: Nancy Roberts
Associate Editor: Nicole Conforti
Development Editor: Ohlinger Publishing Services
Editorial Assistant: Molly White
Marketing Director: Brandy Dawson
Marketing Manager: Kate Mitchell
Marketing Assistant: Paige Patunas
Digital Media Editor: Tom Scalzo
Lead Media Project Manager: Barbara Taylor- Laino
Project Manager: Anne Ricigliano
Full-Service Project Management and Composition: PreMediaGlobal
Design Manager: John Christiana
Art Director: Anne Bonanno Nieglos
Anatomical Illustrations: Joanna Wallington

Interior and Cover Designer: Riezebos Holzbaur/Tim Heraldo
Cover Images: Young orangutan close-up portrait: Christian Aslund/Photographer's Choice/Getty Images; DNA strands: Booka/Shutterstock; Neandertal skull illustration by Joanna Wallington
Text Permissions Specialist: Craig A. Jones
Text Permissions Project Manager: Liz Kincaid, PreMediaGlobal
Manager, Visual Research: Beth Brenzel
Image Permissions Project Manager: Jennifer Nonenmacher, PreMediaGlobal
Senior Operations Specialist: Alan Fischer
Printer/Binder: Courier-Kendallville
Cover Printer: Courier-Kendallville
Text Font: New Baskerville 10/11.5

📖 DK Maps designed and productioned by DK Education, a division of Dorling Kindersley Limited, 80 Strand, London WC2R ORL. DK and the DK logo are registered trademarks of Dorling Kindersley Limited.

Credits and acknowledgments borrowed from other sources and reproduced, with permission, in this textbook appear on the appropriate page within text and on pages 453–454.

Library of Congress Cataloging-in-Publication Data
Stanford, Craig B. (Craig Britton)-
  Exploring biological anthropology : the essentials / Craig Stanford, John S. Allen,
Susan C. Antón. — 3rd ed.
    p. cm.
  ISBN 978-0-205-90733-5 (pbk.)
  1. Physical anthropology—Textbooks.   I. Allen, John S. (John Scott) – II. Antón, Susan C.
III. Title.

GN25.S74 2013
599.9—dc23

2012020319

10 9 8 7 6 5 4 3 2 1

PEARSON

www.pearsonhighered.com

Student Edition:
ISBN 13: 978-0-205-90733-5
ISBN 10:   0-205-90733-4

Instructor's Review Copy: Á la Carte:
ISBN 13: 978-0-205-90763-2   ISBN 13: 978-0-205-90772-4
ISBN 10:   0-205-90763-6   ISBN 10:   0-205-90772-5

To Our Parents

Brief Contents

Contents

Preface

After teaching biological anthropology for twenty years, we felt there was a great need for a new textbook that presents the core information, concepts, and theories of biological anthropology in a modern light. Biological anthropology was once called physical anthropology, because decades ago the field was mainly about human anatomy, human fossils, and the study of racial variation. Over the past twenty-five years, the field has evolved into biological anthropology, the evolutionary biology of humankind based on information from the fossil record and the human skeleton, the genetics of both individuals and populations, our primate relatives, human adaptation, and human behavior, among other topics. This, the third edition of *Exploring Biological Anthropology*, combines up-to-date coverage of the core material with a modern biological approach that includes fields that have become major areas of research by biological anthropologists over the past decade. This core-concepts version of the book is written especially for students needing to obtain a strong grounding in biological anthropology without some of the detail into which our original text delved. We three coauthors conduct our research in the main areas of biological anthropology: the human fossil record (Susan Antón), primate behavior and ecology (Craig Stanford), and human biology and the brain (John Allen). This has allowed us to provide a specialist approach to each of the broad divisions of the field covered by the text. We are biological anthropologists with extensive backgrounds in both biological and social sciences and are both teachers and researchers.

In a field changing as rapidly as human evolutionary science is today, we feel it is critical for active researchers to produce textbooks that serve the needs of students. In addition to the strong biological orientation of the book, we try to frame questions about humankind in light of our understanding of culture and the ways in which culture interacts with biology to create the template for human nature.

Undergraduate enrollment in introductory biological anthropology courses has increased sharply because biological anthropology has become one way to fulfill the basic natural science requirement at many colleges and universities. We believe the changing field and the new audience have created a need for a text such as this one, integrating traditional physical anthropology with a modern Darwinian framework, and presented in a concise, clear format.

We have made an effort in the third edition of *Exploring Biological Anthropology* to present a concise coverage of the core material of the field, while preserving a comprehensive coverage of certain traditionally important topics. For instance, we have included a feature on biomedical anthropology, a large feature (in Chapter 14) on the brain,

and behavior and biology of modern people, from the study of foragers (hunter-gatherers) to that of the human psyche (evolutionary psychology). There is a discussion of the geological background for human paleontology (Chapter 9), and new chapter sections on bioarcheology (Chapter 13) and forensic anthropology (Chapter 15). We have added new double-page features to many chapters to present information in a more visual way, and we have added new information to this edition in the form of new text and figures, as well as special features in some chapters.

In a field famous for intellectual disagreements over the meaning of fossils or interpretations of Darwinian theory, we've tried to present the accepted facts and concise descriptions of debates about evidence. There are places where, because of the introductory nature of the text, we have not delved deeply into the details of some debates, but we have nevertheless tried to balance multiple views of ongoing unresolved questions.

What's New in This Edition

- In this new edition we have moved to the molecular classification system and call humans and our exclusive ancestors hominins, because this is the way that most of the recent literature is constructed.

- New illustration program includes more than 50 new anatomically correct bone drawings.

- New Insights and Advances boxes: Chapter 3, Cloning Controversies, explores the use of cloning for conservation of endangered species or the resurrection of extinct species (the mammoth, for example); Chapter 9, Dating Controversies, now considers applications of new methods to Zhoukoudian *H. erectus* site; Chapter 12, The Denisovans, details a new fossil find in Siberia that is neither human nor Neandertal; Chapter 14, Peopling of the New World, includes the Buttermilk Creek site; Chapter 15, If You Have DNA, Why Bother with Bones, explains the difficulty of using DNA in forensic science.

- New or revised Innovations boxes: Chapter 4, A New Genetic Era, which focuses on genetic counseling and clinical application of genetic knowledge; Chapter 12, Neandertal Genes; and Chapter 13, Symbolism and Human Evolution examines when in human evolution symbolism started to be important for survival.

- New Visual Summaries of each chapter.

- Chapter 4 has updated information on the human genome and the application of DNA sequence information in a wide range of areas, such as obesity and the treatment of genetic disease.

- Chapter 9 has new coverage of cosmogenic radionuclide dating techniques such as ^{26}Al/^{10}Be, and the earth in the Cenozoic section includes updates to the coverage of stable carbon isotope ratios. Chapter 9 also includes information on *Darwinius masillae*, a new, nearly complete primate from Messel, Germany (nicknamed "Ida").

- Chapter 10 discusses the implications of more recently published finds of *Ardipithecus* and the much younger Burtele foot; covers the recent finds of *Australopithecus sediba*.

- Chapter 11 has new coverage of the recently discovered Gona Pelvis and information on the partial mandible from Sima de Elefante; updates on the age of the last surviving *H. erectus*; and inclusion of a discussion of the Flores hominin.

- Chapter 14 includes new research on the evolution of hominin brain size and shape.

Foundation: Organization of the Book

The book is organized in much the same way that we three authors have taught introductory courses in biological anthropology. The theory of evolution by natural selection is the unifying aspect of each chapter, and indeed for the entire discipline. Part I, "Foundations" (Chapters 1 and 2), reflects this. The text begins with an overview of the field of biological anthropology in the larger context of the social and life sciences, including a brief history of the field. Chapter 2 reviews the roots of evolutionary thinking and how it became central to biological anthropology. Part II, "Mechanisms of Evolution" (Chapters 3 through 6), reviews at length the mechanisms of evolution and describes the applications of modern genetic research techniques in unraveling some of the mysteries of human evolution. Chapters 3 and 4 review cellular, molecular, and population genetics. Chapter 5 takes the discussion of genetics into modern evolutionary theory: the formation of species and the central topics of natural selection and adaptation. Chapter 6 surveys the field of human adaptation and the ways in which evolutionary forces mold human populations.

Part III, "Primates" (Chapters 7 and 8), is about the living nonhuman primates. We review their classification, their anatomical and behavioral adaptations, and their social life. We cautiously use the behavior of living monkeys and apes to understand what their ancestors, and therefore ours, may have been like.

Part IV, "The Fossil Record" (Chapters 9 through 13), describes the fossil record for humanity. We begin with the environmental context in which fossils are found and describe both the periods of Earth's history during which primates arose and the fossil primates themselves. We then examine the anatomical transition from an ape to human ancestor and present up-to-date information on the earliest known hominins in Africa. Chapter 11 introduces the genus *Homo* and the causes and consequences of dispersal from Africa.

Chapters 12 and 13 cover the more recent hominin fossils, including Neandertals, and the origins of our own species. We have tried to provide up-to-the-minute information on the discovery of new human fossils, right up to the latest information about the stunningly complete adapoid *Darwinius masillae* and new dating techniques (Chapter 9), the Gona *Homo erectus* pelvis from Ethiopia (Chapter 11), and interpretations of the *Ardipithecus* fossils, Burtele foot, and *Australopithecus sediba* (Chapter 10), the Denisova hominin remains from Siberia (Chapter 12), and a new section on symbolism (Chapter 13) and the earliest peopling of North America (Chapter 13). We have also included interpretive features to understand the significance of all these new finds.

Part V, "Biology and Behavior of Modern Humans" (Chapters 14 and 15), is about the biology of modern people. We include coverage of the brain and biocultural aspects of the lives of traditional foraging people (Chapter 14), and the human brain and biocultural issues of biomedical anthropology, as well as a new half chapter's worth on forensic anthropology (Chapter 15), which explains how scientists use evolutionary theory and the methods of biological anthropology to identify human remains from mass disasters and victims of crime.

The appendices offer a section on the primate skeleton (Appendix A), the Hardy–Weinberg equilibrium (Appendix B), and metric-to-imperial conversion factors (Appendix C).

Student-oriented pedagogy has been maintained in each chapter. We begin each chapter with a short **vignette** depicting the main topic of the chapter. Some of these are quotations taken from famous works by biological anthropologists, such as Dian Fossey describing a day with mountain gorillas at the beginning of Chapter 7. For other chapters, one of the authors has written a short description of how someone studying human fossils, for example, might experience a day in the field. The vignettes should be used as a way to get a feel for the chapter topics and as an enjoyable and informative reflection on the text material.

Other features include a margin **glossary** to define new terms as students encounter them and a complete glossary at the back of the book. Each chapter ends with a visual summary and a summary of the resources available on MyAnthroLab. At the end of the book the **bibliography** contains all the references used and cited in the text.

Innovation: New and Continuing Features

In the first and second editions of *Exploring Biological Anthropology*, we tried to include topics not covered in many of the existing texts while preserving a comprehensive coverage of traditional topics. In this new third edition, we have relied on instructor and student feedback as well as new events in the field to make further changes.

Following the growing scientific consensus in biological anthropology, we have adopted the molecularly based terminology for grouping humans and our ancestors—now referring to us and our exclusive ancestors as hominins rather than hominids. We explain the nomenclatural switch in an Insights and Advances box in Chapter 10.

By popular demand, forensic anthropology (a topic not traditionally covered in introductory biological anthropology texts) has been expanded and included in Chapter 15, "Biomedical and Forensic Anthropology." Bioarcheology, which includes a discussion of the consequences of colonization and agriculture and peopling of the Pacific, is covered in Chapter 13, "The Emergence, Dispersal, and Bioarchaeology of *Homo sapiens*." This section includes a special focus on the newest evidence for a pre-Clovis occupation of North America.

Chapter 1 includes a visual feature that discusses the four fields of anthropology. The text, illustrations, and design all help to make this content come alive for students.

Chapters 3 and 4 include numerous recent updates on human molecular genetics and genomics. Chapter 6 includes updates concerning the recent impact of new molecular genetic studies on aspects of human population genetics and adaptability.

As mentioned, in Part IV, we keep abreast of new fossil discoveries by including figures and discussion of the latest finds. This includes coverage of new fossil primate finds (Chapter 9), including *Darwinius masillae*. A discussion of new fossil hominins (Chapters 11 through 13), including figures and interpretations of the oldest hominins in Europe from the Sima de Elefante, Spain, and the smallest *Homo erectus* from Ileret, Kenya, the new *Homo* erectus pelvis from Ethiopia and the enigmatic Denisova fossil from Siberia.

We have added to our boxes (now called **Insights and Advances**) in each chapter. These insets expand on text material or call your attention to current events connected to our field, to emerging debates, or sometimes just to fascinating side stories. Some chapters feature entirely new boxes (Chapters 9, 12, 13, 15), and others are substantially rewritten and updated as new research has become available (Chapters 10, 11).

A feature called **Innovations** is included in select chapters. This feature provides an intense visual presentation of new, burgeoning areas of research in our field. These research areas include:

Chapter 3: DNA Barcoding

Chapter 4: A New Genetic Era

Chapter 8: Culture in Nonhuman Primates

Chapter 9: Time in a Bottle

Chapter 10: Dikika and Development

Chapter 11: What's Size Got to Do with It?

Chapter 12: Neandertal Genes

Chapter 13: Symbolism and Human Evolution

Chapter 14: Music, the Brain, and Evolution

Chapter 15: Ancestry Genetics

Biological anthropology is a very rich and visual subject, and so we have created a **Visual Summary** at the end of every chapter. Students will be able to easily review the key topics of each chapter, and then refer back into the chapter for a more extensive review.

Illustrations

Illustrations play a major role in any textbook, and they are crucial learning tools in introductory science texts. The publisher and authors have worked together to provide you with the best possible photos and drawings of every topic covered in the book. The third edition features more than 50 new anatomical illustrations especially prepared for this text by medical illustrator Joanna Wallington. These drawings replace our previous versions in Section IV providing superior detail and anatomical accuracy and enhancing student insight into the morphological features of importance in human evolution.

This edition also includes new illustrations in the genetics chapters that were inspired by the tenth edition of *Concepts of Genetics* by Klug, Cummings, Spencer, and Palladino. Illustrations throughout the book have been updated to reflect this new style.

Most of the photographs of living primates, fossils, and fossil sites were taken by one of the authors or were contributed by other biological anthropologists—and many of these have been updated and enhanced in this edition. Pearson has worked hard to produce some of the finest images of everything from molecular genetics to stone tools that have ever been published in a biological anthropology textbook. The maps have been specifically created for this book by Dorling Kindersley, a leading publisher of atlases for both the educational and consumer markets. These maps describe the geography of everything from the distribution of living primates in the world today to the locations of the continents in the distant past. We authors worked with Pearson to be sure everything in this third edition is depicted accurately and clearly, and we hope you will gain a better understanding of the science by studying the visual material as well.

Along with the new *Innovations* features, additional special two-page figures appear in a number of chapters, especially in Part IV, and provide a snapshot of evolutionary development through time. These special figures provide a concise way for the reader to easily grasp the evolutionary changes through a vast sweep of time that are presented in greater detail in the text and they have been updated with new photo imagery and new finds.

A Note about Language

Authors must make decisions about language and terminology, and textbook authors make those choices with the knowledge that they may be influencing the mind-set of a generation of young scholars. Some of these choices are modest. For instance, we use the modern American spelling *Neandertal* instead of the more traditional European spelling *Neanderthal*. Other language choices are more central to the subject matter. Perhaps the most significant choice we have made is with regard to primate classification. Although the primate order historically has been subdivided into anthropoids (the apes and monkeys, including us) and prosimians (the "lower" primates, including lemurs, galagos, lorises, and tarsiers), the majority of scholars today think this dichotomy does not reflect evolutionary reality as well as a subdivision into haplorhines and strepsirhines. Haplorhines include all anthropoids and tarsiers, and strepsirhines include all prosimians except tarsiers. We discuss this distinction in some depth in Chapter 7 and use the terms *strepsirhine* and *haplorhine* rather than *prosimian* and *anthropoid*. We also now use the modern subfamily-level designation *hominin* to refer to humans and our ancestors rather than the older term *hominid*. We discuss this new classification scheme in Chapter 10

Regarding Abbreviations and Time

Because of the plethora of sometimes conflicting abbreviations used to refer to time throughout the text, we have attempted to spell out time ranges (e.g., "millions of years ago" or "thousands of years ago"). Where this is not feasible, such as in tables, we use the abbreviations most common to anthropology textbooks (mya for "millions of years ago" and kya for "thousands of years ago"). However, students should note that the standard usage in geology and paleontology is *Ma* (mega-annum) and *ka* (kilo-annum).

Support for Instructors and Students

The ancillary materials that accompany *Exploring Biological Anthropology, Third Edition* are part of a complete teaching and learning package and have been carefully created to enhance the topics discussed in the text.

Instructor's Resource Manual with Tests (0205907539): For each chapter in the text, this valuable resource provides a detailed outline, list of objectives, discussion questions, and suggested readings and videos. In addition, test questions in multiple-choice, true-false, fill-in-the-blank, and short-answer formats are available for each chapter; the answers are page-referenced to the text. For easy access, this manual is available within the instructor section of MyAnthroLab for *Exploring Biological Anthropology, Third Edition*, or at www.pearsonhighered.com.

MyTest (020590761X): This computerized software allows instructors to create their own personalized exams, to edit any or all of the existing test questions, and to add new questions. Other special features of this program include random generation of test questions, creation of alternate versions of the same test, scrambling question sequence, and test preview before printing. For easy access, this software is available within the instructor section of MyAnthroLab for *Exploring Biological Anthropology, Third Edition*, or at www.pearsonhighered.com.

PowerPoint Presentation for Biological Anthropology (0205907520): These PowerPoint slides combine text and graphics for each chapter to help instructors convey anthropological principles in a clear and engaging way. For easy access, they are available within the instructor section of MyAnthroLab for *Exploring Biological Anthropology, Third Edition, or* at www.pearsonhighered.com.

Strategies in Teaching Anthropology (0-13-603466-7): Unique in focus and content, this book focuses on the "how" of teaching anthropology across all four fields and provides a wide array of associated learning outcomes and student activities. It is a valuable, single-source compendium of strategies and teaching "tricks of the trade" from a group of seasoned teaching anthropologists, working in a variety of teaching settings, who share their pedagogical techniques, knowledge, and observations.

MyAnthroLab *Personalize Learning with New Myanthrolab* The new MyAnthroLab delivers proven results in helping students succeed, provides engaging experiences that personalize learning, and comes from a trusted partner with educational expertise and a deep commitment to helping students and instructors achieve their goals.

- **The Pearson eText** lets students access their textbook anytime, anywhere, and any way they want—including listening online or downloading to iPad.

- **A personalized study plan** for each student, based on Bloom's Taxonomy, promotes critical-thinking skills and helps students succeed in the course and beyond.

- **Assessment** tied to videos, applications, and chapters enables instructors and students to track progress and get immediate feedback. Instructors will be able to find the best resources for teaching their students.

- **Class Preparation Tool** collects the best class presentation resources in one convenient online destination. Resources include PowerPoint slides, streaming audio and video, audio clips for class tests and quizzes, and all illustrations for creating interactive lectures.

Acknowledgments

Textbooks require the collaboration of many people with many areas of expertise, and this book makes good use of all of those involved. The process begins with each author compiling his or her notes from years of teaching biological anthropology and thinking about how the course could be taught more effectively. Over the years, the students in our courses have helped us to assess what did and did not work in conveying the information and excitement of biological anthropology, and for this we are extremely grateful. For her vision and steady guidance over the past nine years, we are most grateful to Nancy Roberts, Publisher of Anthropology at Pearson. We owe a debt of gratitude to our development editor, Monica Ohlinger, for her tireless and careful editing and for her patience and diplomacy in dealing with the logistics of working with three different authors. We also thank Nancy's associate editor, Nicole Conforti, for keeping the chapters flowing, and media editor, Thomas Scalzo, for the media that accompanies this text. The outstanding efforts of Anne Bonanno Nieglos and Riezebos Holzbaur/Tim Heraldo in coordinating and creating all design elements resulted in this beautiful text. Anne Ricigliano, production editor at Pearson, and Nancy Kincade at PMG, did a remarkable job of coordinating the entire production process. We appreciate the creativity of photo researcher Jen Nonemacher. Thanks also to Executive Marketing Manager Kate Mitchell for directing the marketing campaign.

For contributing photos and published or unpublished material to help in writing the text, we thank Brad Adams, Takeru Akazawa, Shara Bailey, Antoine Balzeau, Lee Berger, Jose Maria Bermudez de Castro, Christopher Boehm, David Brill, Peter Brown, Joel Bruss, Jennie Clark, Christian Crowder, Hanna Damasio, Chris Dean, Anna Delaney, Eric Delson, Todd Disotell, Craig Feibel, Jens Franzen, Ken Garrett, Lynn Isbel, Jorn Jurstrum, Rich Kay, Bill Kimbel, John Krigbaum, Meave Leakey, David Lordkipanidze, Laura McClatchy, Melanie McCollum, The National Museum of Kenya, Maria Martinon-Torres, Lisa Matisoo-Smith, William McComas, Monte McCrossin, Salvador Moya-Sola, Jackson Njau, The National Museum of Kenya, Amy Parish, OsBjorn Pearson, Briana Pobiner, Rick Potts, Allysha Powanda, Tim Ryan, Paul Sledzik, Josh Snodgrass, Fred Spoor, Carl Swisher, Judy Suchey, Ian Tattersall, Christian Tryon Brent Turrin, Peter Ungar, Bence Viola, Alan Walker, Mike Waters, Randy White, Tatiana White, Andrea Wiley, and Milford Wolpoff.

All three of us cut our teeth teaching introductory biological anthropology as graduate students apprenticing as teaching assistants (TAs) at the University of California. Our fellow TAs shared their ideas and our tasks, for which we are thankful. We are most grateful to the triumvirate of faculty with whom we apprenticed and from whom we learned much about the subject matter, how to teach it, and how an introductory course can be made a rewarding, enriching experience for undergraduates. Our heartfelt thanks go to Katharine Milton, Vincent Sarich, and Tim White.

Graduate teaching assistants in our own courses at the University of Southern California, the University of Auckland, the University of Florida, Rutgers University, and New York University brought new enthusiasm and ideas, and we are grateful to them all.

In the process of creating this third edition, Pearson held a series of focus groups to query instructors about how they use textbooks and how they use technology in their classrooms. We appreciate the insights provided by:

Janet Altamirano, WCJC and UHD; Douglas Anderson, Front Range Community College; Jennifer Basquiat, College of Southern Nevada; Cynthia Bellacero, Craven Community College; Jacob Boyd, University of Kansas; Victor Braitberg, University of Arizona; Autumn Cahoon, Sierra College; Walter Calgaro, Prairie State College; Bambi Chapin, UMBC; Wanda Clark, South Plains College; Craig Cook, Crown College; Cathy Cooke, Columbus State Community College; Pearce Creasman, Central Texas College.

Douglas Crews, Ohio State University; Stephen Criswell, University of South Carolina Lancaster; Marie Danforth, University of Southern Mississippi; Alexa Dietrich, Wagner College; Anna Dixon, University of South Florida—St. Petersburg; Amy Donovan, UCSF and Santa Clara University; Meredith Dorner, Saddleback College; Arthur Durband, Texas Tech University; David H. Dye, University of Memphis; Alison Elgart, Florida Gulf Coast University; Burhan Erdem, University of Arkansas; Monica Faraldo, University of Miami; Robert Goodby, Franklin Pierce University; Jane Goodman, Indiana University; Mark Gordon, Pasadena City College; Carol Hayman, Austin Community College; Deanna Heikkinen, College of the Canyons; Keith Hench, PhD, Kirkwood Community College.

Kathryn Hicks, The University of Memphis; John Hines, Point Park University; Sarah Holt, Ohio State University; Jayne Howell, CSULB; Kendi Howells Douglas, Great Lakes Christian College; Douglas Hume, Northern Kentucky University; Francisca James Hernandez, Pima Community College; Nick Johnson, Ivy Tech Community College; Sarah Koepke, Elgin Community College; Ailissa Leroy, Florida Atlantic University; Michael Love, California State University, Northridge; Corey Maggiano, Ohio State University; Michael Masters, Montana Tech; Patricia Mathews, Borough of Manhattan Community College; Meghan McCune, Jamestown Community College; Britney McIlvaine, The Ohio State University; Heather McIlvaine-Newsad, Western Illinois University; Susan Meswick, Queens College; Sharon Methvin, Mt. Hood Community College; Krista Milich, University of Illinois at Urbana—Champaign; Jennifer Molina-Stidger, Sierra College; John Navarra, University of North Carolina Wilmington; ChorSwang Ngin, California State University, Los Angeles; Joshua Noah, University of Arkansas; Jana Owen, Ozarks Technical Community College; Amanda Paskey, Cosumnes River College; Elizabeth Perrin, The Ohio State University; Mark Peterson, Miami University; Michael Polich, McHenry County College; Suzanne Simon, University of North Florida; Lakhbir Singh, Chabot College; Burt Siskin, LA Valley College; Micah Soltz, Columbus State Community College; Elisabeth Stone, University of New Mexico & UNM Branch at Gallup; Charles Townsend, LaGuardia Community College/CUNY; Mark Tromans, Broward College; Melissa Vogel, Clemson University; Erin Waxenbaum, Northwestern University; Katherine Weisensee, Clemson University; Leanna Wolfe, Los Angeles Valley College; Cassady Yoder, Radford University.

For their constructive reviewing of the first and second editions, we thank

Robert L. Anemone, Western Michigan University; John R. Baker, Moorpark College; Art Barbeau, West Liberty State College; Anna Bellisari, Wright State University; Wendy Birky, California State University, Northridge; Ann L. Bradgon, Northwest College, Houston Community College System; Pearce Paul Creasman, Blinn College; William Doonan, Sacramento City College; David W. Frayer, University of Kansas; Renée Garcia, Saddleback College; Peter Gray, University of Nevada—Las Vegas; Jonathan P. Karpf, San Jose State University; Sarah A. C. Keller, Eastern Washington University; Roger Kelly, Foothill College; Andrew Kinkella, Moorpark College; Andrew Kramer, University of Tennessee; John R. Lukacs, University of Oregon; Jane A. Margold, Santa Rosa Junior College; Debra L. Martin, University of Nevada—Las Vegas; Paul McDowell, Santa Barbara City College; Peer H. Moore-Jansen, Wichita State University; Leanne T. Nash, Arizona State University; Kaoru Oguri, California State University, Long Beach; Robert R. Paine, Texas Tech University; Jill D. Pruetz, Iowa State University; Ulrich Reichard, Southern Illinois University, Carbondale; Trudy R. Turner, University of Wisconsin, Milwaukee; J. Richard Shenkel, University of New Orleans; Lynnette Leidy Sievert, University of Massachusetts—Amherst; Larissa Swedell, Queens College—CUNY; Salena Wakim, Orange Coast College; Richard E. Ward, Indiana University–Purdue University Indianapolis; Daniel J. Wescott, University of Missouri—Columbia; Bruce P. Wheatley, University of Alabama— Birmingham; Amanda Wolcott Paskey, Cosumnes River College; Leanna Wolfe, Los Angeles Valley College; and Linda D. Wolfe, East Carolina University.

We've made a great effort to produce a comprehensive and fully accurate text, but as is always the case, errors may remain. We would be grateful for comments or corrections from students and instructors using *Exploring Biological Anthropology, Third Edition*. And we hope you find this account of human evolution as fascinating and compelling as we do.

Craig Stanford
stanford@usc.edu
www.craigstanford.org
John S. Allen
Susan C. Antón
Twitter@BioAnthroSAA

About the Authors

CRAIG STANFORD is a Professor of Anthropology and Biological Sciences at the University of Southern California, where he also directs the Jane Goodall Research Center and chairs the Department of Anthropology. He has conducted field research on primates and other animals in south Asia, Latin America, and East Africa. He is well known for his long-term studies of meat-eating among wild chimpanzees in Gombe, Tanzania, and of the ecology of mountain gorillas and chimpanzees in the Impenetrable Forest of Uganda. He has authored or coauthored more than 120 scientific publications. Craig has received USC's highest teaching awards for his introductory Biological Anthropology course. In addition, he has published fourteen books on primate behavior and human origins, including *Significant Others* (2001), *Upright* (2003), and *Planet Without Apes* (2012). He and his wife, Erin Moore, a cultural anthropologist at USC, live in South Pasadena, California, and have three children.

JOHN ALLEN is a research scientist in the Brain and Creativity Institute and the Dornsife Cognitve Neuroscience Imaging Center, University of Southern California. Previously, he was a faculty member in the Department of Anthropology at the University of Auckland, New Zealand, and also taught in the Department of Anthropology at the University of Iowa for several years. His primary research interests are the evolution of the human brain and behavior, and behavioral disease. He also has research experience in molecular genetics, nutritional anthropology, and the history of anthropology, and has conducted fieldwork in Japan, New Zealand, Papua New Guinea, and Palau. He has received several university awards for teaching introductory courses in Biological Anthropology. In addition to this textbook, he is the author of *The Lives of the Brain* (2009) and *The Omnivorous Mind* (2012), as well as *Medical Anthropology: A Biocultural Approach* (with Andrea Wiley, 2nd edition, 2012). John and his wife, Stephanie Sheffield, have two sons, Reid and Perry.

SUSAN ANTÓN is a Professor in the Center for the Study of Human Origins, Department of Anthropology at New York University, where she also directs the M.A. program in Human Skeletal Biology. Her field research concerns the origin and evolution of genus *Homo* in Indonesia and Africa and human impact on island ecosystems in the South Pacific. She is best known for her work on the evolution of the genus *Homo* in Asia and Africa, for which she was elected as a fellow of the *American Association for the Advancement of Science (AAAS)* in 2008. She is past editor of the *Journal of Human Evolution*. She received awards for teaching as a graduate student instructor at the University of California, was Teacher of the Year at the University of Florida, and won the Golden Dozen Award for excellence in undergraduate teaching at NYU. She has been twice elected to *Who's Who Among America's Teachers*. Susan and her husband, Carl Swisher, a geochronologist, raise Anatolian Shepherd dogs.

Chapter 1 Preview

After reading this chapter, you should be able to:

- Identify the subfields of anthropology and explain their applications to the study of the human species.

- Explain the subfields of biological anthropology and discuss how they try to answer key questions about the human species.

- Review the development of biological anthropology in the United States including its change in focus over time.

- Analyze the scope of biological anthropology in light of new discoveries constantly being made about the evolution of the human species.

What Is Biological Anthropology?

On a sunny morning in East Africa, with the temperature already climbing past 90 degrees, a scientist stands in a shallow pit, carefully examining the dusty ground. All around her are the tools of her trade: shovels, dental picks, whisk brooms, and surveying equipment. Something glinting in the morning light catches her eye. She bends over to examine a tiny fragment of whitish bone, then another, and another. Realizing that her week of hard, sweaty work has just paid off, she beckons her assistants to see the prize, then carefully begins to map the location for the work that now begins: unearthing the fossilized skeleton of an ancient primate, perhaps the forerunner of all modern apes. Weeks later, returning to the capital city and its museum, the scientist compares the new fossils with previously collected specimens. She finds that a few of the pieces her team has excavated fit together with the long-neglected bones of a fossil ape discovered at the site in the 1930s. The scientist devotes long hours to studying every detail of the skeleton. A new picture emerges: This ancient ape may have been the first to come down from the trees and venture forth on the ground below.

A few hundred miles away, another scientist sits in the tall grass of a high mountain meadow. All around him are massive, shaggy-haired mountain gorillas, happily munching on wild celery. A bright-eyed baby gorilla ambles up to the scientist and toys with the laces of his boot, then runs quickly back to its mother. Two silverbacks, majestic 400-pound males wearing saddles of gray hair across their backs, sit like enormous statues a few yards away. The scientist uses the tools of his trade: a notebook and checklist to record behavior, plus a handheld global positioning system unit to map the animals' travels. As the gorilla group finishes its lunch, the silverbacks get up and head off into the forest, bulldozing a trail that the females, babies, and scientist obediently follow.

At the same time, half a world away, a third scientist is sitting in a laboratory intently studying a computer monitor. He looks at a three-dimensional, high-resolution image of a human brain. Millimeter by millimeter, he examines the frontal lobe, a region of the brain thought to be of key importance in the evolution of modern people. By moving the screen cursor slightly, he can study the brain's surface from every possible angle, making virtual slices through it to study its internal organization. Unlike skulls, brains do not become preserved as fossils, so the scientist uses images of the brains of living humans and other primates to reconstruct the way in which the brains of long-dead ancestors may have been organized.

What do these three scientists—one studying ancient fossils, another observing primate behavior, and the third studying the evolution of the human brain—all have in common? They are biological anthropologists, engaged in the scientific study of humankind (from *anthropos*, meaning "human," and *-ology*, "the study of"). Despite our exalted intellect, our mind-boggling technology, and our intricately complex social behavior, we are nonetheless biological creatures. Humans are **primates** and share a recent ancestry with the living great apes. Like the apes, we are the products of millions of years of **evolution** by natural selection.

The famed geneticist Theodosius Dobzhansky once said, "Nothing in biology makes sense except in the light of evolution." Biological anthropologists spend their careers trying to understand the details of the evolutionary process and the ways in which it has shaped who we are today. They use a central, unifying set of biological principles in their work, first set down by Charles Darwin nearly 150 years ago. The frequency of a particular trait and the genes that control it can change from one generation to the next; this is evolution. This elegantly simple idea forms the heart and soul of **biological anthropology.**

The evolutionary process usually is slow and inefficient, but over many generations it can mold animals and plants into a bewildering variety of forms. Our ancestry includes many animals that little resemble us today. Biological anthropology is particularly concerned with the evolutionary transformations that occurred over the past 6 million years, as an ape-like primate began to walk on two legs and became something different: a **hominin.** From the perspective of evolutionary theory, humans are like all other biological species, the product of the same long process of **adaptation.**

Anthropology and Its Subfields

Anthropology is the study of humankind in all its forms. But of course, this would not distinguish it from other disciplines that study the human condition, such as psychology, history, and sociology. The critical aspect of anthropology that sets it apart is its cross-cultural, holistic nature. That is, we try to understand the inner workings of a group of people who hold different worldviews, values, and traditions than we do. The unusual thing about the human animal is that we have **culture.** Although it often seems that anthropologists spend their careers arguing about how to define culture, we can say simply that culture is the total of learned traditions of a group of people. Language is culture (although the ability to use language is biological), as is religion, as are the way people dress and the food they eat. These human behaviors vary significantly from one culture to the next. However, what about the universal taboo on incestuous relations with one's siblings, or the observation that across many human societies, women tend to marry older men? Are these common threads of human cultures the result of learned traditions, passed down across the generations, or is there a biological influence at work? As we will see, the interplay between biology and culture provides many of the most intriguing and perplexing clues about the roots of our humanity. It also creates many of the most intense debates; for decades, scholars have debated whether genes or the environment have played the more important role in molding intelligence and other human qualities.

The dichotomy between biological and cultural influences on humankind is a false one, as we examine in detail later in the book. In earliest humans, biological evolution produced the capacity for culture: Intelligence had to evolve before learned traditions such as tool use could flourish, as we see in wild apes today. Our biology produced culture, but culture can also influence biology. We study these patterns under the rubric of **biocultural anthropology.**

Anthropology is divided into four subfields: biological anthropology, cultural anthropology, linguistic anthropology, and archaeology. Some anthropologists consider linguistics and archaeology as subfields within cultural anthropology. In addition, applied anthropology—a method more than a discipline—is sometimes considered a fifth subfield. The majority of practicing anthropologists in the United States are cultural anthropologists, who typically make up more than half of the faculty of anthropology departments in universities and who also are employed in a variety of nonacademic settings, as you will see in this section.

primate   Member of the mammalian order Primates, including prosimians, monkeys, apes, and humans, defined by a suite of anatomical and behavioral traits.

evolution   A change in the frequency of a gene or a trait in a population over multiple generations.

biological anthropology   The study of humans as biological organisms, considered in an evolutionary framework; sometimes called physical anthropology.

hominin   A member of the primate family Hominidae, distinguished by bipedal posture and, in more recently evolved species, a large brain.

adaptation   A trait that increases the reproductive success of an organism, produced by natural selection in the context of a particular environment.

anthropology   The study of humankind in a cross-cultural context. Anthropology includes the subfields cultural anthropology, linguistic anthropology, archaeology, and biological anthropology.

culture   The sum total of learned traditions, values, and beliefs that groups of people (and a few species of highly intelligent animals) possess.

biocultural anthropology   The study of the interaction between biology and culture, which plays a role in most human traits.

THE SUBFIELDS OF ANTHROPOLOGY

Cultural anthropology is the study of human societies in a cross-cultural and focuses on how people lead their daily lives is at the heart of the field. **Ethnology**, one of the subfields of cultural anthropology, is the study of human societies and of the behavior of people within those societies. The practice of ethnology is called **ethnography** (literally, "the describing of culture"). A written account of the initiation rituals of street gangs in Los Angeles and the study of how parents in Boston care for their children relative to parenting among the Sherpas of highland Nepal are also examples of ethnography.

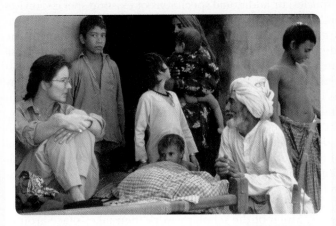

Linguistic anthropology is the study of the form, function, and social context of language. Linguistic anthropologists usually are more interested in language use and the role that language plays in shaping culture than they are in the technical aspects of language structure. An anthropological linguist might study the aspects of Black English that set it apart from mainstream and be interested in the roots of Black English on slave plantations and in West Africa.

Archaeology is the study of how people used to live, based on the materials, or **artifacts**, they left behind.

These artifacts, art, implements, and other objects of **material culture** form the basis for the analysis and interpretation of ancient cultures.

Archaeologists work at sites all over the world, studying time periods from the advent of stone tools 2.5 million years ago until the much more recent past. *Prehistoric archaeologists* study cultures that did not leave any recorded written history—from the early hominins to the preliterate antecedents of modern cultures from Hawaii to Africa. *Historical archaeologists* study past civilizations that left a written record of their existence, whether in the hieroglyphics of Egyptian tombs, the Viking runes scratched onto rock across northern Europe, or the diaries kept by the colonial settlers of New England. Other archaeologists study Revolutionary War battlefields or sites of former slave plantations in an effort to understand how people lived and structured their societies.

Biological anthropology is vastly wider than the study of primates, fossils, and brain evolution. Any scientist studying evolution as it relates to the human species, directly or indirectly, could be called a biological anthropologist. This includes paleoanthropology, skeletal biology and osteology, paleopathology, forensic anthropology, primatology, and human biology.

((•─ **Listen** to the **Podcast** "Richard Leakey Reflects on Human Past—And Future" on **myanthrolab**

The Scope of Biological Anthropology

The scope of biological anthropology is vastly wider than the study of primates, fossils, and brain evolution. Any scientist studying evolution as it relates to the human species, directly or indirectly, could be called a biological anthropologist. This includes a number of related disciplines (Figure 1.1).

Paleoanthropology

When an exciting new fossil of an extinct form of human is found, paleoanthropologists usually are responsible (Figure 1.2). **Paleoanthropology** is the study of the fossil record for humankind, and fossilized remains are the most direct physical evidence of human ancestry that we have to understand where we came from. The discovery of skeletal evidence of new ancestral species, or additional specimens of existing species, revises our view of the human family tree. Discoveries of hominin fossils—some as famous as Peking Man or Lucy (Figure 1.3) but many less known—have profoundly changed the way we view our place in nature. Paleoanthropology also includes the study of the fossil record of the other primates—apes, monkeys, and prosimians—dating back at least 65 million years. These early fossils give us key clues about how, where, and why hominins evolved millions of years later. There are fossil sites producing important fossils all over the world, and with more and more students and researchers searching, our fossil history grows richer every year. In fact, although the first half of the twentieth century witnessed discoveries of new human fossils every decade or so, the pace of discovery of new species of fossil humans has accelerated rapidly in recent years. This is because global and regional political changes have allowed researchers into areas that were long off limits due to civil war or political unrest.

Paleoanthropological research begins in the field, where researchers search the landscape for new discoveries. Much of the scholarly work then takes place around the world in museums and university laboratories, where the specimens are archived and preserved for detailed study. Because we can safely assume that the evolutionary process taking place in the present also took place in the past, the study of the meaning of human and nonhuman primate fossils proceeds from comparisons between extinct and living forms. For example, the presence of large canine teeth in the male specimens of a fossil monkey species implies that when it was alive, the species lived in multiple male groups in which males competed for mates, because major differences in canine tooth size between males and females indicate mate competition in living monkeys.

As the fossil record has grown, we have begun to see that the evolutionary history of our species is extremely complicated; most lineages are now extinct, but many thrived for millions of years. The ladder of progress notion—an older, more linear view of our ancestry in which each species evolved into more complex forms—has been replaced by a family tree with many branches.

paleoanthropology   The study of the fossil record of ancestral humans and their primate kin.

osteology   The study of the skeleton.

paleopathology   The study of diseases in ancestral human populations.

bioarchaeology   The study of human remains in an archaeological context.

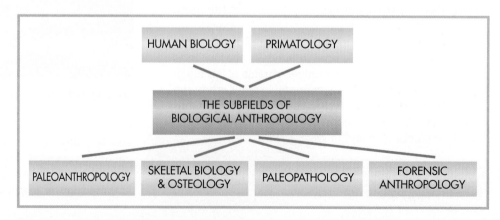

FIGURE 1.1   Subfields of biological anthropology.

Skeletal Biology and Human Osteology

Osteology is the study of the skeleton. The first order of business when a fossil is discovered is to figure out what sort of animal the fossil—often a tiny fragment—may have been in life. Osteologists must therefore possess extraordinary skills of identification and a keen spatial sense of how a jigsaw puzzle—an array of bone chips—fits together when they are trying to understand the meaning of fossils they have found.

FIGURE 1.2 Paleoanthropologist Jane Moore maps sites at Kanapoi, Kenya.

Among the first generation of biological anthropologists (Figure 1.4) were the *anthropometrists,* who made detailed measurements of the human body in all its forms, and their work is still important today. Understanding the relationship between genetics, human growth and stature, and geographic variation in human anatomy is vital to identifying the origins and patterns of human migration across the globe during prehistory, for example. When a 9,000-year-old skeleton was discovered some years ago on the banks of the Columbia River in the Pacific Northwest, osteologists with expertise in human variation in body form were among those who sought to identify its ethnic affinities.

Skeletal biology, like osteology, is the study of the human skeleton. However, because the bones of the body develop in concert with other tissues, such as muscles and tendons, a skeletal biologist must know the patterns and processes of human growth, physiology, and development, not just anatomy.

Paleopathology and Bioarchaeology

Hand in hand with skeletal biology are **paleopathology** and **bioarchaeology:** the study of disease in ancient human populations, and the study of human remains in an archaeological context. When the Neandertal fossils first appeared in the mid-nineteenth century, there was much scientific debate about whether they represented a true species or "race," or whether they were simply modern individuals who had suffered from some pathological condition. It took nearly 30 years and the discovery of several additional specimens to resolve the issue. Today, paleopathologists would help resolve such a debate much more quickly.

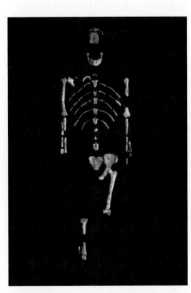

FIGURE 1.3 Lucy, a partial hominin skeleton.

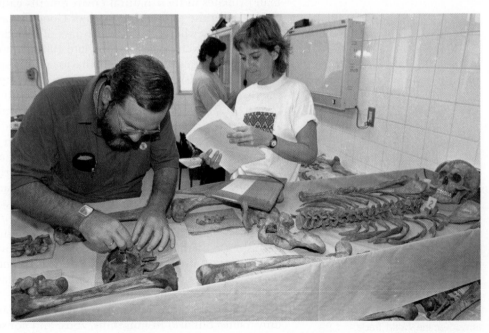

FIGURE 1.4 An osteologist at work.

Bioarchaeologists work with archaeologists excavating ancient humans to study the effects of trauma, epidemics, nutritional deficiencies, and infectious diseases. If archaeologists find evidence that an ancient civilization crashed precipitously, a paleopathologist will study the remains of the bodies for signs of anything from outbreaks of sexually transmitted disease to poor nutrition.

((•—|**Listen** to the **Podcast** "In Texas, A Living Lab for Studying the Dead" on **myanthrolab**

Forensic Anthropology

Although biological anthropology is concerned primarily with basic research into human origins, biological anthropologists also play roles in our daily lives. **Forensic anthropology,** the study of the identification of skeletal remains and of the means by which the individual died, is a contemporary application of biological anthropology. Forensic anthropologists take their knowledge of osteology and paleopathology and apply it to both historical and criminal investigations (Figure 1.5). During the war crime investigations into mass graves in Bosnia, as well as after the September 11, 2001 terrorist attacks in New York, Washington, and Pennsylvania, forensic anthropologists were called in to attempt to identify victims (Figure 1.6). When police were investigating the murder of the ex-wife of football star O. J. Simpson, forensic scientists used the footprints in blood left at the murder scene to try to reconstruct the height and weight of the murderer. This is not so different from what paleoanthropologists did when they discovered a set of tiny human-like footprints imbedded in fossilized ash at Laetoli in northern Tanzania. They used forensic skills to try to reconstruct the likely height and weight of the creatures that had left those prints nearly 4 million years ago.

FIGURE 1.5   Forensic anthropologists use skeletal remains to identify victims of war in Bosnia.

Primatology

Primatology is the branch of biological anthropology that is best known to the public through the highly publicized work of renowned primatologists Jane Goodall and Dian Fossey. Primatologists study the anatomy, physiology, behavior, and genetics of both living and extinct monkeys, apes, and prosimians. Behavioral studies of nonhuman primates in their natural environments gained prominence in the 1960s and 1970s, when the pioneering work of Goodall was publicized widely in the United States and elsewhere. In the early days of primate behavior study, the researchers were mainly psychologists. By the late 1960s, however, biological anthropology had become the domain of primate behavior study, especially in North America.

Primatologists study nonhuman primates for a variety of reasons, including the desire to learn more about their intrinsically fascinating patterns of behavior (Figure 1.7). Within an anthropological framework, primatologists study the nonhuman primates for the lessons they can provide on how evolution has molded the human species. For example, male baboons fight among themselves for the chance to mate with females. They are also much larger and more aggressive than females. Do larger, more macho males father more offspring than their smaller and gentler brothers? If so, these traits appear to have appeared slowly through generations of evolutionary change, and the size difference between males and females is the result of selection for large body size. Then, what about the body size difference between men and women of our own species? Is it the result of competition between men in prehistory, or perhaps a preference by women in prehistory for tall men? The clues we derive about human nature from the behavior and anatomy of living primates must be interpreted cautiously but can be vitally important in our understanding of who we are and where we came from.

FIGURE 1.6   Recovery team at work at the World Trade Center Ground Zero following the September 11, 2001, attack.

Biological anthropologists trained as primatologists find careers not only in universities but also in museums, zoos, and conservation agencies. Many valuable wildlife conservation projects seeking to protect endangered primate species are being carried out around the world by biological anthropologists.

FIGURE 1.7   Jane Goodall is a pioneering primatologist whose studies of wild chimpanzees changed our view of human nature.

Human Biology

In addition to paleoanthropology and primatology, biological anthropologists span a wide range of interests that are often labeled **human biology** Some work in the area of *human adaptation,* learning how people adjust physiologically to the extremes of Earth's physical environments. For instance, how are children affected by growing up high in the Andes mountain range of South America at elevations over 14,000 feet (4,270 meters)? Other human biologists work as *nutritional anthropologists,* studying the interrelationship of diet, culture, and evolution. Biological anthropologists interested in demography examine the biological and cultural forces that shape the composition of human populations. Other biological anthropologists are particularly interested in how various hormones in the human body influence human behavior and how, in turn, the environment affects the expression of these hormones. The study of *human variation* deals with the many ways in which people differ in their anatomy throughout the world.

At an earlier time in history, the scholarly study of physical traits such as height, skull shape, and especially skin color was tainted with the possibility that the researcher had some racially biased preconceptions. Today, biological anthropologists are interested in human variation, both anatomical and genetic, simply because it offers clues about the peopling of the world by the migrations of early people. Understanding when, where, and how people left Africa and colonized Europe, Asia, and eventually the New World can tell us a great deal about the roots of modern languages, diseases, population genetics, and other topics of great relevance in the world today.

Many contemporary biological anthropologists are interested in research problems that require an understanding of both biological and cultural factors. Biological anthropologists with these interests sometimes are called *biocultural anthropologists.* One area in which a biocultural perspective is vitally important is *biomedical anthropology* (Figure 1.8 on page 10). Biomedical anthropologists might study how human cultural practices influence the spread of infectious disease and how the effects of pollution or toxins in the environment affect human growth. Biomedical anthropologists are particularly interested in looking at the effects that adopting an urbanized (and Western) lifestyle has on people who have lived until recently under more traditional, non-Western conditions. The expression of many human diseases is influenced by genetic factors, and biomedical anthropologists often look at the long-term evolutionary consequences of disease on human populations.

Finally, an increasing number of biological anthropologists work in the field of genetics. *Molecular anthropology* is a genetic approach to human evolutionary science

◉─Watch the **Video** "What Makes Us Human (January 23, 2009)" on **myanthrolab**

forensic anthropology   The study of human remains applied to a legal context.

primatology   The study of the non-human primates and their anatomy, genetics, behavior, and ecology.

human biology   Subfield of biological anthropology dealing with human growth and development, adaptation to environmental extremes, and human genetics.

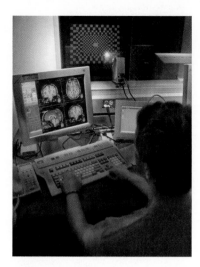

FIGURE 1.8 Biomedical anthropologists study, among other things, the human brain.

that seeks to understand the differences in the genome between humans and their closest relatives, the nonhuman primates. Because genetic inheritance is the basis for evolutionary change, a geneticist is in a perfect position to be able to address some of the fundamental questions about human nature and human evolution. We know that the human DNA sequence is extremely similar to that of an ape, but what exactly does this mean? At which points do the differences result in some key shift, such as language? These are some of the questions that may be answerable in the very near future with the help of anthropological geneticists.

The Roots of Modern Biological Anthropology

In 1856, the fossil of an ancient human ("Neandertal Man") was discovered in Germany (Schaaffhausen, 1858). In England in 1859, Charles Darwin published *On the Origin of Species*. Darwin's work had a greater immediate impact than the Neandertal's appearance because it was some time before scientists agreed that the Neandertal was an ancient human rather than just an odd-looking modern one. Darwin's introduction of an evolutionary perspective made many of the old debates about human origins irrelevant. After Darwin, scientists no longer needed to debate whether humans originated via a single creation or the different races were created separately (*monogenism* versus *polygenism*); the study of the natural history of humans became centered on the evolutionary history of our species. Human variation was the product of the interaction between the biological organism and the environment. Apes and monkeys—the nonhuman primates—became our "cousins" almost overnight.

The field known in North America as **physical anthropology** was established as an academic discipline in the second half of the nineteenth century (Spencer, 1997). In France, Germany, and England, it was called simply *anthropology*. Most early physical anthropologists were physicians who taught anatomy in medical schools and had an interest in human variation or evolution. In the first half of the twentieth century, much of physical anthropology was devoted to measuring bodies and skulls (*anthropometry* and *craniometry*), with particular attention paid to the biological definition of human races. Physical anthropologists also studied the comparative anatomy of nonhuman primates and the limited fossil record of humans and other primates.

By the mid-twentieth century, a new physical anthropology emerged, led by a generation of scholars who were first and foremost trained as anthropologists. In turn, these anthropologists trained hundreds of graduate students who benefited from the expansion of higher education fueled by the baby boom generation. The new physical anthropology, whose main architect was Sherwood Washburn of the University of Chicago and later of the University of California, Berkeley, embraced the dynamic view of evolution promoted by the adherents of the neo-Darwinian synthesis. This synthesis of genetics, anatomy, ecology, and behavior with evolutionary theory emerged in the biological sciences in the 1930s and 1940s. In the new physical anthropology, primates were not simply shot and dissected; their behavior and ecology were studied in the natural environment as well as in the laboratory (Goodall, 1963). The study of human races as pigeonholed categories gave way to the study of evolving populations, with a particular emphasis on how human populations adapt to environmental conditions. The field of paleoanthropology was revolutionized by the introduction of new dating techniques and the adoption of a multidisciplinary approach to understanding ancient environments. Molecular genetics research in anthropology gave us a whole new way to reconstruct the biological histories of human populations and of primate species as a whole (Goodman, 1962; Sarich and Wilson, 1967).

Today, biological anthropology embraces a wide variety of approaches with the goal of answering a few basic questions: What does it mean to be human? How did we become who we are today? How does our biological past influence our lives in the environments of the present? What is the place of human beings in nature?

physical anthropology The study of humans as biological organisms, considered in an evolutionary framework.

What Is Biological Anthropology?

Anthropology

Anthropology and Its Subfields

- Anthropology is the study of humankind in a cross-cultural perspective.
- Anthropologists study cultures in far-flung places, and they also study subcultures in our own society.
- Anthropology has four subfields. **[pp 4–5]**

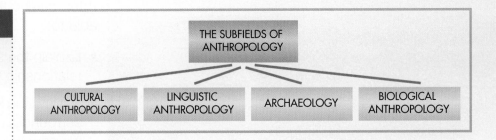

THE SUBFIELDS OF ANTHROPOLOGY

CULTURAL ANTHROPOLOGY · LINGUISTIC ANTHROPOLOGY · ARCHAEOLOGY · BIOLOGICAL ANTHROPOLOGY

Biological Anthropology

The Scope of Biological Anthropology

- Biological anthropology is one of anthropology's four subfields, along with archaeology, cultural anthropology, and linguistic anthropology.
- It is the study of humans as biological creatures: where we came from, our evolution, and how our biology interacts with our culture today. **[pp 6–10]**

The Roots of Modern Biological Anthropology

- Evolution by natural selection is the principle by which biological anthropologists understand the place of humans in the natural world.
- Biological anthropology seeks to answer a few basic questions: What does it mean to be human? How did we become who we are today? How does our biological past influence our lives in the environments of the present? What is the place of human beings in nature? **[p 10]**

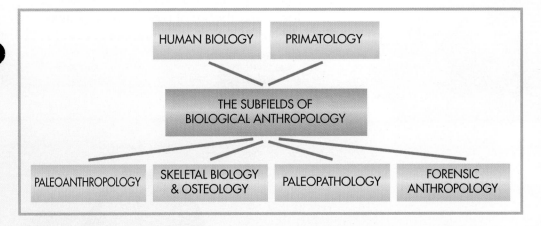

HUMAN BIOLOGY · PRIMATOLOGY

THE SUBFIELDS OF BIOLOGICAL ANTHROPOLOGY

PALEOANTHROPOLOGY · SKELETAL BIOLOGY & OSTEOLOGY · PALEOPATHOLOGY · FORENSIC ANTHROPOLOGY

My AnthroLab CONNECTIONS

Watch. Listen. View. Explore. Read.

MyAnthroLab is designed just for you. Each chapter features a customized study plan to help you learn and review key concepts and terms. Dynamic visual activities, videos, and readings found in the multimedia library will enhance your learning experience.

Resources from this Chapter:

👁─Watch on **myanthrolab**
- ▶ *What Makes Us Human? (January 23, 2009)*

((•─Listen on **myanthrolab**
- ▶ *Richard Leakey Reflects on Human Past—And Future*
- ▶ *In Texas, A Living Lab for Studying the Dead*

✳─Explore on **myanthrolab** In MySearchLab, enter the Anthropology database to find relevant and recent scholarly and popular press publications. For this chapter, enter the following keywords: Evolution, Biological Anthropology, Human Origins, Primatology

📖─Read on **myanthrolab**
- ▶ *Evolution of a Scientist* by Jerry Adler
- ▶ *So You Want to be an Archaeologist* by Brian Fagan

Chapter 2 Preview

After reading this chapter, you should be able to:

- Explain the scientific method and its relationship to anthropology.

- Review the key historical events surrounding the development of what we now call science.

- Analyze the scientific theories developed prior to the Darwinian Revolution and understand how they influenced Darwin's ideas.

- Explain how Darwin's observations in the Galapagos Islands contributed to his theory of evolution by natural selection.

- Show how both Charles Darwin and Alfred Wallace independently developed the same theory of biological evolution.

Origins of Evolutionary Thought

In a courtroom in Pennsylvania, a battle was fought in 2005 over science and religion. A newly elected school board in the town of Dover had passed a policy introducing the teaching of creationist beliefs for the origins of life. The board claimed that, in mandating that intelligent design creationism be taught in high school science classes, they were simply trying to present students with an alternative scientific theory to evolution. Several dismayed parents sued the school board, and the case ended up in a federal court. After a six-week trial that featured impassioned pleas from parents, scientists, and educators, the judge ruled that there was overwhelming evidence that intelligent design is a religious view, a mere relabeling of creationism, and "presents students with a religious alternative masquerading as a scientific theory."

Although some members of the school board said they would appeal the ruling, the next round of local elections saw those members swept from office, and replaced by a school board that favored the teaching of evolution. The battle over evolution was, however, hardly over such legal battles over the separation of church and state loomed in Georgia and Kansas.

The Dover case was only one of the more recent highly publicized battles between evolution and creationism that have occurred in the United States in the past century. The best-known case was the "Scopes Monkey Trial," which pitted two famous lawyers against each other and focused national attention on the issue in 1925 (Figure 2.1 on page 14). The The 1920s was a decade of rapid social change, and conservative Christians, in an effort to preserve traditional values, wanted to ban the teaching of evolution in public schools. The state of Tennessee passed such a ban in 1925.

In the summer of that year, in the small town of Dayton, Tennessee, famed trial attorney Clarence Darrow defended John Scopes, a young schoolteacher charged with illegally teaching evolution. The legendary William Jennings Bryan, a former U.S. secretary of state, represented the state of Tennessee and argued that Scopes should be fired for espousing views that ran counter to literal acceptance of the age of the earth and of humankind as described in the Old Testament. On the witness stand, Darrow forced Bryan to acknowledge that the six-day creation of the book of Genesis, along with the idea that the earth was very young, were powerful myths not meant to be taken literally. In the end, Scopes was found guilty, was fined $100, and lost his job.

It took decades and numerous court battles before all the states dropped laws banning the teaching of evolution from their books. In each case contested before a federal court, the judge has ruled in favor of the separation of church and state, meaning that religious views should not be taught in a public school classroom. The courts have also stated that evolution is the

FIGURE 2.1 The Scopes Trial: William Jennings Bryan (right) represented the state of Tennessee, and Clarence Darrow (left) represented John Scopes.

unifying principle of the life sciences, without valid competition in a science curriculum from theological explanations.

For centuries, people considered the earth to be young, and life on it to be unchanging. Perhaps this is because the reality of evolutionary change is inconceivable to some people. You can't see it, touch it, or sense it happening in any way, unlike more easily perceived physical laws such as gravity. The 80-year human life span is far too short to watch evolution, a process that typically happens on a scale of thousands of years. The enormous time scale of evolution is one reason that religious fundamentalists in the United States can continue to argue that "evolution is only a theory" and therefore campaign for equal time in public schools for biblical explanations for the origins of life and of humankind. As we shall see in this chapter, evolution is a theoretical framework that is the only way to make sense of a tremendous amount of evidence in support of the theory that is all around us. Fossilized dinosaur bones and ancient hominin skulls are evidence of evolution. But so are disease resistance to antibiotics and the need to develop new pesticides in order to cope with the evolution of resistance in insect pests.

In this chapter we will examine the history of ideas about how life came to be and the proponents and opponents of evolutionary theory and fact. We will also consider the issue of creationist opposition to evolutionary science. Biological anthropologists, as human evolutionary scientists, often find themselves on the front line of the debate over science and creation. First, we need to consider what science is and how it works.

Watch the **Animation**
"The Scientific Method"
on **myanthrolab**

What Is Science?

Science is a process, not a result. The process involves **deduction** and **observation;** formulating a **hypothesis,** or preliminary explanation; testing, and **experimentation;** or the collection of evidence (**data**) that either supports or refutes the hypothesis. This is the **scientific method** (Figure 2.2). It is the way scientists proceed when they have a question that needs answering or a possible explanation for a natural phenomenon that needs testing. Suppose a scientist proposes that the reason humans walk upright and apes do not is that walking upright uses less energy (in the form of calories burned) per mile of walking, thereby giving early humans who stood up to walk an advantage over their ape ancestors (Rodman and McHenry, 1980). This is the hypothesis. The scientist would then gather quantitative evidence—the data—to test this hypothesis. He might compare the caloric output of two-legged and four-legged walking by having a human and a chimpanzee walk on a treadmill while measuring the oxygen consumption of each. If chimpanzees were discovered to be less efficient walkers than humans, then the hypothesis would be supported. Of course, there are always alternative hypotheses; perhaps another researcher would argue that chimpanzees are *more* efficient walkers than other four-legged animals, in which case a whole new study that measures walking efficiency of many other animals will be needed before the first researcher can truly stake a claim.

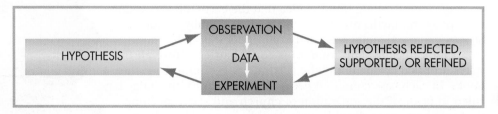

FIGURE 2.2 The scientific method.

Science is an *empirical* process that relies on evidence and experimentation. Science is not perfect, because data can be subject to differences in interpretation. But science has the essential quality of being *self-correcting*. If one scientist claims to have found evidence that the earth is flat, but others claim it is round, this question can be resolved by examining all the data, which can be published for the scientific world to scrutinize. If the data supporting the flat-Earth hypothesis are weak, and the majority of scientific evidence indicates that the earth is round, the flat-Earth research will be ignored or overturned. In other words, the hypothesis that the earth is flat is **falsifiable.** Such falsifiability is a defining trait of science. It means that rarely does a scientist claim to have "proven" anything. Instead, results are presented, and a hypothesis is either supported or rejected. Falsifiability is also a primary reason why science is such a powerful way to understand the world around us: The opportunity always exists for others to come along and correct earlier mistakes. This can be a long, slow process. Once a **paradigm**—an intellectual framework for understanding a given set of information—is in place, it may take a great deal of conflicting evidence and debate between scientists before that paradigm is overturned and replaced by a new one. In the next section we examine the great intellects whose ideas changed the paradigm of how we see the natural world.

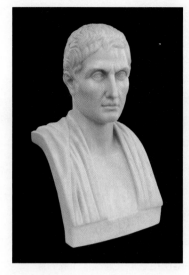

FIGURE 2.3   Aristotle

The Early Thinkers

Although Darwin is the leading intellectual figure in biology and in biological anthropology, his ideas did not reach the public until the publication of his first great work, *On the Origin of Species,* in 1859. For hundreds of years before this event, scholars had been thinking about the nature of life and humanity. The ancient Greeks often are credited with the first written efforts to understand the natural world and our place in it. In the fourth century B.C., Aristotle (Figure 2.3) described the animal and plant life of the Mediterranean region; he believed that each living form possessed an absolutely fixed essence that could not be altered (**immutability** of species) and that all life was arranged in an orderly, hierarchical ladder, with humans at the very top. Ironically, both Aristotle and Plato considered experimental science to be a crude endeavor compared with the innate beauty and elegance of mathematical theory (White, 2001). Although we often think of these natural philosophers as the first real scientists, they did not see themselves this way.

The Roots of Modern Science

The idea of the fixity of species was simply part of the static worldview during the Middle Ages. Theology was a pervasive force during this period, not only spiritually but also legally and politically. The church set doctrine that could be opposed only under penalty of imprisonment, or worse. Part of this doctrine was that the natural world had always existed in the same form as it exists today. Aristotle's Great Chain of Being, the idea that all organisms existed in a hierarchical ladder of sorts, with people at the top rung, was very much in place as both a natural philosophy and a legal code. Under this mindset, it is easy to see why science barely progressed.

During the Renaissance (fourteenth to sixteenth century), when scholars rediscovered the knowledge of the ancient Greeks and Romans their approach to science became more "modern." They also developed a sense of cultural variation as they studied the past and realized that the people of antiquity were not like them. Their discoveries challenged the notions of fixity and hierarchy, ideas reinforced by the powerful religious doctrine that held sway in the Middle Ages. Remarkable advances in the study of human anatomy changed the way scholars looked at the human body. Also, the discovery and exploration of the New World and the circumnavigation of the globe had a significant impact. European naturalists who had begun to be more systematic and accurate about describing the natural world around them got their first look at thousands of exotic plant and animal species.

deduction   A conclusion that follows logically from a set of observations.

observation   The gathering of scientific information by watching a phenomenon.

hypothesis   A preliminary explanation of a phenomenon. Hypothesis formation is the first step of the scientific method.

experimentation   The testing of a hypothesis.

data   The scientific evidence produced by an experiment or by observation, from which scientific conclusions are made.

scientific method   Standard scientific research procedure in which a hypothesis is stated, data are collected to test it, and the hypothesis is either supported or refuted.

falsifiable   Able to be shown to be false.

paradigm   A conceptual framework useful for understanding a body of evidence.

immutability (or fixity)   Stasis, lack of change.

FIGURE 2.4 Carolus Linnaeus

Most natural historians and philosophers before the nineteenth century believed there was a single creation event. Anglican archbishop James Ussher (1581–1656) calculated the date of the creation of Earth using the only evidence of the age of Earth available to him: the Old Testament of the Bible. By counting backward using the ages of the main characters as given in the books of the Old Testament, Ussher arrived at 4004 B.C. as the year of Earth's creation. Although it sounds a bit silly today, Ussher had no other chronological evidence available to him. He knew that Adam had lived to a ripe old age and begat Cain and Abel; the cumulative ages of these founders and all their descendants added up to about a 5,500-year history of the world. Ussher's date provided the time frame for understanding the natural history of Earth for more than two centuries and to this day is accepted by fundamentalist Christian creationists as a reasonably accurate estimate for the age of Earth.

Linnaeus and the Natural Scheme of Life

In the seventeenth and eighteenth centuries, naturalists became more concerned with developing classification schemes for naming and organizing plants and animals. Nevertheless, they did not part company with the theological view of a static, unchanging world. The classification scheme we use in the biological sciences today (now called the *Linnean system*) dates from this period.

Anglican minister John Ray (1627–1705) was the first naturalist to use the terms *genus* and *species* to classify types of animals and plants. Later, Carolus Linnaeus (1707–1778), an eminent Swedish botanist and the author of the *Systema Naturae*, built on Ray's writings to create the most comprehensive classification of the plant world compiled at the time (Figure 2.4). In addition to his work on plants, Linnaeus studied the diversity of animal life, often based on specimens shipped to his laboratory from far-flung corners of the world. He used the physical characteristics of plants and animals to assign them to a scheme of classification. The science of classifying and naming living things that Linnaeus invented is called **taxonomy.** Sorting organisms into categories was a vital way to make sense of their patterns of relationship, so he applied a hierarchy of names to the categories of similarity, which today we call the Linnaean hierarchy. The two-level genus–species labels, or **binomial nomenclature,** were at the heart of taxonomy; a **taxon** is any unit of this formal hierarchy. Linnaeus followed the naming pattern of the ancient Greeks by using Greek and Latin languages for his scheme. But Linnaeus was intellectually hidebound by his theology. He believed firmly in the immutability of species—that each species existed as a completely separate entity from every other species and that these separations were fixed by God. Influenced further by his belief that apes and humans could not be closely related by common descent, Linnaeus assigned people to the family Hominidae and great apes to the family Pongidae. This separation stands to this day although, as we shall see, it may not be justifiable on biological grounds.

👁—⟨**Watch** the **Video** "The Life and Work of Linnaeus" on **myanthrolab**

The Road to the Darwinian Revolution

In the eighteenth and early nineteenth centuries, a number of European natural historians made their mark in explaining the nature of the diversity of flora and fauna on Earth. Some of these directly influenced Darwin's thinking decades later; most were also following in Linnaeus's taxonomic footsteps. Prominent among these were four eminent French natural historians.

Comte de Buffon Georges-Louis Leclerc, Comte de Buffon (1707–1788), accepted the notion of biological change. Buffon (Figure 2.5) observed that animals that migrate to new climates often change in response to new environments, although like others of his day he had no idea about the mechanism of change. He famously claimed that the animals of the New World were weaker and smaller than their counterparts in the Old World, a result of a generally less healthy and

FIGURE 2.5 Comte de Buffon

productive environment. Thomas Jefferson vigorously refuted this claim in his *Notes on the State of Virginia* (1787).

Georges Cuvier By the turn of the nineteenth century, discoveries of dinosaur bones across western Europe had made it difficult for biblically driven scholars to continue to deny the importance of change to the history of Earth. Georges Cuvier (born Jean-Léopold Cuvier; 1769–1832) rose rapidly in the ranks of the world's foremost natural scientists at the Natural History Museum of Paris, where he spent his entire career. Cuvier (Figure 2.6) was a staunch opponent of the modern concept of evolutionary change. The existence of extinct creatures such as dinosaurs was a large problem for Cuvier and other creationist scientists of the day because they presented compelling evidence of a past world very different from that of the present day. Cuvier and his supporters sought to explain away these fossils by embracing the concept of extinction and change, but with a biblical twist. They advocated a theory now known as **catastrophism** in which cataclysmic disasters were believed to have wiped out earlier forms of life on Earth. One such natural disaster that Cuvier had in mind was Noah's flood. After such an event, Cuvier argued, more advanced animals from other regions of the world moved in to repopulate the flooded area. These replacement populations were thought to be more advanced than the originals.

FIGURE 2.6   Georges Cuvier

Geoffroy Saint-Hilaire Cuvier's contemporary Geoffroy Saint-Hilaire (1772–1844) was an anatomist and a strong advocate of evolutionary change. He engaged in acrimonious public debate with Cuvier on the subject after he corrected Cuvier on identification of a crocodile skeleton, which Cuvier called an unknown modern species, but Saint-Hilaire correctly identified as a fossil. Saint-Hilaire's work led him to support his senior colleague Jean-Baptiste Lamarck, who had proposed a system to explain the process of evolution.

Jean-Baptiste Lamarck In 1809, Lamarck (1744–1829) proposed his **theory of inheritance of acquired characteristics,** which is today often called *Lamarckianism.* Lamarck (Figure 2.7) argued that all organisms make adjustments to their environment during their lifetime that could be passed on to their offspring, making those offspring better adapted to their environment. It relied on the concept of *need and use.* For example, if an animal that lived by the seashore spent much of its time swimming in the ocean, its offspring, according to Lamarck, would be better swimmers than its parents had been. In postulating this sort of evolutionary process, Lamarck made one laudable breakthrough and one major error. The breakthrough was seeing the crucial relationship between the organism and its environment. But the fundamental error was thinking that evolutionary change could occur during the lifetime of an individual. This error is easily seen by taking Lamarck's theory to its logical extension: If a mouse loses its tail to a cat, does the mouse later give birth to babies lacking tails? Likewise, no amount of bodybuilding will enable a person to give birth to muscular children.

Lamarck's idea is often ridiculed today, but it was a brilliant notion in light of the evidence of evolutionary change available in the eighteenth century. Lamarck knew nothing about the mode of inheritance—genes—and his theory of the inheritance of acquired characteristics served as a natural antecedent to Darwin's theories (Figure 2.8 on page 18).

FIGURE 2.7   Jean-Baptiste Lamarck

taxonomy   The science of biological classification.

binomial nomenclature   Linnean naming system for all organisms, consisting of a genus and species label.

taxon   A group of organisms assigned to a particular category.

catastrophism   Theory that there have been multiple creations interspersed by great natural disasters such as Noah's flood.

theory of inheritance of acquired characteristics   Discredited theory of evolutionary change proposing that changes that occur during the lifetime of an individual, through use or disuse, can be passed on to the next generation.

The Uniformitarians: Hutton and Lyell

At about the same time that Lamarck's ideas were being debated, a key piece of the evolution puzzle fell into place. Along the rocky Scottish seacoast, James Hutton (1726–1797) spent his career studying, among other things, layering of rock formations. One of the fathers of modern geology, Hutton saw clear evidence of

(a) Lamarck's view

The earliest ancestor possessed a short trunk.

Through continued stretching of the trunk to obtain food, it grew longer and longer. Ensuing generations possessed longer trunks.

(b) Darwin's view

In a population with short-trunked elephants, those individuals with slightly longer trunks obtain more food, therefore leave more offspring.

Many generations later, natural selection has changed the species to an elephant that possesses a long trunk.

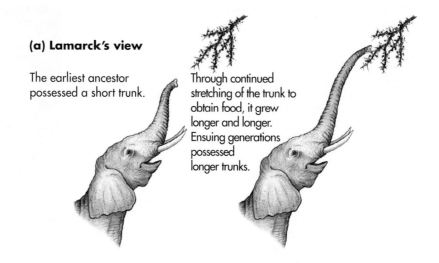
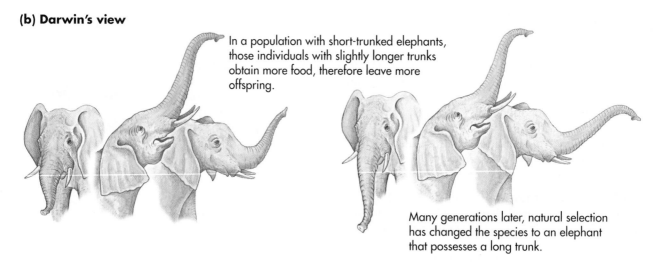

FIGURE 2.8   Lamarckian and Darwinian views of evolution.

FIGURE 2.9   Charles Lyell

past worlds in the upthrusting of the earth. A devout Christian, Hutton attempted to shoehorn his observations into a biblical framework. However, he did assert a central principle that stands to this day: **uniformitarianism.** Hutton asserted that the geological processes that drive the natural world today are the same as those that prevailed in the past. Hutton was not prepared to extend this theory to the living world; that was left for Charles Darwin many years later. But his views of the changing Earth strongly influenced a generation of geologists.

Charles Lyell (1797–1875), another British geologist, was a strong proponent of uniformitarianism, arguing that slow, gradual change was the way of the physical world and that if one looked in older and older rock sediments, one would find increasingly primitive forms of life. Although an ardent creationist, Lyell (Figure 2.9) became the leading geologist of his day; through his research and his prominence in the social hierarchy of nineteenth-century London, Lyell exerted an enormous influence over his academic peers. His acquaintance with Darwin certainly was a strong influence on the latter's evolutionary ideas. His book *Principles of Geology,* published in three volumes beginning in 1830, was a work that Darwin carried and read time and again during his voyage of discovery on the sailing ship HMS *Beagle.* Lyell played a key role in convincing both the scientific world and the public that the earth's history could be understood only in the context of deep, ancient changes in geology, which necessarily cast creationist explanations for life in a different, more dubious light.

The Darwinian Revolution

Charles Darwin (1809–1882) was one of six children born into a life of affluence. His father, Robert Darwin, was a physician; his maternal grandfather was famed pottery maker, Josiah Wedgwood; and his paternal grandfather was Erasmus Darwin (1731–1802), an eminent naturalist and philosopher. His mother, Susana Darwin, died when Darwin was 8 years old. An ardent naturalist from an early age, Darwin wandered the English countryside in search of animals and plants to study. However, he was a lackluster student. When Darwin was 16, his father sent him to study medicine at the University of Edinburgh. Uninterested in his studies and appalled at the sight of surgery, young Darwin did not fare well academically. He did, however, make his initial contacts with evolutionary theory, in the form of Lamarck's ideas about evolutionary change. Darwin subsequently left Edinburgh and headed to Cambridge University, where he planned to study for the ministry in the Church of England (Figure 2.10). In the summer of 1831, while Darwin was on a natural history field trip in Wales, Henslow was meeting with Captain Robert Fitzroy (1805–1865). Fitzroy, an officer in the Royal Navy and himself a keen amateur naturalist, was planning a voyage to map the coastlines of the continents, particularly South America, on the sailing ship HMS *Beagle*. He had invited Henslow to accompany him, but Henslow turned down the offer, as did Henslow's first-choice alternate, his brother-in-law. Henslow then put Darwin's name forward, and Fitzroy accepted. Charles Darwin thus departed in December 1831 as the "gentleman" amateur naturalist aboard the *Beagle,* a journey that changed not only Darwin but also modern science. It also changed Captain Fitzroy, whose deep Christian beliefs eventually led him to regret his decision to take Darwin along on the voyage.

The Galápagos

It's hard for us to appreciate today what a rare gift a trip around the world was for a naturalist in the early nineteenth century. The 22-year-old Darwin, who had left the British Isles only once before his voyage on the *Beagle*, spent 5 years of his life exploring the seacoasts of South America, Australia, and Africa, with many stops along the way (Figure 2.11).

uniformitarianism Theory that the same gradual geological process we observe today was operating in the past.

FIGURE 2.10   Charles Darwin

View the **Map** "*Darwin's Voyage on the HMS Beagle*" on **myanthrolab**

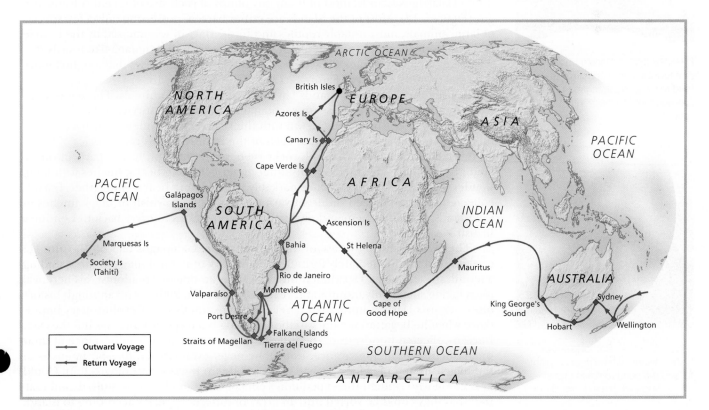

FIGURE 2.11   Map of Darwin's voyage on the HMS *Beagle*.

FIGURE 2.12   Darwin was deeply influenced by his stop in the Galápagos Islands, isolated volcanic rocks off the coast of Ecuador.

FIGURE 2.13   Darwin observed that tortoises on islands that are arid tend to have saddle-shaped shells, allowing them to reach into trees to browse.

FIGURE 2.14   But tortoises on lusher islands, where grass is plentiful and the need to reach into trees not so frequent, have dome-shaped shells.

From 1831 to 1836, unburdened by other distractions, he was able to devote most of his waking hours to observing myriad plants and animals in their natural environment.

Contrary to the popular image of Darwin spending 5 years at sea, most of Darwin's time was spent on land expeditions or in seaside ports in South America. He rode horses in Patagonia, trekked in the Andes, and explored oceanic islands in the Atlantic and Pacific Oceans. Of these oceanic island stops, one had a profound influence on Darwin: the Galápagos Islands. The *Beagle* dropped anchor amid a cluster of rocky islands 600 miles off the coast of Ecuador on September 15, 1835. The two dozen Galápagos Islands, most of them tiny lumps of rock, are of recent volcanic origin (Figure 2.12). Most of the islands are rather barren, possessing only a few species of large animals, most notably reptiles and birds. Darwin was amazed by the bizarre and oddly approachable animal life of the islands, including iguana-like lizards that dived into the sea to forage for seaweeds, and enormous tortoises that weighed more than 400 pounds, shown in Figures 2.13 and 2.14 (Darwin, 1839).

Each of the Galápagos Islands has its own varieties of animals. There was a distinctive variety of giant tortoise on each, many of which still survive today. It was the birds, however, that provided Darwin with the key piece of evidence for his eventual theory of evolution. He found that each of the islands had its own species of finch. To this day, some live on the arid, rocky islets, and others on lusher parts of the island group. There are finches with rather generic-looking beaks; finches with long, slender beaks; and finches with remarkably large, strong beaks. Altogether, Darwin collected at least thirteen different varieties of small, brownish or black finches in the islands, skinning them and packing them into crates to carry back to London's British Museum.

There are many myths about the influence the Galápagos had on Darwin. He certainly did not immediately formulate the theory of natural selection on spending a month there. In fact, Darwin left the Galápagos an uneasy creationist, his heretical ideas taking shape only months and years later (Larson, 2001). And although history often records Darwin immediately recognizing something of evolutionary importance when he began to see the variations among finch species, this was not the case. Darwin collected hundreds of the little birds but never saw the importance of their small differences in appearance. In fact, he never even labeled the specimens as to the specific island on which he had collected them. It was ornithologist John Gould in London who studied the expedition's collection of finches, now stuffed, and realized that they could be sorted into an array of different species according to island.

In his published journal of the voyage of the *Beagle* written the year after he returned home, Darwin said,

> Seeing this gradation and diversity of structure in one small, intimately related group of birds, one might really fancy that from an original paucity of birds in this archipelago, one species had been taken and modified for different ends. (Darwin, 1839)

In light of Gould's discovery of bill differences, Darwin realized the importance of the finches for his budding theory. He surmised that the various animal varieties of the Galápagos, from giant tortoises to mockingbirds, probably descended from a very small number of creatures that had reached the islands (presumably from the South American mainland) long ago and had then diversified in response to the different island habitats they found there (Figure 2.15). This observation was Darwin's first insight into **biogeography,** the distribution of animals and plants on the Earth. Darwin referred to the process of many species emerging from one or few ancient ones, like the spokes of a wheel emerging from the hub, as **adaptive radiation.** The process of biological change in a species in which adaptive radiation occurs, Darwin referred to as **natural selection.** In fact, the Galápagos were the perfect setting for Darwin to see evolution in action. Because these islands are isolated from the mainland, and because they are relatively young, they are biologically simple. Only a few species had managed to reach the islands. Perhaps the ancestors of the finches had been blown off course while flying in a storm and ended up there. Ocean currents probably had carried the tortoises and iguanas there as they floated or clung to pieces of driftwood. Finding rocky islets that had food and shelter with few competitors, the species flourished, and eventually their descendants had radiated into the available space in the archipelago.

biogeography The distribution of animals and plants on the earth.

adaptive radiation The diversification of one founding species into multiple species and niches.

natural selection Differential reproductive success over multiple generations.

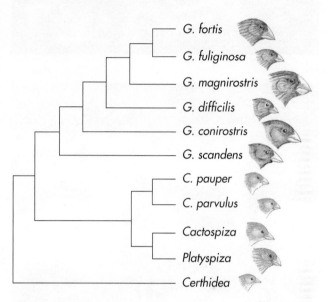

FIGURE 2.15 Darwin's finches: Adaptive radiation of bill types.

Refining the Theory of Evolution by Natural Selection

At home in England, Darwin took up a life of nature study, contemplation, and writing. He married his cousin Emma Wedgwood and purchased a manor house in the village of Downe, some 15 miles south of London (Figure 2.16). Beset by a variety of health problems, he rarely left Downe and was bedridden for long periods. But he spent years developing his theory of natural selection, drawing extensively on the parallel process of artificial selection. When animal breeders try to develop new strains of livestock, they select the traits they want to enhance and allow only those individuals to breed. For example, a farmer who tries to boost milk production in Guernsey cows must allow only the best milk producers to breed, and over many generations, milk production will indeed increase. Darwin developed friendships with some of the local breeders of fancy pigeons and drew on the breeders' work to elaborate on his theory of natural selection. Pigeons, horses, cows, dogs: All are prime examples of what selective breeding can achieve in a few generations. What artificial breeders do in captivity, natural selection does in the wild—with one key exception. The animal breeder chooses certain traits, such as

FIGURE 2.16 Darwin spent most of his life after the voyage of the *Beagle* at Down House in the village of Downe, south of London.

(a)

(b)

(c)

(d)

FIGURE 2.17   Species of horses: (a) zebra, (b) Przewalski's horse, (c) Tibetan kiang, and (d) thoroughbred race horse.

floppy ears or a long tail, and pushes the evolution of the breed in that direction generation after generation (Figure 2.17). He or she has a goal in mind with respect to animal form or function. Natural selection has no such foresight. Instead, it molds each generation in response to current environmental conditions.

Alfred Russel Wallace In 1858, an event occurred that galvanized Darwin into action. He received a letter and manuscript from Alfred Russel Wallace (1823–1913), another field biologist then collecting plant and animal specimens in Indonesia (Figure A in Insights and Advances: Darwin versus Wallace?). Wallace's life paralleled Darwin's only in his citizenship and lifelong fascination with nature. Otherwise, in the class-conscious society of nineteenth-century England, the two men were from different worlds. Whereas Darwin was from wealthy, landed gentry, Wallace grew up in a working-class family, leaving school at an early age. His employment as a specimen collector for wealthy patrons took him on far-flung adventures and set the stage for him to gain many of the same insights that Darwin had gained on the *Beagle*. Wallace had come up with his own version of the theory of evolution by natural selection and was writing to Darwin for advice as to whether the idea was sound and worthy of publication. With prodding from Hooker and Huxley, Darwin wrote down his own theory and readied it for presentation before the Royal Linnean Society and for publication.

Twelve hundred copies of *On the Origin of Species* were published on November 24, 1859, and they quickly sold out of every bookshop in London. Alongside the expected best sellers that autumn—Charles Dickens's *Tale of Two Cities* and Alfred

insights & advances

DARWIN VERSUS WALLACE?

Imagine you are a prominent scientist who has been working day and night for 20 years on a groundbreaking theory that you are certain will revolutionize the life sciences. Then one day you receive a thin parcel in the mail, sent by a colleague who has innocently enclosed a manuscript detailing exactly the same theory. Furthermore, the letter asks your help in improving the theory and your advice on how best to publicize it to the world.

This is the situation in which Charles Darwin found himself one day in June 1858. The mail delivery to his home in England included a package sent by steamship from the remote reaches of the Indonesian islands. The parcel from Alfred Russel Wallace had been 2 months in transit. Darwin and Wallace had corresponded for several years since the publication of a short paper Wallace had written on his early ideas about evolutionary change in animal populations.

Wallace's cover letter described a handwritten manuscript he had enclosed that detailed a theory he had been working on for many years. Wallace titled the manuscript "On the Tendency of Varieties to Depart Indefinitely from the Original Type." We can picture the mailing envelope opening and that cover page sliding before Darwin's eyes. As he no doubt immediately saw, the manuscript proposed a slight variant of the theory of evolution by natural selection. Beginning with a rejection of Lamarckian notions of change, Wallace outlined the way in which some variations in nature are favorable and others unfavorable and the tendency for such variation to produce new forms better suited to their environments. He even paralleled Darwinian thinking in his use of Thomas Malthus's work on populations. Wallace's idea differed in two fundamental ways from Darwin's. Wallace rejected artificial selection—selective breeding—as analogous to natural selection, while Darwin felt animal breeders were essentially mimicking the lengthy process of natural selection. Wallace also placed more emphasis on the replacement of groups and species by other groups and species than did Darwin, who focused on individuals (in this Wallace was certainly wrong).

Although the exact date that Darwin replied to Wallace's letter and manuscript is not known, journals and letters written by the two men suggest that Darwin waited for several weeks, during which he chronicled his worries about receiving proper credit for the theory in his journal. He characterized the similarities between Wallace's theory and his own:

> I never saw a more striking coincidence, if Wallace had my m.s. [manuscript] sketch written out in 1842 he could not have made a better abstract. (Browne, 2002)

Darwin finally wrote back to Wallace, responding politely but with a note of territoriality. He reminded Wallace that "this summer marks the twentieth year since I opened my first notebook on the question how and in what way do species and varieties differ from each other." (Browne, 2002). He apparently spent weeks fretting that his own work had been rendered unoriginal by Wallace. But Darwin's allies, the geologist Charles Lyell and the botanist Joseph Hooker, would have none of this. They insisted that Darwin had priority of place and that he should assert his primacy in responding to Wallace and presenting their ideas before the British scientific community.

Darwin and his ally Hooker proposed in separate letters to Wallace that Darwin be allowed to present a jointly authored paper with an introduction by Lyell and Hooker at a meeting of the Linnean Society of London, announcing both theories simultaneously. Wallace was delighted that his work would receive such prominent attention in the scientific world and that his ideas would be linked to those of such eminent thinkers. Several months later, Wallace received another letter from Hooker, informing him that the joint Darwin–Wallace presentation had taken place and that the two papers had been read: first Darwin's, then Wallace's. The Linnean Society of London then published the papers as one paper in the proceedings of the event, with Darwin as first author and Wallace listed

FIGURE A   Alfred Russel Wallace

second. The title of Wallace's original manuscript had been altered; the term *natural selection,* which Darwin had coined, had been inserted into it.

Three factors may have guaranteed Darwin's fame as the founder of the theory of natural selection. First, Wallace recognized that Darwin had been thinking and writing about his ideas for 20 years and had published a sketch of his theory as early as 1845 (in a revised version of his journal of the voyage of the *Beagle*). Second, Wallace granted enormous respect to Darwin, who was a member of the upper class and had powerful scientific allies. Third, Wallace was living in the jungles of Malaysia and so was unable to argue his own case or present his own paper to the Linnean Society. Had Wallace been in London at the time, and had he been a bit less respectful of his senior colleague, the theory of the origin of species might have emerged quite differently.

((•—Listen to the Podcast "Darwin's Theory of Evolution – or Wallace's?" on **myanthrolab**

Lord Tennyson's *Idylls of the King*—it was a surprise hit. Darwin wrote, as did many scientific authors of his day, with both a scientific audience and the reading public in mind. He was immediately besieged by letters and requests for personal appearances. Darwin was suddenly one of the most famous men in the world.

In presenting his theory of evolution by natural selection as laid out in *On the Origin of Species,* Darwin explained his three observations and two deductions:

Observation 1. All organisms have the potential for explosive population growth that would outstrip their food supply. Darwin took this idea directly from Malthus, who had been concerned with human population growth. A female bullfrog may lay 100,000 eggs every spring, but we don't see bullfrogs hopping everywhere. Even humans, with their very low reproductive potential compared with most animals, can undergo exponential population growth, as evidenced by the global population explosion.

Observation 2. But when we look at nature, we see populations that are roughly stable.

Deduction 1. Therefore, there must be a struggle for existence. That is, the bullfrog's 100,000 eggs may yield no more just one adult frog. This, Darwin labeled *natural selection* to parallel the term *artificial selection* in use by animal breeders of the period.

Observation 3. Nature is full of variation. Even in one animal group, every individual is slightly different from every other individual. If you look closely enough, even a basketful of uniform-looking bullfrogs will resolve into myriad small differences in size, shape, color, and other features.

Deduction 2. Therefore, some of these variations must be favored, and others must be disfavored, in a process we can call natural selection.

This elegantly simple set of ideas is the heart of evolutionary theory. Famed biologist Julian Huxley, the grandson of Darwin's ally T. H. Huxley, referred to the idea as bringing about "the greatest of all revolutions in human thought, greater than Einstein's or Freud's or even Newton's." Far from the eternally static cubbyholes that most earlier thinkers had conceived, species were dynamic units, constantly in flux in response to changing environments and the unceasing pressure of competitors (Figure 2.18). Natural selection was a filtering process in which unfavorable traits

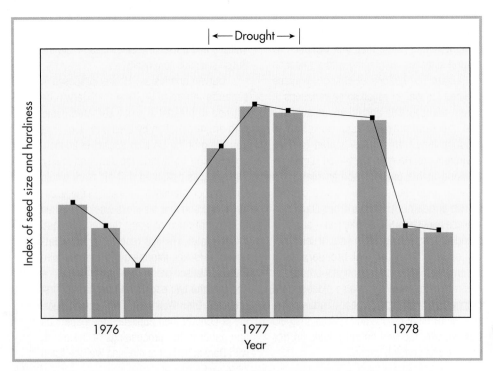

FIGURE 2.18   Index of seed size and hardiness prior to, during, and after drought.

lost the race to more favorable traits. As Darwin saw it, natural selection is all about reproductive success. The time-honored definition of natural selection as "survival of the fittest," a phrase coined by social theorist Herbert Spencer, is misleading. It is much more about the number of offspring that survive to reproductive age, which is a measure we call **fitness**, a biological measure of reproductive success (not a reference to physical fitness). This can be measured, and the qualities that contribute to reproductive success can often be determined. Natural selection can therefore be defined as differential reproductive success across multiple generations and among the individuals of a given population of animals or plants.

For natural selection to work, three preconditions must be met (Figure 2.19):

1. *The trait in question must be inherited.* For example, if you incubate the eggs of some animals, such as reptiles, at temperatures that are too high or too low, the resulting baby will have odd color patterns. These patterns are not genetic and so are not under the control of natural selection.

2. *The trait in question must show variation between individuals.* Natural selection cannot distinguish good from bad traits if all individuals are genetically identical clones. This is rarely the case in nature, where variation abounds and is the key difference between organisms that reproduce by asexual splitting, such as amoebas, and higher animals that reproduce sexually. Higher animals are all genetically unique, so their traits can be selected or not selected.

3. *The filter between the organism and its genetic makeup is the environment, which must exert some pressure in order for natural selection to act.* Many scholars believe that humans evolved rapidly in part because the environment in which our ancestors lived underwent many dramatic fluctuations caused by world climate swings.

Evolution is about change. Although in common English usage *evolution* is sometimes used to describe the changes an individual goes through in the course of a lifetime ("in my evolution as an artist …"), in biology this is never the case. It is a change in a **population** (a breeding group of organisms of the same kind) in the frequency of a trait or a gene from one generation to the next. The currency of change is the genetic material, in which alterations in the DNA sequence provide the raw source of variation—**mutation**— on which natural selection can act. Whereas evolution happens at the level of the population, natural selection occurs at the level of the individual organism. As we will see, this has important implications for understanding how the evolutionary process produces the myriad forms we see in nature.

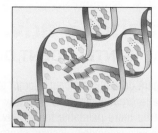

a. Mode of inheritance

b. Variation among individuals

c. Environmental pressure

FIGURE 2.19 The prerequisites needed for natural selection to occur.

Science and Creationism

Ever since the publication of *On the Origin of Species,* a small but vocal minority in the United States (and other countries) have argued against the teaching of the principles of evolution. They argue instead for a biblical, creationist view of the origin of species and of humanity. But what exactly is a *creationist?* A scientist who studies the origins of the known universe but who believes that the universe may have been created 14 billion years ago by a single supernatural force is a creationist. So is a fundamentalist who believes the earth and every living thing on it were created in 6 days, that dinosaurs and other extinct animals never existed, and that we are all descendants of Adam and Eve. Creationism is simply a belief in a single creative force in the universe.

The ongoing conflict between evolution and creationism lies in the claim by some fundamentalist religious groups that the creation story in the book of Genesis is a viable alternative to science as the explanation for how humans came to be. These groups argue that evolution is a theory that has no more scientific validity than biblical explanations for the origins of life and of people. The intellectual centerpiece of their thinking is that the earth is very young (that is, it is approximately the age calculated by Ussher). They believe that the sedimentary layers of the earth that provide scientists with evidence of antiquity, and also yield most of our fossils, are actually the product of Noah's flood and are of very recent origin. They consider the species found alive today and in the most recent fossil beds to be the species that

fitness Reproductive success.

population An interbreeding group of organisms.

mutation An alteration in the DNA that may or may not alter the function of a cell. If it occurs in a gamete, it may be passed from one generation to the next.

insights & advances
WHAT IS INTELLIGENT DESIGN?

Intelligent design is a recent attempt to repackage creationist ideas in a way that might be more palatable for society and the scientific community. Instead of arguing outright for a biblical or divine basis for life, intelligent design advocates claim they have evidence that evolution by natural selection cannot fully explain the diversity of form and function that exists in nature. This school of thought is fond of using the argument of *irreducible complexity*: There are aspects of the design of some organisms that are so complex that gradual, successive small modifications of earlier forms (evolution) could not have produced them. Advocates of intelligent design claim that if removal of one part of an organism's adaptive complex of traits causes the entire complex to cease functioning, then a supernatural force must have been its actual creator. The example of a mousetrap is often cited. Without each essential feature of a mousetrap—the wooden platform, the spring mechanism, and the latch holding it—the device fails to function at all. Intelligent design advocates say that unless the trap were assembled all at once, it would be useless and therefore could not be created by natural selection. Michael Behe, a biologist and an influential advocate of intelligent design who seeks to reconcile evolution with religious faith, has claimed that there are examples of irreducible complexity in biology that make natural selection an inadequate mechanism for all change. For instance, Behe claims that the function of cells at the biochemical level, in which cellular operation can occur only after numerous working integrated parts are in place, might be an example of irreducible complexity (Behe, 1996).

Unfortunately for adherents of intelligent design, their few examples of irreducible complexity have been met with refutations in the scientific literature. Behe himself acknowledges that whereas gradual, Darwinian change by natural selection can be studied and tested using the scientific method, intelligent design cannot. By definition, if the original design is supernatural, understanding this design must be beyond the reach of science or rational explanation. In other words, the intelligent design movement asks us to accept on blind faith that supernatural forces are at work in designing life. Rather than offering rational explanations for features that might challenge Darwinian theory, advocates of intelligent design offer criticisms that cannot be addressed by further research. The whole belief system of intelligent design therefore stands well outside of science—in the realm of faith—rather than offering a scientific alternative to evolution by natural selection.

As described at the beginning of this chapter, the most recent setback to intelligent design came in a landmark federal court case in 2005, in which parents of the Dover, Pennsylvania school district sued to block the teaching of intelligent design in science classrooms. Despite testimony from a range of intelligent design advocates, the judge in that case ruled that intelligent design is simply religion masquerading as science, and as such it has no place being taught in public school science classrooms.

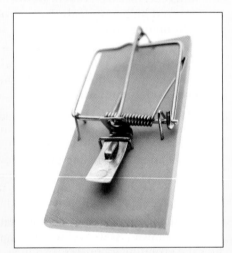

FIGURE A

could swim well enough to escape the rising floodwaters. Not surprisingly, this belief can be easily overturned by quick examination of the fossil record and by the study of radiometric dating of the age of the earth's layers.

A religious belief in a divine creation relies entirely on faith. The sole evidence of this faith in Judeo-Christianity is the book of Genesis in the Old Testament of the Bible. Although the Bible is a profoundly important book, its contents are not testable evidence. Nowhere in the evaluation of the truth of the Old Testament does the scientific method come into play; either you accept the reality of the Old Testament or you don't. A literal interpretation of Genesis would mean accepting a period of creation that lasted only 6 days. However, many Christians accept the Old Testament as a powerful and relevant work that is not intended to be taken literally. The problem that most scientists have with teaching religion in public schools is not due to lack of respect for religion—some are quite religious themselves—but rather that science classes are intended to teach children how to think like scientists.

The political agenda of some American anti-evolution fundamentalist groups belies their stated belief in offering diverse approaches to human origins. Religious fundamentalists often support the teaching of the Judeo-Christian creation story as fact but do not want to allow other creation stories to be taught alongside them in classrooms. Christianity, Judaism, and Islam are creationist faiths: They identify a single creator. Other major religions of the world, such as Hinduism, do not accept a single creator. Fundamentalists fight politically for the right to teach the Judeo-Christian belief system in public schools, but generally do not support and sometimes even oppose teaching other religious points of view.

Repeated state court and Supreme Court decisions have ruled that creationism should not be taught alongside science in public schools. For example, the U.S. Supreme Court ruled that a Louisiana law requiring public school teachers to read a disclaimer about evolution (saying it did not address the validity of biblical accounts of the creation) to their students was unconstitutional. Nevertheless, creationists continue to fight. Many teachers themselves support offering religious views of life in science classes. A local public school board in the suburbs of Atlanta recently approved the teaching of "alternatives to evolution" in science classes only to back down after national and regional condemnation from many quarters (Figure 2.20). Studies have shown that students hold strong private views about evolution and creationism that are not easily changed by education (Lovely and Kondrick, 2008).

All the pieces of evidence for evolution, from fossils to DNA, are facts that add up to a body of evidence for a scientific theory without viable competitors. In recent years, however, challenges have come to evolution in the form of new incarnations of creationism. **Creation science** is one approach taken by fundamentalists. Recognizing that the Old Testament is not scientific evidence for life's origins, many creationists have argued in the negative, trying to refute the voluminous evidence for evolution. They ask why there are gaps in the fossil record; where, they ask, are the intermediate forms that ought to exist between *Homo erectus* and modern humans? Don't these gaps support the notion of a divine power molding our species? The fossil record is fragmentary, and it always will be because of the low odds of fossils being formed, preserved, and then found millions of years later. Creationists seize on the fragmentary nature of fossil records and attempt to portray early humans as apes and later humans as aberrant forms of modern people. In the resulting gap, they argue that God must have played his hand. As we shall see in later chapters, the fossil record for human ancestry is, in fact, quite rich, showing a progression of brain size and anatomical changes bridging the apes, early hominins, and modern humans. Creation science is a denial of science rather than science itself and has not been any more successful in the U.S. court system than were earlier approaches by creationists. In recent years other attempts have been made to resurrect creationism in American education. **Intelligent design** is one such school of thought (Insights and Advances: What Is Intelligent Design?).

Most biological scientists have deep respect for all religious beliefs. Scientists want creationist thinking to be excluded from science curriculum in government-supported schools, because that is the place where children are being trained to think like scientists. In addition, the U.S. Constitution mandates a separation of the influence of church and state in our society, so that the rights of those of other religious faiths, or those without religious faith, can be fully respected. If public schools offered courses in comparative world religion, it would be entirely appropriate to consider Judeo-Christian creation beliefs alongside those of other cultures, from Native Americans to Buddhists.

creation science A creationist attempt to refute the evidence of evolution.

intelligent design A creationist school of thought that proposes that natural selection cannot account for the diversity and complexity of form and function seen in nature.

FIGURE 2.20 A student protesting the teaching of creationism.

Origins of Evolutionary Thought

History of Evolutionary Thought

What Is Science?

- Science is a progressive, self-correcting, evidence-based way of understanding the world.
- Faith's evidence is the Bible, and it is impervious to evidence and hypothesis testing. **[pp 14–15]**

The Early Thinkers

- Carol von Linnaeus revolutionized the study of living things by classifying them according to similarities in form. **[pp 15–16]**

HYPOTHESIS → OBSERVATION / DATA / EXPERIMENT → HYPOTHESIS REJECTED, SUPPORTED, OR REFINED

(a) Lamarck's view

The earliest ancestor possessed a short trunk.

Through continued stretching of the trunk to obtain food, it grew longer and longer. Ensuing generations possessed longer trunks.

The Road to the Darwinian Revolution

- Many pre-Darwinian thinkers accepted evolution and put forward theories for the mechanism.
- Darwin was influenced by three eminent French natural historians: Comte de Buffon, Georges Cuvier, and Geoffroy Saint-Hilaire.
- Lamarck proposed that the use of a trait could influence an offspring's phenotype in the next generation. Darwin showed that change could occur across generations based only on the selective retention of some traits and the filtering out of others. **[pp 16–18]**

(b) Darwin's view

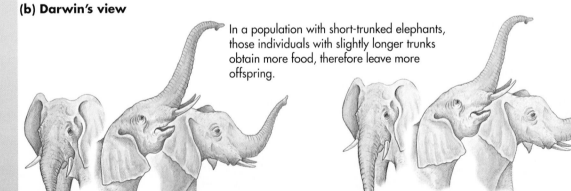

In a population with short-trunked elephants, those individuals with slightly longer trunks obtain more food, therefore leave more offspring.

Many generations later, natural selection has changed the species to an elephant that possesses a long trunk.

After Darwin

The Darwinian Revolution

- Charles Darwin spent his life thinking and writing about evolutionary change, and he developed the theory of evolution by natural selection to account for it.
- Alfred Russel Wallace was a contemporary of Darwin and codiscoverer of the theory of evolution by natural selection.
- Natural selection can occur only if a trait can be inherited, if there is variation within a population, and if there is pressure from the environment. [p 19]

Science and Creationism

- Intelligent design creationism is a recent attempt to repackage old creationist ideas in a way that argues for a divine force without calling it God. [pp 25–27]

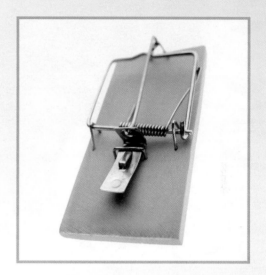

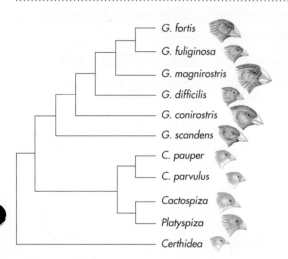

- *G. fortis*
- *G. fuliginosa*
- *G. magnirostris*
- *G. difficilis*
- *G. conirostris*
- *G. scandens*
- *C. pauper*
- *C. parvulus*
- *Cactospiza*
- *Platyspiza*
- *Certhidea*

My AnthroLab CONNECTIONS

Watch. Listen. View. Explore. Read.

MyAnthroLab is designed just for you. Each chapter features a customized study plan to help you learn and review key concepts and terms. Dynamic visual activities, videos, and readings found in the multimedia library will enhance your learning experience.

Resources from this Chapter:

Watch on **myanthrolab**

- ▶ *The Scientific Method*
- ▶ *The Life and Work of Linnaeus*

Listen on **myanthrolab**

- ▶ *Darwin's Theory of Evolution – or Wallace's?*

View on **myanthrolab**

- ▶ *Darwin's Voyage on the HMS Beagle*

Explore on **myanthrolab** In MySearchLab, enter the Anthropology database to find relevant and recent scholarly and popular press publications. For this chapter, enter the following keywords: Evolution, Darwin, Religion, History of Evolutionary Thought

Read on **myanthrolab**

- ▶ *Evolution of a Scientist* by Jerry Adler
- ▶ *Happy Birthday Linnaeus* by Richard Conniff

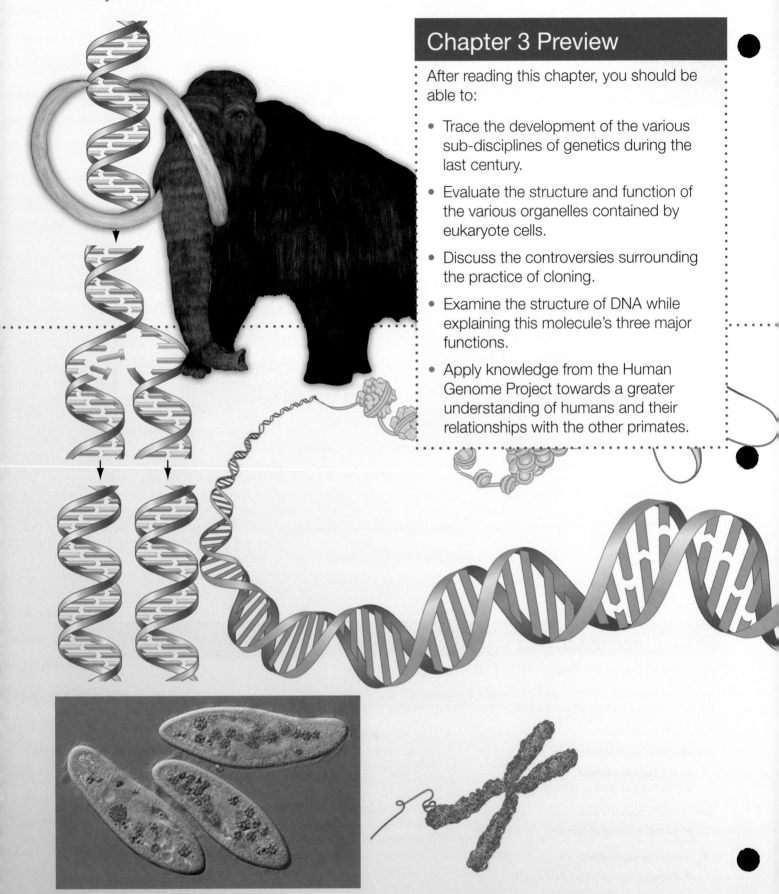

Chapter 3 Preview

After reading this chapter, you should be able to:

- Trace the development of the various sub-disciplines of genetics during the last century.

- Evaluate the structure and function of the various organelles contained by eukaryote cells.

- Discuss the controversies surrounding the practice of cloning.

- Examine the structure of DNA while explaining this molecule's three major functions.

- Apply knowledge from the Human Genome Project towards a greater understanding of humans and their relationships with the other primates.

Genetics: Cells and Molecules

The package the molecular anthropologist had been waiting for finally arrived. After taking it to an isolated part of her laboratory, she opened it carefully. Wrapped inside were ten small vials, each containing a very small piece of bone. She knew that two of the vials held bone fragments from humans who had recently died, and two contained human bone recovered from an archaeological site several thousand years old. There were also single bone samples from a chimpanzee and a baboon. But most exciting of all, the remaining four vials held bone fragments from an extinct kind of person: a Neandertal. Her job was to extract the genetic material of life—DNA—from each of these samples. If the DNA remained in good condition, the information it contained could provide vital clues about the course of human evolution over the past several hundred thousand years.

The vials were labeled only with the letters A to J. The molecular anthropologist's colleagues were well aware of some of the pitfalls in analyzing ancient DNA, and they wanted the experiment to be done blind to see whether her methods and techniques were good enough to deliver reliable results without the knowledge of the source of the samples. This was fine with her. She was thrilled with the opportunity to recover genetic material from people who had lived so long ago. As she gazed at the vials, she reflected on the DNA contained in the bones: The information (or at least some of it) that provided the recipe for these long-dead beings was still there. This was a great responsibility, she told herself, especially given that fossils were so rare, and she would have to destroy the samples to get the DNA out of them.

As she stared at the vials, lost in deep thought, her technician walked up behind her and asked, "Are those the bones?"

"Yes," she said, "they finally arrived."

"When you consider how old those Neandertal samples are," he said, "how they reach back to the dawn of humanity, to the time when people were just beginning to become people, all I can say is, we'd better not screw it up."

One of the most striking examples of the power of modern genetic science is the recovery of DNA from the fossil remains of long-dead organisms. Although the revival of extinct animals (as in the movie *Jurassic Park*) still remains in the realm of science fiction, we should nonetheless be impressed that such a delicate but critical aspect of a living organism can be recovered and observed after tens of thousands of years.

Media outlets today are filled with reports about what genetic science might someday do for us, but a concern with genetics and its applications is nothing new. Ideas about heredity can be found in all human cultures. There is no more basic observation of nature than "like begets like"—it applies to plants, animals, and people. Without some understanding of heredity, the domestication of plants and animals, which began at least 10,000 years ago, would not have been

possible. Over the past hundred years, the modern science of *genetics* has developed to give us a much better understanding of the biological processes underlying heredity. We need to understand genetics if we are to understand how evolution happens, because genetic variation provides the raw material for evolutionary change.

In this chapter, we will begin our exploration of genetics, which will continue in the following chapter with an overview of genetic science today. We will then look at the basic building block of life, the cell, and consider its structure and function. Then we will discuss DNA, the genetic material itself, and how it carries out the important functions of replication and protein synthesis. We will also look at how DNA is packaged into structures called chromosomes, which become visible during the two kinds of cell division, meiosis and mitosis, and conclude the chapter with a discussion of the molecular methods biological anthropologists use to study human and primate evolution.

The Study of Genetics

The first decade of the twentieth century was an exciting time in the history of genetics, with researchers inspired by the rediscovery in 1900 of the groundbreaking research and theories (published in 1866) of Austrian monk Gregor Mendel (see Chapter 4). The term *gene* was coined in the early 1900s by a Danish botanist named Wilhelm Johannsen (1857–1927). Neither Johannsen nor any of his colleagues at that time knew exactly what a gene was in a biochemical sense, but Johannsen thought it was a good little word to describe the "something"—the particulate unit of inheritance—that was being passed on from generation to generation. Ironically for Johannsen, although the word *gene* continues to be used, his own theories about the relationship between genes and evolution have largely been forgotten. The twentieth century saw a steady increase in our understanding of how heredity works, with the gene evolving from a theoretical unit to a well-described biochemical entity.

If a scientist says that he or she works on the genetics of an organism, that can mean several different things. Biological organisms differ greatly from one another, ranging from the very simple (such as a bacterium) to the very complex (such as a mammal). In complex animals, genetics can be approached from several different levels, depending on what aspect of the organism is of interest. These include the following:

- *Cellular and molecular genetics.* Cellular and molecular genetics involves the study of genetics at the level of the basic building blocks of bodies (cells) and at the most fundamental level of genetic transmission (the DNA molecule). Scientists are using molecular genetics to devise genetic therapies for disease or determine the precise makeup of our DNA and that of other animals.

- *Classical or Mendelian genetics.* Classical genetics, such as that done by Mendel or Johannsen, involves looking at the **pedigree** of related individuals (plant or animal) and tracking how various traits are passed from one generation to the next. Although pedigree studies go back to the beginning of genetic science, they are still essential in the age of molecular genetics. After all, we are usually not interested in the variation of the molecules per se but in the observable traits in bodies that they influence. These traits must first be identified as genetic features using pedigree analysis or a related technique.

- *Population genetics.* Biological species usually are divided into populations composed of groups of individuals who associate more with one another than with members of another population. Different populations within species almost always vary at the genetic level. By examining the genetic variation within and between populations (at both the molecular level and the level of observable traits), we can gain insights into the evolutionary history of those populations and of the species as a whole.

- *Phylogenetics.* This field is concerned with determining evolutionary relationships between species, usually by constructing tree-like diagrams that visually indicate how closely or distantly species are related to one another. Although traditionally

pedigree A diagram used in the study of human genetics that shows the transmission of a genetic trait over generations of a family.

prokaryotes Single-celled organisms, such as bacteria, in which the genetic material is not separated from the rest of the cell by a nucleus.

eukaryotes A cell that possesses a well-organized nucleus.

nucleus In eukaryotic cells, the part of the cell in which the genetic material is separated from the rest of the cell (cytoplasm) by a plasma membrane.

cytoplasm In a eukaryotic cell, the region within the cell membrane that surrounds the nucleus; it contains organelles, which carry out the essential functions of the cell, such as energy production, metabolism, and protein synthesis.

somatic cells The cells of the body that are not sex cells.

gametes The sex cells: sperm in males and eggs (or ova) in females.

stem cells Undifferentiated cells found in the developing embryo that can be induced to differentiate into a wide variety of cell types or tissues. Also found in adults, although adult stem cells are not as totipotent as embryonic stem cells.

this has been done by comparing observable traits, over the last 40 years the methods of molecular genetics have come to the forefront of phylogenetic analysis.

- *Behavioral genetics.* When one honeybee transmits information to another honeybee about the location of a flower, the behavior of both honeybees is under strong genetic control. When we look at other animals, especially animals that engage in more complex forms of behavior that may involve learning, the role of genetics is more difficult to ascertain. Behavioral genetics involves trying to understand how the behavior of animals, including humans, is influenced by genetics. It is a controversial field, especially in regard to human behavior, because human behavior is especially complex and the product of multiple influences.

Biological anthropology is concerned with the evolution of the human species in all its aspects. Because genetic variation underlies all evolutionary processes, each of the different approaches to the study of genetics listed here is relevant to understanding human evolution. The field of biological anthropology is also concerned with understanding human biological variability, which arises from both genetic and environmental influences. Biological anthropologists often work at the intersection of biological (genetic) and environmental (cultural) sciences, in their attempt to develop a more comprehensive understanding of human variation and its evolution.

The genetic system underlying the development of life on Earth is a unique and truly extraordinary thing. No simple metaphor can encompass all of its properties and functions. Although our discussion will now turn to the somewhat unromantic realm of cell structure and function, we should not cease to wonder at the exquisite machinery of heredity, which has been shaped by nearly 4 billion years of evolution.

The Cell

The basic building block of life is the cell. A cell is a microscopic organic entity in which genetic material and other structures are separated from the surrounding environment by a semipermeable membrane. Some organisms, such as bacteria or protozoans, are made up of only a single cell. Others, including humans and every other form of life that can be seen with the naked eye, are *multicellular* organisms. Complex multicellular life forms are made up of hundreds of billions of cells, although less complex forms have considerably fewer cells. The marine sea slug (*Aplysia californica*) has long been the object of scientific study in part because its central nervous system consists of a manageable 20,000 cells (Kandel et al., 2000). In contrast, the human brain, which has approximately 10 billion nerve cells, is a bit more complicated.

The basic division of life on Earth is not between single-celled and multicellular creatures but between **prokaryotes** and **eukaryotes.** The prokaryotes, which include bacteria and blue-green algae, are all single-celled organisms with no major compartments within the cell to separate the genetic material from all other components of the cell. The eukaryotes, which include all other forms of life, have a cellular anatomy that separates the genetic material from the rest of the cell in a structure known as the **nucleus.** The outer boundary of the cell is defined by a *plasma membrane,* which regulates the passage of material into and out of the cell and governs communication and coordinated activity between cells. The fluid-filled space within the cell and surrounding the nucleus is known as the **cytoplasm.** The cytoplasm contains a number of structures, known collectively as *organelles,* that help maintain the cell and carry out its functions. Complex organisms have a variety of different somatic cell types. **Somatic cells** are simply the cells of the body that are not **gametes,** or sex cells; gametes are the germ cells that are directly involved in propagation or reproduction. Humans have around 200 different types of tissues, each of which is composed of a characteristic somatic cell type (Klug, Cummings, Spencer, and Palladino, 2009). We have nerve cells (neurons), muscle cells, skin cells, bone cells, cells that secrete hormones, and so on. At the earliest stages of its development, the human embryo contains a population of cells known as **stem cells.** These cells are *totipotent,* which means they can differentiate into any of the somatic cell types found in the fetus

Watch the **Animation** "A Typical Eukaryotic Cell" on **myanthrolab**

or adult. Stem cells are also found in adults, but adult stem cells can differentiate into a more limited variety of cell types (Stewart and Pryzborski, 2002).

Stem cell research has become an important and controversial topic in recent years. Given their totipotent capacity, embryonic stem cells may be useful for treating diseases that are caused by the loss in function of specific cell types. An example of this is *Parkinson disease,* a nervous system disorder characterized by movement problems, which is caused by the loss of a certain population of cells in the brain. It is hoped that embryonic stem cells may be able to replace (i.e., take on the form and function of) the specific cells lost in Parkinson disease. At this time, stem cell scientists have had only limited success converting stem cells into the kind of cells that are lost in Parkinson disease, although progress is being made on this front (Arenas, 2010). The controversy surrounding embryonic stem cell research lies in the fact that human embryos (produced in the laboratory through in vitro fertilization) are our only source of totipotent stem cells; after the stem cells are removed, the embryos are no longer viable (Insights and Advances: Cloning Controversies). To bypass this ethical problem, much research has been devoted to recovering stem cells from adults rather than embryos. Stem cells are found in adults in certain parts of the body. For example, stem cells have been recovered from the olfactory mucosal lining the nasal passages (an area with high cell turnover) and successfully grown in the lab (Mackay-Sim and Silburn, 2008). Nasal stem cells derived from a patient's own nose could conceivably be used to replace dysfunctional cells, with no worry about tissue rejection or the ethical status of the cells used.

Cell Anatomy

Different types of cells have different anatomies that serve the functional or structural needs of a particular tissue. Nonetheless, almost all somatic cells share some basic characteristics (Figure 3.1). Although gametes share some of the characteristics of somatic cells, there are also some fundamental differences, which we'll discuss separately.

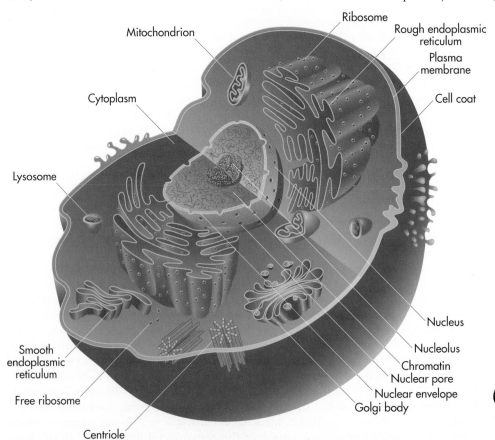

FIGURE 3.1   A typical eukaryotic cell.

insights & advances

CLONING CONTROVERSIES

On July 5, 1996, a sheep was born at the Roslin Institute in Edinburgh, Scotland. This sheep, named Dolly, was as unremarkable as any other sheep with the exception of one fact: She was a clone, an exact genetic copy of another sheep. Dolly was the first mammal ever cloned, and her birth raised many questions about the nature, and even the moral status, of cloning. If a sheep could be cloned, why not a human?

The process of cloning is straightforward but not easy (Solter, 2000). First, the nucleus of a somatic cell (which contains a copy of all of the genetic material of an individual) is carefully removed. The cell often comes not directly from the body but from a cell line that has been established in the laboratory. At the same time, the nucleus of an egg (or *oocyte*) is carefully removed, preserving the cell membrane and the cytoplasm as much as possible. The nucleus from the somatic cell is then transferred, using various methods, to the oocyte. Once the new nucleus is introduced to the egg, the egg is *activated,* which initiates the development of the embryo. In normal fertilization, the introduction of the sperm to the egg causes activation. In cloning, an electrical current applied to the egg (with the new nucleus) activates the egg. Once the embryo begins to develop, the egg can be implanted into a surrogate mother, and the pregnancy proceeds in the usual way.

Sheep, cows, mice, pigs, dogs, and several other mammals have all been cloned. For each group, the success rate of growing a clone (egg with a new nucleus) to adulthood is about 1 percent. The live-birth rate is perhaps twice as high as this, but a number of cloned newborns have problems and die before adulthood. It is likely that one barrier to successful cloning arises in the reprogramming stage after activation (Fairburn et al., 2002).

Another problem that arises with cloned individuals is that even if they survive to adulthood, they do not live as long. In a study of cloned mice, it was found that only two of twelve cloned mice lived as long as 800 days, compared with ten of

FIGURE A   Will we someday see a living mammoth?

thirteen control mice (Ogonuki et al., 2002). The famous cloned sheep Dolly lived less than 7 years, whereas sheep usually live to 11 to 12 years (Coghlan, 2003). One possible cause of the short life span of cloned individuals involves structures called *telomeres.* Telomeres are pieces of DNA that cap the ends of chromosomes. As an individual ages and cells divide, the telomeres shorten. Shortening telomere lengths are a sign of aging in cells. If cloning is done with the genome of an adult, then the short telomeres may be passed on directly to the cloned individual, resulting in accelerated aging or the development of diseases early in life that are associated with aging.

Why do we need cloning? Agricultural scientists are working on cloning in order to develop methods for efficiently propagating animals who have desired characteristics. Sexual reproduction leads to an inefficient genetic mixing (recombination or crossing over) every generation.

Other scientists see cloning as a potential tool to save endangered species, such as the black-footed ferret or the south China tiger (Piña-Aguilar et al., 2009).

The largest wild populations of our closest relatives, the chimpanzee and gorilla, declined by one-half between 1983 and 2000 (Walsh et al., 2003), and the development of efficient cloning techniques may someday help save these seriously threatened species. One of the great hopes is that even some extinct species may be resurrected via cloning. The mammoth, a relative of the elephant that lived in North America and Eurasia, survived in isolated locations as recently as several thousand years ago (Figure A). Many stunningly well-preserved mammoth remains have been recovered from the Siberian permafrost. These bodies are so intact that even the individuals' last meals can be reconstructed. Now, whether or not scientists can reconstruct an entire mammoth via cloning is another matter. Although there are many obstacles, none of them is necessarily insurmountable, so there may be cause for hope (Nicholls, 2008). As Henry Nicholls says, it was not that long ago that many thought that any kind of mammal cloning would be impossible, so "by 2059, who knows what may have returned, rebooted, to walk the Earth?"

deoxyribonucleic acid (DNA)
A double-stranded molecule that is the carrier of genetic information. Each strand is composed of a linear sequence of nucleotides; the two strands are held together by hydrogen bonds that form between complementary bases.

proteins   Complex molecules formed from chains of amino acids (polypeptide) or from a complex of polypeptides. They function as structural molecules, transport molecules, antibodies, enzymes, and hormones.

protein synthesis   The assembly of proteins from amino acids that occurs at ribosomes in the cytoplasm and is based on information carried by mRNA.

ribonucleic acid (RNA)   Single-stranded nucleic acid that performs critical functions during protein synthesis and comes in three forms: messenger RNA, transfer RNA, and ribosomal RNA.

mitochondria   Organelles in the cytoplasm of the cell where energy production for the cell takes place. Contains its own DNA.

endoplasmic reticulum (ER)   An organelle in the cytoplasm consisting of a folded membrane.

ribosomes   Structures composed primarily of RNA that are found on the endoplasmic reticulum. They are the site of protein synthesis.

nucleotide   Molecular building block of nucleic acids DNA and RNA; consists of a phosphate, sugar, and base.

base   Variable component of the nucleotides that form the nucleic acids DNA and RNA. In DNA, the bases are adenine, guanine, thymine, and cytosine. In RNA, uracil replaces thymine.

◉─⎡**Watch** the **Animation** "Nucleotide Structure of DNA" on **myanthrolab**

In most eukaryotic cells, the most prominent structure in the cytoplasm is the nucleus. The nucleus is bounded by its own membrane or envelope, which separates its contents from the rest of the cytoplasm. Within the nucleus, the hereditary material, **deoxyribonucleic acid (DNA),** is found. DNA is a double-stranded complex molecule, and the elucidation of its structure by James Watson and Francis Crick in 1953 launched the modern era in molecular genetics. Two of the primary functions of DNA are making **proteins** for the body, or **synthesis,** and cellular replication. Another complex molecule, **ribonucleic acid (RNA),** which is structurally similar to DNA but is single stranded, is also found in large quantities in the nucleus and in the cytoplasm, as well. RNA is essential for carrying out the protein synthesis function of DNA.

Several other important structures or organelles float in the cytoplasm of the cell (Figure 3.1 on page 34). These structures are like the organs of the body, and they are responsible for functions such as metabolizing nutrients and eliminating waste, energy synthesis, and protein synthesis. The **mitochondria** (sing., *mitochondrion*) are capsule-shaped organelles that number in the hundreds or thousands in each cell. Mitochondria are where a series of metabolic reactions take place, resulting in the production of an energy-rich molecule, *adenosine triphosphate (ATP),* which fuels the activities of the cell. Mitochondria are known as the "powerhouse" of the cell. Another important feature of mitochondria is that they have their own DNA, which is not contained in a nucleus and is distinct from the DNA found in the nucleus of the cell. It is likely that the mitochondria (and their plant analogs, chloroplasts) had their origins as a prokaryotic cell that evolved in symbiosis with a nucleated cell to produce the eukaryotic cell. As we will see later in the chapter, *mitochondrial DNA* (mtDNA) has proved to be a valuable tool in evolutionary and anthropological research.

The **endoplasmic reticulum (ER),** another organelle found in the cytoplasm, is a complex structure, with a folded-sheet appearance. It provides increased surface area within the cell for metabolic reactions to take place. Some of the endoplasmic reticulum has a knobby appearance; this is known as *rough endoplasmic reticulum.* The knobs are **ribosomes,** the structures in the cell responsible for protein synthesis. Ribosomes are made up of RNA molecules (ribosomal or rRNA) and proteins. The synthesis of ribosomes begins in the nucleus but can be completed only in the cytoplasm. Because completed ribosomes cannot pass through the nuclear membrane, protein synthesis always occurs in the cytoplasm.

DNA Structure and Function

Hereditary material—DNA—has to be able to do three things. First, it must be able to make copies of itself, or *replicate,* so that it can be passed from generation to generation. Second, it has to be able to make proteins, which are the most crucial components of cells. Third, it must coordinate the activity of proteins to produce bodies, or at least have some way to translate the information it carries about making bodies into growing actual bodies (i.e., development). As it turns out, the chemical structure of DNA lends itself to self-replication and to carrying the information necessary for making proteins; we will discuss these two DNA functions in detail. However, the third function—directing development—is much more complex and is beyond the scope of this text.

DNA Structure I: The Molecular Level

The structure of the DNA molecule is a double helix, resembling a ladder twisted around its central axis. The basic unit of DNA (and RNA) is a molecule called a **nucleotide** (Figure 3.2). A nucleotide consists of three parts: a sugar (deoxyribose in DNA and ribose in RNA), a phosphate group, and a nitrogenous **base,** a molecule that includes one or two rings composed of carbon and nitrogen atoms. The DNA molecule is assembled from four different nucleotide units that vary according to the base they carry. There are two classes of bases: the *purines* and the *pyrimidines.* The purines are *adenine* (A) and *guanine* (G), and the pyrimidines are *cytosine* (C)

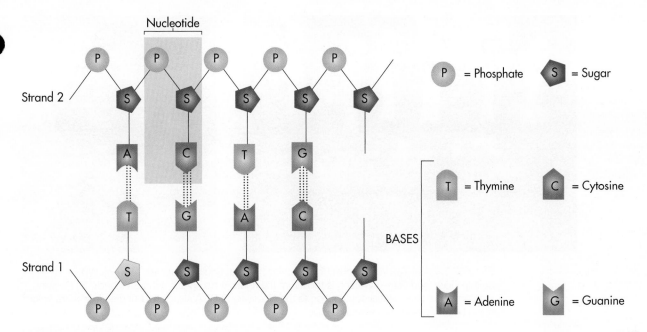

FIGURE 3.2 The nucleotide structure of DNA. The dashed lines between the A-T and C-G pairings indicate hydrogen bonds.

and *thymine* (T). DNA consists of two separate strands, corresponding to the two sides of the ladder, each of which is made up of a chain of nucleotides (Figure 3.3) The sugar of one nucleotide bonds to the phosphate group of the next one; thus, each side of the DNA ladder is composed of alternating sugar and phosphate molecules. The bases point toward the center of the ladder and form its rungs. The rungs are formed by two bases, one projecting from each side of the ladder.

In the late 1940s and early 1950s, biochemist Erwin Chargaff and his colleagues found a curious pattern in the distribution of nucleotides in DNA: The amount of A present in the sample was always about the same as the amount of T, and the amount of C equaled the amount of G. This information, along with an X-ray crystallograph of the DNA molecule provided by physical chemists Rosalind Franklin and Maurice Wilkins, helped Watson and Crick formulate their model of DNA structure (Figure 3.4 on page 38). As they surmised, the rungs of the DNA ladder are composed of two bases, and the base combinations are always A-T or C-G. For example, if there is a sequence of nucleotides on one side of the DNA that goes ATCGATCG, then on the other side of the ladder, the sequence will be TAGCTAGC. The two sides of the DNA double helix complement each other. A purine (A or G) is always opposite a pyrimidine (C or T) because purines are larger molecules than pyrimidines, and the purine–pyrimidine combination is necessary for the two sides of the ladder to maintain a constant distance from each other. The more specific A-T and C-G pairings occur because these combinations form hydrogen bonds (three for G-C and two for A-T), which hold the two sides of the ladder together. Such hydrogen bonding cannot occur between A and C or G and T. Hydrogen bonds are quite weak (compared with the chemical bonds that form between the sugars and phosphates, for example), but in a DNA molecule, thousands of nucleotides line up against thousands of other nucleotides, thus giving strength to the entire molecule.

RNA is similar to DNA except that it is a single-stranded molecule, and ribose replaces deoxyribose as the sugar in the nucleotide. In addition, thymine is not found in RNA but is replaced by another pyrimidine base, *uracil* (U), which also bonds to adenine.

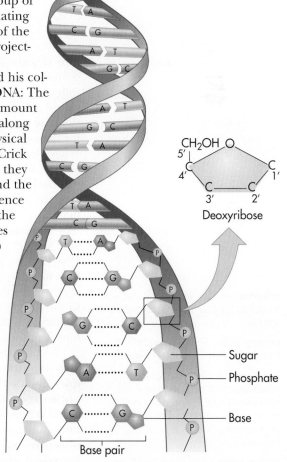

FIGURE 3.3 The double-helix structure of DNA.

FIGURE 3.4   (a) The 1962 Nobel Prize winners. Francis Crick is at far left, Maurice Wilkins is next to Crick, and James Watson is third from the right. At his right is John Steinbeck. (b) Rosalind Franklin made an essential contribution to the discovery of DNA structure, but died four years before these Nobel Prizes were awarded.

DNA Function I: Replication

A complete copy of the DNA is found in the nucleus of almost every cell of the body. When a mother cell divides into two daughter cells, other cell components can be split between the cells, but a faithful copy of the genetic material must be deposited in each daughter cell. After all, once the two cells have split from each other, they no longer have access to the genetic material of the other cell.

The very structure of the DNA molecule suggests a mechanism for its replication (Figure 3.5). Watson and Crick immediately recognized this after they determined the structure of the molecule. In simple terms, DNA replication occurs in the following manner. The DNA molecule (or a portion of it) divides into two separate strands. The two strands can be separated when the weak hydrogen bonds between the base pairs are broken. After separation, each of the strands serves as a template for the assembly, nucleotide by nucleotide, of a new complementary strand of DNA. When the process is completed, there are two copies of the mother DNA molecule, each of which is made up of one original side and one newly synthesized side.

Each step of DNA replication, from the uncoiling of the DNA double helix to "proofreading" and correcting the occasional errors that occur in the process, is mediated by a particular **enzyme.** An enzyme is a complex protein molecule in the body that mediates a chemical or biochemical reaction. One of the first enzymes associated with DNA replication to be discovered is called *DNA polymerase I* (Kornberg, 1960). If you place a single-stranded template strand of DNA in a test tube with all four nucleotide bases (A, T, C, and G) and add DNA polymerase I, you will get synthesis of double-stranded DNA. The observation of its action in the test tube led to the discovery of other DNA polymerases more critical to DNA replication (as it turned out, DNA polymerase I was more critical for proofreading DNA in prokaryotes than for DNA replication).

We will see in this chapter that the proofreading and repair of DNA are critically important because errors in DNA replication can have significant consequences for the survival of an organism. If these errors in DNA replication are not corrected, they can lead to permanent changes, or mutations, in the DNA of a cell. Mutations can alter cell function in many different ways. For example, a mutation can transform a cell, causing it to replicate at an accelerated rate; such uncontrolled cell growth is the basis of cancer. Mutations that occur in gametes can be passed from one generation to the next and may have profound effects on the biology of offspring.

enzyme   A complex protein that is a catalyst for chemical processes in the body.

hemoglobin   Protein found in red blood cells that transports oxygen.

hormone   A natural substance (often a protein) produced by specialized cells in one location of the body that influences the activity or physiology of cells in a different location.

amino acids   Molecules that form the basic building blocks of protein.

DNA Function II: Protein Synthesis

Watch the **Animation** "Schematic Representation of Protein Structure" on **myanthrolab**

Proteins are the workhorse molecules of biological organisms and the most common large molecules found in cells. Structural tissues, such as bone and muscle, are composed primarily of protein. Proteins such as **hemoglobin,** a protein molecule in red blood cells, bind to oxygen and transport it throughout the body, and other transport proteins facilitate the movement of molecules across cell membranes. Some proteins function as **hormones** and hormone receptors and regulate many bodily functions. Antibodies or immunoglobulins are proteins of the immune system, which our bodies use to fight disease or any biochemical invader. The largest class of proteins in the body are the enzymes, such as DNA polymerase I. These proteins *catalyze* (lower the activation energy of) countless biochemical reactions in cells.

Proteins are complex molecules made up of smaller molecules known as **amino acids** (Figure 3.6). Amino acids share a common chemical structure that allows them to bond to one another in long chains. There are twenty different amino

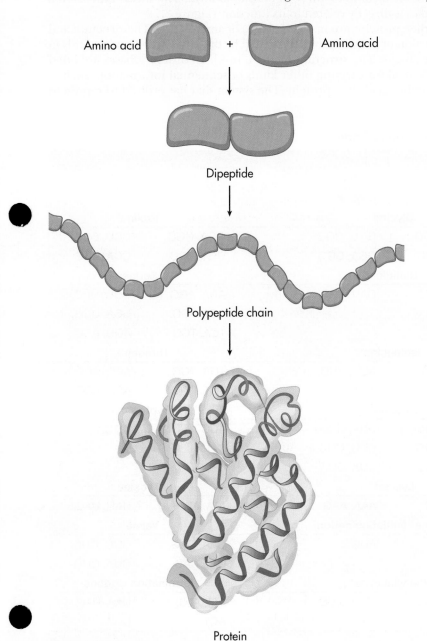

FIGURE 3.6   Schematic representation of protein structure.

= Adenine   = Thymine

= Guanine   = Cytosine

FIGURE 3.5   DNA replication.

acids that function as building blocks for proteins (Table 3.1). Of these twenty, nine are essential amino acids (Laidlaw and Kopple, 1987). This means they cannot be synthesized by the body and must be obtained from protein in the diet. The nonessential amino acids can be synthesized from the essential amino acids.

A typical protein may be made up of a chain of 200 amino acids; such a chain can also be called a **polypeptide.** Any combination of the twenty different amino acids may go into this chain. Thus the number of possible 200 amino acid proteins that may be generated from the twenty kinds of amino acids is immense (20^{200}). At a primary level, proteins differ from each other by length and by the sequence of amino acids in the polypeptide chain. Protein structures generally are much more complex than a simple linear chain, however. The sequence of amino acids in a polypeptide governs how the chain may be folded in space or how it may associate with other polypeptide chains to form a larger, complex protein. For example, the protein hemoglobin is composed of four separate polypeptide chains, which in conjunction assume a complex three-dimensional form. The three-dimensional form a protein takes is directly related to its function (Figure 3.7).

As we saw earlier, proteins are made of chains of amino acids. The structure and therefore the function of proteins are determined by the sequence of amino acids in their polypeptide chains. The structure of DNA, in which different bases are lined up in sequence, is ideal for carrying other kinds of sequential information, such as the sequence of amino acids in a protein. The system that has evolved to represent

TABLE 3.1 The Genetic Code

Amino Acid					
	DNA triplets	mRNA codons	DNA triplets	mRNA codons	DNA triplets
Alanine		**Glycine**		**Proline**	
CGA, CGT, CGC	GCU, GCC, GCA, GCG	CCA, CCG, CCT, CCC	GGU, GGC, GGA, GGG	GGA, GGG, GGT, GGC	CCU, CCC, CCA, CCG
Arginine		**Histidine***		**Serine**	
GCA, GCG, GCT, GCC, TCT, TCC	CGU, CGC, CGA, CGG, AGA, AGG	GTA, GTG	CAU, CAC	AGA, AGG, AGT, AGC, TCA, TCG	UCU, UCC, UCA, UCG, AGU, AGC
Asparagine		**Isoleucine***		**Threonine***	
TTA, TTG	AAU, AAC	TAA, TAG, TAT	AUU, AUC, AUA	TGA, TGG, TGT, TGC	ACU, ACC, ACA, ACG
Aspartic Acid		**Leucine***		**Tryptophan***	
CTA, CTG	GAU, GAC	AAT, AAC, GAA, GAG, GAT, GAC	UUA, UUG, CUU, CUC, CUA, CUG	ACC	UGG
Cysteine		**Lysine***		**Tyrosine**	
ACA, ACG	UGU, UGC	TTT, TTC	AAA, AAG	ATA, ATG	UAU, UAC
Glutamine		**Methionine* (initiation codon)**		**Valine***	
GTT, GTC	CAA, CAG	TAC	AUG	CAA, CAG, CAT, CAC	GUU, GUC, GUA, GUG
Glutamic Acid		**Phenylalanine***		**Termination Codons**	
CTT, CTC	GAA, GAG	AAA, AAG	UUU, UUC	ATT, ATC, ACT	UAA, UAG, UGA

*Essential amino acids

Source: Laidlaw and Kopple (1987).

protein amino acid sequences in the base pair sequence of DNA is known as the **genetic code.**

There are twenty different amino acids in proteins, but there are only four different bases in DNA. Obviously, there are too few bases to uniquely represent each of the 20 amino acids. If two bases in sequence were used to represent an amino acid, there would still be only sixteen possible combinations (4^2), which is not enough to represent the twenty amino acids. However, three bases in sequence produce sixty-four (4^3) unique triplet combinations—more than enough to have a unique triplet sequence of bases represent each of the twenty amino acids. The genetic code therefore consists of three-base sequences, called **codons,** each of which represents a single amino acid. There is *redundancy* in the code: Given that there are sixty-four possible codons and only twenty amino acids, most of the amino acids are represented by more than one codon. Three of the codons (termination codons) do not code for any amino acid but instead signal that the protein chain has come to an end. Another codon (TAC) represents the amino acid methionine and also typically serves as an initiation codon, signaling the beginning of a polypeptide chain.

The information to make proteins is represented, via the genetic code, in the sequence of bases in a portion of a DNA molecule. The part of a DNA molecule that contains the information for one protein (or for one polypeptide chain that makes up part of a protein) is called a **gene.** One DNA molecule can have many genes arrayed along its length. Given the triplet codons of the genetic code, a protein with 300 amino acids would need 900 bases to represent it in a gene (not including initiation or termination signals). If the first twelve bases of that gene were TGA CCA CTA CGA, the first four amino acids of the protein would be threonine, glycine, aspartic acid, and alanine. A single gene can consist of hundreds of thousands of bases, and current estimates are that human beings have no more than 20–25,000 genes in total (Clamp et al., 2008; see also http://www.ornl.gov/sci/techresources/Human_Genome/faq/genenumber.shtml). This figure surprised many scientists because it is not that many more than the 20,000 genes a simple roundworm (*C. elegans*) has, and previous estimates had placed the total number of human genes as greater than 100,000. Only a small proportion of the total DNA is actually made up of genes that code for proteins.

So how does the information to make a protein, encoded in the DNA, actually become a protein? It involves two steps, *transcription* and *translation,* along with the participation of RNA molecules with specialized functions. Transcription occurs in the nucleus of the cell, while translation (protein synthesis) occurs in the cytoplasm. Each step is mediated by specialized enzymes (Figure 3.8 on page 42).

Transcription begins when the two DNA strands split apart in a region where a gene is represented on one of the strands. The whole molecule does not split apart because only the region where the gene is located must be read. When the DNA molecule separates, the strand corresponding to the gene can serve as a template for the synthesis of a single-stranded RNA molecule. As mentioned previously, RNA is a nucleic acid, like DNA, composed of nucleotide bases (C, G, A, and U instead of T). At the site of the gene, a complementary RNA molecule is synthesized: In effect, the information of the gene is transcribed from the language of DNA to the related language of RNA. When an RNA molecule has been synthesized that corresponds to the entire gene, it separates from the DNA and exists as a free-floating, single-stranded molecule. The two strands of the DNA reattach to each other, returning the DNA to its intact double-helix structure. The free RNA molecule is called **messenger RNA (mRNA),** because it carries the information of the gene from the nucleus of the cell to the cytoplasm, which is where protein synthesis or translation takes place.

Protein synthesis occurs at ribosomes, thousands of which are found in the cytoplasm of every cell. At the ribosome, the information the mRNA carries is translated into a protein molecule. The mRNA is read at the ribosome, from beginning

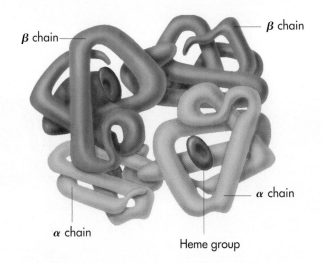

β chain · *β* chain · *α* chain · *α* chain · Heme group

FIGURE 3.7 The complex structure of the hemoglobin protein, which comprises four polypeptide chains in association with iron-based heme groups that are essential for oxygen binding and transport.

polypeptide A molecule made up of a chain of amino acids.

genetic code The system whereby the nucleotide triplets in DNA and RNA contain the information for synthesizing proteins from the twenty amino acids.

codon A triplet of nucleotide bases in mRNA that specifies an amino acid or the initiation or termination of a polypeptide sequence.

gene The fundamental unit of heredity. Consists of a sequence of DNA bases that carries the information for synthesizing a protein (or polypeptide) and occupies a specific chromosomal locus.

messenger RNA (mRNA) Strand of RNA synthesized in the nucleus as a complement to a specific gene (transcription). It carries the information for the sequence of amino acids to make a specific protein into the cytoplasm, where at a ribosome it is read and a protein molecule synthesized (translation).

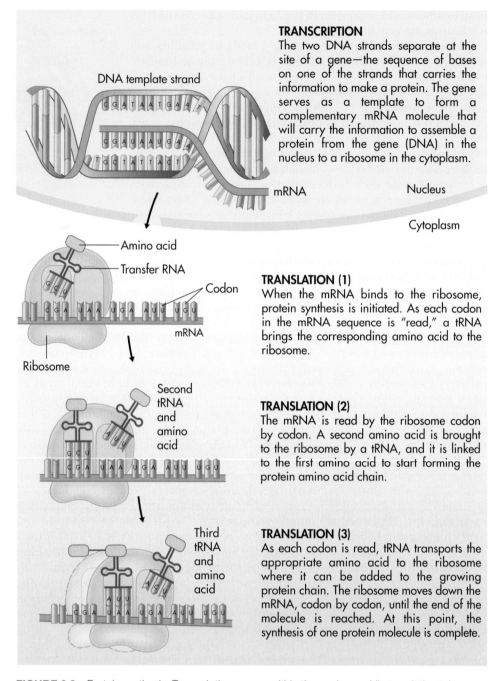

TRANSCRIPTION
The two DNA strands separate at the site of a gene—the sequence of bases on one of the strands that carries the information to make a protein. The gene serves as a template to form a complementary mRNA molecule that will carry the information to assemble a protein from the gene (DNA) in the nucleus to a ribosome in the cytoplasm.

TRANSLATION (1)
When the mRNA binds to the ribosome, protein synthesis is initiated. As each codon in the mRNA sequence is "read," a tRNA brings the corresponding amino acid to the ribosome.

TRANSLATION (2)
The mRNA is read by the ribosome codon by codon. A second amino acid is brought to the ribosome by a tRNA, and it is linked to the first amino acid to start forming the protein amino acid chain.

TRANSLATION (3)
As each codon is read, tRNA transports the appropriate amino acid to the ribosome where it can be added to the growing protein chain. The ribosome moves down the mRNA, codon by codon, until the end of the molecule is reached. At this point, the synthesis of one protein molecule is complete.

FIGURE 3.8 Protein synthesis. Transcription occurs within the nucleus, while translation takes place in the cytoplasm.

to end, two codons at a time. At this point in the process, another critical molecule, **transfer RNA (tRNA),** carries a single, specific amino acid to the ribosome so that it can be attached to the growing protein chain. The tRNA has a three-base region called the *anticodon,* which is complementary to the codon on the mRNA. When an mRNA codon (for example, ACU, which corresponds to the DNA triplet TGA) is read at the ribosome, a tRNA with the anticodon UGA temporarily aligns to the mRNA and brings the amino acid threonine into position. Then the next codon on the mRNA is read, and a second tRNA brings the appropriate amino acid into position next to the first amino acid. Once the two amino acids are next to each other, a chemical reaction requiring energy occurs, and a bond is formed between the two amino acids. The ribosome then moves down one codon, while the growing peptide chain moves in the opposite. This process continues until the entire mRNA has

transfer RNA (tRNA) RNA molecules that bind to specific amino acids and transport them to ribosomes to be used during protein synthesis.

been read, and the complete protein (or polypeptide chain) has been assembled. A single mRNA molecule can be read by several ribosomes at the same time, and thus one mRNA molecule can lead to the synthesis of several copies of the same protein molecule. (Figure 3.9).

Of course in the real world of cells, protein synthesis is a bit more complicated. One complicating factor is that in most cases, after an mRNA is formed but before it reaches the ribosome, it undergoes posttranscriptional processing. As a result, intervening sequences in the mRNA are spliced out, and the mRNA molecule is reassembled. The parts of the gene that correspond to the intervening sequences of the mRNA are called *introns,* and the parts of the gene that are actually translated into a protein (that is, they are expressed) are called *exons.* In some cases, posttranscriptional processing means that a single gene can produce different (but related) protein products depending on which intervening sequences are processed out (Figure 3.10).

The second complicating factor is that most of our DNA, as mentioned above, does not code for anything; in other words, it is not made up of exons. According to results from attempts to determine the complete human DNA structure, only about 1.1 percent of the bases are expressed (Venter et al., 2001). Another 24 percent are introns; they are transcribed into mRNA but are not translated into protein. From the organism's perspective, the rest of the DNA does not do anything but replicate. As we will see later, this noncoding DNA has important ramifications for a variety of genetic processes.

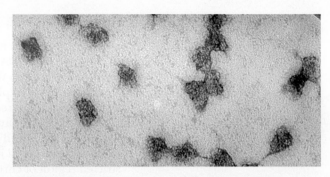

FIGURE 3.9 Electron microscope photo of an mRNA molecule being read by ribosomes (the dark, round structures) with growing polypeptide (protein) chains forming at the ribosomes as the mRNA is read.

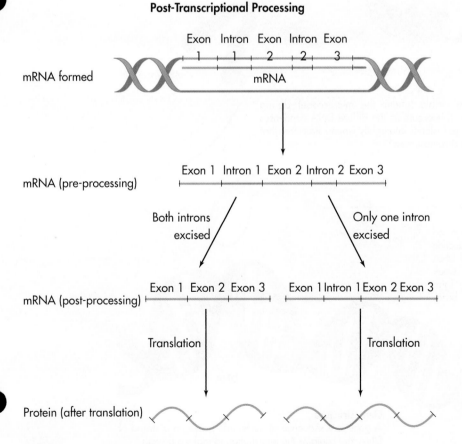

FIGURE 3.10 Processing of an mRNA molecule after transcription.

DNA Structure II: Chromosomes and Cell Division

We have 2 to 3 meters (6 to 9 feet) of DNA in the nucleus of each somatic cell. Most of the time, the DNA in these cells exists in dispersed, uncoiled strands, supported by proteins. DNA in this state is called **chromatin.** However, during the two processes of cell division or replication, **mitosis,** the chromatin condenses and coils into larger, tightly wound, discrete structures called **chromosomes** (which, like chromatin, are composed of DNA and supporting proteins) (Figure 3.11). Each chromosome has a distinctive size and shape, which are observable under the light microscope. The shape is determined in part by the position of the **centromere,** a condensed and constricted region of chromosomes, that is of critical importance during cell replication. The size is determined by the size (in numbers of base pairs) of the DNA molecule that makes up the chromosome.

Except for the gametes, or sex cells, each somatic cell in an individual's body has the same number of chromosomes. In fact, chromosome number is a constant across entire species. Most animals have two copies of each chromosome in each cell; in each of these pairs of chromosomes, one is from the mother and the other from the father. The total number of chromosomes in each somatic cell is called the **diploid number.** Sex cells have only half as many chromosomes as somatic cells

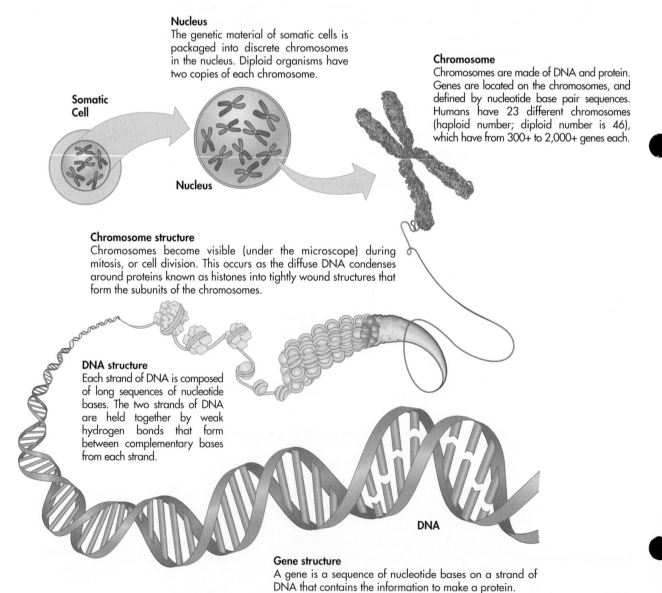

Nucleus
The genetic material of somatic cells is packaged into discrete chromosomes in the nucleus. Diploid organisms have two copies of each chromosome.

Somatic Cell

Nucleus

Chromosome
Chromosomes are made of DNA and protein. Genes are located on the chromosomes, and defined by nucleotide base pair sequences. Humans have 23 different chromosomes (haploid number; diploid number is 46), which have from 300+ to 2,000+ genes each.

Chromosome structure
Chromosomes become visible (under the microscope) during mitosis, or cell division. This occurs as the diffuse DNA condenses around proteins known as histones into tightly wound structures that form the subunits of the chromosomes.

DNA structure
Each strand of DNA is composed of long sequences of nucleotide bases. The two strands of DNA are held together by weak hydrogen bonds that form between complementary bases from each strand.

DNA

Gene structure
A gene is a sequence of nucleotide bases on a strand of DNA that contains the information to make a protein.

FIGURE 3.11   Chromosome structure.

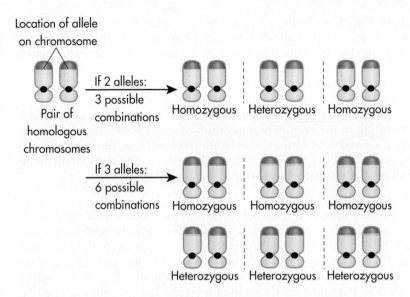

Location of allele on chromosome

Pair of homologous chromosomes

If 2 alleles: 3 possible combinations → Homozygous | Heterozygous | Homozygous

If 3 alleles: 6 possible combinations → Homozygous | Homozygous | Homozygous

Heterozygous | Heterozygous | Heterozygous

FIGURE 3.12   Homozygosity and heterozygosity.

(one copy of each chromosome), so the total number of chromosomes in a sex cell is known as the **haploid number.** In a diploid cell, the members of each pair of chromosomes are known as **homologous chromosomes.**

The genes are distributed across the chromosomes, and the locations of specific genes can be mapped to specific chromosomes (Figure 3.12). Sometimes the term **locus** (pl., *loci*) is used interchangeably with the term *gene*. More specifically, we can think of the locus as the location of a gene on a chromosome. Because somatic cells have two copies of each chromosome, they also have two copies of each gene, one at each locus. Genes come in different versions, called **alleles.** For example, there might be a gene for eye color, but it could have two alleles, one for brown and one for blue; the locus of this gene could be mapped to a specific chromosome. A real example involves the ABO blood type system (which is discussed in more detail in Chapter 4). At that locus (which is on chromosome 9), there are three possible alleles, called A, B, and O that determine blood type. When an individual has the same allele for a gene at each locus on each chromosome, this individual is called **homozygous** for that gene. If the individual has different alleles of the gene at each locus, then he or she is **heterozygous** for that gene. When we consider that each individual has thousands of genes, each of which may be represented by several alleles, it is easy to see that the number of possible different combinations of alleles is enormous.

Mitosis   Mitosis, the process whereby a somatic cell replicates, leads to the formation of two identical daughter cells. Mitosis is the basis of all cell proliferation, which can occur when an organism grows, during healing, or during any physiological process in which new cells are needed to replace the loss of cells (Figure 3.13 on page 47).

The ongoing process of cell division and nondivision sometimes is known as the *cell cycle*. The cell cycle can be divided into several stages. The *interphase* is the stage of a cell's life when it is not involved in mitosis; instead, most of its energies are devoted to metabolism and growth. Although the interphase is not part of mitosis, an important premitotic activity occurs toward the end of interphase: The DNA is replicated in preparation for mitosis. During interphase, DNA is packaged into chromatin, and discrete chromosomes are not visible.

The first stage of mitosis is the *prophase*. Three important things happen during the prophase:

1. The nuclear envelope breaks down and disappears.
2. The diffuse chromatin fibers condense and begin to form dense chromosomes. The individual chromosomes actually are doubled chromosomes, composed of two identical sister *chromatids*.
3. The polar orientation of the cell for the division into two daughter cells is established. The prophase often takes up at least half of the process of mitosis.

chromatin   The diffuse form of DNA as it exists during the interphase of the cell cycle.

mitosis   Somatic cell division in which a single cell divides to produce two identical daughter cells.

chromosome   Discrete structure composed of condensed DNA and supporting proteins.

centromere   Condensed and constricted region of a chromosome. During mitosis and meiosis, location where sister chromatids attach to one another.

diploid number   Full complement of paired chromosomes in a somatic cell. In humans, the diploid number is 46 (23 pairs of different chromosomes).

haploid number   The number of chromosomes found in a gamete, representing one from each pair found in a diploid somatic cell. In humans, the haploid number is 23.

homologous chromosomes   Members of the same pair of chromosomes (or autosomes). Homologous chromosomes undergo crossing over during meiosis.

locus   The location of a gene on a chromosome. The locus for a gene is identified by the number of the chromosome on which it is found and its position on the chromosome.

alleles   Alternative versions of a gene. Alleles are distinguished from one another by their different effects on the phenotypic expression of the same gene.

homozygous   Having the same allele at the loci for a gene on both members of a pair of homologous chromosomes (or autosomes).

heterozygous   Having two different alleles at the loci for a gene on a pair of homologous chromosomes (or autosomes).

After prophase, the chromosomes migrate to the equatorial center of the cell, where they line up in an orderly fashion. When they have reached this position, the cell is in the *metaphase*. The *anaphase* follows the metaphase as the sister chromatids split apart and migrate to opposite ends of the cell. This is usually the shortest part of mitosis. Once the anaphase is completed, there will be a complete diploid complement of *daughter chromosomes* at each end of the cell.

The final stage of mitosis is the *telophase*. During this period, the cytoplasm is split into two, resulting in the complete separation of the two daughter cells, each with its daughter chromosomes. Once the separation is complete, the chromosomes uncoil into chromatin, and the nucleus of the cell forms around the genetic material. The new cell then enters interphase, restarting the cell cycle.

👁 **Watch** the **Animation**
"Mitosis and Meiosis"
on **myanthrolab**

Meiosis   The process of meiosis (Figure 3.13) leads to the formation of the gametes (sperm in males and eggs in females), which are cells that have the haploid number of chromosomes (that is, one copy of each chromosome as opposed to the two copies of each found in diploid somatic cells). Meiosis occurs only in the testes of males and the ovaries of females. Like mitosis, meiosis begins with diploid cells, but through an additional cell division, haploid gametes eventually result. The sex cells must be haploid because when the sperm and egg unite to form the **zygote** (fertilized egg), the resulting zygote should reestablish the diploid number of chromosomes.

The first meiotic prophase is similar in some ways to prophase in mitosis but with some critical differences. It is similar in that the replicated DNA condenses into chromosomes, and sister chromatids form. However, unlike in mitosis, in meiosis the double-stranded homologous chromosomes pair up, forming units that are in effect made up of four chromatids (i.e., two pairs of sister chromatids); this unit is known as a *tetrad*. At this stage, an important event called **crossing over** occurs. Crossing over is the process whereby genetic material is exchanged between pairs of homologous chromosomes, resulting in a **recombination** of alleles on the chromosomes.

Crossing over is extremely important because it enables new genetic combinations (although not new genes) to be assembled along each chromosome. Crossing over increases the available genetic variability in a population, thereby increasing the amount of variability available for natural selection to act on. The rate of evolution in sexually reproducing species therefore is much faster than in asexually reproducing species. Without sexual reproduction, it is likely that the complexity of plant and animal life on Earth could never have been achieved. Only mutation can provide wholly novel new variants in a population, but the new combinations of genes that arise from sexual reproduction are of critical importance in evolution by natural selection.

After crossing over occurs in the first meiotic prophase, a metaphase follows, and tetrads align along the equator of the cell. During the *meiotic division* (also known as the *reduction division*), the chromatid tetrads split, and a double-stranded chromosome is sorted into each daughter cell. This is very different from what happens in mitosis. In mitosis, the doubled chromosomes separate so that each daughter cell winds up with one paternally derived chromosome and one maternally derived chromosome, just as the mother cell had. In the first meiotic division, one daughter cell has two copies of the maternal chromosome, and the other has two copies of the paternal chromosome (although after crossing over, of course, they are no longer identical to the parental chromosomes).

Once the first cell division is complete and after another round of prophase and metaphase, the *second meiotic cell division* occurs. During this division, the paired chromatids split—as they do in mitosis—resulting in a total of four haploid gametes (two from each of the two daughter cells of the first meiotic division) with only one copy of each chromosome.

Different Kinds and Numbers of Chromosomes   As mentioned previously, chromosomes come in different sizes and shapes, and different species have different numbers of chromosomes. During mitosis, when the chromosomes become visible, it is possible to study the chromosomes by taking a photograph of them through a microscope. From such a photograph, a **karyotype** of an individual can be made

meiosis   Cell division that occurs in the testes and ovaries that leads to the formation of sperm and ova (gametes).

zygote   A fertilized egg.

crossing over   Exchange of genetic material between homologous chromosomes during the first prophase of meiosis; mechanism for genetic recombination.

recombination   The rearrangement of genes on homologous chromosomes that occurs during crossing over in meiosis. Source of variation arising out of sexual reproduction; important for increasing rates of natural selection.

karyotype   The complete chromosomal complement of an individual; usually based on a photograph of the chromosomes visualized under the microscope.

autosomes   Any of the chromosomes other than the sex chromosomes.

sex chromosomes   In mammals, chromosomes X and Y, with XX producing females and XY producing males.

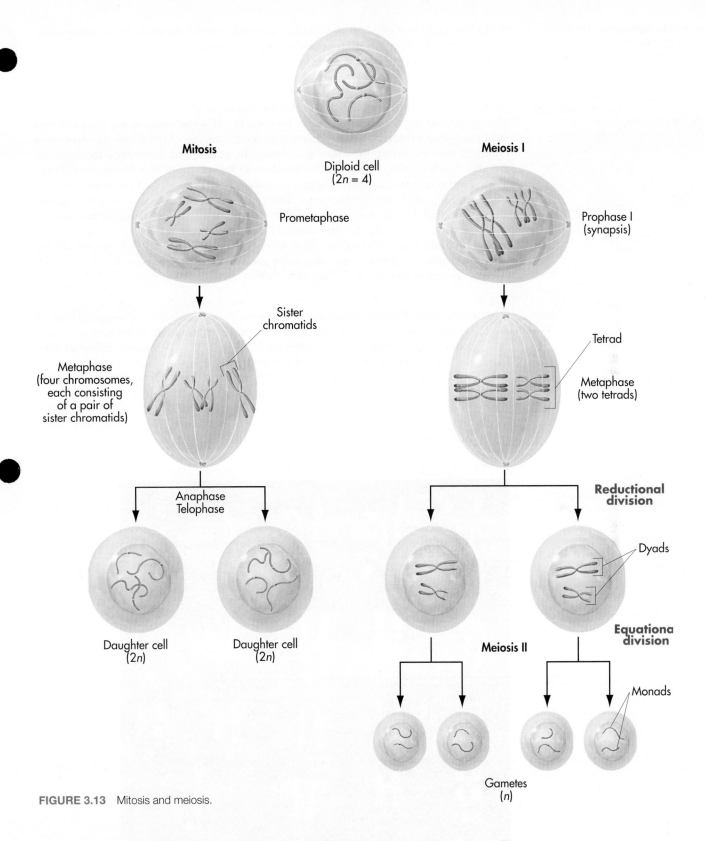

FIGURE 3.13 Mitosis and meiosis.

(Figure 3.14 on page 48). A karyotype shows all the chromosomes in a single somatic cell. Humans have twenty-three different chromosomes (haploid number) and a diploid number of forty-six. Of the forty-six chromosomes in humans, forty-four can be distributed into twenty-two homologous pairs. These are called **autosomes.** The twenty-third pair consists of the **sex chromosomes.** In mammals, the sex chromosomes are labeled X and Y, and the autosomes are numbered (in humans, from 1 to 22). Male mammals have one

nondisjunction error The failure of homologous chromosomes (chromatids) to separate properly during cell division. When it occurs during meiosis, it may lead to the formation of gametes that are missing a chromosome or have an extra copy of a chromosome.

X chromosome and one Y chromosome, whereas females have two X chromosomes. Because females have only X chromosomes, it is the sex cells of the male, who can produce gametes with one X and one Y chromosome, that determine the sex of the offspring.

Even closely related species can have different numbers of chromosomes. In chimpanzees, our closest living biological relatives, the haploid number is twenty-four chromosomes, and the diploid number is forty-eight. At some point since humans and chimpanzees last shared a common ancestor, the packaging of DNA into chromosomes changed. As it turns out, the other great apes, the gorilla and orangutan, to whom we are also closely related, have the same number of chromosomes as a chimpanzee. Thus, along our unique evolutionary lineage, humans had a fusion of two chromosomes, resulting in the loss of one chromosome. Note that this does not mean a reduction in the amount of DNA. Chromosomes are indicative only of the packaging, not the amount, of DNA. We do not know whether the fusion of these two chromosomes was a critical event in human evolutionary history, but these kinds of rare genetic events can potentially be very informative, especially as scientists learn to combine DNA sequence data with knowledge of chromosome evolution (Froenicke, 2005).

Chromosomal Abnormalities In humans, individuals with abnormalities in chromosome number usually suffer from a range of medical and developmental problems; chromosomal abnormalities probably are also a common cause of miscarriages. **Nondisjunction errors** that occur during meiosis result in the misdistribution of chromosomes to the sex cells (that is, one receives both copies of the chromosomes and the sister cell receives none). If fertilization occurs with either of these sex cells, this leads to an inappropriate number of chromosomes in the fertilized egg, or zygote. Two common kinds of nondisjunction errors are *monosomy*, which occurs when one chromosome in a pair is absent, and *trisomy*, which occurs

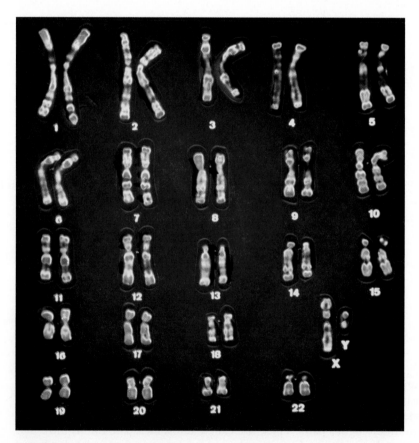

FIGURE 3.14 A human karyotype.

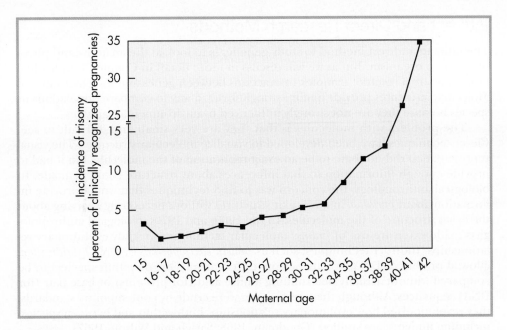

FIGURE 3.15 Increased risk of trisomy with maternal age.

when there is an extra chromosome, resulting in three copies of the chromosomes rather than a pair. An example of monosomy is *Turner syndrome*. Females with Turner syndrome have only a single X sex chromosome (represented as XO) rather than XX or XY. The absence of the second X chromosome leads to a delay or absence of sexual maturation, small physical stature, delayed mental maturation, and other physical abnormalities.

An example of trisomy, *Down syndrome*, or *trisomy 21*, occurs when an individual has three rather than two copies of chromosome 21. Individuals with Down syndrome share a constellation of features, including a common facial anatomy and head shape, short stature, a furrowed tongue, and short, broad hands with characteristic palm and fingerprint patterns. People with Down syndrome also have problems with physical and mental development, and they are also prone to heart disease and leukemia.

It is important to keep in mind that for most chromosomes, monosomy or trisomy is incompatible with life. Down syndrome and Turner syndrome are the exceptions rather than the rule. The rate for Down syndrome is only 0.05 percent in pregnancies in 20-year-old women but rises to 3 percent in women over 45. When you consider that all of the chromosomes are vulnerable to trisomy, it is easy to see why it is so difficult for older women to produce a viable zygote (Figure 3.15). Studies show that about 2 percent of all recognized pregnancies (including those that result in miscarriage) in women 25 years or younger are trisomic for some chromosome; this compares with 35 percent in pregnancies in women over 40 years (Hassold and Hunt, 2001). Nondisjunction errors obviously are more common with increasing maternal age; evidence of an effect of increasing paternal age is not strong (Martin, 2008).

Molecular Tools for Bioanthropological Research

Understanding genetics is critical to understanding evolutionary phenomena such as adaptation and the biological histories of populations and species. Over the years, biological anthropologists have used a variety of molecular genetics techniques to study the natural history of people and other primate species. The application of these techniques to anthropological problems and issues will be considered in later chapters.

Indirect and Direct Research Methods

The ultimate indirect method to study genetics is to look at the anatomy and physiology of an organism. But as we will discuss in more detail in Chapter 4, individual organisms are a result of complex interactions between genes and the environment. Molecular structures provide a more straightforward way to compare populations or species because they are not strongly influenced by environmental variables.

The problem with molecules is that they are very small and difficult to see. Clever techniques have been developed to visualize molecular structures. The visual representation did not have to be an exact replication of the molecule, but it had to provide enough information so that inferences about structure could be made. In biological anthropology, the concern was to find techniques that would provide information about *variation* in molecular structures without necessarily worrying about the exact structure of the molecules. In the 1960s and 1970s, biological anthropologists made extensive use of *indirect* molecular techniques to study evolutionary relationships. Indirect techniques, such as *protein electropheresis* or *DNA hybridization*, allowed protein or DNA structures from different species (or within species) to be compared without actually determining amino acid (for proteins) or base pair (for DNA) sequences. Although these techniques were crude by contemporary standards, they revolutionized how evolutionary relationships both within and between species, including humans, are studied (Goodman, 1963; Sarich and Wilson, 1967).

In recent years, advances in molecular genetics techniques have allowed the direct sequencing of proteins and DNA. Although *protein sequencing* has been used for evolutionary research, *DNA sequencing*—determining the actual base sequence of a gene or stretch of DNA—is by far the most widely used tool in molecular anthropology today. DNA sequencing provides the most direct kind of evidence about the genetic makeup of individuals and species, and it can yield insights about both coding and noncoding regions. The automated methods currently used to directly sequence DNA are beyond the scope of this text, but it is important to know that the development of these methods in the 1970s and 1980s made possible much of the "molecular revolution" of the end of the twentieth century.

View "Human Genome Project" on **myanthrolab**

One of the most spectacular achievements of the molecular revolution has been the sequencing of the entire human **genome**—the sum total of all the genes carried by an individual (International Human Genome Sequencing Consortium, 2001). The Human Genome Project was initiated in the late 1980s with the then-outlandish goal of determining the sequence of all the bases in a single human genome. With increasingly sophisticated and cost-effective DNA-sequencing technology becoming available, the goal of sequencing the human genome—and the genomes of many other organisms—is now achievable. The Human Genome Project has been a massive undertaking, involving thousands of researchers, working in dozens of dedicated research centers throughout the world. But the payoff in scientific terms is potentially immense for the study of development, physiology, medicine, and evolution. The sequencing of the chimpanzee genome (Chimpanzee Sequencing and Analysis Consortium, 2005) demonstrates the potential value of these genomic undertakings for evolutionary studies. We now know that because humans and chimpanzees last shared a common ancestor (5–7 million years ago), over 40 million genetic differences have accumulated between the species. This may sound like a lot, but this number should be considered in the context of the billions of base pairs that make up the human or chimpanzee genomes.

PCR, Mitochondrial DNA, and Ancient DNA

In addition to automated DNA sequencing, the other essential tool of the molecular revolution is a technique known as the **polymerase chain reaction (PCR)** (Mullis, 1990). The key feature of PCR is that an extraordinarily small amount of DNA can be used to make millions or even billions of copies of a specific DNA segment. The technique depends on a specialized enzyme, called *Taq polymerase,* which causes the extension of a single strand of DNA (if free nucleotide base pairs are available). Once the *target sequence,* the specific region of DNA that is to be amplified, has been identified,

genome   The sum total of all the genes carried by an individual.

polymerase chain reaction (PCR) Method for amplifying DNA sequences using the Taq polymerase enzyme. Can potentially produce millions or billions of copies of a DNA segment starting from a very small number of target DNA.

two *primers* must be designed, one for each end of the sequence. These primers are short segments of DNA (about fifteen to twenty base pairs long), which are necessary for the Taq polymerase to begin extension of the two DNA strands. They attach to the DNA at each end of the target sequence because they are designed to complement the DNA sequence in that region.

Here's how the process works (Figure 3.16). DNA containing the target sequence, base pair nucleotides (A,T,C, and G), the two primers, and Taq polymerase are placed in a test tube that is then heated to the point where the DNA strands separate—about 95 degrees Celsius. After this, the solution is cooled to about 55 degrees Celsius. This allows the primers to attach to the single DNA strands at the positions flanking the DNA segment of interest. The temperature is then raised to somewhere around 75 degrees Celsius. At this temperature, the Taq polymerase works to extend the target segment's DNA strands starting at each of the primer positions. Copies of the target DNA are being made during this step in the process. This heating-cooling-heating cycle is then repeated twenty-five or thirty times. Every newly synthesized strand of DNA becomes a target for copying in each new cycle, which results in an exponential increase in the number of target DNA sequences in the reaction tube.

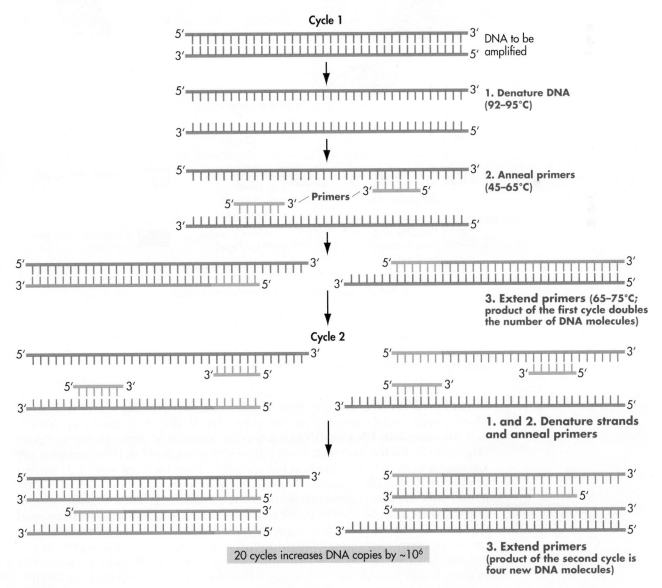

FIGURE 3.16 The polymerase chain reaction (PCR).

mitochondrial DNA (mtDNA)
Small loop of DNA found in the mitochondria. It is clonally and maternally
inherited.

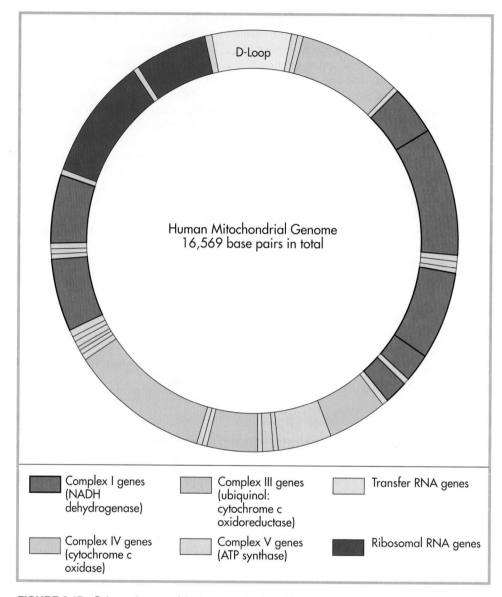

Complex I genes (NADH dehydrogenase)

Complex III genes (ubiquinol: cytochrome c oxidoreductase)

Transfer RNA genes

Complex IV genes (cytochrome c oxidase)

Complex V genes (ATP synthase)

Ribosomal RNA genes

FIGURE 3.17   Schematic map of the human mitochondrial genome.

PCR allows the recovery of DNA sequences from miniscule samples, such as a single hair or dried saliva on an envelope obtained at a crime scene. In biological anthropology, PCR often is used to study evolutionary patterns in mitochondrial DNA and nuclear DNA recovered from bone, or *ancient DNA*.

Mitochondrial DNA The mitochondria are the organelles found in cells in which energy metabolism occurs, but as you recall, they have their own DNA as well. **Mitochondrial DNA (mtDNA)** is a circular structure of about 16,600 base pairs (Figure 3.17). Each mitochondrion may have several copies of its DNA, and each cell can have hundreds or thousands of mitochondria; thus, each cell also has hundreds or thousands of mtDNA copies. Although there are several genes in the mtDNA genome, there are also regions that do not code for anything. These regions (such as one called the D-loop) tend to evolve quickly, so they are highly variable. Because of this, they are very useful for looking at evolutionary patterns between closely related species or even between populations within a single species. These regions are so variable that families may have mutations or sequences specific to them. Sequences of these highly variable mtDNA regions, therefore, are very important in forensic investigation because they allow otherwise unidentifiable pieces of tissue or bodily fluids to be linked to a known individual (provided an appropriate DNA sample from the individual or a relative is available for comparison).

There are two important things to keep in mind about mtDNA. First, unlike nuclear DNA, mtDNA has no exchange (crossing over) between maternal and paternal DNA as it is passed down through the generations. Instead, mtDNA is passed on clonally from generation to generation. Second, mtDNA is passed on only through the mother because an offspring's mtDNA comes from the mitochondria floating in the cytoplasm of the egg. The mitochondria of the sperm are concentrated in the tail region of the cell and are not injected into the egg with the nuclear DNA at fertilization. All of your mtDNA came from your mother, and if you are a male, you are an mtDNA evolutionary dead end. The Y chromosome acts as the male version of the mtDNA: It undergoes minimal recombination and is passed on only through males. It is also being used in evolutionary studies of populations.

Ancient DNA Bones up to 100,000 years old can yield DNA. PCR is essential for recovering ancient DNA sequences, because the DNA in bone is often fragmentary or degraded. In most cases, the "easiest" DNA to amplify from bone is mtDNA. Because there are thousands of copies of mtDNA per cell, there are potentially many more individual copies of mtDNA than nuclear DNA in bony remains, which may be used as a target for amplification (Figure 3.18).

The recovery of DNA, especially nuclear DNA, in bone often involves pushing the PCR technique to its limits, so contamination is a major worry. If the PCR primers find complementary DNA sequences to attach to, amplification of DNA will occur, even if it is not the target sequence. This is especially a concern if one is looking at human bones because the experimenters themselves become the source of contamination: The primers designed to work on the ancient sample might also

(•• Listen to the **Podcast** "5,300 Year-Old Mummy Has No Human Descendants" on **myanthrolab**

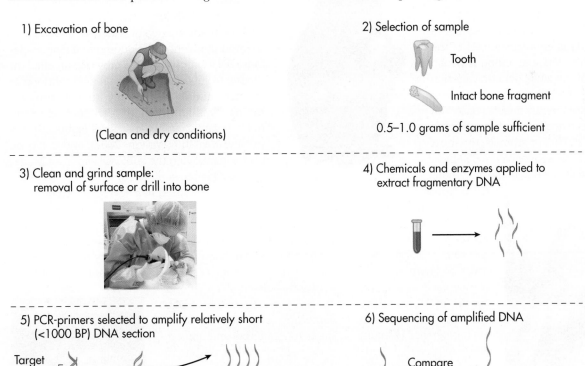

1) Excavation of bone

(Clean and dry conditions)

2) Selection of sample

Tooth

Intact bone fragment

0.5–1.0 grams of sample sufficient

3) Clean and grind sample: removal of surface or drill into bone

4) Chemicals and enzymes applied to extract fragmentary DNA

5) PCR-primers selected to amplify relatively short (<1000 BP) DNA section

Target in intact DNA

DNA fragments from ancient DNA

6) Sequencing of amplified DNA

Compare

Ancient

Contemporary

FIGURE 3.18 Recovery process of ancient DNA.

INNOVATIONS

DNA Barcoding

The taxonomic system we use to identify and name species dates back nearly 300 years. The pioneer taxonomists such as Ray and Linnaeus (see Chapter 2) invented this system with no knowledge about evolution or the mechanisms of genetics. Today, we know a considerable amount about these areas, and some biologists argue that we could make better use of this knowledge as we try to organize and understand the world's biodiversity.

One proposal to modernize taxonomy involves something known as *DNA barcoding* (see the website for the Consortium for the Barcode of Life, (http://www.barcodeoflife.org). Unlike the grocery store, where barcodes are arbitrarily assigned to different items, in DNA barcoding, the source of the identifying code is an intrinsic part of the organism's genome. DNA barcoding is based on the premise that, because genetic variation between species exceeds that within species, it should be possible to identify species based on a short, standardized sequence of the genome (Hajibabaei et al., 2007). For animals, the most commonly used genetic sequence is a 650-base pair fragment found at one end of the mitochondrial gene cytochrome oxidase I.

What are the advantages of using something like DNA barcoding? There are tens of millions of eukaryotic species in the world, the vast majority of which are unidentified (Waugh, 2007). With a standardized, easily reproducible system of biologically meaningful identification, the first step toward understanding species would be significantly streamlined. Naturally enough, critical taxonomic features vary widely among divergent groups of animals. The DNA barcode system provides a common basis for species identification.

It is easy to see where DNA barcoding would be of great value in the identification of insect and microorganismal species (Hajibabaei et al., 2007). The vast majority of these species have yet to be identified, and they are easier to collect than to analyze. Identifying these species is not just a matter of "stamp collecting," however. Understanding species diversity at the microbiotic level is essential for understanding entire ecosystems and how they may be changing in the face of human activity. The taxonomy of larger animals may also benefit from the barcode approach. Indeed, it is only within the last 10 years that molecular evidence has been found to support the claim that there are two distinct species of African elephant (Roca et al., 2005). DNA barcoding may be useful in identifying similar issues in other groups of large animals. Within primates, understanding species diversity within genera such as *Papio* (baboons) and *Macaca* (macaques) is complicated by the existence of hybrids between different species and the maintenance of widely dispersed and isolated populations belonging to a single species. DNA barcoding also provides an efficient means to investigate species designations in extinct animals known only from scrappy remains. This has already been applied to the many recently extinct species of flightless birds in New Zealand (Waugh, 2007), and could be useful in studying the subfossil lemurs of Madagascar (Orlando et al., 2008).

DNA barcoding has several shortcomings. There is no independent way of determining how much DNA change is "enough" to identify a new species; a variety of genetic segments will likely have to be used if all life forms are going to be barcoded. Some critics worry that barcoding conveys an impression of species as fixed and static entities with some essential single quality. But the advocates of DNA barcoding make it clear that it is a taxonomic tool and not a replacement for classic taxonomy. It is meant to be used in conjunction with knowledge about anatomy, behavior, and physiology. DNA barcoding is just one of the many ways that the ready availability of DNA sequencing technology is changing the biological sciences.

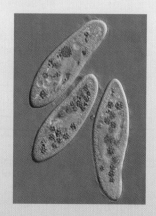

work on the researcher's DNA. Given the sensitivity of PCR, even a single molecule of contamination can distort the results of an experiment. Some molecular archaeologists specialize in looking at the ancient DNA from domestic animals, such as cows, and commensal animals, such as rats, which inevitably share living spaces with humans in many parts of the world (Matisoo-Smith et al., 1998). This tends to limit the possibility of contamination, at least from the excavators or the laboratory workers.

Despite these shortcomings, recovery of DNA from one extinct hominid species, the Neandertals, has shed new light on our evolutionary relationship with this close cousin of modern humans (see Chapter 12). Researchers are always working on new techniques to improve the yield of ancient DNA. One of the most exciting developments involves genetically engineering new versions of the Taq polymerase enzyme, which are more efficient at amplifying heavily damaged or fragmentary DNA (Shapiro, 2008). Although the dream of reviving extinct species is still a long way from being fulfilled, advances in ancient DNA technology are providing exciting insights into the genetic structures of some ancient organisms.

In this chapter, we have reviewed some of the most fundamental aspects of life on Earth: DNA, cells, proteins, and the basics of cell growth and organismal reproduction. Although humans may in some ways be unique among our planet's life forms, molecular genetics reaffirms the evolutionary continuity between us and other organisms, ranging from bacteria to plants to all other animals.

Genetics: Cells and Molecules

Genetics

The Study of Genetics

- There are several kinds of genetic study: cellular and molecular genetics, classical or Mendelian genetics, population genetics, phylogenetics, behavioral genetics. **[pp 32–33]**

The Cell

- The cell is the basic building block of all life—prokaryotes versus eukaryotes.
- All complex life forms are eukaryotes.
- Within the body, somatic cells are the cells of the body that are not gametes (sex cells).
- Stem cells are totipotent cells that can develop into different cell types. **[pp 33–34]**

Cell Anatomy

- Although cells vary tremendously according to function, they have a basic shared anatomy.
- The nucleus sits within cytoplasm and houses the genetic material, deoxyribonucleic acid (DNA).
- Another nucleic acid, ribonucleic acid (RNA), is also essential for cell function.
- The organelles of the cell work to maintain the cell and are analogous to the organs of the body. **[pp 34–36]**

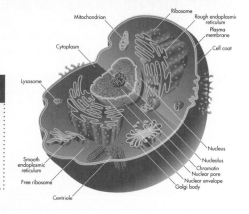

DNA

DNA Structure I: The Molecular Level

- The basic unit of DNA and RNA is the nucleotide, which consists of a phosphate, base, and sugar.
- There are four bases in DNA, and bonds formed between guanine–cytosine and adenine–thymine give the molecule its distinctive double-stranded structure.
- RNA is single-stranded and has the same bases as DNA, except thymine is replaced by uracil (which also binds to adenine). **[pp 36-38]**

DNA Function I: Replication

- A major function of DNA is to make copies of itself, which allows hereditary information to be carried from generation to generation.
- The mechanism of DNA replication was determined by Watson and Crick at the time of their discovery of DNA structure.
- The double-helix structure of DNA provides a template for the synthesis of identical copies of the molecule. **[p 38]**

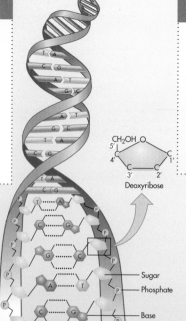

▨ = Adenine ▨ = Thymine
▨ = Guanine ▨ = Cytosine

DNA Function II: Protein Synthesis

- Genes are defined by the sequence of bases in a stretch of DNA—they carry the information necessary to synthesize proteins.
- Proteins are essential molecules in the body that perform a wide range of functions.
- The genetic code converts the information of the sequence of bases in a gene into the sequence of amino acids in a protein.
- There are two steps in protein synthesis: Transcription occurs in the cytoplasm and involves the synthesis of a strand of messenger RNA (mRNA); translation occurs in the cytoplasm, where the mRNA message is read at ribosomes and a protein is assembled. **[pp 39–43]**

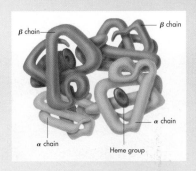

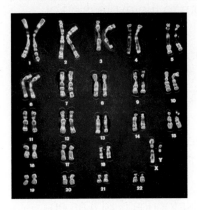

DNA Structure II: Chromosomes and Cell Division

- The DNA in nucleus is packaged into (relatively) large structures called chromosomes.
- In somatic cells, there are two copies of each of the 22 homologous chromosomes, plus the sex chromosomes (females are XX, and males are XY); in gametes, there is only one copy of each chromosome.
- Mitosis is the process of normal somatic cell division, in which the diploid chromosome number is maintained in each daughter cell.
- Meiosis is the process of cell division; in sex cells are created with only one copy of each chromosome (haploid).
- During meiosis, crossing over leads to novel rearrangements of genetic material.
- Nondisjunction errors during meiosis can lead to a variety of chromosomal abnormalities that cause clinical problems (such as Down syndrome). **[pp 44–49]**

Molecular Tools for Bioanthropological Research

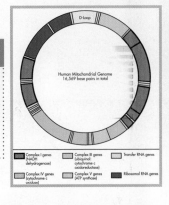

Indirect and Direct Methods

- In the past, researchers used various methods to measure variability at the molecular level, but today new technologies make it possible to study DNA sequence differences at the individual or species level.
- The entire genomes of many species are being sequenced, following the advent of the Human Genome Project. **[p 50]**

PCR, Mitochondrial DNA, and Ancient DNA

- The polymerase chain reaction (PCR) is a method for the amplification of minute quantities of DNA.
- PCR makes possible the recovery of ancient DNA from bone or fossil material, up to about 100,000 years old, provided that preservation conditions were adequate. **[pp 50–55]**

My AnthroLab CONNECTIONS

Watch. Listen. View. Explore. Read.

MyAnthroLab is designed just for you. Each chapter features a customized study plan to help you learn and review key concepts and terms. Dynamic visual activities, videos, and readings found in the multimedia library will enhance your learning experience.

Resources from this Chapter:

Watch on **myanthrolab**

- ▶ *A Typical Eukaryotic Cell*
- ▶ *Nucleotide Structure of DNA*
- ▶ *Schematic Representation of Protein Structure*
- ▶ *Mitosis and Meiosis*

View on **myanthrolab**

- ▶ *Human Genome Project*

Explore on **myanthrolab** In MySearchLab, enter the Anthropology database to find relevant and recent scholarly and popular press publications. For this chapter, enter the following keywords: genetics, DNA, cell, chromosome, protein

Read on **myanthrolab**

- ▶ *Did Life Begin in Ice?* by Douglas Fox
- ▶ *Regulating Evolution* by Sean B. Carroll, Benjamin Prud'homme, and Nicolas Gompe
- ▶ *Evolution Encoded* by Stephen J. Freedland and Laurence D. Hurst

Chapter 4 Preview

After reading this chapter, you should be able to:

- Explain the genetic connection between phenotype and genotype discovered by Gregor Mendel in the 19th century.

- Apply Mendelian genetics to modern concepts of inheritance and show how genes contribute to the expression of specific phenotypes.

- Review the various types of possible mutations and discuss both their possible benefits and negative consequences.

- Reflect on new discoveries in genetics and how polygenic traits interact with the environment to produce complex phenotypes.

- Discuss phenylketonuria (PKU) as an example of both Mendelian genetics and post-Mendelian genetics.

Genetics: From Genotype to Phenotype

On a spring day in 1900, a scientist from Cambridge named William Bateson was riding on a train to London. Although relatively young, Bateson was well known among scientists interested in heredity and evolution. He had conducted field and experimental research on both plants and animals and had been involved in theoretical debates about the nature of evolutionary change. Bateson was heading to London to give a talk to the Royal Horticultural Society. In his talk to the society in the previous year, Bateson had forthrightly argued that if the mechanisms of heredity were ever to be worked out, it would only be through the careful breeding of plants or animals, with precise recording of the expression of characters in parent and offspring generations. The expression of these characters would have to be statistically analyzed to make sense of the patterns of hereditary transmission.

As he rode on the train, Bateson read a scientific paper that he had recently seen mentioned in a new publication by a Dutch botanist named Hugo de Vries. The paper, in an obscure Austrian journal, was not hot off the presses; in fact, it had been published 35 years before. Bateson was not familiar with the author, Gregor Mendel, whom he realized had probably been dead for some time.

As he read, one word came to Bateson: *remarkable.* Mendel had conducted a long series of painstaking hybridization experiments using the common garden pea. Bateson was impressed by the scale of the experiments, his description of them, and, most particularly, the analysis of the results Mendel provided. Bateson immediately recognized that the research program he had so boldly advocated the year before had already been implemented by Mendel more than four decades earlier!

Bateson had prepared his talk to the Royal Horticultural Society before leaving Cambridge, but after arriving in London, he hurriedly added a long section discussing and lauding Mendel's work. During his presentation, he admitted some puzzlement as to how research as significant as Mendel's could be all but forgotten or unnoticed for so many years. He proclaimed that Mendel's ideas would "play a conspicuous part in all future discussions of evolutionary problems." Bateson was confident that the "laws of heredity" were finally within reach.

Bateson returned to Cambridge a self-avowed "Mendelian" and, within 2 years published a book-length defense of "Mendelism." He devoted the rest of his career to the promotion of Mendel's ideas and to explaining what Mendelism meant to understanding evolutionary change. In 1904, Bateson took time out to father a son, Gregory, who grew up to be one of the most famous cultural anthropologists of the twentieth century. Strictly speaking, Bateson did not rediscover Mendel. Rather, he did something that was even more important: He recognized the significance of the rediscovery of Mendel and that a whole new science—*genetics* (a term Bateson coined in 1908)—was at hand.

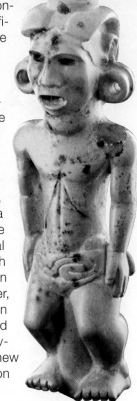

In Chapter 3, we discussed the cellular and molecular bases of heredity. William Bateson (1861–1926) and other scientists had a concept of the gene long before anyone knew what DNA was or how it played its role in heredity. In this chapter, we explore in greater detail the observable effects of genes on the structures of plants and on the bodies and behavior of animals, including humans. As we will see, the relationship between gene and structure sometimes is very simple and straightforward and at other times is much more complex.

Human genetics encompasses a wide range of phenomena. Genetics is vitally important for understanding human evolution, and it has a key role in many contemporary medical and cultural issues. As we cover these diverse topics in this chapter, it is useful to keep in mind the universality of the system of inheritance shared by all forms of life. After all, modern human genetics has its beginnings in research conducted on the common garden pea, a species with whom humans last shared a common ancestor hundreds of millions of years ago.

From Genotype to Phenotype

Little-known Austrian scientist Gregor Mendel (1822–1884), who was "rediscovered" by Bateson and his contemporaries, had a sense of how genes worked almost 90 years before Watson and Crick figured out the structure and function of DNA. This was a striking achievement when you consider that Mendel and his followers could not explore the laws of heredity by looking at the genes themselves. Instead, they had to make inferences about how genes worked based on their observations of how specific plant and animal traits were passed from generation to generation. Such research was painstaking and took years to complete.

How do we make the connection between genes and the physical traits we can observe? As we learned in Chapter 3, DNA functions include replication and protein synthesis. Genes that contain information to make proteins are called **structural genes.** Structural genes are surrounded by *regulatory regions,* sequences of bases that are essential in initiating, promoting, or terminating transcription. If these regulatory regions are altered or missing, the expression of the gene can be affected. Beyond these regulatory regions, however, there must also be **regulatory genes** that further guide the expression of structural genes. Structural genes may be quite similar across different (but related) species, so regulatory genes probably are critical in determining the form an organism, or species, takes. Geneticists estimate that DNA base sequences in humans and chimpanzees are at least 95 percent identical (including coding and noncoding regions) (Britten, 2002).

FIGURE 4.1 Genetically closely related species can have profound anatomical differences, as this movie still from the 1938 film *Her Jungle Love,* featuring Dorothy Lamour and one of her chimpanzee co-stars, indicates.

The 5 percent difference between the two species is accounted for by a variety of insertions, deletions, variable gene copy numbers, and inversions of DNA sequences (Kehrer-Sawatzki and Cooper, 2007). The overall similarity between human and chimpanzee DNA suggests, however, that regulatory rather than structural genes were primarily responsible for the evolution of the physical and behavioral differences we see between the species today (Figure 4.1).

When Wilhelm Johannsen introduced the term *gene* in the early twentieth century (see Chapter 3), he introduced two other terms that remain in use today: **genotype** and **phenotype.** The genotype is the set of specific genes (or alleles) an organism carries; it is the genetic constitution of that organism. The phenotype is the observable physical feature of an organism that is under some form of genetic control or influence. In some cases, the relationship between genotype and phenotype is direct: The observed phenotype is a direct product of the underlying alleles. In other situations, the genotype interacts with factors in the environment to produce a phenotype. In phenotypes that are the result of complex gene-environment interactions, it can be difficult to figure out the contributions each makes to the variation we observe. Two contrasting examples of the relationship between genotype and phenotype in humans are the ABO blood type system and obesity.

The ABO Blood Type System

The **ABO blood type system** illustrates a straightforward relationship between genotype and phenotype. The ABO system (important in typing for blood transfusions) refers to a protein found on the surface of red blood cells, which is coded for by a gene located on chromosome 9. This gene has three alleles: A, B, and O. A and B stand for two different versions of the protein, and O stands for the absence of the protein. Because we are diploid organisms, we have two copies of each gene, one on each chromosome. As we discussed in Chapter 3, if an individual has the same allele of the gene on each chromosome, he or she is said to be homozygous for that gene; if the alleles are different, then the individual is heterozygous. In many cases, the phenotypic expression of the alleles for a gene depends on whether the genotype is heterozygous or homozygous.

An allele that must be present on both chromosomes to be expressed (that is, homozygous) is called a **recessive** allele (or gene). In the ABO system, O is a recessive allele: In order for it to be expressed, you must be homozygous for O (that is, have two copies of it). An allele that must be present at only one chromosomal locus to be expressed is called a **dominant** allele (or gene). Both A and B are dominant to O and **codominant** with each other: Only one copy is needed. As you can see in Table 4.1, there are six possible genotypes and four possible phenotypes. Even though this example illustrates a direct relationship between genotype and phenotype, knowing an ABO blood type does not necessarily tell you what the underlying genotype is if you are type A or B. But no amount of environmental intervention will change your blood type. The phenotype is a direct product of the genotype.

TABLE 4.1   ABO Blood Type System Genotypes and Phenotypes

	Genotype	Phenotype
Homozygous	AA	Type A
	BB	Type B
	OO	Type O
Heterozygous	AO	Type A
	BO	Type B
	AB	Type AB

Obesity: A Complex Interaction

Obesity provides a more complex example of the interaction between genes, environments, and phenotypes (Ulijaszek & Lofink, 2006). Studies have shown that some people with an obese phenotype, defined as some percentage of body weight greater than population norms or ideals, are in some way genetically predisposed to such a condition. Recent research in both lab animals and humans indicates that there are specific genes that are critical to regulating appetite, which may be an important factor in overall body development. Some individuals have alleles for these genes that make it difficult for them to regulate their appetites (Figure 4.2 on page 62); these individuals tend to become morbidly obese at a young age. Genes that regulate fat storage, metabolism, and so on, would also be critical in the development of an obese phenotype. Recent genetic research involving nearly 250,000 subjects has definitively identified a total of 32 genes that are strongly associated with body mass index (Speliotes et al., 2010). Obviously, there is much more work to be done in this area.

Of course, the development of obesity depends on the availability of food in the environment (Figure 4.3 on page 62). No one becomes obese, even those in possession of alleles predisposing them to obesity, if there is not enough food to maintain an adequate body weight. On the other hand, the obese phenotype in some modern populations—characterized by abundant food and inactive lifestyles—is becoming so common that the environment is unleashing the potential for obesity in the majority of people rather than a small number who may be exceptionally prone to developing

structural genes   Genes that contain the information to make a protein.

regulatory genes   Guide the expression of structural genes, without coding for a protein themselves.

genotype   The genetic makeup of an individual. Genotype can refer to the entire genetic complement or more narrowly to the alleles present at a specific locus on two homologous chromosomes.

phenotype   An observable or measurable feature of an organism. Phenotypes can be anatomical, biochemical, or behavioral.

ABO blood type system   Refers to the genetic system for one of the proteins found on the surface of red blood cells. Consists of one gene with three alleles: A, B, and O.

recessive   In a diploid organism, refers to an allele that must be present in two copies (homozygous) in order to be expressed.

dominant   In a diploid organism, an allele that is expressed when present on only one of a pair of homologous chromosomes.

codominant   In a diploid organism, two different alleles of a gene that are both expressed in a heterozygous individual.

Listen to the **Podcast** "Lifestyle Factors May Alter Genetic Traits, Study Finds" on **myanthrolab**

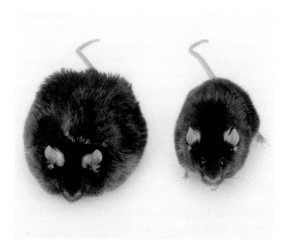

FIGURE 4.2 Laboratory mice demonstrate that genetic differences can have profound effects on the propensity to gain weight.

FIGURE 4.3 Obesity is becoming an epidemic in the United States and other developed countries due in part to a mismatch between genes and the environment.

the condition. This "epidemic of obesity"—which is associated with increased rates of heart disease and diabetes, among other medical conditions— probably is a clear example of the mismatch between the environment in which humans evolved and the environment in which people in developed countries now live. People in general are genetically adapted for an environment where food is not so plentiful and where simply accomplishing everyday tasks uses a substantial amount of energy (Bellisari, 2008). The obesity phenotype is the product of genes and the environment, even in people who do not have an "obesity genotype."

Mendelian Genetics

Many of the basic mechanisms of heredity seem obvious once you know something about DNA structure, chromosomes, meiosis, and mitosis. But what is now obvious was once quite mysterious. In the nineteenth and early twentieth centuries, scientists embraced ideas about heredity that were ill-conceived or were later proved to be simply wrong. Gregor Mendel's careful experimental work demonstrated the nonblending, particulate (that is, genetic) nature of heredity, or **particulate inheritance.** Unfortunately for Mendel, his research was so far ahead of its time that his work was not discovered until 16 years after his death and 35 years after he published it.

Mendel was an Austrian monk who, between 1856 and 1868, conducted plant breeding experiments in the garden of the abbey in which he lived and taught (Figure 4.4). These experiments were conducted on different varieties of the common garden pea (genus *Pisum*) and involved a series of hybridizations or crosses in which Mendel carefully recorded the transmission of several characters across generations. As it turned out, the garden pea was an ideal organism for demonstrating the particulate nature of genetic transmission. Its best feature is that it displays two alternative phenotypes, or *dichotomous variation,* for several different and independent traits: They appear in one distinct form or the other with no apparent blending.

In his breeding experiments, Mendel focused on the following seven features of the pea: seed coat (round or wrinkled), seed color (green or yellow), pod shape (full or constricted), pod color (green or yellow), flower color (violet or white), stem form (axial or terminal), and stem size (tall or dwarf) (Figure 4.5). In his simplest experiments, Mendel looked at the expression of just one trait at a time

FIGURE 4.4 Gregor Mendel.

in the first generation (the F_1 generation) when he crossed two lines that were true-breeding (e.g., wrinkled seeds × smooth seeds, green seeds × yellow seeds, and so on); a true-breeding line is one that reliably produced the same phenotype generation after generation. In the next stage of the experiment, he bred the F_1 generation plants with themselves ($F_1 × F_1$) and looked at the distribution of characters in the second generation (F_2). He obtained similar results for each feature he examined:

1. Although the F_1 generation plants were the result of crosses between different true-breeding lines, only one of the parental generation traits was expressed. For example, when he crossed full pea pod plants with constricted pea pod plants, the F_1 generation consisted entirely of full pea pod plants. For none of the seven traits he examined did Mendel find evidence of blending between the two traits (i.e., a pea pod intermediate between full and constricted).

2. In the F_2 generation, the version of the trait that had disappeared in the F_1 generation returned, but was found in only one-quarter of the offspring plants. The other three-quarters of the plants were the same as those in the F_1 generation. In other words, there was a 3:1 ratio in the expression of the original parental lines. For example, in the cross involving seed color, in which yellow is dominant to green, Mendel counted 6,022 plants with yellow seeds and 2,001 with green, for a ratio of 3.01:1. Similar results were obtained for the other six traits. Mendel called the version of the trait that appeared in the F_1 generation dominant, while the trait that reappeared (as one-quarter of the total) in the F_2 generation was called recessive.

From these basic observations, Mendel developed a series of postulates (or laws or principles) that anticipated the work of later generations of geneticists.

particulate inheritance The concept of heredity based on the transmission of genes (alleles) according to Mendelian principles.

Character	Contrasting traits		F_1 results	F_2 ratio
Seed shape	round/wrinkled	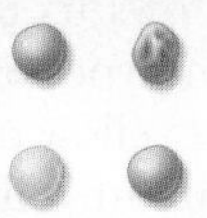	all round	2.96:1
Seed color	yellow/green		all yellow	3.01:1
Pod shape	full/constricted	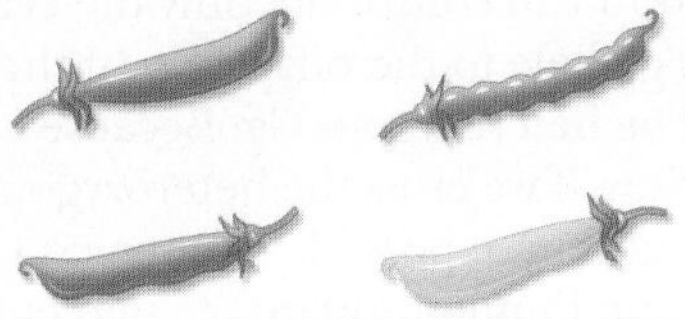	all full	2.95:1
Pod color	green/yellow		all green	2.82:1
Flower color	violet/white		all violet	3.15:1
Flower position	axial/terminal	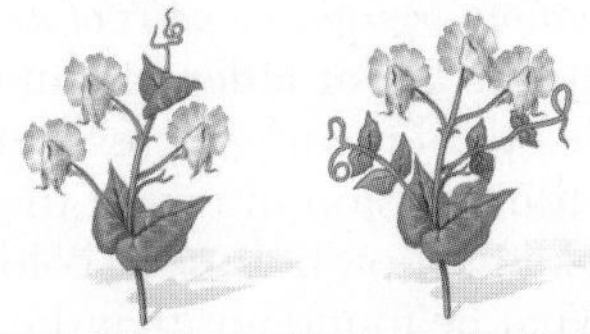	all axial	3.14:1
Stem height	tall/dwarf	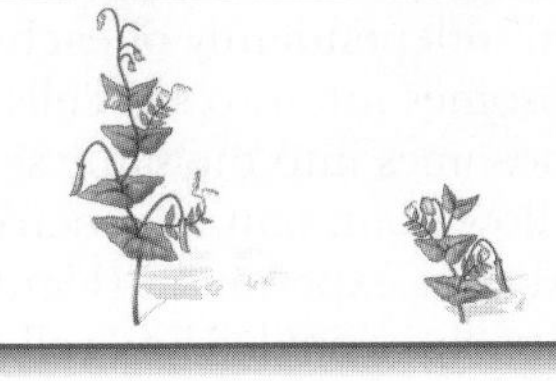	all tall	2.84:1

FIGURE 4.5 The traits Mendel used in his experiments, and the results of the F_1 and F_2 generation crosses.

👁—⌐**Watch** the **Animation** "Mendel's Postulates" on **myanthrolab**

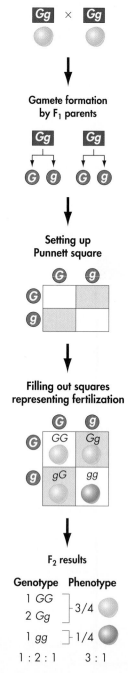

F₁ cross

Gg × Gg

Gamete formation
by F₁ parents

Gg   Gg

G g   G g

Setting up
Punnett square

G g

Filling out squares
representing fertilization

G g

GG Gg

gG gg

F₂ results

Genotype	Phenotype
1 GG	
2 Gg	⎫ 3/4
1 gg	⎫ 1/4
1 : 2 : 1	3 : 1

FIGURE 4.6 The Punnett square demonstrates how the F₂ ratio arises from an F₁ × F₁ cross.

Mendel's Postulates

In the postulates listed (Klug, Cummings, Spencer, and Palladino, 2009), the Mendelian insight is in italics while the modern interpretation of his insight is discussed below it.

1. *Hereditary characteristics are controlled by particulate unit factors that exist in pairs in individual organisms.*

The unit factors are genes, and they exist in pairs because in diploid organisms, chromosomes come in pairs. Each individual receives one copy of each chromosome from each parent: thus, he or she receives one of his or her pair of unit factors from each parent. Different versions of the unit factors (alleles) may exist. An individual may have two that are the same (homozygous) or two that are different (heterozygous).

2. *When an individual has two different unit factors responsible for a characteristic, only one is expressed and is said to be dominant to the other, which is said to be recessive.*

In heterozygous individuals, those who have different versions of a gene on each chromosome, the allele that is expressed is dominant to the allele that is not expressed. Thus in Mendel's experiments, round seed form was dominant to wrinkled seed form, yellow seed color was dominant to green, and so on. Mendel did not examine a codominant character, such as AB in the ABO blood type system.

3. *During the formation of gametes, the paired unit factors separate, or segregate, randomly so that each sex cell receives one or the other with equal likelihood.*

This is known as **Mendel's law of segregation,** and it reflects the fact that in diploid organisms, the chromosomes in a pair segregate randomly into sex cells during meiosis. Mendel formulated this law based on his interpretation of the phenotypes expressed in the F₁ (100 percent of which had the dominant phenotype) and F₂ generations (dominant:recessive phenotype ratio of 3:1). It is easy to understand Mendel's insight if we use a kind of illustration known as a *Punnett square,* named after British geneticist R. C. Punnett (1875–1967).

The Punnett square allows us to illustrate parental genetic contributions to offspring and the possible genotypes of the offspring (Figure 4.6). For example, in the cross between green peas and yellow peas, yellow is dominant to green. Let us call the alleles G and g, for the dominant yellow seed and recessive green seed, respectively. The yellow seed parent can contribute only the G allele, and the green seed parent can contribute only the g allele to the offspring. In the Punnett square, you can see that all of the offspring will be heterozygous Gg. Because G is dominant to g, all of the offspring have yellow seeds. Now, if we cross the heterozygous offspring (Gg) of the F₁ generation with each other, we get three possible genotypes: GG (25%), gg (25%), and Gg (50%). As we can see from the Punnett square, 75 percent of the offspring will produce yellow seeds and 25 percent of them will have green seeds. Thus, the 3:1 phenotypic ratio of Mendel's F₂ generation is obtained. Punnett squares are quite handy and can be used to illustrate the parental contributions to offspring for any gene.

4. *During gamete formation, segregating pairs of unit factors assort independently of each other.*

This is known as **Mendel's law of independent assortment** (Figure 4.7). Mendel did a series of more complex pea-breeding experiments known as *dihybrid crosses* that looked at the simultaneous transmission of two of the seven genetic characters of peas. For example, Mendel looked at how both seed color and seed shape might be transmitted across generations. What he found was that the unit factors (alleles) for different characters were transmitted independently of each other. In other words, the segregation of one pair of chromosomes into two sex cells does not influence the segregation of another pair of chromosomes into the same sex cells. Mendel explored the transmission of seed color (yellow dominant to green) and seed shape (round dominant to wrinkled) in a dihybrid cross experiment (Figure 4.8 on page 66). He started by crossing yellow–round with green–wrinkled and yellow–wrinkled with green–round. In both crosses, he obtained peas that expressed the dominant characters of both traits (yellow and round) but were heterozygous for both as well. So the genotype of these plants (the F₁ generation) was GgWw. He then crossed the F₁ generation (GgWw × GgWw) with

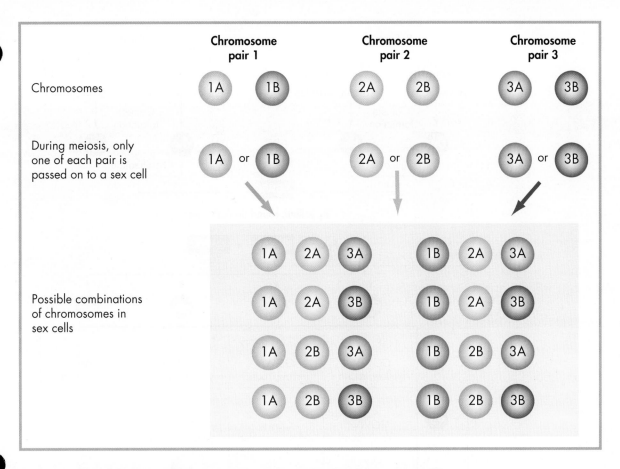

FIGURE 4.7   Mendel's law of independent assortment. Each sex cell receives one chromosome (either A or B) from each of the three paired chromosomes. The assortment of one pair of chromosomes is not influenced by either of the other chromosome pairs, hence "independent assortment." There are eight possible combinations of chromosomes in the resulting sex cells.

itself. There are sixteen possible genotypes resulting from this cross, with four possible phenotypes (yellow–round, yellow–wrinkled, green–round, and green–wrinkled). Mendel found that approximately 9/16 were yellow–round, 3/16 yellow–wrinkled, 3/16 green–round, and 1/16 green–wrinkled. This 9:3:3:1 ratio is what would be expected if the two characters are transmitted independently of each other. Hence, we can say that they are independently (and randomly) assorted during meiosis.

Watch the **Animation** "Using a Punnett Square to Demonstrate the F2 Ratio" on **myanthrolab**

Linkage and Crossing Over

The law of independent assortment applies only to genes that are on different chromosomes. Because the chromosome is the unit of transmission in meiosis, genes that are on the same chromosome should segregate together and find themselves in the same sex cells. This is known as **linkage.** A chromosome may have thousands of genes, and these genes are linked together during meiosis by virtue of being on the same chromosome.

However, decades of genetic research on fruit flies and other organisms have shown that independent assortment of genes on the same chromosome is not only possible but relatively common. How does this happen? It occurs through the process of crossing over, or recombination, which we discussed in Chapter 3. During meiosis, there is a physical exchange of genetic material between non-sister chromosomes (i.e., the chromosomes that originally came from different parents), so that a portion of one chromosome is replaced by the corresponding segment of the other homologous chromosome. Through this process of crossing over, new allele

Mendel's law of segregation   The two alleles of a gene found on each of a pair of chromosomes segregate independently of one another into sex cells.

Mendel's law of independent assortment   Genes found on different chromosomes are sorted into sex cells independently of one another.

linkage   Genes that are found on the same chromosome are said to be linked. The closer together two genes are on a chromosome, the greater the linkage and the less likely they are to be separated during crossing over.

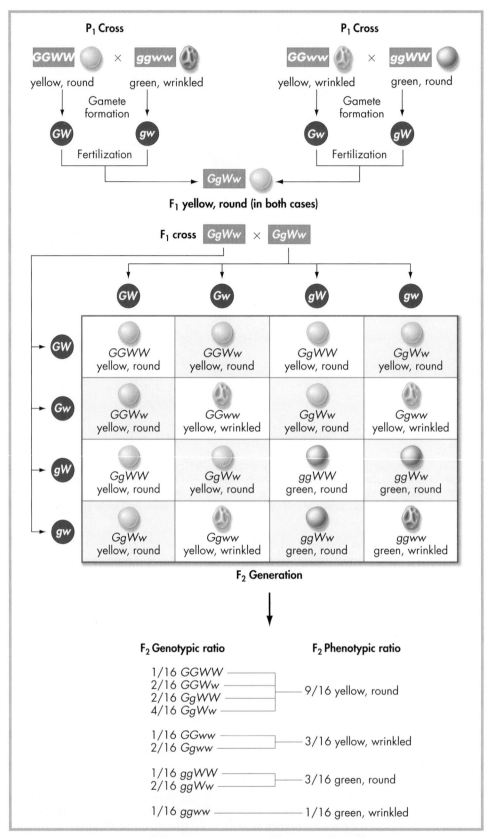

point mutation   A change in the base sequence of a gene that results from the change of a single base to a different base.

sickle cell disease   An autosomal recessive disease caused by a point mutation in an allele that codes for one of the polypeptide chains of the hemoglobin protein.

autosomal recessive disease   A disease caused by a recessive allele; one copy of the allele must be inherited from each parent for the disease to develop.

FIGURE 4.8   The Punnett square of a dihybrid cross demonstrates Mendel's law of independent assortment. The F$_1$ heterozygous plants are self-fertilized to produce an F$_2$ generation. Mendel was able to infer the genotypic ratios from observing the phenotypic ratios.

combinations are assembled on the recombinant chromosomes (Figure 4.9). The likelihood of any two genes on a chromosome being redistributed through crossing over is a function of distance, or how physically far apart they are along the length of the chromosome. Genes that are located near one another on a chromosome are more strongly linked than genes that are far apart and thus are less likely to be separated or "independently assorted" during meiosis through crossing over.

Mutation

A mutation is essentially an error that occurs in the replication of DNA that becomes established in a daughter cell (see Chapter 3). Any time somatic cells divide, a mutation may occur and be passed to the daughter cells. However, mutations that occur in sex cells are especially important because they can be passed to subsequent generations and will be present in all cells of the bodies of offspring. Mutations can occur in any part of the DNA, but obviously those that occur in structural or regulatory genes are much more critical than those that occur in noncoding regions or introns.

Point Mutation and Sickle Cell Disease

There are several different kinds of mutations. A **point mutation** occurs when a single base in a gene is changed. A number of diseases can be attributed to specific point mutations in the gene for a protein. One of the most well-known and anthropologically important is the mutation that results in **sickle cell disease.** Sickle cell disease is caused by an abnormal form of the protein hemoglobin, which is the protein that transports oxygen throughout the body in red blood cells (it makes up 95 percent of the protein found in a red blood cell). Hemoglobin molecules normally exist separately in the red blood cell, each binding to a molecule of oxygen. In sickle cell disease, the hemoglobin molecules are separate from each other when they bind oxygen, but upon the release of oxygen, the abnormal hemoglobin molecules stick together, forming a complex structure with a helical shape. These long helical fiber bundles deform the red blood cells from their normal, plate-like shape to something resembling a sickle, hence the name of the disease (Figure 4.10). During periods of oxygen stress, such as during exercise, oxygen uptake and release increases, leading to an increase in the formation of sickle cells. Sickle cell disease causes chronic anemia, but the secondary effects of the circulation of sickled cells can also be deadly during a crisis.

Hemoglobin (Hb) is a protein that consists of four polypeptide chains (two *alpha* chains and two *beta* chains) (Chapter 3). The *beta* chains consist of 146 amino acids. The normal, adult hemoglobin is called HbA. In the *beta* chain, the sickle cell hemoglobin, or HbS, is one amino acid different from HbA: The sixth amino acid in HbA is glutamic acid, whereas in HbS it is valine (Figure 4.11 on page 68). This amino acid substitution is caused by a mutation in the codon from CTC to CAC. Out of 438 bases, this is the only change. A striking feature of the mutation in sickle cell is that it does not directly affect the ability of the hemoglobin to carry oxygen but rather causes the hemoglobin molecules to stick together, leading to the deformed cell shape. Of course, a mutation that rendered a red blood cell totally incapable of carrying oxygen probably would be directly fatal.

Sickle cell disease appears in people who are homozygous (have two copies) for the HbS allele. A disease of this kind that is caused by being homozygous for a recessive, disease-causing allele is known as an **autosomal recessive disease.** People who are heterozygous HbA HbS produce enough normal hemoglobin to avoid the complications of sickle cell disease under most circumstances, but they are *carriers* of the disease: They do not suffer from the disease but can pass on the allele that causes the disease. If a carrier mates with another individual who is a heterozygous carrier, then following Mendelian laws, there is a 25 percent chance that the offspring will be a homozygous sufferer of the disease. We will discuss the biological anthropology of sickle cell disease in greater detail in Chapter 6.

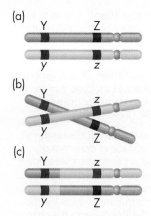

FIGURE 4.9 Crossing over during meiosis leads to allele combinations in sex cells that are not present in the parent chromosomes. (a) A pair of homologous chromosomes is represented, carrying alleles YZ and yz, respectively. (b) Crossing over occurs during meiosis. The more distant from each other two genes are on a chromosome, the more likely they are to be separated during meiosis. (c) Two recombinant chromosomes, with allele combinations of Yz and yZ, may now be passed into sex cells.

View the **Map** "Distribution of Sickle Cell Trait" on **myanthrolab**

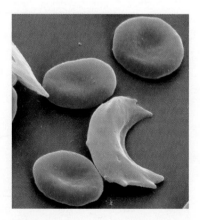

FIGURE 4.10 Comparison of normal and sickle cell red blood cells.

insertion mutation A change in the base sequence of a gene that results from the addition of one or more base pairs in the DNA.

deletion mutation A change in the base sequence of a gene that results from the loss of one or more base pairs in the DNA.

trinucleotide repeat diseases A family of autosomal dominant diseases that is caused by the insertion of multiple copies of a three-base pair sequence (CAG) that codes for the amino acid glutamine. Typically, the more copies inserted into the gene, the more serious the disease.

autosomal dominant disease A disease that is caused by a dominant allele: Only one copy needs to be inherited from either parent for the disease to develop.

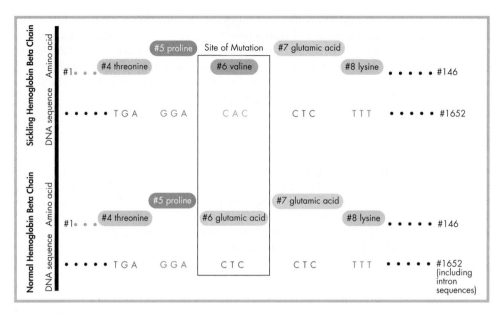

FIGURE 4.11 A single base substitution leading to a single amino acid substitution in the hemoglobin beta chain is the cause of sickle cell disease.

Trinucleotide Repeat Diseases

In addition to point mutations, another common kind of mutation involves the **insertion mutation** or **deletion mutation** of several bases in sequence. At least seventeen genetic diseases have been found to be caused by a specific type of insertion mutation, which involves the multiple, repeated insertion of trinucleotide (three-base) repeat sequences (McMurray, 2010). The best-known of these **trinucleotide repeat diseases** may be *Huntington disease* (which claimed the life of American folksinger Woody Guthrie), a degenerative neurological disorder that is caused by a dominant allele: It is an **autosomal dominant disease.**

The gene that causes Huntington disease (which produces a protein called *huntingtin*) is located on chromosome 4. In normal individuals, a trinucleotide sequence, CAG, which codes for the amino acid glutamine, usually is repeated 10–35 times. In contrast, people who have Huntington disease have 40–180 CAG repeats. Huntington disease usually is thought of as a disease that strikes people in middle age, with a gradual onset of symptoms, including loss of motor control and ultimately dementia. However, there is variability in the age of onset, and it is directly related to the number of CAG repeats a person is carrying. If someone has more than 80 repeats, the age of onset could be in the teenage years, whereas someone with 40 repeats may not show signs of illness until he or she reaches 60 years of age (Figure 4.12). In addition, the more repeats, the more severe the disease. About half of the known trinucleotide repeat diseases are characterized by CAG repeats; they are also known as *polyglutamine expansion* diseases.

Mutations: Bad, Neutral, and Good

The idea that mutations are bad pervades our popular culture. After all, you would probably not consider it a compliment if someone called you a mutant. However, although several diseases arise as a result of mutations in normal genes, it is important to keep in mind that the vast majority of mutations probably are neutral.

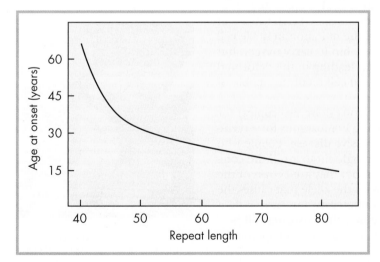

FIGURE 4.12 Relationship between the number of CAG repeats in a gene and the age of onset of Huntington disease.

Mutations that occur in noncoding regions are, by definition, neutral because they make no contribution to the phenotype. Mutations that occur in a gene but do not alter the amino acid in a protein also have no phenotypic effect. These kinds of mutations are common because of the redundancy in the genetic code. For example, if a codon changes from CGA to CGG, alanine is still placed in the corresponding position in the polypeptide chain. On top of that, proteins can endure amino acid substitutions without changes in function. There are usually some parts of a protein that are more critical to function than other parts. Amino acid substitutions in noncritical parts of a protein may not affect the function of the protein at all.

Finally, a mutation may affect the anatomy or physiology of an organism and still have no direct effect on the fitness of an individual. A famous example of such a trait is the *Habsburg face,* which is composed of a characteristic combination of facial features, including a prominent lower lip (hence the name *Habsburg jaw,* by which it is also known) (Figure 4.13). This autosomal dominant trait was found in members of the House of Habsburg and other related European noble families; its transmission has been traced over 23 generations (Wolff et al., 1993). Inbreeding within these European royal families made the expression of autosomal dominant alleles more common (see Chapter 14), and unlike the relatively benign Habsburg face, some of these were likely very detrimental to health and fitness (Alvarez et al., 2009).

Can mutations be good? Absolutely. Mutations are the ultimate source of variation, and variation is the raw material on which natural selection acts. Without mutation, there could be no natural selection. Although chromosomal processes such as crossing over create new allele combinations and thereby increase phenotypic variability, mutation is the only source for new alleles that can be combined in novel ways. "Good" mutations—those that increase an organism's chance of surviving and reproducing—do not have to be common. The process of natural selection makes their spread throughout a population possible. Once this happens, they are no longer considered to be mutations but are the normal or wild type (Figure 4.14).

FIGURE 4.13   King Charles V, Holy Roman Emperor and ruler of Spain from 1516–1556, possessed the distinctive Habsburg jaw.

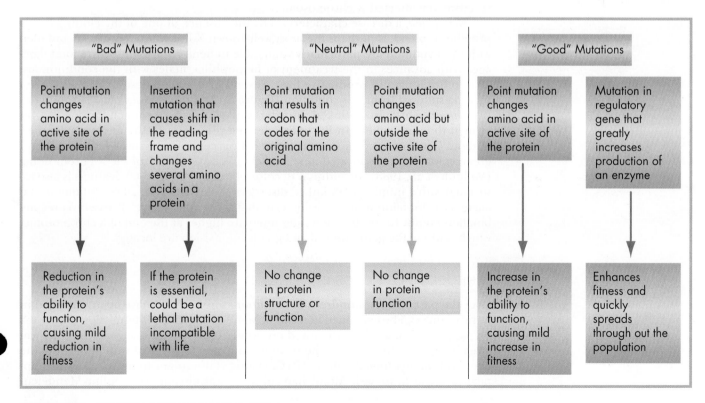

FIGURE 4.14   "Bad," "neutral," and "good" mutations.

X-linked disorders   Genetic conditions that result from mutations to genes on the X chromosome. They are almost always expressed in males, who have only one copy of the X chromosome; in females, the second X chromosome containing the normally functioning allele protects them from developing X-linked disorders.

Many autosomal dominant disorders (such as *achondroplasia,* a disorder characterized by dwarfism caused by impaired long bone growth) occur at rates on the order of 1 in 10,000 births, and they result almost entirely from new mutations. Let us suppose then that the mutation rate in humans for any given gene averages about 1 in 10,000 per generation (mutation rates are very difficult to estimate because they vary by gene and species and other factors). That might not seem very high, but when we consider that humans have two copies each of 20,000–25,000 genes, then it is likely that every individual carries a mutation in some gene. And if we search in a population of individuals, the chance of finding mutations in more than one gene is remarkably high indeed.

X-Linked Disorders

We discussed chromosomal mutations or abnormalities in an earlier section. However, there is one class of gene mutations that is directly related to chromosome structure. These are the **X-linked disorders.** As discussed in Chapter 3, the sex chromosomes in human males are XY, and in human females they are XX (technically speaking, males are the *heterogametic* sex and females are the *homogametic* sex). The Y chromosome is very small compared with other chromosomes and contains a limited number of genes. In contrast, the X chromosome contains a large number of genes.

Because human males have only one copy of the X chromosome, they are susceptible to a host of diseases that are caused by mutations in X chromosome genes. These diseases are much less common in females because they are essentially autosomal recessive disorders and will appear in a female only when they are present in two copies. Female children of affected males are all carriers of the condition because one of their X chromosomes is a copy of their father's (only) X chromosome. Pedigrees of families affected by X-linked disorders show a typical pattern whereby the disorders appear to skip a generation. If a male has an X-linked disorder, he cannot pass it on to his sons because he does not pass an X chromosome to them. His daughters will not have the disease but will be carriers. Their sons then have a 50 percent chance of getting the disorder because they have a 50 percent chance of receiving the affected X chromosome.

Hemophilia, a disease characterized by the absence of one of the clotting factor proteins in blood, is perhaps the most well-known X-linked disorder. Boys and men with this condition are particularly vulnerable to hemorrhage and severe joint damage. With advances in the treatment of hemophilia, males with the condition are able to live long and productive lives. Several of the male descendants of Queen Victoria suffered from this condition (Figure 4.15). Both *red color blindness* and *green color blindness* are also X-linked disorders and therefore are much more common in men than in women. In European-derived populations, the frequency in men is about 7 percent and in women about 0.4 percent. The genes affecting red and green color vision are located next to each other at one end of the X chromosome (Vollrath et al., 1988). In addition to color blindness, congenital deafness is also associated with a number of X-linked disorders (Petersen et al., 2008). Studies of the alleles of color-blind individuals indicate that those alleles have all arisen via recombination events. Recombination rates often are higher at the end of a chromosome, which is where the genes for red and green color vision are located.

Mendelian Genetics in Humans

Over the past century, hundreds of conditions and diseases have been cataloged in humans that can be explained in terms of Mendelian genetic transmission (Table 4.2 on page 72). Besides those discussed previously, there are traits such as earlobe form (free hanging is dominant to the recessive attached form) or the ability to taste the chemical phenylthiocarbamide (PTC; tasting is dominant to nontasting) that appear to conform to basic Mendelian rules of transmission. The Online Mendelian

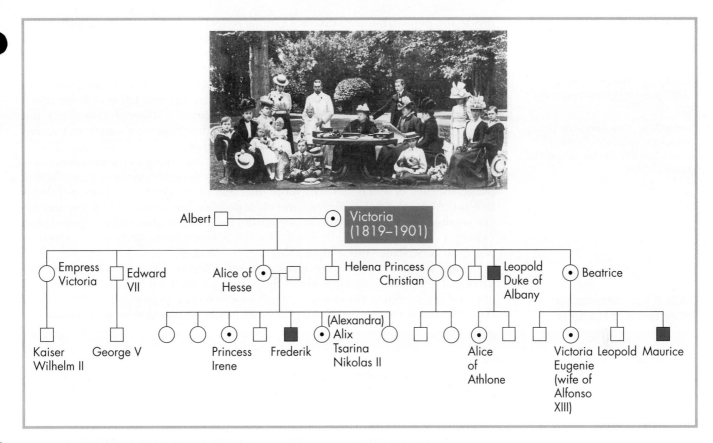

FIGURE 4.15 Queen Victoria and her family and a pedigree showing the transmission of hemophilia in the British royal family.

Inheritance in Man (OMIM) website (http://www.ncbi.nlm.nih.gov/entrez/query .fcgi?db=OMIM.) provides an extraordinary database on genetic conditions in humans, from the most innocuous to the most lethal.

Genetics Beyond Mendel

By studying the Mendelian genetics of phenotypes that are determined by a single gene, each with a small number of alleles, scientists have gained a significant understanding of many other more complex biological phenomena. However, it is important to keep in mind that a single-gene, dominant-recessive model of heredity cannot explain much of the biological world we see around us. As Kenneth Weiss (2002, page 44) has pointed out, although Mendelian genetics provides a foundation for understanding heredity, "a misleading, oversimplified, and overdeterministic view of life is one of the possible consequences." Not long after the rediscovery of Mendel, the overly enthusiastic application of Mendelian principles to human affairs, in combination with certain political and nationalistic movements, had a number of important consequences (Insights and Advances: State Fair Popular Mendelism and the Eugenics Movement).

Mendelian genetics is most useful in examining traits for which there are different and nonoverlapping phenotypic variants. This is called **qualitative variation.** An example of qualitative variation in humans (in addition to some of the Mendelian conditions discussed earlier) is *albinism*, which is the absence of pigmentation in the skin, hair, and iris of the eyes. Although this may be caused by different genes, in each case it is inherited in an autosomal recessive fashion. In contrast, **quantitative variation** refers to continuous variation for some trait, which emerges after we measure a character in a population of individuals. It is not possible to

qualitative variation Phenotypic variation that can be characterized as belonging to discrete, observable categories.

quantitative variation Phenotypic variation that is characterized by the distribution of continuous variation (expressed using a numerical measure) within a population (for example, in a bell curve).

polygenic traits Phenotypic traits that result from the combined action of more than one gene; most complex traits are polygenic.

pleiotropy The phenomenon of a single gene having multiple phenotypic effects.

heritability The proportion of total phenotypic variability observed for a given trait that can be ascribed to genetic factors.

divide the population into discrete groups reflecting one variant or another. For many characters, if we measure enough individuals, we find that there is a normal (or bell-shaped) distribution in the individual expression of the character. Individuals who have extremely high or low measurements are most rare, and those who have measurements near the population mean, or average, are most common. Stature in humans is a classic example (Figure 4.16). Very short and very tall people are much less common than are people of average height. Stature is influenced by genes, but except for rare kinds of dwarfism, the phenotypic distribution of stature in humans does not lend itself to a simple Mendelian explanation.

Stature and other complex phenotypes, such as the timing of puberty, skin color, and eye color are **polygenic traits.** Their expression depends on the action of multiple genes, each of which may have more than one allele. The more genes and alleles that contribute to a polygenic trait, the more possible genotypes—and phenotypes—are possible. Thus when continuous variation for a trait is observed in a population (whether or not it is normally distributed), it is much more likely to be caused by polygenic inheritance rather than a single-gene effect.

Single genes that produce qualitative variants often are referred to as though they produced the whole trait, when in fact the trait in question results from the combined efforts of several genes. For example, Mendel focused on a specific gene and two alleles that influenced the height of pea plants, such that he was able to dichotomize the

TABLE 4.2 Mendelian Inheritance in Humans

Disorders	Descriptions
AUTOSOMAL RECESSIVE DISORDERS Cystic fibrosis	Causes abnormal mucous secretions, which affect several organs, especially in the respiratory system. In European and European-derived populations has a frequency of about 50/100,000 births.
Sickle cell disease	Abnormal hemoglobin molecule causes sickling of red blood cells, impairing oxygen transport in the body. Particularly common in some African and African-derived populations.
Tay–Sachs disease	Most common in Ashkenazi (European) Jews, caused by an abnormal form of an enzyme that breaks down a fatty substance known as ganglioside GM2. When this substance builds up, it is toxic to nerve cells, and death usually occurs before 5 years of age.
Phenylketonuria (PKU)	Defects in the enzyme phenylalanine hydroxylase cause a buildup of the amino acid phenylalanine, which results in mental retardation and physical abnormalities if phenylalanine is not removed from the diet.
AUTOSOMAL DOMINANT DISORDERS Huntington disease	Polyglutamine expansion disease that causes uncontrolled movements, mental and emotional problems, and progressive loss of thinking ability (cognition).
Neurofibromatosis type I	Causes the growth of noncancerous tumors along nerves called neurofibromas, usually in the skin but also in the brain and other parts of the body. Causes mental retardation in about 10% of cases, and about half of afflicted individuals have learning disabilities
Myotonic dystrophy	Most common form of muscular dystrophy in adults. Causes a progressive wasting of the muscles, particularly in the lower legs, hands, neck, and face.
Achondroplasia	Form of dwarfism caused by a failure to convert cartilage to bone, especially in long bones. Individuals have a slightly enlarged head, with prominent forehead, and other physical anomalies in addition to short stature.
X-LINKED DISORDERS Fragile X syndrome	Causes mild to severe mental retardation. Result of the insertion of hundreds of copies of the triplet CGG into a gene on the X chromosome (normal is about 40 repeats).
Hemophilia	Absence of one of the clotting factors in the blood leads to uncontrolled bleeding upon even mild injury. In severe cases, spontaneous bleeding can occur in joints and muscles.
Lesch–Nyhan syndrome	Caused by the overproduction of uric acid, leading to the development of gout-like joint problems, kidney and bladder stones, and involuntary flexing and jerking movements. Self-injury through biting and head banging is common.
Red-green color blindness	Generally benign condition associated with difficulty in discriminating red and green colors.

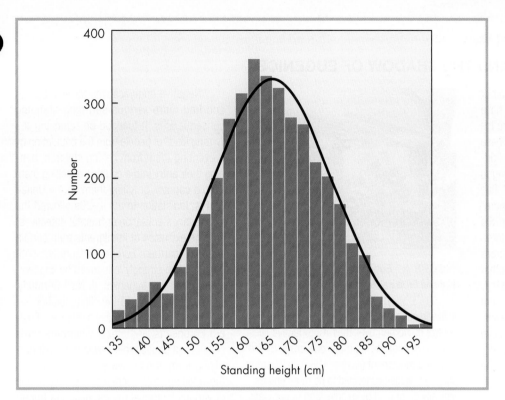

FIGURE 4.16 The normal distribution of height in a sample of 3,808 adult men and women. Mean is 165.2 cm (standard deviation 11.3). (NOTE: Data taken from the National Health and Nutrition Survey 2001–2002, National Center for Health Statistics.)

FIGURE 4.17 Possible achondroplastic dwarf represented in a carved pipe made by Adena Indians who inhabited the central and southern regions of Ohio in the first millennium B.C.

phenotypes as short and tall. However, stem height in peas is really under the control of several genes, some of which have several alleles (Weiss, 2002). Similarly, we often hear that the gene for some disease in humans has been discovered, but that does not mean that the single gene is responsible for the organ system in question. For example, the most common form of short-limbed dwarfism in humans, achondroplasia, is caused by a single dominant gene (Figure 4.17). Although this gene certainly influences stature in a fundamental way, the development of stature in humans is nonetheless a polygenic trait.

Just as one trait can be the result of the interaction of more than one gene, one gene can have multiple phenotypic effects (Figure 4.18). This is called **pleiotropy.** For example, the allele of the gene that causes achondroplasia—the *fibroblast growth factor receptor–3* gene—has the paradoxical effect of shortening limb length while leading to larger than average head size (megalencephaly). Artificial breeding for docility in foxes leads to the development of coat colors not found in wild foxes; this is undoubtedly a pleiotropic effect of whatever genes underlie that behavioral pattern. As we will discuss in Chapter 15, aging patterns in humans may best be explained as resulting from the pleiotropic effects of genes selected for their effectiveness during the earlier, reproductive phase of life.

Polygenic Traits, the Phenotype, and the Environment

Bell curve distributions for the expression of a trait may result from polygenic inheritance. However, phenotypes, especially complex phenotypes, tend to be the result of an interaction between the genotype and the environment. The variation we observe in the expression of a complex trait may result from genetic factors or environmental factors that may influence phenotypic expression.

When scientists investigate the relative contributions of genes and environment to the production of the phenotype, they often use a statistical concept called **heritability.** If we look at variation for some trait in a population, we can be certain that the total variation we observe is caused by some combination of environmental and genetic factors. Heritability is a measure of the proportion of the total

(a) Polygenic trait: many genes contribute to a single effect.

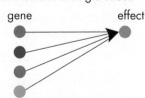

gene　　　　　　　effect

(b) Pleiotropy: one gene has multiple effects.

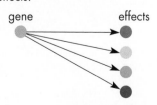

gene　　　　　　　effects

FIGURE 4.18 Contrasting (a) polygenic and (b) pleiotropic effects.

insights & advances

POPULAR MENDELISM AND THE SHADOW OF EUGENICS

In the 1920s, if one attended a state fair or similar public gathering, it would not have been unusual to see a display explaining the finer points of Mendelian inheritance. These displays were not simply meant to be educational; rather, they served as a warning to the dangers and costs of "bad heredity." One might learn that the cross between a "pure" and "abnormal" parent would result in the production of "normal but tainted" children and some "abnormal" grandchildren. A cross between a "tainted" individual and another "tainted" individual would produce the Mendelian F_2 ratio of one "abnormal," one "pure normal," and two "tainted" offspring (Kevles, 1985). Such a display would certainly make a person think twice about the genetic quality of a prospective mate, which was exactly the point of the display.

The popular enthusiasm for Mendelism was directly linked to a broader social and intellectual movement known as *eugenics*. The term was coined in 1883 by Francis Galton (1822–1911), cousin of Charles Darwin and a pioneer in the application of statistical methods to biological phenomena. *Eugenics* was derived from a Greek root meaning "good in birth" or "noble in heredity." In the view of Galton and his followers, eugenics was fundamentally about "the future betterment of the human race." Of course, not everyone can agree on what direction the human race should take.

Eugenics had a remarkably widespread appeal (Figure A). In the first decades of the twentieth century, eugenics societies were founded in countries throughout the world, and the ideals of eugenics could be shaped to serve any number of causes. Women often were

FIGURE A   Eugenics display at the Kansas Free Fair in the 1920s.

active in eugenics societies, and the increasing control of women over their reproductive lives may be one of the ultimate outcomes of the eugenics movement (Kevles, 1985). In Western countries, eugenics tended to be more enthusiastically embraced by middle- and upper-class people, many of whom worried about the decline in the quality of their compatriots caused by the unchecked population growth of lower-class people and other "undesirables."

The eugenics movement called for deliberate intervention in the "natural" evolutionary processes that were ongoing in human populations. This intervention could take either positive or negative forms. In many countries, many upper-class people believed that there was a disturbing trend for the better-educated, more intelligent, and sensitive young people to marry later and to have fewer children than the less-educated, allegedly coarser, and less intelligent lower classes. Positive eugenics was devoted to reaching out to the "right kind" of people and encouraging them, for the sake of the "race," to have more babies.

Negative eugenics was far less benign and had more serious and long-standing consequences. It focused on removing the "wrong kind" of people from the population by preventing them from having children, banning their entry into a country, expelling them from a country, or killing them. In the United States, legislation in the 1920s allowed the involuntary sterilization of "mental defectives" and the exclusion of immigrants from certain (i.e., non-northern European) countries; both actions were strongly influenced by an ideology of negative eugenics. In Nazi Germany, the implementation of the "final solution"—the genocidal killings of Jews, Gypsies, Eastern Europeans, and others whom the Nazis considered undesirable—was the most horrifying form of negative eugenics. Although these killings may represent the culmination of various historical trends, historian Robert Jay Lifton argues that the bureaucratic and practical origins of mass killings in Nazi Germany began with programs to "euthanize" all chronic mental patients and other medical undesirables. It is estimated that 80,000–100,000 chronic mental patients were killed by Nazi doctors as a grisly prelude to the millions killed during the Holocaust.

The popularity of the eugenics movement waned in the United States even before the start of World War II, but the term *eugenics* often arises, usually from critics, any time when human genetics intersects with broader social issues. One can only hope that critics who use "eugenics" as a contemporary pejorative do not have as simplistic and deterministic a view of history as the eugenicists did of human biology, genetics, and behavior.

---

variation observed in a population that can be attributed to genetics rather than to the environment:

$$\frac{\text{Variability caused by genetics}}{\text{Variability caused by genetics} + \text{Variability caused by the environment}}$$

Heritability can range from 0 to 1. It is easy to measure heritability if you can control all the critical factors in the environment, as a scientist working on a short-lived experimental animal might be able to do. In humans, heritability is much more difficult to measure because we obviously cannot use humans in breeding experiments. However, there are several methods for using pedigree data to estimate heritability, especially comparing inheritance of traits in identical (born from a single egg) and fraternal (resulting from two separate eggs) twins. Scientists also use adoption data to estimate heritability in human populations.

Heritability is an extremely valuable tool in trying to understand genetic influences on complex phenotypes. However, the discovery of significant heritability for a trait does not provide information about which or even how many genes are responsible for a phenotype. Heritability is a population statistic and provides no direct insight into individual genetic physiology. Also, it is important to understand that heritability does not provide an absolute measure of the genetic contribution to the development of a phenotype. It is a relative statistic that measures the influence of genetics in a specific environment. If an environment is highly variable, and most of the variation results from environmental factors, then the heritability will be low. However, if the environment is uniform, and all members of the population are affected equally by environmental factors, then heritability will be high. As variation caused by environmental factors decreases, any remaining variation we observe can result only from genetic factors. Thus, heritability changes with changing environments, even as the genetics remains the same.

Heritability and IQ Test Score Performance

Perhaps the most well-known and controversial use of heritability statistics has been in the study of variation in IQ test score performance (Mackintosh, 1998). Scores on IQ tests exhibit continuous variation in human populations, with a normal distribution. Innumerable studies of the heritability of IQ test score in industrial societies have been conducted over the years, and almost all agree that genetics is an important factor in producing the variation observed within populations (heritability ranges from 0.3 to 0.75). Most scientists, although not all, interested in IQ test score would agree that in a population with an absolutely uniform environment, you would still observe variation for IQ test score performance, which would result from genetic factors.

Most people would not argue with the idea that both genetics and environment play some role in IQ test score performance. But what does heritability tell us about an issue of potential anthropological importance: ethnic differences in IQ test score performance? There is much empirical evidence to demonstrate that American Whites score on average about 100 (the designed mean for the test) on IQ tests, with American Blacks scoring substantially lower (7–12 points less), and Asian Americans somewhat higher (about 5 points higher, with most of the difference on the nonverbal portions of the test). Do the heritability studies of IQ test score performance indicate that the ethnic group differences we observe result from genetic differences? No. Heritability scores apply only *within* a population or environment, not *between* populations. Heritability may give us some insight into the production of variation within each ethnic group, but it cannot be used to address issues of population variation between groups. The variation between groups could result from genetics, the environment, or both, but heritability scores, whether high or low, are not relevant to understanding genetic influences for a trait in different populations.

Phenylketonuria: Illustrating Mendelian and Post-Mendelian Concepts

Before the advent of universal neonatal screening for the condition (Lindee, 2000), **phenylketonuria** (**PKU**) was one of the most common causes of mental retardation. Pedigree studies have shown that the transmission of PKU appears to follow classic Mendelian rules. It is caused by a recessive allele and therefore is seen only in people who are homozygous for this allele. People who have just one copy of the allele are heterozygous carriers of the condition.

Individuals with PKU accumulate large quantities of the amino acid phenylalanine in the blood (up to forty times the normal amount) (Scriver et al., 1985). In newborns and infants, a high level of phenylalanine is toxic to the developing nervous system. The most prominent feature of the PKU phenotype is mental retardation, which is a direct result

phenylketonuria (PKU) Autosomal recessive condition that leads to the accumulation of large quantities of the amino acid phenylalanine, causing mental retardation and other phenotypic abnormalities.

INNOVATIONS
....
A New Genetic Era

Genetics touches every life. We all consider our own personal genetic heritages from time to time, when we wonder what it would be like to be shorter or taller, or to look different, and so on. The idea that we are to some extent a product of our genetics is one that has been around a long time, and over the course of a lifetime, we become more or less comfortable with the genetic hands we have been dealt. Although we are not always happy with this state of affairs, we are pretty much used to it.

Things are changing. Recent advances in medical genetics have the power to fundamentally alter the nature of our self-knowledge about our genetic heritages. In the past, the genetic basis of a medical condition was something 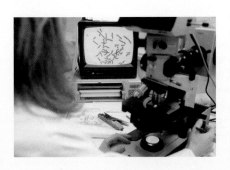 that was usually diagnosed or considered *after* the disease had manifested itself. In the future, many of us may have to deal with genetic knowledge of an impending disease *before* there is any sign of illness. Of course, this is a burden with which many families carrying a serious Mendelian illness or condition have long lived; with new forms of genetic testing, the Mendelian probabilities of inheriting a condition can be rendered as certainties.

Individuals at risk for developing Huntington disease (HD) (see page 68) have been among the first to face the new reality of medical genetics. The location for the gene responsible for HD was discovered in the 1980s, and a genetic test for the HD marker was developed soon after. The HD genetic test today allows at-risk individuals to learn if they have indeed inherited the disease form of the gene, and in addition, learn the number of trinucleotide repeats present, which gives an indication of possible disease severity and age of onset (although these are still variable). This test can be done at any age, perhaps decades ahead of the appearance of symptoms. At present, there is still no cure for HD, although a drug to treat the movement symptoms of HD has recently been approved.

When the genetic test for HD was first announced, it was expected that between 50 and 80 percent of at-risk individuals would have it done. Studies over the last two decades show that the actual figures are more in the range of 3 percent (Germany, Austria, Switzerland) to 24 percent (the Netherlands) (Tibben, 2007). With limited possibility of treatment, it would appear that the vast majority of people at risk for HD choose not to learn if they will or will not develop the condition. Those who do have the test tend to have a psychological profile that indicates high ego

strength/resources (Tibben, 2007); among those who have learned that they will develop HD, risk of suicide or suicide attempt is not markedly elevated, and usually occurs after the onset of symptoms or with a coexisting psychiatric condition (Almqvist et al., 1999).

A quite different situation arises in the testing for mutations in two genes, BRCA1 and BRCA2, which confer a substantially increased risk for developing breast and ovarian cancer (80 percent lifetime risk for developing breast cancer and 20–40 percent for ovarian cancer). The issue at hand is not the absence of treatment options, but rather that the range of treatment options is so extensive, ranging from heightened surveillance to chemotherapy and radiation treatment, to prophylactic removal of the ovaries and/or breasts (Gulati and Domchek, 2008). The psychological burden of testing in this context derives not only from the knowledge of increased risk for a disease, but of the possible necessity to pursue treatment options well in advance of developing it. Women who choose to have BRCA1/2 testing already suffer from significant psychological distress due to the family history of cancer, which prompts their pursuit of testing in the first place (Dorval et al., 2008).

Modern medical genetic testing introduces a host of legal and ethical issues, especially concerning privacy, in addition to the expected clinical ramifications (Minkoff and Ecker, 2008). It is unethical for an individual to be tested for HD or BRCA1/2 status (or other predictive genetic conditions) without formally consulting with a genetic counselor. *Genetic counseling* is a growing health field that will become increasingly important in the coming years. About 30 universities offer masters degrees in genetic counseling, and it is a potentially attractive field for anyone interested in the human side of genetic science (see the National Society of Genetic Counselors website at http://www.nsgc.org). In the future, genetic counselors will be essential to help patients navigate the increasingly complex medical genetics landscape.

of the neurotoxic effects of high levels of phenylalanine. However, people with PKU also tend to have light skin and hair and abnormal gait, stance, and sitting posture, among other characteristic features. It is quite clear that the allele for PKU has pleiotropic effects.

At a biochemical level, PKU is the result of a deficiency of an enzyme, *phenylalanine hydroxylase,* which converts phenylalanine to another amino acid, tyrosine. Phenylalanine builds up in the bloodstream because the PKU phenylalanine hydroxylase either is inactive or has much lower than normal activity. Because the phenylalanine is not converted to tyrosine, people with PKU also tend to have less tyrosine available for metabolic reactions. Tyrosine is the starting point for the body's synthesis of melanin, which is an essential component of skin pigment. This explains one of the pleiotropic effects of the PKU allele: Light skin and hair is a result of low tyrosine levels and low production of melanin.

Over the past 30 years, there have been many advances in our understanding of the molecular genetics of PKU. The gene for phenylalanine hydroxylase has been localized to chromosome 12, and hundreds of different point mutations in the gene have been identified. The effects of these mutations on phenylalanine hydroxylase activity vary tremendously, with some of them rendering the enzyme inactive, whereas others show no effect or only a mild depression in activity (Benit et al., 1999). The variability in the alleles of the phenylalanine hydroxylase gene explains why PKU exhibits a good deal of phenotypic variability. Screening for PKU in newborns is done by assessing phenylalanine levels in the blood not long after birth. Profoundly elevated levels of phenylalanine indicate the presence of PKU and the need for dietary intervention—essentially not letting the child eat any phenylalanine. This is easier said than done because phenylalanine is an important component of proteins found in meat, fish, eggs, cheese and other milk products, legumes, and some cereals. Babies with PKU must take special formula that provides calories and essential nutrients, and children with the condition must adhere to a very limited diet. The good news is that when they become adults, most PKU sufferers can adopt a normal diet because their nervous system is no longer developing. However, if a woman with PKU wants to become pregnant, she must resume the restricted diet, or the elevated levels of phenylalanine in her blood will damage the developing nervous system of her developing child. Other therapeutic interventions are being developed, including novel dietary supplements and treatment with enzymes other than phenylalanine hydroxylase that can metabolize phenylalanine. Even gene therapy is a possibility in the future (van Spronsen, 2010).

PKU provides a striking example of the relationships between genotype, phenotype, and the environment. If people with PKU grow up in a typical dietary environment, their nervous systems will not develop normally, and they will have a seriously dysfunctional phenotype. On the other hand, if we place children with PKU in a different, highly artificial nutritional environment, they will develop normally. Figure 4.19 depicts two sisters with PKU. The older sister was born before there was routine screening of newborns and intervention for PKU, and she suffers from the disease. The younger sister was identified as having PKU immediately after birth, avoided phenylalanine while growing up, developed normally, and later had a healthy child. The sisters have the same PKU genotype, but their divergent phenotypes were shaped by different nutritional environments.

FIGURE 4.19 Two sisters with PKU. The younger sister (left) was diagnosed at birth and followed a strict phenylalanine-limited diet. The older sister (right) was not diagnosed until she was one year of age. She is symptomatic of PKU.

Genes and Environments

When we hear the word *environment* we usually think about the world around us—things such as the air and water, trees and other plants, and all the other critters with which we share the world. But from a gene's perspective, the environment is made up mainly of other genes. Concepts such as pleiotropy and polygenic inheritance emphasize that the genetic environment is just as critical to the production of phenotypes as any other kind of environment.

Mendelian concepts such as independent assortment and segregation were useful in establishing the activities of genes in isolation from one another. But it is clear that the challenge of genetics in the twenty-first century will be to determine how genes work together, not separately, to produce complex phenotypes in the context of complex environments.

Genetics: From Genotype to Phenotype

Mendelian Genetics

From Genotype to Phenotype

- The phenotype of an organism is the product of its genotype and, to a greater or lesser extent, the environment in which it developed and grew.

- Differences in both regulatory and structural genes contribute to the development of unique species characteristics. **[pp 60–61]**

Mutation

- There are several kinds of mutations, including point mutations, deletion mutations, and insertion mutations.

- Mutations can be detrimental to the fitness of an organism or they can enhance it, but many mutations are neutral because they do not lead to a change in protein structure or function.

- Many clinical diseases are classified as Mendelian, meaning that their transmission follows a classical Mendelian pattern. **[pp 67–71]**

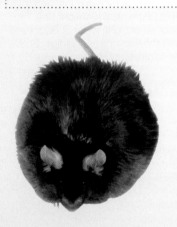

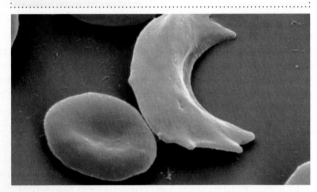

Mendelian Genetics

- Between 1856 and 1868, Gregor Mendel conducted groundbreaking genetic research on the common garden pea.

- Mendel's laws of segregation and independent assortment help describe the particulate nature of inheritance. **[pp 62–67]**

Character	Contrasting traits		F₁ results	F₂ ratio
Seed shape	round/wrinkled		all round	2.96:1
Seed color	yellow/green		all yellow	3.01:1
Pod shape	full/constricted		all full	2.95:1
Pod color	green/yellow		all green	2.82:1
Flower color	violet/white		all violet	3.15:1
Flower position	axial/terminal		all axial	3.14:1
Stem height	tall/dwarf		all tall	2.84:1

Genetics Beyond Mendel

Polygenic Traits, the Phenotype, and the Environment

- Most biological traits we are interested in cannot be studied using simple Mendelian genetics.

- Many traits are polygenic—the combined result of more than one gene, each of which may have more than one allele.

- Many genes are pleiotropic—they have multiple effects, on their own and in their interaction with other genes.

- Continuous quantitative variation (for example, as seen in a normal curve distribution) for a trait is typically seen for polygenic traits. **[pp 73–75]**

(a) Polygenic trait: many genes contribute to a single effect.

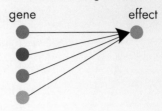

gene   effect

(b) Pleiotropy: one gene has multiple effects.

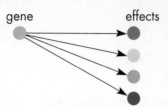

gene   effects

Heritability

- Heritability is a statistic geneticists use to quantify the proportion of all variation observed for a trait that can be attributed to genetic rather than environmental factors.

- For complex phenotypes such as IQ, it is critical to keep in mind that while heritability may indicate a genetic component in its distribution, the heritability value itself may vary among populations according to environmental conditions. **[p 75]**

Phenylketonuria (PKU)

- PKU is a disease whose genetics, diagnosis, and treatment serve to illustrate a host of concepts relating to the complex interaction between genotype and phenotype. **[pp 75–77]**

My AnthroLab CONNECTIONS

Watch. Listen. View. Explore. Read.

MyAnthroLab is designed just for you. Each chapter features a customized study plan to help you learn and review key concepts and terms. Dynamic visual activities, videos, and readings found in the multimedia library will enhance your learning experience.

Resources from this Chapter:

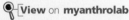 **Watch** on **myanthrolab**

- ▶ *Mendel's Postulates*
- ▶ *Using a Punnett Square to Demonstrate the F2 Ratio Contrasting*

Listen on **myanthrolab**

- ▶ *Lifestyle Factors May Alter Genetic Traits, Study Finds*

View on **myanthrolab**

- ▶ *Distribution of Sickle Cell Trait*

Explore on **myanthrolab** In MySearchLab, enter the Anthropology database to find relevant and recent scholarly and popular press publications. For this chapter, enter the following keywords: sample word, sample word, sample word, sample word

Read on **myanthrolab**

- ▶ *Dental Deduction* by John R. Lukacs
- ▶ *Evolutionary Genetics* by Robert B. Eckhardt

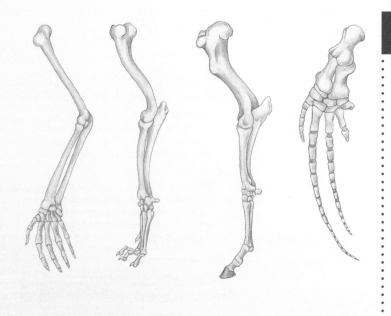

Chapter 5 Preview

After reading this chapter, you should be able to:

- Explain how natural selection works.

- Discuss the evolutionary forces other than natural selection.

- Understand the Biological Species Concept and relate it to natural selection and sexual selection.

- Explain why the **Hardy–Weinberg equilibrium** has proved to be valuable and how it can be used to model complex genetic systems.

- Understand inclusive fitness and kin selection and the role they play in molding animal social behavior.

The Forces of Evolution and the Formation of Species

The little boat sloshes dangerously close to the cliffs of a tiny islet, little more than a rock among the Galápagos Islands. The passengers—biologists and their students—carefully climb the rocky shoreline. For the next six months they live like monks, watching the tiny finches that are the major inhabitants of the island of Daphne Major. They catch the birds in mist nets, measuring their beaks, feet, and wings, and also measure everything in the finches' island habitat.

The scientists come and go for thirty years, spanning about thirty generations of finches and a large portion of their own life spans. The island is subjected to a terrible drought. The drought is followed by several years of plentiful rainfall, turning the island green and lush. Throughout these periods of plenty and famine, the scientists dutifully collect their birds and record their measurements.

Then one day they notice that something astounding is happening. The dimensions of the beaks of the finches have changed in direct relationship to the periods of drought and plenty. When food is scarce, the major available seeds are thick-shelled and very tough to crack. The birds that were born with minutely larger, stronger beaks survive better and leave more baby finches than their smaller-beaked neighbors. When the rains come again and food is plentiful, the trend reverses. The evidence is indisputable: The species is evolving. In the span of just a few years, climate and food conditions have changed the appearance of the tiny finches because finches with stronger beaks are better able to crack open hard-shelled seeds and therefore produce more offspring than their smaller-beaked neighbors.

Demonstrating natural selection in the wild is not easy. It takes many generations and a great deal of tedious field research. However, the results support the reality of Darwinian evolution. The now-famous field study just described, conducted by biologists Peter and Rosemary Grant, is one of the best demonstrations of evolution by natural selection under natural conditions. In this chapter, we will examine the principles of the evolutionary process. These include, but are not limited to, Darwinian natural selection. We will consider where variation in nature comes from and how the forces of evolution act on this variation to mold the form and function of animals and plants. We also examine another important question: What is a species?

How Evolution Works

We speak of the forces of evolution as those factors occurring in natural populations that cause changes in gene frequencies over multiple generations. These include both adaptive and nonadaptive causes. Natural selection is the most cited cause of evolution, and much evidence suggests that it is the most important force. Several

directional selection   Natural selection that drives evolutionary change by selecting for greater or lesser frequency of a given trait in a population.

stabilizing selection   Selection that maintains a certain phenotype by selecting against deviations from it.

((•─Listen to the **Podcast** "Natural Selection Works on Humans, Too" on **myanthrolab**

other causes of evolutionary change exist as well, but evolution can occur only in the presence of a source of variation, which is mutation.

Where Does Variation Come From?

In Chapter 3, we saw that alterations occur in the DNA sequence during the course of replication, changing the allelic expression at a given locus. A change in a base on the DNA molecule is a *point mutation.* Larger-scale errors during replication can result in *chromosomal mutations,* when entire chunks of chromosomes are transposed with one another. Such changes in the genetic material, whether large or small, are the stuff from which new variation springs. Mutations that affect survival occur very rarely. Many mutations are neutral and have no effect on the offspring's viability, survival, and reproduction. Only through the accumulation of mutations do new traits enter a population, allowing natural selection and other evolutionary forces to filter out undesirable traits and perpetuate favorable ones.

How Natural Selection Works

Natural selection is not simply about genes. The mechanism of evolution takes the package of traits each animal or plant inherits from the previous generation and then tweaks it in response to the current environment. The environment is the filter through which traits—and the genes that control their expression—are selected for or against. As we saw in Chapter 4, every organism's genetic makeup, or genotype, is fixed at conception. Natural selection acts on the organism's phenotype, the actual expression of the alleles present in the genotype. The environment can play a critical role in how the genotype is expressed, even when basic Mendelian principles are operating at single gene loci. Such environmental effects include sunlight, nutrition, and exposure to toxins, all of which can have profound biological effect on one's phenotype without affecting the genotype. If you spend years sunbathing to acquire a deep tan, your phenotype—skin color in this case—will change while your genotype stays the same. However, skin cancer from ultraviolet rays in sunlight is a biological effect on which natural selection can forcefully act by removing afflicted individuals from the breeding population. *Natural selection operates on the phenotype of an individual organism.* As individuals who become victims of skin cancer—usually those with the palest skin—are removed from the breeding population, the frequency of genes for pale skin color will decrease. This is evolution, so cultural practices such as sunbathing can potentially have evolutionary effects.

Populations evolve as the frequency of certain genes changes; individual organisms don't evolve. The result is that the frequency at which a gene or a trait governed by genes occuring in a population changes over time. This change generally happens very slowly, although it can be seen easily when researchers study animals with short generation lengths, such as fruit flies or mice, or when animal breeders take selection into their own hands and choose which animals will breed and which will not. In this latter case, selection is not necessarily based on survival and reproductive value of traits. For instance, cattle breeders may select cows for milk production, or they may select them for purely aesthetic reasons such as body size, temperament, or color. This artificial selection is analogous to natural selection, as Darwin himself understood.

When natural selection pushes the size of finch beaks larger and stronger when food is scarce and pushes it back the other way when food is plentiful, we say that **directional selection** has occurred (Figure 5.1). Alternatively, selection for certain beak dimensions may be intense when times are lean, and this pressure is diminished when the rains come again. A relaxation of selection pressure in a population might be difficult to distinguish in nature from selection in the opposite direction from earlier generations.

If natural selection can drive gene frequencies in a certain direction by elaborating or eliminating a certain trait, can it also be responsible for keeping populations uniform? It can, by a process known as **stabilizing selection.** The first demonstration of stabilizing selection was an early study of natural selection in the wild. In the winter of 1898, 136 house sparrows were found lying on the icy ground the morning

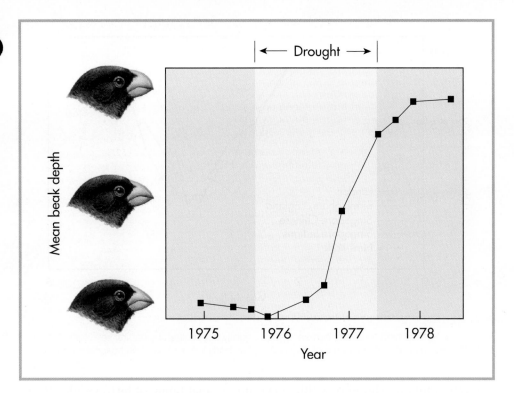

FIGURE 5.1 Directional selection pushes a phenotype one way or another.

after a severe snowstorm in Providence, Rhode Island. They were taken to biologist Herman Bumpus at nearby Brown University. Seventy-two of the birds recovered; the other sixty-four died of exposure to the frigid conditions. Bumpus (1899) then measured nine traits of the birds to see whether there were anatomical differences between the sparrows that survived the storm and those that died. He found that there were anatomical differences between survivors and nonsurvivors. Surviving birds were smaller-bodied and had shorter wings than those that died, and they were more similar to the average size of birds in the local population. In other words, natural selection favored certain *phenotypes* in an environmental crunch. We don't know the exact mechanism—why smaller-bodied birds survived the storm better—but we can say that birds deviating significantly from certain sizes and shapes were not favored by natural selection.

There are many such examples of natural selection in populations of wild animals. Showing natural selection at work in a human population is far more difficult: People reproduce slowly, and the genetic code for specific human traits is rarely known. One well-documented case of natural selection in human populations is birth weight. Producing a healthy baby is a critical precondition for reproductive success (Figure 5.2). Studies have shown conclusively that birth weight of newborns is a key factor influencing the probability of their survival. Babies that are very small have higher mortality rates for a variety of reasons; babies that are very large may not survive the trip down the mother's birth canal. In one study of nearly 6,000 births in a New York City hospital, researchers analyzed mortality rates in relation to a number of anatomical measures of newborns. They found that male and female babies had optimal birth weights of 7.96 pounds (3.62 kg) and 8.5 pounds (3.84 kg), respectively (Van Valen and Mellin, 1967). Other studies have produced similar results (Karn and Penrose, 1951) [Figure 5.3] on page 84). The likelihood of infant mortality was directly related to deviation from the optimal birth weight, even when factors that influence birth weight, such as length of the pregnancy and ethnic background, were controlled for. Natural selection favored

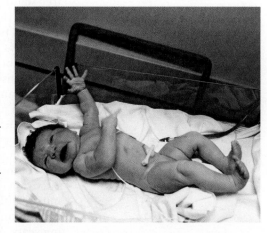

FIGURE 5.2 Human infants are like all other placental mammals, except they are born at a less developed state.

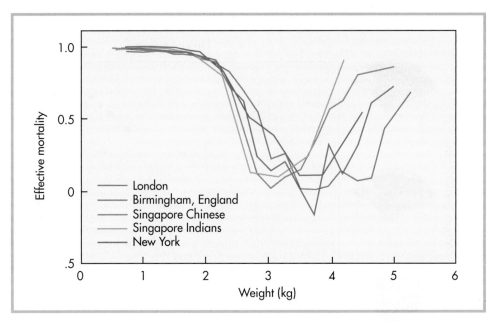

FIGURE 5.3   The birth weight of human infants is tightly constrained by natural selection. Note the high mortality of newborns of very high or low body weight based on hospital records.

survival of infants who were within a certain optimal range of birth weights. Over human history, birth weights that deviated far from the mean were selected against, producing a normal distribution of birth weights with a well-defined optimum.

Other Ways By Which Evolution Happens

The power of natural selection remains a topic of debate. Some scholars argue that natural selection alone cannot account for the rapid evolution of wholesale changes in anatomy that we sometimes observe. These critics are not creationists; they simply question whether natural selection can or should be expected to have produced all the myriad traits we see in nature. There are at least two other important natural processes that produce evolutionary change in populations that are unrelated to natural selection: gene flow and genetic drift.

Gene Flow   When humans or other animals migrate from one place to another, or when wind or water carries airborne seeds hundreds of miles from where the parent tree stands, **gene flow** occurs. *Migration* refers to whole animals on the move; *gene flow* refers to the genetic material they carry with them in their genotypes. The exchange of genes between populations in different geographic locations can produce evolutionary change, as can stopping the exchange of genes between two areas. Movements, both permanent and temporary, of people to new locales have characterized human history. These migrations have become widespread and rapid as regional and global transportation has improved in recent centuries. When migrants produce offspring in new populations, whether they remain in the population long term or not, their genes enter the new gene pool and provide biological diversity and new traits that may eventually change the evolutionary character of the population. An excellent example of how gene flow can change a population occurred in 1789, when the crew of the British sailing ship H.M.S *Bounty* mutinied against Captain William Bligh. Surviving crew members ended up on Pitcairn Island in the South Pacific, and after much battling among the crew (primarily over Tahitian women they brought to the island), one sailor named Adams ended up as a permanent resident. Over the ensuing years, Adams fathered many children, and his genes, including those for his blue eyes, became widespread in the population of Pitcairn.

The end of gene flow can be as important an evolutionary force as gene flow itself. If a population receives genetic contributions (*admixture*) from other nearby populations for a long period of time, it may create one large gene pool spread across two areas through extensive interbreeding. Suppose that interbreeding stops because of changes in social behavior (two neighboring tribes go to war, and all exchange between them is halted for centuries) or changes in geography (a flood creates a wide river barrier between the two populations). In either case, the lack of gene flow means that random mutations that were formerly passed back and forth are now confined to only one population. As they accumulate, the two populations will diverge genetically and perhaps anatomically as well.

Studies of the genetics of human and other populations have generally concluded that despite the long-standing belief that **inbreeding,** or reproduction between close kin, is always bad for the health of a population, very limited amounts of gene flow can eliminate the harmful effects of inbreeding. A study of rhesus macaque monkeys conducted in the mountains of Pakistan showed only limited migration between breeding groups. Nonetheless, very limited gene flow from males who immigrated to the valley where the study was conducted were enough to maintain high levels of genetic diversity (Melnick and Hoelzer, 1996). Studies such as this do not imply that inbreeding is normal and healthy, only that a low level of immigration apparently can offset its harmful effects in a population.

Genetic Drift Despite the importance of selection pressure on animal phenotypes, evolution can also result from nothing more than chance. **Genetic drift** is a change in the frequency of a gene in a population over time caused entirely by random factors. A hurricane that wipes out 99 percent of the population of an island, leaving only a few individuals and their genotypes, is a random event with respect to evolution. The odds that genetic drift will have great importance in changing the frequency of a trait are greatest in very small populations. Consider this analogy: Someone wagers you that if you flip a coin ten times, it will land heads-up nine times. You take the bet, knowing that the odds of a heads-up coin flip are 50 percent on each flip, and ten flips should produce about five heads-ups. But in fact the coin lands heads-up nine times in ten flips. Do you accuse the person making the wager with you of cheating? You do not because we all know that although each flip has a random chance of landing either heads or tails, ten coin flips sometimes produce very skewed results. But suppose the person now wagers that if you flip the same coin a million times, it will land heads-up 900,000 times. This is extremely unlikely to happen, simply because of the very low statistical probability of having the coin land heads-up so many consecutive times.

The comparison between small and large samples of coin flips and small and large populations is apt in the case of genetic drift. Each flip of the coin is analogous to the likelihood that a given allele for a gene is passed to the next generation during reproduction. In small populations, an allele can easily disappear entirely or become prevalent in all individuals (going to *fixation,* in genetic terms). The smaller the population, the larger the potential effect of genetic drift on gene frequencies. Distinguishing drift from the effects of natural selection is not always easily done because selection in a small population would have similar visible results to the gene pool.

There are many examples of genetic drift in human and other mammalian populations, often caused by another aspect of genetic drift, called **founder effect.** When a small subset of a much larger population becomes isolated or cut off from genetic contact with its parent gene pool, its gene pool consists only of the genotypes of the individuals in the new, small subpopulation. Only through a long and slow accumulation of mutations can the genetic diversity of the subset increase. If you and a boatload of fellow travelers were stranded permanently on a desert island, the genetic makeup of the new human population of that island would consist only of the combined genotypes of all the passengers. Founder effect and gene flow often are linked, as in the case of the Pitcairn Islanders receiving new residents in the form of the *Bounty* mutineers. The combination of immigration and very small population size of the island enabled the genes of one British mutineer to become widespread in a short period of time.

Some immigrant groups to the United States who have chosen to live in closed societies experience the effects of genetic drift. The Amish, a well-known religious

gene flow Movement of genes between populations.

inbreeding Mating between close relatives.

genetic drift Random changes in gene frequency in a population.

founder effect A component of genetic drift theory, stating that new populations that become isolated from the parent population carry only the genetic variation of the founders.

FIGURE 5.4 A child with Ellis–van Creveld (EVC) syndrome.

👁—⌐**Watch** the **Animation** "A Single Population Through Time" on **myanthrolab**

sect, immigrated to the United States from Germany and the Netherlands in the 1800s (Figure 5.4). They practice farming with nineteenth-century technology, avoiding contact with the larger American culture around them; until recently very few Amish married outside the Amish community. As a consequence, some genetic diseases that were rare in the parent population in western Europe are common among the Amish in America. *Ellis-van Creveld (EVC) syndrome*, a genetic disease common among the Amish, is a form of dwarfism, and its victims always possess an extra finger on each hand and sometimes extra toes on the feet, a condition known as *polydactyly.* Not only is the EVC gene more common among the Amish than in the larger American gene pool, but it is restricted mainly to the Amish settlements in Lancaster County, Pennsylvania, and is extremely rare elsewhere. It appears that one or a few Amish individuals carried the gene with them from Europe to Lancaster County and, by virtue of their high reproductive rate (the Amish often have ten or more children), spread the gene rapidly through the very small founding population of other Amish (McKusick et al., 1964).

A **genetic bottleneck** is often associated with a founder effect and can bring about evolutionary change. A bottleneck occurs when a large, genetically diverse population undergoes a rapid reduction in size and then increases again (Figure 5.5). When the population size declines, a large percentage of the alleles present may be lost, and after the bottleneck, only the accumulation of mutations will rebuild genetic diversity. For example, Native Americans, Russians, and then Americans hunted the southern elephant seal, a minivan-sized marine mammal, nearly to extinction from the eighteenth to twentieth centuries. By the time complete protection was enacted, there were only a few dozen southern elephant seals left in the wild. But elephant seals breed rapidly, and over the past several decades their numbers have grown exponentially. They are returning to former breeding beaches up and down the California coast (including a few bathing beaches, to the shock of human sunbathers). However, the new elephant seal population has a potential problem. It possesses only the genetic diversity present in the new post-bottleneck population. Should a disease strike the seals, it could well be that a gene for disease resistance that existed in the population before the bottleneck is gone, and the disease could devastate the remaining seals. Hundreds of generations will have to pass before mutations can begin to restore this diversity.

Natural selection is not the only mechanism by which evolution can occur, although it is considered by most researchers to be the predominant way the variation present in nature is molded into new forms.

Darwin and Sexual Selection Although Darwin's *Origin of Species* in 1859 laid the groundwork for all research on evolution by natural selection that followed, he made another contribution in a later book, the importance of which is less appreciated by the general public. In his 1871 book *The Descent of Man*, Darwin extended his evolutionary principles directly to humankind. In it, he explained another major evolutionary force: nonrandom mating brought about by **sexual selection.** Social animals don't mate and bear offspring simply because they bump into each other like balls on a pool table. Females choose particular males as their mates, and they make their choices based on natural variations in male traits (Figure 5.6).

Just as the struggle for existence defined natural selection, Darwin identified two components to sexual selection: the struggle between males to gain access to mates and the struggle by a female to choose the right mate. Sexual selection can be defined as differential reproductive success among the members of the same sex within a given species. Female choice of particular genetically based male traits, such as antlers or large muscles or bright colors, leads to the evolution of males that exhibit those traits because these males enjoy greater reproductive success. Many animal traits that we once

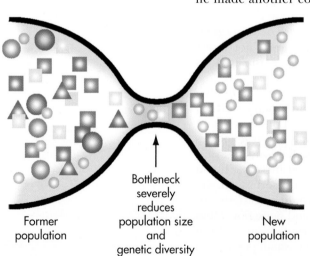

Former population

Bottleneck severely reduces population size and genetic diversity

New population

FIGURE 5.5 A genetic bottleneck reduces a population temporarily to very low levels, removing much of its genetic diversity.

believed had evolved to allow males to defend themselves and their group against predators, such as horns and antlers, are now believed to be the products of sexual selection.

Increased male body size is a common outcome of sexual selection; in a few primate species, males are nearly twice as large as females. This results from female choice for larger body sizes, and implies competition between males for access to females. **Sexual dimorphism,** a difference in size, shape, or color between the sexes, usually is brought about by evolutionary changes in male appearance caused by female mate preferences. But why should females prefer males with large antlers, outlandish tail feathers, or brilliant colors? Females are thought to be under selection pressure to choose a male that offers her a direct benefit, such as help in offspring rearing or protection against predators. She may use physical features of the male to judge his quality in these areas (van Schaik and Kappeler, 2004). If the capacity for judging males on this basis evolves in females, then males are expected to evolve more and more elaborate features to impress females. Or females may choose males by selecting for indirect benefits. In species where males offer nothing to a female except their genes at conception, we expect a female to choose a mate based on his genetic quality.

FIGURE 5.6   A male peacock displays his genetic worth for a female.

To judge a potential mate's genetic quality, a female may use a male's ornamental features as clues (Figure 5.7). Brightly colored feathers may indicate a male's underlying genetic health. Elaborate male ornaments, such as a peacock's enormous tail feathers, may be the result of what famous geneticist R. A. Fisher (1958) called *runaway sexual selection.* In this process, female preference for a trait and subsequent male evolution of that trait reinforce each other. A more recent theory to account for elaborate male traits is *costly signaling,* which derived from the *handicap principle* posed by Israeli biologist Amo Zahavi. Males may display outlandish ornaments in order to state to a female just how vigorous they must be to survive the appendage or brilliant color they bear. Peacocks must escape from tigers and leopards despite their heavy tails; a male who has a large tail may be signaling his genetic quality to females (Zahavi, 1975).

Why is it that males of most social mammals compete for females, and females choose male traits, rather than the other way around? The theory of sexual selection proposes that the sex with the more limited **reproductive potential** should be competed over by the sex with the greater reproductive potential. For nearly all higher animals, this means that females are competed over by males because females are the limited commodity that males need to achieve reproductive success. Whereas a male mammal's fitness often is limited only by access to females, a female must bear most of the costs of reproduction: gestation, lactating, and nurturing. Her level of *parental investment* is far greater than that of males.

The difference in reproductive potential in males and females can be as dramatic in a slow-reproducing animal, such as humans, as in any other organism. Consider the maximum number of children you've ever heard of a woman giving birth to. The *Guinness Book of World Records* cites a woman in Taiwan with twenty-four children born in 33 years as the largest number of offspring of any woman alive (an eighteenth-century Russian woman is alleged to have had sixty-nine children). By contrast, the same source confirms the maximum recorded children for a man to be 888, by the Moroccan ruler Ismail the Bloodthirsty. In addition to the disparity in reproductive potential, males and females often differ significantly in their **reproductive variance**, the degree of variation from the

genetic bottleneck   Temporary dramatic reduction in size of a population or species.

sexual selection   Differential reproductive success within one sex of any species.

sexual dimorphism   Difference in size, shape, or color, between the sexes.

reproductive potential   The possible offspring output by one sex.

reproductive variance   A measure of variation from the mean of a population in the reproductive potential of one sex compared with the other.

"What's the matter? Not puffy enough for you?"

FIGURE 5.7

systematics Branch of biology that describes patterns of organismal variation.

homology Similarity of traits resulting from shared ancestry.

mean of a population in the reproductive potential of one sex compared with the other. One consequence of a female's lower reproductive potential—she can be fertilized only once in each breeding season—is that whereas nearly all the females find mates, many males fail to find females. This reproductive asymmetry between males and females holds major consequences for how males and females behave toward one another during courtship, as we will see in Chapter 8.

Classification and Evolution

To understand the natural world, we categorize plants and animals according to the similarities of their features. The science of taxonomy that Linnaeus devised forms the basis for the study of biological classification today. But as we saw in Chapter 2, Linnaeus's scheme did not incorporate modern notions of evolutionary change. Instead of considering species as dynamic entities that are formed from combination and recombination of gene pools, he saw them as immutable cases of God's handiwork.

Taxonomy and Speciation

Linnaeus classified species in much the same way that we all classify things in our everyday lives, lumping types together based on physical characteristics that were readily apparent to the eye. Presented with an assortment of glasses of wine at a wine tasting, you could quickly sort them into two general taxa: reds and whites. You could then sort the reds into a wide variety of lower-level categories: merlot, cabernet sauvignon, pinot noir, and so on. Each of these could in turn be subdivided based on other descriptive features such as taste (dry or fruity), geographic origin (France or California), vintage (2002 or 1902), and other qualities.

To make sense of all such variations among living things, Linnaeus established a hierarchy of categories to classify all living things (Table 5.1). Each of these levels of the hierarchy is like a set of nested Russian dolls. As one descends the categories, the distinctions between related forms become increasingly small. The only "natural" category is the species. All others are a taxonomist's way of making sense of the evolutionary past of clusters of related species. Notice that humans and chimpanzees are classified in the same taxonomic categories until the level of the family, and if Linnaeus had not been so driven by theology he would have placed us in the same family. Tortoises, on the other hand, are separated from humans and chimpanzees at the level of the class. To Linnaeus, this indicated that tortoises had been created in a different image than primates were in God's plan. Today, we recognize that the class-level distinction indicates distant evolutionary relatedness.

Evolutionary biologists use a variety of methods to determine relationships between related evolutionary groups. Today the study of taxonomy usually is called **systematics.** Systematists rely on the principle of **homology,** the notion that similar features in two related organisms look alike because of a shared evolutionary history. The bones of your arm have homologous counterparts in the flukes of a whale;

TABLE 5.1 **The Linnean Hierarchy**

Linnean Category	Human	Chimpanzee	Tortoise
Kingdom	Animalia	Animalia	Animalia
Phylum	Chordata	Chordata	Chordata
Class	Mammalia	Mammalia	Reptilia
Order	Primates	Primates	Testudines
Family	Hominidae	Pongidae	Testudinidae
Genus	*Homo*	*Pan*	*Geochelone*
Species	*Homo sapiens*	*Pan troglodytes*	*Geochelone platynota*

despite the whale's aquatic lifestyle, its evolution as a land animal is revealed in the bones it shares with all other land animals. On the other hand, some features are similar because of similar patterns of use rather than shared ancestry. Both the wings of a bird and the wings of a bat are used for powered flight, but they evolved independently (Figure 5.8). Although both are warm-blooded vertebrates, bats and birds

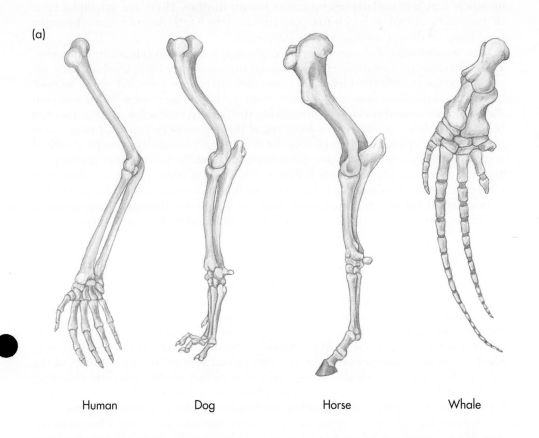

(a)

Human   Dog   Horse   Whale

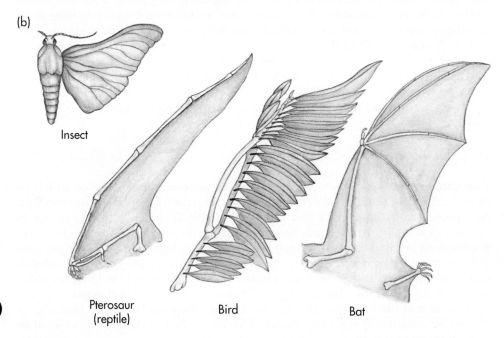

(b)

Insect

Pterosaur   Bird   Bat
(reptile)

FIGURE 5.8   (a) Homologous traits are similar due to shared ancestry. (b) Analogous traits (bat, bird, and fly wings) evolved independently but serve a similar purpose.

analogous   Having similar traits due to similar use, not due to shared ancestry.

convergent (or parallel) evolution   Similar form or function brought about by natural selection under similar environments rather than shared ancestry.

cladogram   Branching diagram showing evolved relationships among members of a lineage.

species   An interbreeding group of animals or plants that are reproductively isolated through anatomy, ecology, behavior, or geographic distribution from all other such groups.

speciation   Formation of one or more new species via reproductive isolation.

biological species concept   Defines species as interbreeding populations reproductively isolated from other such populations.

have not had a common ancestor for tens of millions of years. Bird and bat wings are **analogous** and have evolved through **convergent** (or parallel) **evolution.** The problem of convergence has vexed systematists because natural selection can produce stunningly similar adaptations in distantly related creatures that happen to live in similar environments. Animals with placentas and marsupials that reproduce without a placenta are two distantly related groups of mammals that nevertheless have members that bear striking resemblances to one another. There are marsupial mice in Australia that look so much like placental mice in North America that a biologist would have to dissect them to tell the difference.

We use anatomical *characters*, meaning physical features, to categorize organisms. Two principles are commonly used. First, all organisms are composed of many *ancestral* characters, inherited from ancestors they share with living relatives. Second, organisms also possess *derived* characters: features they alone possess that distinguish them from all related species. By identifying the derived characters, systematists can begin to establish a family tree, or *phylogeny,* of the degree of evolutionary relatedness of one form to another. Phylogenies are the evolutionary histories of groups of related organisms, illustrated in a way that the relationship and the time scale of splitting between ancestors and descendants is shown. A branching order that shows clusters of related forms but does not include a time scale is a **cladogram,** such as the family tree of monkeys in Figure 5.9. A cladogram does not depict the distance in time between the clades, but only the relative degree of anatomical and evolutionary difference.

What Is a Species?

There is no issue more confusing to both students and scientists of evolution than the question: What is a **species?** It is really two questions. First, what does the word *species* mean? Second, how should we identify species in nature? You might think these are easy questions because we all believe we can distinguish a lion from a tiger or a horse from a donkey. In Linnaeus's time the answer was easy: Species were fixed pigeonholes without evolutionary pasts or connections to other species in the present. But ever since Darwin, we recognize that species are dynamic, ever-changing entities, and finding a consensus on concepts of species has proved challenging. The formation of new species, or **speciation,** is a fundamental evolutionary process.

Species are difficult to define because of the amount of variation found in nature. What we call species tend to be overlapping categories, rather than completely distinct units. So taxonomists who apply names to species are superimposing their labeling scheme onto natural variation, and the result can be contrived and subjective. And as a result of the artificial nature of labeling species, there are many concepts and definitions of how species are formed. Whereas earlier generations of scientists had only outward appearance to go by to identify species, modern evolutionary biologists can use DNA analysis and studies of physiology, ecology, and behavior. Yet the problem of unambiguously answering the question "what is a species?" remains.

Species Concepts

Evolutionary biologists have a wide variety of species concepts from which to choose. The most widely used definition of species is the **biological species concept,** first proposed by biologist Ernst Mayr (1942, 1963). Mayr defined species as "groups of actually or potentially interbreeding natural populations which are reproductively isolated from other such groups." This definition has two key phrases. *Reproductive isolation* is at the heart of this concept. If two types of related animals can be distinguished, then they must have been reproductively isolated for some period of time. But the phrase *actually or potentially* indicates that populations of animals that could cross-breed to create hybrid offspring in nature (but don't) should be considered separate species. Therefore, Mayr's definition referred to *natural populations* only.

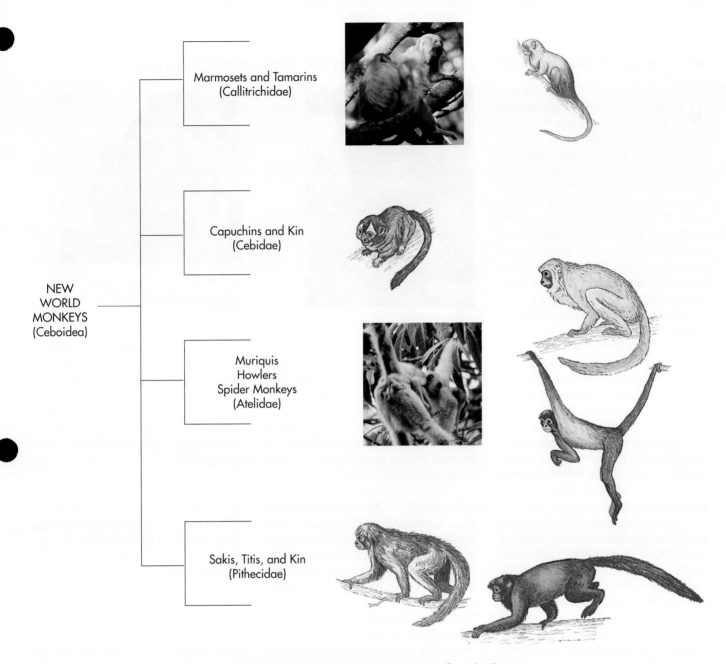

FIGURE 5.9 Example of a cladogram, or branching order, of the New World monkey Superfamily Ceboidea. A cladogram is a family tree but does not show evolutionary time scales.

Consider lions and tigers. They seem to be two obviously distinct species, the lion with its mane and tawny body, the tiger with its bold black stripes and orange fur. But these differences are only skin deep. The two species are closely related, and if housed together in the same zoo exhibit, a male lion and female tiger will produce a hybrid cub (often called a liger), as will a male tiger that mates with a lioness (yielding a tiglon). These hybrid cubs are fully fertile and can be bred to one another or to a lion or tiger to produce another generation of tiger–lion hybrids. In the one natural habitat the two species share (the Gir Forest in western India), lions and tigers have never been seen mating. So are lions and tigers considered separate species according to the biological species concept? The answer is yes, because in nature the species are reproductively isolated: There is no overlap

insights & advances

WHAT'S IN A NAME? SPECIES CONCEPTS, GENETICS, AND CONSERVATION

With many of the world's primate species in danger of extinction, scientists are trying to determine the population size of each remaining species. One factor complicating this effort is confusion about species concepts. Whether one species of primate with a population of 3,000 remaining individuals should be split taxonomically into three with only 1,000 each has critical consequences for conservation efforts. Scientists studying these issues have a new arsenal of genetic research tools at their disposal. But these new tools of an evolutionary biologist's trade have not necessarily resolved species identity problems.

Recent fieldwork has identified numerous populations of great apes across Africa that had not previously been described. With the advances in DNA technologies, it is now possible to collect fecal material from these little-known populations and conduct genetic analysis to tell us how closely related new populations are to other, known ape populations. In some cases the combination of new genetic data and traditional studies of the skeletal anatomy of apes and other primates has led researchers to claim that multiple species exist in places where we previously believed there was one.

Recent genetic studies of gorillas (*Gorilla gorilla*) have revealed an amazing amount of genetic diversity (Gagneux et al., 1996; Jensen-Seaman and Kidd, 2001) and demonstrate how misleading the outward appearance of the animals can be for understanding evolutionary relationships. In eastern Africa, mountain gorillas occur in two populations—the Virungas Volcanoes and in the nearby Bwindi Impenetrable National Park (Figure A). Separated by only 25 miles (40 km), these two populations are genetically indistinguishable. They are similar in appearance but can be distinguished by subtle differences

FIGURE A Only 650 mountain gorillas remain in two tiny forests in East Africa.

in hair color and length (Virungas gorillas are jet black, with longer, shaggier coats). Their behavior differs, too: The Bwindi gorillas climb trees routinely, whereas their Virungas counterparts rarely climb. But despite their geographic separation and differences in appearance and behavior, no one would advocate considering the two variants of mountain gorillas to be separate species.

Meanwhile, lowland gorillas in western Africa also exist in multiple separate populations (Figure B). Unlike their mountain cousins, lowland gorilla populations show a startling degree of genetic divergence. In fact, some western lowland gorilla populations are as different from one another genetically as gorillas are from chimpanzees. Their genetic diversity has prompted some scientists to propose splitting lowland gorillas into at least two species, although this idea remains controversial. This implies a very long history of separation among the populations. However, despite this genetic divergence, western lowland gorillas all look very much alike; in other words, their phenotypes have remained the same.

FIGURE B Most of the world's remaining gorillas are western lowland gorillas.

The lesson vividly illustrated by lowland gorillas is that the genetic distance between two species does not necessarily correspond to the formation of new species. So, learning that two species have been on separate phylogenetic paths for a million years does not necessarily mean that they will look less similar than two other species that have been on separate paths for 100,000 years. This complicates an already thorny conservation question. If gorillas, long considered to be one species across Africa, are really three or more species, how should this change the way we try to protect their future? Splitting one species into three means we would have two additional, even more critically endangered populations. It might also discourage future generations of conservationists from introducing animals to new populations as a means of increasing genetic diversity. On the other hand, creating new gorilla species may help focus world attention on the plight of endangered populations. So when it comes to gorillas, the question, "What is a species?" is far from academic.

between the two species' phenotypes and no evidence of them interbreeding naturally. They also differ ecologically, the lion preferring more open country and the tiger preferring dense thickets. There are many such examples of animals that do not ever meet in nature, because they live thousands of miles apart or occupy different niches in the same habitat, but hybridize readily if placed in the same cage or pond. Nevertheless, these have been traditionally considered separate species (see Insights and Advances: What's in a Name? Species Concepts, Genetics, and Conservation).

TABLE 5.2   Reproductive Isolating Mechanisms (RIMs)

Premating Isolating Mechanisms	
1. Habitat isolation	Species A and B occupy different habitats, such as tree limbs versus the ground beneath the tree.
2. Temporal isolation	Species A and B breed in different seasons or in different months, or are active in day versus at night.
3. Behavioral isolation	Courtship or other behavior or calls by male of species A do not elicit mating response by female of species B.
4. Mechanical incompatibility	Species A and B cannot mate successfully because of anatomical difference, especially in the reproductive organs.
Postmating Isolating Mechanisms	
1. Sperm–egg incompatibility	Mating occurs, but sperm of species A is unable to penetrate or fertilize egg of species B because of biochemical incompatibility.
2. Zygote inviability	Species A and B produce fertilized egg, but it dies at early stage of embryonic development.
3. Embryonic or fetal inviability	Offspring of hybrid mating dies before birth.
4. Offspring inviability	Hybrid offspring is carried to term but dies after birth.
5. Offspring sterility	Hybrid offspring is healthy but reproductively sterile, as in mules born from horse–donkey matings.

reproductive isolating mechanisms (RIMs) Any factor—behavioral, ecological, or anatomical—that prevents a male and female of two different species from hybridizing.

anagenesis Evolution of a trait or a species into another over a period of time.

cladogenesis Evolution through the branching of a species or a lineage.

allopatric speciation Speciation occurring via geographic isolation.

Reproductive Isolating Mechanisms

If species are reproductively isolated from other species, then what factors keep species apart? Such mechanisms can be sorted into two categories: premating isolating mechanisms and postmating isolating mechanisms (Table 5.2). Such **reproductive isolating mechanisms (RIMs)** have been built into the phenotypes of animals to prevent them from accidentally mating with members of another, similar species. Such a mistaken hybrid mating in most cases would be a wasted reproductive effort, and natural selection promotes mechanisms to prevent such matings. Although premating and postmating barriers to accidental cross-species breeding have evolved, premating barriers are prevalent because they prevent lost mating efforts and prevent wasting of sperm and eggs.

Watch the **Animation** "Reproductive Isolating Mechanisms" on **myanthrolab**

How Species Are Formed

The process of speciation can occur in a variety of ways. One species can evolve into another over time, a process known as **anagenesis.** In this mode of change, Species 1 would slowly become Species 2, and Species 1 would no longer exist or be identifiable in the fossil record (Figure 5.10). The question then becomes when taxonomists should stop referring to the species as 1 and begin calling it 2. Species 1 might also branch into two or more new species, a process called **cladogenesis.** In cladogenesis, Species 1 might or might not still exist as one of the new array of species.

Beyond these two general modes of evolutionary change, there are specific processes by which new species are formed. One of these is **allopatric speciation**

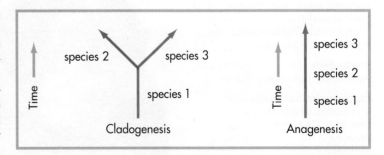

FIGURE 5.10   Two modes of evolutionary change. (a) In cladogenesis, one species branches into multiple new species. (b) In anagenesis, one species evolves into another new species over time.

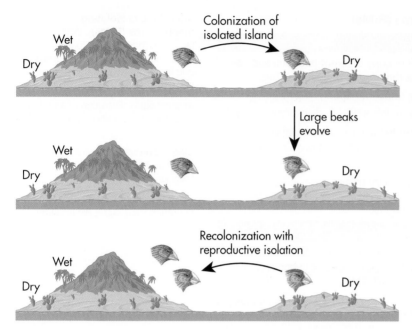

Wet

Dry

Colonization of
isolated island

Dry

Large beaks
evolve

Wet

Dry

Dry

Recolonization with
reproductive isolation

Wet

Dry

Dry

FIGURE 5.11 How allopatric speciation works.

(Mayr, 1942). In allopatric speciation, geographic separation between two populations of the same species triggers the emergence of a new species (Figure 5.11). For example, a river that cuts into its banks grows wider and wider over eons. Eventually the river's course becomes a canyon that separates the populations of animals that live on one side from those on the other side. If the animals are small and unable to cross the chasm, gene flow is interrupted. Over thousands of generations, random mutations accumulate in each population until each is different enough that they can be considered separate species. Such circumstances of isolation and divergence happen frequently in nature; islands and river-course changes both create fragmented animal habitats that lead to allopatric speciation all the time. In fact, one squirrel species is believed to have speciated into two because of the formation of the Grand Canyon in Arizona; as the chasm grew deeper and wider, what had been one species was fragmented into two. Today, the north and south rims of the canyon support separate, closely related squirrel species. Darwin's finches, speciating in isolation on the many islands of the Galápagos, are another good example of allopatric speciation. Scientists studying the great apes believe the closely related chimpanzee and bonobo may have been formed when the great Congo River split and isolated two populations of an ape species that was their common ancestor (Figure 5.12). Apes do not swim, and with a lack of gene flow over thousands of generations, two apes with differing anatomies and behavior emerged where there had been one.

A second process of species formation is **parapatric speciation.** When two populations occur adjacent to one another, with continuous gene flow back and forth between them, speciation of one from the other is nevertheless possible, especially if one or both species occur over a very large geographic area. This can make one part of a population remote enough from another that new traits can appear, and over time parts of the original populations diverge more than others. Often, a zone of overlap remains where the new populations, now two species, continue to interbreed. Such hybrid zones are confusing to evolutionary biologists because they can remain stable, without disappearing or growing, over many years. In northeastern Africa, a hybrid zone exists between savanna and hamadryas baboons. In the strip of arid land that is the hybrid zone, but nowhere outside of it, baboons exist that share a mosaic

parapatric speciation   Speciation occurring when two populations have continuous distributions and some phenotypes in that distribution are more favorable than others.

gradualism   Darwinian view of slow, incremental evolutionary change.

macroevolution   Large-scale evolutionary change over a long time period or evolution of major phenotypic changes over relatively short time periods.

punctuated equilibrium   Model of evolution characterized by rapid bursts of change, followed by long periods of stasis.

(a)

(b)

FIGURE 5.12 Chimpanzees (a) and bonobos (b) likely diverged from a common ancestor due to allopatric speciation in central Africa.

of traits between the two species. These traits are not only morphological ones such as hair color or body size; they include aspects of mating behaviors in hybrids that resemble a mixture of the behavior of both species. Such hybrids therefore allow primatologists to understand better the degree of genetic influence over particular traits.

The Tempo of Speciation

When Darwin considered evolution by natural selection, he considered mainly one kind of change. Lineages of animal and plant species evolve slowly, gradually evolving into new species over vast periods of Earth's history. This is known as **gradualism** and is widely accepted as the most important and prevalent type of biological evolution. Although Darwin knew about the occurrence of "sports," as he called mutations that differed radically in color or shape from their parents, he considered these extremely rare aberrations. Most biologists have since accepted gradualism based on the occurrence of so many intermediate forms in the fossil record and the intricate relationships between an organism's adaptations, which imply small incremental evolutionary changes, because rapid major changes would disrupt the way an organism functions. **Macroevolution,** on the other hand, refers to large-scale phenotypic changes—including species formation—occurring over a long time scale.

Given this evidence of gradual evolution, how do we explain the presence of gaps in the fossil record? Creationists point to these gaps as evidence that a divine power has created at least some species which therefore lack an evolutionary history. Scientists point out that the fossil record is fragmentary, and if complete it would reveal all the gradual changes that evolution has produced.

An alternative explanation for gaps in the fossil record is **punctuated equilibrium** (Eldredge and Gould, 1972). The theory of punctuated equilibrium holds that most species' phenotypes remain static, changing very little over long periods of time. These long periods of stasis are punctuated by bursts of evolutionary change that happen rapidly (Figure 5.13). Such a process would produce gaps in the fossil record because intermediate forms would occur only in brief windows in time. The theory's advocates claim that this may explain large gaps in the fossil record for the most ancient invertebrates, in which wholesale changes in the phenotypes of lineages appear suddenly and without evidence of immediate ancestors.

Adaptation

Adaptations are evolved phenotypic traits that increase an organism's reproductive success. The eye is an obvious adaptation, and the ways in which eyes differ (nocturnal animals possess very different eye adaptations from other animals) are further

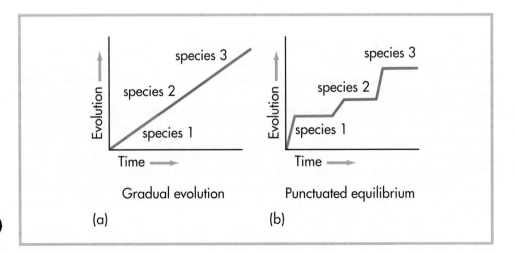

FIGURE 5.13   The tempo of evolution. (a) Gradual evolution involves small, steady changes over a long period. (b) Punctuated equilibrium involves long periods of stasis punctuated by bursts of change.

examples of adaptations. The concept of adaptation is central to modern biology, but it is also much debated. Some evolutionary biologists consider any well-designed trait an organism possesses to be an adaptation. Others use a stricter definition; they consider an adaptation to be a trait that evolved for a purpose and is still serving that purpose. A trait that evolved for a purpose other than what it does today would not be considered an adaptation.

For instance, we can be sure that the wings of birds did not evolve for powered flight. We know this because natural selection sorts among the available adaptive advantages an organism possesses *in each generation.* There would have been no selective advantage to an ancient bird in having wings that were just slightly adapted for flight. Instead, wings must have evolved for another function entirely and then were co-opted for flight. Some evolutionary theorists think that feathered wings were initially adaptive as organs that absorbed solar radiation, allowing a proto-bird to bask in the sun and warm up more effectively (as some birds use them today). As feathered wings evolved, they became useful for gliding and then eventually were modified for powered flight (Figure 5.14). As in other cases of retrospectively explaining the origin of an adaptation, finding intermediate stages of its evolution during which it would have been adaptive is the key.

Is Everything Adaptive?

If you were asked to develop a hypothesis in the next five minutes to describe the evolutionary origin of the human chin, you probably could think of something plausible. The chin, you might argue, evolved to aid our ancestors in the days when they ran across the savanna, protecting their eyes by jutting out from the face to absorb the first shock if they tripped and fell. Or perhaps the chin evolved to provide a place to catch soup as it dribbled out of the mouth. Such scenarios, though silly, are hard to disprove. As we saw in Chapter 2, evolutionary science works by posing a reasonable hypothesis to explain a feature or behavior and then figuring out the sort of data one needs to collect to test that hypothesis. In practice, this means that assuming that a trait may be adaptive at the outset of a study is the way to proceed. The premise of your hypothesis would be that the human chin is an adaptation, evolved for a purpose related to reproduction and survival.

It would be naïve to think that all evolution is adaptive; we saw that genetic drift and its components are notable exceptions. Some scientists tend toward **adaptationism,** accepting that every aspect of an organism is the product of natural selection or sexual selection. Others, including members of one school we can call *holism,* are skeptical that natural selection is all-powerful and consider many apparent adaptations to be merely the by-product of other evolutionary changes. Holists would point out that the chin is only the meeting point of the two halves of the lower jaw, which do not fuse until infancy in human development. The chin exists because of the position of the teeth, not because the chin has any adaptive role of its own.

These two schools of thought represent very different ways of understanding how evolution works. Adaptationists tend toward **reductionism,** trying to understand the function of each component of an organism in order to understand the organism as a whole. They make the working assumption that each part of the organism is adaptive. Holists claim that reductionists oversimplify the nature of adaptation and see natural selection in places where it had not occurred. In a well-known 1979 article, biologists Steven Jay Gould and Richard Lewontin argued that adaptationists overlook or ignore many nonadaptive means by which evolution may occur. They analogized evolution to the arches of a cathedral. As a graceful architectural feature, the spaces between the archways (spandrels) appear to have been created for aesthetic reasons. In fact, spandrels are merely the by-product of building an arch (Gould and Lewontin, 1979; Mayr, 1983).

Adaptationists respond that assuming that traits are adaptive is the only rational starting point for using the scientific method to test their hypotheses. Just as there are both evolved and immediate causes in biology, there are both adaptive and nonadaptive explanations for what an organism looks like. Using an adaptive,

FIGURE 5.14 A feathered dinosaur.

reductionist framework as the way to begin investigating those traits is the best—and perhaps the only—way to conduct scientific research into human evolutionary biology. The holistic approach cautions us against assuming that all features of an organism are adaptive. But in practice, biological anthropologists tend to begin with adaptive hypotheses and test them until they appear to be poor explanations for a phenomenon, and then turn to other possible explanations.

Hardy–Weinberg Equilibrium

What would populations be like if evolutionary change never occurred? Although this is not possible in nature, it can be studied in a mathematician's laboratory, and the experiment is extremely useful for understanding the **null hypothesis,** that natural selection and other evolutionary forces have no effect on a population. In 1908, English mathematician G. H. Hardy (Figure 5.15) published a short article in the journal *Science* that had a peculiarly apologetic beginning:

> I am reluctant to intrude in a discussion concerning matters of which I have no expert knowledge, and I should have expected the very simple point which I wish to make to have been familiar to biologists. However, some remarks of Mr. Udny Yule, to which Mr. R. C. Punnett has called my attention, suggest that it may still be worth making.

In other words, Hardy was saying that the point he had to make was so mathematically elementary that it was almost embarrassing for him to publish it. But we are fortunate that he did, because Hardy's paper played a vital role in the reconciliation of Mendelian and Darwinian views of nature. It also laid the foundations for the modern field of population genetics and other mathematical approaches to understanding evolution.

Before 1908, geneticists struggled with concepts of equilibrium in biological populations. At what point would genetic stability be reached in these dynamic populations? Looking at it from the simplest perspective of one gene with two alleles (one dominant and one recessive), Yule (1902) argued that equilibrium would be reached in a population when there was a 3:1 ratio of the dominant to the recessive phenotype. Most geneticists with practical experience, such as R. C. Punnett, knew this was wrong but did not know how to prove it was wrong. This is where Hardy stepped in.

Suppose we have a population of diploid, sexually reproducing organisms. Assume that this population is not subject to any evolutionary forces that might lead to changes in allele frequencies: no mutation, no natural selection, no migration. Assume that it is infinitely large (that is, no genetic drift) and that mating is random (that is, allele frequencies cannot be influenced by assortive or disassortive mating practices). This is obviously an "ideal" population, but that is not a problem, as we will see. Let us take the case of a single gene A with two alleles, A_1 and A_2. The frequencies of these alleles in the population can be represented by p and q, respectively (see also Appendix C). By definition, $p + q = 1$.

Hardy showed that after one generation, the genotype frequencies in the population can be represented by a simple quadratic equation:

$$(p + q)^2 = p^2 + 2pq + q^2 = 1$$

This means that the frequencies of the homozygous genotypes A_1A_1 and A_2A_2 are p_2 and q_2, respectively, and that the frequency of the heterozygote A_1A_2 is $2pq$. No matter what values p and q have, if the assumptions of no evolution, infinitely large population, and random mating hold, these allele (and genotype) frequencies will not change over generations of breeding. The population is in equilibrium, at least for this single gene or locus.

Despite the fact that ideal populations rarely exist in nature, Hardy's equation, which later came to be known as the **Hardy–Weinberg equilibrium,** has proved to be valuable in many ways. It can be mathematically expanded to model the distribution of more complex genetic systems, including polygenic traits and those for which more than two alleles exist. One can also use it to calculate approximate allele frequencies based on knowledge of the phenotypic frequency of a homozygous

FIGURE 5.15   G. H. Hardy

adaptationism   A premise that all aspects of an organism have been molded by natural selection to a form optimal for enhancing reproductive success.

reductionism   Paradigm that an organism is the sum of many evolved parts and that organisms can best be understood through an adaptationist approach.

null hypothesis   The starting assumption for scientific inquiry that one's research results occur by random chance. One's hypothesis must challenge this initial assumption.

Hardy–Weinberg equilibrium   The theoretical distribution of alleles in a given population in the absence of evolution, expressed as a mathematical equation.

group selection   Notion largely discredited by the rise of Darwinian theory proposing that animals act for the good of their social group or of their species.

kin selection   Principle that animals behave preferentially toward their genetic kin; formulated by William Hamilton.

inclusive fitness   Reproductive success of an organism plus the fitness of its close kin.

recessive trait. For example, there is a chemical called phenylthiocarbamide (PTC), which can be tasted by about 75 percent of the European population but cannot be tasted by the other 25 percent. It is known that this is controlled by a single gene with two alleles, where "tasting" is dominant to "nontasting." Thus the allele frequency of nontasting (homozygous recessive) equals the square root of 0.25, or 0.5.

Finally, although ideal populations rarely exist, the allele distributions of many genes often are found to be in equilibrium. Of course, when we find an allele distribution that is not in equilibrium—this can be the most exciting finding of all: It may mean that an evolutionary force is at work in the population.

Such a hypothetical lack of evolution in a population is known as the *Hardy–Weinberg equilibrium*.

Levels of Selection

A final consideration about the nature of selection and evolution is the level at which evolution by natural selection occurs. Darwin considered an individual's lifetime reproductive success as the bottom line for natural selection. Challenges to this idea have consistently failed. Biologist V. C. Wynne-Edwards (1962) attempted to show that natural selection could sometimes occur for the good of a whole group of animals, which he called **group selection.** He claimed that when animals are overcrowded, they regulate their reproduction rather than overpopulate their range and outstrip their food resources. However, biologist George C. Williams (1966) showed clearly that in such a situation, the individual that is concerned only with itself always prospers evolutionarily. Consider a herd of 100 antelope that are beginning to run out of food because of overpopulation. Ninety-nine antelopes stop bearing offspring for one year because natural selection has a mechanism that is intended to prevent overpopulation, but one antelope continues having babies. That one selfish antelope would eat heartily and pass its genes for selfish behavior to the next generation, whereas its altruistic neighbors did not. In time, *altruism* would be extinguished in favor of selfish behavior. Williams showed succinctly that in the face of selfish behavior, there are few scenarios in which self-sacrifice in the animal kingdom could proliferate.

Inclusive Fitness

More recent evolutionary thinkers argue that selection may operate at other levels as well. Individual selection leads us to believe that all behavior should be selfish; altruism should be very rare. But social animals such as primates behave in ways that benefit their close relatives, often to the detriment of their nonrelatives. Such behavior, called **kin selection,** was first framed by biologist William D. Hamilton (1964). It is part of a larger concept known as **inclusive fitness,** which refers to the sum of the fitness of the individual and all its close kin. Instead of considering only an animal's own reproductive success, evolutionary biologists realized that the reproductive success of one's kin also matters because it can contribute indirectly to the animal's fitness by helping its offspring survive and reproduce. Inclusive fitness predicts that social animals should behave less competitively toward close kin because of their shared genes.

The field of study that incorporates the concepts of inclusive fitness and kin selection is *sociobiology*. The majority of scientists who study animal social behavior in the wild today use an evolutionary framework to understand why animals behave as they do. Because full siblings share more of their genetic material than distant cousins, we can make predictions about how animals will behave in nature. For example, food-sharing between chimpanzees is far more likely to occur between close relatives than between nonrelatives. Ground squirrels sitting near their burrows give piercing alarm calls when hawks or coyotes appear. Isn't this altruistic behavior hard to explain in Darwinian terms because the call attracts attention to the caller, making him more likely to be eaten than his neighbor? Researchers found that alarm calls are given mainly when the nearest neighbor is a close relative; when a squirrel is sitting near nonrelatives, he is the first animal to flee into the burrow when danger approaches (Figure 5.16) (Sherman, 1977).

FIGURE 5.16 Ground squirrel predator warnings illustrate how kin selection may work.

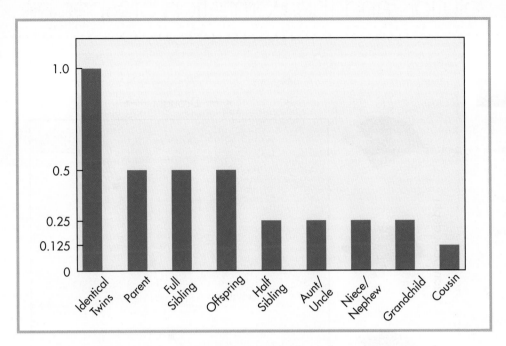

FIGURE 5.17   Coefficients of relatedness: How kin selection works.

Kin selection operates based on a *coefficient of relatedness,* expressed as $rb > c$, or Hamilton's rule, where r is the degree of kinship between two animals, b is the benefit of altruism to the recipient, and c is the cost of altruism to the altruist (the alarm caller, for instance). The closer the degree of kinship, the more likely altruistic behavior becomes, and the more likely an animal is to engage in dangerous behavior to help its kin (Figure 5.17). This principle guides much of the modern-day research into the social behavior of our closest relatives. We will return to the subject of kin selection when we consider the relevance of sociobiology to primate social behavior in more detail in Chapter 8.

The Forces of Evolution and the Formation of Species

Overview of Evolution

How Evolution Works

- There are five primary forces of the evolutionary process:
- Mutation is the only source of new variation.
- Natural selection is the filter that acts on variation.
- Gene flow is the biological name for migration.
- Genetic drift is evolution by random chance.
- Nonrandom mating is about mate selection and what drives it.
- Sexual selection is differential reproductive success within one sex. **[pp 81–88]**

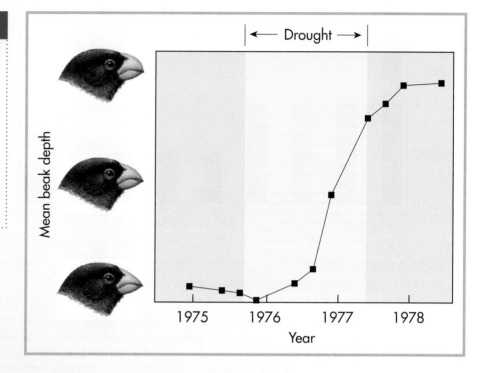

Formation of Species

Classification and Evolution

- Taxonomy is the science of classification, begun in the eighteenth century by Carl von Linnaeus. **[pp 88–90]**

What Is a Species?

- There is no single species concept: Different definitions can be applied depending on the context.
- Species are formed in a variety of ways: allopatric, parapatric, and sympatric.
- Speciation can happen at widely varying speeds. **[pp 90–95]**

Adaptation

- Scientists argue about whether every single trait in an organism is adaptive. **[pp 95–97]**

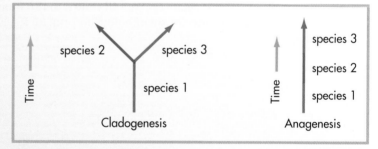

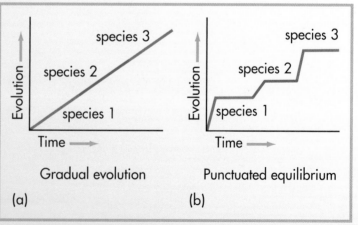

Hardy–Weinberg Equilibrium

- Hardy–Weinberg explains how a population without evolutionary change would look. **[pp 97–98]**

$$(p + q)^2 = p^2 + 2pq + q^2 = 1$$

Levels of Selection

- There are proximate and ultimate explanations for evolutionary change.
- Animals base their behavior toward other animals on potential genetic benefits. **[pp 98–99]**

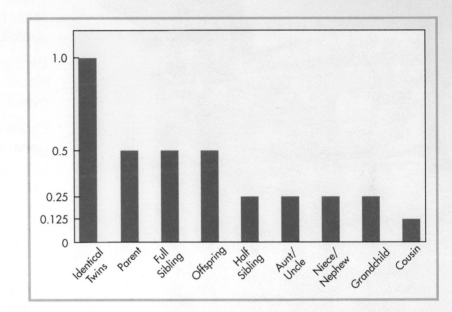

My AnthroLab CONNECTIONS

Watch. Listen. View. Explore. Read.

MyAnthroLab is designed just for you. Each chapter features a customized study plan to help you learn and review key concepts and terms. Dynamic visual activities, videos, and readings found in the multimedia library will enhance your learning experience.

Resources from this Chapter:

Watch on **myanthrolab**

▶ *A Single Population Through Time*
▶ *Reproductive Isolating Mechanisms*

Listen on **myanthrolab**

▶ *Natural Selection Works on Humans, Too*

Explore on **myanthrolab** In MySearchLab, enter the Anthropology database to find relevant and recent scholarly and poplar press publications. For this chapter, enter the following keywords: Forces of Evolution, Natural Selection, Mutation, Gene, Species

Read on **myanthrolab**

▶ *What Is a Species?* by Carl Zimmer
▶ *Testing Natural Selection* by H. Allen Orr

Chapter 6 Preview

After reading this chapter, you should be able to:

- Distinguish the various levels of biological variation (individual, population, species) and be able to discuss differences and similarities between the concepts of subspecies and race.

- Recognize how cultural and scientific views of human variation have evolved over the history of Western Civilization.

- Explain how the field of **population genetics** uncovers and analyzes genetic variation within and between populations of organisms.

- Explain how biological plasticity and adaptability allow humans to survive and thrive in diverse environments. Understand how populations may phenotypically differentiate from one another without any underlying changes to the genotypes.

- Show how polymorphisms, such as those relating to sickle cell disease or lactose digestion, are shaped by natural selection.

Human Variation: Evolution, Adaptation, and Adaptability

6

Down Bromley Kent Nov. 18th

M y dear Gray
It is a horrid shame to trouble you, busy as you always are, but there is one point on which I am very anxious to gain information & possibly it may be gained in the S[outh]. of your country & I can think of no one to apply to but you. Old writers often insist on differences of constitution going with complexion; & I want *much* to know whether there is any truth in this. It has occurred to me that liability to such a disease as yellow-fever would answer my question in the best possible way. Do you know anyone of a scientific mind to whom to apply to ask whether any observations have ever been made or *published*, whether Europeans (without of course any *cross with negro-blood*) of dark complexion & black hair are more liable or less liable to be attacked

with yellow-fever (or any *remittent Fever*), than persons of light complexion. If you could aid me in this it would be of much value to me. But do not trouble yourself to write merely to acknowledge this.—

I have just published a little notice in Gardeners Ch. on the fertilisation of Leguminous plants, which rather bears on our Fumariaceous discussion.

I sincerely hope that you are well & not working yourself to death

Pray believe me | My dear Gray | Yours most sincerely | C. Darwin

A sort of vague feeling comes over me that I have asked you all this before; if I have, I beg very many apologies.— I know I once wrote several letters to various parts of world for similar information.

(letter source: The Darwin Correspondence Project letter 2364, http://www.darwinproject.ac.uk)

In November 1858, Charles Darwin wrote this letter to his American colleague, Asa Gray (1810–1888), professor of natural history at Harvard University. Gray would eventually become known as America's foremost Darwinist, although before the publication of *Origin of Species*, Gray's main service to Darwin was in answering questions from him concerning a wide range of biological topics. In this letter, Darwin asks about the possible adaptive value of darker skin color; he wants to know why people with darker skin—whatever their geographical origins—might be more resistant to tropical diseases compared to people with lighter skin. What is interesting about this letter is that it reveals Darwin's attempt to understand this trait outside of a racial context (he wants to compare lighter- and darker-skinned Europeans). He is not simply taking skin color as an indelible hallmark of race, but as a feature subject to the effects of natural selection.

The origins of biological anthropology go back to the first half of the nineteenth century, an era when evolution had yet to be accepted by most natural historians and fossils representing human ancestors were all but unknown. At that time, biological anthropology was essentially the study of human variation, examined in the context of the 6,000-year history of biblical creation. Like Charles Darwin, who once he completed his voyage on the *Beagle*, never went to the field again, most of the earliest anthropologists

deme   Local, interbreeding population that is defined in terms of its genetic composition (for example, allele frequencies).

subspecies   Group of local populations that share part of the geographic range of a species, and can be differentiated from other subspecies based on one or more phenotypic traits.

race   In biological taxonomy, same thing as a subspecies; when applied to humans, sometimes incorporates both cultural and biological factors.

polytypic species   Species that consist of a number of separate breeding populations, each varying in some genetic trait.

ethnobiology   The study of how traditional cultures classify objects and organisms in the natural world.

did not go into the field to meet their research subjects. Instead, they relied on others' accounts of exotic peoples from faraway places and waited in their universities, hospitals, and museums for specimens, such as skeletal remains, to be sent to them.

Today, we study human variation using the evolutionary approach pioneered by Darwin. The field covers a wide range of topics, encompassing population genetics and the evolutionary history of human populations, how natural selection influences human biology, and how humans biologically and culturally adapt to environmental stress. However, before considering how biological anthropologists today approach the topic of human variation, it is important to examine past approaches, many of which were centered on the concept of race and the goal of racial classification.

Human Variation at the Individual and Group Levels

Modern humans show substantial *individual variation,* but biological anthropologists have generally been interested in variation at the *population level.* Humans have long noticed that people from different populations (or races, as they were sometimes called) may look different from one another. They also noticed that they may behave differently. The science of anthropology developed in order to systematically examine biological and cultural differences observed between different human populations. Population variation is widespread and can be measured using both genetics and morphology (characteristics of the body). As anthropology has developed over the past two centuries, methods for disentangling genetic, cultural, and environmental factors responsible for producing population variation have become more refined. It is important to remember, however, that human variation is not just associated with being a member of a specific population. People vary by age or sex, for example, and in their own particular combination of alleles they possess (Figure 6.1).

What Is a Population?

The word *population* can be a very flexible term. It is typically used to describe a group or community of animals that is identifiable within a species. As we discussed in Chapter 4, the members of a biological population constitute a potentially interbreeding group of individuals. An individual organism will find its reproductive mates from among the other members of its population. Many other terms have also been suggested for groups below the species level. Population geneticists have used terms such as *gene pool,* which emphasize that populations are assemblages of genes as well as individuals (Mettler et al., 1988). In general, geneticists use the term **deme** to refer to populations that are being defined in terms of their genetic composition (such as allele frequencies). All of these terms are meant to suggest that although these groups are in some way stable and identifiable, they are by no means genetically impermeable. After all, we study gene flow *between* populations.

Subspecies is another term some biologists use to describe variation below

FIGURE 6.1   Humans vary according to age, sex, and population of origin.

the species level. A subspecies is defined as a group of local populations that share part of the geographic range
of a species and can be differentiated from other subspecies based on one or more phenotypic traits (in rare
cases, a subspecies could consist of a single local population). Theoretically the identification of a subspecies is
done somewhat more formally than the identification of
a population. In the biological sciences, the term **race**
has been used interchangeably with *subspecies*. As we will
see in this chapter, however, the historical use of the race
concept in anthropology has not been a simple matter
of identifying biological subspecies. Anthropologists
have generally subscribed to the idea that human races,
like biological subspecies, correspond to groups of populations that are found in or derived from a particular
geographic area (Figure 6.2). *Homo sapiens* can be called
a **polytypic species,** one that is divided into local populations that differ by one or more phenotypic traits.

One problem has arisen repeatedly in the investigation
of population variation within our species: The concerns
of some scientists and lay people were centered on identifying "inferior" and "superior" races, and using "racial science" to reinforce and justify the prevailing social order or
impose a new one. The science of anthropology was born
in the nineteenth century, when there were incendiary debates about the moral and scientific correctness of slavery.
Was it the natural right of a "superior race" to enslave the
members of an "inferior race"? In the twentieth century,
Nazi Germany used "racial science" to justify the genocide
of Jews and Gypsies. Increasingly, *race* is viewed as a strictly
cultural or sociological term, denoting group member-
ship by an inconsistently applied range of criteria. Most biological anthropologists thus
avoid using the term altogether, for both scientific and historical reasons.

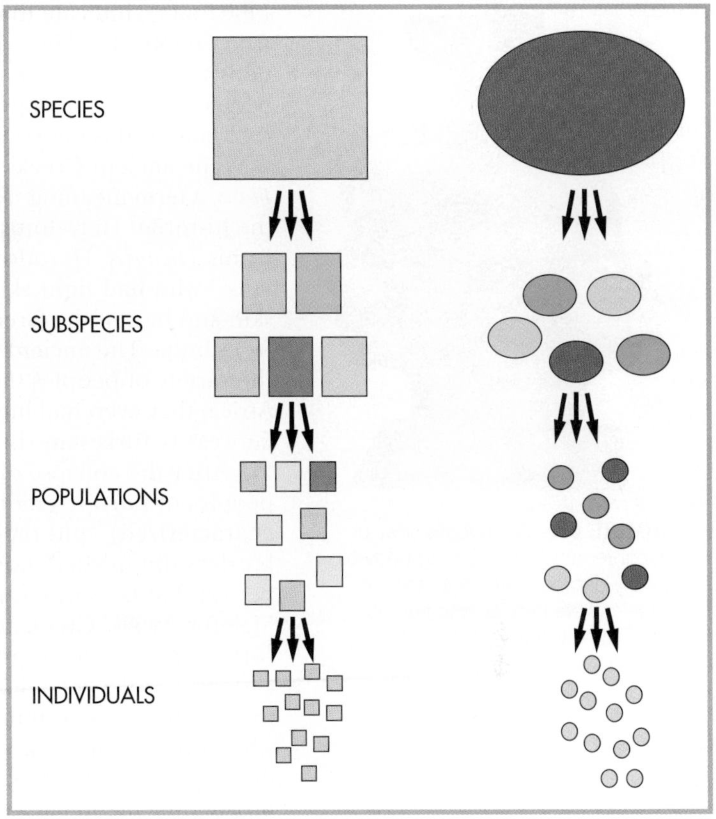

FIGURE 6.2 Species, subspecies, populations, and individuals. Species
are reproductively isolated from one another, but all members of a species
can interbreed.

Historical Perspectives on Human Variation

((•—[**Listen** to the **Podcast** "DNA
Suggests Ancient Hunter
Also Fought Baldness" on
myanthrolab

The most basic and universal classification of human variation at the group level is
"us" and "them." The field of **ethnobiology** is dedicated to understanding the different systems that cultures have developed to classify the objects and organisms in the
world around us (Berlin, 1992; Atran, 1998). One thing that ethnobiology makes
clear is that human beings are masters at making up categories and classifications in
which to place things. It comes as no surprise that humans have made efforts to classify people as well.

Recording Human Variation in Past Civilizations

In the nineteenth century, archaeologists discovered that the ancient Egyptians depicted human variation in some of the hieroglyphic records they left behind (Stanton,
1960). The Egyptians had extensive contacts with peoples to their north and south
and were well aware of the physical differences between them. As the great antiquity
of the Egyptian civilization began to be appreciated, Egyptology figured strongly in
two major nineteenth-century racial debates. One involved the origins of races themselves. Did evidence of human variation (recognized as racial variation by nineteenth-
century scientists) in ancient Egypt, which existed not long after the biblical creation

FIGURE 6.3 An aryballe vase or decanter made for carrying body oils clearly demonstrates that ancient Greeks were familiar with human population variation (520–510 B.C.)

(4004 B.C.), indicate that races were created by God and were therefore immutable (see Chapter 1)? The other debate focused on the physical constitution of the Egyptians themselves: Were they "African Negroes" or a more typically Middle Eastern people? Because the Egyptian civilization was viewed as one of the first great Western civilizations, this was considered to be an issue of some importance.

The ancient Greeks also knew of dark-skinned Africans, whom they called *Ethiopians,* a term meaning "scorched ones" in Greek (Brues, 1977). The poet Homer and the historian Herodotus also make reference to Africans in their work (Figure 6.3). In his *Histories,* Herodotus also made note of nomads from the north, the "Scythians," who had light skin and red or light hair, in obvious contrast to the darker skin and hair of the Greeks themselves, and he was aware of darker-skinned peoples from India. The ancient Romans had at least as extensive knowledge as the Greeks of the variety of peoples that could be found in the western part of Eurasia and north Africa; they even had limited contact with Han Chinese traders who had ventured as far west as Turkestan (Brues, 1977).

After the collapse of the (western) Roman Empire in the fifth century A.D., the peoples of Europe gradually entered the Dark Ages (as the early Middle Ages were characterized), and their knowledge of the world and peoples beyond their local borders diminished along with many other aspects of learning. It was during this period that tales of monsters and other fantastic beasts took center stage (de Waal Malefijt, 1968). Greek and Roman writers had reported the existence of monstrous sorts of people, with greater and lesser degrees of skepticism. There were tales of cyclops, headless people, and people who hibernated or transformed themselves into wolves during the summer (Figure 6.4). These views persisted into the Renaissance, when slowly, a more rational and evidence-based view of the natural world started to develop. Ancient Greek and Roman scholars were rediscovered during this period, broadening the Renaissance scholars' perspectives on people through time and space.

When the European age of discovery began in 1492, Europeans came into contact with many peoples who were new to them, but the basic question was: Were these actually people? Shakespeare's depiction of the strange and brutish Caliban (an anagram of *cannibal*) in *The Tempest* illustrates a common European view of people from the New World. In 1537, when Pope Paul III declared that American Indians were humans, he established a policy that became church orthodoxy for centuries: that all

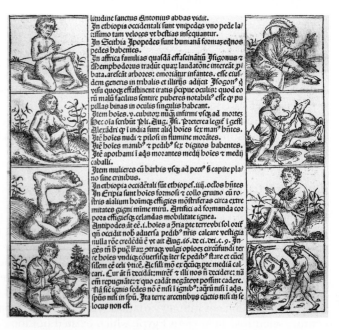

FIGURE 6.4 Monstrous people from distant lands depicted in a fifteenth-century European woodcut.

people, of all races, were the product of a single creation. In later scientific debates, this position became known as *monogenism* (see Chapter 1).

environmentalism The view that the environment has great powers to directly shape the anatomy of individual organisms.

The Monogenism–Polygenism Debate

During the eighteenth century, Linnaeus introduced a biological classification system that formed the basis of the one we use today (see Chapter 1). In the tenth edition of *Systema Naturae* (1758), Linnaeus provided a new name for our species, *Homo sapiens,* and with it he identified five subspecies or races. Linnaeus also identified a second "human" species, *Homo monstrosus,* which included a variety of human- and apelike forms.

German anatomist Johann Friedrich Blumenbach (1752–1840), in many ways the father of physical anthropology, established one of the first large collections of biological anthropological material, including a large number of skulls, for which he carefully noted their place of origin in order to better understand the biological diversity of the human species. Like Linnaeus, Blumenbach was also a monogenist, and he fully recognized the pitfalls of naming races. Despite the fact that he knew the divisions were arbitrary, Blumenbach identified five races for the sake of convenience. He also strongly denied the existence of "wild" or "feral" individuals as representing a distinct variety of humanity. Blumenbach was the first to use the term *Caucasian* to describe the people of western and southern Eurasia because he believed that a likely source of these peoples was to be found somewhere in the Caucasus region in present-day Georgia (Keith, 1940).

A basic problem for the monogenists was how to explain where the racial differences came from if all races had a recent common origin. Many believed in a very strong form of **environmentalism,** which held that the human body was biologically quite plastic and that the environment had great power to shape our anatomy. The Reverend Samuel Stanhope Smith (1751–1819), a president of Princeton University and one of the first American writers to address the natural history of human beings, provided an example of the power of the environment to shape anatomy; Smith (1965 [1810]) looked to the "blacks in the southern states." Smith claimed that the field slaves were darker and retained more of their "African" features, both physical and behavioral, than the domestic slaves, who were more "refined" in appearance, with lighter skin and elegant manners. He argued that the effects of civilization on the domestic slaves shaped their anatomy to make them more like their "civilized" masters (of course, Smith did not acknowledge that the domestic slaves might resemble their masters because they were related to them, or that they were chosen because of their "refined" appearance). By the standards of his day, Smith was not a racist; he believed that exposure to European-based civilization would cause people (African or Indians) to take on a European appearance.

In the early nineteenth century, as more information on the diversity of humanity became available, many scientists found it harder to believe that all of the racial diversity they observed could have arisen within the biblical time frame. Samuel George Morton (1799–1851), an anatomist and physician from Philadelphia, was one of the most prominent advocates of polygenism, or multiple creations or origins (Stanton, 1960). He argued that given only 6,000 years of Earth history and the fact that different races were represented in ancient Egyptian monuments, there was not enough time for the differentiation to occur. The polygenists rejected the idea that the environment had almost unlimited powers to reshape the human body. By the mid-nineteenth century, the polygenist position became increasingly accepted by serious scientists.

The issue of slavery often was associated with debates about racial origins, although not in a consistent way (Figure 6.5). In England, early anthropological societies

FIGURE 6.5 This watercolor depicts the miserable conditions Africans endured as they made the passage across the Atlantic and into slavery in the New World. In the mid-nineteenth century, debates about the abolition of slavery were often focused on concepts of racial origins.

were split on the basis of their adherence to monogenesis or polygenesis, a split that also reflected differing views on the equality of races and the legitimacy of slavery (Stocking, 1987). In the United States, before the Civil War (1861–1865), although the origin of races became an issue in the abolition debates, advocates of polygenism and monogenism did not consistently line up on one side of the debate or the other (Haller, 1970).

Read "American Anthropology Association Statement on Race" on **myanthrolab**

Race and Racism in the Twentieth Century

Throughout the twentieth century, the scientific study of human population variation was shaped by political and cultural forces. Of course, this has always been the case, but an increased recognition of the impact of these factors on "objective" science has developed, especially since the end of World War II (1939–1945). There has also been an increasing awareness of **racism,** scientific and otherwise. At one level, racism is simply prejudice against a person based on his or her racial heritage. The basis of such prejudice is the idea that important qualities of an individual (such as intellect, physical ability, and temperament) are biologically determined by his or her membership in a racial group. *Stereotyping,* in which the qualities of an individual are projected onto a larger group or vice versa, is also an important component of racism, especially of the more "everyday" variety.

Racial issues were of critical importance, in different ways, in three of the principal nations involved in World War II: Germany, Japan, and the United States. In Depression-era Germany, the Nazi party rose to power on the basis of an ideology that was centered on a celebration of *Aryanism,* a form of racism that was, in effect, a mythical rendering of the racial history of northern Europeans. The Aryan myth celebrated the "true" German as being the member of a "superior race" and was used to justify the subjugation and ultimately the extermination of "inferior races," such as Jews and Gypsies (Roma). Nazi ideology tapped into and amplified racial prejudices that had long existed, and the Nazis themselves acted on these impulses on an unprecedented scale. In prewar Japan, the imperial government and military also fostered an ideology of racial superiority, focused on the godlike status of the emperor (Bix, 2000). Some Japanese leaders were particularly attuned to racial issues in conflicts between Japan and Western powers, arguing that they were fueled in part by Western concepts of Japanese racial inferiority. Japanese imperialists justified their invasions of the Chinese province of Manchuria and other Asian nations as being in part a war of liberation from non-Asian colonizers, while asserting their superiority over their subject peoples.

The United States in the first half of the twentieth century was a fundamentally racist country. The conquest of the Native Americans was complete, and their demise was celebrated in the literature and films of the time. Blacks and Whites lived separate and unequal lives; the second-class status of African Americans was reinforced legally by Jim Crow laws and extralegally by lynchings and other violent means of coercion. Immigration laws restricted the entry of "undesirables" such as Asians and southern, central, and eastern Europeans. During World War II, Japanese Americans and Japanese nationals living in the continental United States were interned in "relocation" camps for the duration of the war. After the war, advocates of civil rights and racial equality recognized how ironic it was that the United States had helped to defeat two racist regimes while maintaining racist policies and cultural attitudes at home.

Changing Attitudes toward Race in Anthropology

Anthropologist Franz Boas and his followers instigated a reappraisal of the race concept early in the twentieth century. Unlike modern anthropologists who tend to be quite specialized, Boas conducted research in the cultural, biological, and linguistic realms. Although he did not reject the race concept, he took great pains to emphasize that biology, culture, psychology, and language needed to be carefully studied in any group so that they may be understood in local terms. In *The Mind of Primitive Man* (1911/1938) Boas argued that there was little evidence of a strong relationship

racism   A prejudicial belief that members of one ethnic group are superior in some way to those of another.

anthropometry   The measurement of different aspects of the body, such as stature or skin color.

ethnic group   A human group defined in terms of sociological, cultural, and linguistic traits.

between racial biology and cultural achievement. Boas's biological work focused on craniometry and **anthropometry,** the measurement of different aspects of the body, such as stature or skin, and culminated in his large-scale study comparing head and body form in immigrants to the United States and their U.S.-born children (Boas, 1912/1940; Allen, 1989). The differences he observed between parents and off-spring led Boas to emphasize that there was a good deal of biological plasticity within "racial" types. Boas had a much "softer" view of race than many of his contemporaries. Although the validity of Boas's work on bodily form changes in immigrants continues to be debated (Sparks and Jantz, 2002; Gravlee et al., 2003), there can be no doubt that the critique of race and racism that Boas initiated was one of the greatest scientific achievements of the twentieth century.

A tireless opponent of the use of the term *race* was anthropologist and writer Ashley Montagu (1905–1999). Although he did not invent it, Montagu was a proponent of the term **ethnic group** to describe human populations (Montagu, 1974). Ethnic groups are separated from one another primarily by social barriers, which may lead to biological differentiation or be a marker of biological difference. The term has come into widespread usage, in many cases as a replacement for *race,* but it is far from ideal for use in biologically oriented research because it explicitly incorporates sociocultural factors in group identification. Montagu was the principal author of the United Nations Statement on Race (1950), a far-reaching and influential document in which a powerful argument was made that the "racial science" of the Nazis—and even the term *race*—had no scientific validity. The UN Statement on Race inspired the more recent American Anthropological Statement on Race (1998; http://www.aaanet.org/stmts/racepp.htm), which attempts to summarize contemporary scientific views on race and the cultural and political contexts in which biological variation is shaped and expressed.

Today, biological anthropologists do not typically use the term *race,* preferring almost always to use the term *population.* But if biological anthropologists do not use the term *race,* does that mean that races do not exist? In a formal sense, the answer is "yes," but the word *race* is commonly used every day, by all sorts of people, in all kinds of situations. These people are talking about something, and other people understand what they are referring to, so in that sense races must exist. It *is* possible to sort Scandinavians from Africans or, for that matter, to sort Chinese from Cherokees or Lapplanders from Inuit people. Population-level biological differences do exist and in some cases are quite significant.

FIGURE 6.6 An 1827 portrait by George Catlin of Eeh-Nis-Kin (Crystal Stone), a Blackfoot woman.

Source: George Catlin (1796–1872), Eeh-nis-kim, Crystal Stone, Wife of the Chief. 1832. Oil on Canvas. 29" × 24". Smithsonian American Art Museum, Washington, DC/Art Resource, NY.

Deconstructing Racial Features

A few key traits have loomed large in how both scientists and laypeople have defined different racial groups. Even if the race concept itself is not considered valid in biological anthropology, what about the features people have been focusing on for so many years (Figures 6.6 and 6.7)? What is their biological relevance or irrelevance?

Skin Color Skin color is perhaps the most important morphological feature in cultural racial categories. Variation in human skin color is of no small biological significance. Because humans do not have fur, our skin is more directly exposed to the environment, and skin color likely is influenced by natural selection, as we will discuss later in this chapter. On a global scale, however, skin color is not a particularly good indicator of geographic origins. Populations from different parts of the world may have similar skin colors because they share a common environmental feature, namely the intensity of sunlight exposure. Very dark-skinned populations can be found in Africa, India, and Melanesia, but these populations do not share a recent common ancestry compared with other populations. The amount of variation in skin color of people classified as "White Americans" is substantial and reflects the diverse population origins (in terms of sunlight exposure, among other things) of this "race," which ranges from the Middle East and Mediterranean regions to the far north of Europe.

FIGURE 6.7 A nineteenth-century Japanese portrait of Commodore Matthew Perry, who "opened up" Japan in 1854.

population genetics The study of genetic variation within and between groups of organisms.

microevolution The study of evolutionary phenomena that occur within a species.

polymorphic Two or more distinct phenotypes (at the genetic or anatomical levels) that exist within a population.

cline The distribution of a trait or allele across geographical space.

maternal–fetal incompatibility Occurs when the mother produces antibodies against an antigen (for example, a red blood cell surface protein) expressed in the fetus that she does not possess.

Eye Form North and East Asians, as well as some of their descendant populations in the New World, have a high frequency of a morphological feature known as an *epicanthic fold*. This is the classic racial marker of "Oriental" or "Mongoloid" populations, although it can appear in individuals from other parts of the world. The epicanthic fold is a small flap of skin extending from the eyelid to the bridge of the nose. It has no known biological function. Alice Brues (1977) suggests that it is a secondary anatomical feature that results from a combination of a fatty eyelid and a low nasal bridge, both of which, she argues, may reflect adaptations to cold climates. She points out that epicanthic folds are more common in women than men in some Native American populations and in children rather than adults in European populations; both patterns may be a function of the relative development of the nasal bridge.

Hair Color and Form Human populations vary significantly in the color and form of the hair. There are no generally accepted functional explanations for why hair color, form, or thickness varies. It is clearly a polygenically inherited trait. Hair color is determined in part by the same substance as skin color (melanin), so it is no surprise that the two are correlated. However, some dark-skinned Australian aborigine populations have a large number of individuals with blond hair, especially when they are children. This may indicate that a different set of alleles may be governing hair color in these populations than in others (Molnar, 2002). Hair form varies from straight to tightly spiraled or woolly. Again, although there may be differences in the insulation properties of straight and spiraled hair, arguments can be made that this would be an advantage in either warm or cold climates. African and Melanesian populations both have woolly hair, but at a microscopic level their hair forms are quite different, indicating separate genetic origins.

Head Shape In the 1840s, Swedish anatomist Anders Retzius (1796–1860) introduced a statistic, the cranial or cephalic index (CI), to characterize the shape of the human skull. The CI is simply the width of the skull divided by the length multiplied by 100. Skulls that are narrow, or *dolichocephalic,* have CIs in the 70s, whereas those that are rounder, with CIs in the 80s, are called *brachycephalic*. Despite the fact that the CI was used to categorize skulls (and people) as "long-headed" or "rounded-headed," all normal skulls are longer than they are wide. Retzius's work introduced cranial shape as a marker of racial affiliation, which some late nineteenth and early twentieth century scientists enthusiastically adopted as a "scientific" way to measure race. Although racial schemes based (in part) on cranial shape are not considered valid today, it remains true that human populations show substantial variation in cranial shape and other cranial measures. In an analysis of a large number of skulls from populations around the world, Kenneth Beals and colleagues (1984) found that there is a relationship between skull shape and climate, with skull breadth increasing in colder climates. From a volume-to-surface ratio perspective, this makes sense in terms of the conservation of heat in a cold climate, which will be discussed later in the chapter.

Population Genetics

The field of **population genetics** is concerned with uncovering genetic variation within and between populations of organisms. In Chapter 4 we discussed several evolutionary processes, such as natural selection, gene flow, and genetic drift, which are all studied by population geneticists. Studying the dynamic distribution of alleles across populations can require complex mathematical tools (Cavalli-Sforza et al., 1994), many of which are derived from the Hardy–Weinberg equilibrium (see Chapter 4 and Appendix C). Although discussing these tools in detail is beyond the scope of this text, we will consider some of the results they have produced.

Population genetics is concerned primarily with **microevolution,** or evolutionary processes that occur within a species (in contrast to *macroevolution*; see Chapter 4). With increasingly sophisticated molecular biological techniques now available, the line between microevolutionary and macroevolutionary studies is becoming less clear-cut.

Polymorphisms: ABO and Other Blood Type Systems

View the **Map** "Frequency of the Genes in the ABO Blood-group System" on **myanthrolab**

If we look at a population and find that there are at least two alleles present for a given gene, and the alleles are both present at a frequency greater than 1 percent, then we can say that the population is **polymorphic** for that gene. The term is also used to describe variation at the more observable phenotypic level (see Chapter 4). For example, in a population where both blue- and brown-eyed people live, we can say that it is polymorphic for eye color, assuming that it is a genetic feature and that both phenotypes are present at a frequency of at least 1 percent. Many protein polymorphisms have no phenotypic effect other than the fact that they are slightly different versions of the same protein. The 1 percent figure is used as a cutoff because it is substantially above the level you would expect if a rare allele or phenotype were present simply because of the occurrence of mutations.

In Chapter 3 we discussed the ABO blood type system, which is a classic example of a polymorphic genetic system. Although Karl Landsteiner discovered the ABO system in 1901 (for which he received the 1930 Nobel Prize in Medicine), it was not until 1919 that Polish physicians Ludwik and Hanka Hirszfeld published the first report on "racial" variation in the ABO system. They did this study at the end of World War I on the Macedonian battlefront, where soldiers from Europe, the Middle East, Africa, and southern Asia could be tested. It is interesting to note that ABO distribution initially was of little interest to many anthropologists because it did not correlate particularly well with traditional notions of racial classification (Boyd, 1950), a fact pointed out by the Hirszfelds themselves. In Figure 6.8 on page 112, *clinal* maps of the distribution of the ABO alleles throughout the world's populations are presented. A **cline** represents the distribution of a genotypic or a phenotypic characteristic(s) across geographical space. One worldwide estimate for the frequencies of the three alleles is 62.5 percent O, 21.5 percent A, and 16.0 percent B (Harrison et al., 1988).

The distribution of ABO alleles in populations raises some interesting evolutionary issues. Why are the polymorphisms maintained in different populations? Why do we not see more alleles at fixation in different populations because of the effects of genetic drift or bottlenecks? Why are the A and B allele frequencies always less than 50 percent? Research on A and B antigens strongly suggests that natural selection has influenced their population distribution in some way (Koda et al., 2001). Over the years, several investigators have suggested that infectious disease plays a key role in the distribution of ABO alleles in different populations. Robert Seymour and his colleagues (2004) suggested that a balance between A and B alleles is maintained in populations with a heavy load of bacterial disease, whereas O would be expected to predominate in populations that are more vulnerable to viral disease. Their mathematical genetic models suggest that the relative frequencies of A, B, and O alleles are maintained by the relative impact of bacterial and viral diseases in a population.

The vast majority of Native Americans have type O blood. This has generally been assumed to be the result of a founder effect, reflecting the genetic makeup of the relatively small population(s) that likely settled the Americas from northern Asia. However, alternative possibilities, such as strong selection for type O in the face of exposure to infectious diseases from Europe, could also explain the pattern. However, ancient DNA research seems to confirm the founder effect hypothesis: A study of precontact Native American remains (15 individuals) from the midwestern United States, dating back to 1800 years ago, shows that the allele frequency for O in this population was 0.967 (Halverson and Bolnick, 2008).

Maternal–Fetal Incompatibility Another factor that influences the distribution of ABO alleles in a population arises out of the immune response of a pregnant woman and how it influences the health of her fetus. **Maternal–fetal incompatibility**

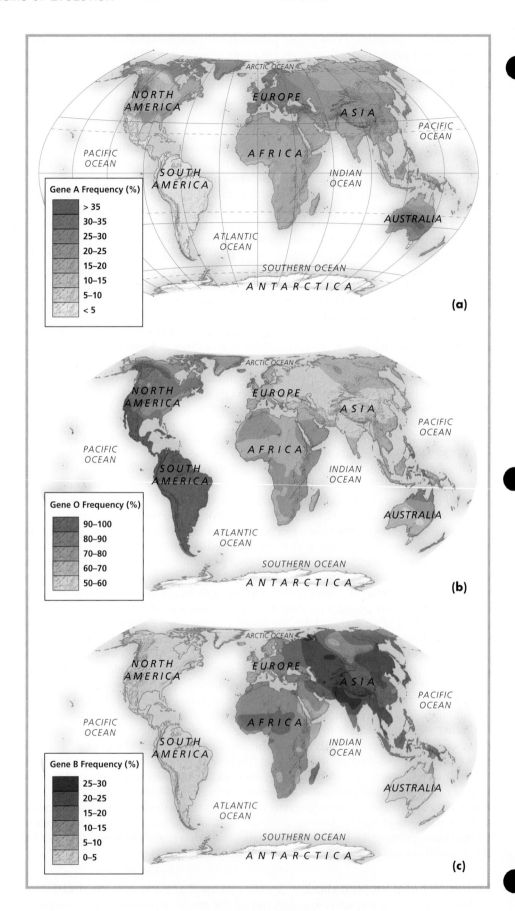

FIGURE 6.8 Clinal maps of ABO allele distributions in the indigenous populations of the world. (a) Frequency distribution of the A allele. (b) Frequency distribution of the O allele. (c) Frequency distribution of the B allele.

Source: Adapted from Mourant et al. (1976). *The Distribution of Human Blood Groups (2nd Edition).* Oxford University Press, London.

occurs when a mother has type O blood and her infant has type A, B, or AB, or when a woman has type A and the infant has type B and vice versa. In the case of a type O mother and a type B infant (the father must carry a B allele), because the mother does not possess the B antigen on her red blood cells, she will make anti-B antibodies on exposure to the fetus's blood. For much of the pregnancy, the maternal and fetal blood do not mix; however, at birth the mother is almost always exposed to fetal blood through ruptures in tissues caused by the delivery or separation of the placenta from the uterine wall. On exposure to the B antigen, the mother's immune system is primed to produce anti-B antibodies. In subsequent pregnancies, the red blood cells of fetuses that carry the B allele are subject to attack by the maternal anti-B antibodies, which can cross the placental barrier. When the infant is born, he or she can be anemic (usually mildly so) because of the reduction in the number of oxygen-carrying red blood cells. This is known as *hemolytic anemia*. There is some evidence that ABO incompatibilities can have a damaging effect early in pregnancy, resulting in a higher rate of spontaneous abortion (Bottini et al., 2001; Bandyopadhyay et al., 2011).

The **rhesus (Rh) system,** another blood group, was originally identified by using antibodies made against rhesus macaque red blood cells. It is of particular clinical importance because maternal–fetal incompatibility in this system leads to the development of a much more severe form of anemia in the newborn, resulting in a disease called *erythroblastosis fetalis,* than does ABO incompatibility. One reason for this is that unlike the Rh factor, the A and B antigens are expressed in tissues other than the red blood cells, so there are fewer maternal antibodies available to attack the fetal red blood cells. The genetics of the Rh system are complex and involve three major genes with at least two alleles apiece (Cavalli-Sforza et al., 1994). For our purposes we can concentrate on one of these loci, which has two alleles, D and d. Individuals who are homozygous DD or heterozygous Dd are called *Rh-positive,* and those who are homozygous dd are *Rh-negative* (Figure 6.9). Similar to cases in which the mother is type O and the infant is type A, B, or AB, maternal–fetal incompatibility arises when the mother is Rh-negative and the infant is Rh-positive. The first pregnancy usually is fine, but subsequent incompatible pregnancies can lead to the development of severe

rhesus (Rh) system Blood type system that can cause hemolytic anemia of the newborn through maternal–fetal incompatibility if the mother is Rh-negative and the child is Rh-positive.

FIRST PREGNANCY

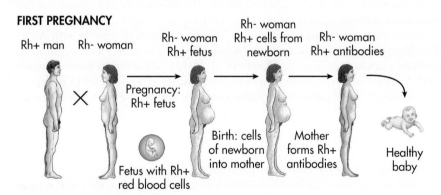

SUBSEQUENT PREGNANCIES

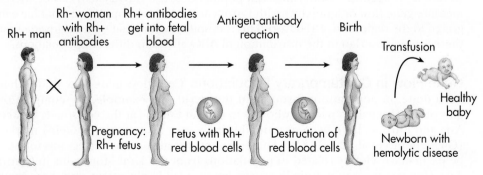

FIGURE 6.9 Maternal–fetal incompatibility in the Rh system.

human leukocyte antigen (HLA) system Class of blood group markers formed by proteins expressed on the surface of white blood cells (leukocytes).

autoimmune diseases Diseases caused by the immune system reacting against the normal, healthy tissues of the body.

haplotypes Combinations of alleles (or at the sequence level, mutations) that are found together in an individual.

Duffy blood group Red blood cell system useful for studying admixture between African- and European-derived populations.

hemolytic anemia in the newborn, which may necessitate blood transfusions. It has been found that giving the mother anti-D antibodies early in pregnancy can suppress her immunological response: The anti-D antibodies "intercept" the fetal red blood cells before the mother's immune system is exposed to them. This prevents development of anemia in the at-risk newborn.

Maternal–fetal incompatibility in both the ABO and Rh systems influences the distribution of their alleles in populations. For example, in the Rh system, only heterozygous offspring of an Rh-negative mother and an Rh-positive father are at risk of developing anemia. In a traditional culture, these infants would be at great risk of dying without reproducing. Simple genetic models indicate that in a population that has a D allele frequency of 50 percent or more, the d allele eventually will be lost. The opposite case is also true if the d allele frequency reaches 50 percent (assuming that no selection or other evolutionary factors are at play) (Cavalli-Sforza and Bodmer, 1971/1999).

The Human Leukocyte Antigen (HLA) System Besides the ABO and Rh systems, several other blood systems are used in population genetic studies. These include the Diego, Duffy, Kell, Kidd, Lewis, Lutheran, and MNS systems. A different class of blood group markers is formed by the **human leukocyte antigen (HLA) system.** These antigens are proteins found on the surface of white rather than red blood cells. There are many classes of white blood cells, all of which are critical in the immune response (an elevated white blood cell count indicates that the body is fighting an infection). As most people know, the ABO antigens are critical for determining who can donate blood to whom. The HLA system is critical in matching donors and hosts for organ and skin transplants. Some HLA alleles are associated with protection from a variety of infectious diseases, including malaria, HIV, hepatitis B, and bacterial diseases (Cooke and Hill, 2001). The high degree of variability within the HLA system is evidence in itself that natural selection and other nonrandom evolutionary forces have been critical in shaping the distribution of its alleles (Meyer and Thomson, 2001).

Certain HLA alleles (along with other gene systems) are associated with the development of **autoimmune disease,** such as rheumatoid arthritis. Autoimmune diseases arise when the immune system reacts to and attacks the normal, healthy tissues of the body. Rheumatoid arthritis affects about 0.5 percent of all people, although there is much population variation in its prevalence, it is less common in people with Asian (0.1–0.5%) rather than European ancestry (0.3–1.1%), but may be most common in Native American populations (5–7%) (Kochi et al., 2010). Variation in the frequency of various HLA alleles underlies differences in rheumatoid arthritis rates in different populations, although these patterns are quite complex and not yet well understood.

Gene Flow and Protein Polymorphisms

Because allele frequencies for countless proteins vary from population to population, genetic polymorphisms can be used to look at patterns of gene flow and migration from one population to another. For example, because the A and B alleles are so rare in indigenous South American populations, the ABO system can be used to measure gene flow or admixture with European or African populations that have migrated to the region since 1500 A.D. This is despite the fact that on a worldwide basis, there is much overlap in the distribution of ABO alleles in different populations.

Gene Flow in Contemporary Populations Countless gene flow studies have been done on populations throughout the world. For example, the complex origins of the Hungarian people, who live in central Europe at the crossroads between Asia and Europe, have been examined using a variety of classic (protein) markers (Guglielmino et al., 2000). One Hungarian ethnic group, the Örség, was found to be particularly closely related to populations from the Ural Mountains in Central Asia. Hungarian is a non–Indo-European language of Uralic origin, and these results confirmed oral histories and traditions that linked the Örség to populations that had migrated from the Ural region in the ninth century.

Numerous studies have also been done to trace the complex genetic history of Jewish populations in western Eurasia and Africa. The migrational history of Jews is complex, dating back to the *diaspora* or dispersal of the Jews from ancient Palestine to Babylonian exile in 586 B.C. The diaspora became a permanent feature of Jewish life and included events such as the expulsion of Jews from Spain in 1492. Gene flow studies have produced conflicting results, some indicating substantial admixture between Jewish and other populations located in an area and others indicating much less gene flow.

More recently, Y-chromosome markers have provided new insights into the histories of some Jewish populations. The Lemba, or "Black Jews," of southern Africa have a long oral tradition of Jewish ancestry (a claim that has been regarded with more than a little skepticism). Consistent with this tradition, genetic studies indicate that about half of the Y-chromosomes in the Lemba population are of Semitic origin (Figure 6.10) (Spurdle and Jenkins, 1996; Parfitt and Egorova, 2005). Michael Hammer and colleagues (2000) looked at Y-chromosome **haplotypes** in Jewish and non-Jewish men from populations throughout Europe, Africa (including a Lemba sample), and the Middle East. Haplotypes are combinations of alleles (or, at the sequence level, of mutations) that are found together in an individual. In many cases, combinations of alleles or mutations are more informative than alleles or mutations considered singly. Hammer and colleagues found that the Jewish populations closely resembled non-Jewish Middle Eastern populations, with whom they are presumed to share a common ancestry, in the distribution of Y-chromosome haplotypes, moreso than non-Jewish populations near which they may currently be living. Thus Jewish populations, despite numerous migrations across a broad geographic area, appear to be more similar to one another and to non-Jewish Middle Eastern populations than to other populations, at least in terms of the Y-chromosome.

Several gene flow studies have been done in African American populations to assess the contribution of European alleles in the composition of their genetic structures. Although for much of U.S. history admixture between African and European Americans has been strongly proscribed, gene flow studies indicate that it was not an unusual occurrence. A classic genetic study using a **Duffy blood group** allele that is largely absent in Africa but common in European populations showed that European admixture in five African American populations ranged from 4 percent in Charleston, South Carolina, to 26 percent in Detroit (Reed, 1969). In a more recent study using autosomal DNA markers, mtDNA haplotypes, and Y-chromosome polymorphisms, Esteban Parra and colleagues (1998) confirmed these high rates of admixture. Looking at nine communities, they found admixture rates ranging from 11.6 percent in Charleston to 22.5 percent in New Orleans (Table 6.1 on page 116).

A sample from a Jamaican population showed a European proportion of only 6.8 percent, indicating a substantial difference between Afro-Caribbean and African American communities. The mtDNA (maternally inherited) and the Y-chromosome (paternally inherited) data indicated that gene flow from European to African American populations was strongly sex-biased, with men making a substantially greater contribution than women. This comes as no surprise, given that sexual contacts between male slave owners and female slaves were not uncommon.

Large-scale immigration of Africans and Afro-Caribbeans into Great Britain occurred during the twentieth century. But an African presence in the British Isles dates back to Roman times, when a division of "Moors" was included among the legions assigned to Hadrian's Wall (along the border of modern England and Scotland).

FIGURE 6.10 Members of the Lemba ethnic group from southern Africa.

TABLE 6.1 **European Genetic Contribution to African American and Jamaican Populations**

Location	Percentage
Detroit	16.3
Maywood, Illinois	18.8
New York	19.8
Philadelphia	13.0
Pittsburgh	20.2
Baltimore	15.5
Charleston, South Carolina	11.6
New Orleans	22.5
Houston	16.9
Jamaica	6.8

Source: Parra et al. (1998)

A Y-chromosome study conducted on males from a family bearing an unusual Yorkshire surname, has found that they possess a Y-chromosome that is clearly derived from a West African source (King et al., 2007). Although these men look like "typical" Yorkshireman, their genetics suggests a more complex history for this lineage. A similar situation is hinted at in a recent study conducted in Iceland using mtDNA (Ebenesersdóttir et al., 2011). These Icelandic researchers have identified a unique mtDNA lineage in Iceland that is clearly not derived from Scandinavia, but which appears most likely to have a Native American origin dating back to before the time of Columbus. This suggests contact between Icelanders and Native Americans arising from the tenth century Viking exploration of North America. These two studies illustrate, at the level of the individual perhaps, the dynamic forces that shape the genetic histories of human populations.

Polymorphisms and Phylogenetic Studies

Allele frequencies, haplotype frequencies, and DNA and protein sequence information can all be used to construct an evolutionary tree, or **phylogeny,** relating populations (if frequency data are used) or individuals from different populations (if sequence data are used). The statistical mathematics underlying the construction of these trees is beyond the scope of this text, but the basic principles are not.

Constructing a Phylogenetic Tree Any phylogenetic tree aims to cluster closely related populations together compared to less closely related populations (Figure 6.11). Closely related populations share a *branch*: a lineage or a clade (see Chapter 4). Branching points, or *nodes,* in the tree represent the separation or division of any pair (or groups) of populations. For example, a particular genetic mutation may be found in some populations but not others; possessing that particular mutation could serve as the basis for putting those populations together on one branch of the tree separate from the others. The node in the tree where that branch begins represents when the ancestral population possessing the mutation split off from the other populations. Longer branches and deeper nodes indicate that more change has occurred along the evolving lineages, and thus that more time has elapsed since the separation of the two populations (assuming the rate of genetic change is relatively constant). A phylogenetic tree produced from a genetic data set should incorporate the fewest number of evolutionary steps or events; in other words, the tree should be constructed parsimoniously.

A Genetic Tree of the World's Populations Geneticist Luigi Luca Cavalli-Sforza and colleagues (1994) provided an extensive analysis of the distribution of 120 alleles (29 of which come from the HLA system) in 42 populations throughout the

phylogeny An evolutionary tree indicating relatedness and divergence of taxonomic groups.

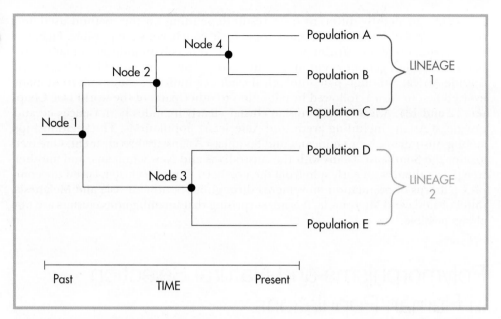

FIGURE 6.11   A generic phylogenetic tree. Populations A, B, and C share a lineage (or clade) and are more closely related to each other than populations D and E of lineage 2. Populations A and B share a more recent common ancestor (at node 4) with each other than they do with population C. The last time all five populations shared a common ancestor was at node 1.

world. The selection of these 42 populations was based on several criteria, not the least important of which was the availability of genetic data for inclusion in the analysis. They provide a good sample of the world's populations as they were distributed at the arbitrary cutoff date of 1492 A.D. The phylogenetic tree of these 42 populations divides into 9 major clusters: Africans (sub-Saharan), Caucasoids (Europeans), Caucasoids (non-Europeans), northern Mongoloids (excluding arctic populations), northeast Asian arctic populations, southern Mongoloids (mainland and island Southeast Asia) (Figure 6.12), New Guineans and Australians, inhabitants of the minor Pacific islands, and Americans.

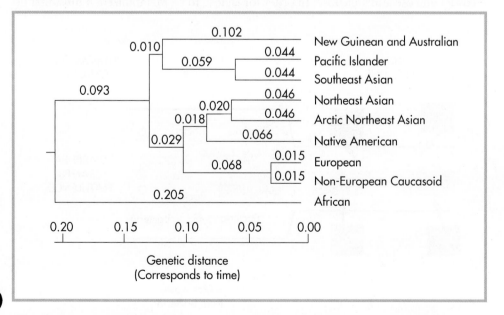

FIGURE 6.12   Phylogenetic tree based on the distribution of 120 alleles in 42 populations from around the world, clustered into 9 major groups.
Source: Cavalli-Sforza et al. (1994).

lactose intolerant The inability to digest lactose, the sugar found in milk; most adult mammals (including humans) are lactose intolerant as adults.

Although slightly different trees result depending on the method used and how the populations are constructed, some basic conclusions are possible. First, the deep separation of the African populations from others is an indication that this reflects the earliest genetic event in human history. This event could have happened outside Africa, although paleontological evidence indicates that modern humans evolved first in Africa, followed by migration to other parts of the world (see Chapters 12 and 13). A northern Eurasian cluster clearly includes both Caucasoid and northeast Asian (including arctic and American) populations. The relationships among Australians, New Guineans, and Southeast Asians are less clear-cut. One tree groups the Southeast Asians with the Australians and New Guineans, and another tree places them as an early split from the northern Eurasian cluster. Given the complex patterns of population movements throughout Southeast Asia and Melanesia into Polynesia and Micronesia, it is not surprising that unambiguous clusters are not always possible.

Polymorphisms and Natural Selection in Human Populations

Many polymorphisms in human populations have come about as a result of genetic drift or gene flow, but it is also clear that some have been shaped by natural selection. An obvious example of negative selection can be seen in maternal–fetal incompatibility, which has led to polymorphisms in the ABO and Rh blood type systems. But positive selection for new genetic variants has also shaped the distribution of some human polymorphisms.

The Evolution of Lactose Tolerance

One of the main characteristics of mammals is that newborns and young animals suckle milk from their mothers. After weaning, young mammals are no longer directly dependent on their mothers for food, and they never drink milk again. The main carbohydrate in mammal milk is a sugar called *lactose*. Lactose is actually a *disaccharide*—or a sugar made up of two smaller sugars—composed of the monosaccharides glucose and galactose. In order for lactose to be metabolized, it must first be

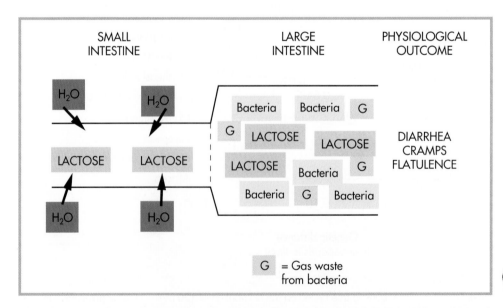

FIGURE 6.13 Physiological effects of the accumulation of lactose in the intestines of a lactose-intolerant individual.

split into glucose and galactose; this is done by an enzyme called *lactase* (coded for by a gene on chromosome 2 [Hollox et al., 2001]), which is present in the small intestine of most young mammals. As mammals get older, their bodies shut down production of lactase, so older mammals cannot digest lactose. As adults, they are *lactose malab-sorbers*. Indeed, many older mammals suffer gastric distress if they consume milk, with symptoms such as abdominal distention, flatulence, cramps, acidic stools, and diarrhea. These digestive problems are caused by the accumulation of lactose in the small intestine, which changes the osmotic activity in that part of the gut, leading to an influx of fluid (that is, diarrhea), and excess lactose in the large intestine, which is fermented by bacteria in the colon (that is, gas production). An individual who has these symptoms after consuming milk products is **lactose intolerant** (Figure 6.13).

It was once thought that humans were unique among mammals in the continued production of lactase through adulthood, which allows humans to digest lactose (milk products) as adults. However, research in the 1960s on European and African Americans demonstrated that only *some* humans were lactose tolerant as adults (Cuatrecasas et al., 1965). Indeed, as more research was done, it was discovered that most people in the world are lactose intolerant as adults and that lactase production is a highly polymorphic trait across the human species (Allen and Cheer, 1996). Table 6.2 presents lactose absorption rates for populations throughout the world. High-absorber populations are concentrated in Europe or in populations with a high degree of European admixture (such as Polynesian populations in New Zealand). In addition, some African ethnic groups, such as the Tussi, Fulani, and Hima, also

TABLE 6.2   Lactose Absorption Rates in Different Populations

Population	Percentage Lactose Absorbers
AFRICA	
Bantu (West Africa)	4
Watutsi (East Africa)	83
Nilotic (Sudan)	39
South Africa	17
ASIA	
South India	33
Japan	0
Thailand	2
Taiwan Chinese	0
EUROPE	
Britain	94
Germany	85
Sweden	100
Italy	25–50
NORTH AMERICA	
European American	80–94
African American	25–30
Apache	0
Chippewa	30
PACIFIC	
Fiji	0
New Zealand Maori	36
Australian Aborigines	16
Papua New Guinea	11

Sources: Allen and Cheer (1996), Molnar (2002).

balanced polymorphism   A stable polymorphism in a population in which natural selection prevents any of the alternative phenotypes (or underlying alleles) from becoming fixed or being lost.

frequency-dependent balanced polymorphism   Balanced polymorphism that is maintained because one (or more) of the alternative phenotypes has a selective advantage over the other phenotypes only when it is present in the population below a certain frequency.

heterozygous advantage   With reference to a particular genetic system, the situation in which heterozygotes have a selective advantage over homozygotes (for example, sickle cell disease); a mechanism for maintaining a balanced polymorphism.

have high rates of lactose tolerance. Other populations, such as many in Asia, some African, and many Native American groups, have very low frequencies of lactose absorbers.

Lactose-tolerant individuals are found at high frequency in populations with a long history of dairying and using milk products (Simoons, 1970; McCracken, 1971; Wiley, 2011). There has been strong selection for LCT*P in these populations. In nondairying populations, the distribution of haplotypes associated with lactase non-persistence are consistent with evolution primarily by genetic drift (Hollox et al., 2001). The *cultural historical hypothesis,* suggested by Simoons and McCracken independently, proposes that in populations where animals were domesticated and milk products used (dating back to about 9000 B.C. in the Middle East), there has been strong selection for lactose-tolerant individuals. Milk is a valuable food providing both carbohydrates and proteins, and in an environment where other nutritional resources might be scarce, individuals who could digest milk as adults would have a substantial survival advantage. Modest selective advantages (relative increases in fitness) of 5–10 percent could account for the high frequencies of lactose tolerance found in northern European populations over a period of about 6,000 years (Aoki, 1986; Feldman and Cavalli-Sforza, 1989).

There are populations in which dairying is present but lactose tolerance frequencies are low, such as those in central and southern Asia. In many of these populations, milk is not drunk raw but is processed into yogurt or cheese. In the making of yogurt and cheese, bacteria are used to convert lactose to lactic acid. Thus the ability to digest lactose is not critical in obtaining the nutrients from these products, and lactose tolerant individuals historically have had no selection advantage in these populations.

The evolution of lactose tolerance is a clear-cut example of the interaction of biological and cultural factors in shaping biological variation within our species.

Balanced Polymorphisms: Sickle Cell and Other Conditions

In any population, the polymorphism for lactose digestion ability in adulthood can be explained in terms of cultural practices, natural selection, gene flow, and genetic drift. However, when we look at other genetic systems and populations, it appears that there are polymorphisms that are quite stable and are not the result of obvious historical factors. Something is preventing alleles from going to fixation or being lost. This is called a **balanced polymorphism.** A fascinating aspect of microevolution is the attempt to explain mechanisms underlying balanced polymorphisms.

The large number of variants present in the HLA system may be evidence of a balanced polymorphism in this genetic system. If HLA variants are useful for conferring resistance to infectious diseases, then some HLA polymorphisms may be maintained as a **frequency-dependent balanced polymorphism** (Cooke & Hill, 2001). In this situation, an allele (or trait) has an advantage in a population relative to other alleles until it reaches a certain frequency in the population. If it becomes more common than this frequency, it loses its advantage, and the balanced polymorphism is maintained. In the HLA system, an HLA variant may confer resistance to a specific infectious disease. While it is rare in the population, it will have an advantage because the infectious agent itself has not evolved to overcome whatever defense it confers. However, as the resistant variant becomes more common in the population, there will be selection on the infectious agent to adjust to it. Eventually, a frequency will be reached at which the disease-resistant variant loses its advantage. A high degree of polymorphism in a population may result as this process is repeated for multiple alleles, and the resulting polymorphism is stable or balanced.

View the **Map** "Distribution of HbS in Africa" on **myanthrolab**

Heterozygous Advantage   It has been noted that genetic diversity in breeding plants and animals often results in improved yields; this is called hybrid vigor or *heterosis.* It is assumed that this may result from a high frequency of heterozygosity at many loci underlying a complex genetic trait. However, **heterozygous advantage** has been observed in much simpler genetic contexts. In a one-gene, two-allele situation, a balanced polymorphism will be maintained if the heterozygotes have a selective advantage over both of the homozygotes. This is just the opposite of what happens in cases of maternal–fetal incompatibility, which actually works against the maintenance of a polymorphism.

The classic example of a balanced polymorphism maintained by heterozygous advantage is the high frequency of the *sickle cell trait* in some populations with endemic *malaria*. In Chapter 3 we discussed the molecular and cellular genetics of sickle cell disease, which is caused by an abnormal hemoglobin protein, HbS (as opposed to the normal HbA), that impairs the ability of red blood cells to deliver oxygen to the tissues of the body. It is an autosomal recessive disease, and people who are heterozygotes are carriers of the condition. In a nonmalarial environment, the carriers show few signs of illness, although they may be slightly at risk in low-oxygen environments.

Malaria may have killed more people—especially children—than any other infectious disease. According to the World Health Organization, more than 40 percent of the world's population lives in malarial regions. It affects 300–500 million people per year, and it kills a million children per year under the age of 6 in Africa alone. In addition, chronic malaria has incalculable negative economic, social, and political effects. There is no doubt that malaria has exerted a strong selection pressure on human populations for many thousands of years.

Malaria is caused by protozoa from the genus *Plasmodium*. Of the 120 species in this genus, 4 cause malaria: *P. malariae*, *P. vivax*, *P. falciparum*, and *P. ovale*. The symptoms of malaria include fever, anemia, inflammation of the spleen, and headache. Cerebral malaria is especially serious and may lead to insanity, unconsciousness, and death. Humans are infected with the *Plasmodium* parasite via the bite of a female *Anopheles* mosquito, which is an essential carrier or *vector* of the disease. The *Plasmodium* life cycle requires both human and mosquito hosts. Because malaria depends on the mosquito for its spread from human host to host, the ability of the mosquito to survive and breed is a critical factor in local patterns of malarial expression. For example, in regions that have a pronounced dry season, mosquito breeding is highly seasonal, and malaria does not become a stable and constant aspect of life. In contrast, malaria is endemic in wet, equatorial climates in Africa and Southeast Asia, where mosquito breeding continues year-round.

Although human intervention has worked to limit the range of malaria, human cultural practices have also helped to increase its impact on human populations. The development of slash-and-burn agriculture in Africa led to clearing of tropical forests; an increase in the amount of standing, stagnant water; and higher human population densities (Figure 6.14) (Livingstone, 1958). All of these worked to increase the disease's spread. In addition, the disrupted tropical forest conditions favored breeding of a particular species of mosquito, *A. gambiae*, which is the vector for *P. falciparum*, which in turn causes the most lethal form of malaria. This was the context for the evolution of high frequencies of the HbS allele (Allison, 1954).

In malarial environments, individuals who are heterozygous HbS HbA have higher reproductive fitness than either HbA HbA or HbS HbS homozygotes (Figure 6.15 on page 122). Individuals who are homozygous HbS HbS have sickle cell anemia, a disease that, in traditional settings, drastically shortens the life span, precluding reproduction. However, heterozygous individuals with sickle cell trait are more resistant to developing malaria than homozygous HbA HbA individuals. This is because the presence of

FIGURE 6.14 Slash-and-burn agriculture in Africa.

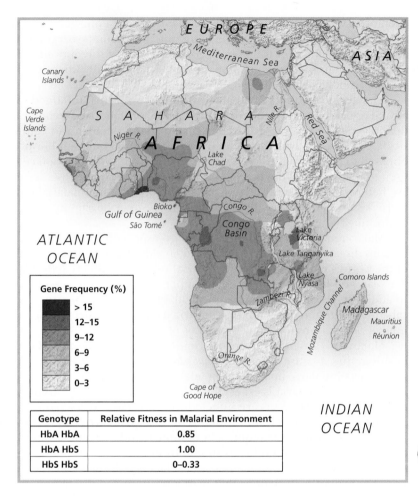

Genotype	Relative Fitness in Malarial Environment
HbA HbA	0.85
HbA HbS	1.00
HbS HbS	0–0.33

FIGURE 6.15   Clinal map of the distribution of HbS in Africa.

abnormal hemoglobin in the red blood cells of heterozygous individuals seriously affects the life cycle of the *P. falciparum* parasite, though not enough to affect human physiology in any meaningful way. In these malarial regions, heterozygote individuals are overrepresented in populations over age 45, indicating their enhanced survival. The HbS allele cannot go to fixation because the homozygotes are seriously impaired. Thus the HbA–HbS polymorphism is maintained by heterozygous advantage.

Sickle cell carrier frequencies are almost 40 percent in some African populations. High HbS frequencies are also found in Mediterranean, Middle Eastern, and Indian populations, reflecting former and present malarial loads in these regions. African Americans also have a high frequency of HbS, which reflects their ancestral populations. However, without malaria in the environment, heterozygotes are no longer at an advantage, and the frequency of HbS is declining because of the reduced fitness of HbS homozygotes.

Several other alleles that directly or indirectly affect red blood cell physiology (such as the thalassemias, which directly affect the structure of hemoglobin, and G6PD polymorphisms, which affect key metabolic pathways) are also found in high frequency in malarial areas. These conditions, along with sickle cell trait, are compelling evidence of the importance of malaria as a selective force in human evolution.

Other Possible Disease-Associated Balanced Polymorphisms   The sickle cell polymorphism is the best example we have of a balanced polymorphism maintained by heterozygous advantage. The high frequencies in some populations of alleles responsible for two other autosomal recessive diseases—*Tay–Sachs disease* and *cystic fibrosis*—have led some to suggest that a similar mechanism may be underlying

their polymorphisms (M. T. Smith, 1998). For both of these genetic diseases, the hypothesized selective agent in the environment was *tuberculosis,* a bacterial disease (usually but not always affecting the lungs) that was once one of the main causes of death in urban populations in Europe and the United States.

Tay–Sachs disease (TS) causes the accumulation of a fatty substance in the nerve cells of the brain. There is no treatment for the disease. Although a child with TS is normal for the first few months of life, as the disease takes hold there is a progressive loss of mental and physical function, resulting in death within a few years. Tay–Sachs is found at high frequency in Ashkenazi (European) Jewish populations and occurs at a rate of about 0.2–0.4 per 1,000, which makes it about 100 times more common in these populations than in others. A rate of 0.4 per 1,000 would indicate a TS allele frequency of 2 percent and a heterozygote carrier frequency of 3.9 percent (0.98 * 0.02 * 2) in Ashkenazi populations. Several geneticists have argued that given the ancient origins of the TS allele in Palestine, some selection advantage—specifically resistance of the heterozygotes to tuberculosis or typhoid (Myrianthopoulos & Aronson, 1966; Chakravarti & Chakraborty, 1978)—must be working to maintain its presence in the historically isolated and diverse Ashkenazi populations.

Cystic fibrosis (CF) is the most common autosomal genetic disorder in northern European–derived populations (Ratjen & Döring, 2003). Although it is found in other populations, the rates are much higher in populations with European ancestry. Cystic fibrosis is a disease of the mucus- and sweat-producing glands, characterized by symptoms such as excessive sweating (leading to mineral imbalances in the blood, which can in turn lead to heart problems) and the accumulation of thick mucus in the lungs and intestine. Lung disease is the most common cause of death in CF; today, with medical treatment, the average life span of a CF sufferer is about 30 years (although it can be significantly longer than this with aggressive treatment). In European populations, the rate of cystic fibrosis is about 0.5 per 1,000 births. As with Tay–Sachs, given the obvious reduction in fertility of the homozygous sufferers, several investigators have suggested that the heterozygote CF carriers may be more resistant than normal homozygotes to developing disease. Meindl (1987) argued specifically that CF carriers have a greater ability to resist damage caused by pulmonary (lung) tuberculosis and that there has been selection for the CF allele in European populations since tuberculosis first became a public health problem in the sixteenth century. Other investigators have suggested that the CF allele may confer a resistance to intestinal bacteria that are known to induce diarrhea, which can pose a serious health risk, especially to children (Hansson, 1988).

Although intriguing and plausible cases can be made for heterozygous advantage in CF and TS, it is important to keep things in perspective: HbS carrier frequencies approach 40 percent in some malarial populations, compared with 3–5 percent for CF and TS carriers in their high-frequency populations. The HbS heterozygous advantage may simply be that much greater, or its allele frequencies may have had more time to evolve. It seems likely that heterozygous advantage is an important factor in determining CF and TS allele frequencies, but we do not know whether sickle cell disease is a particularly accurate model for the maintenance of these other polymorphisms.

Adaptation and Adaptability

A variant that can be demonstrated to increase fitness in a specific environment (such as the ability to digest lactose as an adult) is an adaptation in the classic evolutionary sense. However, adaptation is a more general phenomenon. All organisms exhibit some degree of *biological plasticity:* an ability on the part of individuals to physiologically respond to changes in the environment. This is obvious in poor environments; for example, if there is not enough food, an animal will become thinner. When the phenotype of an organism reflects *positive* changes that arise in the context of short- or long-term exposure to a set of environmental conditions, this is called **adaptability.** Differences in environments can thus lead to population-level differences, as

adaptability The ability of an individual organism to make positive anatomical or physiological changes after short- or long-term exposure to stressful environmental conditions.

acclimatization *Short-term changes in physiology that occur in an organism in response to changes in environmental conditions.*

individuals within the populations biologically adapt to local conditions. Because of biological plasticity and adaptability, populations may phenotypically differentiate from one another without any underlying changes to the genotypes. Adaptation and adaptability are not always separate and distinct issues. The ability of a phenotype to respond differently to different environments an organism may encounter in a lifetime may in itself be an adaptation.

Levels of Adaptability

The process of very short-term changes in physiology that occur in response to changes in environmental conditions is called **acclimatization.** We are all familiar with acclimatization. When people from sea level move to high altitude, they have to cope with a reduction in the amount of oxygen available in the atmosphere. Initially, the body physiologically adapts by breathing more quickly and increasing heart rate. Over time, more profound changes in the body occur, such as an increase in red blood cell production, which allows the individual to cope with a lower-oxygen environment. Tanning is another example of acclimatization, which will be discussed later in this chapter.

In contrast to acclimatization, adaptability refers to the physiological changes that arise in individuals who have lived their entire lives under a certain set of environmental conditions (Figure 6.16). Thus their bodies reflect the influence of the environment on development as they were growing up and the long-term effects of continued exposure to such an environment.

Again, acclimatization, adaptability, and genetic adaptation are all interacting forces in the production of individual phenotypes. They reflect different mechanisms that organisms possess to adapt to the environments in which they live. Humans also use cultural adaptations to cope with the environment (see Insights and Advances: Technology and Extreme Environments). These cultural adaptations can interact with biological adaptations to shape patterns of human variation.

Heat and Cold

From the arctic to the desert, humans live in a vast array of thermal environments, some of them with marked seasonality. One way we cope with changes in ambient temperature is through the cultural adaptation of wearing more or less clothing. But in addition to clothing, humans display a variety of physiological adaptations to heat and cold, some of which reflect adaptations of a genetic kind, whereas others are better described in terms of acclimatization and adaptability (Moran, 2000; Beall & Steegman, 2000; A. T. Steegman, 2007).

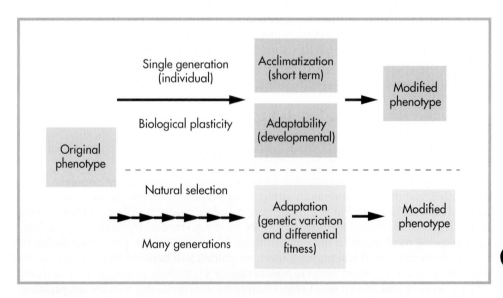

FIGURE 6.16 *Adaptability and adaptation.*

insights & advances
TECHNOLOGY AND EXTREME ENVIRONMENTS

Human beings have had thousands of years to adapt to certain kinds of natural environments. However, our technological prowess allows us both to exploit and to create new environments. These new environments require a physiological response from our bodies if we are to survive within them.

A *zero-gravity* or *microgravity* environment is one of the most exotic to which any human being would have to adapt (Figure A) (D. R. Williams, 2003). Since the advent of extended (weeks and months) stays in space, with the Skylab and Mir programs and the development of the International Space Station, dozens of people have had to deal with how their bodies react to an environment essentially free of the effects of gravity. Over time, people in a microgravity environment have muscle atrophy and loss of muscle strength. There are also cardiovascular changes, which can affect the ability to maintain blood pressure after one returns to Earth. The most critical change may be the loss of calcium in bone. In certain bones, prolonged microgravity exposure causes calcium levels to drop two standard deviations below normal levels. Although this loss is mostly reversible when one returns to gravity, it is not known what the effects would be after a very long-range flight, such as would be needed for a manned mission to Mars. Another medical issue that arises

FIGURE A   A human in a microgravity environment.

with prolonged microgravity exposure involves how the symptoms of various diseases might be influenced by bodily changes. For example, physicians recognize appendicitis by the presence of pain in a certain part of a patient's abdomen (although it varies widely). In space, the effects of microgravity on both the structure and function of the gastrointestinal tract could totally change how appendicitis presents to physicians (Williams, 2003).

In contrast to the small numbers of people affected by the space environment, billions of people around the world are subject to the effects of industrial pollution in the environment. Lawrence Schell and Elaine Hills (2002)

argue that polluted environments, as much as high altitude or hot or cold climates, should be considered extreme environments to which humans must adapt. Industrial pollution has been a problem for some human populations for more than 150 years, and even as some parts of the developed world clean up their air and water, people living in developing countries are increasingly being exposed to toxic substances in their environments. Air pollutants, such as carbon monoxide, sulfur dioxide, and ozone, contribute to increased mortality rates and may also affect prenatal and postnatal growth. Exposure to lead, mercury, and other substances may also affect growth and have cognitive effects. Schell and Hills point out that people with the highest exposure to one pollutant are also likely to have high exposure to others. These people also tend to be the poorest in a society, thus the human biology of pollution exposure interacts with social issues such as access to food, health care, and adequate housing.

Human technological achievements can be characterized as triumphant, as in the "conquest of space," or tragic, as in the "poisoning of the environment" by pollution. In either case, technology places individual human bodies into new environments to which they are not well adapted. It will be interesting to see what the long-term effects of exposure to these environments will be.

When people get too hot, the body responds through a process of *vasodilation* and sweat. Vasodilation (which appears as flushing in lighter-skinned people) increases blood flow to the surface of the body, which allows heat from the core of the body to be dissipated into the environment. The primary mechanism for dissipating heat at the surface of the body is sweating. The human body is unusual (although not unique) among mammals in having more than a million specialized sweat glands distributed over the skin. Despite the great range of thermal environments in which people live, there is almost no population variation in the number of sweat glands per person. This may reflect the fact that we are ultimately of tropical origin and that our bodies are well adapted to this kind of environment.

The evaporation of 1 liter of sweat removes 560 kcal of heat from the body, and people can sweat up to 4 liters/hour (Beall & Steegman, 2000). Heat stroke—when the core temperature of the body reaches 41°C (105.8°F)—is a serious condition, with the depletion of fluid from the body unleashing a cascade of events that ultimately leads to the coagulation of blood and the death of brain tissue. Even today, heat waves in urban environments kill hundreds or even thousands of people. Heat is a strong selective force.

Bergmann's rule   Stipulates that body size is larger in colder climates to conserve body temperature.

Allen's rule   Stipulates that in warmer climates, the limbs of the body are longer relative to body size to dissipate body heat.

Cold is also a strong selective force in environments where temperatures go significantly below freezing. Death from hypothermia is likely to result if the body's core temperature falls to 31–32°C (88–90°F). Because the body's reaction to cold is to decrease blood flow to the periphery—*vasoconstriction*—in order to maintain core temperature, frostbite, resulting in serious damage to the appendages and face, is another serious consequence of prolonged exposure to cold. Another basic acclimatization mechanism to cold is shivering. A decline of the body's core temperature by 2–3°C brings on the shivering response, which generates heat.

Human populations show significant variation in response to cold. In the Korean War, U.S. soldiers of African ancestry suffered higher rates of frostbite than those of European ancestry (Schuman, 1953). However, there is no particular evidence that European-derived populations are particularly cold-adapted; the difference between European American and African American soldiers in frostbite susceptibility may have resulted from the fact that African Americans in general show a more acute sympathetic nerve response to stress, which may lead to a more pronounced vasoconstriction response to cold (Beall & Steegman, 2000).

Humans can cope with temperatures in the freezing range via a combination of shivering and vasoconstriction. Subcutaneous fat also helps insulate the core of the body from the external cold. Populations vary in how these mechanisms are used to deal with cold. Arctic Inuit populations, who must deal with extreme cold, use cultural adaptations such as clothing, combined with biological adaptations, such as subcutaneous fat storage and vasoconstriction, to cope with cold on an ongoing basis. In addition, research involving hand immersion in a cold water bath indicates that Inuit maintain higher hand temperatures than do European or African Americans after prolonged exposure to cold (Meehan, 1955). At the other extreme, desert-dwelling Australian aborigines must cope with a great range of temperatures on a daily and seasonal basis. In winter, they sleep in near-freezing temperatures uncovered and without shelter. They cope with the cold by using an extreme vasoconstriction response, which causes the skin surface temperature to fall 2.5°C. Given that the temperatures they must cope with are not severely cold, frostbite does not occur, and they conserve energy while maintaining adequate core body temperatures. It is assumed that the adaptive responses seen in these populations are a result of both genetic adaptation and the process of developmental adaptability.

Body Size and Shape

In the nineteenth century, two biologists, Carl Bergmann (1814–1865) and Joel Asaph Allen (1838–1921), looked at the relationship between body size and climate in a wide range of mammals. They found that within polytypic species, there were predictable relationships between body form and proportions and temperature. **Bergmann's rule** (1847) focuses on body size. He found that the colder the climate, the larger the body. This makes geometric sense in that as volume increases, surface area decreases as a proportion of the volume. This would decrease the rate of heat dissipation through the surface, which helps to maintain a higher core temperature. **Allen's rule** (1877) focuses on the appendages of the body. For example, limbs should be longer relative to body size in warmer climates because that would help to dissipate heat, whereas shorter limbs in colder climates would conserve body heat. An example of Bergman's and Allen's rules can be found in comparing snowshoe and desert hares (Figure 6.17). The ears of the desert hare are much longer than those of the arctic hare and the body much leaner and rangier; both are features that dissipate heat.

Do Allen's and Bergmann's rules hold for human populations? Body forms of peoples living in some extreme environments are consistent with the rules. If we look at the Inuit in the Arctic and Nilotic peoples from East Africa, we see that the stocky, short-limbed Inuit body seems to be structured to conserve heat, whereas the long-limbed Nilotic body is designed to dissipate heat (Figure 6.18). Looking at a broad range of populations, there is a general trend among humans for larger body size and greater sitting height (that is, body length) to be associated with colder climates, whereas relative span (fingertip to fingertip length divided by height) tends to be greater in warmer temperatures (that is, longer appendages relative to body size) (Roberts, 1978).

Because it seems unlikely that an Inuit person raised in East Africa would grow up with drastically modified limb and body proportions, should we assume that the associations between body form and climate in humans always result from genetic differences? The evidence that body-size proportions reflect developmental adaptability is not particularly strong. The results of a classic study conducted in the 1950s on U.S. soldiers showed a relationship between state of origin (that is, warmer or colder) and body proportions (Newman & Munroe, 1955) and was interpreted to represent an example of adaptability or acclimatization rather than adaptation. However, a recent analysis of updated Army data shows that if one takes into account whether the soldiers are of African or European ancestry, the climate association disappears (Steegman, 2007). European-Americans have shorter legs and longer trunks than African-Americans, and warmer (that is, southern) states may have had a higher representation of African-Americans than the colder states in these Army data.

One study shows that climate change may affect primate phenotypes in accordance with Allen's and Bergmann's rules (Paterson, 1996). In the 1960s, two troops of Japanese macaques (*Macaca fuscata*) were transferred from one location in Japan to an Oregon primate center. Subsequently, one of the troops was moved to a facility in Texas. Analysis of long-term records (more than 20 years) on body size and proportions in the troops showed that by the 1990s, the Oregon monkeys

(a)   (b)

FIGURE 6.17 Bergmann's and Allen's rules expressed in two rabbit species. (a) A snowshoe hare. (b) A desert-living black-tailed jack rabbit.

(a)   (b)

FIGURE 6.18 Bergmann's and Allen's rules expressed in two human populations. (a) Sudanese tribesmen have body types adapted to warm climates. (b) Inuit people have body types adapted to cold climates.

melanocytes Cells in the epidermis that produce melanin.

were significantly larger than their Texas cousins, whereas the Texas monkeys had significantly longer limbs. The Oregon monkeys lived at latitude 45° N, whereas the Texas troop was at 28° N; the Texas site was substantially warmer. Thus the results were in accordance with predictions based on Allen's and Bergmann's rules. Although natural selection could have been responsible for the body changes, it would be surprising to see such effects after only two generations and in the absence of any obvious differences in fertility.

Living at High Altitude

Humans originally evolved in a warm, humid climate, which was at low altitude. But millions of people today live at very high altitudes of 3,500–4,000 m (11,600–13,200 ft), in environments that are typically dry and cold (Figure 6.19). Another major difference between high- and low-altitude environments is that atmospheric pressure is much less at high altitude. Although oxygen makes up the same proportion of the air at high and low altitude (21%), the lower pressure means that hemoglobin molecules in red blood cells take in fewer oxygen molecules with each breath—about one-third less at 4,000 m than at sea level (Harrison et al., 1988; Beall, 2001). The effects of altitude on oxygen availability start to become a physiological issue at around 2,500 m.

Any person accustomed to breathing at sea level who goes to one of these high-altitude locations is at risk of *hypoxia,* or "oxygen starvation." Immediate acclimatization to hypoxia involves increasing heart and breathing rates in order to increase circulation of oxygen. This is only a temporary solution, and the long-term effects of increased lung ventilation include headaches, tunnel vision, and fainting. Hemoglobin concentrations are increased by initially reducing the volume of blood plasma, followed by an increase in the production of red blood cells. Over time, the maximal oxygen consumption capacity reduces, which is an adaptation to the reduction in oxygen available. There are few indications that high altitude alone poses any particular long-term health problems. Growth is slower in children, but the total growth period is prolonged, so overall size is not decreased (Frisancho & Baker, 1970). High altitude has been no barrier to the development of large-scale, well-populated civilizations.

The inhabitants of three high-altitude populations have been extensively studied to determine the mechanisms underlying adaptation to hypoxia. These include

FIGURE 6.19 Anthropologist Andrea Wiley with friends from Ladakh, a high altitude area of the Himalaya.

Andean populations in South America, Tibetans in South Asia, and Ethiopians in Africa (Beall, 2001; Beall et al., 2002). A striking result of these studies is that there does not appear to be a single way in which humans adapt to high altitude: A variety of mechanisms or combinations of mechanisms are observed. For example, the increase in ventilation induced by hypoxia, the *hypoxic ventilatory response* (HVR), is initially quite elevated in lowland people who go to high altitude, although it reduces significantly over time as they acclimatize. Andean and Tibetan populations show significant differences in HVR. The Andean populations show a marked blunting in HVR, resembling the acclimatization response of lowlanders at high altitude. In contrast, Tibetan populations maintain a higher ventilation response, which is close to those observed in sea level populations and twice that of Andean populations.

We mentioned that hemoglobin concentrations increase in low-altitude individuals going to high altitude. Another difference between Andean and Tibetan populations is that whereas increased hemoglobin concentration is seen in Andean individuals, it is not seen in Tibetans. Cynthia Beall's (2001) analysis of several studies shows that at a mean elevation of 3,859 m, the hemoglobin concentration for acclimatized lowlanders was 18.2 g/dL, for Andean men it was 18.1 g/dL, and for Tibetan men it was only 16.9 g/dL. Ethiopian males have a concentration of 15.9 g/dL, which is within 2 percent of the U.S. male sea level value of 15.3 g/dL (Beall et al., 2002). Ethiopians living at only 2,400 m have similar hemoglobin concentrations to those living at about 3,500 m, indicating that there is no increase of hemoglobin with altitude in this population. Although Ethiopian and Tibetan populations have similarly low (for high altitude) levels of hemoglobin, they differ in the extent of oxygen saturation in arterial blood. Tibetans have low oxygen saturation compared with sea level populations, which is not surprising because they do not produce more hemoglobin to deal with the reduced atmospheric pressure. However, the Ethiopians have oxygen saturation percentages similar to those seen in sea level populations. Basically, the Ethiopian population at high altitude has a blood oxygen profile that resembles most other populations at sea level.

Over-production of red blood cells and high hemoglobin levels are associated with a debilitating condition called *chronic mountain sickness* (or *Monge's disease*), which can result after living for extended periods of time at high altitude. Tibetans are notably resistant to developing chronic mountain sickness, and they avoid the overproduction of red blood cells and high hemoglobin levels associated with it. Beall and her colleagues (2010) have identified variants of a gene (*EPAS1*) associated with red blood cell production that appears to have undergone strong natural selection in Tibetan populations. They propose that the gene variants may have been selected for specifically because they made individuals less likely to develop chronic mountain sickness.

Skin Color

The skin is one of the largest and most complex organs of the body (Robins, 1991; Molnar, 2002). It has two main components: the thick *dermis* and the much thinner *epidermis,* which covers it (Figure 6.20 on page 130). The dermis is a connective tissue layer consisting of collagen and other fibers, sweat and sebaceous glands, hair follicles, and hair. The epidermis is a thin layer of tissue consisting 95 percent of epithelial cells called *keratinocytes,* with 5 percent pigment cells, or **melanocytes.** Keratinocytes are synthesized at the base of the epidermis and migrate over the course of 4 to 6 weeks to the surface, where they are shed. Thus the epidermis is a continually renewing tissue layer.

Skin has several important functions. It is a fluid barrier, keeping the body protected from most chemicals in the environment. It is extremely important in thermoregulation (maintaining body temperature in the normal range) thanks to blood vessels located in the dermis and the cooling effects of the evaporation of sweat on the surface of the body. Skin also plays a critical function in the metabolism of various vitamins. This function may be critical to our understanding of the evolution of skin color in human populations.

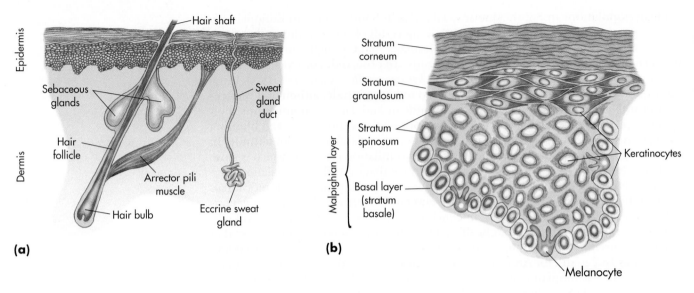

FIGURE 6.20 The structure of skin (a) and epidermis (b) at the microscopic level.

Skin color is produced primarily by two substances. *Oxidized hemoglobin* in red blood cells contributes red, and its contribution can be seen in heavily vascularized structures, such as the nipples. By far the most important component of skin color is **melanin,** a dark pigment produced by the melanocytes of the epidermis. Like neurons, with which they share a common embryonic origin, melanocytes are cells that consist of a cell body and long projections known as dendrites. The melanin in melanocytes is packaged into an organelle in the cytoplasm known as the *melanosome.* Through its dendrites, the melanocyte deposits mature melanosomes in the keratinocytes surrounding it. Skin color is produced by a combination of melanosome size, the density of melanosomes within each keratinocyte, and the distribution of keratinocytes (Robins, 1991). People with darker skin have more melanin in their epidermis than people with lighter skin.

The distribution of skin color in the populations of the world follows a fairly orderly pattern, especially in the Old World (Africa and Eurasia). People with the darkest skin live at the equator or in the tropics (Figure 6.21). As you go north or south to higher latitudes, skin color becomes progressively lighter. In the New World, skin color does not follow such an orderly distribution, probably because of the recent migration (likely less than 15,000 years ago) of peoples to the New World from temperate Asia. Migration patterns over the past few hundred years have further disrupted this orderly picture, with people from higher latitudes moving to places with an abundance of sun (for example, people of northern European ancestry living in Australia) and people from equatorial regions moving to places where there is not so much sun (for example, people of west African ancestry living in the northeast United States). Such migrations and mixings are nothing new. For example, Khoisan peoples have lived in the temperate climate of south Africa for thousands of years and have substantially lighter skin color than Bantu-speaking Zulu people, who came to the area from equatorial Africa only 1,000 years ago (Jablonski & Chaplin, 2002).

Reconstructing the evolution of skin color depends on explaining the advantages of dark skin in more abundant sunlight and of light skin in less abundant sunlight. Many attempts to explain this pattern have been based on diseases or conditions associated with having the "wrong" skin color for the environment.

Advantages and Disadvantages of Light and Dark Skin Color Electromagnetic energy from the sun comes to the earth not only in the form of visible light but also in the form of *ultraviolet radiation* (UVR), which is below the wavelength for visible light. Although much of the UVR is absorbed by the ozone layer, enough

melanin A dark pigment produced by the melanocytes of the epidermis, which is the most important component of skin color.

reaches the earth to profoundly affect the biology of many organisms, including human beings.

In humans, the two most visible effects of UVR are *sunburn* and *skin cancer.* Sunburn causes congestion of subcutaneous capillaries, destruction of skin cells, and edema (collection of fluids under the skin), and it can permanently damage skin. Besides being uncomfortable, sunburn can be very serious because it may interfere with the body's ability to cool itself and lead to the development of wounds that are highly vulnerable to infection. Ultraviolet radiation also damages DNA, which in turn leads to the development of skin cancer. Most skin cancers, though unsightly, are benign. However, cancer of the melanocytes, *malignant melanoma*, spreads easily throughout the body and must be treated early.

Melanin blocks or filters out incoming UV waves. Thus people with more melanin or the ability to temporarily produce more melanin in response to light (that is, *tanning*) are less susceptible to the effects of UVR than people who have less melanin. As most of us know, very light-skinned people who cannot tan are very susceptible to sunburn. They are also more susceptible to skin cancer. People from the British Isles who have migrated to sunnier climates provide an example of the effects of increased UVR on light skin. In Britain, the skin cancer rate is 28 per 100,000 in males and 15 per 100,000 in females. In Queensland, Australia, much of which is tropical, the rates are 265 and 156 per 100,000. Despite the health risks of skin cancer in light-skinned peoples today, for most of human history, when most people did not enjoy long lives, it was probably protection against sunburn that provided the greater fitness benefit because cancer typically takes its toll later in life.

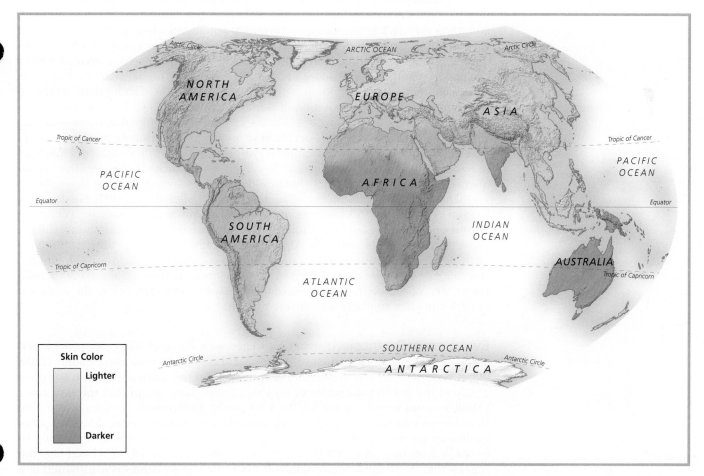

FIGURE 6.21   World map of the distribution of skin color. Note that darker skin colors are found near the equator, especially in the Old World.

Another important factor that may influence the evolution of skin color is *vitamin D synthesis*. Vitamin D is an essential compound in calcium metabolism and is necessary for the normal development of bones and teeth. Dietary sources of vitamin D are not common, although it is present in large quantities in some fish oils and to a much lesser degree in eggs and butter. Most people get their vitamin D from the sun, or, more accurately, UVR in the sun causes a photochemical reaction in the epidermis, converting *7-dehydrocholesterol* (7-DHC) into a precursor of vitamin D, which is transformed in the kidney into vitamin D over a period of 2 to 3 days. Vitamin D deficiency leads to the development of a serious medical condition known as *rickets*. Because calcium metabolism is disrupted, children with rickets have bones that are severely weakened. The bones can become deformed or are prone to breakage. Rickets can range from very mild to quite severe and can even result in death. On the other side of the coin, vitamin D toxicity can also have important health consequences, but it is almost impossible to get enough vitamin D via exposure to sunlight to cause toxicity (Robins, 1991).

Because melanin blocks the effects of UVR, people with darker skin cannot synthesize vitamin D as efficiently as people with lighter skin. Dark skin takes six times longer to make vitamin D as light skin (Holick et al., 1981). In the tropics, this is not an issue because intense sunlight is readily available and seasonality is minimal. At the higher latitudes, the sunlight is less intense, and seasonality means that during certain times of the year, access to sunlight is nearly cut off. Cold weather necessitates covering the skin, further limiting the skin's exposure to direct sunlight. Vitamin D synthesis in the skin is very efficient, however, so even the exposure of a limited amount of skin (as little as 20 cm^2) to sunlight can provide sufficient vitamin D.

Rickets was first recognized to be a major health problem in the industrialized cities of northern Europe and North America at the beginning of the twentieth century. The cities' northern location and smoky pollution limited exposure to sunlight, and it was very dark in the dingy, overcrowded tenements where factory workers and their children lived. Up to 90 percent of children in these cities suffered from some degree of rickets (Robins, 1991). In the 1920s, rates for rickets in African American children in the United States were two to three times higher than for European American children. The epidemiology of rickets led to the development of the *vitamin D hypothesis* for the evolution of skin color (Murray, 1934; Loomis, 1967). In a nutshell, this hypothesis proposes that the evolution of lighter skin color—starting from darker-skinned ancestry—occurred in areas with less sunlight as a direct result of selection for more efficient vitamin D synthesis. Impaired movement or childbearing ability (if the pelvis is affected) in rickets would provide the negative consequences of vitamin D deficiency that would drive the selection for light skin color.

Skin color also influences the metabolism of *folate* (folic acid). Folate is a B vitamin essential for DNA synthesis and cell replication, and exposure to UVR in the dermis causes the breakdown of folate in the bloodstream. This effect is particularly pronounced in people with light skin, who do not filter out UVR as efficiently as people with dark skin (Branda & Eaton, 1978). Deficiencies in folate during pregnancy can cause neural tube birth defects in the developing embryo. Jablonski & Chaplin (2000, 2002) propose that retention of folate may be a critical factor in the evolution of dark skin color in places with strong sunlight.

Evolutionary Synthesis Diseases associated with skin and skin color provide several potential insights into the evolution of skin color. Jablonski and Chaplin (2000, 2002) have mapped out the distribution of UVR on the earth and used it to create a map of the predicted distribution of skin color. They found that the skin color prediction was very accurate for the Old World. Indigenous peoples of the New World tropics do not have skin as dark as predicted. However, as we discussed previously, they are recent arrivals to that region, and thus we can explain the mismatch between skin color and UVR exposure by historical factors. Jablonski and Chaplin suggest that the distribution of skin color in human populations is maintained by a balance between the contrasting effects of UVR on vitamin D synthesis and on folate degradation. Jablonski and Chaplin focus on the role of vitamin metabolism, but factors such as resistance to sunburn may have also contributed to the evolution of the distribution of skin color. Although there may have been some primary driving force in the evolution of skin color, the different evolutionary models are not mutually exclusive.

Human variation is a truly multifaceted topic. It goes right to the heart of what it is to be a human being. Although in the past some scientists looked at human variation as a means of dividing our species into competing groups, contemporary views emphasize differences without resorting to division. Human diversity is a beautiful thing, and that diversity reflects our extraordinary ability to adapt to different environments and our penchant for migrating across great swaths of the planet. Our individual biologies reflect where we came from, in both a genetic and environmental sense. We are all products of a dual heritage.

Human Variation: Evolution, Adaptation, and Adaptability

Human Variation

At the Group Level

- Species are generally composed of different populations, which may vary genetically or phenotypically.
- Subspecies or races are identified when population variation combined with geographic separation reaches a certain level, which is not formally defined.
- The formal identification of "human races" began in the eighteenth century.
- The race concept in anthropology was heavily critiqued during the twentieth century, when anthropologists responded to the need to combat racism at the political and cultural levels. **[pp 104–110]**

Population Genetics

- The microevolutionary changes that can be observed within and between species can be measured using the tools of population genetics.
- Specific genetic polymorphisms are often best understood in terms of their clinal variation across populations.
- Understanding the evolution of human polymorphisms is a critical part of biological anthropology.
- Polymorphisms provide important information that can be used for the phylogenetic reconstruction of population relationships. **[pp 110–118]**

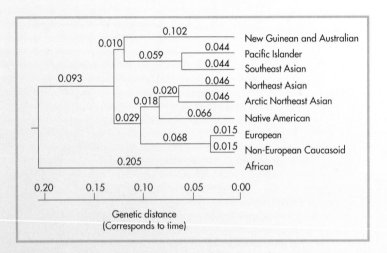

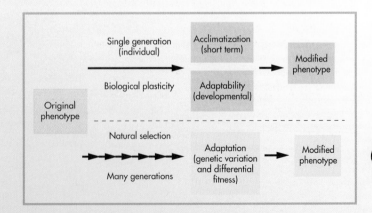

Polymorphisms

Lactose Intolerance and Sickle Cell

- The evolution of lactose tolerance in some human populations demonstrates clearly how positive natural selection acts on human polymorphisms.
- Balanced polymorphisms, such as that observed for sickle cell trait, demonstrate how polymorphisms are maintained via positive and negative selection. **[pp 118–123]**

Adaptation and Adaptability

Levels of Adaptability

- Organisms must make adjustments to cope with long- and short-term changes in their environments.
- **Acclimatization**, **adaptability**, and **adaptation** are terms used to describe the different physiological levels at which these adjustments may be made. **[pp 123–124]**

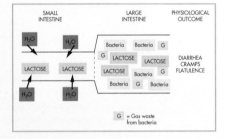

Extreme Environments

- Studying human biology in extreme environments allows us to understand adaptation at both the individual and population levels.
- The stresses associated with hot, cold, dry, and high-altitude environments contribute to population variability in body size, shape, and physiology. **[pp 124–129]**

Skin Color

- Although it has been of critical importance in classic and popular concepts of race, skin color is best understood in the context of human adaptation and adaptability.
- Clinal variation in skin color suggests an interaction between population history and sunlight exposure. **[pp 129–133]**

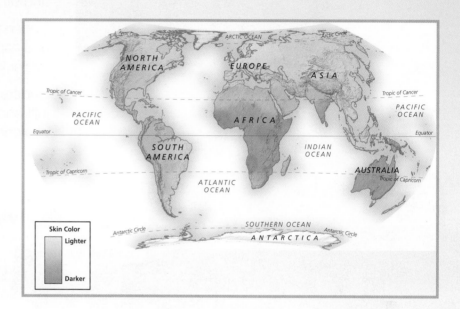

My AnthroLab CONNECTIONS

Watch. Listen. View. Explore. Read.

MyAnthroLab is designed just for you. Each chapter features a customized study plan to help you learn and review key concepts and terms. Dynamic visual activities, videos, and readings found in the multimedia library will enhance your learning experience.

Listen on **myanthrolab**

▶ *DNA Suggests Ancient Hunter Also Fought Baldness*

View on **myanthrolab**

▶ *Frequency of the Genes in the ABO Blood-group System*
▶ *Distribution of HbS in Africa*

Explore on **myanthrolab** In MySearchLab, enter the Anthropology database to find relevant and recent scholarly and popular press publications. For this chapter, enter the following keywords: race, variation,

adaptability, altitude, skin

Read on **myanthrolab**

▶ *American Anthropology Association Statement on Race*
▶ *Does Race Exist* by Michael J. Bamshad and Steve E. Olson
▶ *Skin Deep* by Nina G. Jablonski and George Chaplin
▶ *Are We Still Evolving* by Kathleen McAuliffe

Chapter 7 Preview

After reading this chapter, you should be able to:

• Describe the suite of traits that characterize each major primate group.

• Distinguish between the Primate order and other mammalian groups.

• Understand the taxonomy of strepsirhines and haplorhines, and the place of the tarsier in the Primate order.

• Understand how primate behavior is influenced by diet, predation, and other ecological factors.

The Primates

Ranomafana National Park in Madagascar is a range of rugged, rain-soaked hills and rushing streams, and is home to some of the world's most unusual, beautiful, and endangered primates. We've come here to spend a few days looking for them.

Unlike monkeys and apes, which are active in the daytime and sleep all night, many of the most interesting primates in Madagascar are nocturnal. Finding them means hiring a guide who can lead us with his headlamp along muddy trails in the rainy dark. We have high hopes of seeing some of the forest's more exotic residents, such as aye-ayes, dwarf lemurs, and avahis. For several hours we follow in our guide's footsteps as the beam of his light falls across prehistoric-looking chameleons clinging to tree limbs along our path.

Around midnight we cross our umpteenth muddy ravine, and I am cold and tired and beginning to privately curse my guide for leading me on this wild primate chase. Just then he stops and points at the tree branches overhead.

Looking up, I see movement in the foliage and spot several small rat-sized creatures bounding about. We stare at them, and one stares back. It's a mouse lemur, one of the world's smallest primates, weighing in at only a few ounces.

If I were not in Madagascar, I would assume it was a rodent. But due to Madagascar's isolation, natural selection took the primate path in an idiosyncratic direction, and primates evolved along some bizarre lines. I reflect on the difference between a mountain gorilla, with a close genetic kinship to me, and this little creature that seems more rat than primate. But the mouse lemur is just as much a primate as the gorilla is; the two species share an ancestor that lived over 60 million years ago before they and the monkeys and apes went separate evolutionary ways. If we look back far enough into Earth's past, this tiny mammal's ancestor and my ancestor are the same.

The mouse lemur takes a last look at us, its eyes glowing in the beam of our headlamps, then turns and bounces off into the rainy night.

Craig Stanford, Madagascar

Biological anthropologists are interested in nonhuman primates for three reasons. First, as our closest living kin, nonhuman primates share with us a recent ancestry. By carefully testing hypotheses about their diet, social behavior, and anatomy, we can reconstruct aspects of how extinct primates, including hominins, probably behaved. In other words, studying nonhuman primates offers us a window onto our own evolutionary past.

Anthropologists also want to know how the forces of natural selection and sexual selection molded our ancestors after the human lineage split from the rest of the primate order. Therefore, when we study nonhuman primates we are studying not just the animals but also the evolutionary process itself.

Finally, biological anthropologists study nonhuman primates simply because they are intrinsically fascinating animals. Most living nonhuman primate species are under threat of extinction because human activities are destroying their habitat and the animals themselves. To develop

FIGURE 7.1 Kangaroos and other marsupials lack a placenta; they give birth to poorly developed offspring that grow and develop in a pouch.

FIGURE 7.2 Most modern mammals are placentals.

View the **Map** "A World Map of Living Nonhuman Primates" on **myanthrolab**

strategies for primate conservation, we must first have detailed information about their habitat needs and behavioral biology. Only with this knowledge can we hope to ensure their survival.

This chapter introduces the nonhuman primates, their habitat, and their anatomical and ecological adaptations. After considering the place of the order Primates among the mammalian orders, we examine the suite of traits that characterizes the order. We then survey primate taxonomy and general traits of the major primate groups. In the latter part of the chapter, we turn to the topic of primate ecology—the role of nonhuman primates in tropical ecosystems—and look at the ecological factors that have molded primate behavior.

The Primate Radiation

About 5 to 10 million species of animals and plants inhabit Earth today. Only a tiny fraction of these, about 4,000 species, are mammals. Taxonomists divide the mammals into three groups:

1. The **metatheria,** or marsupials, reproduce without use of a placenta. Instead, their offspring are born in an almost embryonic state. They leave the mother's reproductive tract and crawl into her pouch, where they attach themselves to a nipple. After a further period of development, the offspring leave the pouch at a well-developed stage. Metatheria include the kangaroos (Figure 7.1), koalas, opossums, and a wide variety of other mammals, most of which are confined to Australia and nearby islands.

2. The **prototheria** are the monotremes, a small and unusual taxonomic group that includes only the Australian platypus and echidna. These species reproduce by egg-laying, but they nurse their young with milk in the manner of other mammals. Paleontologists believe that monotremes were more diverse and numerous in the past than they are today.

3. The **eutheria,** or placental mammals, include some two dozen orders, one of which is the order Primates. Primates and other placental mammals reproduce by means of internal fertilization, followed by implantation of the fertilized zygote on the wall of the uterus. The developing embryo is nourished via thickened tissue that connects the circulatory system of the mother with that of her offspring. The pattern of reproduction, length of gestation, and degree of development of the newborn offspring vary widely among placental forms (Figure 7.2).

The Extraordinary Diversity of Nonhuman Primates

Some 300 species of nonhuman primates are currently recognized (Table 7.1), but including all the minor taxonomic variations of these species, there are more than 400 varieties, or *taxa* (Groves, 2001). This is a small percentage of overall mammalian diversity, but nonhuman primates nonetheless exhibit an amazing variety of size and

TABLE 7.1 **Some Mammalian Orders and the Number of Species in Each**

Order	Number of species
Chiroptera (bats)	1,000
Rodentia (rodents)	1,700
Insectivora (hedgehogs, tree shrews, and kin)	380
Carnivora (dogs, cats, weasels, raccoons, and kin)	240
Marsupials	270
Nonhuman primates (strepsirhines, monkeys, and apes)	300

Source: Adapted from Nowak and Paradiso (1983).

FIGURE 7.3   Primate body size and shape vary widely from the 440-lb (200-kg) gorilla to the 2-oz (40-g) mouse lemur.

form. Adult body weights range from less than 2 ounces (40 g) in mouse lemurs to more than 450 pounds (200 kg) in gorillas. Body shapes range from the graceful arm-swinging gibbon to the bizarre aye-aye.

What Exactly Is a Primate?

Primates are mammals with grasping hands, large brains, a high degree of learned rather than innate behavior, and a suite of other traits. However, the primates are a diverse group, and not all species share the same set of traits. The order Primates is divided into two suborders: the **Strepsirhini,** or **strepsirhine** primates (lemurs and lorises), and the **Haplorhini,** or **haplorhine** primates (tarsiers, monkeys, apes, and humans) (Figures 7.3 and 7.4). We should not consider strepsirhines more primitive than haplorhines; both groups have been evolving on their own paths for more than 60 million years. But many of their adaptations are clear holdovers from the early days of the

metatheria   Mammals that reproduce without a placenta, including the marsupials.

prototheria   Mammals that reproduce by egg-laying and then nurse young from nipples. The Australian platypus and echidna are the only living monotremes.

eutheria   Mammals that reproduce with a placenta and uterus.

strepsirhine (Strepsirhini) Suborder of the order Primates that includes the prosimians, excluding the tarsier.

haplorhine (Haplorhini)   Suborder of the order Primates that includes the anthropoids and the tarsier.

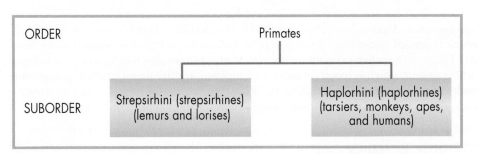

FIGURE 7.4   The major groupings of living primates.

Indri

(a) Skeleton of a vertical clinger and leaper

Gibbon

(b) Skeleton of a brachiator

FIGURE 7.5 The Primate order displays a diversity of ways of moving around.

Primate order (Figure 7.5). The strepsirhine–haplorhine classification system reflects genetic relationships and was developed by St. Hilaire in the late eighteenth century, long after Linnaeus's earlier primate taxonomy. Many taxonomists use another traditional naming system, which is based on aspects of anatomy, for the major primate groups: the **prosimian** and **anthropoid** suborders. We'll see how the strepsirhine–haplorhine classification differs from the prosimian–anthropoid classification later in the chapter.

Anatomical Traits

We distinguish primates from other mammals by a set of traits that all primates share.

prosimian   Member of the primate suborder Prosimii that includes the lemurs, lorises, galagos, and tarsiers.

anthropoid   Members of the primate suborder Anthropoidea that includes the monkeys, apes, and hominins.

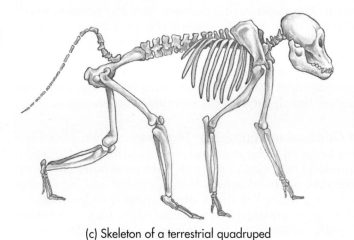

(c) Skeleton of a terrestrial quadruped

Baboon

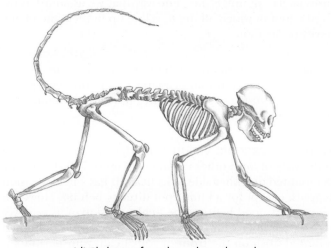

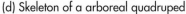

(d) Skeleton of a arboreal quadruped

Uakari

FIGURE 7.5   (Continued)

Generalized Body Plan The primate body plan is generalized, not specialized. Many mammals have extremely specialized body designs; consider a giraffe's neck, a seal's flippers, or an elephant's trunk. Primates typically lack such specializations. Their generalized body plan gives them versatility; most primate species engage in a wide variety of modes of travel, for instance, from arm-swinging (in apes) to running, leaping, and walking (Figure 7.5).

Because primates evolved from ancient mammalian stock, they have inherited the many traits of that lineage. All nonhuman primates are quadrupeds, designed for moving about using all four limbs, but there is great variation in the way they use their limbs. Many strepsirhines move by *vertical clinging and leaping* (VCL, Figure 7.5a). Their hind limbs are longer than their front legs. This allows them to sit upright against a tree trunk or bamboo stalk, then launch themselves from a vertical posture through the air, turning as they leap and landing upright against a nearby upright support. For instance, sifakas bound from tree trunk to tree trunk at high speed using this locomotor technique.

Contrary to the commonly depicted image of them swinging through treetops, monkeys actually walk and run (on the ground and in trees) in much the same way that dogs, cats, and other four-legged mammals do (Figure 7.5d). Rather than arm-swing, monkeys run and leap along branches, their arms and legs moving in a limited plane of motion. The palms of the hands and feet make contact with the surface they are walking on. The skeleton of a monkey such as a baboon, which lives both on the ground and in trees, shows this clearly (Figure 7.5c on page 141). By contrast, an ape's arm has a full range of motion (Figure 7.5b on page 140). As we shall see, this is an adaptation to arm-hanging for feeding. Arm-hangers need a scapula that is oriented across the back rather than on the sides of the upper arms to allow this freedom of motion. Apes also possess a cone-shaped rib cage and torso; long, curved digit bones; small thumbs; and long arms to aid in arm-swinging.

Grasping Hands with Opposable Thumbs or Big Toes The grasping hand with opposable thumb is believed to be the fundamental primate adaptation, although some prosimians don't fully exhibit this trait. Like most other mammals, primates typically have five digits per hand or foot. Having a thumb and big toe that are anatomically opposed to the other four digits allows primates to grasp objects with greater precision than other mammals. In some primates, such as colobine monkeys, gibbons, and spider monkeys, the four fingers are so elongated or the thumb is so reduced that the digits do not meet, rendering them less useful for gripping. Nonhuman primates also have an opposable hallux (the big toe).

For example, an ape uses its feet in much the same way that we use our hands. Humans have instead evolved a foot in which all the toes line up in the same plane, at the cost of a loss of dexterity of the foot.

Flattened Nails The primate grasping hand has flattened nails at the ends of the digits instead of claws. This is the case for all primates except one group, the marmosets and tamarins. In addition, many strepsirhines have a combination of nails and a single clawed digit on their hands and feet.

Forward-Facing Eyes with Stereoscopic Vision Consider the way you see the world and compare it with the view of most other mammals (Figure 7.6). For example, a horse has eye sockets mounted on either side of its head. It has a field of vision that extends nearly 360 degrees, except for a blind spot directly behind. However, the horse's forward vision is not very good because the fields of vision of its two eyes don't fully overlap in front. Now consider your own vision. Like those of nonhuman primates, your eyes are mounted flush on the front of your head; your peripheral vision to the sides and behind you is severely constrained by this anatomy. But your forward field of vision is covered by both eyes. This stereoscopic view enables you

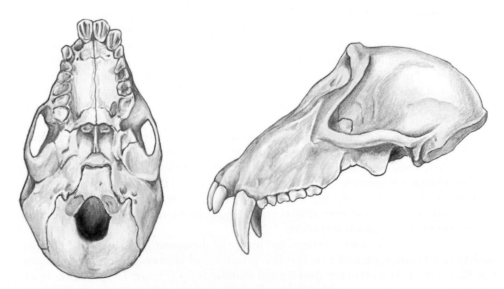

FIGURE 7.6 The primate skull is generalized compared to many other mammals.

to have excellent *depth perception* because the overlapping fields of vision provide a three-dimensional view of the world.

Stereoscopic vision, grasping hands, opposable thumbs, and nails rather than claws seem like an obvious suite of adaptations to life in the trees. This was the thinking of Frederic Wood-Jones and George Elliot-Smith, two British anatomists who proposed the idea in the 1920s. Their **arboreal hypothesis** was widely accepted and stood unchallenged for half a century. But in the 1970s, Matthew Cartmill pointed out some key flaws in that model. Squirrels, he noted, lack the primate stereoscopic vision and grasping hand with nails, yet they scamper up and down trees with great agility. To understand primate origins, Cartmill argued, we should consider how the very earliest primates and their close kin lived. The fossil record shows that early on, primates were anatomically very much like modern insectivores. Today, such small creatures live in the tangled thickets that grow around the base of tropical forest trees, where they live by stalking and capturing insects and other fast-moving prey. Cartmill hypothesized that these creatures are a useful analog for early primates; his **visual predation hypothesis** proposed that forward-facing eyes, depth-perceptive vision, and grasping hands for catching their prey, not for climbing in trees, were the key adaptations of ancient primates (Cartmill, 1974). Many predators have forward-facing eyes—eagles, owls, and cats, for instance—and this is thought to aid them in precisely homing in on their prey.

Teeth are an extraordinarily important part of a nonhuman primate from an anthropologist's perspective. Their shape tells us a great deal about everything from a species' diet to its mating system (Figure 7.7). Fossilized teeth also allow us to cautiously infer patterns of behavior and diet in extinct primates we study. Most nonhuman primates eat a diet that is some combination of leaves, fruit, and other plant products, with occasional animal protein in the form of insects, small mammals, or other animals. Only one, the tarsier, eats mainly animal protein.

Nonhuman primates do not possess enormous canine teeth for tearing food, as carnivores do, nor do they have the heavy grinding molars that grazing animals have. Scientists believe that nonhuman primates have undergone an evolutionary reduction in the degree of specialization of the teeth, evident in the small canines and incisors, and the rounded molars of most of them. If we consider the **dental arcade,** the arc of teeth along either the bottom or top of the mouth, beginning at the midline of the mouth there are four types of teeth arranged in the following dental formula: two incisors, one canine, two premolars (what your dentist calls bicuspids), and three molars. The exceptions to this pattern are most of the New World monkeys, which have a third premolar, and the strepsirhines, which have varying dental formulas.

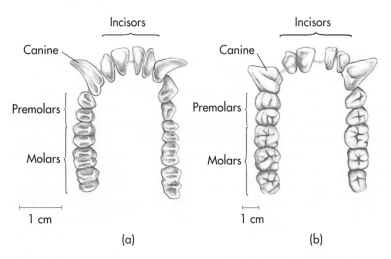

FIGURE 7.7   The primate dental formula illustrated for (a) the lower dentition of an Old World monkey and (b) the upper dentition of a gorilla.

neocortex The part of the brain that controls higher cognitive function; the cerebrum.

ontogeny The life cycle of an organism from conception to death.

diurnal Active during daylight hours.

Petrosal Bulla The petrosal bulla is the tiny bit of the skeleton that covers and protects parts of the inner ear. Its importance to primate taxonomists is that this is the single bony trait that is shared by all primates, living or extinct, that occurs in no other mammalian group. When a fossil of questionable status is uncovered, researchers examine the ear portion carefully in search of the petrosal bulla.

Enclosed Bony Eye Orbits in the Skull Primates also have an apparent anatomical adaptation that emphasizes the importance of vision: enclosed (or partially enclosed) bony eye orbits in the skull, which may protect the eye more effectively than the open orbit of lower mammals (Figure 7.6 on page 142). This orbital closure is more complete in haplorhines than it is in strepsirhines.

Life History Traits

The life history of mammals—their trajectory from conception to death—varies widely. In general, mammals that reproduce slowly, live long lives, and acquire information about their world through learning and not their genes, have delayed maturation and drawn-out life histories. Primates take this trend to an extreme.

Single Offspring Nearly all primates give birth to single offspring. Many mammals, especially smaller species, give birth to litters or twins. The only exception among nonhuman primates is the marmosets and tamarins, which give birth to twins. Single births, combined with the long maturation period and the amount of time and energy mothers invest in their offspring, represent a strategy in which investment of time and energy in a few babies has replaced the more primitive mammalian pattern of litters of offspring that receive less intensive care.

Large Brains Primates have large brains. They possess a high degree of *encephalization,* or an evolved increase in the volume of the **neocortex,** or cerebrum, of the brain, which is involved in higher cognitive processes. This is more obvious in the brains of haplorhine primates than in strepsirhines, and we see it in the greater number of convolutions that compose the ridges and fissures (sulci and gyri) of the brain's surface. These convolutions increase the effective surface area of the brain and are believed to contribute to higher cognitive function.

There is much debate among scientists about the reasons for the evolutionary expansion of brain volume in primates and for the survival value of a big brain itself. The primate brain is such a large, metabolically expensive organ to grow and maintain that it must have important survival and reproductive benefits. We will consider these in Chapter 8.

Extended Ontogeny Primates live by learned behaviors as much as they do on hardwired instinct. For example, many primates live in social groups, so a baby monkey or ape must learn how to be a member of a social group if it intends to successfully court a mate and rear offspring itself; these are largely learned behaviors. Thus, it is important for primates to be socialized within their communities, a process that can take up a large proportion of their infancy and maturation.

Many animals live much longer life spans than primates. Giant tortoises may live 150 years, and even among mammals some whale species may live more than 100 years. But primates are notable for the extended length of each stage, from infancy to adulthood, of their life cycle. The life cycle is also called **ontogeny** (Figure 7.8). The gorilla life span is about 20 times longer than that of a mouse, but the time it takes from gestation to sexual maturity is almost 80 times longer (about 15 years, compared with 10 weeks). Why?

Consider the sort of information a growing primate must learn in order to survive in the world. In addition to learning how to find food and water, the primate

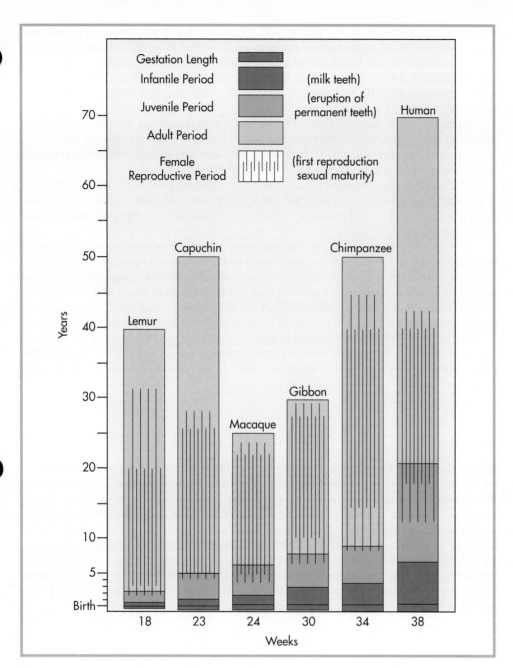

FIGURE 7.8 Primates exhibit prolonged life histories, spending more time in each stage of life than most other mammals do.

must learn how to live in a social group. The process of learning to live in a group is a long one, and the behaviors involved tend not to be purely instinctual. An infant monkey or ape reared in isolation will end up severely deficient in the social skills it needs to be part of a social group. Parental investment in the infant is dramatically greater in primates than it is in rodents or most other mammals because social skills require years of maturation and practice.

Behavioral Traits

Activity Patterns Most primate species are **diurnal** (active during daylight hours) possess color vision, and have limited olfactory senses. Many mammal species are nocturnal and rely on their sense of smell to negotiate their physical and social

nocturnal   Active at night.

sociality   Group living; a
fundamental trait of haplorhine
primates.

environment. Consider a cat, rat, or wolf, all of which are primarily nocturnal and
have a sense of smell thousands of times more powerful than that of any haplorhine
primate. Many strepsirhines are **nocturnal,** but all haplorhines except one—the
night monkey *Aotus*—are diurnal. Primates made a fundamental shift from an
olfactory-based lifestyle to a visually based one. This entailed shifting from being
primarily nocturnal to being diurnal.

Sociality, or the characteristic of living in groups, is perhaps the most fundamental social adaptation that characterizes most primates. It is the adaptation by which a
primate survives and reproduces because it provides the animal with ready access to
mates and may help it find food and avoid predators.

Of the haplorhine primates, only one—the orangutan—is not normally found in
a social group of some sort. There are many variations in sociality among the nonhuman primates, and we will examine the diversity of social grouping patterns in detail
in Chapter 8.

Not all the characteristics in the previous descriptions apply to every primate
species. Many strepsirhines are nocturnal and solitary, navigating by olfaction,
whereas others are highly social, diurnal, and visually oriented. Strepsirhines often
possess a mixture of primate traits, such as a combination of claws and nails on the
hands. Don't make the mistake of thinking that lemurs and their kin are necessarily "less evolved" or more primitive than monkeys. The simple fact is that, as we
will examine in detail in Chapter 11, monkeys and strepsirhines share a common
ancestor, and after the split between the two lineages, each group evolved in separate
lines. Natural selection favored diurnality and sociality more in monkeys than it did
in strepsirhines.

A Guide to the Nonhuman Primates

As discussed, we consider the nonhuman primates as two major groups within the
order Primates: the suborders Strepsirhini and Haplorhini (Figure 7.9). Alternately
the primates can be subdivided into suborders Prosimii and Anthropoidea. Recall
that the Linnaean system for naming includes not only order, family, genus, and
species but also higher and lesser categories (see Chapter 5). So primate families
that are anatomically similar are lumped in the same superfamily, and subgroups
of families are called subfamilies. Not all taxonomists agree on how to classify the
primates, and one nonhuman primate, the tarsier, straddles the two suborders.
The geographic distribution of nonhuman primates is presented in Figure 7.10 on
pages 148–149.

The Strepsirhines

The primates of the suborder Strepsirhini include the lemurs of Madagascar and
the lorises and galagos of mainland Africa and tropical Asia. Linnaeus originally
subdivided the primates into two major groups—the prosimians (sometimes called
the lower primates) and the anthropoids (higher primates)—based on a number
of anatomical features. *Strepsirhine* and *prosimian* are not completely synonymous;
one prosimian primate, the tarsier, is a haplorhine, not a strepsirhine. But all
strepsirhines and prosimians share some common anatomical features: a reliance
on olfaction, nocturnality, and a lack of complex social behavior patterns. Their
incisor teeth protrude from the front of the mouth to form a comb-like surface,
known as the *tooth comb,* used for grooming. Many also have specialized clawed toes
that serve as grooming tools. Some lemurs violate these general traits, however, as
we shall see next.

View the **Map** "Modern
Lemurs" on **myanthrolab**

The Lemurs   The superfamily Lemuroidea is found only on Madagascar and
consists of the families Lemuridae (true lemurs), Cheirogalidae (dwarf lemurs),
Indriidae (the sifakas and indri), and Daubentoniidae (the aye-aye). The fourth

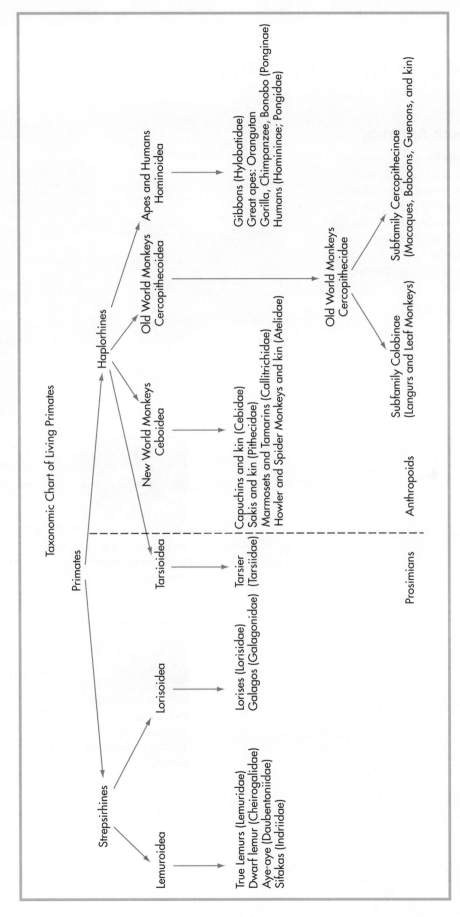

FIGURE 7.9 A taxonomic chart of the living primates.

FIGURE 7.10

A World Map of Living Nonhuman Primates

North and South America

Primates in the New World tend to be small-bodied compared to those elsewhere. All species are primarily arboreal, and some have grasping tails to aid in tree-top feeding. New World primates are found from central Mexico to Argentina, and in some equatorial forests, numerous species can be found sharing the same habitat.

UAKARI   Native to seasonally flooded rain forests

MURIQUI   Highly endangered, the largest new world monkey

GOLDEN LION TAMARIN   One of Brazil's endangered primates

Europe and Asia

Nonhuman primates are found across tropical Asia, occurring as far north as central Japan (the Japanese macaque). They occur in only the tiniest bit of Europe, on the island of Gibraltar (where they may have been introduced by people). Asia is the home of gibbons and orangutans, many species of Old World monkeys (the langurs, leaf monkeys and macaques) plus numerous strepsirhines.

DEBRAZZA'S GUENON A diverse group found in African forests

GALAGO Live in many African forests; Also called Bushbabies

GOLDEN SNUB-NOSED MONKEY One of China's beautiful and endangered primates

CHIMPANZEE Found in suitable habitat across equatorial Africa

SAVANNA BABOON Baboons are found across subsaharan Africa

HANUMAN LANGURS Found all across the Indian Subcontinent

LAR GIBBON Found in forests from India through Southeast Asia

LORISES The only Strepsirhine primates in Africa and mainland Asia

TARSIER The only entirely carnivorous primate, found in Southeast Asia rain forests

GORILLAS Live in both lowland and mountain forests

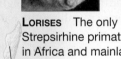
RED-BELLIED LEMUR Found only on Madagascar

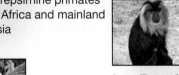
LION-TAILED MACAQUE One of the world's most threatened primates, found in hilly forests of Southern India

ORANGUTAN Live only on the islands of Sumatra and Borneo in Indonesia

Africa

Primates are found across sub-Saharan Africa and also in small areas of northwestern Africa and in the Arabian peninsula. Primate biodiversity peaks in the central African Congo Basin, where more than fifteen species can be found in the same tropical rain forest habitat. Africa provides primate habitat ranging from rain forest to savanna to high-mountain meadows, across a vast area. Moreover, because humans evolved in Africa, we can study African primates with an eye toward learning something about the environment of the human past.

FIGURE 7.11   Lemurs are found only in Madagascar.

FIGURE 7.12   A sifaka, a member of the lemur family.

largest island on Earth, Madagascar is home to perhaps the best example of an adaptive radiation we know of among living nonhuman primates (Figure 7.11). Madagascar broke away from the eastern coast of the continental mainland of Africa, through the process of continental drift, beginning some 100 million years ago. By the time the separation was complete, the earliest members of the primate order had evolved in Africa. As Madagascar drifted slowly out of contact with the rest of Africa, the primitive primates stranded on its landmass began to evolve without gene flow from other primates. Some researchers believe that lemurs may have other, more ancient origins as well, but the bulk of evidence indicates an African ancestry, and that all modern lemurs are descended from a single origin of Madagascar primates.

Over time, these animals developed a wide range of adaptations to exploit the many available habitats and niches on Madagascar (Figure 7.12). In the absence of large predators (there are no big carnivores or large eagles on the entire island), a diverse array of forms radiated from the ancestral colonizing forms. Sadly, many of those species are now extinct, presumably because of hunting by people, who arrived on the island beginning 1,500–2,000 years ago. We know about the extinct forms through the skeletal remains we have found; we call these remains *subfossils* because they are found as bones, rather than fossils, due to the recent date of the animals' disappearance (in about the past 1,000 years).

There was once an adaptive radiation on Madagascar of large-bodied, slow-moving lemurs, both arboreal and terrestrial. Many of the extinct species were quite large; *Archaeoindris* and *Megaladapis* ambled along the ground like large bears (Figure 7.13). One entire subfamily, the Paleopropithecines, were sloth lemurs; some of these species apparently hung upside down from tree limbs, as New World sloths do. Lacking natural predators, they would have been plentiful prey for the human colonizers. The species still alive today may be those that were simply too small

FIGURE 7.13   A subfossil lemur, *Megaladapis*.

or too elusive for human colonizers to bother hunting (see Insights and Advances: The Rarest of the Rare on pages 152–153).

The four families of lemurs alive today range in size from the 2-ounce (40-g) mouse lemur to the 20-pound (8-kg) indri. The families are quite distinct from one another. The dwarf lemurs are small, dull-colored insect- and fruit-eaters and tend to be nocturnal and solitary. True lemurs tend to be diurnal and social, living in social groups like those of many haplorhine primates. The well-studied ring-tailed lemur (Figure 7.14) lives in groups of up to 25 in which, as among many true lemurs (Figures 7.15 and 7.16), females are dominant to males (Ganzhorn and Kappeler, 1993). The indri and several sifaka species are the largest living prosimians. The indri is noted for its monogamous social system; its loud, haunting call; and its diet of leaves. The aye-aye is nocturnal and largely solitary. It feeds on bird eggs, fruit, and insect larvae that it locates by tapping fallen tree trunks with its long middle finger. Grubs respond to the tapping by wriggling, and the aye-aye then digs under the bark to find its meal.

The Lorises   The lorises are a diverse group of strepsirhines in tropical Africa and Asia (Figure 7.17 on page 154). They include the various species of galago, or bush baby, which occur only in Africa and are now considered to be in their own family,

🔍 **View** the **Map** "Galagos and Lorises" on **myanthrolab**

FIGURE 7.14   The ring-tailed lemur is the best-known of the Madagascar primates.

FIGURE 7.15   This red-bellied lemur shows clearly the traits that characterize strepsirhine primates.

FIGURE 7.16   The endangered ruffed lemur.

insights & advances

THE RAREST OF THE RARE

Although extinction has always been a natural event in the history of life on Earth, humans have dramatically increased the odds of extinction for many species. Of the 300 living nonhuman primate species, the majority are threatened with extinction. For perhaps half of these, the new century may bring an end to their existence on Earth.

At least fifty species are critically endangered. Many of these endangered species live in one of several hotspots of biodiversity, geographic regions known for a unique assortment of highly diverse animals and plants (Mittermeier et al., 2002). Not surprisingly, these areas are centered in equatorial regions, where large tracts of forests in the Amazon Basin of South America and the Congo Basin of central Africa remain. In these strongholds it is still possible to find fifteen or more nonhuman primate species in a single tract of forest. Other areas, such as Madagascar, harbor whole ecosystems full of primates that exist nowhere else on Earth.

These vanishing treasures include the following:

• **Golden bamboo lemur** Discovered only in the late 1980s, this beautiful 5-pound (2-kg) prosimian (*Hapalemur aureus*) lives in Ranomafana National Park, a densely forested preserve of lemur biodiversity in eastern Madagascar (Figure A). It feeds on bamboo, which it shares with two other species of bamboo lemur in the same forest. The golden bamboo lemur eats the inside of the stem of the bamboo, whereas the other two species eat the leaves. The pith contains high levels of cyanide; every day the lemur consumes enough cyanide to kill a horse (Meier et al., 1987; Glander et al., 1989). An estimated 300–400 of the animals exist in the only remaining forest habitat left to this species.

FIGURE A   The golden bamboo lemur.

• **Zanzibar red colobus** Zanzibar, a palm-covered tropical island just off the coast of the East African nation of Tanzania, is home to a small and dwindling population of red colobus monkeys (*Procolobus badius kirkii*) (Figure B). They are gorgeous animals, with a crimson back and black face fringed with white tufts of hair. A remnant population lives in tiny patches of forest amid villages and palm groves on both Zanzibar and neighboring islands. Their long-term prospects are bleak in the face of land development and human population increase.

• **Golden snub-nosed monkey** Snub-nosed monkeys are still little known to Western science because their several species live in China and Vietnam, which until recently were closed to foreign scientists. The golden snub-nosed monkey (*Rhinopithecus roxellanae*) has the largest population, about 20,000, centered in the high-mountain ranges of Sichuan and Hubei Provinces in central China (Figure C). Males can weigh nearly 50 pounds (22 kg) and possess a thick mane of golden-orange hair that drapes across its back. This, combined with a pale blue face, gives the species

a dramatic appearance. In Shennongjia Nature Reserve, it lives in pine and fir forest not unlike the Rocky Mountains of the United States, and it survives the snowy winters eating pine needles and lichens. Two close relatives, *Rhinopithecus bieti* and *R. brelichi*, are more critically endangered, with populations of only a few hundred each.

• **Lion-tailed macaque** The western Ghat mountains of southern India are home to a number of rare primates. Among these is the lion-tailed macaque (*Macaca silenus*), so named for its long tail ending in a tuft and its mane of white hair (Figure D). The species has never been common, and its limited habitat of lush mountain valleys is threatened by construction of a controversial hydroelectric project by the Indian government, that will flood part of the macaque's range.

FIGURE B   The beautiful Zanzibar red colobus.

the Galagonidae. Recent behavioral and genetic studies have warranted the splitting of many new species from this group (Bearder et al., 1995; Groves, 2001).

Lorises (Figure 7.18 on page 154) and galagos (Figure 7.19 on page 154) probably resemble the primitive ancestors of modern haplorhines. They communicate both vocally and olfactorily, by scent-marking objects in their environment. Although lorises and galagos were long thought to be exclusively solitary and nocturnal, recent research has shown that many species are in fact social

FIGURE C   The golden snub-nosed monkey.

• *Muriqui* The largest nonhuman primate in the Western Hemisphere is also one of the rarest (Figure E). The muriqui, or woolly spider monkey, lives in forest fragments in the Atlantic coastal forest of Brazil, where ranching has eaten up almost all its remaining

FIGURE D   The lion-tailed macaque.

FIGURE E   The muriqui.

habitat. Conservation efforts have focused on preserving existing habitat on private lands; roughly 1,000 animals may remain.

• *Golden lion tamarin* This flame-colored, 1-pound (0.4-kg) monkey lives in the same region as the muriqui and is also critically endangered because of habitat loss (Figure F). A novel project has reestablished golden lion tamarins by releasing monkeys that have been reared in zoos and then "rehabilitated" to survive in the wild in forests in which they had gone extinct. After years of shaky progress, this project has restored healthy populations of golden lion tamarins to some former habitats and shows how sound knowledge of a species' needs in nature can be essential for its long-term conservation.

The current approach to nonhuman primate conservation is to try to protect hotspots of nonhuman primate diversity that are home to species such as these and to prevent people from exploiting the forest resources at unsustainable levels. The threat is clear: If we do not act now, a large proportion of the diversity of nonhuman primates will be gone within a generation.

Nearly all threatened nonhuman primate species live in developing countries. The challenge is to help these countries develop without casting aside regard for the health of the environment.

In the entire twentieth century, not one primate taxon went extinct. It seems very unlikely we will be able to make the same statement about the twenty-first century. Indeed, in the few years since the new century opened, one species, Miss Waldron's red colobus, has already been reported to be on the brink of extinction in West Africa.

FIGURE F   The golden lion tamarin.

at certain times and under certain circumstances (Radespiel, 2006). In a classic study, Pierre Charles-Dominique (1977) found that in West African forests, multiple species of lorises and galagos shared their habitat by dividing up the available food items and by foraging at different heights within the forest canopy and understory. During the daylight hours, many lorises and galago species stay curled up in a nest in a tree cavity, and some species also park their offspring in such nests when they are out searching for food.

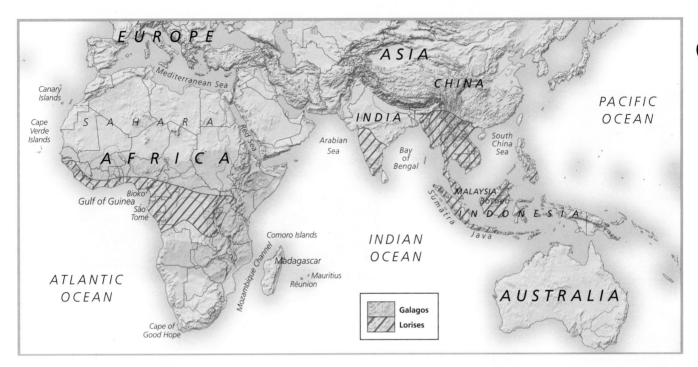

FIGURE 7.17 The distribution of lorises and galagos.

The Haplorhines

The nonhuman primates of the suborder Haplorhini include the tarsier, New World monkeys, Old World monkeys, apes, and hominins. The tarsier is a haplorhine but also a prosimian. It is closely related to the anthropoids but occupies an evolutionary status intermediate between the lower and higher primates. All the other haplorhines can also be called anthropoid primates. Haplorhines possess the full suite of adaptations that characterize the living primates. Without exception haplorhines are guided more by vision than by olfaction. This emphasis on vision is reflected in the full closure of the back of their eye orbits, providing bony protection for the eye that strepsirhines and most other mammals lack. Living haplorhines also possess a lower jaw that is fused at the midline in adulthood; in prosimians and most other mammals the jaw is two pieces joined in the middle with cartilage.

With few exceptions (the owl monkey and tarsier), haplorhines are diurnal. And with one exception (the orangutan), they live in social groups. The ratio of brain to body size in haplorhines is higher than in strepsirhines; cognition is part of the

FIGURE 7.18 A loris.

FIGURE 7.19 A galago, or bushbaby.

haplorhine suite of adaptations. Cognition also is related to the degree of social complexity we observe among haplorhines, greater than what we usually see among the strepsirhines. The haplorhines include all extinct forms of hominins, as well as humans.

Platyrrhini Infraorder of the order Primates that is synonymous with the New World monkeys, or ceboids.

The Tarsiers Tarsiers are haplorhine primates that are thought to occupy an evolutionary position between the prosimian and anthropoid primates. Tarsiers possess a mixture of traits of anthropoid and prosimian primates, but they are generally considered to be closer to anthropoids (Figure 7.20). Frederick Szalay and Eric Delson (1979) tried to resolve the status of tarsiers by classifying them as both prosimians and haplorhines to indicate their mixed evolutionary bridge. That is, they are haplorhines but have anatomical links to the strepsirhines.

The several species of tarsier recognized today live in Indonesia and nearby island groups (Figure 7.21). They occupy an owl-like ecological role as nocturnal predators on small vertebrates and are the most highly carnivorous of all nonhuman primates, eating small prey such as lizards, frogs, and insects. They live in monogamous pairs, are exclusively nocturnal, and park their young in tree nests while out foraging (Gursky, 1994, 1995).

View the **Map** "Tarsiers" on **myanthrolab**

The New World Monkeys

The New World monkeys are classified in the infraorder **Platyrrhini** (referring to the flat shape of the nose) and are all in the superfamily Ceboidea. They live in the tropical and subtropical forests of the Western Hemisphere, from Argentina northward to within a few hundred miles of the U.S. border in the state of Veracruz, Mexico (Figure 7.22 on page 156). All the New World monkeys share three features:

- *Small body size.* The largest New World monkey, the muriqui (Figure 7.23 on page 156), weighs only about 25 pounds (12 kg). The smallest, the marmosets and tamarins, range from 1.5 pounds (0.6 kg) down to just a few ounces.

View the **Map** "New World Monkeys (Ceboidea)" on **myanthrolab**

FIGURE 7.20 The tarsier is a haplorhine, and may represent an evolutionary bridge between lower and higher primates.

FIGURE 7.21 The distribution of the tarsier.

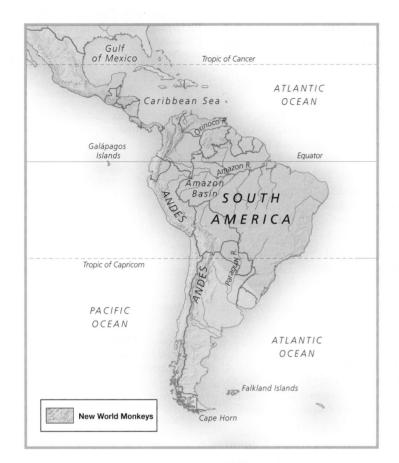

FIGURE 7.22   Distribution of the Ceboidea, or New World monkeys.

FIGURE 7.23   The muriqui of Brazil, the largest New World monkey.

- *Three premolar teeth.* Whereas all other haplorhine primates have two premolars (bicuspids) and three molars in each quadrant of the mouth, New World monkeys have three. (The ceboid monkeys possess three molars and the Callitrichidae only two.)

- *Arboreality.* There are no primarily terrestrial New World nonhuman primates, even though there are large stretches of grassland in parts of South America (as opposed to Africa, where baboons and other nonhuman primates make use of open country). In addition, some New World monkeys have grasping **prehensile tails;** this trait occurs in some members of the families Cebidae and Atelidae (Figure 7.24). The prehensile tail is an adaptation to feeding, allowing a monkey to hang beneath slender branches to reach food.

The Ceboidea are usually classified as four families: Cebidae (capuchins), Pithecidae (sakis and related species; (Figure 7.25), Atelidae (howlers, spider monkeys, and muriquis), and Callitrichidae (marmosets and tamarins; Figure 7.26). The callitrichids are unique among primates for their suite of traits that resemble those of lower mammals: small body size, claws instead of nails, and the routine birthing of twins rather than a single offspring. In some species a **polyandrous mating system,** in which one female has more than one male mate, occurs. The evolutionary reasons behind these traits are complex; we will discuss them further when we consider the diversity of nonhuman primate mating systems.

The Old World Monkeys

View the **Map** "Old World Monkeys" on **myanthrolab**

The Old World monkeys, along with the apes and humans, are in the infraorder **Catarrhini** (or primates with downward-facing nostrils). Old World monkeys occur in many parts of Africa and Asia and also in small areas of the Middle East

FIGURE 7.24 A prehensile tail is an adaptation to grasping branches for support while feeding.

FIGURE 7.25 The red-faced uakari, a bizarre-looking New World monkey.

(Figure 7.27 on page 158). They are in the superfamily Cercopithecoidea, which contains the single family Cercopithecidae. Old World monkeys have exploited a wider variety of habitats than their New World counterparts, occupying every ecological setting from tropical rain forest to savanna to desert.

As a family, the Old World monkeys share *ischial callosities:* thickened calluses on the rump that presumably make sitting on rough surfaces more comfortable. They also possess double-ridged molar teeth. These *bilophodont molars* are believed to be an evolutionary advance for biting through fibrous plant material. Old World monkeys

FIGURE 7.26 The rare golden lion tamarin is the largest callitrichid monkey.

prehensile tail Grasping tail possessed by some species of the primate families Cebidae and Atelidae.

polyandrous mating system Mating system in which one female mates with multiple males.

Catarrhini Infraorder of the order Primates that includes the Old World monkeys, apes, and hominins.

estrus Hormonally influenced period of sexual receptivity in some female mammals that corresponds to the timing of ovulation.

hylobatid (Hylobatidae) Member of the gibbon, or lesser ape, family.

pongid (Pongidae) One of the four great apes species: gorilla, chimpanzee, bonobo, or orangutan.

brachiation Mode of arm-hanging and arm-swinging that uses a rotating shoulder to suspend the body of an ape or hominin beneath a branch or to travel between branches.

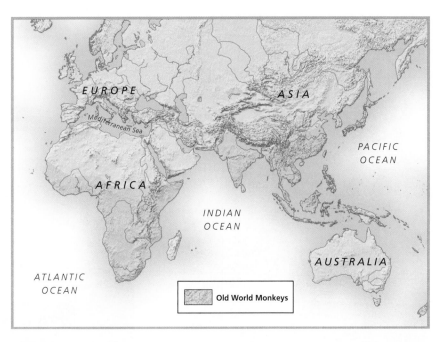

FIGURE 7.27 Distribution of the Old World monkeys.

display a greater size range than New World monkeys, from 2-pound (0.8-kg) talapoins (*Miopithecus talapoin*) to 70-pound (32-kg) baboons (*Papio* spp). Some groups also display a greater degree of sexual dimorphism than we see in any New World monkey species.

Two subfamilies within the Cercopithecidae merit special attention. Colobines are the so-called leaf-monkeys, langurs, and odd-nosed monkeys of Asia (Figure 7.28) and the colobus of Africa (Figure 7.29). They have evolved a semi-chambered stomach that resembles that of a cow and can digest tough, cellulose-laden foods in an organ called a foregut, using a community of microbes that break down the cellulose compounds in their food for them. This adaptation enables colobines to live at high population densities in forests where they would otherwise be hard-pressed to find edible foods. The gruesome but intriguing behavior of infanticide also occurs more widely among colobines than any other monkey taxonomic group (see Insights and Advances: The Impending Extinction of the Great Apes? on pages 164–165).

The cercopithecines include the macaques of Asia and the baboons, guenons, drills, mangabeys, and patas monkeys of Africa (Figures 7.30 and 7.31). They share

FIGURE 7.28 The Hanuman langur, a widely distributed Asian colobine.

FIGURE 7.29 The black-and-white colobus is an African colobine.

FIGURE 7.30 Baboons are African cercopithecines.

FIGURE 7.31 De Brazza's monkey and its fellow guenons are in the subfamily Cercopithecinae.

the presence of cheek pouches for food storage. Females of some Old World monkey species undergo a regular period of sexual receptivity, or **estrus,** during which skin around the genital area inflates with fluid and serves as a billboard of her fertility. Sexual dimorphism is generally more pronounced in cercopithecines than in colobines. Some of the cercopithecines—the baboons of Africa and the rhesus macaque in Asia—are among the most studied species of all primates.

The Hominoids

The apes and humans, past and present, are classified in the superfamily Hominoidea. This includes the ape families **Hylobatidae** (the gibbons, or lesser apes) and **Pongidae** (the chimpanzee, bonobo, gorilla and orangutan, or great apes). As we saw earlier, had Linnaeus not been so bound by his theology, humans and apes more properly would have been placed in the same family, based on their many shared anatomical traits. Recently, based on genetic evidence, taxonomists have begun to place humans and the African apes in their own separate subfamily (Homininae; see Insights and Advances: A Rose by Any Other Name: Hominins versus Hominids on page 246).

The hominoids extend many haplorhine traits: increased brain volume and intelligence, extended ontogeny, increased complexity of social interactions, and large body size. Apes and humans share several key postcranial anatomical traits. Foremost among these is the suspensory, rotating shoulder apparatus that allows for arm-hanging and arm-swinging, or **brachiation.** The anatomy that allows a quarterback to throw a football or a gymnast to perform on the high bar is the same as that which allowed fossil apes to hang from branches in the canopy of ancient forests (Figure 7.32), although it probably did not evolve for the purpose. Instead, researchers believe that arm-hanging initially was adaptive for suspending a large-bodied ape underneath a tree limb from which ripe fruit was growing. A branch that could not support the weight of an ape walking on top of it could support the same weight hung beneath it. In this way, the rotating shoulder of the ape may have an evolved function similar to that of the prehensile tail of many New World monkeys.

The four great apes move about by a modified form of quadrupedalism called knuckle-walking (Figure 7.33 on page 160) or, in the case of the orangutan, fist-walking. Apes also lack tails.

The social complexity of the hominoids does not apply to all taxa. We see it to its greatest extent in chimpanzees, bonobos, and human societies. Anthropologists study ape behavior because, in addition to being intrinsically fascinating, apes are among the most intelligent animals with which we share the planet. Only in great apes do we see tool technologies that resemble simple versions of human tool industries; lethal aggression between communities that resembles human warfare; and cognitive development, including language acquisition, that parallels that of children.

FIGURE 7.32 All living apes possess rotating, suspensory shoulders, as do humans.

FIGURE 7.33 Great apes knuckle-walk when traveling on the ground.

View the **Map** "African Great Apes" on **myanthrolab**

Listen to the **Podcast** "Orangutans Aren't Lazy, Just Evolved To Hang Around" on **myanthrolab**

frugivorous An animal that eats a diet composed mainly of fruit.

Gibbons Gibbons are fourteen species of closely related apes, all currently classified in the genus *Hylobates* (although some taxonomists divide the genus into three or four genera). Gibbons live in Asian tropical and subtropical forests from easternmost India and Bangladesh through mainland Southeast Asia and the Indonesian archipelago (Figure 7.34). They range in size from the 10-pound (4-kg) Kloss's gibbon of the Mentawai Islands to the 25-pound (12-kg) siamang of peninsular Malaysia.

Gibbons are rain forest canopy inhabitants, their bodies well adapted for a highly arboreal existence of brachiating among and hanging beneath tree limbs (Figure 7.35). They possess long arms, extremely elongated fingers, shortened thumbs, and a suspensory shoulder designed for tree-top life. Most gibbon species are highly **frugivorous,** or fruit-eating, using their high-energy diet to engage in a high-energy lifestyle of brachiating and singing. They are among the most vocal of all nonhuman primates; their whooping songs are given from morning until night and serve as declarations of territorial boundaries for other members of their species. Mated pairs also sing duets that reinforce the bond between male and female.

Orangutans Orangutans (*Pongo pygmaeus*) are the most enigmatic of all the hominoid primates. These red apes are among our closest living kin and among the largest-brained animals on Earth. But compared with other apes, they are largely solitary. Found in the rapidly disappearing rain forests of the Indonesian islands of Sumatra and Borneo (Figure 7.36), orangutans are large-bodied and extremely sexually dimorphic. Males may weigh 200 pounds (78 kg), more than twice the size and weight of adult females (36 kg) (Figure 7.37).

Orangutan densities and grouping patterns seem to be based on the local abundance of fruits; in some forests, they are quite solitary, and in others, groups of three or four may form when fruit is ripe (van Schaik, 2004). Adult females and their dependent offspring occupy territories that they defend from other adult females. Adult males attempt to maintain control over a number of female territories, moving over a much larger area to attempt to monopolize them for mating purposes. Surplus males that cannot obtain access to their own females live as transients, attempting to approach females without being detected by the resident adult male. Resident adult males use resonating, loud calls to warn transients away. Birute Galdikas (1985), who did pioneering field research on Bornean orangutans in the

FIGURE 7.34 Distribution of the gibbons.

FIGURE 7.35 Gibbons are lesser apes and live in the forests of south and southeast Asia.

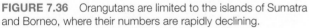

FIGURE 7.36 Orangutans are limited to the islands of Sumatra and Borneo, where their numbers are rapidly declining.

FIGURE 7.37 Orangutan males are twice the size and weight of females.

1960s, first observed transient males trying to forcibly mate with females, sometimes successfully. It became clear only recently that these transient males, long assumed to be adolescents because of their small size and lack of adult male physical features, often are adult males that have retained adolescent features. In fact, these "pseudo-adolescents" possess the physical features of immature males but produce male sex hormones and sperm (Maggioncalda et al., 1999). This appears to be a case of sexual selection for *bimaturism*, in which adults can take two different forms, allowing males to approach females by "posing" as adolescents without arousing the ire of resident adult males.

Orangutans share the extended ontogeny of the other great apes; females reach sexual maturity at age 11–15 and males not until 15. The interval between successive births is longer in orangutans than in any other primate, nearly 8 years (Galdikas and Wood, 1990). When females mature, they disperse from their mother's territory to a nearby area to establish themselves as breeding adults. Males disperse more widely and often are alone for long periods (Delgado and van Schaik, 2000).

Gorillas The largest primates, weighing more than 400 pounds (200 kg) in the wild, gorillas today have a severely fragmented geographic distribution (Figures 7.38 and 7.39 on page 162). Most of the estimated 80,000 gorillas in equatorial Africa are lowland gorillas and live in forests across central and western Africa. Lowland gorillas are extraordinarily diverse genetically, and some isolated populations are being elevated to full species status on the basis of the degree of their divergence from other gorillas (Gagneux et al., 1996). In eastern Africa, mountain gorillas also live in a highly fragmented distribution, but their overall numbers are far lower. Only 750 remain in the wild in two mountain ranges, the Virunga Volcanoes and the Bwindi Impenetrable Forest, along the border of Uganda, Rwanda, and the Democratic Republic of the Congo (see Insights and Advances: The Impending Extinction of the Great Apes? on pages 164–165). An exciting recent discovery of a large lowland gorilla population living in the forests of the Republic of Congo means that gorillas may be more numerous in the world today than any other ape species (Stokes et al., 2008).

Gorillas are extremely sexually dimorphic, with males outweighing females by more than 50%. In their mid-teen years, males reach sexual maturity and acquire a gray saddle of hair on their backs, hence the label *silverback* for an adult male gorilla

View the **Map** "Orangutans" on **myanthrolab**

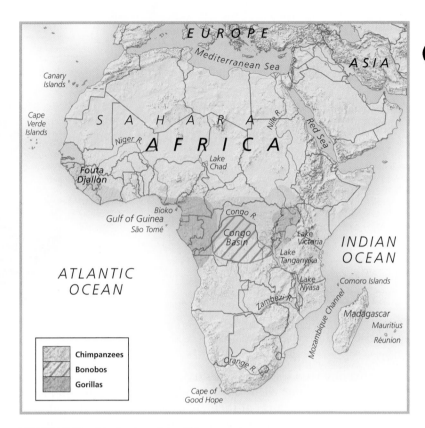

FIGURE 7.38   Distribution of the African great apes.

and *blackback* for an adolescent male. Females give birth about every 4 years. At or after sexual maturity, females tend to migrate to other groups, often in the company of sisters or close female kin (Figure 7.40). Life can be difficult for a female if she migrates with offspring; infanticide by silverbacks is a leading cause of mortality among mountain gorillas (Watts, 1989). Researchers in central Africa recently reported the first instances of tool use in wild gorillas, such as the use of a large stick to assist in wading across a watery swamp (Breuer et al., 2005).

Gorillas live in highly cohesive groups, ranging in size from several animals to several dozen. Males have two reproductive options. They can remain in their birth

FIGURE 7.39   Gorillas are the largest living primates.

FIGURE 7.40   Gorillas live in one or multimale groups, from which females emigrate at sexual maturity.

group, waiting to join the ranking silverback as a breeding adult male some day (or wait for him to die or be driven out). Alternatively, they can emigrate and attempt to find mates elsewhere. Young silverbacks often spend months or years on their own or live in bachelor groups of other silverbacks. Such bachelors wait for opportunities either to take over a male–female group by driving out the resident silverback or to steal a female or two away from an established group. Female gorillas are prone to emigrate just after encounters between groups occur; they may be sizing up the males in the new group to assess whether the time is right to leave with them (Harcourt, 1978). Contrary to the image of a "harem" of females led by a single silverback male, many gorilla groups have two or more silverbacks.

Our view of gorillas as slow-moving, terrestrial leaf-eaters living in one-male harems was shaped by the pioneering study of mountain gorillas begun by Dian Fossey in the Virunga Volcanoes. Following early work by George Schaller, Dian Fossey gave up her training as an occupational therapist to begin the first long-term study of wild gorillas. She established a research camp in the mountains of Rwanda and began to document the daily lives of her study subjects. Fossey's mountain gorillas ate a diet that was nearly 100% high-fiber, poor-quality plants, for which they foraged slowly, almost exclusively on the ground (Fossey, 1983).

As more recent studies of gorillas elsewhere in Africa have been carried out, it has become clear that most wild gorillas do not behave much like those in the Virungas. It appears that gorillas all over Africa prefer to eat fruit but can fall back on fibrous leaves as a staple when fruit is not widely available. Contrary to their terrestrial image in the Virungas, gorillas in other forests, including mountain gorillas in the Bwindi Impenetrable Forest (Uganda), climb trees readily and often are seen feeding on fruits more than 100 feet (30 m) from the ground. Socially, lowland gorillas appear to forage in a more dispersed way than mountain gorillas and may live in less cohesive groups (Remis, 1997a). In some sites in central Africa, lowland gorilla groups use open swampy clearings to gather and feed, even wading into water in search of aquatic plants to eat.

Chimpanzees Along with bonobos, chimpanzees (*Pan troglodytes*) are our closest living relatives (Figure 7.41). The genetic similarity between a chimpanzee and us is greater than the chimpanzee's evolutionary affinity to a gorilla. The most abundant of the three living African apes, with a total wild population estimated at 150,000–200,000, chimpanzees are extraordinarily adaptable animals, found across equatorial Africa from lowland rain forest to nearly open grasslands. Males may weigh up to 150 pounds (68 kg) and are 10%–15% larger and heavier than females.

Unlike most nonhuman primates, chimpanzees live not in cohesive, stable social groups but rather in a multimale, multifemale community called a **fission–fusion** mating system. A community may number 20–120 individuals, in which the only stable unit is a mother–offspring pair. Its members come together in unpredictable social groupings to form foraging subgroups, the size and composition of which seem to be determined by a combination of fruit distribution and the presence of fertile females (Figure 7.42 on page 166). The community occupies a territory, which is defended by its males with great ferocity. Males band together to patrol the territorial boundaries on a regular basis and may attack and attempt to kill any chimpanzee, male or female, that is found encroaching on their land. The only exception occurs when male patrols encounter sexually receptive females from other communities, in which case the female may be coercively brought back to the home community (Goodall, 1986).

Within the community, males and females have very different social behavior patterns. Males tend to be highly social with one another, forming strong, long-lasting coalitions that they use to try to control females, patrol, and hunt. Females travel more independently, apparently in order to avoid feeding competition from other adults. After an 8-month pregnancy, a 4-year infancy, and a prolonged juvenile period, a female chimpanzee reaches sexual maturity around age 12. After this time, most females begin to visit neighboring communities, eventually settling there as

fission–fusion Form of mating system seen in chimpanzees, bonobos, and a few other primates in which there are temporary subgroups but no stable, cohesive groups.

FIGURE 7.41 Chimpanzees and humans share a very close genetic and evolutionary kinship.

insights & advances
THE IMPENDING EXTINCTION OF THE GREAT APES?

For more than 20 million years, apes have flourished in the tropical forests of the Old World. But today, throughout their geographic distribution in equatorial Africa and Southeast Asia, the great apes are in grave peril of extinction. For the most critically endangered, the orangutan and bonobo, this could mean extinction in the wild within your lifetime. Can this be prevented? Conservation efforts must begin with an understanding of the threats to the endangered species. These threats exist in several key areas:

• **Habitat destruction** The loss of tropical forest habitat is the single greatest factor causing the decline in nonhuman primate populations worldwide (Figure A). From Congo to Indonesia, forest clearing is accelerating, and with it comes the loss of thousands of animal and plant species. Forests are cut by local farmers so they can plant crops, but forests are also cut by government-sanctioned logging companies in many regions.

FIGURE A   The destruction of tropical forests, the habitat of living great apes, continues at an alarming rate.

Recent estimates on the Indonesian island of Sumatra place the loss of orangutan habitat at 80% in the past two decades, and the population declined 45% just from 1993 to 1999 (van Schaik et al., 2001). At current rates of habitat loss, the 20,000 orangutans remaining in the wild face extinction within 15 years.

• **Bushmeat** A major cause of population decline among apes in central and western Africa is the bushmeat trade. Bushmeat is simply the meat of any wild animal that is eaten by people.

In Africa, the smoked flesh of gorillas, chimpanzees, and bonobos is highly valued. People have been hunting and eating apes for thousands of years, but recently the pattern has changed. No longer is ape hunting practiced only by local villagers trying to put some protein in their children's stomachs. As international logging companies from Europe cut logging roads deep into pristine rain forests, they create a pipeline by which ape carcasses can be easily transported from remote areas. Businessmen in towns and cities pay hunters to send them as many apes as they can kill, the meat of which is sold on the black market (and sometimes in the open market) for several times the price of beef. In Africa, government officials and wealthy people exhibit

breeding adults. The result is that adult females tend to be unrelated immigrants with few bonds in the new community (Goodall, 1986). Males remain in their birth community their entire lives, reaching maturity at 15 years of age. In the wild, chimpanzees live to a maximum age of 45; in captivity, some have been known to reach 60 years of age.

Chimpanzees eat a highly diverse diet that is composed mainly of ripe fruit. In addition, they eat leaves and other plant products, plus insects such as termites and ants, which they extract from termite mounds using hand-fashioned tools (Figure 7.43 on page 166). Some West African chimpanzee populations use stones and clubs collected from the forest floor to crack open hard-shelled nuts. Researchers recently observed one chimpanzee population extracting **galagos** from tree cavities using sharp sticks (Pruetz & Bertolani, 2007). More than any animal other than humans, chimpanzees live by learned traditions and pass these traditions on to their offspring. Tool use is not genetically based, although the intellectual capacity to understand how a tool is used certainly is.

Chimpanzees also relish meat, in the form of monkeys, wild pigs, young antelope, and other small animals. In some forests, chimpanzees kill and eat hundreds of animals every year (Stanford, 1998a). Meat-eating patterns vary from site to site and seem to be subject to the same learned traditions that characterize tool use and other behaviors. Anthropologists find chimpanzee hunting behavior intriguing as a model for how early hominins may have behaved. Jane Goodall's pioneering research on chimpanzees, followed by research by Toshisada Nishida (1990), set the stage for much modern primate research.

galago   Live in many African forests; Also called Bushbabies.

their affluence by serving ape meat to visitors, including stunned foreigners.

Apes have withstood low levels of hunting for millennia, but the recent intense pressure, combined with the very slow reproductive rate of the great apes (perhaps one baby every 4 years), has resulted in dramatic population decline even in forests that have seen little human use. Stopping the bushmeat trade entails not only law enforcement but also a change in cultural values so that Africans do not consider the eating of apes to be a status symbol.

• **International zoo, laboratory, and pet trade** Despite increased public awareness of the evils of taking apes from the wild, poaching for the live animal trade still occurs. Hundreds of baby orangutans are caught every year to be sold illegally as pets in Southeast Asia.

Some years ago, conservationists estimated that there were more baby orangutans being kept as household pets on the island of Taiwan than were being born in all of Borneo each year. For every baby entering the pet trade alive, many others die before reaching the market.

Poaching has been outlawed, but the practice continues. Although most labs in Europe and the United States now use captive-bred apes, gorillas and chimpanzees sometimes are poached for their value as laboratory animals in other countries and for sale to unscrupulous zoos.

• **Disease** Emerging viruses, including ebola and anthrax, have recently been discovered in wild ape populations and pose a great threat.

What can we do? The first step is habitat protection. Many conservation organizations work in Africa to preserve ape populations. This goal can be achieved only by providing local people with an economic incentive to protect the animals and other forest resources. Because apes are valued as tourist attractions, ecotourism sometimes provides that incentive.

In Bwindi Impenetrable National Park in southwestern Uganda, tourists pay up to $500 per hour to view wild mountain gorillas. A percentage of this fee goes to local villages for building hospitals and schools. Ecotourism does not work everywhere, however, and is highly vulnerable to the political instability that plagues much of Africa. In addition, close contact between tourists and apes increases the risk of disease transmission from us to them. Most wild ape populations have no immunity to flus, colds, and other human diseases that, because of their genetic kinship with us, they easily catch.

Conservationists must provide a simple economic rationale for local people and governments: How will protecting the forest and its inhabitants, rather than destroying them, help people living near great apes? The answer to nonhuman primate protection lies in improving the living conditions of people. Scientists from wealthier countries help to train students to become conservation leaders themselves in countries where apes live. In this way, we hope to help people in Asia and Africa preserve their natural heritage for future generations.

Bonobos Bonobos (*Pan paniscus*), sometimes called pygmy chimpanzees because of their slightly more slender build, are close relatives of chimpanzees and are classified in the same genus (Figure 7.44 on page 166). They exhibit more modest sexual dimorphism than the other great apes. Males and females have similar body sizes, but males have larger skulls and canine teeth. They occur only in a limited region south of the Congo River in the Democratic Republic of the Congo (formerly Zaire), mainly in lowland rain forest habitat. Their total population is estimated at only about 25,000 (Insights and Advances: The Impending Extinction of the Great Apes?). Far less is known about bonobos than about chimpanzees; the first detailed field studies were conducted only in the 1980s, and political turmoil in Congo has repeatedly disrupted long-term research.

Bonobos eat a largely fruit diet but rely more on leafy plant material from the forest floor than chimpanzees do. Their more consistently available food supply may allow bonobos to live in larger parties than do chimpanzees (Malenky et al., 1994). Although they hunt and kill other mammals, bonobos do not necessarily eat them. At Lilungu, bonobos have been observed to capture young monkeys and use them as playthings, releasing them unharmed after they become bored with their prey (Sabater-Pi et al., 1993). At other sites, however, bonobos catch and eat small antelopes (Hohmann and Fruth, 1993); the degree to which bonobos eat meat may be underappreciated (Hohmann and Fruth, 2008).

Like chimpanzees, bonobos live in large, fluid social groupings called communities. Males remain in the community of their birth, whereas females migrate between communities after sexual maturity. Males engage in border clashes with males from

FIGURE 7.42 Chimpanzees live in complex kin groups in which lifelong bonds and individual personalities play key roles, as in human societies.

neighboring communities (Kano, 1992). But there are some striking differences between bonobo and chimpanzee societies. Unlike female chimpanzees, female bonobos forge strong bonds and use female coalitions to prevent males from dominating them. Females engage in *genital-genital (or GG) rubbing*, a sociosexual behavior that reduces tensions between individuals. Immigrant females ally themselves with individual resident females and slowly extend their social network (Furuichi, 1987). Females achieve dominance status in bonobo communities far beyond that of female chimpanzees (Parish, 1996).

Bonobos have become well known to the public because of reports of their hypersexuality. The contrast between their behavior and that of chimpanzees has led to a debate over which species is the better model for how early humans may have behaved. Bonobos are said to be closer in sexual behavior and biology to humans than any other animal. Whether this is fully accurate has been questioned by a number of researchers.

FIGURE 7.43 Wild chimpanzees make and use simple tools to obtain food, learning tool-making from one another.

FIGURE 7.44 Bonobos are close relatives of chimpanzees and humans.

In addition to their interesting behavior patterns in the wild, bonobos have been the subjects of exciting research on the origins of human language. Kanzi, a male bonobo at the Great Ape Trust in Iowa, understands several hundred words in spoken English and communicates using a symbol board (Savage-Rumbaugh and Lewin, 1994).

ecology The study of the interrelationships of plants, animals, and the physical environment in which they live.

Primate Ecology

It's important to remember that despite their interesting social behavior, primates are first and foremost parts of ecosystems. A revolution has taken place in the way we see primates and other animals in their natural habitat, as a result of advances in the field of ecology.

Ecology is the study of the interrelationships of animals, plants, and their physical environment. The environment provides the template on which natural selection molds behavior. At the same time, primates influence the ecology of many tropical forests, as dispersers of seeds and even as pollinators of flowering plants. Primate behavior evolved in direct response to environmental pressures, and we can understand most aspects of primate behavior only in the context of the natural environment in which the primate evolved.

Several key ecological factors have shaped the evolution of nonhuman primates and continue to shape them today. Finding and eating food is a constant, chronic concern that occupies much of the day for nonhuman primates. They are bound by the same equation that faces all other wild animals: The energy that is expended to find food (calories burned) must be balanced by the quantity (calories consumed) and quality (nutrients such as fats, proteins, and carbohydrates) of the food eaten. This need is even greater for females because of the physical cost of reproduction. To understand how nonhuman primates live, we must therefore understand something about the nature and distribution of their favorite foods and how that affects aspects of their behavior. In this section we consider primate ecology, which will allow us, in Chapter 8, to understand how primate social systems may be adapted to the environment.

Diet

Most primates are *herbivores,* living largely on a plant food diet (Figure 7.45). Exceptions to this pattern are many of the lower primates, which eat insects as a substantial portion of the diet, and a few higher primates (including humans) that also eat meat. Only one primate group is entirely carnivorous: the tarsier of Southeast Asia, which subsists on insects, lizards, frogs, and other small animals. For the rest, much of the diet is composed of two items: fruits and leaves.

We tend to think of the natural world in a very human-centric way. But for a moment, consider a tropical forest from the point of view of a tree. As a tree, you produce several products that are highly valued by the animals you share the forest with: fruit, leaves, flowers, seeds, and so forth. All around you there are birds, monkeys, and small mammals that hunger after the fruit you produce. There are also millions of leaf-eating insects, monkeys, and other animals that eat your leafy foliage. But fruit and leaves have very different values to the potential herbivore. Leaves are the factories of a tropical tree; they take in sunlight and synthesize energy for the tree by the process of photosynthesis. For this reason, if a horde of insects or leaf-eating monkeys comes along and eats all its leaves, the tree will be unable to produce energy or obtain the nutrients it needs. At best it will have to endure a difficult period until new leaves can be grown, and at worst it could die. So ecologists predict that natural selection should endow trees with the means to protect their leaves.

Fruits have a very different value. They are the vessels that hold the seeds, which are the reproductive opportunities for the tree—its embryos for the next generation. Therefore, a tree "wants" its fruit to be eaten by animals, carried away

FIGURE 7.45 Like all animals, primates must balance their calories expended searching for food with calories, protein, fat, and other nutrients obtained.

somewhere, and then excreted out so that its seeds can germinate on the forest floor some distance away from their parents. Whereas trees and leaf-eaters, or **folivores,** are in a constant evolutionary battle, trees and fruit-eaters, called *frugivores,* are in a long-running symbiosis. So ecologists predict that natural selection should build traits into fruit that encourage frugivores to seek out the fruit crop and eat it.

There is abundant evidence that this is exactly what has happened. Consider how you choose a peach in the market that is ripe and ready to eat. First you look at it; is it orange and red, or is it still green? Then you touch it; is it soft, or is it still rock hard? Finally, you may smell it; does it have a pleasant, sweet smell? Wild primates use exactly the same criteria for choosing their fruits in tropical forests. And all these qualities—bright color, soft texture, and a good smell—were built into fruits by natural selection to convince frugivorous animals that they are delicious, nutritious, and ready to be eaten. These signals show a foraging primate that the fruit contains high levels of carbohydrate in the form of sugars, providing a caloric boost for an active day of foraging. Certainly brightly colored fruit did not evolve solely in response to primates; many birds eat fruit too, and their ancestors pre-date those of modern primates. But like birds, many primates are color-visioned fruit foragers. A primate must be able to efficiently locate fruits and then compete successfully for access to them as fruit availability is far less predictable than leaf availability.

Leaves are an entirely different story when it comes to foraging. Leaves are found everywhere in a tropical forest, so you might think all a monkey has to do is reach out and pluck its breakfast. But a tropical forest is not the cornucopia of food that it might appear. Leaves tend to be poor sources of nutrients and calories compared with fruits, but they can contain large amounts of protein. Because leaves are such a valuable and dependable resource, trees protect them against folivores in a variety ways. First, many leaves are coated with bristles, spines, or hairs that make it difficult or painful to ingest them. A primate must also have a digestive system designed to cope with *fiber.* Fiber is a barrier to digestion, as anyone who eats raw corn or other high-fiber vegetables knows. Young tender leaves contain minimal fiber because the cell walls in each leaf have not yet built up layers of cellulose and hemicellulose that later become the structural support of the plant (Figure 7.46). Mature leaves are tougher and highly fibrous.

You Are What You Eat: Dietary and Digestive Strategies

In general, the largest-bodied primates rely the least on insect prey, although a few primates, such as chimpanzees and capuchin monkeys, forage for insects very intensively and at times consume large numbers of them. Gorillas don't eat many insects, and very small-bodied primates rarely eat large quantities of leafy matter. This is because of the time and energy needed to make a living on these diets in relation to the time and energy needed to properly digest leaves, fruits, and live prey. The very largest primates tend to be folivorous, although there are exceptions. So gorillas are able to subsist on a diet of high-fiber plants, which they slowly pass through a very

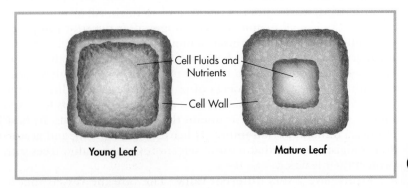

FIGURE 7.46 Comparison of a tender and mature leaf. As leaves mature, they become fiber-filled and harder to digest.

long digestive tract that provides the space for maximal breakdown of food before excretion. The smallest primate that is highly folivorous is a species of dwarf lemur (*Lepilemur mustelinus*).

Diet and Feeding Competition

In nature, there are only so many hours of daylight during which a diurnal primate can make its living. A primate's **activity budget** allows it to compensate for calories expended with calories consumed. Diurnal primates forage during the day, nocturnal primates come out of hiding at night, and *crepuscular* primates forage at dawn and dusk. *Cathemeral* primates have irregular active periods during both the day and night. Each activity period has its share of foods available and predators lurking to catch unwary prey.

Activity budgets are tightly linked to dietary quality. Primates that live on high-fiber, low-calorie diets also tend to be more sedentary than those living on a high-fruit diet; compare the fission–fusion social system of the chimpanzee or spider monkey with the slowly moving cohesive groups in which howlers or mountain gorillas live. Gibbons brachiate acrobatically through Asian forests, eating fruit as their dietary staple. Muriquis of the Atlantic coastal forest of Brazil wake up late, go to sleep early, and in between forage slowly through their tree-top habitat for a diet that consists largely of leaves. Mountain gorillas in Rwanda move at a glacial pace, walking as little as a few hundred yards in a day. Their high-mountain habitat contains practically no fruit trees, so their diet is mainly wild celery and other highly fibrous plants. But lowland gorillas a few hundred miles to the west live in tropical forests with a high diversity of fruiting trees, and they eat a great deal of fruit. Lowland gorillas travel up to 2 miles (3 km) per day. They travel such great distances to find widely scattered fruit trees, and the energy they burn in their travels is replaced by the high carbohydrate value of their fruity diet.

Katharine Milton (1980) conducted a field study of howler and spider monkeys that illustrates the contrasts between frugivore and folivore activity patterns and what they may mean for primate evolution. On Barro Colorado Island in Panama, Milton observed howlers eating a diet high in leaves. The howlers carefully selected the most tender, young growing parts, but their diet contained little other than fiber. They were also very sedentary, moving very slowly through the forest canopy in a cohesive group. Meanwhile, spider monkeys ate a diet high in ripe fruit and traveled many times further per day than howlers. Milton (1981) further considered the relative brain sizes of the two species; spider monkeys have larger brain–body size ratio than do howlers. She hypothesized that the evolutionary pressure of finding and remembering the changing locations of ripe fruit trees had placed a premium on cognition in spider monkeys, leading to brain-size increase in this primate but not in the related howlers.

Territories and Ranges

All mammals, including nonhuman primates, live in defined places called **home ranges** (Figure 7.47 on page 170). This area can be very limited—smaller than a football field in the case of some nocturnal strepsirhines—or many square kilometers in the case of some apes and monkeys. The range must contain all the resources needed by a nonhuman primate or a social group: water, food, shelter, and mates. Home ranges often overlap, either slightly or entirely. Parts of the home range that are used most intensively are called the **core area.** In some species, such as gorillas, home ranges overlap greatly, and groups encounter one another often. In other species, such as chimpanzee, community ranges overlap only slightly, and aggressive encounters occur in the overlap zone. In some species, the home range is defended against other members of the same species, in which case we call it a **territory.** The defended portion of the home range usually is the part in which critical resources are located.

Territorial defense can take the form of vocalizing, such as the songs of gibbons. By setting up loudspeakers within, at the border of, and outside the territorial boundaries

folivores Animals that eat a diet composed mainly of leaves, or foliage.

activity budget The pattern of waking, eating, moving, socializing, and sleeping that all nonhuman primates engage in each day.

home range The spatial area used by a primate group.

core area The part of a home range that is most intensively used.

territory The part of a home range that is defended against other members of the same species.

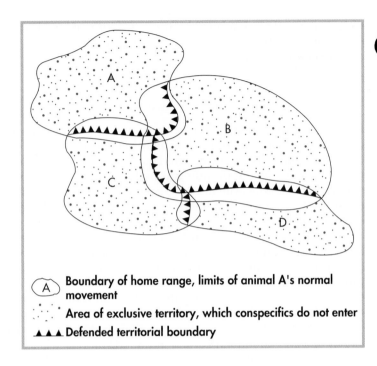

A — Boundary of home range, limits of animal A's normal movement

Area of exclusive territory, which conspecifics do not enter

▲▲▲ Defended territorial boundary

FIGURE 7.47 Primates use their space in a variety of ways: home ranges, core areas, and territories.

of gibbon pairs, John Mitani (1985) showed that gibbons use their songs as territorial markers. As Mitani predicted, gibbons that heard the calls of strange gibbons coming (via loudspeakers) from within their territory responded most vigorously, calling and approaching the site of the call in obvious territorial defensiveness. Territorial defense can also result from visual encounters along territorial borders, in which males, females, or both (depending on the species) intimidate and chase the potential intruders. Among many Old World monkeys, females rather than males engage in territorial disputes. In some species, territorial disputes may be settled through physical contact, including lethal contact in rare cases, such as chimpanzees.

Predation

Nonhuman primates in the wild face the difficult challenge of finding food while avoiding attacks by predators. Failing to find food on a given afternoon will leave a monkey hungry the next day, but failing to avoid an attack by an eagle or leopard will leave it dead or injured. So we should expect that nonhuman primates have evolved behavioral defenses against predators. But actually observing predation is difficult because the predators are stealthy and usually nocturnal and solitary (Figure 7.48). Most often a member of a nonhuman primate group being studied disappears one day, and the researcher has no idea whether disease, accidental death, or a predator was responsible.

Despite a lack of field observations, we can make a few generalizations about predation. First, small-bodied nonhuman primates are more vulnerable to predation than larger species. In Madagascar, owls have been reported to kill up to one-quarter of the mouse lemur population each year (Goodman et al., 1993). Even a much lower predation rate could be a major source of mortality in a population of monkeys. Second, many nonhuman primate species exhibit behaviors that appear to have evolved in response to the threat of predation. Alarm calls are often given when a predator approaches, and experimental studies using loudspeakers to play the calls of leopards and eagles have shown that monkeys respond

FIGURE 7.48 Primates face a wide variety of predators in the wild, including birds of prey.

in a variety of ways. Vervet monkeys studied in Amboseli National Park, Kenya, by Dorothy Cheney and Robert Seyfarth (1991) give alarm calls that vary depending on the type of predator spotted; different calls are given for eagles, leopards, and pythons. Red colobus monkeys studied by Ronald Noë and colleagues in the Taï Forest of Ivory Coast responded to the calls of wild chimpanzees by moving toward other monkey species nearby; the chimpanzee calls seemed to be acting as early warning systems that the colobus could capitalize on (Noë and Bshary, 1997).

One of the few cases in which we can directly observe predation on nonhuman primates is in African forests in which chimpanzees prey on other nonhuman primates. We saw earlier that chimpanzees are avid meat eaters, and red colobus monkeys are their most frequent prey. In Gombe National Park, Tanzania, chimpanzees kill 18% of the red colobus population living in their home range in some years (in other years, predation is much lighter; Stanford, 1998a). Chimpanzee predation was overall such a major source of colobus mortality that the colobus population would have been in serious decline at Gombe were it not for the fact that in some years predation was infrequent.

Primate Communities

If you were to walk through some tropical forests, you would see not one but many species of primates. In the Congo Basin of central Africa or the Amazon Basin of Peru, it's possible to see more than a dozen primate species in a single acre of forest. If you were to take a walk through the same forest at night, you would see a different, nocturnal community of primates. With so many closely related and often morphologically similar primates sharing the same forest, why isn't there more intense competition between them for food and other resources? The answer is that there is or was competition in the evolutionary past of the species. Ecological theory predicts that when two or more organisms with very similar needs are sympatric, sharing the same space, they will diverge from one another in some critical aspect of their *niche,* or ecological role. For example, two monkeys that seem to eat the same foods will be found to eat different diets when food is scarce. One species might forage high in trees, whereas the other finds its food on the ground. Without such *niche separation,* species would drive each other into extinction far more often than they are observed to.

Niche separation occurs among all primates that are sympatric, and such divergence often is evident only during ecological crunch times. What's more, it can be very difficult to demonstrate feeding competition in the wild—simply overlapping strongly with another species' ecology is not evidence that the two species compete—so field studies more often record the nature of ecological overlap than the occurrence of ecological competition. Gorillas and chimpanzees share forests across central Africa, and both species prefer a diet heavy in ripe fruit. But during lean seasons, gorillas fall back on fibrous plants as their staple, while chimpanzees continue to forage widely for fruit. Although the diets of the two ape species overlap extensively, direct contest competition over food is rare (Stanford, 2007).

As you can see, primates are a highly diverse group of mammals that are subject to many of the same evolutionary and ecological principles that guide the lives of other mammals. However, nonhuman primates have two adaptations—sociality and large brains—that set them apart from nearly all other animals. In the next chapter, we will examine nonhuman primate social behavior and cognition to see what they tell us about human evolution.

The Primates

Primate Radiation

Mammalians and Primate, Diversity

- Mammals are categorized as placental (eutherian), marsupial (metatherian), or monotreme (prototherian). **[pp 138–139]**

What Is a Primate?

Anatomical traits that characterize the primate order:

- Generalized body plan
- Grasping hand and opposable thumb
- Forward-facing eyes with stereoscopic vision
- Flattened nails
- Generalized teeth
- Petrosal bulla
- Enclosed bony eye orbit

Life history traits that characterize the primate order:

- Single births
- Large brain–body size ratio
- Extended ontogeny

Behavioral traits that characterize the primate order:

- Visually oriented daytime activity
- Sociality **[pp 139–146]**

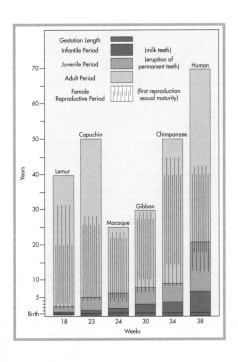

The Nonhuman Primates

Strepsirhines

- This group includes lower primates.
- Lemurs, lorises, and galagos are also part of this group. **[pp 146–153]**

New World Monkeys

- This group is also called platyrhines or ceboids.
- Small-bodied anthropoids of the western hemisphere can be found in the New World monkey group.
- Capuchins, uakari, and spider monkeys are a part of the New World monkeys. **[pp 155–156]**

Old World Monkeys

- Another name for this group is catarrhines or cercopithecoids.
- They live in Africa and Asia.
- It is a large, diverse group.
- It includes langurs, colobus, macaques, and baboons. **[pp 156–159]**

Haplorhines

- This group is made up of the tarsier, New World monkeys, Old World monkeys, apes, and hominins.
- It occupies an evolutionary status intermediate between the lower and higher primates. **[pp 154–155]**

The Hominoids

- Hominoids include ape families Hylobatidae (gibbons, or lesser apes) and Pongidae (chimpanzee, gorilla, bonobo, orangutan, or great apes) [pp 159–167]

Primate Ecology

- Primates select food to balance an energy budget of nutrients and calories that requires them to forage all day long.
- Nonhuman primates engage in feeding competition and use well-defined areas of their habitat to find food and shelter.
- Primate communities, like communities of other animals, are integral parts of tropical forest ecosystems. [pp 167–171]

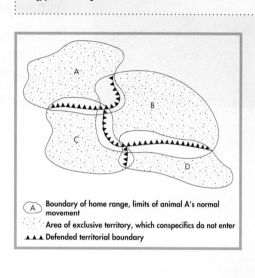

Ⓐ Boundary of home range, limits of animal A's normal movement

Area of exclusive territory, which conspecifics do not enter

▲▲▲ Defended territorial boundary

My AnthroLab CONNECTIONS

Watch. Listen. View. Explore. Read.

MyAnthroLab is designed just for you. Each chapter features a customized study plan to help you learn and review key concepts and terms. Dynamic visual activities, videos, and readings found in the multimedia library will enhance your learning experience.

Resources from this Chapter:

 **Listen** on **myanthrolab**

▶ *Orangutans Aren't Lazy, Just Evolved to Hang Around*

View on **myanthrolab**

▶ *A World Map of Living Nonhuman Primates*
▶ *Modern Lemurs*
▶ *Galagos and Lorises*
▶ *Tarsiers*
▶ *New World Monkeys (Ceboidea)*
▶ *Old World Monkeys*
▶ *African Great Apes*
▶ *Orangutans*

 **Explore** on **myanthrolab** In MySearchLab, enter the Anthropology database to find relevant and recent scholarly and popular press publications. For this chapter, enter the following keywords: Primates, Taxonomy, Strepsirhine, Haplorhine, Apes

Read on **myanthrolab**

▶ *Chimpanzee Technology* by William C. McGrew
▶ *Are We in Anthropodenial?* by Frans B.M. De Waal

Chapter 8 Preview

After reading this chapter, you should be able to:

- Explain both the theory and techniques for studying primate behavior.

- Discuss the evolutionary paradox of primate sociality.

- Review male primate reproductive strategies and contrast them with female reproductive strategies.

- Distinguish among the major forms of primate social systems.

- Compare bonobo and chimpanzee social behavior.

Primate Behavior

8

The following day I tracked Group 8 [a group of gorillas] into the saddle area west of Visoke and contacted them from a distance of about sixty feet. They gave me the calmest reception I had ever received from an unhabituated group. The first individual to acknowledge my presence was the young silverback, who strutted onto a rock and stared with compressed lips before going off to feed. I named him Pugnacious, Pug for short. He was followed by the extremely attractive blackback, who nipped off a leaf to fold between his lips for a few seconds before spitting it out, a common displacement activity known as symbolic feeding and indicative of mild unease. After whacking at some vegetation, the magnificent male swaggered out of sight into dense foliage, seemingly quite pleased with himself. I named him Samson. Next, the two young adults scampered into view and impishly flipped over on to their backs to stare at me from upside-down positions, giving the impression they were wearing lopsided grins. In time

they were named Geezer and Peanuts. When the elderly female came into view, she gazed briefly at me in a totally uninterested manner before sitting down next to Peanuts and maneuvering her patchy rump almost into his face for grooming. I named her Coco because of her somewhat light chocolate-colored hair. Lastly, the old silverback came forward. In all my years of research I never met a silverback so dignified and commanding of respect. His silvering extended from the sides of his cheekbones, along the neck and shoulders, enveloped his back and barrel, and continued down the sides of both thighs. Having little to go by in comparison, except for zoo gorillas, I estimated his age as approximately fifty years, possibly more. The nobility of his character compelled me to seek a name for him immediately. In Swahili, *rafiki* means "friend." Because friendship implies mutual respect and trust, the regal silverback became known as Rafiki.

—Dian Fossey, *Gorillas in the Mist* (1983)

Watching nonhuman primates is one thing; understanding their behavior is another. Observation of behavior is at the heart of the subfield of biological anthropology known as *primatology*, as pioneering researcher Dian Fossey understood.

Primates are intrinsically fascinating animals that serve as illustrations of evolutionary principles of natural selection, adaptive radiation, convergent evolution, and sexual selection. They also inform us about human evolution, offering a window into how early humans may have behaved. In this chapter, we will consider how biological anthropologists study nonhuman primates and their social evolution. We will see that evolutionary principles that you learned in Chapter 5, such as natural selection and sexual selection, play key roles in shaping primate behavior. You'll also examine the diversity of societies in which nonhuman primates may live and explore the reasons these societies evolved the way they did. And you will read about some of the current controversies over the form and function of primate social behavior.

FIGURE 8.1   Sociality is the most fundamental behavioral adaptation of the primates.

FIGURE 8.2   Jane Goodall pioneered the modern approach to studying primates in the wild, involving close-up observation of known individuals over many months.

◉ **Watch** the **Video** "Dr. Jane Goodall: Primatology and The Leakey Foundation" on **myanthrolab**

Studying Primates

As we saw in Chapter 7, *sociality* is the most fundamental primate behavioral adaptation (Figure 8.1). It is the hallmark of nearly all the haplorhine primates, and its study is an essential component of nearly all nonhuman primate behavior research. Primatologists want to learn why nonhuman primates are social. To do this, they study the costs and benefits of group living and examine how the same evolutionary processes that promoted sociality in nonhuman primates may have promoted the emergence of humankind.

The modern approach to the study of nonhuman primate behavior occurred when we began to study the animals systematically. The earliest field researchers spent only a few days or weeks watching nonhuman primates in the wild. Jane Goodall (1968) was the first researcher to immerse herself in the lives of the animals, following her subjects year after year and learning intimate details of their lives (Figure 8.2). What Goodall did in the early 1960s is now the norm for primatologists; graduate students typically spend 1–2 years living in the habitat of the primates for a doctoral thesis project. Many field studies of more than 10 years' duration have been carried out. In extended studies, multiple primate generations can be followed and individuals' lives more fully understood. Studies of nonhuman primate demography have revealed aspects of the evolution of life histories and the ways in which long-term patterns of mating success are related to reproductive success. Primatologists have also added new research tools to their arsenal: paternity tests using DNA, studies of endocrine influences on behavior using hormones extracted from feces or urine, and studies of communication using sophisticated sound recording equipment (Figure 8.3).

We can study nonhuman primates in several different settings, each of which strongly influences the sort of research that is possible. A **captive study** allows us to closely observe nonhuman primates up-close and personal, because they won't hide in dense trees for hours on end. We often study captive populations over many generations and know their family histories in great detail. We can also manipulate the study group; the researcher might move a new male into the social group in order to observe the effect on the rest of the group. A valuable use of captive studies is to confirm and refine the results of studies done in the wild.

Some nonhuman primate studies are conducted in a more spacious **semi-free-ranging environment.** Very large enclosures, or even small islands, sometimes have nonhuman primate populations. Cayo Santiago, an islet off the coast of Puerto Rico onto which rhesus macaques from India were

FIGURE 8.3   Modern primate study sometimes involves high-tech methods. This golden lion tamarin is having a battery changed in its radio transmitter collar.

introduced in the 1930s, is one example. The animals in a semi-free-ranging setting can establish territories, form their own groups, and forage for food, even though they are in captivity. Because they are confined (though in a large area), we can easily study kinship and follow many generations of the animals. Semi-free-ranging primates exhibit a more natural pattern of behaviors than they would in a zoo, but not so natural as in the wild.

A modern study of primate behavior called **field study** is conducted in the habitat in which the species evolved. Only in the field can researchers see patterns of behavior that evolved in response to environmental variables (Figure 8.4). As we saw earlier, the interplay between genes and behavior depends on a third critical variable: the physical environment. Studies of nonhuman primates in the wild focus on various aspects of ecology, such as diet and its influence on grouping patterns and social behavior; *positional behavior,* or the relationship between locomotor morphology and the physical environment; and social interactions within and between primate groups.

FIGURE 8.4   Field research on free-living primates allows primatologists to study patterns of behavior in the setting where the behavior evolved.

There are significant difficulties in studying nonhuman primates in the wild. First, the primatologist must accustom the animals to his or her presence. This is a slow process that can take months or even years. Only once habituated can the primates be identified as individuals and observed closely. However, habituation may also allow other people, including poachers intending to kill the animals, to approach. Therefore, habituation can be undertaken only in areas where the animals' lives will not be placed in danger should the scientists pack up their project and go home. And even well-habituated primates are difficult to watch because so much of their behavior takes place behind dense foliage and rocks or in tall trees. Some nonhuman primates have huge home ranges, and just locating the group every day can be a challenge. A year spent in the wild watching monkeys may produce a small fraction of the observation hours that a scientist could obtain in a zoo in one month. Manipulations of the social and physical environment that can be done easily in captivity, such as changing the diet or taking DNA samples, are rarely possible in the wild.

The Evolution of Primate Social Behavior

We can understand and study behavior at different levels. All behaviors we see in the wild have immediate causes: hunger, fear, sexual urges, and the like. The immediate, or *proximate,* causes involve the hormonal, physiological reasons for the animal to act. At the same time, behaviors reflect deeper, evolved tendencies that have been shaped over millions of years of natural and sexual selection to promote reproductive success. A baboon mates because of immediate impulses that are both hormonal and social. But ultimately, the urge to mate reflects deeper, evolved strategies that arise through natural selection to enhance the baboon's odds of reproduction. In Chapter 5 you saw how these evolutionary forces mold an organism's phenotype. In this chapter, you will examine how the same forces shape primate behavior as a phenotype.

The value of an evolutionary approach to nonhuman primate behavior and ecology is that it allows us to test hypotheses. Using an evolutionary framework, we can study mating as one of many behaviors that has fitness consequences. The pattern of mating may be related to everything from dominance relationships and coalitionary networks to female physiology, which may in turn reveal something important about the evolution of the **social system.** In other words, behavior can be seen as an adaptation, one aspect of the primate's phenotype. Although the genetic basis for a specific trait remains largely unknown, we can study the consequences of the behavior.

⊙⌐**Watch** the **Animation** "Taxonomy of Primate Social Systems" on **myanthrolab**

captive study   Primate behavior study conducted in a zoo, laboratory, or other enclosed setting.

semi-free-ranging environment Primate behavior study conducted in a large area that is enclosed or isolated in some way so the population is captive.

field study   Primate behavior study conducted in the habitat in which the primate naturally occurs.

social system   The grouping pattern in which a primate species lives, including its size and composition evolved in response to natural and sexual selection pressures.

For example, if being aggressive promotes reproductive success for a baboon compared with less aggressive baboons in the group, we may infer that aggression is subject to evolutionary forces. We can use such studies to test our interpretations of the evolution of human social behavior too.

Social Behavior and Reproductive Asymmetry

The reproductive asymmetry between males and females plays a key role in our understanding of the evolution of nonhuman primate social strategies. Females have a lower reproductive potential and lower variance in reproductive output than males. Females invest far more energy and time in offspring, during both gestation and offspring rearing, than males do. In accordance with Darwinian sexual selection theory (Chapter 5), females tend to be competed for by males rather than the other way around. As a result, we expect females of all social mammals to prioritize obtaining adequate food supplies for themselves and their offspring. Females do not need to be particularly concerned about finding a male; because of their lower reproductive potential, they will always be the sought-out sex, and males will find them. Because the availability of females is the single factor that most limits a male's opportunity to achieve reproductive success, we expect that males will go where females go and will map themselves onto the landscape in accordance with the distribution of females.

The form the social system takes therefore depends on the way females distribute themselves. The social system of nonhuman primate species in which females form the core of the group is called **female philopatry.** This means that females do not migrate at maturity; they stay in the group of their birth to reproduce and rear offspring. In such groups, males typically migrate. Females in female-philopatric groups often form tight bonds, based partly on the likelihood of their kinship. Such matrilines of mother, daughters, grandmother, and so on, can form the core of the group. In **male philopatry,** males remain in their natal home range throughout life, and females migrate. The two types of social systems are closely connected to other important aspects of behavior, so each bears closer examination.

When female kin live together, they share a strong incentive to cooperate or at least to limit their competition over food resources. Studies have shown that in female-philopatric groups, territorial defense is done mainly by females, and the degree of affiliation among females is far greater than among females in male-philopatric species. For instance, in Gombe National Park, Tanzania, female baboons, which are female philopatric, spend much time sitting together and grooming one another. In the same forest, female chimpanzees, which are male-philopatric, rarely engage in social grooming or contact (Figure 8.5). Competition among females can

(a)

(b)

FIGURE 8.5   (a) Savanna baboons live in female-philopatric groups, among which males migrate. (b) Chimpanzees live in male-philopatric communities, among which females migrate.

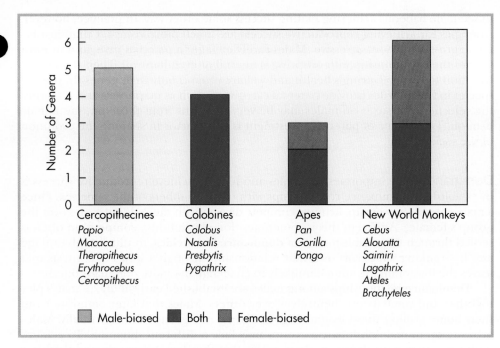

female philopatry Primate social system in which females remain and breed in the group of their birth, whereas males emigrate.

male philopatry Primate social system in which males remain and breed in the group of their birth, whereas females emigrate.

FIGURE 8.6 Male and female philopatry. The internal dynamics of primate societies differ greatly depending on which sex emigrates from the group at sexual maturity.

be fierce, with nutrients and calories for bearing and rearing offspring at stake. But on the whole, females in female-philopatric societies—such as most macaques, baboons, and numerous other Old World monkey taxa—socialize in ways that females in male-philopatric species do not.

Females in male-philopatric societies, on the other hand, may not show a high degree of affiliation, perhaps because of their lack of kinship (Figure 8.6). They are still, however, the driving force in the mating process (Figure 8.7). In chimpanzee society, females rarely groom one another, and they often engage in competitive aggression, including infanticidal aggression in which a female may attempt to kill the offspring of another female. Bonobos are an exception to this pattern in that immigrant females in a community, though unrelated, establish close bonds with one another. These bonds are used to protect females from harassment by males.

The form of the social system cannot be entirely explained by the behavior of females, however. Some researchers have linked the number of males in a primate group to other factors, such as the intensity of the risk of predation. In separate studies, Carel van Schaik and Marc Hörstermann (1994) and John Mitani and colleagues (1996) hypothesized that the number of males in a primate group, though subject to multiple factors, depends most strongly on the number of females and also on the presence of predators in the species' habitat.

Male Reproductive Strategies

Within a primate society, both males and females seek the same goal: reproductive success, or fitness. The ways each sex tries to enhance its fitness differ dramatically, however. A male baboon should be expected to fight with other male baboons over females if fighting improves his opportunities to place his genes into the next generation. If fighting and aggression were counterproductive, we should expect

FIGURE 8.7 Despite the traditional focus on males, females actively choose mates and are the driving force in the reproductive process.

dominance hierarchy   Ranking of individual primates in a group that reflects their ability to displace, intimidate, or defeat group mates in contests.

sexual receptivity   Willingness and ability of a female to mate, also defined as fertility.

to see male baboons achieving mating success some other way. In practice, however, strategies for achieving reproductive success are much more complex than just being aggressive or nonaggressive. Males rarely engage in paternal care, and in most species their relationship with offspring is neutral or even harmful. Their direct contribution to their offspring's health and welfare often is only their genes. In the few species in which males provide parental caregiving, such as marmosets and tamarins, the selection pressures on males may be very different from those on, say, a male baboon. The degree of parental investment is a key factor in shaping the evolution of the social system.

Dominance   One important way males and females achieve reproductive success is by establishing dominance relationships with other members of the same sex. Once a male enters a new group, he must compete directly with the resident males over the group's females. Although this is sometimes done by fighting, competition often is settled through the establishment of **dominance hierarchies,** in which high-ranking and low-ranking males sort out their relationship through a series of contests that leaves the lower-ranking animal unlikely to challenge the more dominant one.

Dominance relationships among males are established early in life, as males play together and some assert themselves over others. Males that later emigrate from their home group cannot assume high rank in a new group, at least initially. Males growing up in male-philopatric groups may face a different dilemma. To achieve high rank, they must demonstrate to males that they have grown up and that they are now a force to be reckoned with. In chimpanzee society, all the adult males in the community are dominant to all the females. An adolescent male climbs the dominance hierarchy by taking on and dominating (fighting with or supplanting at fruit trees) each of the adult females. Once he has risen to the top of the female hierarchy, he will begin to challenge the lowest-ranking males and so on, until he has risen as high as he will go. These challenges illustrate the political nature of life among nonhuman primates.

However, males are not the dominant sex in all primate species. Among many lemur species, females are dominant to all males, displacing them at food sources and choosing newly immigrated males to mate with (Sauther et al., 1999). Male lemurs do not engage in the sort of complicated dominance interactions that we see in anthropoid primates, perhaps because social dynamics are strongly influenced by high-ranking females.

Female Reproductive Strategies

Females invest much more time and energy in reproduction than males do, and their reproductive strategies reflect this. Instead of competing for males, female nonhuman primates typically are competed over. But females do not mate with whichever male is the winner of the competition. Sexual selection theory predicts that females should choose their mates carefully because a given mating may result in years of investment in gestation, lactation, and offspring rearing. A nonhuman primate must undergo years of socialization to learn how to behave successfully as an adult, and this socialization is closely connected to the development and growth of its brain. During the socialization period, the maturing offspring is utterly dependent, physically and psychologically, on its mother. And we know from Jeanne Altmann's (1980) long-term study of mother and infant baboons that when they are carrying fetuses or young infants, females suffer high mortality rates, presumably because they are less able to escape predators and more likely to suffer nutritional stress, leading to disease.

Dominance   Although dominance rank usually is not as important to female primates as it is to males, dominance may nonetheless have important consequences for female reproductive success. A study of the relationship between dominance and reproductive

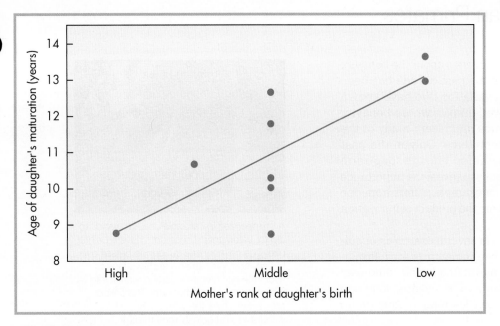

FIGURE 8.8 In some species, dominant females have more surviving offspring that mature earlier, indicating an adaptive value for high social status.

success among Gombe chimpanzees showed that there was a small but significant influence of rank on the number of surviving offspring a mother bore (Figure 8.8). The daughters of high-ranking females also matured slightly more rapidly than did those of low-ranking females (Pusey et al., 1997). And, as we have seen, females form matrilineal kin groups in Old World monkeys such as baboons, macaques, and langurs, within which a female's status may influence her reproductive success.

Primatologists think females choose dominant males more often than low-ranking males because dominant animals are so often in better health, with priority of access to food. Females appear to receive mating interest from males in direct relation to how reproductively fertile they are (Thompson and Wrangham, 2008). The offspring of dominant animals also tend to grow up to be high-ranking; we can't say whether this reflects a genetic predisposition to become dominant or is the proximate result of having a mother who is dominant herself and whose alliance network and socialization perpetuate high status.

Sexual Receptivity Signals Female primates use sexual signals to promote their reproductive success. These signals can be behavioral, anatomical, or physiological. Such signals are intended to advertise a female's **sexual receptivity,** or willingness to mate. They also make a female more attractive to males. Some nonhuman primates use body posture to indicate receptivity; female Hanuman langurs arch their tails over backs and shake their heads side to side to indicate willingness to mate. Females of many other species simply move in front of a male and present their rumps as a solicitation for mating. As we saw in Chapter 7, behaviors associated with such a willingness to mate constitute *estrus.*

Nearly all female mammals are fertile during only a restricted part of each reproductive cycle. The time around ovulation often produces changes in female appearance and behavior that incite males to compete to mate with them. Only during this time are females likely to conceive, and only then are they willing to mate. Around the time of ovulation, the rump of a female primate may change color, produce a fluid-filled swelling, or emit odors, any of which signal males in the vicinity that she is ready and willing to mate (Figure 8.9). Although it was long thought that such female features existed for the convenience of

FIGURE 8.9 Sexual swellings are one way for females to advertise their mating availability, thereby inducing male competition for them.

INNOVATIONS
Culture in Nonhuman Primates

One of the most important discoveries about the behavior of higher primates made in the past decade has been the importance of cultural variation. We have known for decades that, unlike many lower animals whose behavior patterns are largely innate, primates must learn many of the skills they need to survive and reproduce. Only in the past few years, however, have we gathered enough long-term information on many primate societies to reveal the importance of culture. Chimpanzee behavior, for example, differs from one forest to another in many ways that are the product of innovation and learning, not genetics.

On these two pages you can see several examples of cultural traditions in apes and other nonhuman primates. Primatologists believe these behaviors originated in the same way that human behaviors often do—they were invented long ago and then spread through observational learning to other group members.

A chimpanzee in Tanzania uses a "wand" to dip for safari ants. These ants have a painful bite. The chimpanzee suspends herself over the ant nest with an arm and two legs to avoid the bites, while inserting a stick into the nest using the other arm. The solider ants swarm over the wand, which she withdraws and quickly runs through her lips.

(a)

(b)

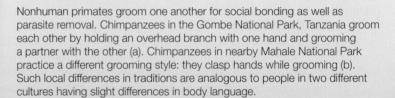

Nonhuman primates groom one another for social bonding as well as parasite removal. Chimpanzees in the Gombe National Park, Tanzania groom each other by holding an overhead branch with one hand and grooming a partner with the other (a). Chimpanzees in nearby Mahale National Park practice a different grooming style: they clasp hands while grooming (b). Such local differences in traditions are analogous to people in two different cultures having slight differences in body language.

Perhaps the first documented example of culture in a wild nonhuman primate was Imo. In the late 1940s, Japanese scientists began studying Japanese macaques on the island of Koshima. They put sweet potatoes on the beach to lure the monkeys within easy observation distance. A few years into the study, a young female named Imo began carrying her sweet potatoes to the water's edge to rinse it in seawater. The tradition spread, and within a decade most of the monkeys washed their potatoes before eating them.

Although chimpanzees are the best-known tool users among nonhuman primates, they are by no means the only ones. The capuchins of the New World are also highly adept tool users. Studies in Brazil have shown that they use stones, sometimes as large as they are, to crack open palm nuts in much the same way that chimpanzees in some populations do.

In 2007, primatologists studying chimpanzees in Senegal reported something amazing; chimpanzees were using sticks to catch bushbabies. The chimpanzees stripped the tip of the stick to taper it to a point, then jabbed it into holes in trees in which bushbabies were hiding. When successful, the result was a mortally injured bushbaby, which was then extracted by hand and eaten by the chimpanzee. Although chimpanzees have often been observed to use sticks to extract food from tree holes, this was the first observation of systematic use of a "weapon" to catch prey.

Although most observations of chimpanzee tool use involve sticks or stones, other natural materials are used as well. Jane Goodall first observed Gombe chimpanzees chewing leaves, then dipping the chewed-up "wadge" into tree cavities containing rain water. The wadges acted like sponges, soaking up drinking water, which the chimpanzee would not have been able to reach otherwise.

((•—[Listen to the **Podcast** "Chimps with Spears Captivates Photographer" on **myanthrolab**

males, we now realize that females evolved these traits to aid their own reproductive strategy. Because females choose their mates, using vivid sexual signals to excite males is a good way to persuade them to compete with one another. This competition may allow a female to assess the quality of her potential mates.

The adaptive function of sexual swellings and other such signals of fertility lies in the information it conveys to males. They may confuse paternity, in that many males are attracted to the swollen female, who mates with as many males as possible during this brief period. This leaves each male in the group with a chance of being the father of the ensuing offspring and may discourage them all from being aggressive toward the infant or its mother. Alternatively, the swelling may increase the investment a male makes in the female and her offspring by establishing paternity (Nunn et al., 2001). Sexual swellings may also play a role in male mate choice by advertising a female's potential quality as a mate (Domb and Pagel, 2001).

Why Are Nonhuman Primates Social?

Primatologists choose their study subjects according to the evolutionary principles they intend to investigate. Sociality is one of the most fundamental primate adaptations, and primatologists study the evolution of the types of primate societies that exist. A primatologist wanting to understand how monogamy works in nonhuman primates, with an eye toward understanding the origins of monogamy in human societies, might study a monogamous primate such as the gibbon. The gibbon certainly is an animal of great intrinsic beauty and interest, but to a primatologist it is also an illustration of how natural and sexual selection operate in the wild.

We are limited in our ability to extrapolate likely patterns of behavior in ancient primates, including hominins, by the small number of nonhuman primate species living. Not including the largely solitary strepsirhines, we have perhaps 150 species from which to reconstruct likely patterns of the evolution of primate social behavior. By contrast, biologists seeking to understand the evolution of bird social behavior have more than 9,000 species from which to draw examples of how adaptation and natural selection work. Nevertheless, we have made much progress in recent years in understanding the evolutionary and ecological influences on sociality.

Watch the **Video** "Social Learning in Primates" on **myanthrolab**

The Paradox of Sociality

Nonhuman primates, like all other social mammals, tend to behave in ways that maximize their individual fitness. But this creates a paradox: Why would any animal live in a group if its evolutionary goal is individual mating success? Group living is an evolved primate adaptation, which improves access to mates, food, and protection from predators (see Innovations: Culture in Nonhuman Primates on pages 182–183). Each of these benefits has, however, a significant downside.

Access to Mates Access to multiple potential mates is an obvious benefit of living in a group. Nonhuman primates exhibit a variety of grouping patterns, but in each mating system, male and female goals are the same: enhancing their reproductive success. The behavioral strategies employed by each sex is, however, quite different.

Group life may provide access to mates, but it also means that males must compete for mating. Among nonhuman primates that live in large social groups, many males lose out due to the enormous amount of energy and time they must expend in the quest for mating success. When access to a female is at stake, male baboons are more willing to engage in highly aggressive behavior toward one another, inflicting injury (Figure 8.10). Males also form alliances when females are ovulating and sexually receptive; if a male is not in an alliance, his ability to obtain matings may suffer.

The intensity of male–male competition, and the importance of female choice of male traits, is also reflected in the level of sexual dimorphism we see among

polygyny Mating system consisting of at least one male and more than one female.

(a)   (b)

FIGURE 8.10   (a) Male competition can be fierce. (b) This male baboon has bite wounds suffered in competition with other males.

primates. Species in which males compete aggressively for females tend to feature high degrees of sexual dimorphism because male size and strength help to determine mating success. Species exhibiting sexual dimorphism in body size also tend to live in **polygynous** groups, which have multiple females living with either one or multiple males. Monogamous and solitary species tend to be less dimorphic. In baboons, for instance, males compete fiercely with other males for mating opportunities and are about 30% larger and heavier than females. Gibbons, on the other hand, live in monogamous pair bonds and are not dimorphic with respect to body size (Figure 8.11). There are exceptions to this pattern, however, such as the highly dimorphic but largely solitary orangutan.

Food   One benefit of living in a group is exploiting the food-finding abilities of others. But the feeding and foraging benefits of living in a group are offset by the need to compete for food once food is found. If a monkey is led to a bonanza of fruit by the

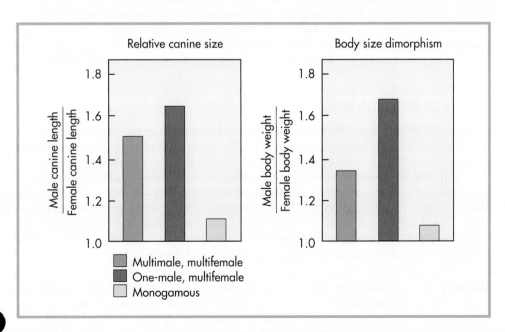

FIGURE 8.11   The most polygynous primates live in groups with many more females than males. In such species, the degree of sexual dimorphism tends to be pronounced.

other members of its group, the individual must then compete with its group mates. Much evidence supports the notion that feeding competition strongly affects group life in nonhuman primates, lowering the nutrition and survival of animals that don't compete successfully. Females are particularly dependent on the availability of food resources in their habitat because they must nourish themselves adequately to bear the costs of reproduction.

Avoiding Predators As we saw in Chapter 7, many species of predatory animals hunt nonhuman primates. In tropical forests, attacks by birds of prey, big cats, large snakes, and humans are all potential causes of mortality. Predation can have a major impact on nonhuman primate populations, even when it occurs rarely. We should therefore expect evolved responses to predation in any nonhuman primate species prone to being hunted. However, little direct evidence of predation exists because of the difficulty of observing predation. Predators themselves tend to be silent, stealthy, and often nocturnal, so a primatologist records only the sudden disappearance of one of his or her study subjects from its group. Whether the disappearance resulted from disease, migration, infanticide, or predation often is unclear.

There is abundant indirect evidence, however, that group living helps nonhuman primates avoid predators. In larger groups, there are more eyes to act as sentinels, warning group members about danger approaching. For example, Michelle Sauther studied the response to predation risk by small and large groups of ring-tailed lemurs in Beza Mahafaly Reserve in southern Madagascar. She found that lemurs in small groups avoided foraging on the ground in areas where predator pressure was intense. Therefore, those animals found less food. On the other hand, small groups tended to associate with other lemur species when feeding and during the birth season, when highly vulnerable infants were present. Sauther reasoned that small ring-tailed lemur groups compensate for their lack of numbers by combining with other species. Larger groups entered new and unknown areas of the forest and therefore encountered predators more often than smaller groups did but reaped more food. Sauther (2002) showed that lemurs face trade-offs between predation risk and food intake that vary according to social factors such as group size.

Most nonhuman primate species have an alarm call of some sort that they use to warn group members of approaching danger. This suggests that predation is a strong evolutionary pressure molding their behavior. Nonhuman primates also tend to be very vigilant, scanning the ground and trees around them continually while feeding. Many studies of primates and other mammals have shown that animals of many species spend less time scanning their surroundings when they live in larger groups, which suggests a greater margin of safety when more eyes are present to look for danger.

Types of Nonhuman Primate Societies

Nonhuman primates number only 300 species but exhibit great diversity in grouping patterns. We call the type of group in which nonhuman primates live their **social system.** Earlier generations of primatologists viewed social groups as male-centered; they believed that females wanted to live with or near males, and so males determined the form that social systems took. However, the consensus today is that females have evolved strategies, behavioral and ecological, to cope with the need to balance limited food supplies while avoiding predators with the demands of mating and rearing offspring. Males then use their habitats to maximize their access to females. This section outlines the types of nonhuman primate social systems.

Solitary Most strepsirhines live in a social system similar to that of the earliest primates. They are largely solitary. females occupy individual territories along with their dependent offspring, which they defend by scent-marking objects (Figure 8.12). Of course, no mammal is truly solitary; it must locate mates during the breeding season. Males occupy territories that overlap a number of female territories; they attempt to maintain exclusive mating access to all these females and keep transient males away.

monogamy A mating bond; primates can be socially monogamous but still mate occasionally outside the pair bond.

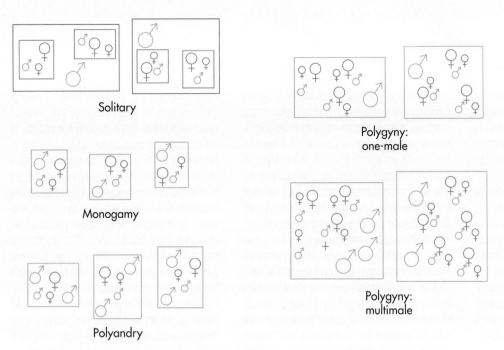

FIGURE 8.12 A taxonomy of primate social systems. Larger symbols indicate adults. (Adapted from Strier 1994)

Males use scent-marking and a variety of calls to communicate with one another and to warn intruders to stay out. This social system characterizes many of the strepsirhines, especially the nocturnal galagos and lorises.

When females live solitary lives, males must choose whether to try to defend them from all other males or to share access to them with other males. Most solitary nonhuman primate species feature males that attempt to maintain exclusive access, as is the case in **monogamy.** Monogamy is a social system in which a male and female live in a pair bond for an extended period of time, perhaps years (Figure 8.12). Recent studies have shown that our notion of monogamy needs some adjusting because members of pair bonds sometimes mate secretly outside the pair bond as well. In some cases, a pair of gibbons may live as a socially monogamous pair bond, but both male and female may secretively mate with other gibbons. Social monogamy thus is not necessarily strict reproductive monogamy.

Monogamy is best understood as a female reproductive strategy. Monogamous female primates establish and hold territories, and on each territory a single male attaches himself to the resident female. The female therefore tolerates the presence of a male. The male may provide some essential services to the female, such as aiding in territorial and food defense or protecting the female's offspring from infanticide by marauding males. In a few species, males actually aid in the rearing of infants by carrying young and shielding them from harm. In exchange for this service, they receive a high degree of certainty that they fathered the offspring (though not absolute certainty, as females are prone to sneaking off to mate with other males).

Because males in monogamous pairs don't appear to compete as directly with other males as those in social groups need to, we expect that sexually selected aspects of male competition, such as large canines or big body size, would be deemphasized. And we find this to be the case. For instance, gibbons exhibit little sexual dimorphism except in hair color.

Polygyny The majority of haplorhine nonhuman primate species live in groups composed of one or more males and more than one female (Figure 8.11 on page 185). We call this social system polygyny. Of course, many animals, from geese to deer, live in large social groups comprising both males and females. What characterizes

insights & advances

THE INFANTICIDE WARS

Infanticide is the killing of infants. Scientists have observed infanticide in many different animal species, from birds to monkeys to humans. Most of the debate among scientists has centered around infants that are killed by a male other than the biological father.

Scientists once believed that the ultimate goal of animals living in a social group was the attainment of group harmony. Events that disrupt the harmony, such as fights or sexual jealousy, were thought to disrupt the balance of the group in a negative way. But the rise of Darwinian theory to explain social behavior changed that. Scientists recognized that individuals seek to reproduce themselves, often at the expense of other, unrelated individuals.

FIGURE A   Infanticide in nonhuman primates has been best-documented in Hanuman langurs.

In the early 1970s, Sarah Blaffer Hrdy was planning a doctoral thesis on Hanuman langur monkeys, a large and graceful monkey ubiquitous across the Indian subcontinent (Figure A). Hrdy had heard reports from the arid western regions of India that langurs living at high population density committed infanticide. She set off to investigate, settling in Mount Abu, a town nestled among the red hills of southernmost Rajasthan.

At Abu and elsewhere, langurs live in two types of social groups: one-male and multi-male. One-male groups predominate at Abu, and in this social setting the lone resident male becomes a target for attack by bands of males that lack a group of females of their own. As it turned out, some of the Abu langurs were killing infants, and they did not seem to be acting pathologically. Instead, Hrdy observed bands of males invading established social groups, ousting the resident male, and in some cases killing infants sired by him. She observed four infanticides and strongly suspected numerous others over a 5-year period.

Hrdy viewed the killings in a Darwinian light. Instead of pathological reactions to overcrowding or stress, Hrdy saw infanticide as a reproductive strategy by otherwise bachelor males. By ousting a resident male and then fending off other competitors, a marauding male langur reaped a sudden windfall of mating opportunities with the group's females, except that some or all of the females

were preoccupied, reproductively speaking, because they were pregnant by the previous resident male or were nursing his infants. In either case, the females would not be cycling, rendering them unavailable for a new male eager to sire his own progeny. Hrdy reasoned that if the tendency toward infanticide were inherited, males who engaged in the behavior would have greater reproductive success than other, noninfanticidal ones. This suggested that infant killing was an adaptive strategy evolved through sexual selection to promote a male's genes, at the expense of other males. Female langurs who preferred noninfanticidal males as mates lost in the evolutionary arms race because by failing to kill rivals' offspring, their sons would leave fewer descendants.

The results of Hrdy's long-term field research at Abu appeared in her 1977 book *The Langurs of Abu: Female and Male Strategies of Reproduction.* The reaction from the scientific community was swift and angry. Many primatologists initially denied that the infanticides she reported had occurred at all. When it became clear that the infant killing had occurred in this and other populations of langurs, the critics argued against its evolutionary relevance. The critics noted that most reported cases of infanticide were only circumstantial; the prime evidence often was an infant found dead with bite wounds shortly after a group takeover. Critics charged that

nonhuman primate polygyny is the complexity of social interactions. In a few species, sociality has accompanied the evolution of brains capable of remembering a long history of interactions with group mates—the debts and favors an animal owes and is owed by others—and of strategizing accordingly.

The complexity of social interactions in nonhuman primate groups is influenced by the social system. A male in a multiple-male group must by necessity use a far more complex set of tactics to obtain mates than a male living in a group in which he is the only male or living monogamously with just one female.

One-Male Polygyny   *One-male polygynous groups* are what primatologists used to call harems. One male lives with as many females as he can monopolize (Figure 8.12 on page 187). The term *harem* implies male control over females and is obsolete because it dates from a time when primatologists did not appreciate the role that females play

FIGURE B Some scientists believed that langur infanticide was influenced by human disturbance.

the explanation for langur infanticide at Abu was social pathology, not reproductive strategy (Curtin and Dolhinow, 1978). Perhaps the high langur population density and level of human disturbance in and around Abu had made it impossible for males to take over new groups in a gradual, nonaggressive fashion (Figure B). Instead, in the melee of male–male encounters, aggression directed at other males and at females sometimes injured or killed infants accidentally.

The debate over langur infanticide continued to rage as other researchers produced field data supporting the reproductive strategy theory. Primatologist Volker Sommer studied langurs living in the arid scrubland of Jodhpur, Rajasthan, in collaboration with an Indian team led by S. M. Mohnot (Figure C). Between 1969 and 1985, they documented fourteen cases of infanticide, plus twenty other suspected killings and fourteen nonfatal attacks on infants. They also showed that the pattern of aggression was consistent with the sexual selection hypothesis. Females whose babies were killed by incoming males began to cycle again significantly sooner than those whose infants survived, thus rewarding a marauding male with procreative opportunities months earlier than he would have gotten by waiting for the infants to mature (Sommer, 1994).

Reports of infanticide mounted for a wide range of species. David Watts (1989) showed that among the mountain gorillas of the Virunga Volcanoes, infanticide by silverback males is a leading cause of infant mortality. In species as different as marmosets and macaques, the killing of infants was witnessed, often in scenarios that were consistent with the Darwinian model.

For the past two decades, researchers have produced increasingly strong evidence that infanticide among social animals often is carried out strategically in accordance with Darwinian predictions. Opponents of the adaptationist approach argue that unless a gene or complex of genes can be found that causes infanticidal behavior, we should not speak of infant killing as an evolved trait.

Although there are a few examples of direct gene–behavior relationships (some captive-bred strains of mice commit infanticide, whereas other strains do not), higher social animals are too complex genetically and behaviorally for simple gene–behavior links to be made. No doubt infanticide occurs in a variety of scenarios and for a variety of reasons, and not all episodes of infanticide can be linked to reproductive benefits to the infant killer. However, the weight of current evidence lends support to the reproductive strategy theory.

FIGURE C Primatologist Volker Sommer and his colleagues showed that langur infanticide had adaptive value and is likely an evolved reproductive strategy.

in the mating system. In some cases, one-male groups are driven by choices made by females, not males. For example, Robin Dunbar showed that in the multitiered social system of the gelada baboon, females bond to one another, and the male, despite all appearances of being the central hub of the social system, is simply hoping to be accepted by "his" females (Dunbar, 1983). Among mountain gorillas, half of all groups are one-male. But females often transfer between groups, and resident silverbacks appear to regard other males with fear and anxiety mainly because of the risk that their own females may emigrate for a new silverback in a different group.

When one-male polygynous groups exist, males who are not able to obtain females usually live as extragroup males, either alone or in all-male "bachelor" groups. In some species, these all-male groups attack one-male groups and attempt to evict the resident male from his females (Figure 8.13 on page 190; Insights and Advances: The Infanticide Wars).

(a)

(b)

FIGURE 8.13   (a) A group of capped langurs. (b) In one-male group species, extra males typically reside in all-male "bachelor" groups. These are Hanuman langurs.

Multimale Polygyny   A male nonhuman primate would like to have as many females to himself as he can monopolize. The downside of this is that he may have to constantly fend off intruding males who want to mate with his females. As the number of females in a one-male group increases, it becomes impossible for a male to prevent other males from joining the group. A better option for him may be to allow other males to enter the group but continue to obtain the majority of matings with the females by being socially dominant. So in many species, we see multimale–multifemale polygynous groups.

Instead of competing for sole access to females, males in multimale groups may compete for priority of access. Priority often takes the form of a dominance hierarchy, in which a top-ranking, *alpha male* allows other males access to the females in the group but may attempt to exclude his rivals when females are in estrus and may conceive. In this way he strikes a balance between the goal of maximizing mating success and the burden of spending all his time and energy fending off other males. In species living in multimale groups, females are not typically all in estrus at the same time. When one female enters estrus, she becomes a focus of competition among the group males. That such competition is far more intense than among monogamous primates is reflected in polygynous primates' canine tooth size and body size sexual dimorphism. Both body and canine tooth size may contribute to male success in mate competition.

Some nonhuman primate species maintain both one-male and multimale groups in the same population. Hanuman langur monkeys live across the Indian subcontinent in populations that can be mainly one-male or multimale. Why this variation occurs is unclear. Primatologists have tried to explain it as a response to the local physical environment, local demographic trends, or the number of females and the overall population density (Newton, 1987; Sommer, 1994). In any case, populations featuring a preponderance of one-male groups also tend to exhibit higher levels of intergroup aggression and especially a tendency for strange males to attempt group takeovers of existing groups, with accompanying **infanticide** of the group's infants (see Insights and Advances: The Infanticide Wars).

Fission–Fusion Polygyny   One additional form of polygyny is perhaps the most complex social system found in nonhuman primates. A few species do not live in cohesive groups; instead, temporary associations of individuals come together and split up repeatedly (Figure 8.14). This is called **fission–fusion polygyny,** and it is seen in species as different as chimpanzees, bonobos, and spider monkeys (see Insights

infanticide   The killing of infants, either by members of the infant's group or by a member of a rival group.

fission–fusion polygyny   Type of primate polygyny in which animals travel in foraging parties of varying sizes instead of a cohesive group.

polyandry   Mating system in which one female mates with multiple males.

FIGURE 8.14   Chimpanzees and a few other primates live in fission–fusion polygynous communities.

and Advances: Are Chimpanzees from Mars and Bonobos from Venus?). Instead of forming a well-defined stable group, populations divide into communities. These communities have distinct home ranges and community membership within which the community members join and part with one another unpredictably in temporary foraging units called parties. The same chimpanzee may be in a party of two at dawn, of ten an hour later, and of thirty later in the day. The only stable unit in the social system is a female and her young offspring. Males often travel together, forming coalitions among themselves.

Fission–fusion polygyny is believed to be an evolved response to reliance on ripe fruit in the diet. Because of the patchy and seasonal distribution of fruits in a tropical forest and the daily variation in fruit availability, foraging for food in large cohesive groups would incite intense competition for resources. Females forage on their own to optimize their access to fruit, and males attempt to control access to females by forming bonds with one another.

Polyandry   When one female lives in a reproductive or social unit with multiple males, we say the social system is polyandrous (Figure 8.11 on page 185). **Polyandry** is quite rare in nonhuman primates; it is better known in birds, where it has demonstrated key rules of sexual selection. Among nonhuman primates, only a few species of marmosets and tamarins in New World tropical forests exhibit this social system, and it remains poorly understood. In some species of these monkeys, males bond together and help females to rear offspring. This is probably a reproductive strategy by males. Marmosets and tamarins are very small (<1 kg) monkeys and are vulnerable to a wide range of predators. Females boost their reproductive output by producing twins, but these twins weigh an extraordinary 20% of the mother's body weight. Males assist in infant caregiving by carrying babies and may help in antipredator defense as well. Males may opt to assist a female for the opportunity to achieve reproductive success; if two males mate with the same female, each has a 50% chance of being the father of the twins. It should be noted that, although some marmoset and tamarin species live polyandrously, they don't necessarily all mate polyandrously. The females of some species may mate mainly with one male of the several who help

insights & advances
ARE CHIMPANZEES FROM MARS AND BONOBOS FROM VENUS?

Jane Goodall shocked the scientific world in 1961 when she reported that chimpanzees relish meat and hunt other mammals eagerly; they are not the vegetarian pacifists they had always been thought to be. As observations in the wild accumulated, it became clear that there is a brutal side to chimpanzees (Figure A).

Males strive to ascend a rigid dominance hierarchy, and on reaching high rank they wield their political power with Machiavellian cunning. They patrol the perimeter of their territory, attacking and sometimes killing their unwary neighbors (Goodall, 1986).

FIGURE A Chimpanzees are far better studied than bonobos.

Chimpanzees are also efficient predators, consuming hundreds of prey animals including monkeys, antelope, and wild pigs at some study sites. Colobus monkeys are attacked by hunting parties of chimpanzees, and the male colobus defend their groups by courageously counterattacking the ape marauders. Male chimpanzees make nearly all the kills and after a successful hunt, high-ranking males control the distribution of meat.

Only since the mid-1980s has the closely related bonobo become well known to science (Figure B). Studies of bonobo behavior have revealed a society contrasting sharply with the hierarchical nature of chimpanzee society. Bonobo social life is marked by female cooperation, sex as social communication, and alliance formation rather than aggression. Female bonobos band together in coalitions to dominate males, avoiding the sort of domination and sexual coercion that male chimpanzees routinely inflict on females. Such coalitions among females are nearly unknown in chimpanzees (Parish, 1996).

Bonobos often are said to be the "make love, not war" ape. They mate in more positions, seemingly for recreation as much as procreation, than any mammal other than humans. They engage in same-sex pairings, in which two females rub their genital swellings together ("GG rubbing"). This behavior eases tensions between

individuals and may allow them to feed near one another without undue stress. This female bonding is absent in chimpanzee society.

An even more striking difference between female chimpanzees and female bonobos exists in reproduction. Females of nearly all mammalian species are reproductively active only during a constricted time period surrounding ovulation. This estrus period characterizes all the higher primates except humans (see Chapter 7). Females of our species, though more likely to conceive around the time of ovulation, are free of the bonds of a strictly defined period of "heat." As a result, sex serves not only for procreation but also as a mechanism of social communication and reinforcement of long-term pair bonds. This release from the constraints of estrus means that the timing of ovulation is no longer advertised to males and is thought to have been a pivotal event in the evolution of early human society.

FIGURE B Bonobo females form close alliances, maintained through sex, that are lacking in chimpanzees.

her; that makes her reproductively monogamous, but socially polyandrous with male helpers (Strier, 2006).

In Chapters 7 and Chapters 8, you have seen how the lives of nonhuman primates inform us about ourselves and our ancestry. In this chapter, we examined social behavior, but social behavior and ecology cannot be fully separated from each other. Natural selection has molded primate social behavior, with the environment as the filter. These same natural forces shaped human ancestry, human anatomy, and perhaps aspects of human behavior. Now that you have seen the context for the roots of human evolution, it's time to turn to Chapter 9 to examine the fossil record and what it tells us about the context of primate evolution.

Bonobo females often are said to be the only mammals other than humans to be released from the bonds of estrus (de Waal and Lanting, 1997). They maintain their sexual swellings for a much longer portion of their menstrual cycles than chimpanzees do and therefore mate nearly throughout the cycle, as humans do. Being released from estrus, bonobos have come to use sex as much for communicating with males as for conceiving offspring, as in our own species.

In conflict as in mating, bonobos and chimpanzees appear to be strikingly different. Bonobo researcher Takayoshi Kano (1992) observed that when two bonobo communities meet at a range boundary, not only is there no lethal aggression, but there may be socializing and even sex between females and the enemy community's males.

In hunting and meat eating, which chimpanzees so relish, we see another apparent contrast between the two apes. Bonobos capture baby monkeys and then use them as dolls or playthings for hours, only to release the monkey unharmed (though worse for the wear) without eating them, as a chimpanzee would (Sabater-Pi et al., 1993).

The close genetic kinship between these apes and humans and the behavioral differences between them have led anthropologists to debate which species is the better model for understanding the evolution of human behavior. Were our ancestors violent, meat-eating, male-dominated creatures or more gentle, female-bonded vegetarians?

While this debate rages, some researchers have pointed out that the differences between chimpanzees and bonobos may not be as stark as they are usually depicted. Many behavioral contrasts reported between chimps and bonobos have been based on comparisons between wild chimpanzees and captive bonobos (Stanford, 1998b). Animals in captive settings are well known for their tendency to display greater frequencies of the whole gamut of social behavior, from fighting to sex, than do their wild counterparts. Therefore, their behavior patterns do not necessarily reflect those that evolved for living in an African forest.

Field data show that in two important respects, female bonobos are not more sexual than their chimpanzee counterparts. First, the frequency of copulating, in which captive bonobos show a markedly higher rate than wild chimpanzees, is no different between wild bonobos and wild chimpanzees (Stanford, 1998b). Second, the idea that bonobo females are released from estrus is derived from data on the duration of sexual swelling taken mainly from bonobos in captivity. In captivity, female bonobos maintain their sexual swelling for up to 23 days, nearly half of their 49-day (captive) cycle. This dwarfs the receptive period of wild female chimpanzees, who swell for about 10 days of their 37-day cycle. However, this comparison changes completely if we consider wild bonobos rather than captive specimens, whose excellent nutrition may enhance the reproductive system. Wild bonobos from Wamba in the Democratic Republic

of Congo, are swollen for only 13 days of a 33-day cycle, numbers that are much closer to those of wild chimpanzees than they are to captives of their own species. A report of captive bonobos in Belgium shows that even in captivity, bonobos do not necessarily have longer swelling durations than chimpanzees (Vervaecke et al., 1999).

Meat eating, though certainly less common than among chimpanzees, may be quite common among bonobos as well, but it has been underrated because little field research has been done on this ape. German researchers Gottfried Hohmann and Barbara Fruth (2008) have observed extensive meat eating and meat sharing by bonobos at Lui Kotale, indicating that our view of bonobos being too "peaceful" to hunt for meat is simplistic.

Finally, the idea that bonobos are somehow more closely linked to humans has been based on the claim that they walk upright more often than chimpanzees do (Kano, 1992). But this may also be a myth: In a recent study that compared bipedal walking captive bonobos and captive chimpanzees, Elaine Videan and William McGrew (2001) found that bonobos were no more bipedal than chimpanzees.

Before we tar ourselves with the legacy of the male-chauvinist, carnivorous, warring chimpanzees or congratulate ourselves for leaning toward the sisterhood-is-powerful bonobos, we would do well to consider how our depiction of primate societies sometimes becomes intertwined with our own political views.

Primate Behavior

The Study of Nonhuman Primates

Settings

- Captive studies allow close observation, study of several generations, behavioral experiments, but they are limited because the setting is unnatural.

- Some studies are set in semi-free-ranging environments that allow animals to establish territories, form their own groups, and forage for food; it is a compromise between the confines of a captive study and a field study.

- Field studies are conducted in the habitat in which the species evolved, so researchers can see patterns of behavior that evolved in response to environmental variables. **[pp 176–177]**

Evolutionary Basis of Primate Behavior

- Males and females of most social animal species have evolved mating strategies that are so different that we refer to a reproductive asymmetry between the sexes.

- The social system of nonhuman primates depends on the way females distribute themselves.

- In female philopatry females remain and breed in the group of their birth; the males emigrate.

- In male philopatry males remain and breed in the group of their birth; the females emigrate.

- Male reproductive strategies tend to involve competition and attempts to entice females.

- Female reproductive strategies involve choosing the best males to mate with, and obtaining the best nutrients needed by their offspring.

- The paradox of sociality: Why would any animal live in a group if its evolutionary goal is individual mating success? **[pp 177–184]**

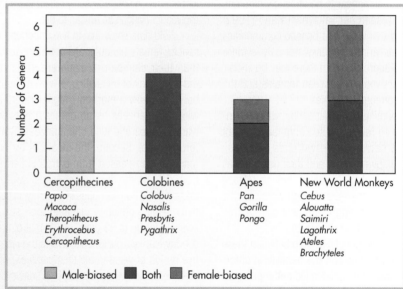

Primate Societies

Solitary

- It is the social system of some strepsirhines.

- Females occupy individual territories along with dependent offspring.

- In a solitary society, it is most common for males to attempt to maintain exclusive access to females. **[pp 186–187]**

Monogamous

- Males and females live in a pair bond for an extended period of time.

- Social monogamy is not necessarily strict reproductive monogamy.

- It is a female reproductive strategy.

- There is little sexual dimorphism. **[p 187]**

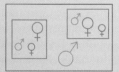

Solitary

Monogamy

Polygynous

- It is the social system of majority of haplorhine, nonhuman primate species.
- One or more males and more than one female live in this type of society.
- There are complex social interactions.
- One-male polygyny may be driven by female choices; sometimes "bachelor" groups will attack and try to evict the resident male.
- In multimale polygyny, males compete for priority of access, which often takes the form of a dominance hierarchy.
- In the most complex social system, fission–fusion polygyny, temporary associations of individuals come together and split up repeatedly. **[pp 187–191]**

Polygyny:
one-male

Polygyny:
multimale

Polyandrous

- The social system where one female lives with multiple males is quite rare; a few species of marmosets and tamarins in New World tropical forests exhibit this social system. **[pp 191–192]**

Polyandry

My AnthroLab CONNECTIONS

Watch. Listen. View. Explore. Read.
MyAnthroLab is designed just for you. Each chapter features a customized study plan to help you learn and review key concepts and terms. Dynamic visual activities, videos, and readings found in the multimedia library will enhance your learning experience.

Resources from this Chapter:

Watch on **myanthrolab**

▶ *Dr. Jane Goodall: Primatology and The Leakey Foundation*
▶ *Social Learning in Primates*
▶ *Taxonomy of Primate Social Systems*

Listen on **myanthrolab**

▶ *Chimps with Spears Captivates Photographer*

Explore on **myanthrolab** In MySearchLab, enter the Anthropology database to find relevant and recent scholarly and popular press publications. For this chapter, enter the following keywords: Sociality, Primates, Aggression, Mating, Evolution.

Read on **myanthrolab**

▶ *Bonobo Sex and Society* by Frans B.M. De Waal
▶ *Why Are Some Animals So Smart?* by Carel Van Schaik

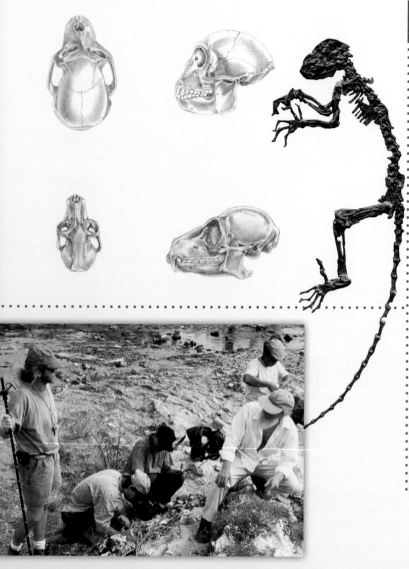

After reading this chapter, you should be able to:

- Describe the processes necessary for fossilization and the importance of context in relationship to understanding the information fossils contain.

- Describe the many relative and chronometric dating techniques used in the sciences.

- List the temporal and anatomical characteristics of the different groups of fossil primates from the Cenozoic to Pleistocene.

- Analyze the climate of the Cenozoic as to its impact on animal and primate evolution, especially the origin and evolution of both monkeys and apes.

- Explain both molecular phylogeny and the molecular clock in relationship to our understanding of primate evolution.

Geology and Primate Origins

9

Doom was coming out of the sky in the form of an enormous comet or asteroid—we are still not sure which it was. Probably 10 km across, traveling tens of kilometers a second, its energy of motion had the destructive capability of a hundred million hydrogen bombs.

It is worth pondering the realization that each of us is descended from unknown ancestors who were alive on that day when the fatal rock fell from the sky. They survived and the dinosaurs did not, and that is the reason why we are here now—as individuals and as a species. That one terrible day undid the benefits which 150 million years of natural selection had conferred upon the dinosaurs, making them ever fitter to be the large land animals of Earth. Evolution had not equipped them to survive the environmental disasters inflicted by a huge impact and when the holocaust was over, they were gone.

Evolution had not provided impact resistance for the mammals either, but somehow they did survive. No one knows why, but it must have helped that they were smaller and therefore much more numerous than the dinosaurs, so that there was a better statistical chance that some would live.

When the environmental disruptions from the impact had waned and the mammal survivors emerged into a new world they must have faced great dangers and great opportunities.

—W. Alvarez, *T. rex and the Crater of Doom* (1997, p.130)

As the vignette suggests, geological forces have had a critical impact on mammalian evolution, including primate evolution. **Paleontology,** a field that takes its name from the Greek words for "old" (*paleos*) and "existence" (*ontos*), is devoted to finding, studying, and understanding **fossils,** the preserved remnants of once-living things. Paleontologists want to know how old the fossil is, what kind of organism it represents, how it lived, and how that fossil came to be preserved where it was.

In this chapter, we will set the stage for understanding human evolution by looking closely at the fields of **geology,** the study of the earth, and primate paleontology. We will see how materials fossilize and look at what we can learn from both the fossils themselves and the surroundings in which they are found. We'll introduce and compare some of the most important dating methods in use today, and we'll explore conditions on Earth during the Cenozoic Era, the time period in which primates evolved. We also consider what we know about the origin and evolution of the Primate order. We will look at three of the major events in primate evolution: the strepsirhine–haplorhine split, the origin of Old World and New World monkeys, and finally the origin of the apes. To help organize the fossils, you will want to refer to the family tree of living primates in Chapter 7 (Figure 7.9 on page 147) and review the bony characteristics that allow us to recognize animals at different levels of that tree. In each case, we focus on the anatomical characters of the fossils and the ecological circumstances in which they evolved, and we discuss possible scenarios for what this evidence tells us about the natural selective factors that favored the origin of each group.

197

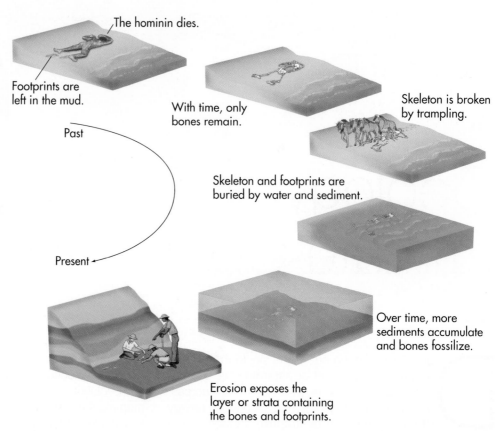

The hominin dies.

Footprints are
left in the mud.

With time, only
bones remain.

Skeleton is broken
by trampling.

Past

Skeleton and footprints are
buried by water and sediment.

Present

Over time, more
sediments accumulate
and bones fossilize.

Erosion exposes the
layer or strata containing
the bones and footprints.

FIGURE 9.1   Fossils are formed after an animal dies, decomposes, and is covered in sediment. Minerals in ground water replace bone mineral, turning bone into stone that may later be discovered if the surrounding rock erodes away.

👁 Watch the **Animation** "Fossil Formation" on **myanthrolab**

How to Become a Fossil

You might think that fossils are abundant. After all, every organism eventually dies, and natural history museums are filled with fossils of dinosaurs and other prehistoric creatures. In reality, very few living things become fossils and only an exceedingly small proportion of these fossils are discovered, collected, and studied. Thus, the fossil record is not entirely representative of the composition of past biological communities (Behrensmeyer and Hill, 1980). Instead, the fossil record preserves some organisms in abundance, whereas others are seldom preserved.

Taphonomy, the study of what happens to remains from death to discovery, reveals some of the factors that determine whether an organism becomes a fossil (Shipman, 1981). These include both biological and geological processes. Death might come to a human ancestor or any other animal in a number of ways, such as old age, injury, disease, or predation (Figure 9.1). In many instances, the agent of death may leave marks on the skeleton, such as the bite marks of a predator. After death, the carcass begins to decompose and numerous microbes, bacteria, mold, and insects, accelerate this process. While this is happening, scavengers may ravage the carcass, consuming its soft tissues and perhaps even chomping on its bones. Eventually, only the most durable tissues remain, especially the densely constructed middle shafts of the limb bones, the jaws, and the teeth (Brain, 1981). Even these durable remains can disappear through various means including erosion and trampling.

To become a fossil, part of the organism must be preserved by burial, a natural process in which the carcass or part of it is covered with sediment. Burial interrupts the biological phase of decomposition, protecting the skeleton from further trampling.

Burial often occurs in the floodplains of rivers, along the shores of lakes, and in swamps where uplift, erosion, and sedimentation are occurring. Once buried, skeletal remains may absorb minerals from the surrounding soil or ground water, which eventually replace the organism's original inorganic tissues. The result is *petrifaction* the process of being turned to stone. On occasion soft parts such as skin, hair, or plant parts may be preserved. In very exceptional circumstances, the original tissues of an organism are preserved largely intact. For example, whole mammoths have been found frozen in permafrost and naturally mummified people have been found, especially in arid places. Finally, *trace fossils* such as the tracks left by animals may provide impressions of their activities, and *coprolites*, or fossilized feces, also tell us about the presence of past animals.

paleontology   The study of extinct organisms, based on their fossilized remains.

fossils   The preserved remnants of once-living things, often buried in the ground.

geology   The study of the earth.

taphonomy   The study of what happens to the remains of an animal from the time of death to the time of discovery.

strata   Layers of rock.

stratigraphy   The study of the order of rock layers and the sequence of events they reflect.

The Importance of Context

A fossil without its context is useless, except perhaps as a pretty object on the mantelpiece. In this section we review the important principles used in geology to understand the position of a fossil in its rock layers and the relationship of different fossil sites to each other.

Stratigraphy

Imagine driving through a road cut where you see what looks like layers or bands of rock. These are **strata,** literally "layers" in Latin. In some road cuts these layers are basically horizontal, but in others they may be more vertical or even quite deformed (Figure 9.2). **Stratigraphy** is the study of the distribution of these layers. In 1830, Charles Lyell, whose work influenced Darwin (see Chapter 1), synthesized a number of accepted geological principles including the principles of stratigraphy. Four of these principles are critical to an understanding of the context of a fossil: original horizontality, superposition, cross-cutting relationships, and faunal succession.

The *principle of original horizontality*, formulated by Nicolas Steno, says that layers of rock (strata) are laid down parallel to the earth's gravitational field and thus horizontal to the earth's surface, at least originally (Figure 9.3 on page 200). All the deformations and upendings that you see in road cuts are caused by later activity such as earthquakes and volcanic eruptions (Figure 9.2b).

(a)

(b)

FIGURE 9.2   (a) Rock layers (strata) usually look like the layers in a cake, but geological processes such as earthquakes and mountain building can deform these once horizontal layers. (b) The paleoanthropologist must understand these deformations in order to figure out which strata a fossil comes from and how old it is.

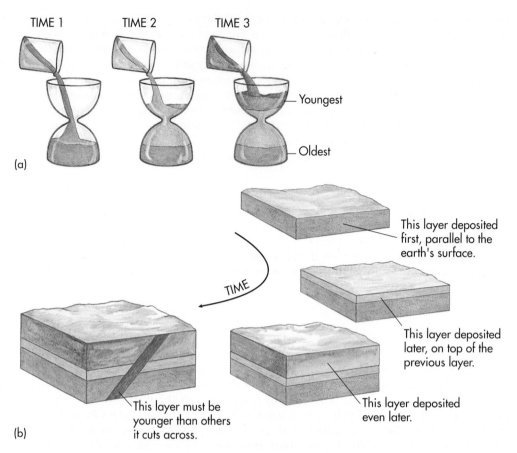

TIME 1   TIME 2   TIME 3

Youngest

Oldest

(a)

This layer deposited first, parallel to the earth's surface.

TIME

This layer deposited later, on top of the previous layer.

This layer must be younger than others it cuts across.

This layer deposited even later.

(b)

FIGURE 9.3 (a) The principles of stratigraphy help us understand the relative age of rock layers. (b) Layers are deposited parallel to Earth's surface (horizontality). Younger layers are deposited on top of older layers (superposition). A layer that cuts across others is younger than those it cuts (cross-cutting relationships).

Building on the principle of original horizontality is the principle of superposition, also proposed by Steno. The *principle of superposition* (Figure 9.3) states that, with all other factors equal, older layers are laid down first and then covered by younger (overlying) layers. Thus older sediments are on the bottom, and the fossils found in them are older than those found above. However, stratigraphy is not always so straightforward, and in the late 1700s James Hutton added the *principle of cross-cutting relationships*, which says simply that a geological feature must exist before another feature can cut across or through it, and that the thing that is cut is older than the thing cutting through it (Figure 9.3), just as the layers of a cake must exist before you can stick a candle into them.

Using the principles of stratigraphy, we can determine which strata are older and younger. Comparisons between sites can provide a sequence of rocks from older to younger for both areas. By comparing the stratigraphy of sites from around the world, especially for marine sediments that are very continuous, geologists have assembled a great geological column from the very oldest to the very youngest rocks on Earth (Figure 9.4 on pages 202–203). This geological column, with age estimates provided by dating techniques discussed later in this chapter, is called the geologic time scale.

Finally, the *principle of faunal succession*, first proposed in 1815 by William Smith (whose nickname was "Strata" because of his passion for stratigraphy), addresses the changes or succession of fauna (animals) through layers. Smith recognized not only that deeper fauna is older, but also that there are predictable sequences of fauna through strata, that successive layers contain certain types of faunal communities and types of fossils that follow one another in predictable patterns through the strata (Figure 9.5 on page 204). Certain kinds of these animals that typify a layer are called *index fossils*. Furthermore, Smith noted that once a type of fossil leaves a section, it does not reappear higher in the section. With the benefit of Darwin's work, we know this is because once a type of animal goes extinct, it cannot reappear later (and so cannot be fossilized in younger sediments).

geologic time scale (GTS) The categories of time into which Earth's history is usually divided by geologists and paleontologists: eons, eras, periods, epochs.

The Geologic Time Scale

Watch the **Animation** "Geological Time Scale" on **myanthrolab**

The **geologic time scale (GTS)** is divided into nested sets of time. From most inclusive to least inclusive these are eons, eras, periods, and epochs (Figure 9.6 on page 205). The earth itself is approximately 4.5 billion years old, and the GTS covers this entire time, although human and primate evolution occurs only in the Cenozoic Era, or about the last 65 million years.

The scale is divided into two eons, the Precambrian and Phanerozoic. The Precambrian dates from 4.5 billion to 543 million years ago and is divided into three eras: the Hadean, Archean, and Proterozoic. The Phanerozoic Eon dates from 543 million years ago to the present. "Zoic" in each of these names refers to the presence of animals.

Although we will spend the next several chapters discussing the fossil record of only the last 65 million years (the Cenozoic Era), take a moment to consider the enormity of time represented by the entire history of the earth, 4.5 billion years (Figure 9.6 on page 205). Primates are present for a little less than 1.5% of that tremendous span, and humans and our closest ancestors are present for only about 0.1% of that time. To put this in perspective, think about your 7-day spring break. On this scale, the Primates have existed for about 2.4 hours, and the human lineage for only about 11 minutes and 20 seconds!

Mammals arose in the Mesozoic Era; *Mesozoic* literally means "middle age of animals," but the era is often called the "age of reptiles" because of the abundance of dinosaurs. The Mesozoic spans 248–65 million years ago and has three periods: the Triassic, Jurassic, and Cretaceous. The Cenozoic, or recent age of animals, spans from 65 million years ago to present and has two periods: the Tertiary and Quaternary. The Tertiary Period, from 65 to 2.5 million years ago spans parts of five epochs: the Paleocene (65–54.8 million years ago), Eocene (54.8–33.7 million years ago), Oligocene (33.7–23.8 million years ago), Miocene (23.8–5.3 million years ago), and the first part of the Pliocene (5.3–2.5 million years ago). The Quaternary Period from 2.5 million years ago to present, spans parts of three epochs: the remainder of the Pliocene (2.5–1.8 million years ago), the Pleistocene (1.8 million years ago to 10,000 years ago), and Holocene (10,000 years ago to present). We live in the Holocene Epoch of the Quaternary Period of the Cenozoic Era of the Phanerozoic Eon.

The lengths of epochs, periods, and eras are not evenly spaced in the GTS. Boundaries are placed at points in the time scale where large shifts are evident in the geological column. For example, the boundary between the Cretaceous Period of the Mesozoic and the Tertiary Period of the Cenozoic Era (or the Cretaceous/Tertiary [K–T] boundary) records a great change in animal taxa: the drastic decrease of dinosaur species and increasing number of mammals. The boundary between the Tertiary and Quaternary periods signals the onset of glacial events in the Northern Hemisphere, and was recently moved from 1.8 to 2.5 million years ago to reflect evidence for glaciations becoming severe at that time. Some geologists have argued that the lower boundary of the Pleistocene should also be moved to 2.5 million years ago (Gibbard et al., 2010). But because this is a source of much debate we use the traditional boundary of 1.8 million years for the Pleistocene (Gradstein et al., 2004).

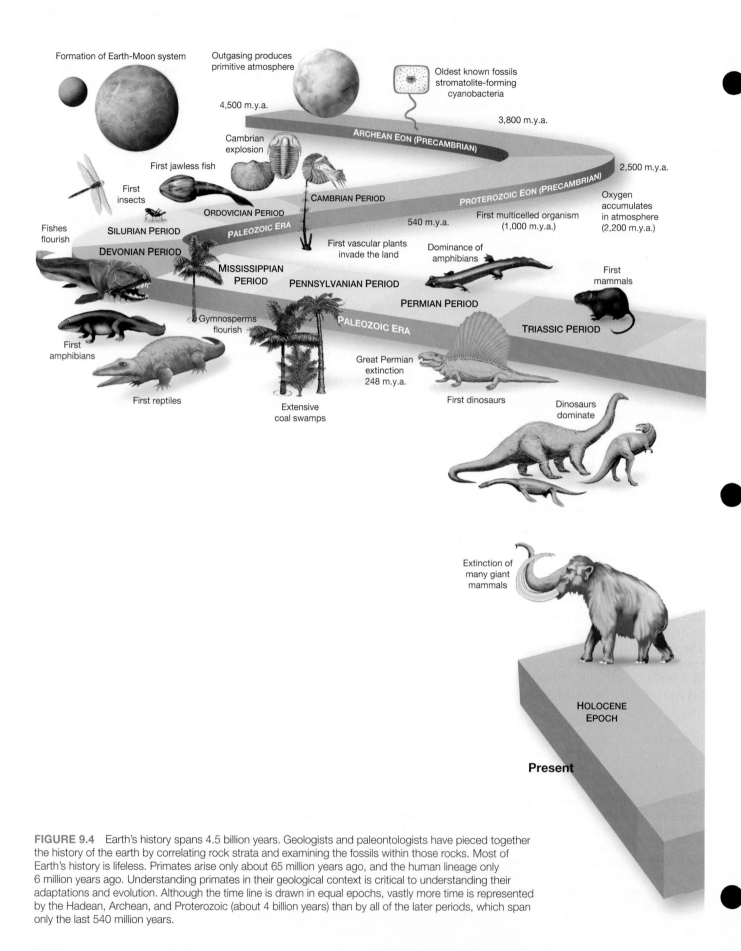

FIGURE 9.4 Earth's history spans 4.5 billion years. Geologists and paleontologists have pieced together the history of the earth by correlating rock strata and examining the fossils within those rocks. Most of Earth's history is lifeless. Primates arise only about 65 million years ago, and the human lineage only 6 million years ago. Understanding primates in their geological context is critical to understanding their adaptations and evolution. Although the time line is drawn in equal epochs, vastly more time is represented by the Hadean, Archean, and Proterozoic (about 4 billion years) than by all of the later periods, which span only the last 540 million years.

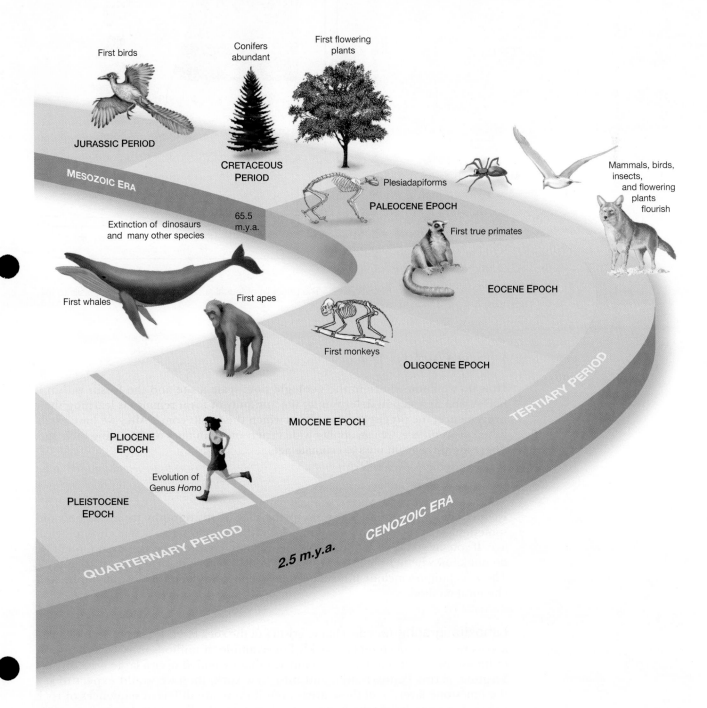

First birds

Conifers abundant

First flowering plants

JURASSIC PERIOD

MESOZOIC ERA

CRETACEOUS PERIOD

Plesiadapiforms

PALEOCENE EPOCH

Mammals, birds, insects, and flowering plants flourish

65.5 m.y.a.

Extinction of dinosaurs and many other species

First true primates

EOCENE EPOCH

First whales

First apes

First monkeys

OLIGOCENE EPOCH

TERTIARY PERIOD

MIOCENE EPOCH

PLIOCENE EPOCH

Evolution of Genus *Homo*

PLEISTOCENE EPOCH

QUARTERNARY PERIOD

2.5 m.y.a.

CENOZOIC ERA

203

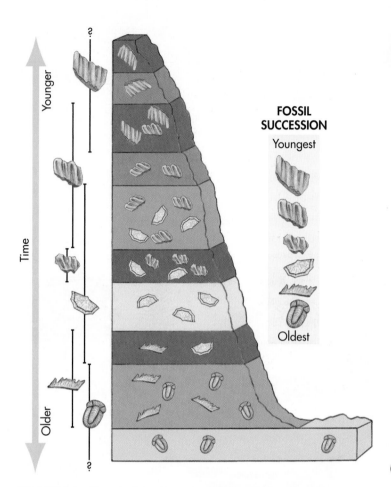

FIGURE 9.5   The principle of faunal succession uses animal fossils to tell relative time.

How Old Is It?

How do we know where in the geologic time scale a site and the fossils within it fall? A vital first step in determining the antiquity of fossil remains is learning their **provenience,** the precise location from which the fossils come. After we have established provenience, we can apply a wide variety of techniques to estimating their age. There are three main ways to estimate age.

Relative Dating Techniques

Relative dating techniques use the principles of stratigraphy to tell us how old something is in relation to something else without applying an actual chronological age. If you say you have an older brother, we know your relative ages even though we do not know whether the two of you are 6 and 16 years old, 19 and 25, or 60 and 65. These techniques include lithostratigraphy, tephrostratigraphy, biostratigraphy, and chemical methods.

Lithostratigraphy uses the characteristics of the rock layers themselves to correlate across regions (*litho* refers to rock). For example, if millions of years ago a layer of limestone was formed by an inland sea that extended over a large area of West Virginia, across Pennsylvania, and into New York, then we would expect to see the limestone layer in all these areas even if there are different sequences of rock layers above and below the limestone. Therefore, the limestone layer allows us to correlate the widely separated sequences of rock layers (Figure 9.7 on page 206).

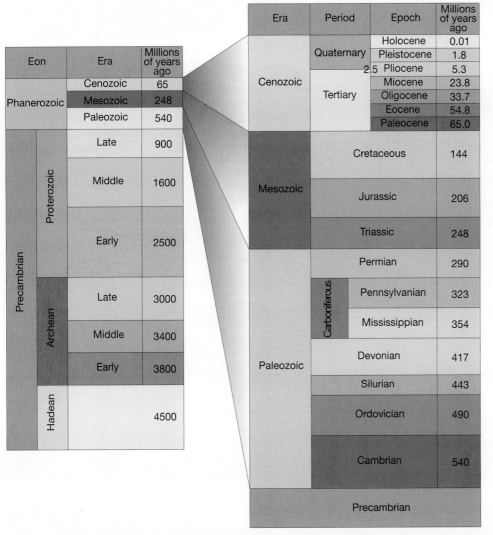

Eon	Era	Millions of years ago
	Cenozoic	65
Phanerozoic	Mesozoic	248
	Paleozoic	540
		Late	900
	Proterozoic	Middle	1600
		Early	2500
Precambrian		Late	3000
	Archean	Middle	3400
		Early	3800
	Hadean		4500

Era	Period	Epoch	Millions of years ago
		Holocene	0.01
	Quaternary	Pleistocene	1.8
Cenozoic		Pliocene	5.3
		Miocene	23.8
	Tertiary	Oligocene	33.7
		Eocene	54.8
		Paleocene	65.0
	Cretaceous		144
Mesozoic	Jurassic		206
	Triassic		248
	Permian		290
	Carboniferous — Pennsylvanian		323
	Carboniferous — Mississippian		354
Paleozoic	Devonian		417
	Silurian		443
	Ordovician		490
	Cambrian		540
Precambrian			

provenience The origin or original source (as of a fossil).

relative dating techniques Dating techniques that establish the age of a fossil only in comparison to other materials found above and below it.

lithostratigraphy The study of geologic deposits and their formation, stratigraphic relationships, and relative time relationships based on their lithologic (rock) properties.

tephrostratigraphy A form of lithostratigraphy in which the chemical fingerprint of a volcanic ash is used to correlate across regions.

biostratigraphy Relative dating technique using comparison of fossils from different stratigraphic sequences to estimate which layers are older and which are younger.

FIGURE 9.6 Earth's history is divided into nested sets of time—eons, eras, periods, and epochs—and is called the geologic time scale.

Volcanic deposits can be identified by the chemical components of their strata using **tephrostratigraphy,** and can be used to demonstrate time equivalence even in widely separated sites. This technique has been used with great success in the Turkana Basin of northern Kenya and southern Ethiopia, where researchers have made many important discoveries of ancestral human fossils.

Biostratigraphy uses Smith's principle of faunal succession (Figure 9.5), to correlate age between sites and across regions based on the index fossils found at those sites. The presence of certain index fossils, such as pigs or rodents, tells you only how old the site is relative to other sites with similar or different animals. An absolute age (i.e., 1.6 million years old) can be assigned only if other sites with these index fossils have absolute ages. For example, the rodent fossils found at the Dmanisi *Homo erectus* site in the Republic of Georgia tell us the site must be older than 1.6 million years because these rodents go extinct in Europe after this time.

Chemical Techniques within Sites rely on the fact that two bones buried in the same sediments for the same amount of time should have similar chemical signatures. For example, as bones and teeth lie buried in sediment, they take up fluorine and other elements from the soil, roughly in proportion to the amount of time they have been buried (Oakley, 1963). These chemical techniques can be used to test

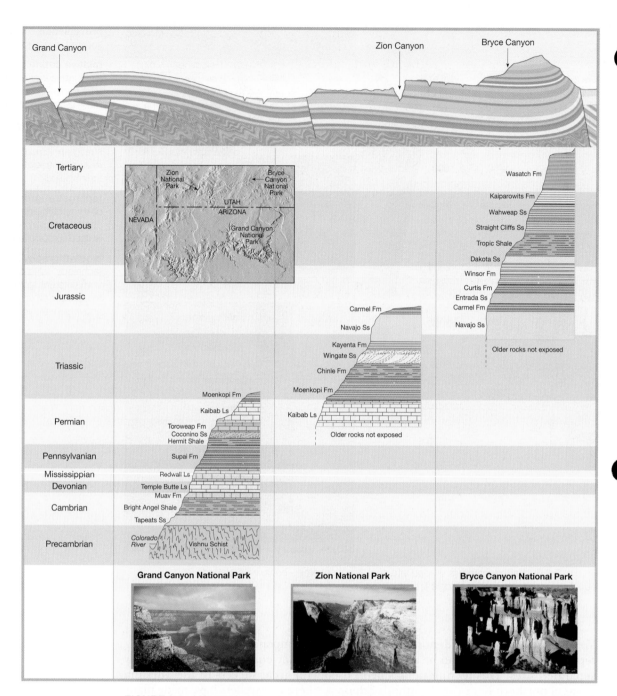

FIGURE 9.7 Lithostratigraphy uses the correlation of rock units to estimate the relative age of different areas. The overlapping rock units for U.S. parks show that the Grand Canyon contains strata that are mostly older than those at Zion National Park, and that Bryce Canyon National Park is the youngest.

associations within sites but are not useful between sites because these elements vary locally. Such techniques become important when the association between different fossils or between the fossils and their sediments is in question.

Chemical techniques were responsible for exposing the greatest fraud in paleoanthropology, the case of the Piltdown Man. Fossilized remains uncovered in a gravel pit at Piltdown Common, in southern England (Figure 9.8) appeared to show that the cradle of humankind was in the United Kingdom. The key finds were part of a modern-looking skull, with a brain size smaller than that of a Neandertal, and a large mandible with apelike teeth (Spencer, 1990). Because he fit the preconceived notions of how human evolution occurred, when Piltdown Man was announced

calibrated relative dating techniques Techniques that can be correlated to an absolute chronology.

geomagnetic polarity time scale (GPTS) Time scale composed of the sequence of paleomagnetic orientations of sediments through time.

to the world in 1912 he was accepted as the first European even though two far better-documented fossil humans, Neandertal and Java Man (*Homo erectus*), were disputed and even dropped from the human family tree by some prominent scientists of the day.

Beginning in 1950, British scientists conducted chemical relative dating tests on the fossil. These tests revealed that the level of fluorine in the Piltdown skull did not match that of the mandible or the animals from the site; Piltdown was a fraud. The "fossils" were really a modern human brain case, artfully stained to appear ancient, and an orangutan mandible whose teeth had been filed down to appear more human like (the file's scratches were clearly visible under a microscope) and whose connecting points with the skull had been broken off to disguise the fact that the two did not belong together. A cleaning of the attic of the Natural History Museum in London in the 1980s revealed clues to who forged the Piltdown fossils. A trunk with the initials of a former museum clerk, Martin Hinton, was filled with an assortment of hippo and elephant teeth, stained to the exact color of the Piltdown fossils as well as human teeth that had been stained in different ways, as though by someone practicing the best way to fake an ancient appearance. It appears that Hinton and Charles Dawson, the fossils' collector, were the likely perpetrators of one of science's greatest hoaxes.

Calibrated Relative Dating Techniques

Calibrated relative dating techniques make use of geological or chemical processes that can be calibrated to a chronological scale if certain conditions are known. One such technique, paleomagnetism, is important in the time scale of primate evolution.

Geomagnetic Polarity Although we take for granted the current position of Earth's north and south magnetic poles, the polarity of the magnetic field has alternated through geologic time (Brown, 1992). At times in the past, magnetic north has been the opposite or reverse of today, that is, in the South Pole. Such reversals occur quickly, perhaps over thousands of years, and do not last for set periods of time. As rocks are formed, their magnetic minerals orient themselves toward magnetic north. Rocks laid down today would have a polarity, or orientation, similar to today's magnetic field. Such polarities are called *normal*. Rocks formed under a reversed field have a *reversed polarity*.

The **geomagnetic polarity time scale (GPTS)** records the orientation of sediments from different intervals (Figure 9.9). The GPTS is divided into long intervals of similar polarity (normal or reversed) called chrons. Here we are most concerned with the last four chrons, the Gauss (reversed, 4.2–3.5 million years ago), Gilbert (normal, 3.5–2.6 million years ago), Matuyama (reversed, 2.6 million–780,000 years ago), and Brunhes (normal, 780,000–present), and some of their subchrons. The present-day interval is the Brunhes Chron, which began about 780,000 years ago.

The sequence of polarities measured from sediments at a site can be a critical test of absolute ages because scientists can use the GPTS to predict what the polarity should be for a given chronological age. For example, the site of Dmanisi, mentioned previously, yielded *H. erectus* fossils in association with rodents known to have gone extinct by 1.6 million years ago. The hominins and rodents also overlay a basalt layer dated to 1.8 million years ago. The GPTS predicts that the basalt was laid down during a period of normal polarity that ended 1.79 million years ago. Alternatively, sediments dated from 1.79 million years and younger are of reversed polarity. Systematic evaluation of the polarity of the Dmanisi deposits tested these predications and found that the basalt was of normal polarity, coinciding with its chronometric age, and that the hominins and rodents were from reversed-polarity deposits, confirming that they must be younger than 1.79 million years (Figure 9.10 on page 208).

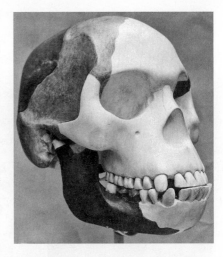

FIGURE 9.8 The Piltdown hoax was exposed by fluorine analysis, a relative dating technique that can test whether two bones have come from the same paleontological site. The mandible and skull fragment were shown to have different fluorine compositions than one another and animals at the site.

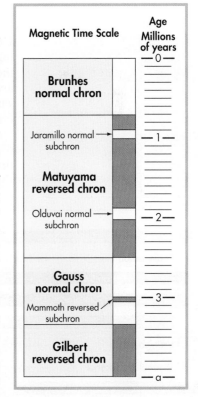

FIGURE 9.9 The geomagnetic polarity time scale shows how Earth's magnetic pole has changed through geologic time. Orange bands indicate periods of reversed polarity and white bands indicate normal polarity.

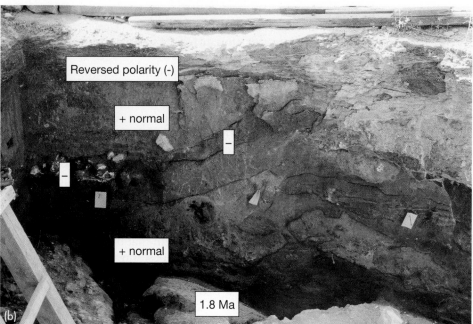

FIGURE 9.10   (a) The site of Dmanisi, in the Republic of Georgia, has produced some of the earliest *H. erectus* outside of Africa. (b) The basalt below the hominins is dated to 1.8 million years ago using argon–argon techniques, and the geomagnetic polarity of the sediments is recorded by pluses and minuses on the wall of the excavation.

Chronometric Dating Techniques

Unlike relative dating methods, **chronometric dating techniques** provide a chronological age estimate of the antiquity of an object in years before the present. These methods rely on having a clock of some sort to measure time. Such clocks include annual growth rings on trees and the recording of annual cycles of glacial retreat, which date very recent events. Radioactive clocks date more distant events. The most famous of the radioactive decay clocks is Carbon-14 (^{14}C, or radiocarbon).

We focus on the clocks most useful for providing age estimates from about 65 million years ago to perhaps as recently as 100,000 or 50,000 years ago, the time scale of primate, including human, evolution. Figure 9.11 illustrates the relative age ranges of the different chronometric techniques discussed in this chapter,

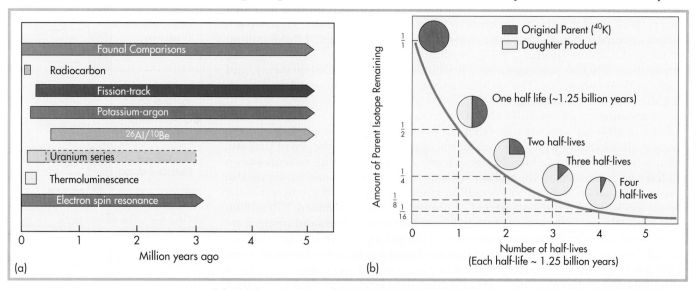

FIGURE 9.11   (a) The relative age ranges of different dating techniques depend upon the half-life of the system used. (b) For example, potassium–argon can date very old events because of its long half-life.

TABLE 9.1   Comparison of Chronometric Techniques

Technique	Age Range	Materials Dated
K–Ar	Recent to 4.5 billion years	Potassium (K)-bearing minerals and glass
$^{40}Ar/^{39}Ar$	Same as for K–Ar	K-bearing minerals (can date single grains)
Fission track	Tens of millions of years	Uranium-bearing, noncrystalline minerals, zircon, apatite, and glasses
$^{26}Al/^{10}Be$	Hundreds of thousands to 6 million years	Quartz grains that have been deeply buried
Uranium series	Thousands to 500,000 years, depending on material	Uranium-bearing minerals, $CaCo_3$, flowstones, corals, shells, teeth
Radiocarbon	Recent to 40,000 years	Organic materials such as wood, bone, shell
TL	100–500,000 years depending on material	Quartz, feldspars, pottery, stone tools
OSL	1,000–400,000 years	As above
ESR	Typically to 500,000 years and possibly to a few million years depending on material	Uranium-bearing materials in which uranium has been taken up from external sources

View "Radiometric Dating Overview" on **myanthrolab**

Table 9.1 compares the materials dated, and the two-page spread on pages 212–213 summarizes the systems.

Radiometric Dating relies on the natural, clock-like decay of unstable isotopes of an element to more stable forms. *Elements* are chemically irreducible categories of matter such as carbon (C), hydrogen (H), and oxygen (O) that form the building blocks of all other matter, such as molecules of water (H_2O) and carbon monoxide (CO). Elements often occur in nature in more than one form, differing slightly on the basis of their atomic weights, which reflect the number of neutrons and protons in the nucleus. These different forms are called **isotopes.** For example, there are three isotopes of carbon, ^{12}C, ^{13}C, and ^{14}C, each with six protons (positively charged) but with six, seven, and eight neutrons (neutral particles), respectively (Figure 9.12 on page 210). Although ^{12}C and ^{13}C are stable (they do not naturally decay), the extra neutron of ^{14}C makes it unstable or prone to decay. The rate at which this radioactive decay takes place is constant, and the **half-life** of the isotope is the amount of time it takes for one-half of the original amount to decay. To determine the age of a sample we measure the amount of **parent isotope,** the original radioactive isotope the sample started with, and the amount of **daughter isotope (product)** in the sample, which is the isotope formed by radioactive decay of the parent isotope (Figure 9.11b). The total of these two is the amount of total parent that existed before radioactive decay started. The amount of daughter as a percentage of total parent tells you the number of half-lives expended. Knowing the length of the half-life yields an age (number of half-lives × length of half-life = age estimate) (Figure 9.11b). For example, the half-life of ^{14}C is about 5,730 years; if we know that two half-lives have passed in our sample, then we know that the sample is 11,460 years old.

Potassium–argon (K–Ar) and **argon/argon ($^{40}Ar/^{39}Ar$) dating** use the decay of the isotope ^{40}K (potassium) to ^{40}Ar (argon) and require potassium-bearing minerals to work. Unlike the short half-life of ^{14}C, the decay from potassium to argon has a half-life of 1.3 billion years (Deino et al., 1998). As a result, this decay series has been used to date some of the oldest rocks on Earth and has also dated events as recent as the eruption of Mt. Vesuvius in Italy in A.D. 79. These methods are

chronometric dating techniques Techniques that estimate the age of an object in absolute terms through the use of a natural clock such as radioactive decay or tree ring growth.

radiometric dating Chronometric techniques that use radioactive decay of isotopes to estimate age.

isotopes Variant forms of an element that differ based on their atomic weights and numbers of neutrons in the nucleus. Both stable and unstable (radioactive) isotopes exist in nature.

half-life The time it takes for half of the original amount of an unstable isotope of an element to decay into more stable forms.

parent isotope The original radioactive isotope in a sample.

daughter isotope (product) The isotope that is produced as the result of radioactive decay of the parent isotope.

potassium–argon (K–Ar) dating Radiometric technique using the decay of ^{40}K to ^{40}Ar in potassium-bearing rocks; estimates the age of sediments in which fossils are found.

argon–argon Radiometric technique modified from K–Ar that measures ^{40}K by proxy using ^{39}Ar. Allows measurement of smaller samples with less error.

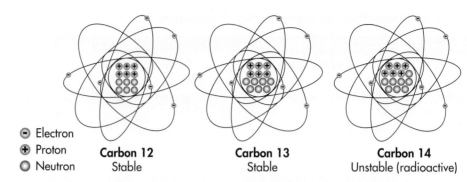

⊖ Electron
⊕ Proton
◯ Neutron

Carbon 12
Stable

Carbon 13
Stable

Carbon 14
Unstable (radioactive)

FIGURE 9.12 Isotopes may be stable or radioactive depending on the arrangement and number of neutrons in the nucleus. ^{14}C is heavier than ^{12}C or ^{13}C because it has more neutrons, and it is radioactive (or unstable) for the same reason.

useful in dating the timing of the eruption of volcanic sediments because heating during the eruption drives off all argon gases, and at the time the volcanic material cools, the clock is effectively set to zero (there is no argon and only potassium in the system).

Fortunately, there are many situations in which fossil hominins are in sediments sandwiched between volcanic tuffs, so we can estimate the fossil ages by their association with the age of the volcanics. K-Ar and the $^{40}Ar/^{39}Ar$ methods have been widely used in paleoanthropology for dating volcanic sediments associated with hominins in Africa, Georgia, and Indonesia. For example, they provide the maximum age estimate of 1.8 million years for the volcanic rock that underlays the Dmanisi hominins discussed earlier.

Fission track dating provides age estimates for noncrystalline materials (such as volcanic glass) that contain uranium (U). The method relies on counting the small tracks produced each time an atom of ^{238}U decays by fission (hence its name). Fission track dating provides a viable age range from about 100 years to the oldest rocks on Earth, although the low density of tracks makes it difficult to date very young samples (<100,000 years), and old samples have too many tracks to count accurately. In the Nihewan Basin in China, tektites (glasses formed by the impact of a meteor) are found in association with early evidence of stone tool manufacture. The age of these tektites is about 780,000 years, and thus the stone tools with them would be among the earliest stone tools in China.

Cosmogenic radionuclide techniques such as $^{26}Al/^{10}Be$ are relatively new methods that provide radiometric age estimates of the length of time sediments have been buried. The ratio of the nuclide ^{26}Al to the nuclide ^{10}Be is a fixed or known ratio that appears to change with a half-life of around 1.52 million years. The method requires deeply buried sediments that have been shielded from cosmogenic (sun-generated) sources of radiation, and it is necessary that quartz grains be present. The technique is useful in dating non-volcanic sediments such as those fossils at the South African *Australopithecus* site of Sterkfontein and the Peking Man *H. erectus* site from Zhoukoudian, China (Shen et al., 2008; see Insights and Advances: Dating Controversies).

Uranium series (U-series) techniques use the decay chain of ^{238}U, ^{235}U, and ^{232}Th, all of which decay to stable lead isotopes, to provide age estimates for calcium carbonates, such as flowstones precipitated in caves, shells of invertebrates, and sometimes teeth. U-series techniques usually date strata associated with a fossil, not the fossil itself. Associations therefore are critical to providing the correct age estimate for a fossil. It may be possible to date a fossil directly with u-series techniques, but the method is more complicated. Flowstones and teeth at Chinese hominin sites have established ages for the famous Peking Man site that suggest a time range between about 200,000 and 400,000 years ago, although the ages on teeth may be too young (see Insights and Advances: Dating Controversies).

fission track dating Radiometric technique for dating noncrystalline materials using the decay of ^{238}Ur and counting the tracks that are produced by this fission. Estimates the age of sediments in which fossils are found.

cosmogenic radionuclide dating Radiometric dating technique that uses ratios of rare isotopes such as ^{26}A, ^{10}Be, and ^{3}He to estimate the time that sediments and the fossils in them have been buried.

uranium series (U-series) techniques Radiometric techniques using the decay of uranium to estimate an age for calcium carbonates including flowstones, shells, and teeth.

insights & advances

DATING CONTROVERSIES

Although modern radiometric dating techniques provide some of the most rigorous scientific data available to biological anthropologists, the resulting age estimations often are highly controversial. A number of variables introduce uncertainty into our attempts to estimate the age of fossils. One vexing problem is the absence of material suitable for chronometric dating. A number of chronometric dating techniques (including potassium–argon, argon/argon, and fission track) are incredibly useful in areas with volcanic sediments such as East Africa and Indonesia, but can't be used in areas that are primarily made of sedimentary rocks such as Europe, Continental Asia during certain times, and South Africa. In these areas other techniques, such as uranium series, the newer cosmogenic radionuclides, and nonradiometric techniques such as paleomagnetism and biostratigraphy are often used and sometimes provide conflicting age estimates.

A recent example is the famed Peking Man site of Zhoukoudian near Beijing, China (Figure A). The site was discovered and most of the excavation was undertaken in the 1920s and 1930s. Once thought to represent the cave sites in which *H. erectus* lived, recent analysis has shown that the site is a series of in-fillings into deep fissures in the limestone bedrock. The "lower cave" of Zhoukoudian consists of more than 15 layers of deposits, many of which

contain fossil hominin and animal remains. Dating these layers has proven challenging since China lacks Pleistocene volcanic sediments. Older volcanics provide good age control of Jurassic and Cretaceous sites in China such as those in which the feathered dinosaurs of Liaoning are found. But younger volcanics are missing. Thus Chinese hominin ages are established by relative methods such as biostratigraphy or lithostratigraphy, loess stratigraphy, or, more recently, uranium series, ESR, and cosmogenic radionuclide ages like $^{26}Al/^{10}Be$.

At Zhoukoudian, U-series and ESR age estimates on faunal remains and U-series and $^{26}Al/^{10}Be$ on flowstones suggest that the multiple layers at the site were accumulated over a time span of several hundred thousand years. However, the absolute age range covered by the site differs amongst the methods. U-series and ESR ages on faunal remains suggest a range of 200,000–400,000 years ago (Grün et al., 1997), but the flowstone and $^{26}Al/^{10}Be$ ages are substantially older, around 770,000 years ago for the oldest set of fossils (Shen et al., 2008). Because U-series on flowstones can only effectively date specimens up to about 500,000 years ago, new dating systems such as $^{26}Al/^{10}Be$ were necessary to suggest this older age. Still, these ages rely on the correct association of the sediments dated and the fossils of interest, which leaves some level of uncertainty especially for sites excavated so long ago.

Dating controversies will continue to exist, but securely establishing provenience and applying multiple methods of age estimation should almost always lead us to the correct determination of antiquity.

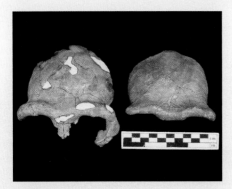

FIGURE A The famous Peking Man site is a deep series of fissure-fills that span hundreds of thousands of years from top to bottom and contains many *H. erectus* cranial fossils.

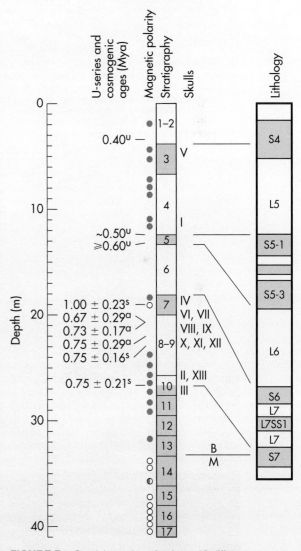

FIGURE B Cranial remains of at least 12 different individuals have been recovered from Zhoukoudian. New dating techniques suggest that the majority of them are around 770,000 years older, far older than had been previously thought. After Shen et al., 2009.

Time in a Bottle

K-Ar and Ar/Ar

Some radiometric or "absolute" dating methods use the accumulation of a daughter product from the radioactive decay of a parent element to estimate age. For example, the Potassium-Argon (K-Ar) and Argon/Argon ($^{40}Ar/^{39}Ar$) methods use the amount of ^{40}Ar accumulated from the decay of ^{40}K to estimate age. To make this estimate we must know that the system starts with no ^{40}Ar gas and that all the accumulated argon has occurred since the formation of the rock. An ideal situation for this is when a volcano erupts; the molten lava releases all its argon gas and effectively sets the clock to zero age (or time zero, T_0).

We can estimate the age since the time of eruption by considering how much argon has accumulated after T_0. As the molten lava solidifies into rock, any newly formed ^{40}Ar will be trapped inside the rock. Estimating the age then relies on measuring the ^{40}Ar and the remaining ^{40}K, and calculating how much of a half life has passed since the rock formed.

^{40}K → ^{40}Ar

Ash

The longer the time since the lava or ash cooled to rock, the greater the amount of ^{40}Ar, the less ^{40}K present, and the greater the age.

Ash

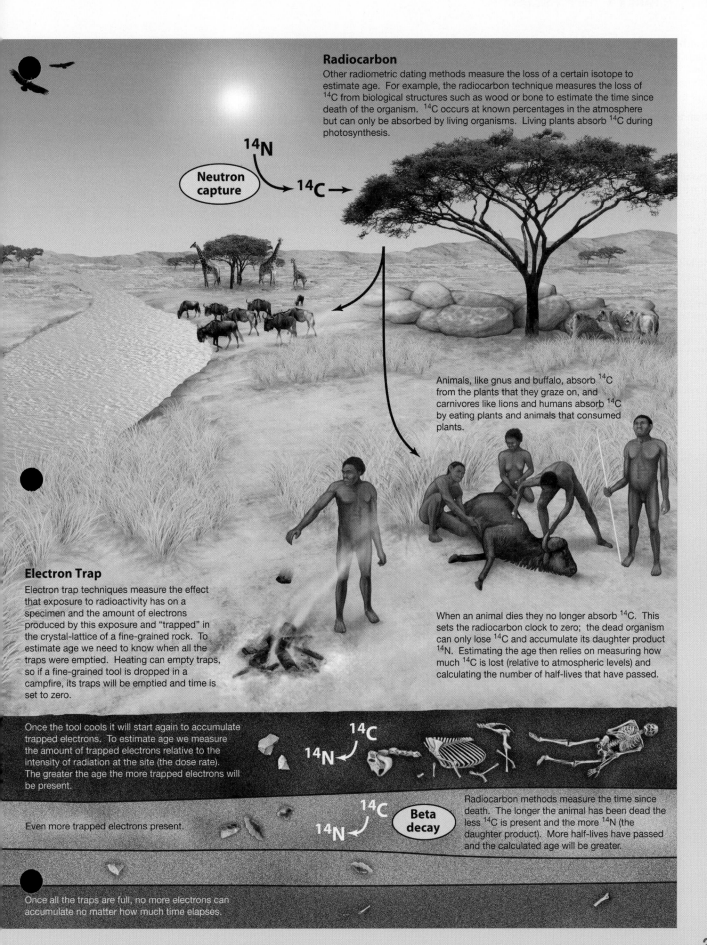

Radiocarbon

Other radiometric dating methods measure the loss of a certain isotope to estimate age. For example, the radiocarbon technique measures the loss of ^{14}C from biological structures such as wood or bone to estimate the time since death of the organism. ^{14}C occurs at known percentages in the atmosphere but can only be absorbed by living organisms. Living plants absorb ^{14}C during photosynthesis.

^{14}N

Neutron capture → ^{14}C →

Animals, like gnus and buffalo, absorb ^{14}C from the plants that they graze on, and carnivores like lions and humans absorb ^{14}C by eating plants and animals that consumed plants.

Electron Trap

Electron trap techniques measure the effect that exposure to radioactivity has on a specimen and the amount of electrons produced by this exposure and "trapped" in the crystal-lattice of a fine-grained rock. To estimate age we need to know when all the traps were emptied. Heating can empty traps, so if a fine-grained tool is dropped in a campfire, its traps will be emptied and time is set to zero.

When an animal dies they no longer absorb ^{14}C. This sets the radiocarbon clock to zero; the dead organism can only lose ^{14}C and accumulate its daughter product ^{14}N. Estimating the age then relies on measuring how much ^{14}C is lost (relative to atmospheric levels) and calculating the number of half-lives that have passed.

Once the tool cools it will start again to accumulate trapped electrons. To estimate age we measure the amount of trapped electrons relative to the intensity of radiation at the site (the dose rate). The greater the age the more trapped electrons will be present.

^{14}C
^{14}N ↝

Even more trapped electrons present.

^{14}C
^{14}N ↝ **Beta decay**

Radiocarbon methods measure the time since death. The longer the animal has been dead the less ^{14}C is present and the more ^{14}N (the daughter product). More half-lives have passed and the calculated age will be greater.

Once all the traps are full, no more electrons can accumulate no matter how much time elapses.

radiocarbon dating   Radiometric technique that uses the decay of ¹⁴C in organic remains such as wood and bone to estimate the time since the death of the organism.

electron trap techniques
Radiometric techniques that measure the accumulation of electrons in traps in the crystal lattice of a specimen.

thermoluminescence (TL)
Electron trap technique that uses heat to measure the amount of radioactivity accumulated by a specimen, such as a stone tool, since its last heating.

optically stimulated luminescence (OSL)   Electron trap technique that uses light to measure the amount of radioactivity accumulated by crystals in sediments (such as sand grains) since burial.

electron spin resonance (ESR)
Electron trap technique that measures the total amount of radioactivity accumulated by a specimen (such as tooth or bone) since burial.

Radiocarbon dating is the primary technique for estimating the antiquity of organic items from the latest Pleistocene through the present, including primate and human fossils as well as artifacts from archaeological sites. All living organisms are composed of molecules that contain carbon. Recall that three isotopes of carbon, ^{12}C, ^{13}C, and ^{14}C, exist in the atmosphere, only one of which, ^{14}C, is radioactive. As plants photosynthesize carbon dioxide they take up these isotopes at atmospheric levels. Animals that eat plants then take up carbon, as do animals that eat other animals. Uptake of carbon ceases at the death of the organism. At this point, the atoms of ^{14}C begin to decay and are not replenished by additional ^{14}C from the atmosphere. We estimate age in the usual way by comparing the amount of daughter product (in this case ^{14}N) with the amount of original parent in the material and then multiplying this percentage by the half-life. Because the half-life of ^{14}C is short, about 5,730 years (Taylor, 2000), the technique is useful for organic remains from the last 30,000 to 40,000 years. The age range of the ^{14}C technique limits its paleoanthropological applications to the latest part of the Neandertal lineage and their overlap with anatomically modern humans (Jöris and Street, 2008).

Electron Trap Techniques rely on the effect that exposure to radioactivity has on a crystalline specimen, not on the decay of radioactive isotopes within the specimen. If the amount of radiation an object is exposed to is constant, then the number of trapped electrons will be proportional to the age of the material. The main electron trap techniques are **thermoluminescence (TL), optically stimulated luminescence (OSL),** and **electron spin resonance (ESR).** TL and OSL can date things over hundreds of thousands of years but are used mostly in the range of the past 100,000 years, which is older than ^{14}C can measure. The age range of ESR is about the same as that for the U-series techniques, and the two are often used together if U-series is being conducted on tooth rather than on flowstone. TL and ESR analyses have been critical in corroborating the early age of the Tabun Neandertals (about 100,000—150,000 year) and of the Skhul and Qafzeh modern human sites (about 100,000 years) in the Near East (Stringer et al., 1989; Grun et al., 1991) (Figure 9.13). In conjunction with the U-series techniques, these data suggest that the modern humans and Neandertals alternated their use of the region (see Chapter 12).

FIGURE 9.13   In the caves of the Mt. Carmel region of Israel, electronic spin resonance, uranium series techniques, and thermoluminescence have shown that modern humans and Neandertals alternated their use of the region.

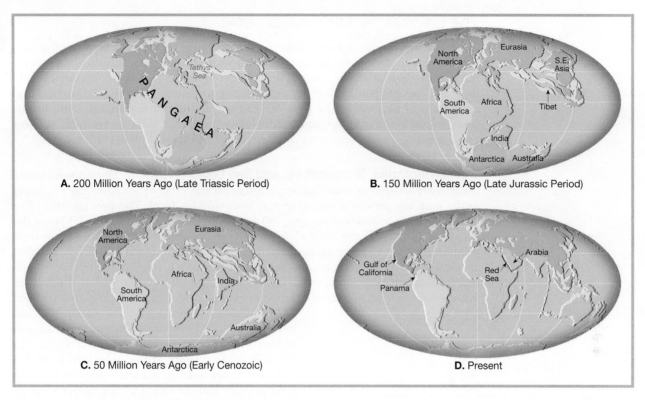

FIGURE 9.14 The continents were not always in their present positions. The position of the continents is important for understanding movements of primates in the past.

The Earth in the Cenozoic

Having established the various ways we might assess the age of a paleontological site and the fossils within it, we now turn to other issues of understanding the context in which fossil primates are found. Most importantly, we will look at the position of the major land masses during the Cenozoic, which has implications for how animals moved from one place to another, and then we consider the various methods scientists use to reconstruct the habitat in which animals once lived.

Continents and Land Masses

As you may be aware, the continents have not always been in their current locations. Approximately 200 million years ago the earth was divided into two major land masses that we now call Laurasia and Gondwanaland. Laurasia was composed of most of present-day North America and Asia, and Gondwanaland included Africa and South America (Figure 9.14). By 50 million years ago North America and Asia were beginning to spread apart, and both South America and Africa had separated from one another and from the other continents. Africa eventually became connected to Asia via the Near East, North America and Asia were separated by a chain of islands (but remained connected during low sea levels), and South America was an island continent until well into the Pliocene (~3.5 million years ago), when the Central American land bridge connected it to North America. These movements are critical for understanding early primate evolution, particularly the distribution of the Eocene primates and the conundrum of the origin of the South American primates (which appeared while that continent was still an island). Once the continents were in their present positions, the onset of severe glacial events in the late Pliocene and Pleistocene periodically lowered sea levels, exposing additional land and sometimes resulting, as is the case between continental Asia and Indonesia, in land bridges between otherwise isolated areas (see Chapter 11).

The Environment in the Cenozoic

As we saw in Chapter 2, conditions in the environment naturally select individuals most suited to them, and because of their favored traits, these individuals reproduce more than others in the population. So, studying past environmental conditions is critical to understanding the selective pressures affecting the survival and extinction of animals in the past. We can reconstruct environmental conditions from several kinds of geological and biological evidence. Here we consider ways for reconstructing past temperature, sea levels, and animal and plant communities.

Oxygen Isotopes, Temperature, and Sea Level Perhaps the best-known climate proxies are oxygen isotope curves that rely on the ratio of stable oxygen isotopes in the past as a proxy for global temperature and sea level. The process works like this. Two stable isotopes of oxygen, ^{16}O and ^{18}O, differ in weight, with ^{18}O being the heavier of the two. These isotopes exist as oxygen in water molecules and other compounds. In water they are incorporated into the shells of marine invertebrates that are composed of calcium carbonates. Water molecules formed of the lighter isotope tend to float nearer the ocean surface, and water molecules formed of the heavier isotope tend to sink; therefore, the lighter isotope of oxygen tends to evaporate from ocean surfaces sooner than does ^{18}O. During cold periods when ^{16}O evaporates from the ocean, it is not returned to the world's water reserves via rain but is locked up in ice at the poles and northern latitudes. Consequently, sea levels are lower during cold periods and contain a greater percentage of ^{18}O than during warmer periods. Therefore, the $^{18}O/^{16}O$ ratio increases in sea water during cold periods and in the shells of the marine animals formed in them at that time (Figure 9.15).

The Pliocene and Pleistocene epochs are characterized by oscillations in temperature from colder (glacial) to milder (interglacial) periods (Figure 9.15). Oxygen isotope curves have been important for reconstructing climate patterns in the mid- and late Pleistocene and correlating the movements of Neandertals and modern humans in relation to climate change (see Chapter 12). Global climate patterns can help us understand what kinds of conditions animals lived in during the past. But local differences in climate would also exist within these global patterns—for example, think of the differences in climate between the beach and the mountains today. Plant and animal fossils from specific paleontological localities help us understand these more local environmental conditions.

Vegetation Fossilized plants, pollens, and plant impressions can show us what the local environment was like at the time a paleontological site was formed. Plants are less often preserved than bones, but under certain circumstances, such as in peat bogs or very fine-grained sediments, plant fossils are abundant. These fossils can be used to compare the environments that animals once lived in with those of today. For example, the recovery of fossil pollens can tell us about the presence of certain kinds of plants in an area. As we'll see in Chapter 12, the Neandertal site of Shanidar was thought to show

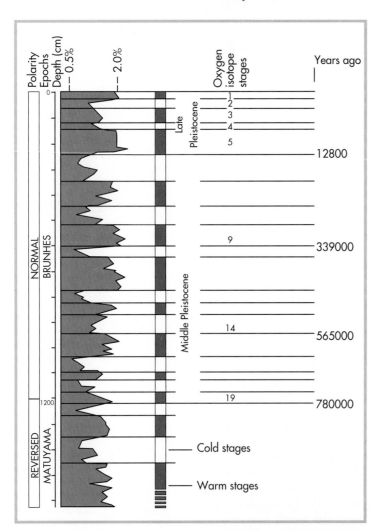

FIGURE 9.15 The oxygen isotope curve illustrates the ratio between ^{16}O and ^{18}O. More of the heavy isotope indicates colder periods (even-numbered stages); more of the lighter indicates warmer periods (interglacials, odd-numbered stages; After Klein, 1999).

the ritual burial of a Neandertal on a blanket of flowers (based on the plentiful pollen around the skeleton). But it is also possible that modern pollens were introduced to the site, either as the archaeologists excavated or as the wind blew over local plants.

paleosol   Ancient soil.

Stable Carbon Isotope Ratios in Teeth and Soil Stable carbon isotope ratios are also used to reconstruct the types of vegetation in a region. We can use carbon isotopes to differentiate between plants using different photosynthetic pathways because these different pathways lead to the retention of different amounts of carbon isotopes. Trees and shrubs, different kinds of grasses, and arid-adapted plants use different photosynthetic pathways. By examining ratios of stable carbon isotopes in ancient soils (**paleosols**), scientists can identify if an ancient environment was, for example, an open grassland or a shady woodland. Analyzing paleosols in this way has been important in reconstructing environments in Africa during hominin evolution (Figure 9.16). We used to think bipedality arose in an open savanna environment, perhaps implicating heat stress or other selective factors in its origin. However, we are learning that many of the early hominin environments were more wooded, suggesting that another selective factor was at work; perhaps bipedality was an efficient means of crossing short distances between food patches while also carrying food. The recent publications on *Ardipithecus ramidus* have used soil carbonates as one piece of evidence to argue for a moister and more wooded environment for this early putative hominin (White et al., 2010); however, other analysts argue that these data indicate less than 25% tree cover (Cerling et al., 2010).

Animal Communities Animal bones can also be used to infer local environment. Although some types of animals seem to be able to live just about anywhere, most have preferred types of habitats. Hippos and crocodiles live near water sources, and the presence of monkeys usually indicates wooded areas. Animals that are adapted to running long distances over open terrain tend to have longer, slighter limbs; those adapted to life in forested areas often have shorter limbs. Based on comparisons with the adaptations in living animals of known habitat preference, paleontologists infer the climatic and environmental preferences of past animals associated with fossil primate and hominin sites and thus the paleoenvironmental conditions in which these primates lived.

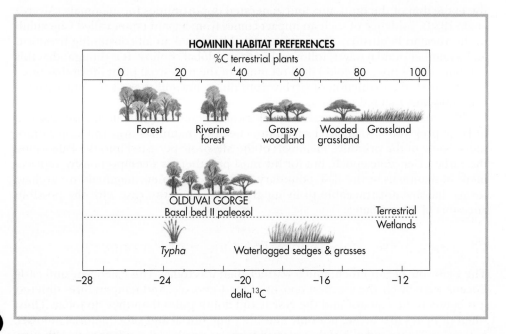

FIGURE 9.16 Habitat reconstruction is possible based on the kinds of plants present at past sites. The kinds of plants present are reflected in the ratios of stable carbon isotopes in soils, fossils, and fossil carbonates.

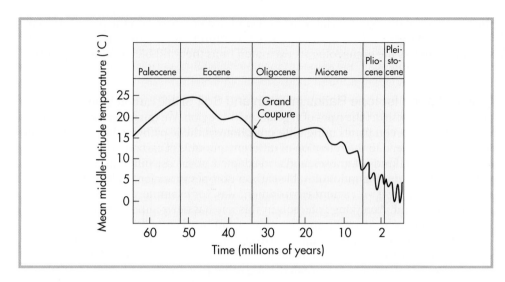

FIGURE 9.17   Climate has cooled substantially during primate evolution.

**View** the **Map** "Primate Evolution" on **myanthrolab**

Climate Change and Early Primate Evolution

Using the kinds of reconstructions described here, scientists have drawn a general picture of the climate during the evolution of the Primate order. Figure 9.17 provides an overview of temperature changes throughout the Cenozoic. The story of Cenozoic climate change is generally one of cooling and drying. By combining these reconstructions of ancient climate change with information from the Primate fossil record, we can begin to understand how our lineage evolved.

The origin of primates is tied first to the origin of mammals, which began in the Mesozoic Era (225–65 million years ago), an age dominated by dinosaurs. At the end of the Mesozoic, drastic environmental changes, probably arising from an asteroid or comet crashing into the surface of the earth, caused or contributed to the extinction of the dinosaurs and generated opportunities for mammals (Alvarez et al., 1980). Evidence of such an impact comes from a giant crater called Chicxulub in the Yucatán Peninsula. The impact probably caused an all-consuming firestorm and a number of tidal waves, followed by abrupt global cooling. It is thought that this combination of fire and cold killed off much of the terrestrial plant life at that time, which caused the extinction of herbivorous dinosaurs and then also of the carnivorous dinosaurs that fed on them.

The ensuing environmental and ecological circumstances, including the absence of large prey animals, favored small, insect-eating mammals over the larger dinosaurs. Some of the primitive mammals of the Mesozoic persisted into the Paleocene, the earliest Cenozoic epoch, but for the most part there is a comprehensive replacement of mammals at the K–T boundary. Many of these new mammals are archaic forms that are not traceable to living groups. Such is the case with the possible ancestors of the primates.

Changes in the Paleocene: The Origin of Primates?

The Cenozoic began much, much warmer than it is today. The Paleocene and early Eocene were by far the warmest epochs of the Cenozoic, and temperatures differed less between the equator and the North and South poles than they do today. Thus, when primates first arose, not only were they equatorial and subequatorial animals, as they largely are today, but they existed fairly far north and south as well. Although it was warmer than today, there was some climatic fluctuation during each epoch. As the era proceeded, the climate cooled and dried but still fluctuated somewhat.

During the Paleocene Epoch, many archaic groups of mammals arose that are not precisely like any living group. Based on comparisons of DNA from living mammals, the order Primates should originate in the Paleocene because the molecular divergence of the group (which should pre-date the appearance of fossil primates) began about 63 million years ago.

Among the new arrivals at the beginning of the Paleocene are primate-like mammals, the **plesiadapiforms,** either a separate order of mammals or a suborder of the primates, on equal footing with strepsirhines and haplorhines (see Chapter 7). The controversy over whether plesiadapiforms are early primates arises because they are anatomically more primitive than any living primate. They had small brains, a **prognathic face** that projected well in front of their braincase, and small eye sockets positioned on the sides rather than on the front of their face. They lacked a **postorbital bar,** a bony ring encircling the eye, a key feature of primates that indicates the importance of vision to the order. Many plesiadapiforms possessed large, rodent-like lower incisors that were separated from the premolars by a large **diastema,** or gap between their anterior teeth. Some had claws (rather than nails) and lacked an opposable big toe. In all these ways plesiadapiforms do not look like modern primates.

One well-known Plesiadapid genus from Montana, *Purgatorius*, has less specialized, less spiky teeth, a dental formula (see Chapter 7) of 3:1:4:3, suggesting a diet of both insects (the spikes help break into the insect shell) and fruit. *Purgatorius* is generalized enough to have given rise to the first clear primates that appear in the fossil record of the Eocene (about 54 million years ago).

Why Primates?

As we saw in previous chapters, environmental conditions shape the characteristics of a group by favoring individuals who exhibit certain traits and selecting against individuals without those traits (see Chapter 2). So what environmental change or problem favored the origin of the primate trends? The Paleocene was warmer than today and was a period of recovery from the giant meteor impact described earlier. In the Paleocene flowering plants evolved, insects increased in number and diversity as pollinators for these plants, and the plants evolved visual cues to lure these insects. The plesiadapiform fossils suggest that primate ancestors took advantage of these changing resources by eating insects (remember the spiky teeth of the plesiadapids that are good for crunching the hard bodies of insects) and possibly fruit from new plants (remember also that the teeth of *Purgatorius* are slightly less spiky than rodents of the Cretaceous, better for mashing fruit). We know that living primates emphasize vision over olfaction and have tactile pads on their fingers not hard pads and claws (see Chapter 7).

In the past, scientists thought that primates evolved these features in response to life in the trees rather than on the ground. However, the fossil record of early proto-primates such as the plesiadapiforms has helped us to understand that early primate forebears probably were visual predators dependent on sighting and catching insects to survive rather than clambering on branches for fruit (see Chapter 7 for a review of the *visual predation hypothesis*). In the Eocene, the first true primates expand on this early primate adaptation.

True Primates of the Eocene

Climate warmed significantly at the beginning of the Eocene, around 54 million years ago (see Figure 9.17), resulting in the replacement of the archaic mammals of the Paleocene by the first representatives of a number of modern orders of mammals, including Primates. Throughout the Eocene there would be a precipitous drop in global temperature that would also influence Primate evolution. The fossil primates of the Eocene include the first true primates, those that possess the bony characters by which we identify living primates (Figure 9.18 on page 220). We also see the origin of the strepsirhine-haplorhine split during this epoch.

plesiadapiforms   Mammalian order or suborder of mammals that may be ancestral to later Primates, characterized by some but not all of the primate trends.

prognathic face   Projection of the face well in front of the braincase.

postorbital bar   A bony ring encircling the lateral side of the eye but not forming a complete cup around the eye globe.

diastema   Gap between anterior teeth.

adapoids   Super family of mostly Eocene primates, probably ancestral to all strepsirhines.

omomyoids   Super family of mostly Eocene primates, probably ancestral to all haplorhines.

The two main superfamilies of Eocene primates, the Adapoidea and Omomyoidea, appeared at the beginning of the Eocene, but declined during the Oligocene (Covert, 2002). We recognize these Eocene fossils as true primates because, unlike the plesiadapiforms, they possess the full suite of primate trends. In particular, they possess slightly larger brains than plesiadapiforms, eye sockets positioned on the front of the face (allowing stereoscopic vision and depth perception), a complete postorbital bar for greater protection of the eye, an opposable big toe, and nails (rather than claws) at the ends of their fingers and toes. At the same time, the reduction of their snouts and whiskers suggests that smell was less important for locating food than was sight (Figure 9.18). Based on other anatomical evidence discussed in this chapter, we think the adapoids and omomyoids gave rise to the lineages that became the living strepsirhines (lemurs and lorises) and haplorhines (tarsiers, monkeys, and apes), respectively.

Adapoids (strepsirhine ancestors)   **Adapoids** resemble modern strepsirhines mainly in primitive ways. Therefore, the adapoids are best considered the most primitive group of early modern primates known. The adapoids probably gave rise to strepsirhines before the evolutionary divergence of lemurs and lorises (Figure 9.19). This interpretation is consistent with the molecular evidence that suggests lemurs and lorises diverged around 45 million years ago (later than the first appearance of the adapoids) but that strepsirhines and haplorhines had already split by about 58 million years ago. There is, however, an alternative argument linking adapoids to haplorhines. For instance, those who discovered the remarkably complete adapid skeleton *Darwinius masillae* (Figure 9.20) consider it a haplorhine ancestor.

The adapoids were mostly small to medium sized and weighed approximately 3.5 oz to 15 lb (100 g to 6.9 kg). They were slow-moving arboreal quadrupeds that were active by day and probably ate fruit and leaves (Figure 9.18). Many had long broad snouts with teeth that suggest some may have eaten a fibrous diet. Although they occur in both North America and Europe, adapoids are most abundant in the Old World.

Omomyoids (haplorhine ancestors)   **Omomyoids** are best regarded as Eocene primates that had recently diverged from the adapoids and may have given rise to the common ancestor of both tarsiers and anthropoids (Figure 9.19). This view is consistent with the molecular evidence that suggests that the strepsirhine–haplorhine split occurred around 58 million years ago. Previously, the omomyoids had been widely

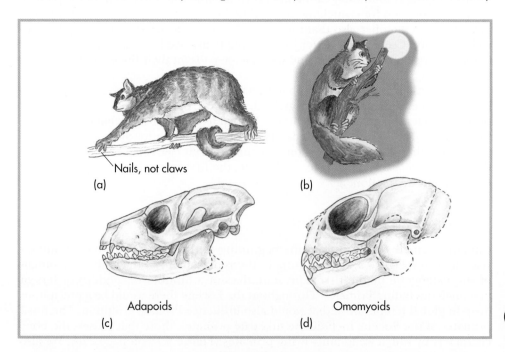

FIGURE 9.18   Adapoids and omomyoids are the first "true" primates. Both have a postorbital bar. Omomyoids have shorter snouts.

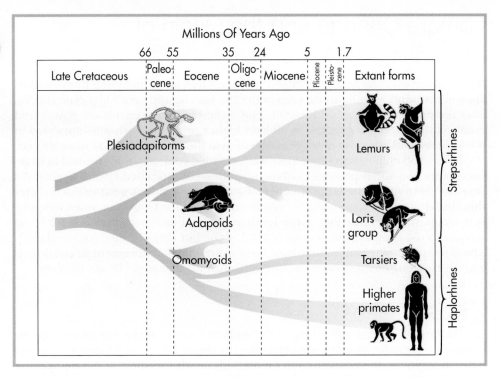

FIGURE 9.19 Possible relationships between fossil and living primates: Plesiadapiforms may or may not be primates. Adapoids are probably ancestral to living strepsirhines, and omomyoids to living haplorhines.

regarded as the ancestors of tarsiers. However, omomyoids are similar to tarsiers and other haplorhines, suggesting that omomyoids may have been ancestral to all haplorhines rather than only to tarsiers.

The omomyoids were even more diverse than the adapoids. Omomyoids were smaller-bodied primates weighing 1 oz to 5 lbs (30 g to 2.2 kg) that ate diets of insects and fruit and had larger orbits, probably indicating that they were active at night. Their limb bones probably were evolved for active arboreal quadrupedalism and leaping, like those of living mouse lemurs and galagos (Godinot & Dagosto, 1983). Although they occur in both Eurasia and North America, omomyoids are more abundant in North America.

The geographic distribution of the adapoids and omomyoids in North America and Europe is understandable if you recall the position of the continents in the Eocene. Europe and North America were joined by a broad band of land, and there was little difference in climate from north to south or east to west (see Figure 9.14 on page 215). Thus the distribution of primates from North America to Europe makes sense given that they could have freely walked (or leaped or scampered) between Europe and North America.

Selective Pressures Favoring the Strepsirhine–Haplorhine Split

Again, we may ask what aspects of the environment (what selective pressures) may have favored the divergence of strepsirhine (adapoid) and haplorhine (omomyoid) lineages. We know from molecular data that the groups diverged around 58 million years ago, but anatomically they are similar in some aspects throughout the Eocene Epoch. Clues from teeth and bones suggest that adapoids and omomyoids (that is, early strepsirhines and haplorhines) divided up the available food resources, thus avoiding competition. Adapoids ate fruit and leaves and relied more on their sense of smell (remember their longer snouts). Omomyoids focused on fruit and insects and had a shorter snout. From these original differences, the haplorhines eventually diverged quite far from the original primate niche.

FIGURE 9.20 *Darwinius masillae* is a remarkably complete adapoid primate from Messel in Germany. The discoverers argue that it is a haplorhine ancestor. Photo courtesy of Jørn H. Hurum: Copyright Per Aas, Natural History Museum, Oslo, Norway.

Climate Change and the Origin of Monkeys and Apes

Representatives of the higher primates (monkeys and apes, including humans) first appeared around 34 million years ago in the late Eocene and early Oligocene epochs, after the strepsirhine–haplorhine split. The earliest higher primates are generalized monkeys that probably gave rise to all later higher primates. Early apes appeared in the Miocene and were also more generalized than their living apes and more diverse.

Around 36 million years ago, there was a decided cold snap that resulted in large-scale extinction and replacement of many species—the so-called *Grande Coupure* (or "big cut" because of the large number of animal groups that went extinct). After this, the temperature continued to decline until late in the Oligocene when temperature rose just a bit, returning to the levels at the beginning of the epoch (so it was still quite cold compared with most of the Eocene but warm by modern standards). These temperature changes may have been caused by the movement of continents and the resulting changes in ocean and wind currents that alter climate patterns.

The First Monkeys?

Like all large-scale climatic changes, the marked cooling at the end of the Eocene created both challenges and opportunities for the animal populations alive at the time. In response, the adapoids and omomyoids nearly vanished, as did many other mammals. Monkeys first appeared in the Oligocene. Remember from Chapter 7 that all monkeys, apes, and humans share certain anatomical characters, including greater enclosure of the orbits, smaller snouts, fewer teeth, a fused frontal bone and a fused mandible, and larger body size (Figure 9.21). The molecular evidence tells

HAPLORHINE (Cebus Monkey)

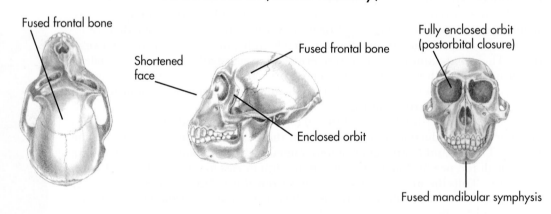

Fused frontal bone

Shortened face

Fused frontal bone

Enclosed orbit

Fully enclosed orbit (postorbital closure)

Fused mandibular symphysis

STREPSIRHINE (Lemur)

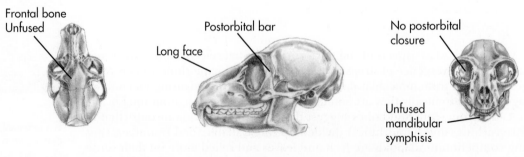

Frontal bone Unfused

Postorbital bar

Long face

No postorbital closure

Unfused mandibular symphisis

FIGURE 9.21 The skulls of living haplorhines differ from those of strepsirhines by having enlarged brains, an enclosed orbit, and a fused frontal and mandible among other differences. Not to scale.

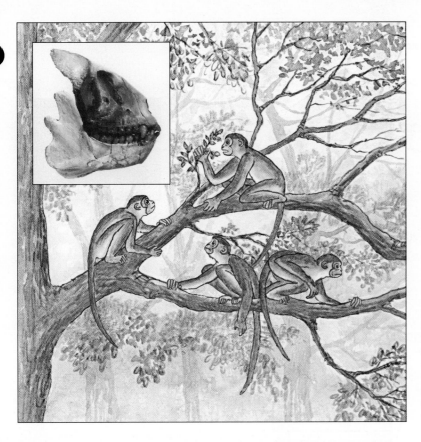

FIGURE 9.22 *Apidium* may be ancestral to all later higher primates and is reconstructed as looking like a small-bodied monkey. The genus has the skeleton of an arboreal quadruped and a 2:1:3:3 dental formula. A fossilized skull of *Apidium phiomense* (inset), a primitive anthropoid and a relative of monkeys and apes, shows a surprisingly powerful mandible and a saggital crest on top of its cranium.

us that the first monkeys occurred between 58 and 40 million years ago, after the split between tarsiers and anthropoids and before New World and Old World monkeys diverged.

The fossil record provides two windows into the origin of anthropoids. One is in the Eocene of China, the other in North Africa and the Middle East. A strong candidate for ancestor of the earliest anthropoids is the Eocene *Eosimias* from China (Beard et al., 1994). These are very small tarsier-sized (about 3.5 oz, 100 g) animals that include several genera living from about 45 million years ago in China to about 32 million years ago in Pakistan. The anatomy of the jaws, teeth, and ankle bones suggest they form the very base of the anthropoid radiation, before its diversification into platyrrhines (New World monkeys) and catarrhines (and between Old World monkeys and apes, including humans). A possible basal member of this family, *Anthrasimias,* was recently discovered in India and is perhaps as much as 55 million years old (Bajpai et al., 2008). The African anthropoids may be descended from those in Asia (Seiffert et al., 2005).

Much of what we know about the evolution of higher primates in the late Eocene and early Oligocene comes from the research of Elwyn Simons' team at the Fayum depression in Egypt. The Fayum region today is in the inhospitable Sahara Desert, but during the Eocene and Oligocene it was a lushly forested area surrounding a large river system that supported a great diversity of tropical fauna and flora. At the end of the Eocene and the early Oligocene we find at least three families of early anthropoids at the Fayum: the Parapithecidae, the Oligopithecidae, and the Propliopithecidae. Like living monkeys, these early anthropoids possessed advanced features of the skull and jaws, including a fused frontal bone, a fused lower jaw, and postorbital closure, that distinguish them from strepsirhines (Figures 9.21 and 9.22).The Parapithecidae includes the genus *Apidium* (Figure 9.22), which possessed three premolars in each quadrant of its jaws, suggesting that it predated the split between New World monkeys (with three premolars) and Old World monkeys (with two premolars). Unlike the parapithecids, both the oligopithecids and the propliopithecids had the 2:1:2:3 dental formula of living Old World higher primates,

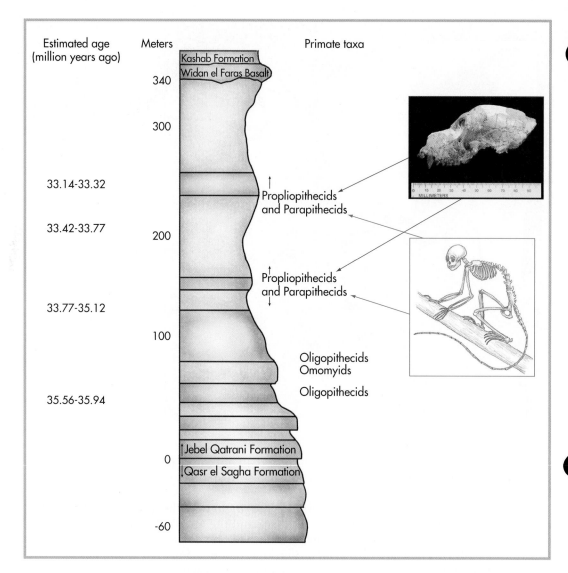

FIGURE 9.23 Stratigraphic section of the Fayum shows the relative age of early anthropoid fossils. The primates include the potential ancestor for all anthropoids (*Apidium,* a parapithecid) and the potential ancestor for all Old World monkeys and apes (*Aegyptopithecus*, a propliopithecid).

suggesting that they postdate the split (Figure 9.23). One propliopithecid, *Aegyptopithecus*, could have been ancestral to later Old World monkeys and apes. Thus, the early anthropoids of the Fayum reveal a radiation of early monkeys, some of which (*Apidium*) may have been ancestral to all later anthropoids, but others (*Aegyptopithecus*) may have been early representatives of the Old World higher primates, before the divergence of Old World monkeys, apes, and humans (Figure 9.24).

New World Monkeys

How monkeys got to South America is still something of a mystery. When these primates first appear around 25–40 million years ago, there is no easy route to the New World. South America was an island continent during the early part of the Cenozoic; the connection to Central and North America, via the Panamanian Isthmus, was established less than 5 million years ago by sea level changes (see Figure 9.17 on page 218). New World monkeys could have originated from Eocene adapoids or omomyoids in North America or from the most primitive anthropoids of Africa. Both required a water crossing. Because the Atlantic Ocean was not as wide in the late Eocene as it is today and because molecular evidence suggests that the two groups split recently (40 million

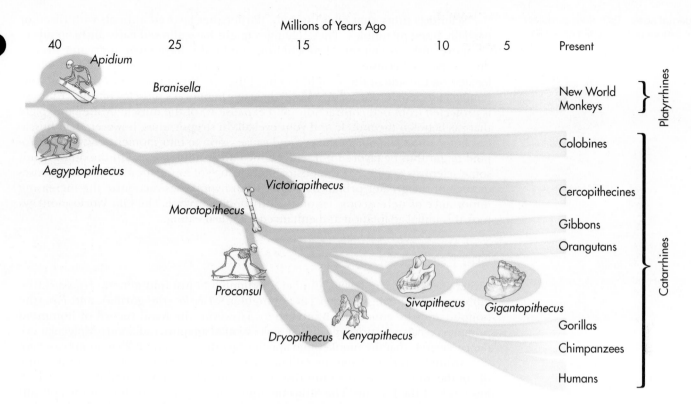

FIGURE 9.24 Proposed relationships between living and fossil platyrrhines and catarrhines.

years ago), most scientists currently support a model that supposes an *Apidium*-like ancestor "rafting over" from Africa to South America during the late Eocene or early Oligocene (Hartwig, 1994). We know that during floods animals get isolated on floating mats of vegetation and are carried to sea. This even happened to humans during the recent tsunamis in Indonesia (2004) and Japan (2011). Early monkeys could have reached the New World in this way. However they got there, in the early and middle Miocene we see an increasingly rich fossil record of monkeys in the New World.

Old World Monkeys

According to DNA comparisons, Old World monkeys and apes shared a common ancestor about 25 million years ago. The fossil record tells us that ancestor had anatomical features shared by both monkeys and apes, such as a bony ear tube and presence of two rather than three premolars, but lacked characters unique to each group, such as the bilophodont molars characteristic of modern Old World monkeys and the suspensory shoulder characteristic of modern apes.

The earliest fossil evidence of a lineage leading just to Old World monkeys is the family Victoriapithecidae from Uganda and Kenya that lived between 19 and 15 million years ago, thus predating the split between the subfamilies of the modern leaf-eating Colobinae and fruit-eating Cercopithecinae (Benefit, 1999). Approximately 12 million years ago, Victoriapithecids were replaced by true Colobines and Cercopithecines.

What Favored the Origin of Anthropoids?

The fossil evidence seems to suggest the early monkeys, such as *Victoriapithecus*, were successful because they were able to chew a tougher diet and better protect their eyes; their mandibles were fused into a single bony unit, and their orbits were completely enclosed by bone. What selective pressures could these changes reflect?

dental apes   Early apes exhibiting Y-5 molar patterns but monkey-like postcranial skeletons.

Scientists think that chewing on a harder diet favored animals with fused or partially fused mandibles. These changes might have allowed early anthropoids to eat more and grow larger. More chewing might also have favored greater protection of the eye because one of the main chewing muscles, the temporalis muscle, is located on the side of the skull just behind the eye. If you place your finger on your temple and clench your teeth you will feel your temporalis muscle contract. Your eye is protected from that contraction (and expansion) of the muscle by the bone plate that sits between the muscle and your eyeball. In strepsirhines, however, that muscle can bulge into the globe of the eye and cause vision to blur momentarily. An anthropoid might thus be favored if it had a bone cup around its eye. On the other hand, some scientists argue that the postorbital closure of anthropoids arose as a consequence of the greater orbital frontality. Both hypotheses recognize the increasing importance of stereoscopic vision to anthropoid survival. The Old World monkeys took this initial adaptation and enhanced it for leaf eating.

The Earliest Apes

Living ape species are few in number and limited to just four genera: *Hylobates* (the gibbons and Siamangs), *Pongo* (the orangutan), *Gorilla* (the gorilla), and *Pan* (the bonobo and the common chimpanzee). However, the fossil record of hominoid primates reveals a surprisingly diverse succession of adaptive radiations. Molecular evidence suggests that the monkey and ape lineages diverged about 25 million years ago.

Around this time, from the end of the Oligocene (around 24 MYA) to the middle of the Miocene, temperature rose again gradually, although it remained well below levels of the Eocene. The Miocene hominoids provide a picture of the ape and human family tree before it was so drastically pruned back to just the few branches that exist today (See Figure 9.24 on page 225). Fossil apes first appeared during the early Miocene, approximately 23–16 million years ago. At that time, hominoids were almost totally restricted to Africa, where they are well known from sites in Kenya, Uganda, Ethiopia, and Namibia.

On the forested continent of Africa lived dozens of genera of early apes with very monkey-like postcranial skeletons. In fact, we might call them **dental apes** to show that we recognize them as apes based mostly on their teeth (Figure 9.25). Unlike the specialized, high-crested bilophodont molars of Old World monkeys, all apes, including the dental apes possess molars with five rounded cusps, connected by a pattern of Y-shaped fissures or grooves (Figure 9.26). The dental apes were small-bodied compared with modern apes, they lacked a suspensory shoulder for brachiating, and they walked on the soles of their feet rather than on their knuckles. The best known of the early dental apes is the genus *Proconsul* (Figure 9.25), which lived in Africa about 18–20 million years ago and ranged in size from approximately 33 to 110 lb (15–50 kg). But another 20-million-year-old ape, *Morotopithecus bishopi*, may be a

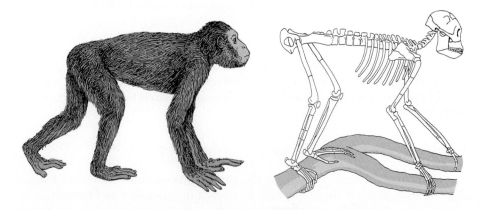

FIGURE 9.25   The dental ape *Proconsul* has an apelike dentition but monkey-like skeleton.

better candidate for the last common ancestor of apes and humans (Gebo et al., 1997). Unlike *Proconsul, Morotopithecus* possessed the short and stiff back and suspensory shoulder anatomy of the modern living apes (MacLatchy et al., 2000) (Figure 9.27).

The first fossil apes linked to living African apes appear in the middle Miocene, and approximately 12–5 million years ago (in the middle and late Miocene), larger-bodied hominoids diversified and dispersed into Europe and Asia. For example, the recently discovered *Pierolapithecus* appears in Spain about 12.5 million years ago (Figure 9.27). *Sivapithecus* (after the Hindu figure Siva) from the late Miocene of India and Pakistan is a relative of the modern orangutan (Figure 9.28 on page 228). A distant relative of *Sivapithecus* named *Gigantopithecus* roamed in Asia from the late Miocene until the middle Pleistocene. *Gigantopithecus* was the largest primate that ever lived, perhaps as large as 660 lb (300 kg), and co-existed with *Homo erectus* for a time (Figure 9.29 on page 228).

Although we have identified many apes from the Miocene, we have little fossil evidence for the direct ancestors of orangutans, gorillas, chimpanzees, or bonobos. The dearth of ape fossils is related in part to the moist tropical forests in which they live. In these climates, biological processes often completely destroy the skeleton after death.

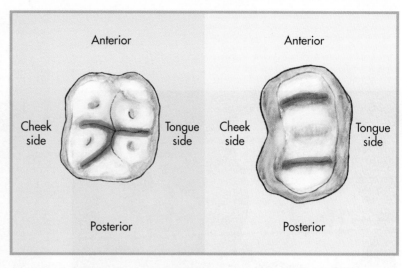

FIGURE 9.26   The Y-5 molar pattern (left) characterizes the ape, whereas bilophodont molars (right) characterize the Old World monkey. Both have a 2:1:2:3 dental formula.

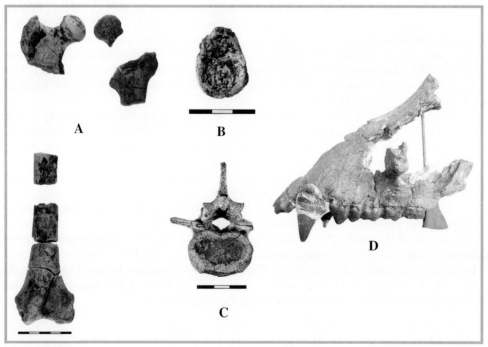

(a)

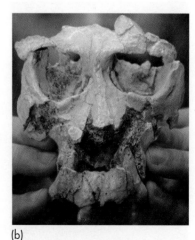

(b)

FIGURE 9.27   (a) *Morotopithecus* is the earliest fossil ape to show postcranial adaptations similar to those of living apes. (b) *Pierolapithecus catalunicus* may be an ancestor of great apes and humans. Its postcranial skeleton shows adaptations for suspensory locomotion, and its skull shows some features of living apes.

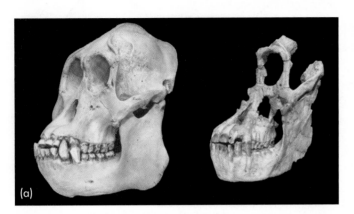

FIGURE 9.28   (a) *Sivapithecus* is a Miocene ape (right) with anatomical similarities to orangutans (left). (b) Siwaliks, Pakistan, where *Sivapithecus* was found.

Selection Pressures and the Divergence of Monkeys and Apes

Monkeys and apes differ in specific anatomical ways related to their form of locomotion, so their origin is likely to be related in part to this shift in locomotor pattern. Monkeys have bodies shaped more or less like your dog or cat: The thorax is narrow from side to side but deep from back to front. Apes are the opposite, having wide but not very deep thoraxes. This change may be related to the origin of a particular kind of suspensory locomotion called *brachiation* that is used by living gibbons and siamangs and probably by the common ancestor of all apes. Because it is advantageous for a brachiator to have an arm positioned well to the side of its body, apes with a wide thorax (and longer clavicles or collar-bones) were favored. And because the arm is often over the animal's head, the humeral head is round. The scapula is rotated from the animal's side onto its back and elongated from head to tail (Figure 9.30). And the ape's back is stiff.

The apes appear to have evolved their specialized locomotor capacity in the early middle Miocene (remember *Morotopithecus*), when forests were widespread. Later the African apes modified this brachiating anatomy for knuckle-walking so that in the middle Miocene, when body size increased and apes became more terrestrial, we see evidence of knuckle-walking anatomy. Orangutans eventually become quadrumanous, using all four hands in locomotion.

Although part of the origin of the living hominoid pattern is related to locomotor shifts, you will recall that the first distinctive evidence of apes in the fossil record is from the detention of the groups we call *dental apes.* This suggest that the initial change in the ape lineage was a dietary shift, probably to eating more fruits. In the changing environment of the Miocene we see monkeys focusing increasingly on more leafy diets and early apes focusing more on fruits. Later apes, such as the gorilla, return to a fibrous diet, modifying the original ape niche.

The Monkey's Tale: What Happened to Primate Diversity in the Miocene?

FIGURE 9.29   Reconstruction of *Gigantopithecus,* a fossil ape, towers over artist Bill Munns.

What selective factors might explain the decreasing diversity of apes and the increasing diversity of monkeys during the Miocene? During the Miocene, new niches became available in grasslands and wooded grasslands. Animals that once lived in the forest had a few possible routes to survive: Stick with the same old pattern but reduce numbers of individuals (after all, the forested areas were smaller) or strike out into a new area with new resources that might favor different adaptations. Animals that reproduce more quickly (i.e., those that are **r-selected,** with each female having many offspring during her lifetime at short interberth intervals, and making less maternal investment per offspring) could colonize areas faster and rebound from population declines more quickly. Monkeys reproduce more quickly than apes and so had an advantage in colonizing new areas. Apes are strongly **k-selected,** exhibiting the opposite reproductive characteristics of r-selected animals. In addition, the shape of the monkey thorax and limbs is more conducive to evolution of quick terrestrial locomotion. These attributes seem to have favored the monkeys over the apes during the late Miocene (Figure 9.31 on pages 230–231). Only one group of apes seems to have overcome the issues of locomotion and reproduction to move into new, more open habitats. This lineage eventually evolved into humans.

Molecular Evolution in Primates

Throughout the chapter we have presented the picture of primate evolution that can be drawn from fossil remains and augmented it with estimated divergence times based on molecular evidence. A *molecular phylogeny* is a tree of relatedness among species, or larger taxonomic groupings, based on a gene or protein or even large portions of the entire genome. The structure of the tree provides a visual summary of how similar or dissimilar a given molecule is in any two or more of the taxa represented on the tree.

In 1967, a key advance in molecular phylogenetics occurred when anthropologist Vincent Sarich and biochemist Allan Wilson demonstrated that it was possible to use molecular relationships between species to determine divergence dates in the past; in other words, there existed a **molecular clock,** or a systematic accumulation of genetic differences through time that, if measured, could be used to estimate the amount of time since two groups shared a last common ancestor. A molecular clock needs two things in order to work. First, the clock must be calibrated with a date from the fossil record that corresponds to one of the nodes in the tree. The date for this one node can be used to determine the rate of change in the molecule, which then allows us to date each node in the tree (Figure 9.32 on page 232).

Second, there must be a demonstration of *rate constancy* in the molecule that is used to make the tree: A molecular clock can work only if the molecule is changing at a similar rate in each branch or lineage represented in a phylogeny. Sarich and Wilson proposed a way to demonstrate rate constancy for any protein or gene—a **relative rate test,** or a comparison of the amount of genetic difference between each

r-selected Reproductive strategy in which females have many offspring, interbirth intervals are short, and maternal investment per offspring is low.

k-selected Reproductive strategy in which fewer offspring are produced per female, interbirth intervals are long, and maternal investment is high.

molecular clock A systematic accumulation of genetic change that can be used to estimate the time of divergence between two groups if relative rates are constant and a calibration point from the fossil record is available.

relative rate test A means of determining whether molecular evolution has been occurring at a constant rate in two lineages by comparing whether these lineages are equidistant from an outgroup.

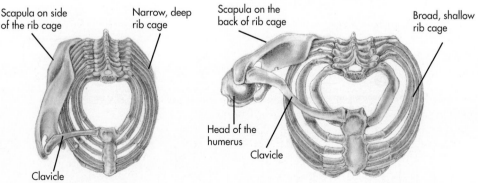

FIGURE 9.30 The thorax of apes, including humans, is broad but shallow in contrast to the narrower, deeper chest of the monkey.

FIGURE 9.31

Primate Evolution

Primates or primate ancestors appear around 63 million years ago and diversify into niches created by the extinction of the dinosaurs but do not show most of the anatomical characteristics of living primates. Strepsirhine and haplorhine lineages appear in the early Eocene. The first monkeys with postorbital closure appear in the Oligocene. Apes diversify in the Miocene but are rare by the Pliocene.

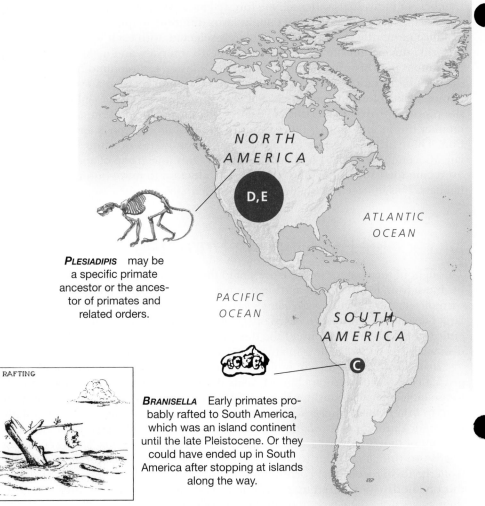

PLESIADIPIS may be a specific primate ancestor or the ancestor of primates and related orders.

RAFTING

BRANISELLA Early primates probably rafted to South America, which was an island continent until the late Pleistocene. Or they could have ended up in South America after stopping at islands along the way.

ISLAND STEPPING STONES

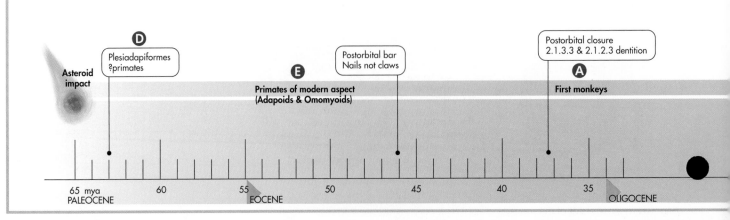

D Plesiadapiformes ?primates

Asteroid impact

E Primates of modern aspect (Adapoids & Omomyoids)

Postorbital bar Nails not claws

Postorbital closure 2.1.3.3 & 2.1.2.3 dentition

A First monkeys

65 mya — 60 — 55 — 50 — 45 — 40 — 35
PALEOCENE   EOCENE   OLIGOCENE

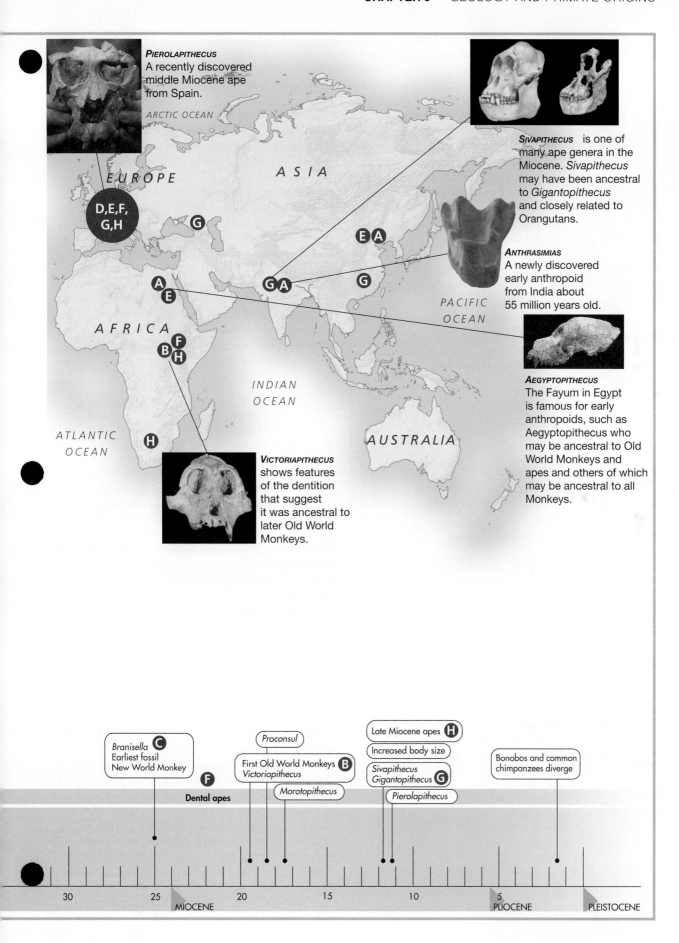

PIEROLAPITHECUS
A recently discovered middle Miocene ape from Spain.

SIVAPITHECUS is one of many ape genera in the Miocene. *Sivapithecus* may have been ancestral to *Gigantopithecus* and closely related to Orangutans.

ANTHRASIMIAS
A newly discovered early anthropoid from India about 55 million years old.

AEGYPTOPITHECUS
The Fayum in Egypt is famous for early anthropoids, such as Aegyptopithecus who may be ancestral to Old World Monkeys and apes and others of which may be ancestral to all Monkeys.

VICTORIAPITHECUS shows features of the dentition that suggest it was ancestral to later Old World Monkeys.

ARCTIC OCEAN

EUROPE

ASIA

AFRICA

PACIFIC OCEAN

INDIAN OCEAN

ATLANTIC OCEAN

AUSTRALIA

Branisella **C**
Earliest fossil New World Monkey

Proconsul

Late Miocene apes **H**

Increased body size

First Old World Monkeys **B**
Victoriapithecus

Sivapithecus **G**
Gigantopithecus

Bonobos and common chimpanzees diverge

F

Morotopithecus

Pierolapithecus

Dental apes

30   25   20   15   10   5

MIOCENE   PLIOCENE   PLEISTOCENE

primate species of interest and a member of an outgroup, such as a dog. If the DNA of each primate is equally different from a dog's DNA, then there must be rate constancy within primates; if there had been a slowdown in the rate of change on one lineage, then that lineage would have shown fewer differences from the outgroup DNA than the others did.

Not all genetic systems can be used as molecular clocks because some systems are influenced by natural selection, lineage-specific rate changes, and other factors that make them inappropriate for timing evolutionary events. A study by Navin Elango and colleagues (2006) examined the effect of generation length difference on evolutionary rates for long DNA sequences of several human and chimpanzee chromosomes. Using either the rhesus monkey or baboon as an outgroup, the relative rate test showed that the rate of evolution in humans was slightly slower than for chimpanzees, a difference Elango and colleagues attributed to the fact that humans have a longer generation length (i.e., there have been fewer "human" than "chimpanzee" generations since the two lineages split). Several different proteins, genes, and noncoding regions of DNA have proven to be useful as molecular clocks. Molecular phylogenies sometimes have been controversial, especially when they do not agree with phylogenies determined by traditional anatomical and paleontological methods. However, only one history is being reconstructed and ultimately molecular and paleontological phylogenies must agree with each other.

A Primate Molecular Phylogeny

In 1998, Morris Goodman, a pioneer of molecular anthropology, published a comprehensive phylogeny of primates based primarily on evolution in the *beta-globin* gene cluster on chromosome 11 (in humans) (Goodman et al., 1998; Goodman, 1999). Beta-globin is one of the polypeptide chains that make up hemoglobin. Goodman's phylogeny is based on gene sequences from more than 60 primate species, calibrated with several dates from the fossil record (Figure 9.33). In terms of the largest branches and major nodes, this molecular phylogeny, which relies on multiple calibrations from the fossil record, fairly accurately represents current ideas about the major phylogenetic events in primate evolution. However, controversy still remains regarding the synthesis of fossil and molecular data in determining primate phylogenetics of closely related groups of primate species (Stewart & Disotell, 1998).

We have referred to these divergence time estimates in earlier sections and bring them together here as an overview of the timing of primate evolution. Goodman's phylogeny places the last common ancestor (LCA) of all primates at 63 million years ago. It is at this point that we get the deepest split within primates, that between the strepsirhines and the haplorhines. Within the strepsirhines, there was a split between the lemurs and lorises 45 million years ago. Within the haplorhines the tarsiers branched off from the anthropoid lineage at 58 million years ago, and the major split within the anthropoids, that between the platyrhines and the catarrhines,

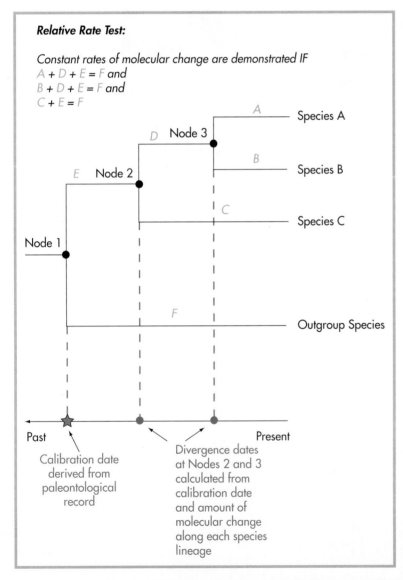

Relative Rate Test:

Constant rates of molecular change are demonstrated IF
$A + D + E = F$ and
$B + D + E = F$ and
$C + E = F$

FIGURE 9.32 Relative rate test, calibrating the molecular clock, and calculating divergence dates. Letters *A–F* correspond to amounts of molecular change or molecular distance along each lineage.

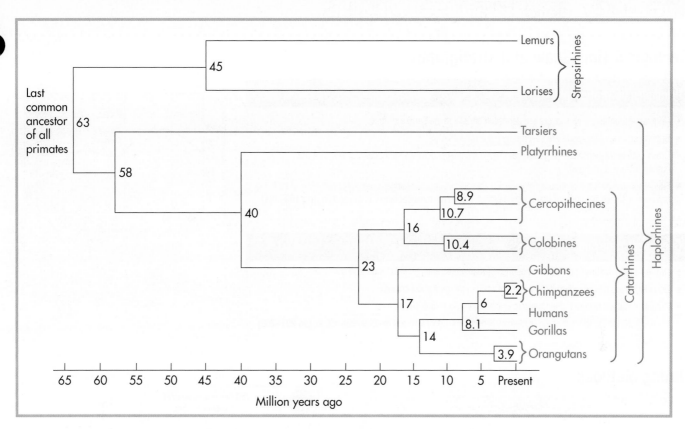

FIGURE 9.33 Relationships and dates of divergence of living primate groups based on molecular and DNA comparisons (Data from Goodman, M., 1999).

occurred 40 million years ago. Within the catarrhines, the division between the cercopithecoids and the apes occurred 25 million years ago, just at the beginning of the Miocene. Within the Old World monkeys, cercopithecines and colobines split about 16 million years ago. Within the apes, lesser apes (gibbons and siamangs) split about 17 million years ago from the great apes. African and Asian great apes split around 14 million years ago, gorillas split from the chimp–human clade about 8 million years ago, and human and chimp lineages split about 6 million years ago. Chimps and bonobos split about 2.2 million years ago.

The fossil record of primate evolution provides a full view of the history of primate relationships, adaptations, and ecology. In addition to documenting the evolutionary history of nonhuman primates, this record sets the stage for the emergence of the lineage that ultimately led to humans. In the next four chapters we explore the fossil record for hominin evolution and the selective pressures that shaped the evolution of our ancestors.

Geology and Primate Origins

Geological Time Scale and Stratigraphy

Principles of Stratigraphy

- Original horizontality—rock layers are deposited parallel to the Earth's surface.
- Superposition—older layers are covered by more recent layers.
- Cross-cutting relationships—a geological feature must exist before another can cut across it (the cutting feature is younger).
- Faunal succession—the community of fossilized animals in a section changes predictably with time; older fauna are lower in the section; once a species goes extinct, it does not reappear higher in the section. **[pp 199–201]**

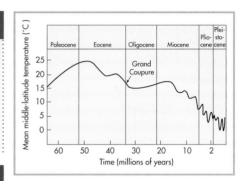

Geological Time Scale

- Divides Earth's history into nested categories of time: eons, eras, periods, and epochs.
- Boundaries are placed where large shifts are seen in the geological column.
- Primate evolution occurs in the Cenozoic Era (the past 65 million years).
- We live in the Holocene epoch of the Quaternary period of the Cenozoic era of the Phanerozoic Eon. **[pp 201–203]**

Dating Methods

Relative Dating

- Uses the principles of stratigraphy to estimate age relative to something else.
- It includes lithostratigraphy, tephrostratigraphy, biostratigraphy, and chemical techniques within sites. **[pp 204–207]**

Calibrated Relative Dating

- Uses geological or chemical processes that can be calibrated to a chronological age if certain conditions are known.
- One technique is paleomagnetism. **[p 207]**

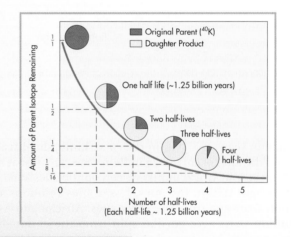

Chronometric Dating

- Chronometric dating uses a clock of some sort to measure age in years before the present.
- Radiometric clocks are based on the radioactive decay of isotopes.
- Radiometric techniques include radiocarbon, potassium-argon, argon/argon, fission track, cosmogenic radionuclides, U-series, and electron trap techniques. **[pp 208–214]**

Reconstructing Ancient Environments

Climate Reconstructions for the Cenozoic

- Global climate has cooled and dried dramatically during primate evolution.
- The Paleocene and Eocene epochs were substantially warmer than today.
- In the Oligocene there was a colder shift in climate (but still warmer than today).
- The Miocene Epoch saw cooling, drying, and disruption of forests.
- The Pliocene and Pleistocene epochs began glacial periods.
- Climate shifts imposed selective pressures on the primates and other animals alive at the time. **[pp 215–218]**

Origin of Primates

Plesiadapiforms

- Questionable primates that lack certain primate features: no postorbital bar, many have specialized teeth and a diastema, and they probably had claws rather than nails.
- They appear in the Paleocene of Montana and elsewhere. **[pp 218–220]**

Selective Forces at Work

- The visual predation hypothesis suggests primates originated as arboreal quadrupeds preying on insects, possibly specializing in using the smallest branches of the trees. This niche selected for depth perception and grasping hands. **[p 221]**

Adapids and Omomyids

- Adapids and Omomyids are the true primates of the Eocene Epoch.
- They possess primate features such as a postorbital bar, greater orbital frontality, nails not claws, and an opposable big toe.
- Adapids occur in both the New and Old World but are most abundant in the Old. The opposite is true of Omomyids.
- Adapids probably gave rise to strepsirhines (lemurs and lorises).
- Omomyids probably gave rise to haplorhines. **[pp 220–221]**

Monkeys and Apes

Early Anthropoids

- Primitive anthropoids first appear in the Eocene to the Oligocene epoch.
- Many possess fused mandibles and fused frontal bones, postorbital closure.
- Genera possibly ancestral to all later anthropoids include *Eosimias* (China), *Apidium* (Africa).
- Genera possibly ancestral to all later Old World monkeys (OWM) and apes include *Aegyptopithecus* (Africa). **[pp 222–224]**

Platyrrhines (New World Monkeys)

- Platyrrhines appear at 25–30 MYA when South America is an island.
- Platyrrhines may originate from either African or Asian anthropoids or North American primates of the Eocene. **[pp 224–225]**

Old World Monkeys (OWM)

- *Victoriapithecus* may be ancestral to all later OWM.
- Colobines and cercopithecines diverge about 12 MYA (based on DNA).
- Monkeys are few in the early Miocene and abundant by the late Miocene. **[pp 225–226]**

Apes

- The early apes appear around 23–16 MYA in Africa and Asia.
- Early dental apes such as *Proconsul* have postcranial skeletons similar to monkeys and the Y-5 dental pattern of apes.
- True apes show wide, not deep, chests, and a suspensory shoulder probably reflecting brachiation or a brachiating ancestor.
- Apes are abundant in the early Miocene and very few by the late Miocene. **[p 226]**

Selective Forces at Work

- The origin of anthropoids in the Oligocene may reflect adaptations to a tougher.
- Changing patterns of monkey and ape diversity in the Miocene seems to reflect drying climate and loss of forested areas; r-selected monkeys take advantage of new opportunities, but k-selected apes are more sensitive to change. **[pp 228–229]**

My AnthroLab CONNECTIONS

Watch. Listen. View. Explore. Read.

MyAnthroLab is designed just for you. Each chapter features a customized study plan to help you learn and review key concepts and terms. Dynamic visual activities, videos, and readings found in the multimedia library will enhance your learning experience.

Resources from this Chapter:

Watch on myanthrolab

- ▶ *Fossil Formation*
- ▶ *Geological Time Scale*

View on myanthrolab
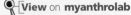
- ▶ *Radiometric Dating Overview*
- ▶ *Primate Evolution*

Explore on myanthrolab In MySearchLab, enter the Anthropology database to find relevant and recent scholarly and popular press publications. For this chapter, enter the following keywords: Dating, Geology, Stratigraphy, Primate evolution, Climate

Read on myanthrolab
- ▶ *Radiocarbon Dating's Final Frontier* by Michael Balter
- ▶ *Dating Archaeological Materials* by R.E. Taylor
- ▶ *Planet of The Apes* by David R. Begun

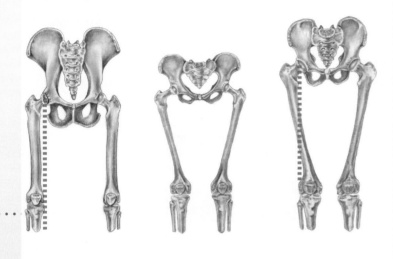

Chapter 10 Preview

After reading this chapter, you should be able to:

- Outline the anatomical changes necessary for hominin bipedalism.

- Discuss the behavioral differences from ape to human.

- Analyze the anatomical features that define the hominins.

- Detail the various species of the genus *Australopithecus*, including their anatomical characteristics, temporal and geographic range.

- Discuss the evolutionary relationships among the species in the genus *Australopithecus* and begin to explain their evolutionary radiation in Africa.

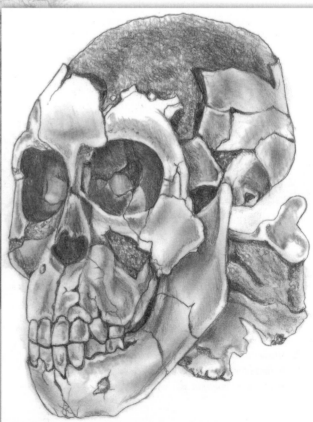

Early Hominins and *Australopithecus*

10

As the sun rose over the treetops, the young hominin opened her eyes reluctantly, rolled over in her leafy nest, and yawned. By the time the sun had moved fully above the horizon, she was climbing out of the tree and shimmying down the trunk. Watching her do this, you might easily have mistaken her for a chimpanzee. But as she reached the ground and stepped away from the tree, she assumed an upright posture. She walked purposefully on two legs across a clearing to some fruit trees. There she joined a small cluster of others like her, some of them perched in branches, others collecting fruits that had fallen to the ground. She sniffed a fruit for ripeness and popped it in her mouth. She looked over at the alpha male of the group, an imposing creature much bigger than she was with large canine teeth, a prominent brow above his eyes, and a muscular body carried about on equally muscular legs.

As the day warmed up, the group headed toward some low, densely forested hills a kilometer away. There were patches of grassland amid the expanse of forest, but they stuck to the comforting safety of the trees. Only last month, in this same spot, a lion had ambushed a young female. She had screamed in fear and tried to escape to the safety of the tree, and the group came to her aid, but too late: The lion had caught and eaten her.

Although predators were a constant worry, so too was the possibility that when they reached the fruiting trees, a neighboring group of their own species would have gotten there first. The battles that raged between the two groups were as dangerous for them as any lion, and many family members and allies had been brutally injured. Today they reached the trees without competition and settled in for a meal of ripe fruits.

We will never know exactly how the earliest humans looked or behaved. But biological anthropologists have a number of lines of evidence that help them reconstruct the likeliest path from an ape ancestor to a hominin. These include anatomy, living primate behavior, and genetic relationships. Recall from Chapters 7 and 9 the adaptations that characterize the living African apes, our closest relatives, and the fossil apes. These adaptations include a large brain–body size ratio and extended growth period compared with monkeys, anatomical features related to knucklewalking, and those related to a brachiator ancestor (including thorax shape, a highly mobile shoulder, and the absence of a tail). In a remarkable adaptive shift at the end of the Miocene, this combination of features gave way to a new suite of traits in a new tribe, the Hominini (Hominins include humans and our extinct ancestors after the split from the last common ancestor with chimps.) The most noticeable anatomical development in the early hominin lineage is in a suite of traits related to bipedality, along with slightly smaller canine teeth. The dramatic expansion of the brain that characterize living humans came millions of years later.

This chapter is about the quest to understand the origin of the earliest humans. First we review the basic anatomical changes that natural selection produced in the bipedal skeleton. Then we explore scenarios for why such a bipedal primate might have evolved. Many of the time-honored assumptions about human origins have been challenged in recent years, and we review some of the controversy. We identify the adaptations of the very earliest hominins, including *Ardipithecus,* and how we can recognize their fossils. Then we explore the radiation of the genus *Australopithecus*, the newest discoveries, and the diverse array of dietary adaptations and favored habitats these species exhibit. At the end of the chapter we consider who the likely candidates are for the last common ancestor of *Homo* to set the stage for Chapters 11–13, in which we explore the evolution of our own genus.

((•─Listen to the **Podcast** "Study: Human Ancestors Walked Upright Early" on **myanthrolab**

Becoming a Biped

Walking upright is an extremely rare way to move about. In the entire history of life on Earth, truly bipedal posture and walking have appeared in just a few lineages. Of some 4,000 living mammals, only humans are habitual striding bipeds today. Although a number of other primates, from sifakas to chimpanzees, stand upright occasionally while walking or feeding, only hominins exhibit bipedal behavior and the extensive morphological adaptations for striding on two legs.

Anatomical Changes

An animal walking on two legs has to solve several problems not encountered by our four-legged friends. Critical among these is the issue of balancing the body's weight over two limbs (while standing) and often over one limb (while walking) (Figure 10.1). Think of the quadruped as a four-legged table: The center of gravity falls in the area between the four legs, and the body weight is distributed equally over all four limbs (while standing). Remove one leg and it is still possible to balance the table's weight by shifting it to the area between the three legs. But take away two legs, and the task becomes extremely difficult. When an animal that evolved to walk on four legs walks on its two hind limbs instead, it compensates for this lack of support by constantly moving its weight between the remaining limbs. Imagine your dog dancing on its hind limbs for a treat, constantly in motion forward and backward (trying to move under that center of gravity) and standing only briefly, tiring quickly from the constant muscular work. But when you stand,

(a)   (b)   (c)   (d)

FIGURE 10.1   Becoming a biped changes the way an animal balances. The quadruped's center of gravity goes right through its back to the ground, balancing its weight over four legs (a). If the quadruped stands on two legs, it either must bend its knees (b) or fall forward (c). A habitual biped has structural changes in the skeleton so that the center of gravity falls between the two feet when standing with legs extended (d). (After Wolpoff, 1999)

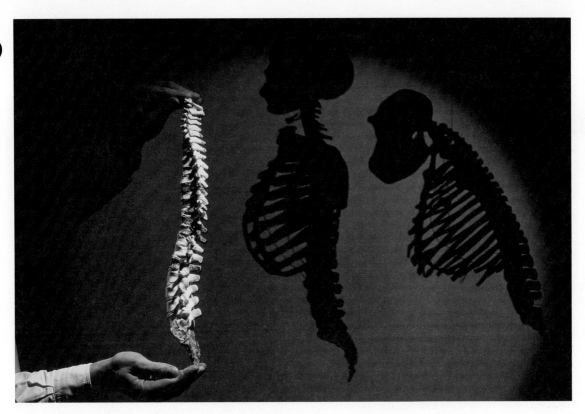

FIGURE 10.2   The spine of a biped has two additional curves in it at the neck and lower back to move the center of gravity over two feet. The ape (quadruped) has a C-shaped spine (far right).

your body weight falls naturally between your two feet—no dancing required. And when you walk, your foot naturally falls directly under your center of gravity. This greater efficiency means that while standing at rest, you burn only a few more calories than you would when lying down. The reasons for these differences are found in the structural changes in our skeleton that directly affect the skull, spine, pelvis, leg, and foot.

The Vertebral Column and Skull

The spine, or **vertebral column,** is made up of a series of bones in the neck (**cervical vertebrae**), thorax (**thoracic vertebrae**), lower back (**lumbar vertebrae**), and pelvic (**sacrum** and **coccyx**) regions (Figure 10.2; Appendix A on page 422). The quadruped has a gently C-shaped curve that makes the thoracic region of the spine slightly convex. The biped has an S-shaped spine made by adding two secondary and opposing curvatures (in the cervical and lumbar regions) to the C-shaped curvature of the quadruped. If you stand a quadruped up on its back legs, the C-shape of its spine tends to put the center of gravity in front of its feet, causing the animal to fall forward (or dance to avoid falling). The secondary curvatures in the bipedal spine compensate for that C-curve and bring the center of gravity back closer to the hips, ultimately resting over the biped's two feet.

The weight of the biped is borne down the spine to the sacrum, where it passes to the hips, and from there through the two legs. The amount of weight increases as you go down the spine, so the vertebrae of a biped get increasingly large as you approach the lumbar region or lower back. In contrast, weight-bearing doesn't increase along the quadruped's spine, and the vertebral bodies are of nearly equal size in different regions of the spine. These differences can have adverse effects on the biped's body. Lower back problems, especially among pregnant women, are a result of the changes wrought by natural selection on our ancestral skeleton.

vertebral column   The column of bones and cartilaginous disks that houses the spinal cord and provides structural support and flexibility to the body.

cervical vertebrae   The seven neck vertebrae.

thoracic vertebrae   The twelve vertebrae of the thorax that hold the ribs.

lumbar vertebrae   The five vertebrae of the lower back.

sacrum   The fused vertebrae that form the back of the pelvis.

coccyx   The fused tail vertebrae that are very small in humans and apes.

Human

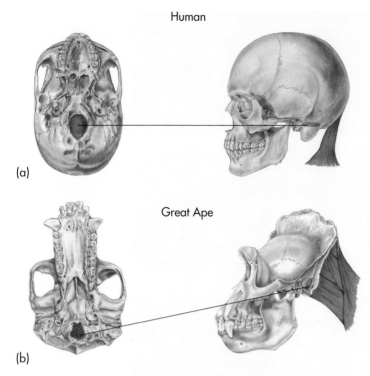

(a)

Great Ape

(b)

FIGURE 10.3 (a) The spine meets the skull from below in a biped, so the foramen magnum, in blue, is directly beneath the skull and the neck muscles run down from the skull. (b) In the ape the spine meets the skull from the back so the foramen magnum is positioned posteriorly and the neck muscles also run posteriorly from the skull.

foramen magnum Hole in the occipital bone through which the spinal cord connects to the brain.

innominate bones (os coxae) The pair of bones that compose the lateral parts of the pelvis; each innominate is made up of three bones that fuse during adolescence.

ischium Portion of the innominate bone that forms the bony underpinning of the rump.

ilium The blade of the innominate to which gluteal muscles attach.

pubis Portion of the innominate that forms the anterior part of the birth canal.

gluteal muscles Gluteus maximus, medius, and minimus, the muscles of walking, which have undergone radical realignment in habitual bipeds.

femoral condyles The enlarged inferior end of the femur that forms the top of the knee joint.

tarsals Foot bones that form the ankle and part of the arches of the foot.

metatarsals Five foot bones that join the tarsals to the toes and form a portion of the longitudinal arch of the foot.

phalanges Bones that form the fingers and toes.

The vertebral column attaches to the bottom of the skull of a biped rather than to the back as it does in quadrupeds. So the junction of the spinal cord and the brain, which occurs through a hole called the **foramen magnum** in the occipital bone, is positioned underneath the skull in bipeds but toward the back of the skull in quadrupeds (Figure 10.3 and Appendix A, page 422). Thus, the occipital bone is a clue for paleoanthropologists about the way in which an extinct animal may have stood and walked.

The Pelvis and Birth Canal The pelvis of hominins was modified by natural selection to keep the body's center of gravity over one foot while walking. The bony pelvis consists of two **innominate bones (os coxae)**, each composed of three other bones (the **ischium**, **ilium**, and **pubis**) that fuse during adolescence, and the sacrum, part of the vertebral column (Figure 10.4 and Appendix A on page 422). The ischium is the bone you sit on. The ilium is the bone you feel when you put your hands on your hips. And the pubis is the anterior bony portion of the pelvis in the pubic region.

The pelvis of a biped is basin-shaped with a short, broad ilium that runs from the posterior to the anterior of the animal. The quadruped ilium is long and flat and situated on the back of the animal. The basin shape supports abdominal organs that tend to be pulled downward by gravity, and it places key locomotor and postural muscles in a better mechanical position. Most important are the anterior **gluteal muscles** (gluteus minimus and medius), which attach to the ilium and are rotated around to the side of the biped. In this position, they connect the ilium to the top of the femur (thigh bone), and when you stand on one limb they contract, pulling the ilium (and the rest of your trunk) toward the support side, so your center of gravity balances over the single foot. The gluteus maximus runs from the back of the ilium to the back of the femur, and when it contracts it keeps your pelvis (and you) from tipping forward in front of your feet (Figure 10.5 and Figure 10.1 on page 238). The shortening and

Human   Great Ape

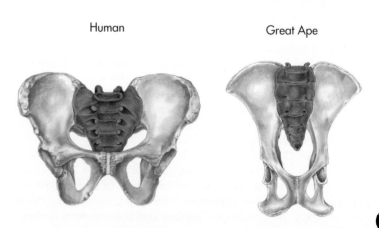

FIGURE 10.4 To maintain balance the bipedal pelvis has a foreshortened ilium and is broader and bowl-shaped. The quadrupedal (ape) pelvis has a long ilium positioned on the back, not the side, of the animal.

broadening of the ilium also moves the hip joint closer to the sacrum. This is good for balance but narrows the birth canal, a problem with which later hominins including ourselves have to contend.

The Leg The broad pelvis places the top of the femur far to the side of the biped. However, when you walk your foot must fall directly below your center of gravity. A straight femur, like that of a quadruped, would place the foot far to the side of the center of gravity. Natural selection favored bipeds with a femur that was angled from the hip into the knee because the angle places the foot below the center of gravity, which saves energy while walking (Figures 10.1 on page 238 and 10.6). However, this configuration creates problems at the knee because the musculature attached to the femur must also act at an angle. When the biped flexes its muscles on the front of the femur in an effort to extend the knee, the muscles pull both superiorly (up) and laterally (out). The patella (knee cap) sits in the tendon of this muscle and is likewise displaced outward. To avoid dislocating the patella, the groove on the femur that the patella sits in is deep, and the outside edge or lip is enlarged in a biped. In addition, to help support the excess body weight going through each limb, the bottom of the femur (**femoral condyles**) is enlarged. The top of the tibia or shin bone is similarly enlarged.

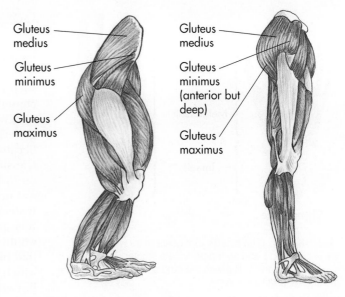

FIGURE 10.5   The gluteal muscles are repositioned in the biped and aid in support. (After Wolpoff, 1999)

The Foot The foot skeleton is composed of three types of bones: **tarsals**, which form the heel and ankle region; **metatarsals;** and **phalanges** (the toes) (Figure 10.7 on page 242). In bipedal walking, the heel strikes first, followed by the rest of the foot. The main propulsive force comes at toe-off, when the big toe pushes off from the ground, and the toes bend strongly backward (dorsiflex). To accommodate toe-off and dorsiflexion, the big toe moves in line with the other toes and becomes much, much larger than the other toes, and all the phalanges shorten and change joint orientation. Imagine the advantage to the biped of shorter toes; it is rather like the difference between walking in floppy clown shoes and wearing shoes with regular-sized toes.

((•─ Listen to the **Podcast** "Fast Feet: A Springy Step Helps Humans Walk" on **myanthrolab**

A biped's foot is stouter than a quadruped's and has arches that accommodate the immense weight put on the two feet. The tarsal bones and big toe are robust and bound tightly together by ligaments, providing stability but decreasing overall flexibility of the foot. The foot has two arches that act as shock absorbers that store and return some of the energy during walking and help to reduce the incidence of fatigue fractures to the biped's lower leg.

Chimpanzee   *Australopithecus*   Human

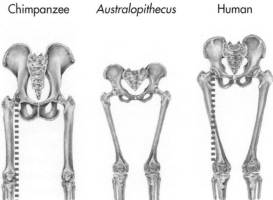

The Arm One advantage of walking on two legs is that it frees the arms to do other things. Carrying objects and tool-making are two activities often associated with the hominin lineage (although they are not exclusive associations). Throughout human evolution, the arm and hand skeleton have changed as a result of their release from locomotor activities and their new use, particularly in tool making. Although early hominins have relatively long arms, through hominin evolution the arms shortened relative to trunk length and assumed modern human proportions sometime after the origin of *Homo erectus*. The thumb and phalanges shorten and become less curved.

FIGURE 10.6   To keep the foot under the center of gravity, the biped's femur is angled from hip to knee. The quadruped femur is not.

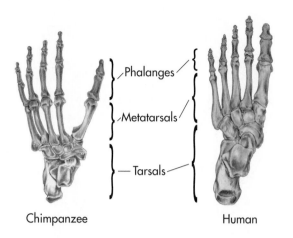

FIGURE 10.7 The biped's foot bears more weight than the quadruped's and so the bones are stouter. The big toe is especially big and in line with the others, and the phalanges are shorter and less curved.

Constructing the Bipedal Body Plan

It is easy to make the mistake of thinking that once the shift from quadrupedalism to bipedalism began, it was somehow preordained that an efficient biped would result. But remember that such master plans do not exist in evolution: All the anatomical changes we've discussed occurred like the construction of a mosaic, with interlocking pieces driven by natural selection in every generation. Natural selection drove the evolution of bipedalism because in each subsequent generation once the shift began, each transitional stage conferred survival and reproductive benefits on individuals. The mental image of a shuffling prehominin that was neither an efficient quadruped nor biped is certainly wrong. Instead, in each generation the emerging biped must have been very good at surviving and reproducing, or else natural selection would not have pushed the process further. This strongly suggests that bipedalism arose in a variety of forms and functions, some of which may have died out while others succeeded. Ultimately, one lineage of bipeds—our own—succeeded, and we are the product of that lengthy process.

Why Bipeds?

By now you are probably wondering why bipedalism evolved. What was it about bipedalism that helped our distant ancestors to survive? Were they more energy efficient? Were they able to get more food? Did standing on two legs make them more attractive to mates? Many scenarios have been proposed for what selective pressures favored bipeds (Figure 10.8).

Energetic Efficiency Bipedal walking is a more efficient way of traveling than walking on all fours, at least if we compare human and chimpanzee walking. Peter Rodman and Henry McHenry (1980) pointed out that although humans do not necessarily walk more efficiently than all quadrupeds, they certainly walk more efficiently than knucklewalking apes. In other words, if hominins evolved from a knucklewalking ancestor, then the shift to upright posture would have made perfect energetic sense. Although there is still some argument about the relative efficiency of early hominin walking, most studies suggest that bipedal walking (but not running) is a more efficient means of locomotion than knucklewalking (Leonard & Robertson, 1997). Recent experiments suggest that oxygen consumption is greater in chimpanzees than in humans when walking bipedally, and models for early *Australopithecus* suggest even they would be substantially more efficient than were chimpanzees (Pontzer et al., 2009). This greater efficiency in getting between food patches may have had other advantages as well. Greater efficiency in moving between patches of food would have allowed hominins to maintain group size even as the Miocene forests dried (Isbell and Young, 1996).

Another way in which the body plan of a biped may have been more efficient than its ape ancestor is in its ability to dissipate heat. Overheating poses a greater risk to the brain than to other parts of the body. Dean Falk and Glenn Conroy (1983, 1990) suggest that successful hominins in open (unforested) areas had a means of draining blood (the vertebral plexus) that also cooled the brain. The idea is provocative: the circulatory system as a radiator designed to keep a growing brain cool, enabling more and more brain expansion in one lineage but not in another. However, the correlation between this drainage system and environments in which there is little shade isn't perfect, and modern humans don't all have this adaptation. In addition, Pete Wheeler (1991) has shown that bipeds dissipate heat faster than quadrupeds because they stand slightly taller above the ground, and when exposed to midday sun they present less surface area to be heated. Although hominins may

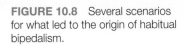

Carrying tools, food, or infants

Ecological influences: traveling between trees or seeing over tall grass

Preadaptation from a change in feeding postures

Energy efficiency

Provisioning family

have been better at dissipating heat from their bodies and brains than their last common ancestor this doesn't necessarily mean that this was the advantage that led to bipedalism. It could be that better heat dissipation was a side benefit enjoyed by hominins once bipedalism arose for other reasons, or that it was one of many advantages that led to the origin of bipedalism.

Ecological and Dietary Influences on Bipedalism Environmental changes between 5 and 8 million years ago may have favored the ability to walk upright. In the late Miocene of Africa, grasslands expanded and forests decreased in size. This trend culminated in the widespread savannas we find in East Africa today. Increased grassland resulted in a wider scattering of the food trees that protohominins needed for their meals, so they had to forage over longer distances across more open country. With increased travel across open country, natural selection may have driven the evolution of a more energy-efficient mode of transport, namely bipedalism.

Many researchers have observed that standing upright would have offered greater ability to see over tall grass or to scan for potential predators. Gaining a better view of one's surroundings by walking upright has long been advocated as the selective advantage necessary to drive the evolution of bipedalism. But other researchers ask why the enormous changes to the anatomy that allow habitual bipedalism would have taken place, when an occasional look over tall grass might have been just as effective without requiring these fundamental anatomical changes.

And there may have been dietary advantages to bipedalism as well. Perhaps a lineage of fossil apes became bipedal because of the value of standing upright for feeding in fruit trees. Researchers from the 1970s to the present all envision a protohominin that became increasingly bipedal for the feeding advantages that this posture offered, whether it be to pluck ripe fruits more efficiently (Hunt, 1990; Stanford, 2002), to shuffle between food patches (Jolly, 1970), or to walk atop tree limbs (Tuttle, 1981). Whether such feeding benefits would have favored the conversion to full-time bipedalism remains to be answered.

Sexual Selection, Mating Strategies, and Bipedalism Perhaps bipedalism arose because it conferred mating benefits on protohominins that walked upright. Nina Jablonski and George Chaplin (1993) argued that bipedalism would have been beneficial to males engaging in social displays. Male chimpanzees often stand upright briefly when they assert their dominance over other males during charging displays. Walking upright would allow males to look impressive and therefore get more matings with females. It is unclear why this benefit would lead to habitual bipedalism and all the accompanying anatomical alterations rather than just a temporary behavioral bipedality.

In the 1980s, C. Owen Lovejoy proposed a model that tied together information about ancient climate, anatomy, and reproductive physiology to explain the evolution of bipedalism. He argued that the slow reproductive rate of the hominin lineage, like that of many of the fossil ape lineages, would have led to our extinction if we had not found some means of increasing reproduction. He also argued that the evolution of the monogamous mating system offered a way to increase the likelihood of infant survival, and he saw male provisioning of females and their young as critical to this system. However, males needed to ensure their paternity and females needed to ensure continual male support. As forests contracted, males had to walk farther to find food to carry back to the females they were guarding from the attentions of other males. Bipedality raised the energy efficiency of walking and enabled the male to carry food in his arms. If female protohominins did not "announce" through swellings on their rears that they were ovulating, they would have had an advantage because the provisioning male would need to remain in the near vicinity or return constantly to increase his chances of mating when the female was fertile. The female's physiology, fortified by the extra nutrition she received from her now-attentive mate, could produce more offspring. The interval between births shortened, and the emerging hominins not only staved off extinction but also invaded a new grassland niche.

A number of faults might be found with Lovejoy's model; for example, bipedality arose millions of years before hominins moved into the grassland niche and the earliest hominins may not have had monogamous mating systems as they were likely to have been highly sexually dimorphic (see Chapter 7). It is important to emphasize, however, that a complex evolutionary change like bipedality is more likely to be brought about by a web of factors, such as those proposed by Lovejoy, than by a single cause.

The Transition to Human Behavior

How did the behavior of emerging hominins change as they developed more upright posture and a new mode of travel? Although the behavior of extinct primates is not preserved in their fossilized remains, we have every reason to assume that primates living in the past followed the same guiding principles of natural selection and sexual selection that primates do today. Thus, inferences from living primates allow us to reconstruct diets, modes of locomotion, and other aspects of primate lives that inform us about the ways extinct hominins likely behaved. Because of the evolutionary relationship between humans and nonhuman primates, we look to the higher primates first when we want to reconstruct aspects of the behavior of our ancestors. We are therefore using the principle of homology that shared ancestry allows us to infer how we once used to be (see Chapter 2).

What Made Humans Human?

Although there is no single explanation for the behavioral shift from apes to humans, we can be sure of a few facts. First, the anatomical shift from quadrupedalism came after a behavioral shift began. Whether for feeding or carrying or any other reason, natural selection favored individuals possessing slight anatomical differences that made them better bipeds.

Second, the transition to bipedality happened only because at every stage of the process, natural selection favored the form the evolving protohominin took. At each intermediate stage in our evolution the emerging hominin had to be very good at what it did, or bipedalism would not have been the result. We can be sure that the earliest hominins were agile, powerful creatures, combining elements of ape and human behavior and morphology. Even if they were not as efficient at walking upright as modern people are, they were, without doubt, highly effective foragers.

Third, at the earliest stages of hominin evolution brain size and intelligence were quite apelike. Paleoanthropologists debate exactly when hominins became more like people than like apes, but certainly the very earliest hominins (and also *Australopithecus*) were still quite primitive. Terry Deacon (1990) points out that the notion of linear progression in brain size from the most primitive to the brainiest primates is largely a fiction. A good deal of the variation in brain-to-body size ratio in the Primate order results from body size differences between taxa, with the brain being scaled in size accordingly, rather than from natural selection operating directly on brain size itself. The bigger-is-naturally-better notion may be the product of outdated thinking about the evolution of intelligence. Natural selection will select for a bigger brain only if other, less costly solutions are not available.

Will You Know a Hominin When You See One?

Recognizing a hominin in the fossil record may not be easy because all we have to work with are skeletal remains. Molecular evidence suggests that humans and chimpanzees diverged from our last common ancestor about 6 million years ago. The anatomical characters that distinguish human bipeds from quadrupedal apes can help us to recognize the fossilized skeletons of bipeds and hence hominins. (Currently, there is a debate over the best name for the group that includes humans and our ancestors; the traditional classification calls them hominids, but the classification we use based on molecular evidence calls them hominins [Insights and Advances: A Rose by Any Other Name: Hominins versus Hominids on page 246]).

In addition to skeletal differences due to bipedality humans and apes also differ in other features of the skull and dentition. We infer that a fossil possessing the human condition of these traits—or an intermediate condition tending toward the human condition—is a hominin. For example, the modern human dental arcade is shaped differently than an ape's. The human tooth row forms a rounded, parabolic arch reflecting the smaller anterior teeth (canines and incisors) and posterior teeth (premolars and molars). The dental arcade of a primate with large canines, such as

insights & advances

A ROSE BY ANY OTHER NAME: HOMININS VERSUS HOMINIDS

The traditional classification system of the hominoids—humans, the great apes, and the lesser apes—is based on morphological characteristics. In this traditional system, the superfamily Hominoidea contains three families: Hominidae, Pongidae, and Hylobatidae (Figure A Part [a]). In this view, the Hominidae, or hominids, are humans and our extinct ancestors; the Pongidae includes the African and Asian great apes; and the Hylobatidae are the lesser apes (gibbons and siamangs). This system reflects how startlingly different we bipeds are from our closest quadrupedal relatives. However, genetic distances suggest a slightly different classification system. Recall from Chapter 9 that genetically humans and chimpanzees are more closely related to one another than either is to the gorilla. Therefore, humans and chimps should be grouped together, despite their morphological differences. And both African apes are more closely related to humans than either is to orangutans.

In the new classification system that reflects these genetic distances (Figure A Part [b]) the superfamily Hominoidea contains two families: Hominidae and Hylobatidae. The Hominidae now includes humans and our extinct ancestors as well as the great apes and their ancestors. Within the family Hominidae are two subfamilies that separate African apes including ourselves (Homininae) from the orangutans (Ponginae) because of our genetic differences. And within the subfamily Homininae, humans and our ancestors are in the tribe Hominini, or hominins for short. In this book we use the molecular classification system and call humans and our exclusive ancestors *hominins* because this is the way that most of the recent literature is constructed. But you should be aware that earlier literature and some current papers use the term *hominids*. So always be sure to check your definitions!

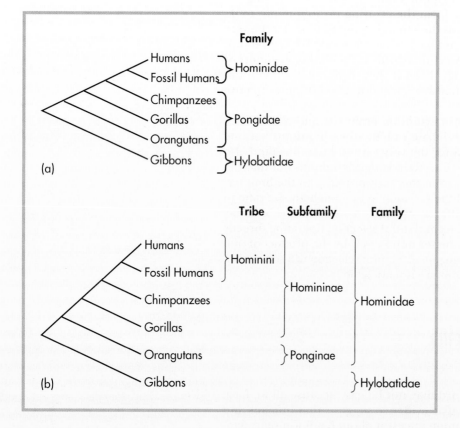

(a)

(b)

FIGURE A   Taxonomic classification of hominids versus hominins. (a) A traditional classification system recognizes only humans and our fossil ancestors in the family Hominidae, which we refer to as hominids. (b) A classification system that reflects molecular relationships groups African great apes and humans together at the subfamily level in the Homininae and humans and our ancestors in the tribe Hominini or hominins.

an ape or baboon, is broader in front (Figure 10.9) and U-shaped, with the teeth behind the canines forming two parallel rows. Early hominins tend to have somewhat smaller anterior teeth than such primates, but the arcade remains relatively U-shaped. Large anterior teeth also contribute to greater facial prognathism, the degree to which the face projects in front of the braincase. Like that of apes, the face of most early hominins is relatively prognathic.

The sizes and shapes of the teeth also differ between apes and humans. One aspect of the dental pattern that paleoanthropologists use to differentiate fossil apes from fossil hominins is the size and shape of the canine and premolar teeth (Figure 10.10). In a monkey or ape, the enormous canines of the upper jaw (the maxilla) must fit into a space or *diastema* in the tooth row of the lower jaw (the mandible) where they slide past the third premolar, The back of the upper canine is sharpened,

CP$_3$ honing complex Combination of canine and first premolar teeth that form a self-sharpening apparatus.

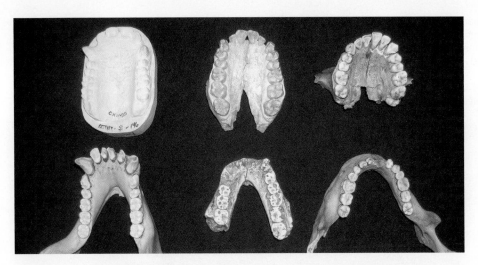

FIGURE 10.9 Upper and lower jaw shapes differ between chimpanzees (left), *Australopithecus,* and humans (right). Notice the U-shaped dental arcades of the ape with large anterior teeth, the parabolic arcades and smaller anterior teeth of humans, and the intermediate appearance of *Australopithecus.*

or honed, by the bladelike premolar (this is called the **CP$_3$ honing complex**). As canines shorten during evolution, the blade on the premolar disappears, and the tooth gains a cusp and becomes broader. The very earliest *Australopithecus* show some reduction of the canine, the absence or reduction of a diastema, and at least partial loss of the CP$_3$ honing complex, often including the presence of a two-cusped premolar.

Another aspect of the teeth that differs between humans and apes is the thickness of the enamel, the white outer coating of our teeth. Living African apes have thin enamel, but our enamel is thick. Thus thick enamel has been used to identify hominins. However, thicker enamel probably arose several different times during primate evolution as an adaptation to certain kinds of foods, so the presence of thick enamel alone does not guarantee that we are looking at a hominin tooth.

So fossil hominins, including human ancestors since the split from the chimpanzee lineage, can be recognized by anatomical characters related to bipedalism, and by reduction of the canine teeth and CP$_3$ complex, and by changes in palate shape. The very earliest of the hominins show these features to only a very slight degree and therefore are often difficult to differentiate from fossil apes. Other changes that we associate with humans, such as our very large brain and extremely small face and jaws, appear only later in human evolution.

The First Hominins?

The majority of the fossil evidence of the earliest hominins has come from the Great Rift Valley of East Africa, a broad expanse that runs north to south from the Horn of Africa at the Red Sea southward to Zambia (Figure 10.11 on page 248). The valley contains a series of ancient volcanoes and a string of lakes—Lake Victoria, Lake Turkana, Lake Tanganyika, and Lake Malawi, among others—that are often called the Great Lakes of Africa. The Rift Valley's tectonic history resulted in the creation and disappearance of lakes and streams during hominin evolution. These waterways provided likely habitats for species of early hominins, and the volcanic sediments allow radiometric assessment of fossil ages.

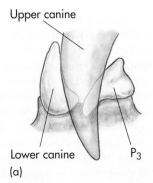

Upper canine

Lower canine   P$_3$

(a)

(b)

FIGURE 10.10 (a) A canine/premolar or CP$_3$ honing complex consists of a large, projecting upper canine passing across the bladelike edge of the lower premolar. Hominins lose this complex as the anterior teeth decrease in size. (b) Monkeys and apes such as this chimpanzee can be recognized in the fossil record by the anatomy of their teeth.

FIGURE 10.11 Geographic distribution of early hominins. Hominins are limited to the continent of Africa until about 1.8 million years ago. Some of the important sites for *Australopithecus* and other early hominin fossils are located on the map. Although most known sites are in eastern and southern Africa, *Australopithecus* likely inhabited most of the African continent.

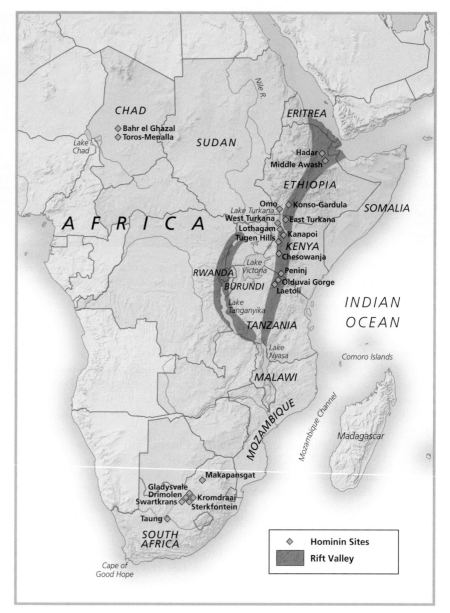

During the later Miocene (10–5.5 million years ago) and early Pliocene (5.5–4 million years ago) at least one lineage of apes made the adaptive shift to a terrestrial niche and became increasingly bipedal. The shift to bipedality came about partly in response to major climatic changes that were occurring in equatorial Africa and was accompanied by anatomical changes to the pelvis, vertebral column, and other body systems of hominins. Molecular evidence suggests that the first hominins emerged from lineages of late Miocene apes. Unfortunately, between 10 and 6 million years ago, the fossil record for the roots of our lineage is poorly represented. Between 7 and 4.4 million years ago, we have several candidates for the earliest hominin remains, but all or some of them may represent fossil apes rather than hominins. Some of these sites (Lothagam, Tabarin, Djurab, and Tugen Hills) have produced evidence too fragmentary for an unambiguous answer. The others (Aramis and several Middle Awash sites) have produced a plethora of remains that have just recently begun to be published (Table 10.1). Two recently discovered fossils from 7 to 6 million years ago may be the very earliest hominin remains known. However, whether they are primitive hominins or fossil apes is hotly debated.

TABLE 10.1   **Candidates for the Earliest Hominin (some could be fossil apes).**

Site	MYA*	Species
Toros-Menalla, Chad	7.0–5.2	*Sahelanthropus tchadensis*
Tugen Hills, Kenya	6.0	*Orrorin tugenensis*
Middle Awash, Ethiopia	5.8–5.2	*Ardipithecus kadabba*
Lothagam, Kenya	5.8	??
Tabarin, Kenya	5.0	??
Aramis, Ethiopia	4.4	*Ardipithecus ramidus*

*MYA = millions of years ago

Sahelanthropus tchadensis (7.0–6.0 MYA)

A French expedition led by Michel Brunet discovered a fossilized skull, which the team nicknamed Toumai ("hope of life"), in the sands of the Djurab Desert in northern Chad in 2001 (Brunet et al., 2002) (Figure 10.12a). Formally named *Sahelanthropus tchadensis* ("the Sahara hominin from Chad"), the fossil was estimated to be between 5.2 and 7 million years old based on biostratigraphic correlations with East African sites, with 6–7 million years considered most likely by Brunet. This age would make it the oldest hominin and one of only two found in West Africa. The site where Toumai was found was a dry, lightly forested area near a lakeshore in the late Miocene, when *S. tchadensis* lived.

The Toumai fossil consists of a fairly complete skull, mandibular fragments, and isolated teeth. Surprisingly, the face is less prognathic than expected for an early hominin. Other characters that argue for Toumai being a hominin are a large browridge, somewhat smaller canine teeth, a non-functional CP_3 honing complex, no diastema, and possibly an anteriorly placed foramen magnum, which may indicate bipedality. However, Toumai also exhibits a number of apelike characters, including small brain size (cranial capacity is 320–380 cc), a U-shaped dental arcade, and somewhat thin

(a)

(b)

FIGURE 10.12   (a) The skull of *Sahelanthropus tchadensis* is argued to be the earliest of the hominins and one of only two species known from western Africa. (b) The femur from the Tugen Hills belongs to *Orrorin tugenensis*—possibly an early hominin. The significance of both specimens is hotly debated.

enamel (but intermediate between chimps and *Australopithecus*). Milford Wolpoff, Brigitte Senut, and Martin Pickford (2002) argue that Toumai is just a fossil ape that has been deformed after burial. Alternatively, some of those who accept Toumai as a hominin prefer to place it in the genus *Ardipithecus*, thus making it closely related to the somewhat later group from Ethiopia. In either case, Toumai is profoundly important because it fills key gaps in the fossil record in the 6-million year range and pushes the distribution of fossil Homininae far to the west of the Rift Valley.

Orrorin tugenensis (6.0 MYA)

In 2001, Martin Pickford and Brigitte Senut announced the discovery of "Millennium Man" (Pickford & Senut, 2001), so named because the discovery was made in the year 2000. The approximately 6-million-year-old fossils were found in the Lukeino Formation of the Tugen Hills of Kenya and consist of fragmentary cranial and postcranial remains, most importantly multiple femoral (thigh bone) fragments (Figure 10.12b on page 249). Pickford and Senut thought that the new fossils were so different from other known hominins that they chose a new genus name, *Orrorin tugenensis* ("hominin from the Tugen Hills"). They argue that *Orrorin* is a hominin because of a suite of postcranial characters that indicate it was a biped, but the anatomy they use is not a conclusive indicator of bipedality. The remains do indeed indicate a larger body size than expected for a late Miocene ape and internal femur anatomy may support bipedality (Galik et al., 2004). Also linking *Orrorin* to the hominins is the fact that its small teeth possess thick enamel. However, the upper canine is large and a bit more apelike. Because we typically define hominins based on anatomy related to bipedality, more fossilized remains and clearer indications of bipedality will be needed before we can make a final determination about the place of *Orrorin tugenensis* in our family tree.

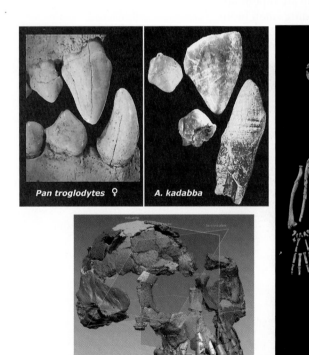

FIGURE 10.13 *Ardipithecus kadabba* has large canine teeth that are only slightly smaller than those of living apes. The oldest of the Ethiopian hominins at 5.7 million years old, *Ar. kadabba* was ancestral to the 4.4 million-year-old *Ar. ramidus* and perhaps the rest of the hominin lineage. The *Ar. ramidus* fossils include a partial skeleton with a divergent big toe. The skull, seen here, was reconstructed from a large number of fragments and the digital image shows each of the pieces in different colors.

Ardipithecus ramidus (4.4 MYA) and *Ardipithecus kadabba* (5.8–5.2 MYA)

In 1994, an international team led by Tim White, Berhane Asfaw, and Gen Suwa, announced the discovery of fossilized remains of a very primitive hominin in the northeastern part of Ethiopia near the Red Sea (Figure 10.13). In 2009, an entire issue of the journal *Science* was devoted to additional finds of *Ardipithecus*. The finds come from a site called Aramis in the Middle Awash region of an ancient river delta called the Afar Triangle. In the late Miocene and early Pliocene, the team thinks that Aramis was a dense forest home to ancestors of modern colobine monkeys and forest antelopes. This is very interesting because we expected to find the earliest hominins living in open savanna habitat, not closed forests similar to those in which apes live today (see Chapter 9). There is some debate as to just how forested the area was, but it seems clear that it was not an uninterrupted grassland (see Chapter 9; Cerling et al., 2010; White et al., 2010).

Ardipithecus ramidus ("ground-living root hominin") is a primitive hominin. The presence of more primitive traits, including relatively thin enamel and little postcanine enlargement or **megadontia**, as well as possible locomotor differences (such as an abducted big toe) with

Australopithecus, led the Middle Awash team to assign the fossils to a new genus, *Ardipithecus*. However, the molars are apelike in size but exhibit little dimorphism. In 2004, a team led by Yohannes Haile-Selassie announced new specimens that had lived much earlier than *Ar. ramidus*, around 5.7–5.8 million years ago. On the basis of more apelike dentition, the researchers propose calling them a new species *Ardipithecus kadabba* (Figure 10.13).

The bipedal nature and hominin status of *Ardipithecus* are still questioned by some scientists. The hominin status of *Ardipithecus* is based on the smaller canine, absence of CP_3 honing, and several features of the cranial and postcranial skeleton that are argued to indicate some level of bipedality. The Middle Awash group argues that the evidence from *Ardipithecus ramidus* suggests that some of the traits that we have taken for granted as primitive for the African apes and our ancestors (such as knucklewalking, great sexual dimorphism, etc.) evolved several different times in different ape lineages. Alternatively, other researchers think *Ardipithecus* could as easily be just one of many of the apes that radiated in the Miocene (Wood and Harrison, 2011). For now, there seems to be more certainty that *Ardipithecus* was a biped and therefore a more likely candidate for the stem hominin than either *Orrorin* or *Sahelanthropus*. All of the genera mentioned so far share the absence of a functional CP_3 honing complex. However, the possibility remains that *Ardipithecus* may not be directly ancestral to later hominins. A newly discovered foot skeleton from Burtele, Ethiopia dated to 3.4 million years ago is similar to *Ardipithecus* but a contemporary of *Australopithecus afarensis* (Haile-Selassie et al., 2012). The Burtele foot seems to suggest that hominins evolved more than one way of being bipedal; the lineage represented by *Ardipithecus* and Burtele retained extensive grasping capabilities of the foot, whereas *Australopithecus* was a more committed terrestrial biped.

megadontia Enlarged teeth.

Australopithecus and Kin

Recognizing the very earliest members of a group in the fossil record is difficult because the record is fragmentary and incomplete. Also the more ancient the ancestor, the less it will look like its living descendants. So it will be very hard to differentiate an early hominin from an ape, for example. The hominins just discussed fall into this nebulous category.

However, most of the early members of the hominini do not suffer from this ambiguity and are assigned to the genus *Australopithecus*. The name *Australopithecus*, meaning "southern ape," was coined by Raymond Dart in the 1920s for the very first specimen of the genus ever discovered. Since that time, fossil discoveries have revealed an adaptive radiation of *Australopithecus* species that filled a variety of habitat types in eastern, southern, and central Africa and are now known to have lived from 4.2 to about 1.0 million years ago. The genus *Australopithecus* can be usefully thought about as species of bipedal apes that are small bodied (64–100 lbs; 29–45 kg) and small brained (340–500 cc), had moderately prognathic faces, and a mosaic of primitive and derived cranio-dental anatomy (Figure 10.14). As we discover new specimens and new taxa, we will no doubt expand both the geographic distribution and the time span for this group and raise additional questions about their origins and descendants (Figure 10.15 on pages 252–253).

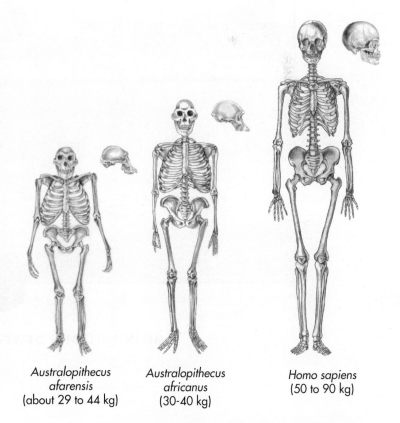

Australopithecus afarensis (about 29 to 44 kg)

Australopithecus africanus (30-40 kg)

Homo sapiens (50 to 90 kg)

FIGURE 10.14 Comparison of hominin skeletons. The *Australopithecus* species were short bipedal primates, most with relatively long arms. Compared to modern humans (right) the *Australopithecus* torso was broad and funnel shaped.

FIGURE 10.15

Early Hominin Evolution

The earliest hominins appeared around 6 million years ago in western and eastern Africa. About 4 million years ago large jaws and small body size arose. *Australopithecus* is probably the first stone tool maker, and one species is likely to have given rise to *Homo*.

Several species of the genus overlapped with one another in time and space, probably avoiding competition by relying on slightly different food resources. In the robust *Australopithecus* lineage (*Au. aethiopicus, Au. robustus,* and *Au. boisei*), several species evolved massive jaws, molar teeth, and cranial skeletons optimized for producing large chewing forces. These hominins probably relied on hard-to-open food items during times of nutritional stress.

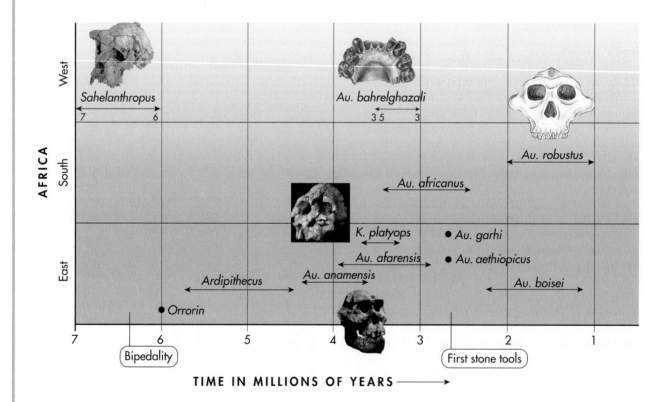

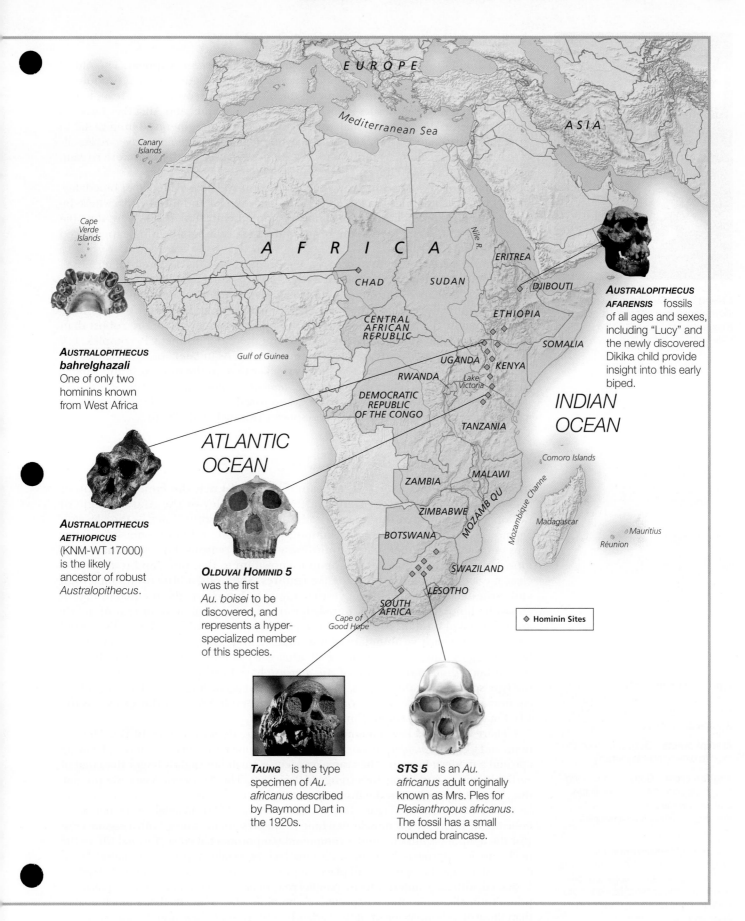

AUSTRALOPITHECUS bahrelghazali One of only two hominins known from West Africa

AUSTRALOPITHECUS AETHIOPICUS (KNM-WT 17000) is the likely ancestor of robust *Australopithecus*.

AUSTRALOPITHECUS AFARENSIS fossils of all ages and sexes, including "Lucy" and the newly discovered Dikika child provide insight into this early biped.

OLDUVAI HOMINID 5 was the first *Au. boisei* to be discovered, and represents a hyper-specialized member of this species.

◆ **Hominin Sites**

TAUNG is the type specimen of *Au. africanus* described by Raymond Dart in the 1920s.

STS 5 is an *Au. africanus* adult originally known as Mrs. Ples for *Plesianthropus africanus*. The fossil has a small rounded braincase.

Australopithecus anamensis (4.2–3.9 MYA)

Around 4 million years ago, members of genus *Australopithecus* appear. The oldest and most primitive of these is *Australopithecus anamensis* (Figure 10.16). Announced in 1995, *Au. anamensis* ("southern ape of the lake") was discovered by a team led by Meave Leakey. At separate sites near Lake Turkana, Kanapoi, and Allia Bay, Leakey's team uncovered dozens of cranial and postcranial bone fragments, dating to 4.2 to 3.9 million years ago, or just 200,000 years younger than *Ardipithecus ramidus*. Fossils of fish and aquatic animals found with *Au. anamensis* indicate the sites were streamside forests in the early Pliocene.

Australopithecus anamensis provides early incontrovertible evidence of bipedality. In particular, its tibia has thickened bone at its proximal and distal ends, where bipeds place stress on their lower legs. Furthermore, the tibial plateau, where the tibia meets the femur, is enlarged as the result of the greater weight-bearing experienced by the bipedal lower limb.

The *Au. anamensis* teeth and jaws are more primitive than those of later hominins but more derived than those of early hominins such as *Ardipithecus*. The dental arcade is U-shaped, with parallel sides and large anterior teeth, and the palate is shallow, all features that are more apelike than human. Although the canine is smaller than in *Ardipithecus*, the root of the canine is longer and more robust than in the slightly later *Australopithecus afarensis*, and there is a distinct CP$_3$ complex, but the molars of *Au. anamensis* are shorter and broader. As in later *Australopithecus*, the molar enamel of *Au. anamensis* is distinctly thicker than in the more primitive *Ardipithecus ramidus*, all characters that make *Au. anamensis* a hominin. In general, *Au. anamensis* is more primitive than *Au. afarensis*, and based on its mandible and dentition, may be ancestral to later *Australopithecus* species (Kimbel et al., 2006).

Australopithecus afarensis (3.9–2.9 MYA)

In 1974 Donald Johanson and his team discovered Lucy, the famed skeleton of *Australopithecus afarensis*, at Hadar in the Awash Valley of the Afar Triangle of Ethiopia. (They named the specimen after the Beatles song "Lucy in the Sky with Diamonds.") The discovery of the diminutive A.L. 288-1, as Lucy is known from her museum catalog number, was extraordinary for two reasons. First, her anatomy is more primitive than that of any hominin known up to that time, and it includes a clear mosaic of humanlike and apelike features. She stood a little over a meter tall and possessed a cranial vault suggesting a modest brain size about equal to that of an adult chimpanzee. Second, her skeleton is more complete than that of nearly any other fossil human. Although more primitive hominins have been discovered since, none is nearly so abundant or well studied, and *Au. afarensis* has remained the benchmark by which the anatomy of all other early hominins is interpreted. In addition to Lucy, thousands of finds of *Au. afarensis* have been made in the Afar. In fact, the **type specimen** of the species, the specimen that according to the laws of zoological nomenclature serves as the original anatomical reference for the species, is the LH 4 mandible from Laetoli, Tanzania.

There are several key anatomical features of *Au. afarensis* (Figure 10.17). The cranium and teeth of *Au. afarensis* are intermediate in appearance between those of a living ape and a modern human. The cranial capacity is small but slightly larger than that of earlier hominins and living apes (range 350–500 cc). The *Au. afarensis* face was prognathic, but not so much as in the living apes, and the cranial base was relatively flat, similar to that of living apes (Figure 10.18) (Kimbel et al., 2004). **Cranial crests**, flanges of bone on the braincase for muscle attachment, are present, including both a **sagittal crest** (for the temporalis muscle) and a **compound temporonuchal crest** (formed where the neck muscles approach the temporalis muscles), especially in presumed males. These crests tell us that *Au. afarensis* still placed a premium on chewing. The dental arcade is U-shaped, with large anterior teeth, parallel rows of cheek teeth, and a shallow palate, all primitive, apelike traits. But as expected of a hominin, the canine teeth are much smaller than those of a chimpanzee or of the earlier hominins *Ardipithecus* and *Au. anamensis* but

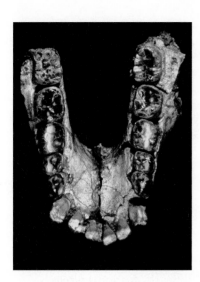

FIGURE 10.16 The remains of *Australopithecus anamensis* from Kenya date to about 3.9 to 4.2 million years old.

type specimen According to the laws of zoological nomenclature, the anatomical reference specimen for the species definition.

cranial crests Bony ridges on the skull to which muscles attach.

sagittal crest Bony crest running lengthwise down the center of the cranium on the parietal bones; for the attachment of the temporalis muscles.

compound temporonuchal crest Bony crest at the back of the skull formed when an enlarged temporalis muscle approaches enlarged neck (nuchal) muscles; present in apes and *Au. afarensis*.

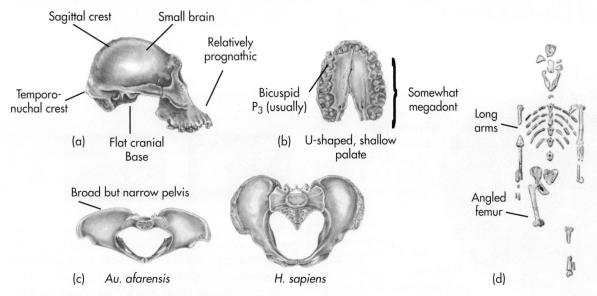

FIGURE 10.17   Key features of *Australopithecus afarensis* include (a) a small cranial capacity, and cranial crests (b) a shallow, U-shaped palate with reduced canines and (c, d) features of the postcranial skeleton that indicate habitual bipedality.

larger than those of more recent hominins or other *Australopithecus* species. With smaller canine teeth, no CP_3 honing complex is present in *Au. afarensis,* and many specimens have premolars with two cusps. The molar and premolar teeth are modest in size compared with those of later *Australopithecus* but much larger than those of the earliest hominins and *Au. anamensis.*

In its postcranial skeleton, *Au. afarensis* is clearly an accomplished biped. *Au. afarensis* possesses a pelvis with short, broad iliac blades that curve around the side of the animal. The femur is angled in toward the knee to keep the foot under the center of gravity, the condyles on the lower end of the femur are enlarged, and the groove for the patella is deep. The tibia is modified to bear more weight, and the big toe is in line with the other toes. Indirect evidence of bipedal walking in *Au. afarensis* comes from the Laetoli footprint track that, on the basis of its age and location, is thought to have been made by *Au. afarensis.*

The postcranial skeleton also differs from that of modern humans, however (see Figure 10.14 on page 251). The thorax is more funnel shaped, similar to an ape's, perhaps indicating that *Au. afarensis* had a large gut and a largely vegetal diet. Their arms are somewhat longer relative to leg length than in modern humans, but their arm and wrist anatomy is unlike that of modern apes who use their arms for walking. *Australopithecus afarensis* has more curved phalanges of the toes and fingers; smaller, perhaps more flexible tarsal bones; and aspects of the shoulder and hip joints that may indicate some level of arboreality. The remarkably complete skull and skeleton of a 3-year-old *Au. afarensis* girl that were discovered from the site of Dikika in Ethiopia has a scapula similar to a gorilla and curved phalanges (Figure 10.19 and Innovations: Dikika and Development on pages 256–257). These characters suggest that *Au. afarensis* may have retreated to the trees to escape from predators and to forage for fruits and leaves during the day and to sleep at night.

It is likely that *Au. afarensis* lived in groups, and because they were very sexually dimorphic, they probably were not monogamous. The largest adults from Hadar are, in some measures, nearly twice the size of the smallest *Au. afarensis* (Lucy is one of the very smallest). *Au. afarensis* shows a level of sexual dimorphism more similar to that of the living apes than to living humans although there is some debate about this (McHenry, 1991; Gordon et al., 2008) (Table 10.2 on page 258). From this we infer that *Au. afarensis* had a polygynous mating strategy because in living primates great sexual dimorphism usually is associated with multiple mates (see Chapter 7).

FIGURE 10.18   A complete skull of *Au. afarensis* from Hadar, Ethiopia, shows a prognathic face and small braincase.

FIGURE 10.19   The Dikika baby. A recently discovered three-year-old *Au. afarensis* girl has a scapula and phalanges that suggest possible adaptions to life in the trees and a developmental pattern similar to living apes.

INNOVATIONS
Dikika and Development

Evolution often proceeds by modifying the pattern of development. Slight modifications during growth can lead to large anatomical differences between adults. Such modifications might alter the rate and timing of growth, or they might alter growth processes; for example depositing bone at a certain spot in one species while resorbing bone in that same spot in another species. New technologies such as X-rays, scanning electron microscopy, computed tomography (CT), and microCT are being used to understand growth in fossil hominins. First, however, fossil children must be discovered.

In 2006, Zeresenay Alemseged and his team announced a spectacular discovery of an infant skeleton of *Australopithecus afarensis* from Dikika in Ethiopia dated to about 3.3 million years old. This child's bones were retrieved over several field seasons in three different years. The work included the careful survey of an entire slope and the screening of excavated sediments. Most of the skull and part of the postcranial skeleton, especially the arm,

was recovered, but many of the bones were cemented together by sediment. The analyses would include CT scanning to determine which bones and teeth were present and how old the child was. Although you would suppose that children's remains are rarely preserved in the fossil record,

almost every fossil hominin species has at least one fairly well-preserved subadult specimen. Indeed, the first *Australopithecus* species ever discovered was the Taung Child from South Africa.

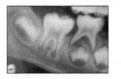 

The first step in understanding development of any fossil specimen is to evaluate its developmental age. If the fossil has teeth, dental development is the best means for assessing age (see also Chapter 15). Radiographs, X-rays like the ones your dentist takes, and CT scans can be used to visualize the relative development of the tooth crown and its roots (Dean, 2007). Using comparative standards for apes and humans a developmental age can be assigned. In the case of Dikika, only baby teeth were visible externally, but adult teeth could be seen developing in the jaw. An ape developmental standard suggests the child was about 3 years old when she died. The same techniques can be applied to other species. For example, the three-dimensional CT scan of King Tut reveals his third molars (wisdom teeth) were unerupted, which is consistent with his reported age of 19 years at the time he died.

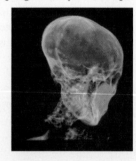

More detailed information about growth rate and timing is revealed by examination of the microstructure of tooth crowns and roots. Tooth enamel is laid down in daily increments, with darker bands accumulating about once a week. By counting these bands and the space between

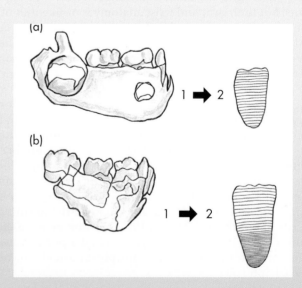

them, relative rate of growth can be assessed. Beynon and Dean (1986) used crown development to show that robust

Australopithecus developed their incisors more quickly than did non-robust species like Dikika. And both groups erupt their teeth at earlier ages than do living humans.

Robust and non-robust *Australopithecus* of similar dental ages also show different patterns of facial growth. Using scanning electron microscopy (SEM), scientists can see whether bone in a particular region of the skeleton was being deposited or resorbed at the time of death (Bromage, 1987). Melanie McCollum (2007) has analyzed growth in the face of recent chimpanzees and

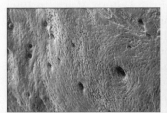

human children, and compared this with patterns in fossil children, including non-robust species such as the Taung Child (*Au. africanus*) and the Hadar Baby (A.L. 333-105, *Au. afarensis*), the same species as the Dikika three-year-old, and *Au. robustus* (SK-66). Robust *Australopithecus*

show bone resorption on their anterior maxilla, while non-robusts of the same age do not. This response may in some small way influence the facial differences in these species.

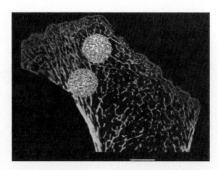

The most recent technology to be applied to understanding growth is microCT—or computed tomography able to visualize structures of very, very small scale. Using this technology Tim Ryan and Gail Krovitz (2006) have established how the spongy bone in the top of the femur changes in density and organization during growth. They looked at the changes in humans from fetal to about 9 years old to understand how becoming bipedal might influence bone structure. Around two or three years of age, the three-dimensional structure of the top of the femur reorganized in ways that were consistent with changes in loading caused by unassisted walking as opposed to crawling. Their work establishes a baseline for understanding how changes in behavior influence structure—an understanding that one day may help us understand fossil specimens such as the Dikika three-year-old.

FETUS   3 - 6 MONTHS

6 - 12 MONTHS   24 - 36 MONTHS

5 mm

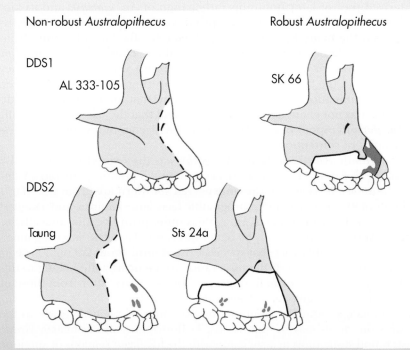

Non-robust *Australopithecus*   Robust *Australopithecus*

DDS1

AL 333-105   SK 66

DDS2

Taung   Sts 24a

TABLE 10.2   Comparisons of *Au. afarensis*, Great Apes, and Modern Humans (data from McHenry and Coffing, 2000 and Smith and Jungers, 1997).

	Cranial Capacity (cc)	Sexual Dimorphism (Male weight/Female weight)
Au. afarensis	450	1.6
Au. africanus	450	1.4
Au. robustus	500	1.2
Au. boisei	500	1.4
Bonobo	350	1.3
Chimpanzee	400	1.1–1.3
Gorilla	500	1.7–2.4
Orangutan	400	2.0–2.2
Modern human	1,350	1.18

East and West African Hominins (3.5–2.5 MYA)

As we have seen, most early fossil hominins have come from eastern Africa. In 1995, Michel Brunet announced the discovery of the first hominin from West Africa, *Au. bahrelghazali* ("the hominin from Antelope Creek"). The species dates between 3.5 and 3.0 MYA and is known from a single fossil: the front of a mandible with seven teeth (Figure 10.20a). Most researchers think that *Au. bahrelghazali* is either a member of *Au. afarensis* or at least that it is too fragmentary to form the basis of a new species. Until additional fossils are known, the major importance of this find is its confirmation that hominins lived over much of the African continent, not only in East Africa.

Similarly aged remains in East Africa have been assigned to a new genus, *Kenyanthropus*. Working on the arid western shore of Lake Turkana in northern Kenya, Meave Leakey and her team discovered an early hominin dated to 3.5 million years ago (Leakey et al., 2001). Leakey and Fred Spoor thought the specimens, particularly a nearly complete but crushed cranium, were sufficiently different from members of the genus *Australopithecus* that they should be given a new genus name (Figure 10.20b). The researchers based their argument on the specimen's surprisingly flat face, a derived trait of later hominins rather than of *Au. afarensis* and its kin, and its small molar teeth, a condition more primitive than the other *Australopithecus*. They proposed the name *Kenyanthropus platyops* ("the flat-faced hominin from Kenya"). Some researchers think *Kenyanthropus* should be considered just another species of *Australopithecus* or even a member of *Au. afarensis*, especially because they argue that the shape of the face was highly deformed during fossilization. However, a recent detailed examination of the face seems to show that the fundamental anatomy of the maxilla was not changed by deformation and that the face is substantially flatter than *Au. afarensis* (Spoor et al., 2010). Given the recency of the find, this question remains a point of contention.

Another enigmatic *Australopithecus*, *Au. garhi*, was discovered by the Middle Awash team at Bouri, Ethiopia. These fossils are about 2.5 million years old (Asfaw et al., 1999). *Australopithecus garhi* ("the unexpected southern ape from the Afar") had a small brain (450 cc), a prominent prognathic face, large canines, and a sagittal crest (Figure 10.21). In most respects *Au. garhi* is quite primitive anatomically, although some workers argue that it may be better interpreted as a late surviving member of *Au. afarensis*; remember that that species existed until about 2.9 million years ago in the same geographic area. If the postcrania from a nearby site belong to this species, then, surprisingly, *Au. garhi* limb proportions seem to differ from those of *Au. afarensis*, by having a longer, more humanlike lower limb.

Regardless of its taxonomic attribution, the proximity of *Au. garhi* fossils to the earliest known stone tools may be significant. At Bouri, and also at nearby Gona, archaeologists found stone tools in association with the fossilized remains of antelope and other likely prey species. These animal bones show cut marks and percussion

breccia   Cement-like matrix of fossilized rock and bone. Many important South African early humans have been found in breccias.

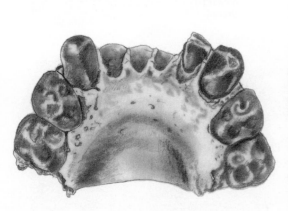
(a)

(b)

FIGURE 10.20   (a) The mandible of *Au. bahrelghazali*. The first hominin found in western Africa, *Au. bahrelghazali* dates to about 3.5 million years ago. (b) The cranium of *Kenyanthropus platyops* dates to about 3.5 million years ago in Kenya. The species takes its name from the very flat face.

marks, unmistakable evidence that early hominins had been using stone tools to butcher carcasses. We cannot say whether *Au. garhi* was the butcher, but no other early hominin fossils have been found in the same strata. At the time of their discovery these were the earliest evidence for stone tool use by *Australopithecus*. However, recently another set of marks from 3.4 million years ago at Dikika, Ethiopia have been argued to be evidence of even earlier tool use (McPherron et al., 2010). The jury remains out on these marks with some archaeologists arguing the marks were not made by tools at all but by natural forces.

Australopithecus africanus (3.5–<2.0 MYA)

Southern Africa also saw a major radiation of hominin species during the Pliocene. In fact, the first *Australopithecus* ever discovered, the Taung Child, was found in southern Africa, which is why the genus is called *Australopithecus*, or "southern ape-man."

There are a few key differences between the study of fossils in southern and eastern Africa. Unlike the open-air sites of East Africa, most South African fossil sites are in cave and cliff deposits. Hominins and other animal remains are found in a mixture of ancient marine limestone and bone cemented into a **breccia.** The hominins did not live in the caves in which they were found, although the caves could easily be misinterpreted this way because natural processes can produce fossil deposits that look very much like they were created by humans. Careful taphonomic study of the caves and their fossils reveals instead that the skeletal remains probably fell into the South African caves, which themselves are the result of dissolution of the bedrock by groundwater (see Chapter 9). South African caves often appear as sinkholes in the ground, similar to those seen in parts of Florida, and often have trees growing along their rims (Figure 10.22 on page 260). Animals are thought to have fallen into these caves by accident or in some cases to have been introduced after having been killed by carnivores, such as leopards, which cache their kills in the branches of trees overhanging the sinks to protect them from larger carnivores (Brain, 1981).

There is another key difference between the East and South African fossil record. Volcanic ash that forms the matrix in which many East African fossils are embedded can be dated quite precisely using the argon-argon techniques you read about in Chapter 9. However, South African deposits cannot be dated using these techniques. Although some uranium series dates have been attempted and cosmogenic radionuclides are starting to be used, paleontologists mostly rely on geomagnetic polarity data and relative dating methods to provide an estimate of the age of the deposits. Since the stratigraphy of the South African caves is

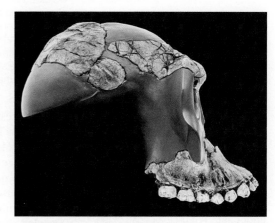

FIGURE 10.21   *Australopithecus garhi* dates to about 2.5 million years ago in Ethiopia and was found in the same beds as early stone tools. It is slightly younger than *Au. afarensis,* and its cheek teeth are more robust.

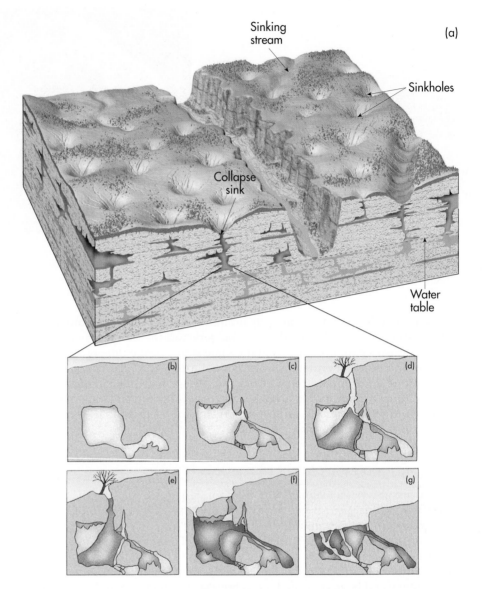

FIGURE 10.22   South African cave sites were formed by the dissolution and collapse of (a) bedrock that later trapped sediments and animals, including hominins. (b) Initially, bedrock is dissolved by groundwater. (c) When the water table lowers, there may be roof collapse into the chamber and stalagmite/stalactite formation. (d) With time, the chamber may erode further, eventually connecting to the surface. (e) Vegetation and trees often grow near these wet openings and sediments and animals may fall into the chambers. (f) Over time other openings to the surface may form introducing new sediments and bones. (g) Erosion of the surface exposes the stratigraphy of these sediments, the relative ages of which are difficult to interpret because of their complex history.

complex, establishing the sequence of which fossil species lived contemporaneously with others is not always possible.

In 1924, Raymond Dart, a young professor of anatomy in Johannesburg, South Africa, received a shipment of crates loaded with fossils collected from the Taung limestone quarry. One of the crates held a tiny partial skull of a primitive hominin, and a juvenile at that (Figure 10.23). The face and teeth were attached to a fossilized impression of the interior of the braincase as well, a so-called natural **endocast** that revealed the general appearance and size of the juvenile's brain. "The Taung Child" appeared to be a very young, apelike hominin who retained some baby teeth, which suggested an age of 5 or 6 years, based on modern human growth rates. Recent research suggests *Australopithecus* followed an apelike developmental rate and that the child was really about 2 or 3 years old at the time it died.

endocast   A replica (or cast) of the internal surface of the braincase that reflects the impressions made by the brain on the skull walls. Natural endocasts are formed by the filling of the braincase by sediments.

When Dart first published his findings, the majority of scientists thought that Taung was merely a new variety of ape and implied that Dart, who had a reputation as a grandstander, had sought attention for himself in his bold assertions about the fossil. Because of the controversy surrounding Taung and the entrenched view about the fraudulent Piltdown Man (see Chapter 9), it was not until nearly 1950 that *Australopithecus* was given its rightful place as a South African forerunner of modern humans. The discovery of an adult *Au. africanus* skull from Sterkfontein in 1947 by Robert Broom made it impossible for skeptics of Taung to insist that *Au. africanus* was an ape because the adult was clearly a bipedal hominin (Broom, 1947).

Other *Au. africanus* sites include Sterkfontein, Taung, Gladysvale, and Makapansgat, and most date between about 3.5 and 2.4 million years ago, although some may be about 1 million years old (Figure 10.24). Phillip Tobias made important contributions to understanding *Australopithecus* anatomy, and hundreds of *Au. africanus* specimens of various ages and probably both sexes have been found since Broom's initial work. A nearly complete skeleton of *Au. africanus* is being extracted from the deposits at Sterkfontein.

Australopithecus africanus is more derived than *Au. afarensis* in several aspects of its cranial skeleton (Figure 10.25). *Au. africanus* has a larger braincase (about 450–550 cc, still quite small by modern standards), a rounded vault that lacks cranial crests, a less prognathic face, and a more flexed cranial base. The teeth of *Au. africanus* are more generalized and the molars smaller than in later, more specialized forms such as *Au. robustus* and *Au. boisei*. This has led to a classification into "gracile," including *Au. africanus*, and "robust," including *Au. robustus*, *Au. boisei*, and *Au. aethiopicus*, species. *Australopithecus africanus* has small anterior teeth, especially canines, compared with earlier hominins such as *Au. afarensis*. However, the molars of *Au. africanus*, although clearly larger than in earlier forms, are smaller than the enormous molars of the robust species.

Australopithecus africanus was a small-bodied biped that possessed the broad and short iliac blade of the pelvis and structural adaptations in the spine, leg, and foot that characterize habitual bipeds. Based on an extensive collection of postcranial remains, body size has been estimated at about 65–90 pounds for *Au. africanus* (which is slightly smaller than the robusts). *Australopithecus africanus* has the same general body plan as *Au. afarensis*, with a more funnel-shaped thorax than in humans, although *Au. africanus*' arms may be shorter (Figure 10.14 on page 251).

Like the hominins in East Africa, *Au. africanus* seems to have been living in woodland and open woodland environments (Reed, 1997). Perhaps these wooded areas provided some protection from predators. There are currently no earlier hominins in South Africa than *Au. africanus*, but it is generally assumed that *Au. africanus* evolved from a population of East African hominin, probably *Au. afarensis*, that migrated to the south.

FIGURE 10.23   The Taung Child, the first of the *Australopithecus* species to be discovered, is the type specimen for *Australopithecus africanus*. It has been suggested that large birds of prey may have been responsible for some of the predation on this early species.

FIGURE 10.24   The site of Gladysvale in South Africa is excavated for *Australopithecus* remains.

Australopithecus sediba (1.97–1.78 MYA)

A newly discovered South African hominin named *Australopithecus sediba* was announced in 2010 by a team led by Lee Berger of the University of the Witswatersrand (Figure 10.26 on page 262). The geological age of the site, based on uranium-lead dating, is between 1.977 and 1.78 million years, although the team thinks that the fossils are likely nearer the older end of this range. Importantly, the remains include both

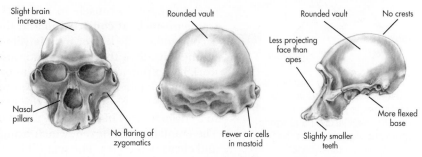

Slight brain increase

Nasal pillars

No flaring of zygomatics

Rounded vault

Fewer air cells in mastoid

Rounded vault

Less projecting face than apes

No crests

Slightly smaller teeth

More flexed base

FIGURE 10.25   Key features of *Australopithecus africanus* include a rounded vault without cranial crests, a slightly flexed cranial base, and moderate facial prognathism.

FIGURE 10.26 *Australopithecus sediba* shares small brain size with other members of *Australopithecus* but also has a relatively broad braincase that some think links it to the genus *Homo*.

👁 **Watch** the **Animation** "Key Anatomical Features of Robust Australopithecines" on **myanthrolab**

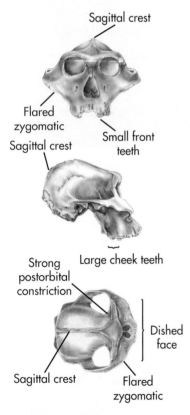

Sagittal crest

Flared zygomatic

Sagittal crest

Small front teeth

Large cheek teeth

Strong postorbital constriction

Dished face

Sagittal crest

Flared zygomatic

FIGURE 10.27 Key features of robust *Australopithecus* include adaptations to heavy chewing such as a large sagittal crest and flaring zygomatics, a dished face, and strongly flexed cranial base.

cranial and postcranial bones, of both an adult and juvenile. Like other *Australopithecus* fossils, the brain size is small, around 420–435 cc, and the body size is small with long arms. But unlike other fossils, these also show some characteristics similar to genus *Homo* and sometimes even *H. erectus* (a more advanced form than the earliest members of the genus). In particular, these characters include dental size and shape, particularly of the molars and canines, a broad frontal, a derived face, and features of the pelvis. Berger and colleagues have argued that these shared characters imply that *Au. sediba* is uniquely related to *Homo* and perhaps even *Homo erectus* (Berger et al., 2010). However, the features could be independently acquired in *Au. sediba* and *Homo* (that is they could be homoplasies) and thus not tell us about close relatedness at all. Many scientists favor this explanation. Or, the characters could tell us about relatedness but could indicate that *Au. sediba*, is a species of *Homo* and not *Australopithecus*. Much more work is needed to differentiate amongst these hypotheses.

"Robust" *Australopithecus* (or *Paranthropus*)

The "robust" group of *Australopithecus* includes several species of early hominins that appear to have been an evolutionary dead end because of their extreme anatomical specializations. The group is united by a suite of cranial features related to their feeding adaptation that made them extremely efficient at producing a great deal of force at their molars (Figure 10.27). These cranial features often are thought of as an adaptation to **hard-object feeding,** chewing tough food items such as hard-shelled nuts or fibrous vegetation. In fact, early fossils were nicknamed "nut-cracker man" for this reason. Scientists think that these cranial adaptations allowed the robust species to survive during times when not much food existed, because they were specialized for eating a kind of food that other hominins could not eat. Most of the time robusts probably ate a lot of different things, but when food was scarce they relied on their "fallback food." What that fallback food was remains much debated. Isotopic research on South African robusts shows that they were omnivores, probably eating some kind of animal protein (perhaps termites) at some times of the year. There is also evidence in South Africa that they may have used bone tools to access this food, and they have been found with stone tools, as well, suggesting that they were fairly intelligent creatures. But new isotopic work from East Africa suggests that *Au. boisei* could have fed on low quality foods, like grasses and sedges, (Cerling et al., 2011). Their reliance on tough foods, whether hard objects or sedges, during times of resource scarcity, seems to become more specialized through time. Eventually, this overspecialization would lead to their demise when food resources changed too dramatically and their fallback foods disappeared.

Whatever the food items and however often they were employed, they seem to have favored an anatomy to produce large bite forces. The **muscles of mastication** that produce chewing force are maximized in size and placement for mechanical efficiency (Figure 10.28). One of these muscles, the temporalis, which sits on the side of the braincase, lifts the mandible. (You can feel your own temporalis doing the work of chewing if you touch your temples while closing your jaw.) The size of the temporalis muscle in robust *Australopithecus* results in the presence of extreme **postorbital constriction** and the flaring of the **zygomatic arches** laterally to accommodate the bigger muscle (Figure 10.27). Another muscle, the masseter, sits on the outside of the jaw and also raises the mandible. (You can feel your masseter work if you put your fingers on the outside and rear of your lower jaw and clench your teeth.) The masseter is moved forward in robusts in two ways. First the zygomatic (cheek) bones, to which the masseter attaches are moved forward (resulting in a "dished face" in which the cheeks extend farther forward than does the nose). The cranial base is flexed, which brings the face (and the teeth) up under the vault and chewing muscles. The mandible is large and deep, and the face is tall to counter

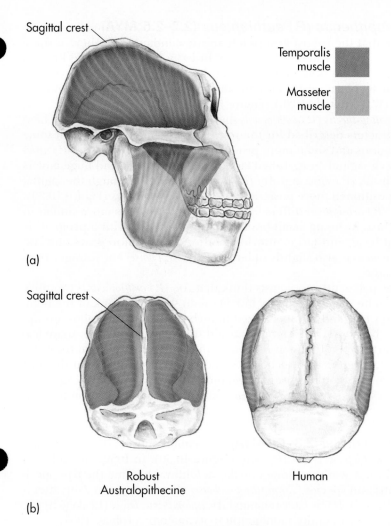

Sagittal crest

Temporalis muscle

Masseter muscle

(a)

Sagittal crest

Robust Australopithecine

Human

(b)

FIGURE 10.28 Muscles of mastication in robust *Australopithecus*. (a) The temporalis muscle (red) attaches to the sagittal crest and the mandible, and the masseter muscle (pink) attaches to the zygomatic bone, which is moved directly over the molar teeth. (b) From above we can see that robust *Australopithecus* had much greater muscle attachment area on their skulls than do modern humans (right).

hard-object feeding   Chewing tough, hard-to-break food items such as nuts or fibrous vegetation.

muscles of mastication   The chewing muscles: masseter, temporalis, medial and lateral pterygoids.

postorbital constriction   The pinching-in of the cranium just behind the orbits where the temporalis muscle sits. Little constriction indicates a large brain and small muscle; great constriction indicates a large muscle, as in the robust groups of *Australopithecus (Paranthropus)*.

zygomatic arch   The bony arch formed by the zygomatic (cheek) bone and the temporal bone of the skull.

these muscle forces. The molars and premolars are enormous, further indicating that at least at some times of the year these hominins relied on a diet that included tough objects. The premolars are like small molars and are called molarized. In contrast, the anterior teeth are tiny, indicating what little importance they had in the dietary habits of the robusts.

Some scientists think that the robust species differ so much from other *Australopithecus* that they should be placed in their own genus, *Paranthropus*. The decision to define a new genus in the fossil record rests on the evidence that a sufficiently different adaptive plateau exists for a given group of species, in this case the robusts, than for other closely related species. Scientists who use the term *Paranthropus* argue that the highly specialized chewing adaptions seen in the skull of the robusts are evidence that, as a group, these species had a substantially different way of making a living and had reached a different adaptive plateau. By using this separate genus name, these scientists also accept that all the robust species are more closely related to one another than they are to species outside of *Paranthropus* and thus that they descend from a recent common ancestor. As we shall see, other scientists disagree as to how closely related the robust species are to one another, so in this book we take a conservative approach and include them in *Australopithecus*.

FIGURE 10.29 *Australopithecus aethiopicus,* called the "Black Skull" because of its manganese staining, is an early robust form dating to about 2.5 million years ago in Kenya.

FIGURE 10.30 Olduvai Hominin 5 (OH 5) is a hyper-robust member of *Australopithecus boisei* discovered in Tanzania by Mary Leakey.

FIGURE 10.31 *Australopithecus robustus* is a South African "robust" species first discovered in 1938.

Australopithecus (P.) aethiopicus (2.7–2.5 MYA)

There is no evidence that the robust groups left any descendants, but there is some tantalizing evidence about their origin. In 1985, Alan Walker and Richard Leakey found the skull of a very primitive robust species that is a good candidate for the ancestor of both later species, *Au. (P.) boisei* and *Au. (P.) robustus* (Walker et al., 1986) (Figure 10.29).

Australopithecus (P.) aethiopicus shares the suite of masticatory (chewing) characters described for the robust group generally but with some modifications and some more primitive characters as well. *Au. (P.) aethiopicus* has a sagittal crest, dished face, flared zygomatics, and huge molars that both *Au. (P.) boisei* and *Au. (P.) robustus* possess, although the sagittal crest is positioned more posteriorly in *Au. (P.) aethiopicus* (Figure 10.30). But *Au. (P.) aethiopicus* differs from other robusts and is more similar to *Au. afarensis* by being small-brained (about 400 cc), with a prognathic face, flat base, and large anterior teeth. At 2.5 million years old, *Au. (P.) aethiopicus* is also slightly older than *Au. (P.) boisei* but younger than *Au. afarensis.*

Many paleoanthropologists think that *Au. (P.) aethiopicus* is primitive enough to be the evolutionary link between the early trunk of the hominin family tree and the specialized branch that led to the robust group. However, because *Au. (P.) aethiopicus* and *Au. (P.) boisei* uniquely share features (such as a heart-shaped foramen magnum) that differentiate them from *Au. africanus* and *Au. (P.) robustus,* some scholars still consider it possible that the East and South African robusts could represent two more distantly related lineages that have converged on a shared anatomy based on a similar dietary adaptation to hard-object feeding.

Australopithecus (P.) boisei (2.3–1.2 MYA)

The culmination of the lineage that started with *Au. (P.) aethiopicus* is *Au. (P.) boisei* (Figure 10.30). In 1959, the skull that Mary Leakey found while working alone one day at Olduvai became the type specimen for a new genus and species, *Zinjanthropus boisei* ("hominin from Zinj; after a benefactor named Boise"). It was later renamed *Australopithecus boisei* (Leakey, 1959), and Philip Tobias devoted an entire monograph to its anatomy (Tobias, 1967).

Since 1959, East African sites in Kenya, Tanzania, and Ethiopia have yielded a plethora of *Au. (P.) boisei* remains, both cranial and postcranial. Although the Leakeys did not know it at the time, Zinj represented the most specialized end of this East African species of robusts. The species spans the time period from about 2.3 to about 1.2 million years ago, based mostly on radiometric ages. The brain size is about the same as that of the robusts from South Africa, and the postcranial skeleton is large, with an estimated body size between 75 and 110 pounds (McHenry, 1992, 1994). The cranial skeleton of *Au. (P.) boisei* reflects the suite of masticatory adaptations discussed previously and some features shared with *Au. (P.) aethiopicus* but not shared with the South African forms.

Australopithecus (P.) robustus (2.0–1.5 MYA)

When Robert Broom discovered the first robust species in 1938 at Kromdraai in South Africa, most of the scientific community still doubted the presence of early hominins in Africa. However, Broom recognized that the forward location of the foramen magnum indicated a biped and thus a hominin rather than a robust ape skull (Figure 10.31). This was also a species quite different from the more gracile *Australopithecus* fossil from Taung. The characters that led Broom to his conclusion are the suite of masticatory characters discussed previously. These characters led Broom to name the genus *Paranthropus* ("next to man"), and the species *robustus.* Later the Swartkrans remains were reassigned to genus *Australopithecus.*

Australopithecus (P.) robustus is known principally from Kromdraai, Swartkrans, and Drimolen; and based on biostratigraphy it dates to about 2.0–1.5 million years ago. Its cranial capacity is between 500 and 550 cc, and the postcranial skeleton indicates a body size of about 70–90 pounds (McHenry, 1993, 1994). *Australopithecus (P.) robustus* differ from their East African counterparts in several minor characters, including the shape of the nasals and browridge and the presence of bony pillars next to the nose.

Understanding the *Australopithecus* Radiation

Just as the Miocene Epoch was a time of great diversification of the apes, the Pliocene was a time of adaptive radiation and diversification of the early hominins. We still do not know how large this radiation was, but frequent new discoveries suggest that many more species of *Australopithecus* and other hominins remain to be found.

Cohabitation

It is difficult for us to imagine today that at various times in the past, two or even three hominin species lived in the same regions of the African continent (Table 10.3). In some of these cases, two species occurred contemporaneously in the same habitat. When two or more species with similar diets and behaviors coexist in the same habitat, we predict that some key aspects of their biology will diverge as a result of competition. If this did not occur, then one species or the other probably should become rare or extinct in the face of direct competition with the other. In the case of the *Australopithecus* species that appear to have shared the same habitat at the same time, they show striking morphological differences that probably reflect differences in dietary adaptations. This suggests that natural selection molded them to avoid feeding competition. Such is the case with living chimpanzees and gorillas who share habitats. Both species prefer fruit to all other forest foods; however, gorillas fall back on high-fiber leafy foods in lean seasons, whereas chimpanzees forage far and wide to continue eating fruits (Tutin, 1996; Stanford and Nkurunungi, 2003).

In addition to *Au.(P.) africanus* and *Au. (P.) robustus* in southern Africa, potential cases of sympatry in the hominin fossil record include *Au. (P.) boisei* (robust) and early genus *Homo* in eastern Africa, *Au. garhi* and *Au. (P.) aethiopicus* in eastern Africa, and *Au. afarensis* and *K. platyops* in eastern Africa.

Tools and Intelligence

We used to think that only members of our own genus *Homo* were clever enough to make tools. *Australopithecus* was considered dim-witted in comparison and without tools. However, until the 1960s tool-making was also unknown in the living great apes. We

TABLE 10.3   Examples of Potentially Contemporaneous Hominins by Region

Age (MYA)*	West Africa	East Africa	South Africa
~6	*Sahelanthropus tchadensis*	*Orrorin tugenensis*	
3.9		*Australopithecus afarensis, Au. anamensis*	
3.5	*Au. bahrelghazali*	*Au. afarensis, Kenyanthropus platyops*	*Au. africanus*
2.5		*Au. garhi, Au. aethiopicus*	*Au. africanus*
2.5–2		*Au. boisei, Au. garhi*	*Au. africanus, Au. robustus*
2–1.5		*Au. boisei, Homo sp.*	*Homo sp., Au. sediba, Au. robustus*

*MYA= millions of years ago

osteodontokeratic culture A bone, tooth, and horn tool kit envisioned by Raymond Dart to be made by *Australopithecus*.

know that tool-making is common in the great apes and even some monkeys, although none make stone tools. Chimpanzees make and use probes to extract insects and other food items, make sponges to soak up liquids, use hammers to crack open nuts, and wield branches as weapons against prey and other chimpanzees (see Chapter 8). Other apes and even Capuchin monkeys use organic tools, although they may not make them (see Chapter 8 Innovations: Culture in Nonhuman Primates on pages 182–183). We might expect, then, that early hominins such as *Australopithecus* fashioned tools, perhaps out of organic materials, but did not necessarily make stone tools.

The archaeological record for *Australopithecus* is quite limited, but there is tantalizing evidence that these hominins were smarter than we think. South African paleontologist Raymond Dart proposed a so-called **osteodontokeratic culture** in which he envisioned *Au. africanus* using the bones, teeth, and horns of animals as tools (hence the name he gave the culture). Although his evidence has not held up under more recent scrutiny, Dart may have been right in thinking that *Australopithecus* made and used tools. The earliest definite evidence of tool use in the genus is the possible association between *Au. garhi* and the butchered remains of animals about 2.5 million years ago in Ethiopia. Recent suggestions of cut-marked bone at 3.4 million years ago are more contentious, but if true, would point to *Au. afarensis* as the maker. At other sites in eastern and southern Africa, stone tools are found in the same beds and even at the same localities as the remains of robust *Australopithecus*. No other hominin genera are known from these particular contexts, so this may indicate the production and use of stone tools by robust *Australopithecus*. And bone tools, probably used for unearthing termites, are found at South African robust sites. It seems likely that *Australopithecus* was at least as sophisticated as living great apes, although it is not until around 2.5 million years ago, well into their radiation, that we see the first certain use of stone tools.

Ancestors and Descendants

There are several ways to envision the evolutionary relationships among the early hominins we have examined in this chapter (Figure 10.32). There is no single consensus model, and a number of plausible models exist. Based on anatomy, many scientists derive *Au. afarensis* from the more primitive *Au. anamensis* and then see *Au. afarensis* as the base of the radiation of *Au. africanus*, *Au. garhi*, *Au. aethiopicus*, and possibly the *Homo* lineage. Each of these lineages takes the *Au. afarensis* anatomy in a slightly different direction depending on the environmental conditions in which it lived and by which individuals were selected for or against. Many see *Au. (P.) aethiopicus* giving rise to the robust radiation of *Au. (P.) boisei* and *Au. (P.) robustus*, whereas others derive the East African robusts from *Au. (P.) aethiopicus* but the South African robusts from *Au. africanus*. This splitting into South and East African lineages means that these scientists don't think the robusts shared a last common ancestor exclusive of other species of *Australopithecus* and therefore are not part of a separate genus, *Paranthropus*. *Australopithecus africanus*, *Au. afarensis*, and *Au. garhi* have all been implicated as possible ancestors for the genus *Homo*, and *Au. sediba* is even considered a possible ancestor to *H. erectus*, although this seems unlikely. However, one thing that almost all scientists agree on is the idea that the robust species are too specialized to be ancestral to genus *Homo*. The key to a good potential ancestor is that it exists early enough to give rise to the later groups, is not more derived than those groups, and has characters that look as if they could give rise to later groups.

Because the fossil record is sparse, each new fossil discovery throws the tree into brief disarray, after which paleoanthropologists try to sort out the most likely phylogeny suggested by the sum of the evidence. This may seem as though scientists cannot agree, but disagreement is a healthy feature of any science. Each new find tests previous hypotheses and produces new interpretations, new research, and new results that push the state of our understanding of human ancestry forward.

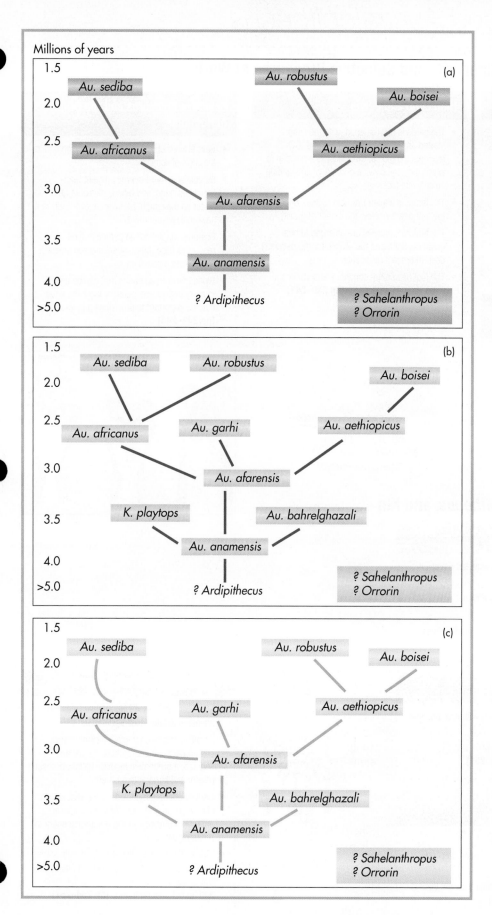

FIGURE 10.32 Three possible phylogenies for *Australopithecus* with *Au. anamensis* as the stem ancestor and recognizing a small number of species and close relationships between (a) *Au. robustus* and *Au. boisei*, (b) a larger number of species and only distant relationship between *Au. robustus* and *Au. boisei*, or (c) a large number of species and a close relationship between *Au. robustus* and *Au. boisei*.

Early Hominins and *Australopithecus*

Anatomical Adaptations to Bipedality and Selective Pressures at Work

Axial Skeleton

- The foramen magnum is placed on the inferior of the cranium.
- Vertebral bodies bear progressively more weight lower in the column and so are largest in the lumbar region.
- The spinal column acquires two secondary curvatures (in the cervical and lumbosacral regions) that keep the center of gravity directly above, rather than in front of, the feet of the biped. **[pp 238–240]**

Forelimb Adaptations and Changes Not Directly Related to Bipedality

- The arm is not weight-bearing and as a result is relatively gracile and eventually foreshortened.
- Fingers are shortened and not curved.
- The canine is reduced in size and lacks a CP$_3$ honing complex.
- Eventually the dental arcade is relatively parabolic in shape. **[p 242]**

Hind Limb and Pelvis

- The pelvis is bowl-shaped, with the ilium rotated around the side of the biped. This reorients the gluteal muscles into a position in which they can provide support while standing on only one foot.
- The femur is angled from hip to knee bringing the foot directly below the center of gravity.
- The femoral condyles are enlarged to bear greater weight, and the groove for the patella is deep to prevent dislocation.
- The foot has arches for shock absorbing and short, straight phalanges. **[pp 240–241]**

Energy efficiency

Selective Pressures and the Origin of Hominins

- Several kinds of scenarios have been proposed for the origin of hominins.
- Bipedality is more energy efficient than knucklewalking, and bipeds dissipate heat faster so they might be favored, especially in a savannah environment.
- Postural adaptations to particular food resources (from trees, or specialized grasses) might favor bipedalism.
- Bipeds have freed hands that can be used to carry infants, weapons, or food; the latter may be important to provisioning by males. **[pp 242–244]**

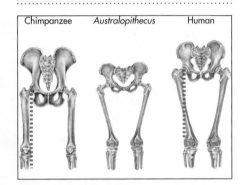

Chimpanzee   *Australopithecus*   Human

Earliest Hominins, *Australopithecus,* and Kin

Earliest Hominins

- The earliest potential hominins appear in Africa between 5 and 7 million years ago.
- They include *Sahelanthropus, Orrorin,* and *Ardipithecus.*
- They all lack a functional CP$_3$ honing complex.
- Controversy surrounds whether many of the genera are hominins. **[pp 244–251]**

Australopithecus Characters

- Small-bodied, small-brained, bipedal African apes with both primitive and derived characters.
- Less well-known species between 2.5 and 3.5 MYA are: *Au. bahrelgazali,, Au. garhi,* and *K. platyops..* **[p 251]**

Au. anamensis (4.2–3.9 MYA)

- This early form is likely ancestral to *Au. afarensis.*
- Primitive characters include a shallow, U-shaped palate and large anterior teeth.
- Derived characters include somewhat smaller canine crown, thick enamel, and adaptations to bipedalism. **[p 254]**

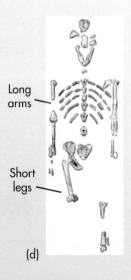

Long arms

Short legs

(d)

Au. afarensis (3.9–2.9 MYA)

- More derived than *Au. anamensis;* may be ancestral to later *Australopithecus.*
- Primitive cranial characters include cranial cresting (compound temporo-nuchal and sagittal); a prognathic face; a shallow, U-shaped palate; and large anterior teeth.
- Derived characters include somewhat smaller canine crown and root, somewhat smaller anterior dentition, and slight enlargement of the posterior dentition.
- The postcranium is that of a biped, with some primitive retentions such as curved phalanges, a wide pelvis, short hind limb, long forelimb, and funnel-shaped thorax. **[pp 254–257]**

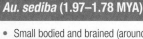

Au. africanus (3.5–<2.0 MYA)

- More derived than *Au. afarensis*, this hominin may have a unique relationship to *Au. robustus* or *Homo*.
- Derived characters include a rounded vault (absence of cranial cresting), a somewhat flexed cranial base, and a more parabolic dental arcade.
- The postcranial skeleton is similar to *Au. afarensis*. **[pp 259–261]**

Au. sediba (1.97–1.78 MYA)

- Small bodied and brained (around 420 cc), this species had long arms.
- A broad braincase and derived face, and some changes to the pelvis are like *Homo*.
- Its discoverers argue that this species may have a unique relationship to *Homo* or even *H. erectus*. **[pp 261–262]**

Robust Australopithecus (Paranthropus)

- The robust group appears to have been an evolutionary dead end.
- They show a suite of craniodental adaptations for producing high bite forces.
- Species include the East African *Au.(P) aethiopicus*, *Au. (P) boisei*, and South African *Au. (P) robustus*. **[pp 262–263]**

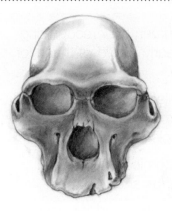

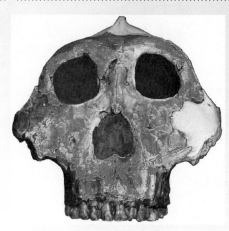

Geological Context of East and South African Hominin Sites

East African Sites

- Often associated with volcanic ashes or tephra.
- ^{40}Ar/^{39}Ar (chronometric) dating is possible as are relative dating techniques such as biostratigraphy, tephrostratigraphy, and calibrated relative techniques such as paleomagnetism. **[pp 252–253; 258]**

South African Sites

- Usually fissure fills in karst (limestone) systems that lack volcanic sediments.
- Site ages are mostly based on biostratigraphy and paleomagnetism, with U-series offering a few age estimates. **[pp 252–253; 259]**

My AnthroLab CONNECTIONS

Watch. Listen. View. Explore. Read.

MyAnthroLab is designed just for you. Each chapter features a customized study plan to help you learn and review key concepts and terms. Dynamic visual activities, videos, and readings found in the multimedia library will enhance your learning experience.

Resources from this Chapter:

👁 **Watch** on **myanthrolab**

▶ *Key Anatomical Features of Robust Australopithecus*

🔊 **Listen** on **myanthrolab**

▶ *Study: Human Ancestors Walked Upright Early, by Jon Hamilton*
▶ *Fast Feet: A Springy Step Helps Humans Walk*

✳ **Explore** on **myanthrolab** In MySearchLab, enter the Anthropology database to find relevant and recent scholarly and popular press publications. For this chapter, enter the following keywords: *Australopithecus*, Bipedality, Hominin, *Paranthropus*

📖 **Read** on **myanthrolab**

▶ *Morning of the Modern Mind* by Kate Wong
▶ *An Ancestor to Call our Own* by Kate Wong

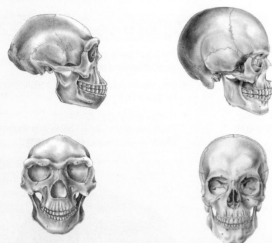

Chapter 11 Preview

After reading this chapter, you should be able to:

- Detail the evolution of *Homo* in the Pliocene and Pleistocene.

- Discuss the anatomical characteristics that define the genus *Homo* and its earliest members *(H. habilis, H. rudolfensis)*.

- Discuss the arguments for recognizing one species of early *Homo* vs those for recognizing two.

- Analyze the intellectual abilities necessary for producing Oldowan tools and what the tools may be used for.

- Discuss the anatomical differences between *H. erectus* and *H. habilis*.

- Outline the distribution and life ways of *Homo erectus*.

- Discuss the arguments for recognizing *H. erectus* as one species or two.

EUROPE
1.0 mya

GEORGIA
1.7 mya

ASIA
1.6–1.2 mya

AFRICA
1.8 mya

INDIAN
OCEAN

JAVA
1.6–1.8 mya

ATLANTIC
OCEAN

Rift Valley

Rise of the Genus *Homo*

For the following few weeks, the excavating brought nearly nonstop excitement, but there was some meticulous scientific work behind the celebrations....The bones kept coming, right up to the last moment, so we knew we would have to come back. Nearly everything we found was part of our skeleton.... When we closed down the site for the season, on September 21, 1984, we had found more of *Homo erectus*—the classic missing link—than anyone had ever seen. The next four field seasons laboring in the pit, as we came to call the enormous excavation, would see 1,500 cubic yards of rock and earth moved by hand. Our schoolboys, who worked with us faithfully year after year, grew from adolescents to young men while the Nariokotome boy, as we took to calling the specimen, grew from a fragment of skull to the most complete early hominin skeleton ever found.

—from *The Wisdom of the Bones,*
by A. Walker and P. Shipman

The discovery of the skeleton of the Nariokotome boy, the remains of most of a *Homo erectus* skeleton, dramatically changed our understanding of early *Homo.* The lanky body proportions of the Nariokotome youth suggested that the transition from the apelike body of *Australopithecus* to that of modern humans occurred in the short time interval between 2.3 and 1.7 million years ago. What we know about the transition from *Australopithecus* to earliest *Homo* rests ultimately on the fossil record. And what we know of the fossil record, including the discovery of the Nariokotome boy, rests in equal parts on skill, perseverance, planning, and sheer luck. In fact, the early fossil record of genus *Homo* is remarkably sketchy in comparison to that of *Australopithecus,* making the task of understanding the origin of the genus that much more difficult.

In this chapter, we examine the early members of the genus *Homo,* from their beginnings in apelike African hominins to the first migrations out of Africa and into other parts of the Old World. We discuss how climate fluctuations may have influenced the origin and evolution of *Homo.* We discuss the appearance of *Homo erectus,* whose larger brain and body size may signal an adaptive shift in diet, who makes increasingly sophisticated tools, and who may use fire. Then we examine early tool technologies and subsistence. And finally we consider the debate over later stages of *H. erectus,* setting the stage for the discussion of other hominins outside Africa in Chapters 12 and 13.

Climate and the Evolution of *Homo* in the Pliocene and Pleistocene

The origin and evolution of our genus seems to be related to fluctuations in climate. During the early Pliocene, ice sheets became permanent features at both the north and the south poles. Cyclic glaciation began about 3 million years ago and became increasingly intense throughout the Pleistocene. The first appearance of fossils of the genus *Homo* coincides with the period of greatest variability in the fossil record (that is, when we see the most changes in the occurrence of different species of mammals). A later period of climatic fluctuation is linked to the appearance of early stone tools, and during a still later period of fluctuation, some *Australopithecus* species went extinct.

It may be that humans are adapted to such periods of climatic instability and that our intelligence and adaptability may have been honed as a result (Potts, 1996). Around 2.5 million years ago, glacial cycles began to become more severe, some lowered sea levels enough to connect island Southeast Asia to mainland Asia. These intermittent connections allowed animals and *H. erectus* to cross back and forth between the two areas at times and to be isolated from one another at other times. Before hominins left Africa, however, the selective pressures of changing climate and diet resulted in changes to their skeleton that we can see in the fossil record.

Defining the Genus *Homo*

The first species of genus *Homo* are not all that different from some *Australopithecus*. Recall that a genus name implies a certain adaptive strategy, so that with the switch from *Australopithecus* to *Homo*, you should expect to see a suite of adaptive differences between the two genera. In general, genus *Homo* differs from *Australopithecus* by having a larger, more rounded braincase; a smaller, less projecting face; smaller teeth; and eventually a larger body and shorter arms and perhaps more efficient striding bipedalism. These features may be related to an adaptation that includes more meat and animal fat in their diet, greater ranging, and greater food processing through tool use. However, early members of the genus *Homo* differ less strongly from *Australopithecus* than later members and therefore are harder to distinguish from them.

There is much debate over the application of names to the fossil record for genus *Homo*. Depending on the scientist, earliest *Homo* is conceived of either as a single, variable species (*H. habilis*) or as multiple, less variable species (usually *H. habilis* and *H. rudolfensis*). Similarly, *H. erectus* is seen as either a single species or two species (*H. ergaster* and *H. erectus*), and the presence of any of these species in Europe is hotly debated. All this disagreement results in part from the paucity of the fossil record, differences in species concepts (lumpers versus splitters), and the inherent difficulty of applying a static classification system to the dynamic process of evolution. Some scientists think that the variability that we see in these species is in part related to the climate in which they evolved.

View the **Map** "The Genus *Homo* Through Time" on **myanthrolab**

Earliest Genus *Homo*

In the 1960s, Louis and Mary Leakey discovered a nearly 2-million-year-old juvenile partial skull at Olduvai Gorge. Olduvai Hominid 7 (OH 7) possessed a brain larger than any known *Australopithecus* and differed markedly from the "robust" *Australopithecus*, *Zinjanthropus boisei*, also from Olduvai (see Chapter 10). Louis Leakey, Philip Tobias, and John Napier included OH 7 in the new species *Homo habilis*, or "the skilled human or handy man," referring to the use and manufacture of stone tools (Figure 11.1).

In the early 1970s at Koobi Fora on the eastern shore of Lake Turkana, Richard Leakey's team discovered a more intact skull of *H. habilis*, known by its National Museums of Kenya catalog number KNM-ER 1470, which is approximately 1.8 million years old (Figure 11.2). KNM-ER 1470 has a large cranial capacity of 775 cc. Additional finds of *H. habilis* from Koobi Fora range in geological age from about 1.4 to 1.9 million years old and vary greatly in size (Figure 11.2). A recently discovered palate from Ileret Kenya extended the time range of *H. habilis* to 1.4 million years ago (Spoor et al., 2007) indicating some temporal overlap with *H. erectus*.

Many scholars think that the differences between the largest (1470) and smallest Koobi Fora early *Homo* crania are too great to fall within the variation of a single species. The smallest has a brain almost one-third smaller (only 510 cc) than the largest specimen, smaller teeth, and a differently proportioned face. Most who separate these fossils into two species place OH 7, the type specimen and name-bearer of the species, with the smaller-brained specimens, calling this grouping *H. habilis*. They

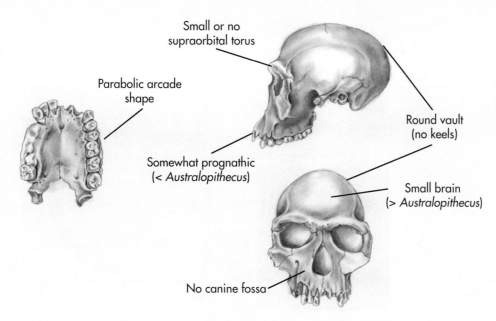

Small or no supraorbital torus

Parabolic arcade shape

Round vault (no keels)

Somewhat prognathic (< *Australopithecus*)

Small brain (> *Australopithecus*)

No canine fossa

Oldowan The tool industry characterized by simple, usually unifacial core and flake tools.

tool industry A particular style or tradition of making stone tools.

core The raw material source (a river cobble or a large flake) from which flakes are removed.

flake The stone fragment struck from a core, thought to have been the primary tools of the Oldowan.

hammerstone A stone used for striking cores to produce flakes or bones to expose marrow.

FIGURE 11.1 Key anatomical features of *Homo habilis* include reduced facial size, a parabolic palate, and some brain enlargement.

then use 1470 as the type specimen for *H. rudolfensis*. If true, this would mean that there were two species of genus *Homo* living sympatrically in East Africa between 1.5 and 2.0 million years ago along with sympatric *Australopithecus*. If this is the case, it would be unclear which of the two species of early *Homo*—*H. habilis* or *H. rudolfensis*—gave rise to later species of *Homo* such as *H. erectus* and *H. sapiens*. Is the larger-brained group linked to *H. erectus* through brain size? Or are the dental and facial similarities between the smaller-brained group and *H. erectus* evidence of an evolutionary relationship between these two? There are still too few fossils to distinguish between these two options with any certainty.

Alternatively, other researchers think the largest and smallest early *Homo* fossils are a male and a female of the same species. This single species would be known as *H. habilis* and may ultimately have given rise to *H. erectus*. Whatever you call these fossils, there is clear evidence that they made and used stone tools. Whether they were the first or the only hominins to make stone tools is debated, but we know that this practice began in earnest around 2.5 million years ago.

Early Tool Use

Whoever the first tool-maker was, stone tools occur in the record starting about 2.5 million years ago. The earliest tools are known as the **Oldowan** industry, so named for their first discovery at Olduvai Gorge in Tanzania. We refer to stone tools made in a particular way or tradition as a **tool industry** (Figure 11.3 on page 274). Oldowan tools consist mainly of **cores,** lumps of stone, often river cobbles modified from the original rock by flaking pieces off it, and **flakes,** the small fragments taken from the core. Archaeologists used to think the core itself was the cutting tool, but experimental evidence suggests the flakes were used as tools. The cores probably were used to produce flakes until they became too small and were discarded (Schick and Toth, 1993). Flakes can be extremely sharp and are effective at cutting through tough animal hides and removing meat from bones. Other Oldowan tools called **hammerstones**

FIGURE 11.2 Crania of KNM-ER 1813 and 1470 differ enough that some scientists include them in two different species.

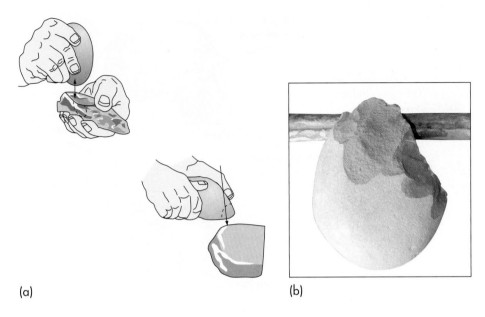

(a) (b)

FIGURE 11.3 (a) Oldowan tools are simple flake tools struck from a core using a hammerstone or an anvil technique. The flakes are often removed from only one side of the core and are useful for cutting through hides, muscle, and plant material. (b) An experimentally made Oldowan-type core is shown at right.

butchering site A place where there is archaeological evidence of the butchering of carcasses by hominins. The evidence usually consists of tool cut marks on fossilized animal bones or the presence of the stone tools themselves.

quarrying site An archaeological site at which there is evidence that early hominins were obtaining the raw material to make stone tools.

home base Archaeological term for an area to which early hominins may have brought tools and carcasses and around which their activities were centered.

were used to crack open the bones of large animals to extract marrow and to remove flakes from cores. Oldowan tools are deceptively simple in appearance; if you held one you might not be sure whether it was human-made or naturally created. However, archaeologists, some of whom are proficient stone tool-makers, can distinguish human manufacture patterns from natural breakage of stone.

Tool-making was first and foremost an adaptation to the environment of the late Pliocene. Through the use of tools, hominins could eat animal meat and access fat resources in their bones. The use of animals as food became an increasingly important adaptive strategy for early humans. Based on the archaeological record, early *Homo* probably carried tools with them rather than constantly discarding or continually making them anew. If early hominins carried tools with them, they must have been using these tools as an important part of their daily routine. Just think about the things you choose to put in your backpack each day—like your cell phone and wallet— and what that means about their importance in your routine.

Archaeologists specializing in the study of stone tools have categorized the patterns of tool use at various Oldowan sites in East Africa. Some of these are believed to have been **butchering sites:** A variety of mammal bones, some with direct evidence of butchering, such as cut and percussion marks, are found in association with stone tools. One such site at Olduvai Gorge contains the remains of a hippo with cut marks on its bones along with scores of flakes, suggesting the hippo had been butchered. Some sites, where stone implements are found in great abundance, are **quarrying sites,** where hominins went to obtain the raw material for the tools. A third type of site is what the archaeologist Glynn Isaac (1978) called a **home base.** Isaac hypothesized that hominins repeatedly brought butchered carcasses back to a central place, possibly with a particular amenity such as a shade tree or a water source nearby, where they slept and ate in greater safety than at the site where the animal was killed. At such a home base, the hominins would have been manufacturing or refining tools as well. Other archaeologists are skeptical of this idea, arguing that natural processes, such as movement of remains by water, wind, and animals, may account for what look like human-created bases of activity. Still others think that the accumulations may represent caches of material made by hominins for their later use rather than campsites.

We don't know for certain which early hominin made which tools because we don't find hominin fossils actually holding the tools. We can only infer tool use by the association between tools and hominin remains in the same excavations. Even this is dangerous because antelope are the most abundant fossils found in association with stone tools, and we are quite sure the antelope are not the tool-makers! Despite the enormous amount of evidence of meat and marrow eating, in the form of butchered bones, we don't know how often a group of early *Homo* might have actually eaten these or how important meat (or marrow) was in their diet. Did a group of *H. habilis* butcher and consume one large mammal per week? Per month? Per year? Did all members of the group participate in this butchering activity and in the feast? How much did the incorporation of stone tool manufacture and annual consumption affect other aspects of early hominin behavior, ecology, physiology, and biology? It seems that after 2.5 million years ago, animal resources took on increasing importance, but the method of measuring that importance has been contentious.

Hunting and Scavenging

The debate about the role of meat and marrow in the early human diet has a long and tumultuous history, beginning with Raymond Dart's recognition of an "oste-odontokeratic" culture that he attributed to South African *Australopithecus'* carnivorous diet (Dart, 1925; see Chapter 10). The earliest hominins almost certainly ate most of the same foods that modern apes eat: fruit, leaves, seeds, insects, and some animal prey. The first indisputable evidence of animal foods is stone tool use for carcass butchery (based on cut marks on fossilized bones of antelope), probably by earliest genus *Homo* but possibly also by *A. garhi*, at about 2.5 million years ago or perhaps even earlier. Before this time, if emerging humans were making and using tools, they were using materials such as wood or unmodified bone that did not accumulate or preserve in the fossil record. And if they were eating meat or marrow without the assistance of stone tools, we have no visible archaeological record of their activity.

We would like to know whether our own lineage arose with the help of a hunting or scavenging way of life because each of these entails a different set of behavioral adaptations. There are currently three main models for how early hominins acquired carcasses. Bands of early humans may have courageously attacked and slaughtered large and dangerous game (hunting). Or they could have fought off large predators such as saber-tooth cats to gain access to significant amounts of meat and marrow (confrontational scavenging). Or perhaps they crept nervously up to decomposing, nearly stripped carcasses to glean a few scraps of meat and fat (passive scavenging). Mostly, however, discussion focuses on differences between hunting and scavenging.

Although interpretations of "Man the Hunter" were popular in the 1960s, many anthropologists took issue with this perspective, particularly because in some of the traditional societies that are most vaunted for the man's role in hunting, up to 85% of the protein obtained by a household comes not from men but from women gathering foods such as nuts, tubers, and small animals (Tanner and Zihlman, 1976). Also, there was evidence at some fossil sites that *H. habilis* had been butchering animal carcasses that had first been chewed on by carnivores. When anthropologists Rick Potts (1988) and Pat Shipman (1986) studied the bones of animals from Old-owan sites, they saw that in some cases the human-made cut marks were on top of the carnivore tooth marks, evidence that humans were cutting flesh from the bones after they had already been chewed by a predator. The implication was clear: On at least some occasions, hominins were scavengers rather than hunters.

To be a scavenger rather than a hunter affects every aspect of daily life. Instead of depending on an ability to chase down and kill elusive prey, a scavenger relies on finding the kills made by hunters and then somehow taking some of the meat. Many scavengers, such as vultures and jackals, are tolerated by larger carnivores at a kill, but would early hominins have been? Through the 1980s, archaeologists adopted

Listen to the **Podcast** "Food for Thought: Meat-Based Diet Made Us Smarter" on **myanthrolab**

new experimental approaches to understanding the role that the hominins may have played in those ecosystems. These studies suggested that ample scavenging opportunities existed for hominins 2 million years ago (Blumenschine, 1987). By the 1990s, field studies of meat eating by wild chimpanzees showed that even without tools, apes can capture and consume large quantities of small mammals (Boesch and Boesch, 1989; Stanford, 1998). John Yellen (1991) showed that modern hunter-gatherers consume large amounts of small mammals, none of which would leave any archaeological evidence had early hominins done the same. Archaeologists began to reinterpret the models for hominin scavenging behavior, arguing that aggressive, active carcass piracy was far more likely than passively locating dead animals that were already mostly consumed by primary predators (Bunn and Ezzo, 1993).

Early views of the hunting and scavenging debate tended to emphasize a black-or-white approach, which is rarely the way that living creatures behave. Instead, perhaps *H. habilis* acquired animal resources in any form they could, through both hunting for small animals and scavenging carcasses. Modern foragers do the same. Cultural diversity in modern chimpanzee populations (see Chapter 10) suggests that some populations of early genus *Homo* could have hunted, whereas others may have preferred scavenging, and both strategies probably were included in a flexible behavioral repertoire. Regardless of whether meat and marrow was obtained by hunting or scavenging, the archaeological record shows that hominin stone-tool–assisted consumption of large animals began about 2.5 million years ago and gradually increased through time. The two innovations of stone tool manufacture and animal resource exploitation undoubtedly shaped much of subsequent human evolutionary history.

Who Was *Homo erectus*?

Sometime around the Plio-Pleistocene boundary, about 1.8 million years ago, hominins underwent a major adaptive shift. This is reflected in the fossil record by body and brain size increases and tooth size decreases that may signal an increase in diet quality and a larger home range perhaps similar to that of modern humans. These changes may have been this group's response to environmental and climatic changes during that time period. Remember, however, that while the early *Homo* lineage was responding to these climate changes by adaptive shifts, another lineage—the "robust" *Australopithecus* species—responded not by changing but by intensifying its previous adaptation to hard object feeding.

Homo. erectus appeared in Africa more than 1.8 million years ago and was the first hominin to leave the continent, probably by about 1.7 million years ago (Figure 11.4). Some paleoanthropologists call these earliest *H. erectus* by another name, *Homo ergaster* (Wood and Collard, 1999). Whatever you call them, these hominins quickly left Africa. Why hominins left Africa when they did is a source of debate. What is certain is that dispersal probably was the result of multiple movements of small groups of hominins into new territories. The last members of the species exist more than 1.5 million years later, being found in the late Pleistocene of Indonesia.

Anatomical Features

Homo erectus is characterized by a somewhat larger body and brain and a uniquely shaped skull. *H. erectus* shows the beginnings of a modern human body plan, with a larger body size than the average *Australopithecus* and perhaps a less funnel-shaped thorax than in earlier hominins and living apes.

The Skull and Teeth *H. erectus* crania are easily identified by their shape (Figure 11.5 on page 278). The skull is thick-boned and robust, much longer than it is wide, relatively low and angular from the side, and pentagonal in rear view. The angularity of the skull is enhanced by a series of cranial superstructures, regional thickenings of bone along certain sutures and across certain bones. These include

supraorbital torus Thickened ridge of bone above the eye orbits of the skull; a brow ridge.

angular torus A thickened ridge of bone at the posterior angle of the parietal bone.

occipital torus A thickened horizontal ridge of bone on the occipital bone at the rear of the cranium.

sagittal keel Longitudinal ridge or thickening of bone on the sagittal suture not associated with any muscle attachment.

metopic keel Longitudinal ridge or thickening of bone along the midline of the frontal bone.

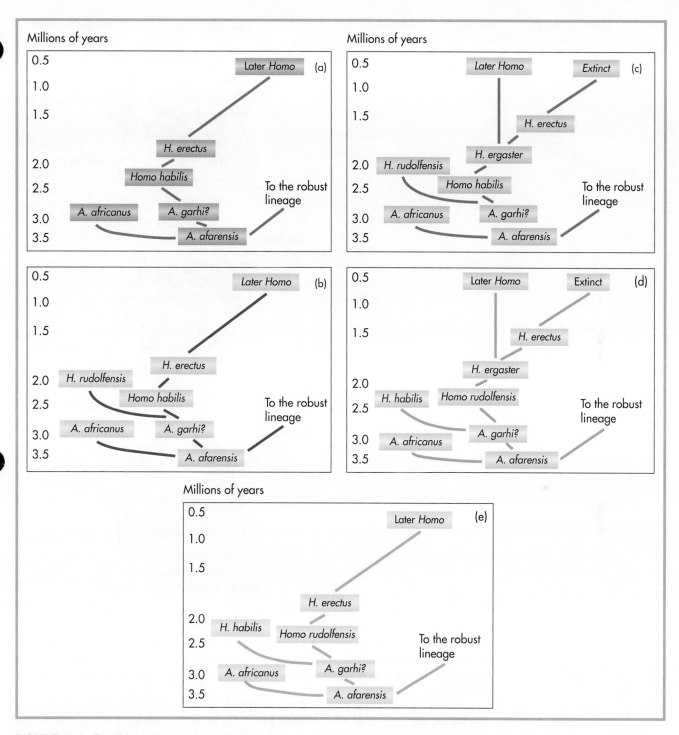

FIGURE 11.4   Possible phylogenies for early *Homo*.

thickenings such as the prominent **supraorbital torus** or brow ridge on the frontal, a thickened **angular torus** on the back of the parietal, and the **occipital torus,** a ridge of bone that runs horizontally across the occipital. In addition, the forehead has a low, sloping or receding appearance. The pentagonal rear view is formed by other thickenings including those along sutures such as the **sagittal keel,** along the sagittal suture that joins the two parietals, and the **metopic keel** along the midline frontal. The pentagon is widest at its base; the sides slant inward from there to the lateral part of the parietal and then turn in to meet at the tip of the pentagon, which is formed by the sagittal keel. Although it is easy to see these anatomical changes,

FIGURE 11.5 Major features of *Homo erectus* include increased brain size, an angular vault, and cranial superstructures (such as tori and keels).

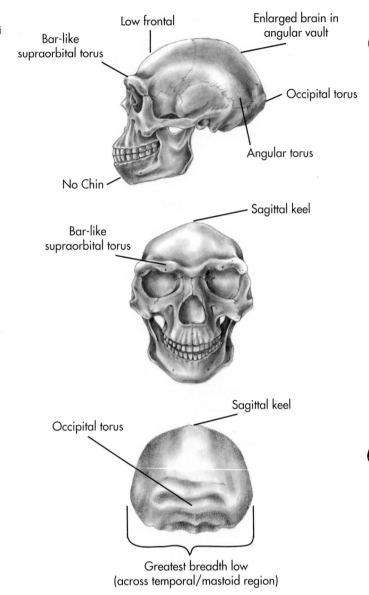

Low frontal

Bar-like supraorbital torus

Enlarged brain in angular vault

Occipital torus

Angular torus

No Chin

Sagittal keel

Bar-like supraorbital torus

Sagittal keel

Occipital torus

Greatest breadth low (across temporal/mastoid region)

it is not so clear why they might have evolved. Unlike the cranial crests of earlier hominins, these thickenings of bone are not related to muscle attachments. And their function, if any, is unclear. Possibly they were a way to strengthen the braincase as brain size increases.

H. erectus brain size ranges from something less than 700 to 1,200 cc, averaging about 900 cc (Table 11.1; Figure 11.6). Partly as a result of this expansion, the degree of postorbital constriction is less than in *Australopithecus* but still marked compared with later forms. Early brain size increases in *H. erectus* may occur simply in proportion to body size increases in the species, and real (i.e., disproportionately large) brain size evolution may not occur until archaic *H. sapiens,* just a few hundred thousand years ago. Of course, not only sheer volume but also organization of the brain are key factors in determining how smart a species is. Certainly in absolute brain size, *H. erectus* was less well-endowed than modern humans. However, the brain size of *H. erectus* also shows regional and evolutionary variation, indicating progressive but slow increase in the lineage through time (Leigh, 1992; Antón and Swisher, 2001) (Figure 11.7 on page 280). Because there are so few associated skeletons, it is difficult to know whether the increased brain size of *H. erectus* was a unique adaptation or simply a result of larger body size.

shovel-shaped incisors Anterior teeth that, on their lingual (tongue) surface, are concave with two raised edges that make them look like tiny shovels.

TABLE 11.1   Dmanisi Hominins Compared with Other Early Hominins

Taxon	Brain size (cc)	Body height (in.)	Body weight (lb.)
Dmanisi	650–780	58	105
H. sapiens	1,350	63–69	108–128
African *H. erectus*	700–1,067	63–71	123–145
Asian *H. erectus*	800–1,250	—	—
Earliest *Homo*	500–750	39–63	70–132
A. africanus	448	45–54	66–90

Source: Gabunia et al. (2001).

The jaw of *H. erectus* was as robust and powerfully built as the rest of the cranial complex. The proportions of the mandible contrast with the small teeth in some of the earlier *H. erectus* specimens from Africa (Wolpoff, 1999). The lingual (tongue) sides of the incisors are concave, with ridges along their edges forming the shape of a tiny shovel, referred to as **shovel-shaped incisors.** This shape is thought to prevent tooth damage when the front teeth are exposed to heavy wear from food or other activities. Some researchers have attempted to link ancient Asian *H. erectus* populations with modern Asian populations, based on this apparent continuity of incisor shape (see Chapter 13). However, because most *H. erectus* specimens from all regions possess this trait, as do Neandertals, it seems more likely that it is a primitive trait for the genus that may or may not suggest a link between modern and ancient Asian populations.

Body Size and Shape Despite the large numbers of *H. erectus* skulls and teeth that have been found over the past century, what we know of the postcranial skeleton comes from just three partial skeletons and some isolated bones, mostly from East Africa and some recently discovered remains from the Republic of Georgia. The

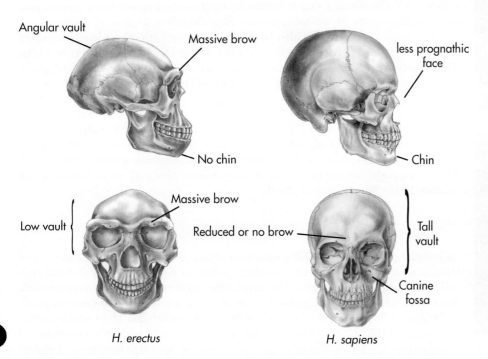

H. erectus   *H. sapiens*

FIGURE 11.6 Compared with modern humans, *Homo erectus* has a larger face, lacks a chin, and has a more angular vault and smaller brain.

platymeric A bone that is flattened from front to back.

platycnemic A bone that is flattened from side to side.

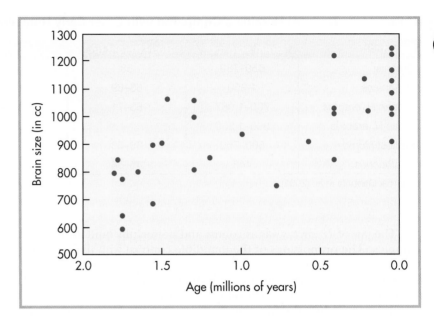

FIGURE 11.7 Although average brain size increases gradually through time in *H. erectus*, individuals with small brains are present even late in time. Dots represent individual fossils.

most important of these is the remarkably complete KNM-WT 15000 skeleton—the Nariokotome boy—found in 1984 on the western side of Lake Turkana in Kenya by Alan Walker and Richard Leakey, whose discovery is described at the beginning of this chapter (Figure 11.8). These specimens suggest not only that *H. erectus* was robustly proportioned but also that some individuals were quite tall as adults, between five and a half and six feet (Walker, 1993; McHenry and Coffing, 2000). The long bones of the arms and legs are thick; the femur is **platymeric,** which means it is flattened from front to back, and the tibia is **platycnemic,** flattened from side to side. These features are distinctive to *H. erectus* but not to *H. sapiens,* and do not differentiate *H. erectus* from later Neandertals or archaic *H. sapiens.*

H. erectus in Africa may also have been narrow-hipped, at least based on reconstructions of pelvis shape in KNM-WT 15000 by Chris Ruff (Figure 11.9). These body proportions—long and linear—seem to follow the latitudinal gradient seen in modern humans adapted to tropical environments (see Chapter 6) and suggest that *H. erectus* was dissipating heat in much the same way that we do, that is, by sweating. This ability to dissipate heat may have allowed *H. erectus* to be more active during midday. However, a recently described pelvis from Gona, Ethiopia contests this view. The Gona pelvis, which is more complete than that of KNM-WT 15000, is broad, suggesting that if this was an *H. erectus* female, we still have a great deal to learn about *H. erectus'* adaptations (Figure 11.9b; Simpson et al., 2008).

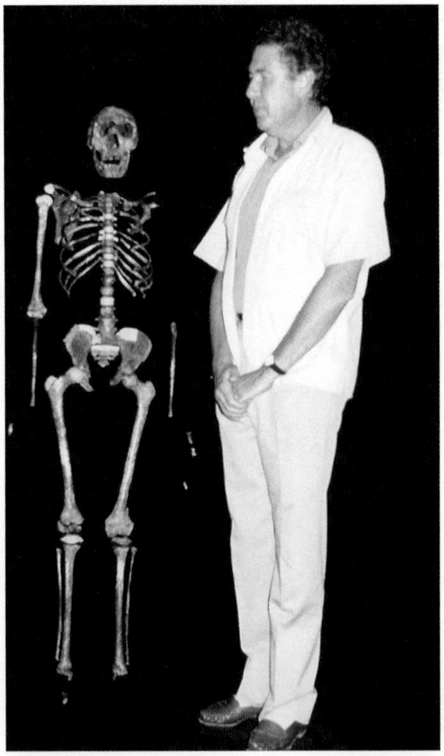

Homo erectus versus Homo ergaster

As was the case with *H. habilis,* opinions differ about whether *H. erectus* constitutes one widely dispersed, variable species or two (or more) distinct species, *H. erectus* and *H. egaster.* The argument centers mainly around the early African (and Georgian) forms of *H. erectus* that some researchers recognize as *H. egaster.* The main differences between *H. egaster* and *H. erectus* are summarized in Table 11.2 and include more gracile crania with less pronounced brow ridges in African forms and more robust and thicker-browed Asian forms, with larger teeth and more pronounced cranial superstructures (keels and tori, discussed previously). There are also archaeological differences,

FIGURE 11.8 Dr. Alan Walker stands next to the skeleton of the Nariokotome *H. erectus* boy.

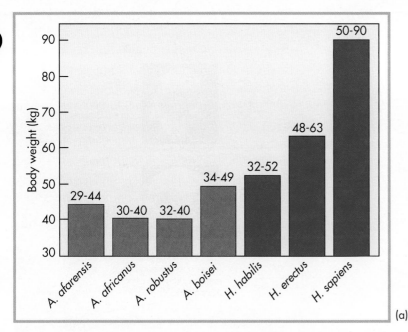

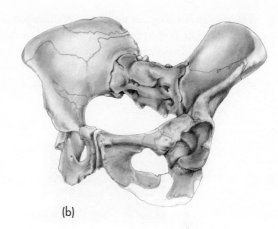

(a)   (b)

FIGURE 11.9   (a) Body weight estimates from fossil remains show that *H. erectus* had a larger body than earlier hominins. (b) The Gona pelvis may be a small female *H. erectus*.

with some of the African forms found in association with somewhat more advanced tools, whereas even later forms of Asian *H. erectus* continue to make Oldowan-like tools (see the section, The Lifeways of *Homo erectus* on page 291). In practice, *H. egaster* is used to refer to early African *H. erectus* specimens and is considered by many to be only a regional variant of the pan–Old World species *H. erectus* (Rightmire, 1993; Antón, 2003). Here we will consider *H. egaster* as a regional variant or subspecies of *H. erectus*.

Homo erectus Around the World

View the **Map** "*Homo erectus* Migration" on **myanthrolab**

If we accept *H. erectus* as a single, widely dispersed species, then it represents more than 1.5 million years of time and a broad geographic range (Figure 11.10 on pages 282–283). *H. erectus* sites range in age from about 1.8–1.6 million years to 100,000 years (and perhaps younger in Indonesia). *H. erectus* is found first in Africa (where it persisted until about 1.0 million years ago), in the Republic of Georgia by 1.7 million years ago, in island Southeast Asia by about 1.8–1.6 million years ago (persisting until perhaps 100,000 years ago), and only later in continental Asia from about 800,000 to about 200,000 years ago although there are earlier archaeological sites. There is controversy as to whether *H. erectus* is found in Western Europe, with many researchers arguing that the fossils that appear there from about 800,000 until 200,000 years ago belong to a lineage other than *H. erectus* (see later in this chapter and Chapter 12).

TABLE 11.2   **Comparison of *H. ergaster* and Classic *H. erectus***

	Region	Skeleton	Date (MYA)*
H. ergaster	East Africa	Thinner cranial bones	1.8–1.0
	Republic of Georgia	Less pronounced browridges	
H. erectus	Asia	Thicker cranial bones	1.8–0.05
		More pronounced browridges	

*MYA = millions of years ago.

FIGURE 11.10

The Genus *Homo* Through Time

The genus *Homo*, characterized by changes in the dentition, first appeared in the fossil record about 2.3 million years ago. The genus eventually developed larger brain and body sizes and spread out of Africa around 1.8 million years ago.

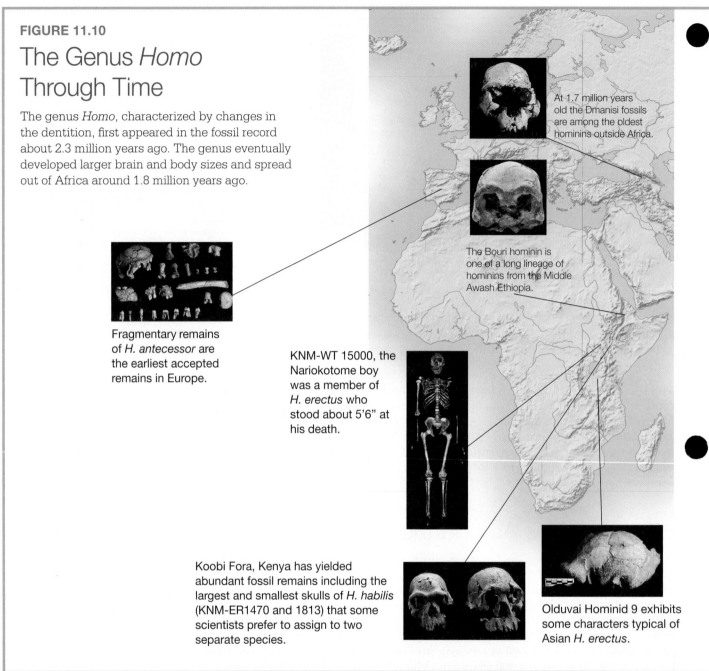

At 1.7 million years old the Dmanisi fossils are among the oldest hominins outside Africa.

The Bouri hominin is one of a long lineage of hominins from the Middle Awash Ethiopia.

Fragmentary remains of *H. antecessor* are the earliest accepted remains in Europe.

KNM-WT 15000, the Nariokotome boy was a member of *H. erectus* who stood about 5'6" at his death.

Koobi Fora, Kenya has yielded abundant fossil remains including the largest and smallest skulls of *H. habilis* (KNM-ER1470 and 1813) that some scientists prefer to assign to two separate species.

Olduvai Hominid 9 exhibits some characters typical of Asian *H. erectus*.

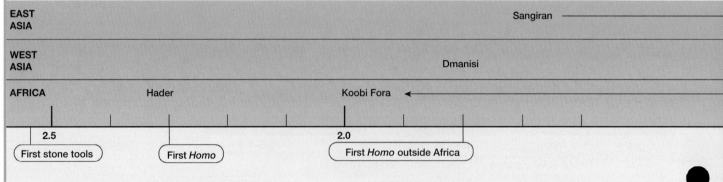

EAST ASIA			Sangiran	
WEST ASIA			Dmanisi	
AFRICA	Hader		Koobi Fora	

2.5

First stone tools

First *Homo*

2.0

First *Homo* outside Africa

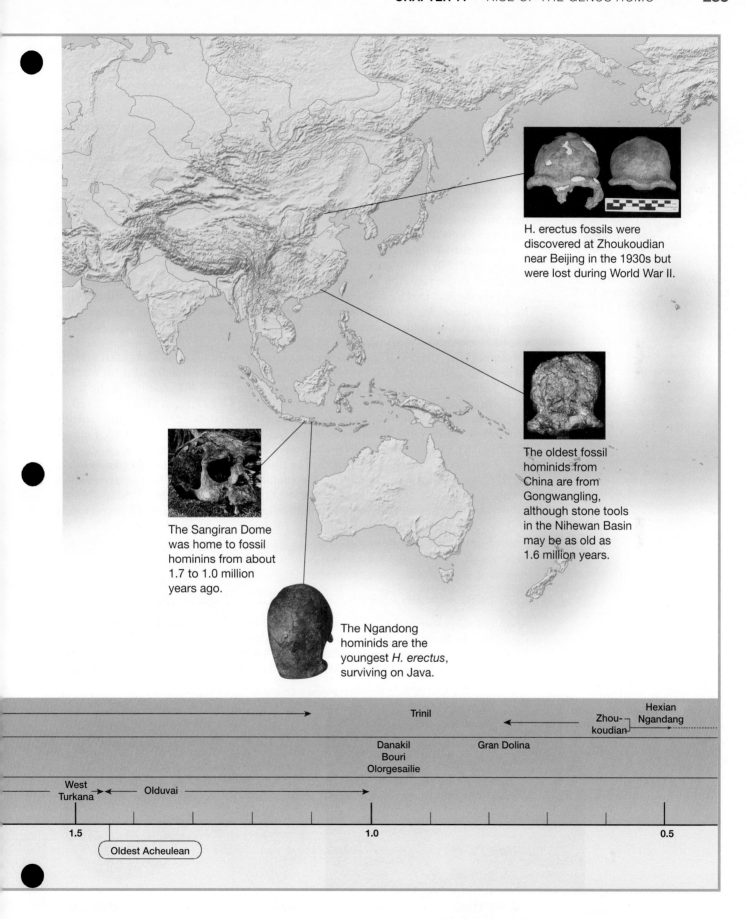

H. erectus fossils were discovered at Zhoukoudian near Beijing in the 1930s but were lost during World War II.

The oldest fossil hominids from China are from Gongwangling, although stone tools in the Nihewan Basin may be as old as 1.6 million years.

The Sangiran Dome was home to fossil hominins from about 1.7 to 1.0 million years ago.

The Ngandong hominids are the youngest *H. erectus*, surviving on Java.

Hexian
Ngandang
Zhou-
koudian
Trinil

Danakil
Bouri
Olorgesailie

Gran Dolina

West
Turkana

Olduvai

1.5

1.0

0.5

Oldest Acheulean

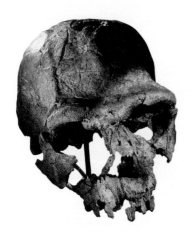

FIGURE 11.11   The cranium of early African *H. erectus* KNM-ER 3733 is nearly 1.8 million years old.

African Origins

The earliest fossil evidence for *H. erectus* comes from Koobi Fora in Kenya 1.8 million years ago. The oldest remains are a largely complete cranium, KNM-ER 3733, dated at 1.78 million years old and with a cranial capacity of only about 850 cc (Figure 11.11). Slightly older remains from Koobi Fora of 1.89 and 1.95 million years ago may also be *H. erectus* but are too fragmentary or are parts of the postcranial skeleton that cannot be identified to species with certainty. Other fossils from East Turkana provide an age range for the species of about 1.5–1.78 million years or older. The most exciting recent find is the partial cranium from Ileret, Kenya (part of the Koobi Fora Formation), dated to 1.55 million years ago, that has a very small cranial capacity and some characteristics more typically found in Asian *H. erectus*, suggesting that African and Asian *H. erectus* should be included in a single species (Figure 11.12; see Innovations: What's Size Got to Do with It? on pages 286–287; Spoor et al., 2007).

From the western side of Lake Turkana between 1.5 and 1.6 million years ago comes the nearly complete and quite tall Nariokotome *H. erectus* skeleton of a boy described in the vignette. The youth was between 8 and 11 years old when he died based on the fact that he had just gotten his permanent premolars but still retained his baby canine. We do not know if the timing of his tooth eruption was more like ours (if so, he would be about 11 years of age) or more like that of an ape (if so, he would be closer to 8 years of age).

Important African *H. erectus* fossils also come from Olduvai Gorge, where the largest-brained African *H. erectus*, OH 9, with a cranial capacity of a little more than 1,000 cc, dates to about 1.47 million years ago. In addition, some of the latest *H. erectus* in Africa are also the smallest, including OH 12 from Oldvuai, dated to perhaps as little as 780,000 years ago, with a capacity of only 727 cc, and the recently discovered Olorgesailie hominin at about 900,000 years old (Figure 11.13; Potts et al., 2004). These fossils highlight the differences in size in *H. erectus*.

H. erectus from the Bouri Formation of the Middle Awash, Ethiopia (Asfaw et al., 2002; Gilbert and Asfaw, 2008), and the Danakil Depression in Eritrea are around 1 million years old (Abbate et al., 1998) (Figure 11.14). Another Ethiopian site, Konso-Gardula, has very ancient (1.8 million years old) fragmentary *H. erectus* fossils and the oldest known *H. erectus*–associated stone tools. The oldest of the *H. erectus* fossils from Africa are found with Odowan type tools. By about 1.5 million years ago in Africa, *H. erectus* is making a new type of tool as well.

The First African Diaspora: Republic of Georgia

About 50 miles southwest of Tbilisi, the capital city of the Republic of Georgia, lies the village of Dmanisi. Nearby, beneath a medieval village built at the confluence of two rivers, a stunning series of finds in the 1990s changed our understanding of when humans left the cradle of Africa (see Figure 9.9 on page 207). Excavations

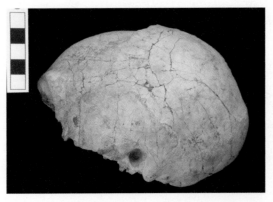
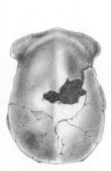

FIGURE 11.12   The recently discovered Ileret calvaria from Kenya is the smallest *H. erectus* and shares many traits with Asian *H. erectus*.

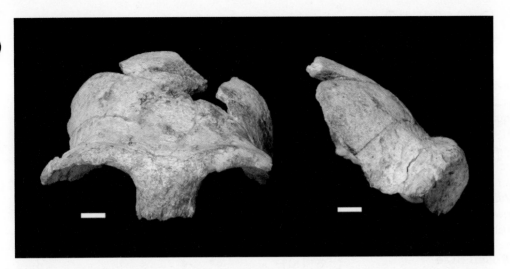

FIGURE 11.13 A small adult *H. erectus* from Olorgesailie, Kenya, is also one of the youngest in Africa at about 900,000 years old.

headed by Leo Gabunia and David Lordkipanidze discovered evidence of early *H. erectus*–like hominins outside Africa at greater than 1.7 million years ago and associated with Oldowan-like stone tools. Since 1991, at least five crania and some postcranial remains have been found in a small area (16 m²) beneath the medieval village (Figure 11.15).

The Dmanisi hominins are very similar to early African *H. erectus*, or so-called *H. ergaster* (Table 11.2 on page 281). They are small-brained (less than 800 cc) but differ in anatomy from *H. habilis*. The Dmanisi hominins are linked to *H. erectus* by their premolar and molar tooth structure, the development of browridges, and their high cranial vault. And they share with Nariokotome the lengthening of the hind limb, even though they are much shorter than the Nariokotome boy (Lordkipanidze, 2007). They are markedly more similar to the early African *H. erectus* fossils than they are to early Asian *H. erectus* (Gabunia et al., 2000). They are also interesting because they show a number of health issues not normally seen in fossil crania: One is entirely toothless, which poses interesting questions about how he prepared his food, whether he could survive on his own, or if he needed the assistance of others of his group (Figure 11.15b).

The Dmanisi skulls show conclusively that early humans had migrated out of Africa at nearly the same time that *H. erectus* first appears in Africa. Thus, shortly after the emergence of *H. erectus* in Africa, the species moved out of the African continent and into other regions and other ecosystems.

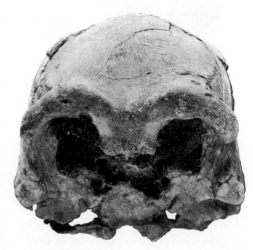

FIGURE 11.14 *Homo erectus* from the Bouri Formation of the Middle Awash, Ethiopia, is about 1 million years old.

(a)

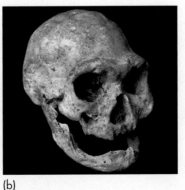

(b)

FIGURE 11.15 (a) The Dmanisi cranium (right) shows similarities to early African *H. erectus*, including the Nariokotome boy (left). (b) One individual from Dmanisi lost all his teeth before he died.

What's Size Got to Do With It?

*H*omo erectus were bigger, in some cases much bigger, than *H. habilis*. On average, they had bigger brains and bigger bodies, an increase perhaps due to their ability to access a higher-quality diet. However, there was also a lot of size variation in *H. erectus*, and a number of new fossils suggest that some *H. erectus* individuals were no bigger than some of the larger members of *H. habilis*, and one new *Australopithecus afarensis* is somewhat larger than expected (Haile-Selassie et al., 2010).

Fossil Size

The smallest of the new fossil *H. erectus* is a calvaria from Ileret, Kenya, that, at 1.5 million years old, is about the same geological age as the largest of the African *H. erectus*, OH 9 from Olduvai Gorge, Tanzania (Spoor et al., 2007). The Ileret specimen, discovered by Meave and Louise Leakey's Koobi Fora Research Project, has a cranial capacity of just 690 cc, and external vault dimensions that are even smaller than those of the Dmanisi fossils (see Figure 11.15 on page 285). The Ileret specimen is even tinier in comparison with the largest of the early African *H. erectus* Olduvai Hominid 9. Yet the specimen has all the cranial characters typical of *H. erectus*: cranial superstructures, an angulated vault, and so on. In fact, the Ileret specimen is more similar to some Asian *H. erectus* than are other Koobi Fora specimens. And this makes a good argument for Asian and African specimens belonging to a single species.

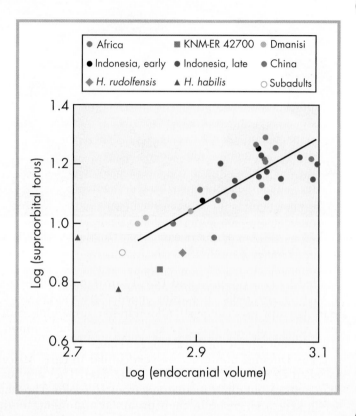

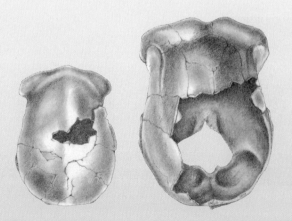

Scaling of Size to Other Traits

The Ileret and Dmanisi specimen are examples of small, early *H. erectus;* however, there appear to have been small individuals through the entire time range of the species (see Figure 11.7 on page 280). At the younger end of the *H. erectus* range in Africa lived some relatively small individuals at Olduvai (OH 12; Antón, 2002) and one recently discovered at Olorgesailie (Potts et al., 2004), which are both larger than the Ileret specimen. With all these specimens, we can test to see whether some anatomical features are more exaggerated in larger crania. Larger-brained *H. erectus* have thicker cranial walls and their brow ridges are larger as well. But other anatomical characters, such as keels and dental proportions, do not vary with overall size, and these differentiate even small-brained *H. erectus* individuals, like Ileret and Dmanisi, from *H. habilis*.

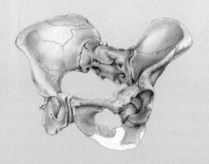

Sexual Dimorphism

The new fossils from Ileret, Dmanisi, and Olorgesailie change our understanding of size variation in *H. erectus*. Until recently, size variation wasn't considered to be that great and the amount of sexual dimorphism in *H. erectus* was thought to be less pronounced than in earlier hominins and about the same as that seen in our own species (Aiello and Key, 2002). In living humans, males tend to be larger on average than females, but their size range overlaps substantially (see graph). Because the decrease in dimorphism in *H. erectus* was thought to be due mostly to the larger size of female *H. erectus*, it had important implications for the size and costs of bearing newborns. However, the new fossils expand the size range of *H. erectus*. Taken as a group, the amount of variation in African *H. erectus* is larger than that seen in living humans or chimpanzees, but smaller than that seen in gorillas today and in earlier hominins like *A. afarensis*. We do not know for sure which fossils are male and female, but if these size differences are caused by sexual dimorphism, they might give us clues about a nonmonogamous mating system in *H. erectus* (see Chapter 6).

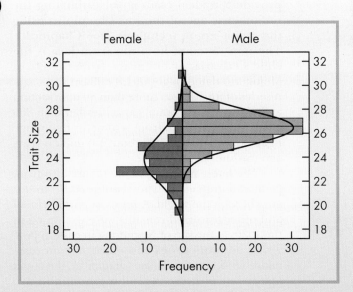

Regional, Populational, or Nutritional Size Differences

It is also possible that the size differences do not reflect differences between males and females but reflect individual differences in genetic background, diet, or other factors such as predation levels. For example, humans in industrial societies have undergone an increase in height related to improvements in nutrition (see Chapter 15), and body size and proportions in human populations are scaled to climatic and other selective factors. In addition, high mortality rates in early development also often lead to smaller adult body size. So it is possible that the size variation in *H. erectus* also reflects intraspecific variation in body size based on regional conditions. There is some evidence for this because it appears that both males and females are present in the best preserved of the small populations, the fossils from Dmanisi, Georgia (Lordkipanidze et al., 2007), yet all the individuals are small for *H. erectus*. Perhaps the size differences in the Dmanisi group tell us about local resource scarcity in the early Pleistocene rather than sexual dimorphism.

287

calotte The skullcap, or the bones of the skull, excluding those that form the face and the base of the cranium.

calvaria The braincase; includes the bones of the calotte and those that form the base of the cranium but excludes the bones of the face.

Dispersal Into East Asia

The oldest Asian *H. erectus* are from island Southeast Asia, particularly the island of Java, and date to about 1.8–1.6 million years ago. At 1.8 million years ago sea level was substantially lower than it is today, and Java and nearby islands were part of mainland Asia (Figure 11.16). Thus, colonizing the far reaches of Asia meant only walking a long distance, not crossing water.

Indonesia The very first *H. erectus* fossil ever found—and thus the type specimen for the species—was discovered in 1891 in Indonesia (Figure 11.17). A few years earlier, a young doctor named Eugene Dubois left Amsterdam by steamship in search of human fossils in the Dutch East Indies (now called Indonesia). Following Darwin's lead, Dubois considered the tropics a likely cradle of humankind. But he also thought that Asia was a more likely spot for the origin of humans than Africa because African apes, with their primitive appearance and robust facial features, seemed unlikely human antecedents, whereas the slender-bodied, monogamous Asian gibbons and modern humans seemed more similar (Shipman, 2001). Dubois went to Indonesia to find the missing link between the two.

In October 1891, in the banks of the Solo River near the village of Trinil, Java, Dubois's team unearthed the **calotte,** or skullcap, of an early human (Figure 11.17). Although only the top of the skull was found, Dubois could see that it was hominin and that in life it possessed a large brain in a robust cranium more primitive than that of any hominin known at that time. He named the species *Pithecanthropus erectus* ("the upright ape-man"), and this specimen, Trinil 2, also nicknamed Java Man, became the type specimen for the species.

The volcanic sediments of Java have yielded a wealth of other *H. erectus* fossils and also provide the ideal context for estimating the radiometric age of the fossil hominins using the argon–argon technique (see Chapter 9). The most ancient hominin from Java is the child's **calvaria,** or braincase, from the site of Mojokerto dated to about 1.8 million years ago. A series of fossils from more than 80 m of section at Sangiran have cranial capacities between 800 and 1,000 cc and are from sediments that range in age from about 1.7 to about 1.0 million years ago (Swisher et al., 1994).

The latest surviving *H. erectus* are also from Java and represent the youngest *H. erectus* anywhere in the world. A series of partial crania and other fossilized remains were excavated in the 1930s at the site of Ngandong in eastern Java. Using uranium series and electron spin resonance (ESR) methods (see Chapter 9), the fauna associated with the Ngandong hominins are estimated to a remarkably young 27,000–53,000 years ago (Swisher et al., 1996). And using a nondestructive spectrometric U-series technique two of the Ngandong hominins recently yielded ages around 70,000 years (Yokoyama et al., 2008). Thus, *H. erectus* may have survived in this island refug even while going extinct in other parts of the world (Figure 11.18). Recent finds on the island of Flores dating to 18,000 years ago may also support a young age for the last surviving *H. erectus* (see Insights and Advances: The Little

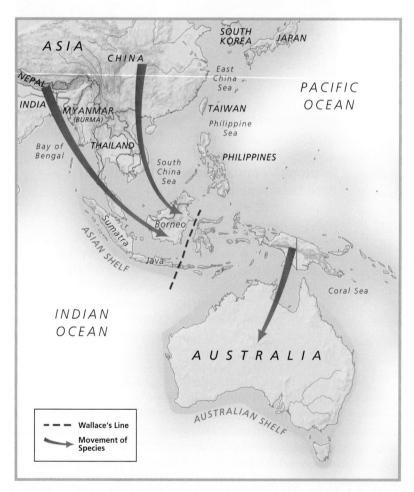

FIGURE 11.16 Land-bridge connections between continental Asia and Indonesia during glacial periods (and low sea level) extend as far as Wallace's line.

(a)   (b)

FIGURE 11.17   (a) The skull cap from Trinil, Java, is the type specimen for *H. erectus* and is about 900,000 years old. (b) Outcrops near Trinil, Java.

People of Flores on page 292). However, scientific work continues on the Solo River sites, and a group led by Etty Indriati and dating experts Swisher, Feibel, and Grün has conducted more extensive excavation and exploration (Indriati et al., 2001). This group has found evidence of pumices dating to 550,000 years ago at Ngandong, while the fossil teeth yield U-series ages similar to those found previously. This conundrum may mean either that the pumices are not in stratigraphic position, or that the U-series ages of the teeth are recording another event that influenced uranium migration, such as a change or drop in the water table. Despite the many fossil finds from Java, tools are rare. Tools of an Oldowan-like technology have been found, but none were found in association with fossil hominins.

China   Perhaps the best known of the *H. erectus* remains, the fossils from China are younger than those in Africa or earliest Indonesia, spanning only from about 800,000 to about 200,000 years ago. However, stone tools found at sites in the Nihewan Basin indicate there was likely an early Pleistocene (approximately 1.6 million years old) hominin presence, although there are no fossils from these sites (Zhu et al., 2004). The earliest Chinese fossils, fragmentary and crushed remains from Gongwangling, are not of much help in

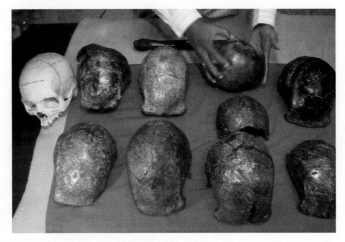

(a)   (b)

FIGURE 11.18   (a) The site of Ngandong Java was excavated in the 1930s and excavations continue today. (b) Ngandong calottes and calvariae from Java may be the youngest *H. erectus* fossils at perhaps 27,000–50,000 years old, or they may be significantly older.

FIGURE 11.19   The site of Zhoukoudian outside Beijing, China, spans several hundred thousand years.

understanding evolution in *H. erectus*. Even more ancient finds from Longuppo with an age of perhaps 1.8 million years ago are of uncertain taxonomic status and may not even be hominins. The most numerous and best preserved are the so-called Peking Man fossils discovered in the 1930s and dated between about 600,000 and 300,000 years ago.

The story of the famed Peking Man fossils is one of discovery and loss. Chinese paleontologist Pei Wenshong discovered the original skull in December 1929 at a quarry site, Chou Kou Tien (now transliterated as Zhoukoudian), not far from present-day Beijing (Figure 11.19). Along with Davidson Black, a Canadian anatomist, he described and initially named the fossil *Sinanthropus pekinensis* ("Chinese human from Peking"). After Black's untimely death, Franz Weidenreich took over anatomical work on Zhoukoudian. In the mid-1930s, Japan invaded China before the American entry into World War II, and work at Zhoukoudian stopped. Fear spread that the *H. erectus* fossils, objects of great cultural and historical value, would be confiscated, destroyed, or taken as gifts to the Japanese emperor, a noted naturalist. So Weidenreich made extensive measurements, drawings, and plaster casts of the fossils. The fossils were then placed in the care of the U.S. Marines, who guarded them on a train from Beijing to the coast, where they were to be put on a ship for San Francisco. The train arrived at the Chinese coast on December 7, 1941, the day of the Japanese attack on Pearl Harbor. The marines were taken prisoner, and the crates of fossils have never been found (Shipman, 2001).

Because of Weidenreich's careful molding and measuring of the Zhoukoudian fossils, at least we have replicas of more than a dozen calvaria and hundreds of associated teeth and bone fragments (Weidenreich, 1943). They represent as many as forty individuals who lived near Zhoukoudian between 800,000 and 250,000 years ago (see Chapter 9 Insights and Advances: Dating Controversies on page 211). Although it was originally described as a cave where *H. erectus* lived, used fire, and cooked meals, more recent archaeological work at the site has found that it is not a cave at all but a series of sediment-filled cracks in the rock (Goldberg et al., 2001).

The Status of *Homo erectus* in Europe

Early humans that somewhat resembled *H. erectus* lived in Europe during the same time period as *H. erectus* in Asia. However, most of the fossils discovered so far differ from the typical *H. erectus* seen in Africa, Asia, or Southeast Asia. Many of the European fossils resemble *H. sapiens* as well as *H. erectus* and Neandertals, and they may well be transitional, or archaic, forms of *H. sapiens*. The later middle Pleistocene European fossils, those dated between 500,000 and 200,000 years ago, are likely to be ancestral only to Neandertals and are discussed in Chapter 12.

The oldest European hominin, announced in 2008, is 1.2 million years old (Carbonell et al., 2008). This partial mandible is from Sima de Elefante in the Sierra de Atapuerca, Spain (Figure 11.20a). Slightly younger are the fossils from Gran Dolina in the Sierra de Atapuerca that date to nearly 800,000 years ago, more than 200,000 years older than any other known hominins in western Europe (Figure 11.20b). The Sima de Elefante and Gran Dolina fossils were found by a team led by J. M. Bermúdez de Castro, E. Carbonell, and J. L. Arsuaga (1997) in the oldest of a series of deposits in the Sierra de Atapuerca that were exposed when a road cut was made for a now abandoned rail line. Younger deposits from the same region are discussed in Chapter 12. The fossils from Gran Dolina include young individuals, between 3 and 18 years of age at the time they died, that exhibit a mix of characteristics, some of which appear to foreshadow Neandertals, others of which seem to link the fossils to modern humans. In particular, the presence of a **canine fossa** (an indentation on the maxilla above the canine root) has been used to argue that the Gran Dolina fossils represent a previously unknown hominin species, *Homo antecessor,* which may have been the common ancestor of both Neandertals and modern *H. sapiens* (Arsuaga et al., 1999). However, many researchers are skeptical of this new classification because the species *H. antecessor* was based largely on characters

canine fossa   An indentation on the maxilla above the root of the canine, an anatomical feature usually associated with modern humans that may be present in some archaic *Homo* species in Europe.

Acheulean   Stone tool industry of the early and middle Pleistocene characterized by the presence of bifacial hand axes and cleavers. This industry is made by a number of *Homo* species, including *H. erectus* and early *H. sapiens*.

Early Stone Age (or Lower Paleolithic)   The earliest stone tool industries including the Oldowan and Acheulean industries, called the ESA in Africa and the Lower Paleolithic outside Africa.

biface   A stone tool that has been flaked on two faces or opposing sides forming a cutting edge between the two flake scars.

hand axe   Type of Acheulean bifacial tool, usually teardrop-shaped, with a long cutting edge.

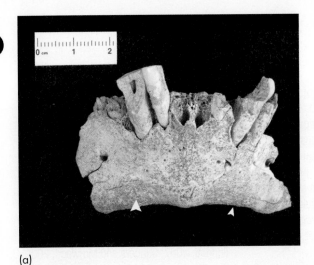

(a)

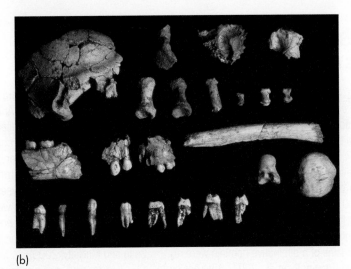

(b)

FIGURE 11.20   (a) The mandible from Sima de Elefante, Atapuerca, Spain is the oldest European hominin at about 1.2 million years old. (b) The Gran Dolina locality in Atapuerca, Spain has yielded some of the oldest fossil hominins in Europe.

exhibited in a child's partial cranium, characters the child might have lost as it aged. Another adult calvaria, Ceprano, from Italy is said to be 800,000 years old and a member of *H. antecessor,* but it lacks the critical facial bones that define that species. It also differs anatomically from typical *H. erectus* and, more important, is probably not nearly as old as is claimed. Only the discovery of more complete adult fossils will settle the question of the identity of *H. antecessor.* Regardless of whether *H. antecessor* is a valid taxon or part of *H. heidelbergensis* or archaic *H. sapiens* (see Chapter 12), anatomically they cannot be classified as *H. erectus,* suggesting that this species may never have made it into Europe. Whatever its name, its discoverers argue that the broken bits of bone from Spain are evidence of cannibalism.

The Lifeways of *Homo erectus*

From the fossils and stone tools associated with *H. erectus* and from their own anatomy, we can begin to piece together how these early species lived. The fossils themselves are evidence of the physical adaptations of the species, and the tools are a window into their activities and how their minds worked. *H. erectus* is associated with two different tool technologies that show the species possessed advanced cognitive skills. *H. erectus* appears to have undergone a dietary shift to perhaps a more heavily animal-based diet than its predecessors, and this shift seems to have fueled both its dispersal from Africa and a different pattern of growth.

Homo erectus and the Early Stone Age

From 1.8 to about 1.5 million years ago in Africa, only Oldowan-type tools are found. And the earliest tools found outside Africa, at Dmanisi in the Republic of Georgia, are also Oldowan-like assemblages (Gabunia et al., 2001). However, starting at about a million and a half years ago in Africa, some *H. erectus* are found with a different tool technology called the **Acheulean** tradition. This tradition persists until about 250,000 years ago and is made by a number of different species of the genus *Homo.* Together, the Oldowan and Acheulean are known as the **Early Stone Age** or **Lower Paleolithic.**

Acheulean assemblages are characterized by specifically shaped tools called hand axes and cleavers that are worked on two sides. Both are thus **bifaces,** tools whose cutting edge is formed by the removal of flakes from opposing sides of the piece. The scars left by the removal of these flakes meet to form the sharp edge. A **hand axe** is a bifacially worked, symmetrical, teardrop-shaped tool

View "Later Acheulian Stone Tools (Circa 500,000 to 100,000 Years Ago)" on **myanthrolab**

insights & advances
THE LITTLE PEOPLE OF FLORES

Homo sapiens never coexisted with *Homo erectus*. Or did they? Conventional wisdom has held that *H. erectus* went extinct in the middle Pleistocene after giving rise to *Homo sapiens*. Controversial discoveries on the island of Flores suggest that another group of hominins may have survived until 18,000 years ago. At the cave of Liang Bua, where Indonesian archaeologists led by R. P. Soejono have been excavating since 1976, the remains of a diminutive hominin were recovered (Brown, P., et al., 2004). Analyses by Peter Brown show that the skull had a cranial capacity of 380 to 420 cc (Figure A) (Falk D., et al., 2005), and the postcranial skeleton suggests a female biped that stood just about a meter tall—the size of the *A. afarensis* skeleton "Lucy." Stone tools at the site may be associated with the hominin.

Although some scientists call it a new species, *H. floresiensis*, Brown's description of the skull makes it difficult to distinguish from *H. erectus*, except on the basis of its small size. And the shoulder skeleton is also reminiscent of *H. erectus* (Larson et al., 2007, 2009). But other aspects of the postcranial skeleton look more primitive (Morwood et al., 2005; Jungers et al., 2009a, b). The hand skeleton in particular suggests to Matt Tocheri that the hominins from Flores were more primitive than even earlier *Homo* (Tocheri et al., 2007; Larson et al., 2009). And limb proportions are certainly not those of modern humans. Alternatively, Teuku Jacob and colleagues (2006) argue the Flores remains are just those of a short human with an abnormally small brain. And it is the case that some aspects of the skeleton are diseased—for example, one arm shows evidence of a healed fracture. Jacob's initial claim has gained support from studies of the relationship between brain and body size by Bob Martin (Martin et al., 2006) and Tom Schoenemann (Schoenemann and Allen, 2006). Their studies suggest that the relationship between brain and body size in the Flores specimen is more similar to humans with a condition known as microceph-

aly, or perhaps to some kind of dwarfism, than it is to fossil hominins. And recent work by Israel Hershkovitz and colleagues (2007) argues the Flores material represents modern individuals with a congenital deficiency in insulin-like growth factor production. However, other scaling analyses suggest the Flores remains are what you would expect of a scaled-down version of *H. erectus* or some other form of *Homo* (Gordon et al., 2007; Baab and McNulty, 2009).

A common phenomenon for large mammals that colonize small islands (Flores is about 1400 km², or 540 square miles) is to become smaller over many generations. In fact, the fossil record of Flores yields the remains of a dwarfed elephant as well. This size reduction (called insular dwarfism) is related to two selective pressures on large island mammals: Fewer resources favor smaller individuals who need less food to survive, and fewer predators mean that having a small body doesn't increase the chance of being eaten. If the Flores hominin is a new species, it may represent such a process. Perhaps a few members of *H. erectus* were washed onto the island on natural rafts during a storm. Stranded there, they were isolated from other members of their species. Their isolation may explain not only their small size but also their survival. In their island refuge, they did not come into competition for resources with and were not replaced by modern humans until much later than other archaic hominins.

There is so much disagreement over the interpretation of the Flores individual because only a single skull has been found, and

the critical characters (such as cranial capacity) for assessing what species a hominin belongs to are found in the skull; however, most of the new studies of the postcrania all seem to support the idea that the Flores specimens are not modern humans and may be even more primitive than *H. erectus*. In the short time since its discovery, two special volumes of papers and many individual studies have been wholly or partly dedicated to its identity (Indriati, 2007; Jungers and Morwood, 2009). Yet disagreement abounds, and much about how morphology scales with very small size is not yet well understood (Holliday and Franciscus, 2009).

The growing consensus seems to favor the idea that the Flores remains are not pathological human remains (Aiello, 2010), and that they represent a distinct type of hominin. Many studies favor associations from *H. erectus*, but aspects of especially the postcranial anatomy may favor another form of early *Homo*. More evidence is needed to assess this, but for the moment the remains remind us that it may have been only a few thousand years since we last shared the earth with another hominin species.

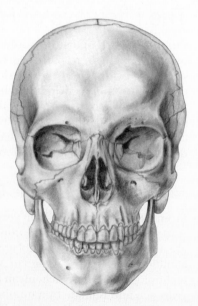

FIGURE A   The skull from Flores is tiny, less than one-third of the capacity of a modern human skull.

(Figure 11.21). A **cleaver** has a broader working end where the point of the teardrop would have been in a hand axe.

For the first time in human prehistory, we see hominins making standardized tools that clearly indicate they had a plan or mental template in mind. Hand axes and cleavers were highly uniform in appearance. Indeed, one of the most extraordinary aspects of the Acheulean industry is its persistence and uniformity over great spans of time and space. We first see hand axes at about 1.5 million years ago, and they persist almost unchanged until about 250,000 years ago. In comparison, how many of our tools do you think will still be in use 1.2 million years from now and in nearly the same form they have today? This conservatism is

FIGURE 11.21   The Acheulean industry is typified by hand axes and cleavers.

also found across vast geographic areas. Hand axes appear in western and northern Europe, in East and North Africa, and in the Near East. (However, as we saw, they are very rare or absent in the East Asian *H. erectus* sites.) The uniformity of hand axe appearance suggests that they were used for specific purposes and in standard ways.

The advantages of the hand axe and cleaver over the simple flake are their ability to hold a sharp edge for a long period of time, the greater length of their working edge, and their generally convenient size, which allows them to be used for holding and cutting without fatigue. Hand axes and cleavers may have been developed for the butchery of large animals. The circular pattern of flaking around the perimeter of the axe leads some scholars to consider them primitive versions of a circular saw in which more flaking was done as earlier edges became worn and dull. But other hypotheses for the use of hand axes cannot be discounted. A recent study found evidence of fossilized phytoliths, microscopic mineral particles from plants (see Chapter 9), on the cutting edge of some hand axes. Their presence suggests that the tool was used to scrape plant material. This could have meant that the users of the tools were sharpening a wooden spear, or perhaps stripping bark from wood for building or eating. Alternatively, hand axes might also have been used as digging implements or as projectiles thrown at prey animals or even at hominin enemies.

Whatever their use, the Acheulean industry presents an innovative technology that extended over much—but not all—of *H. erectus*' Old World range. As mentioned, East Asian sites yield Oldowan-like tools but no true hand axes, at least not until late in time. The division between hand–axe–bearing areas and those without hand axes is called the **Movius line,** after Hallam Movius, a renowned archaeologist who first recognized this puzzling distribution (Figure 11.22 on page 294). There are two not necessarily mutually exclusive hypotheses for the Movius line. The first suggests that the absence of hand axes reflects a loss of hand axe technology in Asia caused by differences in selective pressures and raw materials between Asia and Africa. In particular, organic materials such as bamboo are inferred to have been used by the hominins. In this view, African *H. erectus* left the continent with Acheulean technology but reverted to Oldowan technology in their new environment. Alternatively, other scientists suggest that the hominins that inhabit Asia left Africa before Acheulean tools were developed, so their absence is not so much a loss of technology as a difference in the technological paths taken in Asia and Africa. This difference may result from differences in available resources and selective pressures as well.

However, it is important to recognize that there is no one-to-one correlation between a species and a technology. Oldowan tools are used by both *H. habilis* and *H. erectus* (and perhaps any number of *Australopithecus*), and different groups of *H. erectus* use Oldowan or Acheulean tools or both. *H. erectus* continued to make and use Oldowan industry tools in Africa and elsewhere even after Acheulean tools came into widespread use, and later hominins used Acheulean tools in Africa and Europe.

cleaver   Type of Acheulean bifacial tool, usually oblong with a broad cutting edge on one end.

Movius line   The separation between areas of the Old World in which Acheulean technology occurs and those in which it does not; named by archaeologist Hallam Movius.

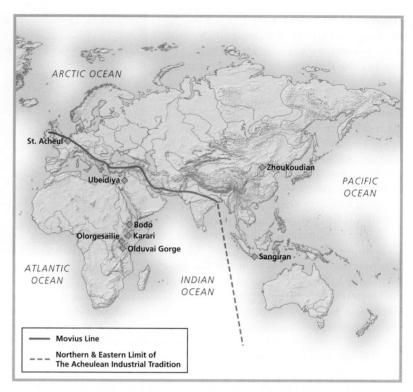

FIGURE 11.22 The Movius line separates regions of the world where Acheulean hand axes were made from regions where they were not.

A Higher-Quality Diet: *Homo erectus* Subsistence

We assume that *H. erectus*, like modern foragers, ate mostly plant foods, but there is no mistaking the archaeological evidence that *H. erectus* also ate meat and marrow. About 1.8 million years ago, an important biological shift apparently occurred in the hominin lineage; the human form became much more modern, a bit taller, perhaps more linear, and with a larger brain. Shortly after this time, hominins left Africa and began their worldwide expansion. Both these things tell us that the shift probably was associated with a major increase in the quality of the diet, which was needed to maintain a larger body and brain (see Innovations: What's Size Got to Do with It? on pages 286–287; Leonard and Robertson, 1997; Antón et al., 2002).

Most scientists argue that the adaptive shift happened at the emergences of *H. erectus,* around 1.8 million years ago and that *H. erectus* was the first truly predatory human species. As meat and marrow became a more important part of their diet, their small intestine would have lengthened while the large intestine shortened because meat takes less time in the large intestine for processing. The amount of leisure time would have increased as the time needed to forage for plants decreased. Population density would have been low because predators sit atop the food chain and must exist at low densities to avoid outstripping their prey supply. But the ability to disperse may have increased as hominins became less dependent on specific plant resources and more dependent on animal resources. Migrating herds might have led hominins to follow them, and in new areas meat is fairly safe, regardless of species, whereas new plants might be poisonous or inedible. Dental studies suggest changes in tooth shape from *Australopithecus* to *H. erectus* that are consistent with such a dietary shift (Figure 11.23).

Once meat or marrow was obtained, there is only equivocal evidence that *H. erectus* was the first hominin to prepare it for consumption by cooking it. Archaeologists working in East Africa at Koobi Fora and Chesowanja have found associations of hominin fossils, animal fossils, and burnt earth to suggest the presence of fire as early as 1.6 million years ago (Bellomo, 1994). However, it is unclear whether this was hominin-controlled fire, perhaps collected from a natural fire, or hominin-made fire, or even just a natural fire. To date, most researchers think this may be evidence of brush fires that were not human-made. The best unequivocal evidence of hominin-controlled fire comes much later in the middle Pleistocene. Although the evidence of controlled fire is questionable, some researchers hypothesize that the advent of cooking created whole new adaptive niches for *H. erectus*. They suggest that eating potato-like tubers rather than meat could have provided the higher-quality diet necessary for expansion of the human brain (Wrangham et al., 1999). However, during the same time period, evidence of meat eating is overwhelming, whereas the evidence of tuber cooking is scanty at best.

Homo erectus Life History

As adults, modern humans and *H. erectus* look remarkably different, but are they more similar as children? The discovery of the Nariokotome boy (KNM-WT 15000), the remarkably complete *H. erectus* youth discussed earlier, highlighted how little we know about growth in fossil hominins. At first this may seem unimportant, but

A. afarensis

H. rudolfensis

H. erectus

FIGURE 11.23 Dental topography differs between *A. afarensis* and *H. erectus*, suggesting that *Australopithecus* was better suited to chewing brittle food objects.

consider this basic fact: Evolution often proceeds by modifying the developmental pattern. In small ways and in larger ways, modifications of this pattern produce the differences we see in adult forms. So understanding the developmental pattern is critical to understanding hominin evolution.

As you saw in Chapter 7, and we will explore further in Chapter 14, because of our large brain, humans grow slowly and mature late compared with nonhuman primates, even chimpanzees. When this human pattern arose is a question of interest for interpreting hominin behavior. Teeth have been the most informative structures from which we learn about development in fossil hominins because their internal structure forms by layers deposited in cyclical patterns in daily increments during dental development. Thus, from a tooth crown we can glean something about the age and rate of development of the individual. Work on dental micro-structure by Chris Dean and colleagues suggests that early development in *H. erectus* was fast. Dean's group concluded that the Nariokotome boy would have been no more than about 8 years old at the time of death, even though a modern human with similar development would be closer to 11 or 12 years of age. And *H. erectus* probably reached adulthood earlier than we do, perhaps around the age of 15 years. Although this seems fast by modern standards, it is slower than what we know of *Australopithecus* developmental rates. In humans, the tempo of maturation and the size attained is sensitive both to nutritional challenges and mortality risks. Thus, growth rates in *H. erectus* may be another indication of a slightly higher-quality diet than in *Australopithecus*.

Homo erectus Leaves Africa

The most important adaptive shift *H. erectus* made was the first migration out of Africa (Figure 11.24). This emigration meant moving across a variety of ecosystems, climates, and ecological settings. Each of these would have presented *H. erectus* with new challenges never encountered by a hominin. Most notable was the move from tropical and subtropical Africa into the more seasonally cold regions of the Northern Hemisphere in Eurasia and the Far East. This change alone demonstrates the remarkable adaptability and behavioral flexibility our lineage had evolved by just

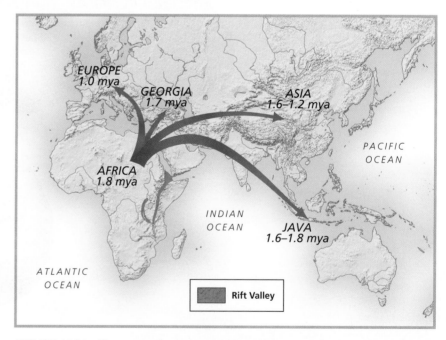

FIGURE 11.24 *H. erectus* migrated out of Africa beginning about 1.8 million years ago and is first known from Georgia and Java.

under 2 million years ago. The ability to adapt to a wide range of novel environments is a hallmark of the human species.

One question remains: Why did hominins remain in Africa for more than 4 million years, only to disperse rapidly after the origin of *H. erectus*? Some of the likely causes we have suggested in this chapter form a web of ecological and morphological advantages that facilitated *H. erectus* dispersal. First, recall that world climate was beginning to undergo some severe fluctuations at the origin and slightly before the rise of *H. erectus*. The African area was cooling and drying around 2 million years ago, leading to diminished forests with larger grasslands between them. The rise of grasslands saw the increase in the quantities of herbivorous animals and the evolution of a new niche for animals (including hominins) that could eat them.

H. erectus seems to have taken advantage of these opportunities by using Oldowan tools to access animal resources it was not physically adapted to acquire. The higher-quality animal diet that resulted allowed the growth of larger bodies, and their more linear body shape probably allowed greater midday activity because they coped better with the heat. Larger bodies allowed greater ranging (home range, the area an animal traverses over a year, is positively correlated to body size in mammals). As animals such as antelope migrated, hominins may have followed.

In the late Pliocene, at about the time that we see other African fauna migrating into the Near East and western Asia, we also see *H. erectus* migrating. Were they following this food resource? Earlier hominins had not migrated during earlier faunal migrations out of Africa. Perhaps they remained in place because of their greater reliance on plant foods. It does seem that at this point *H. erectus* was able to do something that earlier hominins were not capable of doing. It seems reasonable to assume that tool use and the access to previously inaccessible animal resources it allowed were fundamental to the ability to migrate. However, a complex web of factors is implicated in dispersal. Even though the entire dispersal seems a long one, consider that an average change in home range of just 1 km a year (less than a mile), over a period of 10,000 or 15,000 years, would have led to a slow dispersal, yet it would look geologically instantaneous.

Having moved into many parts of the Old World using a combination of technology and physical adaptation, and having made a shift in foraging strategy to a higher-quality diet, early *H. erectus* was poised to begin the brain size expansion and intellectual development characteristic of the genus. Intelligence is a survival strategy of enormous evolutionary importance to the human lineage. In *H. erectus*, we see the beginning of what intelligence meant for the hominin lineage. Now we turn to Neandertals and *H. sapiens*, in which cognition and culture take on far more importance.

Rise of the Genus *Homo*

Defining *Homo habilis*

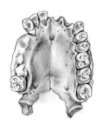

Defining the Genus

- Members of *Homo* differ from *Australopithecus* by increases in brain and eventually body size, and decreases in tooth and jaw size. **[p 272]**

Anatomical Features of *H. habilis*

- Their brain size was from 500 to 750 cc.
- They had smaller molar teeth and jaws than the *Australopithecus*. **[pp 272–273]**

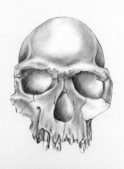

One Species or Two?

- Some scholars divide the species into a larger-brained and smaller-brained groups.
- Usually, the smaller is called *H. habilis*, and the larger is called *H. rudolfensis*. **[p 272]**

Time, Geography, and Behavior

- So far, *H. habilis* is restricted mostly to eastern Africa.
- The species appears about 1.9 million years ago, and the last is dated to 1.4 million years ago.
- *H. habilis* is associated with Oldowan stone tools. **[pp 273–276]**

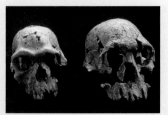

Homo erectus

Anatomical Features

- They possessed a larger average brain and body size than *H. habilis*; however, there is a great deal of size variation in *H. erectus*.
- Members have long, low, and relatively angular cranial vaults, often with well-developed supraorbital and occipital tori, and other superstructures.
- Their teeth suggest a different diet that *Australopithecus* and a slightly different diet than *Homo*. **[pp 276–281]**

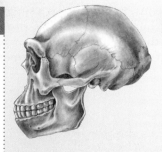

Time and Geography

- First appear about 1.8 to 1.9 million years ago and persist until perhaps 100,000 years ago.
- Initially an African species, they disperse into Asia and Southeast Asia by about 1.7–1.8 million years ago.
- Only the African members appear to have made Acheulean tools.
- Some scholars divide the species into two—*H. ergaster* in Africa and *H. erectus* in Asia—based on cranial anatomy. **[pp 281–283]**

Life History, Size, and Dimorphism

- Dental evidence suggests that *H. erectus* grew more quickly than we do but more slowly than do living African apes or *Australopithecus*.
- Their average body size was larger than earlier hominins.
- But there was a great deal of variation in body size, which may be related to sexual dimorphism, regional differences, or differences in nutrition or climate. **[pp 286–287]**

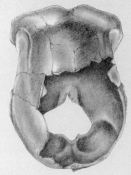

Diet, Body Proportions, and Dispersal

- The archaeological record suggests that meat and marrow became a more consistent part of the diet of *Homo* and *H. erectus* providing a high-quality resource in addition to gathered plants.
- The larger body size suggests an expansion of home-range size.
- A web of interrelated factors, including a shift to greater animal resource use, larger ranging, and body size, may be related to this hominin's ability to disperse from Africa. **[pp 284–291]**

Tools and Behavior

Core and Flake Industries

- Also known as the Oldowan industry, these tools first appear around 2.6 million years ago.
- Flakes struck from cores have sharp edges useful for cutting.
- Hammerstones were used for flaking and to smash open animal bones to access marrow.
- Made by *H. habilis*, *H. erectus*, and possibly some *Australopithecus* species. **[p 291]**

Acheulean Industries

- Typical tools include bifacial handaxes and cleavers.
- They appear around 1.6 million years ago and persist until about 140,000 years ago.
- These tools retain their cutting edges longer, are easier to hold than simple flakes, and may be adaptations to carcass processing.
- Made by *H. erectus* and archaic *H. sapiens*. **[pp 291–293]**

Hunting, Scavenging, Gathering, and Diet Quality

- Broken and cutmarked bones found at butchering sites provide evidence that early hominins were sometimes eating meat and marrow.
- We do not know whether those animal resources were hunted or scavenged, but we do know that they provided high-quality resources.
- Studies of modern carnivores suggest that scavenging carcasses would have been a possible source of nutrition for early hominins.
- Many scenarios of the evolution of genus *Homo* consider these new animal resources important (but not necessarily exclusively responsible) for brain expansion.
- However, evidence from recent hunter-gatherers shows that the vast majority of the hominin diet must have come from gathered plants. **[pp 297–297]**

My AnthroLab CONNECTIONS

Watch. Listen. View. Explore. Read.
MyAnthroLab is designed just for you. Each chapter features a customized study plan to help you learn and review key concepts and terms. Dynamic visual activities, videos, and readings found in the multimedia library will enhance your learning experience.

Resources from this Chapter:

View on **myanthrolab**

- ▶ *The Genus* Homo *Through Time*
- ▶ Homo erectus *Migration*
- ▶ *Later Acheulean Stone Tools (Circa 500,000 to 100,000 Years Ago)*

Listen on **myanthrolab**

- ▶ *Food for Thought: Meat-Based Diet Made Us Smarter*

Explore on **myanthrolab** In MySearchLab, enter the Anthropology database to find relevant and recent scholarly and popular press publications. For this chapter, enter the following keywords: *Homo*, *Homo erectus*, Early Stone Age, Oldowan, Acheulean

Read on **myanthrolab**

- ▶ *The Fellowship of the Hobbit* by Elizabeth Culotta
- ▶ *Were our Ancestors Hunters or Scavengers?* by John D. Speth
- ▶ *Stranger in a New Land* by Kate Wong

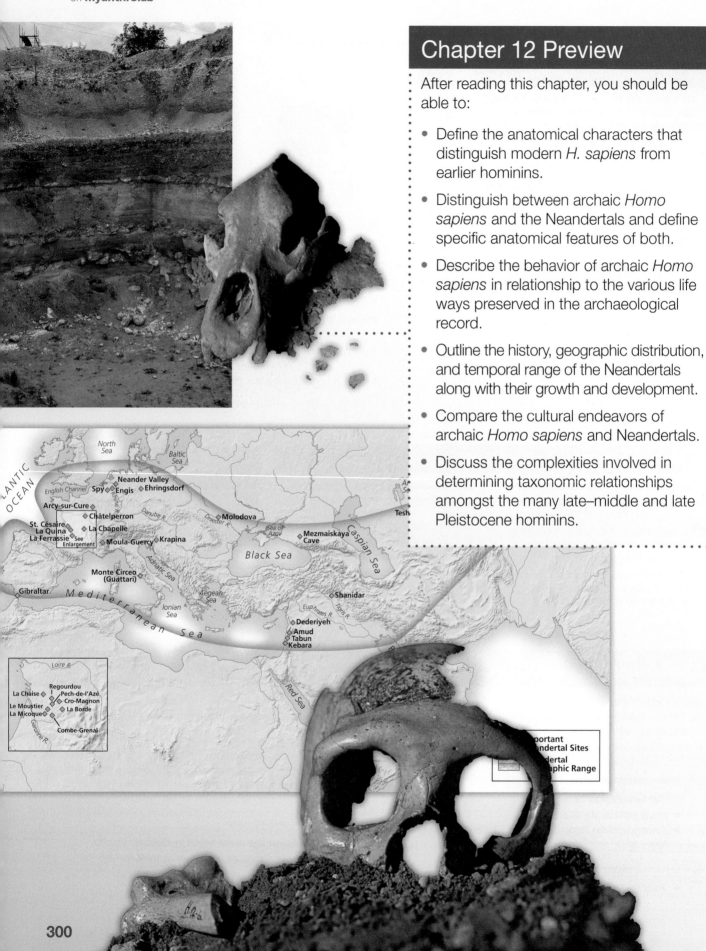

Chapter 12 Preview

After reading this chapter, you should be able to:

- Define the anatomical characters that distinguish modern *H. sapiens* from earlier hominins.

- Distinguish between archaic *Homo sapiens* and the Neandertals and define specific anatomical features of both.

- Describe the behavior of archaic *Homo sapiens* in relationship to the various life ways preserved in the archaeological record.

- Outline the history, geographic distribution, and temporal range of the Neandertals along with their growth and development.

- Compare the cultural endeavors of archaic *Homo sapiens* and Neandertals.

- Discuss the complexities involved in determining taxonomic relationships amongst the many late–middle and late Pleistocene hominins.

Archaic *Homo sapiens* and Neandertals

In an open coal pit in Schoeningen, Germany, a huge mechanical shovel grinds away at the earth, stripping away not only vast amounts of coal but also Holocene and Pleistocene deposits. Over the years, archaeologists have identified a number of Lower Paleolithic sites in the pit that are located several meters below the ground. The sites date to about 400,000 years ago: the middle Pleistocene. The material found at these sites includes flint tools and flakes, combined with the remains of extinct elephants, bovids, deer, and horses. No hominin remains are found, which is unfortunate given the scarcity of fossils from this critical period in human evolution. But after several years of excavation, archaeologist Hartmut Thieme discovered something that was even more scarce—and perhaps more significant—than additional fossil remains: four large wooden spears.

The spears are impressive: Two of them measure more than 2.25 m (7 ft) in length. Three of them are sharpened at one end. They are carefully shaped, and their weight is distributed to make them aerodynamically efficient when thrown; it is also possible that they could have been used as lances and thrust at prey. The fourth, perhaps a throwing stick or a small thrusting spear, is smaller (less than 1 m long) and sharpened at both ends. These wooden spears, which show us how hominins of the middle Pleistocene used organic materials, provide us with a window to the past that is typically shuttered, and remind us that hominin behavior during this period may have been more sophisticated than we sometimes think.

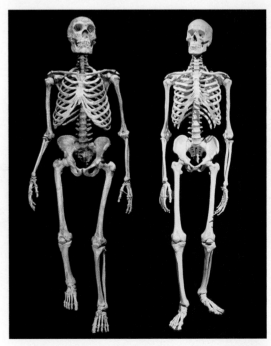

To understand the evolution of our genus during the Pleistocene, we need to consider both the anatomical and behavioral traits of our ancestors. The discovery of tools made from organic material, such as the wooden spears at Schoeningen, reminds us just how much information is missing from the archaeological record of early humans. Hominins definitely have an African homeland, but *Homo erectus*, the presumed ancestor of all later hominin species, lived throughout the Old World in regions that were later occupied by modern humans. So it is not immediately clear which populations, if any, are directly ancestral to us.

In this chapter, we look at the anatomy and behavior of the hominins of the middle to late Pleistocene. Hominin fossils from this evolutionarily dynamic period have been found throughout much of the Old World, but taxonomic assignments for the fossil specimens remain controversial. How many species were present? What constitutes enough variation to differentiate them from one another? Are the famous Neandertals simply another type of human or something more distinct? How did they behave, and what does that tell us about the selective pressures and evolutionary changes that led to the origin of our species?

⚲ View the **Map** "Hominin Evolution in the Mid-to-Late Pleistocene" on **myanthrolab**

Hominin Evolution in the Mid- to Late Pleistocene

As we saw in Chapter 9, the middle Pleistocene dates from about 900,000 years ago (corresponding to the earliest glaciation of continental Europe) to about 125,000 years ago (Conroy, 1997). The period from 125,000 to 10,000 years ago corresponds to the late Pleistocene. In the latter half of the middle Pleistocene, we begin to find fossils that exhibit features often interpreted as being more "advanced" or derived in the direction of *H. sapiens* than was *H. erectus*. To indicate their transitional nature, these specimens often are informally labeled "archaic *Homo sapiens*" or "advanced *H. erectus*," designations that distinguish them from anatomically modern *H. sapiens* and classic *H. erectus*. In addition to archaic *H. sapiens*, classic *H. erectus* survived in China and Indonesia until at least 250,000 years ago and maybe later (see Chapter 11). In Europe, the earliest representatives of the Neandertals make their first appearance, and it is possible that the earliest modern humans made their first appearance, at the very end of the middle Pleistocene in Africa (see Chapter 13).

Defining Anatomically Modern *Homo sapiens*

Archaic *H. sapiens* are intermediate between classic *H. erectus* and anatomically modern *H. sapiens*. To understand what this means, let us first consider the features that distinguish modern humans from other hominins (Clark, 1975).

Compared with those of other members of genus *Homo*, the anatomically modern *H. sapiens* skull is large (mean capacity 1,350 cc), bulbous, and gracile (Figure 12.1). Muscular ridges on the cranium are not strongly marked. Supraorbital (brow) ridges are not strongly developed or are absent altogether. The occipital region of the

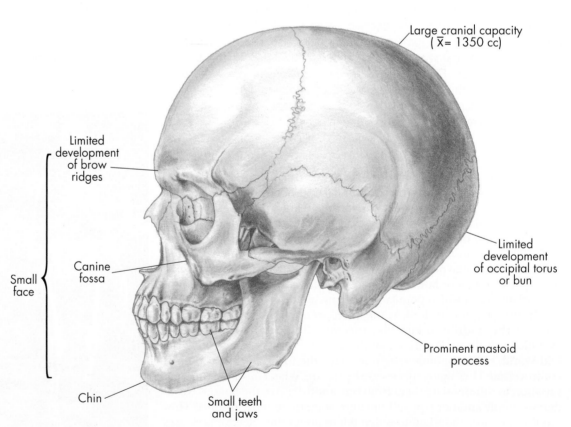

FIGURE 12.1   Features of the skull of anatomically modern *Homo sapiens*.

cranium is rounded, without development of an occipital torus and usually without an **occipital bun** (a backward-projecting bulge on the occipital bone). The forehead is rounded and more vertical than in other groups of *Homo*. Seen from behind, the maximum breadth of the skull is high (in the parietal region), and the vault is parallel-sided in rear view. The **mastoid process,** a protrusion from the temporal bone of the skull located behind and below the ear, is large and pyramidal. The jaws and teeth are small. Following jaw size, the face is smaller and retracted under the braincase to a greater degree than in previous hominins because the cranial base is more flexed. A canine fossa (a depression in the maxilla above the root of the upper canines) also develops. There is marked development of a chin. The limb bones are straight and slightly built.

Archaic *H. sapiens* typically exhibit a mosaic of *H. erectus* (see Figure 11.7 on page 280) and *H. sapiens* features, in many cases retaining the robustness of classic *H. erectus* but with a larger cranial capacity and a shape more similar to anatomically modern *H. sapiens*. As we will see, the intermediate or transitional nature of archaic *H. sapiens* can pose problems for determining how these specimens should be classified.

occipital bun   A backward-projecting bulge on the occipital part of the skull.

mastoid process   A protrusion from the temporal bone of the skull located behind the ear.

Archaic *Homo sapiens*

Archaic *H. sapiens* specimens reflect an important transitional period during human evolution. Anatomically the group is diverse, but it seems to consistently differ from *H. erectus* by having larger brains (1,000–1,400 cc); more parallel-sided, taller, and less angular cranial vaults; robust but arching rather than straight supraorbital tori; and in some instances wide nasal apertures (Figure 12.2). Archaic *H. sapiens* differ from modern humans by retaining large faces and thicker-walled, lower cranial vaults. As we review the individual fossils, keep in mind that, although we may call them archaic *H. sapiens*, that does not mean we consider them ancestral to later anatomically modern *H. sapiens* (although that may be a reasonable hypothesis), nor do they necessarily all represent the same species, although many scientists argue that they do.

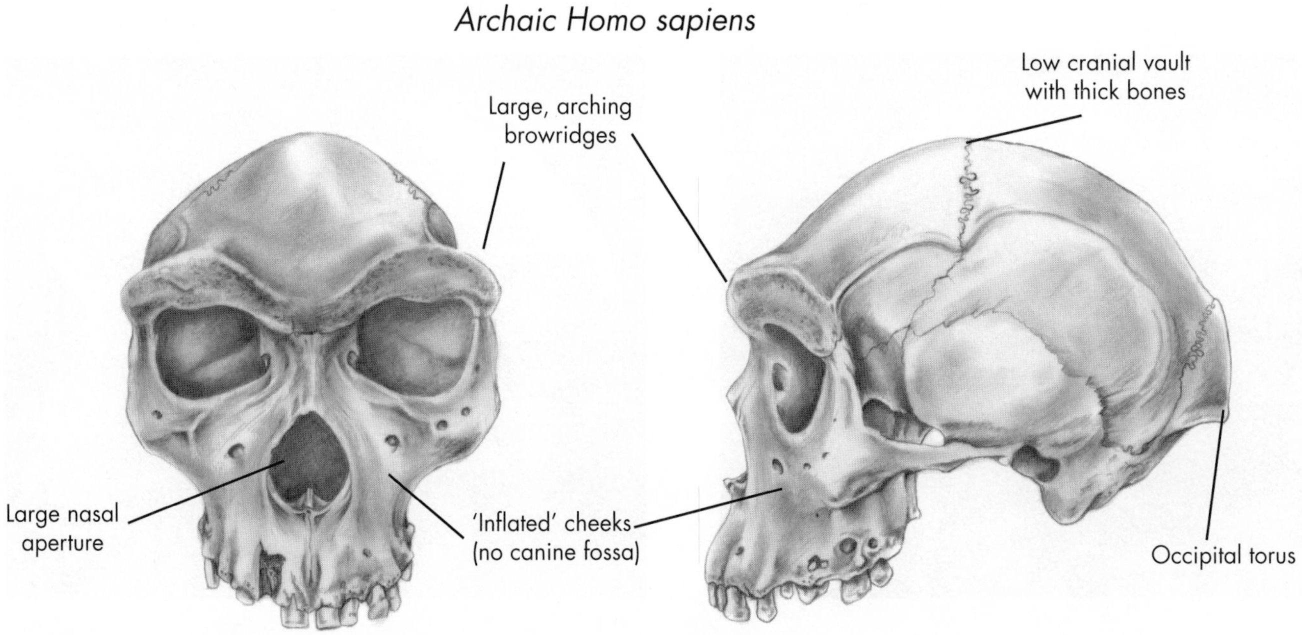

Archaic Homo sapiens

Large, arching browridges

Low cranial vault with thick bones

Large nasal aperture

'Inflated' cheeks (no canine fossa)

Occipital torus

FIGURE 12.2 Features of the skull of archaic *Homo sapiens*.

FIGURE 12.3   The Mauer mandible, discovered in Germany in 1907.

European Archaic *Homo sapiens*

Although the oldest hominins in Europe are those found at the Sima de Elefante site of the Sierra de Atapuerca in Spain, from about 1.2 million years ago (described in Chapter 11), the first of the European middle Pleistocene remains to be discovered was a mandible found in 1907 in a sandpit in the village of Mauer, near Heidelberg, Germany (Figure 12.3; Schoetensack, 1908). Based on biostratigraphy and lithostratigraphy (absolute dating is impossible at the site, see Chapter 9), the mandible was assigned a middle Pleistocene age of 400,000–500,000 years. Because the Mauer mandible is clearly not modern—it is quite robust and lacks a chin—it was correctly identified in 1908 as a hominin species distinct from our own. The Mauer mandible was given the name *Homo heidelbergensis*. For the many researchers who think that the informal label "archaic *H. sapiens*" should be replaced with a formal species designation, the species name *H. heidelbergensis* would have priority because the Mauer mandible was the first of the group to be discovered and named.

More complete fossils provide a more detailed picture of European hominins in the middle Pleistocene (Figure 12.4). These include the Petralona cranium from Greece (150,000–300,000 years ago), the Steinheim cranium from Germany (200,000–250,000 years ago), the Arago 21 partial cranium from France (300,000–600,000 years ago), and the rear portion of a cranium from Swanscombe, England (200,000–250,000 years ago). Less complete remains of archaic *H. sapiens* are known from several other sites in Europe, such as Bilzingsleben and Véretesszöllös in Hungary. The greatest number of archaic *H. sapiens* fossils recovered from a single locality comes from the middle Pleistocene part of the same cave system where *H. antecessor* was discovered, the Sierra de Atapuerca, Spain (Arsuaga et al., 1997; Arsuaga, 2002) (Figure 12.5). This cave (or pit) known as "Sima de los Huesos" (literally, the "bone pit"), is about 500,000–600,000 years old and yielded around thirty individuals, ranging in age from 4 to 35 years at their death, and probably included both males and females (Bischoff et al., 2007; Arsuaga et al., 1997).

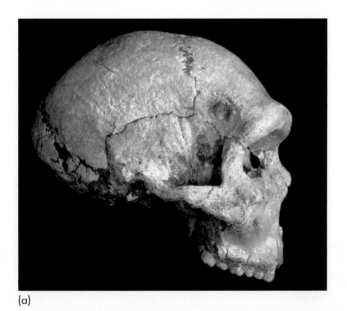

(a)

(b)

FIGURE 12.4   (a) The Petralona cranium from Greece. (b) The Steinheim cranium from Germany.

FIGURE 12.5 Skeletal remains from the Sima de los Huesos, Sierra de Atapuerca, Spain.

All these archaic *H. sapiens* specimens differ from classic *H. erectus* in vault shape and size, brow ridge conformation, and facial morphology, although they are similar in having thick cranial bones and less round cranial vaults and have similar postcranial skeletons. Cranial capacities are between 1,100 and 1,390 cc, making them larger-brained than typical *H. erectus* specimens. They have taller vaults with the greatest cranial breadth higher on the parietal than in *H. erectus*, yet their vaults remain lower than those of modern humans. The 500,000-year-old tibia from Boxgrove in southern England, along with extensive postcranial remains from Sima de los Huesos, suggest that, like other premodern *Homo*, archaic *H. sapiens* skeletons were robust with strong muscle markings and thick cortical bone, large joint surface areas, and strongly buttressed pelves (Arsuaga et al., 1997; Stringer et al., 1998; Arsuaga, 2002).

These middle Pleistocene European hominins are too primitive to be considered full Neandertals, but those from the Sima de los Huesos exhibit several cranial features that are very Neandertal-like. These include a double-arched supraorbital torus and **midfacial prognathism,** the forward projection of the middle facial region, including the nose, and an incipient fossa on the occipital. These features suggest that the Sima de los Huesos hominins and other European archaic *H. sapiens* may be directly ancestral to the later Neandertals and not ancestral to modern humans.

African Archaic *Homo sapiens*

The African continent has yielded at least four crania that are generally regarded as archaic *H. sapiens* because of their large cranial capacities; massive but more arching, non-bar-like supraorbital tori; and less angular vaults, with their greatest width higher on the cranium. Two are perhaps large males. The oldest of these is likely

midfacial prognathism The forward projection of the middle facial region, including the nose.

FIGURE 12.6 The Kabwe cranium (left) and the Bodo cranium (right) from Ethiopia, which shows signs of having been defleshed with stone tools.

to be the partial cranium from Bodo, Ethiopia (Figure 12.6) that dates to as much as 600,000 years ago. The Bodo cranium has a capacity of about 1,300 cc (Conroy et al., 1978). Its most extraordinary features are cut marks on the face that appear to be made by stone tools (White, 1986). The Kabwe cranium and several postcranial elements (also known as Rhodesian Man or Broken Hill for their find spot) were discovered in northern Rhodesia (present-day Zambia) at the Broken Hill limestone mine in 1921 and represent a more complete but slightly smaller (1,280 cc) individual than that from Bodo (Figure 12.6). Dating of the site is uncertain, although a late middle Pleistocene age of 125,000 years, based on faunal remains, is suggested. Both Kabwe and Bodo have somewhat prognathic midfaces with massive brows. The previous classification of Broken Hill as an African Neandertal, although now discarded, may indicate an ultimate ancestry to the Neandertal lineage.

Two smaller archaic *H. sapiens* crania also exist in Africa. The Ndutu partial cranium from near Olduvai Gorge in Tanzania has a cranial capacity of about 1,100 cc (Rightmire, 1990). Dates for the Ndutu cranium range from 200,000 to 400,000 years ago. The Salé partial cranium from Morocco has a smaller cranial capacity (900 cc) and dates to about 200,000–250,000 years ago (Hublin, 1985). Like the Steinheim cranium from Germany, these crania may be from small females, with small cranial capacities. Although not particularly large, Ndutu and Salé share features of the cranial vault with other archaic *H. sapiens*, including a high maximum cranial breadth and rounder vaults.

The European and African archaic *H. sapiens* specimens share many features and have a similar overall appearance. However, unlike the Sima de los Huesos hominins in Spain, no African archaic *H. sapiens* have been found that possess the specific derived features reminiscent of the Neandertals.

Asian Archaic *Homo sapiens*

Archaic *H. sapiens* specimens from Asia differ from *H. erectus* in vault size and shape as well as supraorbital toral shape. Reasonably complete crania have been found in China from the sites of Dali, Maba, and Jinniushan (Figure 12.7) that range in age from 130,000 to 200,000 years ago. Two other crania from Yunxian probably also represent archaic *H. sapiens*. However, both are heavily distorted and difficult to interpret (Li and Etler, 1992). The oldest hominin remains on the Indian continent come from the Narmada Valley, where a partial calvaria dates to the latest part of the middle Pleistocene (125,000–150,000 years ago). The Narmada specimen has an estimated cranial capacity of 1,150–1,400 cc, more vertically sided vault walls, and a double-arched brow ridge (Kennedy et al., 1991).

Although dating is a problem for the Chinese and Indian archaic *H. sapiens*, evidence indicates that archaic *H. sapiens* probably were present in Asia by 200,000 years ago. Given some of the late dates for classic *H. erectus* in Asia (see Chapter 11), if you accept that archaic *H. sapiens* is a different species from *H. erectus*, it is possible that two distinct hominin species were present in Asia in the latter part of the middle Pleistocene.

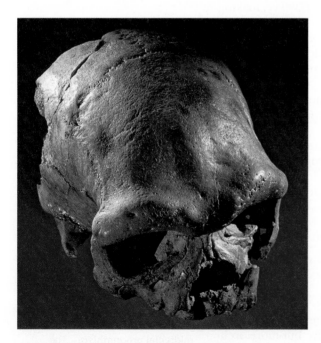

FIGURE 12.7 Dali, a Chinese archaic *Homo sapiens*.

Behavior of Archaic *Homo sapiens*

Reconstructing the behavior of archaic *Homo sapiens* poses a somewhat different problem from reconstructing the behavior of earlier hominins. Given their large brain size and probable close relationship to modern humans, we are compelled to consider archaic *H. sapiens* behavior from the perspective of what we know about the behavior of contemporary humans. Unfortunately, as we have seen, the material culture of archaic *H. sapiens* doesn't provide a comprehensive rendering of late middle Pleistocene behavior. Nonetheless, archaeological excavations at many sites in the Old World dating from 150,000 to 500,000 years ago indicate this was a period of evolutionary, although perhaps not revolutionary, change in behavior.

Stone Tools

Middle Pleistocene archaeological sites yield the same stone tool types that characterized the early Pleistocene, but also tell us of new technological developments. In Africa and Europe, where the Acheulean was well represented, Acheulean traditions—including production of bifaces (hand axes)—continued until about 150,000 years ago. In China, where hand axes were never associated with *H. erectus*, archaic *H. sapiens* are found in association with simple flake tools and cores.

Middle Paleolithic (Middle Stone Age) industries that used prepared-core technologies originate in the middle Pleistocene (Figure 12.8). Prepared-core technologies require that the toolmaker modify the original core by a number of flake removal steps in order to prepare it to produce a flake of a prescribed size and shape. Although wasteful of raw material in one sense, prepared-core technology allows great control of production of a main tool type, the so-called Mousterian point. Such preparation in pursuit of a particular flake indicates increasing forethought and abstract thinking. Prepared-core techniques include the **Levallois technique,** named for a French site near Paris where it was first discovered by scientists, even though the technique was developed in Africa between 200,000 and 300,000 years ago. In addition to prepared cores, Middle Paleolithic industries also used other flaking methods, characterized by a greater reliance on soft hammer techniques (in which materials such as bone, antler, or limestone were used as hammerstones), more retouched tools, and a larger variety of possibly stylized tool shapes. Tools

Middle Paleolithic (Middle Stone Age) Stone tool industries that used prepared-core technologies.

Levallois technique A Middle Paleolithic technique that made use of prepared cores to produce uniform levallois flakes.

THE LEVALLOIS TECHNIQUE

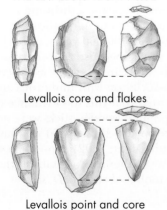

Levallois core and flakes

Levallois point and core

(a)

5 cm

(b)

(c)

FIGURE 12.8 (a) The Levallois technique for making uniform flakes from a prepared core. (b) A levallois core from the Kapedo Tuffs, Kenya, dates to about 130,000 years ago. (c) Levallois points and flakes from the Kapthurin Formation date to between 200,000 and 280,000 years ago.

FIGURE 12.9 F. Clark Howell with excavated dremains at Torralba, Spain.

FIGURE 12.9 F. Clark Howell with excavated dremains at Torralba, Spain.

include a number of different kinds of scrapers, made from flakes, and the previously mentioned points. The advantage of Middle Paleolithic industries, beyond the predictability of flake size and shape, is that from a given amount of raw material, they produce more cutting surface than Early Paleolithic techniques. Once these tool types appeared in the late middle Pleistocene, no new tool types were introduced until the late Pleistocene.

Tools from Organic Materials

Based on the behavior of living nonhuman primates and humans, we assume that hominins also used tools made from organic materials that would rarely be preserved in the archaeological record. Chimpanzees fashion tools from twigs and leaves, and it is likely that early hominins did as well. Although we have seen evidence of bone tool use by the robust *Australopithecus* species in Chapter 10, modified bone or antler tools are absent from the archaic *H. sapiens* archaeological record. However, there is indirect evidence, from flake scars on stone, that these items were used as soft hammers to produce stone tools (Stringer et al., 1998).

As described at the beginning of this chapter, wooden spears, a throwing stick, and three other worked branches were recovered in 1997 from excavations in an open-pit coal mine in Schoeningen, Germany, dated to 400,000 years ago. The three worked branches may be as significant as the spears because they may have formed the handles of stone–wood composite tools, a technologically advanced technique. Because the spears were found in close association with numerous animal remains, their discoverer, Hartmut Thieme, argued that this was evidence of large-game hunting. Some researchers believe these pointed wooden sticks were not spears but only thrusting lances or that, if they were spears, they would not have been very effective for large-game hunting (Klein and Edgar, 2002). Nonetheless, the discoveries of well-crafted wooden implements at Schoeningen establish that wooden tools probably were an important part of the toolkit of archaic *H. sapiens*.

Big-Game Hunting

There is little doubt that big-game hunting would have been advantageous for some archaic *H. sapiens* (or *H. erectus*) occupying northern latitudes in Europe or Asia. In those locations, there would have been a seasonal dependence on animal food, and the ability to hunt big game would have made it easier to expand into colder areas, even if scavenging were still done. In numerous middle Pleistocene archaeological sites, such as the Spanish sites of Ambrona and Torralba dating to 200,000–400,000 years ago (Howell, 1966), skeletal remains of large game have been found in association with Acheulean artifacts. In the 1960s and early 1970s, several middle Pleistocene archaeological sites were interpreted as demonstrating that archaic *H. sapiens* or advanced *H. erectus* (as they were more likely to be considered then) were capable of big-game hunting (Figure 12.9). Critics point out that associations such as this do not constitute proof of hunting because they could have resulted from the activity of other animals or other nonhominin depositional forces. Perhaps the Ambrona and Torralba animals were scavenged not hunted (Shipman and Rose, 1983), or perhaps finding large fauna in proximity with hominin artifacts near water sources simply means that water was important for both hominins and other animals (Klein and Edgar, 2002).

However, excavations at two sites in the 1990s provide increasing evidence in support of the hypothesis that middle Pleistocene hominins hunted big game. The Schoeningen spears were found in direct association with the butchered remains of ten horses and flake tools that could be used to deflesh the carcasses. Although it is impossible to be certain that the spears were used to bring down the horses, it seems reasonable to conclude they were made to be thrown at large, living animals. Excavations at the Boxgrove site in England (Figure 12.10) provide further evidence of big-game hunting (Stringer et al., 1998; Roberts and Parfitt, 1999). In addition to a hominin tibia and tooth, numerous remains of small and large animals in association with stone tools, mostly hand axes, have been excavated. Mark Roberts and his colleagues have shown that hominins got to the animal remains before carnivores or scavenging animals; stone tool cut marks always underlay carnivore teeth marks, and butchering marks indicate that eyes and tongues were removed by hominins ahead of bird scavengers. Furthermore, a horse scapula (shoulder blade) recovered from the site has a clear projectile wound, a hole about 50 mm (2 inches) in diameter; it is the kind of wound that spears of the kind found at Schoeningen would produce. Thus, the evidence seems to be mounting that archaic *H. sapiens* were capable of bringing down large game and that they did so in a cooperative manner, using Acheulean technology.

Fire, Campsites, and Home Sites

Evidence of the use of fire and campsites by archaic *H. sapiens* is rare. No proper hearths have been discovered, but ash deposits and charred bones recovered from a number of sites indicate that fire may have been used by both *H. erectus* and archaic *H. sapiens*. Archaic *H. sapiens* did not make a particularly strong impact on the landscape. Although it is reasonable to assume that they had campsites and home bases, there are few signs of them in the archaeological record, and no middle Pleistocene postholes or storage pits have been found, for example. It has been claimed that there is evidence of Acheulean "beach huts" at the site of Terra Amata in the South of France. However, disruption of the "living floor" of the site and the somewhat random scatter of bone and stone remains make this interpretation difficult to accept (Stringer and Gamble, 1993), and the use of caves as shelter was also limited.

The Neandertals

Compared with the little we know of archaic *H. sapiens*, we know much more about the anatomy and culture of the late Pleistocene fossil hominins informally known as Neandertals. The complete or

FIGURE 12.10 Evidence for big-game hunting by archaic *H. sapiens* is suggested by the excavations at the Boxgrove site, England. Here the stratigraphic layers of the site that have been meticulously excavated can be seen.

FIGURE 12.11 A scientific reconstruction of a Neandertal man.

partial remains of several hundred Neandertal individuals have been discovered from sites dating between 27,000 and 150,000 years ago in Europe, the Near and Middle East, and western Asia (Stringer and Gamble, 1993; Trinkaus, 1995). As you will recall from Chapter 9, this time period is one of extreme oscillations in temperature caused by strong glacial and interglacial cycles (see Figure 9.14 on page 215). One of the results of this increasing cold and glacial cycling is that latitudinal variation in climate became quite significant (remember that temperature varied little from north to south early in primate evolution). As a result of these cycles and the northern location of Neandertal sites, climate is a particularly important variable for understanding the origin and evolution of this group (Howell, 1964). At the end of their existence, Neandertals and anatomically modern *H. sapiens* overlap in time and space. How they share the landscape—and indeed the relationships between them—are points of some debate.

Scientists disagree as to whether Neandertals should be considered a species within the genus *Homo* (*H. neanderthalensis*) or a subspecies within *H. sapiens* (*H. s. neanderthalensis*). As was the case for archaic *H. sapiens*, choosing a taxonomic name for the Neandertals depends on how we define a species and on the phylogenetic model for the emergence of anatomically modern *H. sapiens* to which we subscribe. There is little disagreement that western "classic Neandertals" are an anatomically distinct group of hominins that lived during a short period of time and occupied a circumscribed portion of the Old World (Figure 12.11, see Figure 12.12). However, there is much disagreement as to whether these anatomical differences mean that Neandertals are a separate species or simply a geographic variant of living humans.

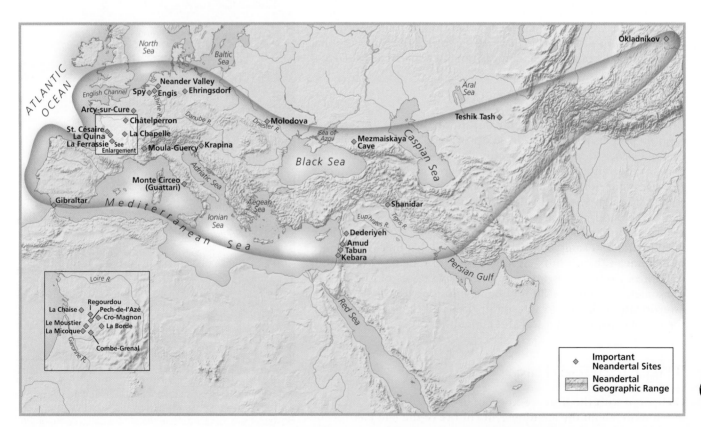

FIGURE 12.12 Distribution of Neandertal sites in Europe and western Asia.

Geographic and Temporal Distribution

The largest number of Neandertal sites, including the oldest (more than 150,000 years ago) and the youngest (about 30,000 years ago), are located in western Europe (Figure 12.12). Fossil-bearing sites are plentiful in Germany (Neandertal, Ehringsdorf), Belgium (Spy, Engis), Spain (Zafarraya, Gibraltar), Italy (Guattari), and France (La Quina, La Ferrassie, St. Cesaire, La Chapelle). However, the Neandertal range extends into central Asia at the site of Teshik Tash in Uzbekistan; and, based on DNA evidence, into Siberia at the site of Okladnikov; the Near East (Kebara, Amud, and Tabun, Israel; Dederiyeh, Syria); and the Middle East (Shanidar, Iraq). In addition to fossil-bearing localities, archaeological sites of the same ages span the entire region, telling us about site distribution and Neandertal movements relative to time and climate.

History of Neandertal Discovery

View the **Map** "Neandertal Sites" on **myanthrolab**

From the mid-1800s until the 1930s, when *H. erectus* became a more widely accepted taxon and South African *Australopithecus* started to come to light, Neandertals were the core of the hominin fossil record. In the popular imagination, "Neandertal" and "caveman" became synonyms, and the Neandertals became the focus of negative portrayals and feelings.

The significance of the first Neandertal finds was not fully appreciated at the time of their discovery. The first Neandertal was discovered at the Engis cave site in Belgium in 1830: the cranium of a small child aged 2–3 years, who even at that young age shows slight development of a double-arched Neandertal brow ridge. The second Neandertal discovery, in 1848, was a nearly complete cranium from the British colony of Gibraltar on the southern coast of Spain. It took nearly 20 years for the Gibraltar cranium to be recognized as a Neandertal; although considered from the time of its discovery to be an ancient specimen, and the Engis child was not "rediscovered" to be a very young Neandertal for more than a century.

The Neandertal specimen for which the group was named was not found until 1856 in a limestone quarry in the Neander Valley (in German, *Neanderthal*) near Düsseldorf. The Neandertal bones, including a skullcap and partial skeleton (Figure 12.13), were discovered in clay deposits removed from a limestone cave that was being quarried. The owner of the quarry saw the large bones, and thinking that they were from cave bears, contacted a local schoolteacher and natural historian, Johann Carl Fuhlrott, who identified them as human. Recognizing the potential significance of this find, Fuhlrott then contacted anatomy Professor Herman Schaafhausen, who led the scientific analysis of the discovery. Although the original cave was destroyed by commercial quarrying, the deposits removed from the cave were recently rediscovered through study of the archives of the mining company (Schmitz et al., 2002). So, more than 140 years after the initial find, additional bones and artifacts from Neandertal indicate that there were at least three individuals in the cave. Almost unbelievably, additional remains of the original Neandertal specimen were discovered. This re-excavation allowed dating of the finds for the first time, giving them an age of 40,000 years.

Professor Schaafhausen presented his initial analyses of the Neandertal remains in 1857, a full 2 years before Darwin published *On the Origin of Species*. Schaafhausen noted the long and low shape of the skullcap, the large brow ridges, and the development of an occipital bun. All these distinguished this specimen from modern humans. Furthermore, the postcranial bones were very robust and marked with ridges for the attachment of large muscles; the ribs were rounded, indicating a barrel-chested individual. Thus, Schaafhausen argued that the Neandertal remains were probably those of a different species than living

FIGURE 12.13 The original Neandertal remains from the Neander Valley, Germany.

humans. Critics argued, however, that the Neandertal remains were simply those of an odd or pathological human, perhaps a Cossack who had died during the Russian invasion of Germany in 1814 or possibly an unfortunate individual who suffered from a variety of pathological conditions, thus explaining his obviously injured left arm. These arguments would not be disproven until more fossils were discovered; by the 1920s, Neandertals were known throughout Europe and even Asia and accepted as more than just modern humans.

Aside from modern humans, Neandertals are by far the most thoroughly represented hominins in the fossil record. Given the large number of Neandertal remains available, it is possible to study aspects of their growth, development, and demography, population-level variables that are impossible to examine in earlier hominins. It is likely that compared with earlier hominins, the cultural behavior of Neandertals was more complex, so it is more difficult to interpret in the context of the archaeological record.

👁 **Watch** the **Animation** "Anatomical Features of Neandertal Skull and Teeth" on **myanthrolab**

Neandertal Anatomy and DNA: Built for the Cold

Neandertals possess some derived features that are not present in either anatomically modern humans or archaic *H. sapiens* such as *H. heidelbergensis* (Figures 12.14 and 12.15). Therefore, many scientists think that they represent a unique evolutionary trajectory in the context of middle and late Pleistocene hominin evolution.

Although the Neandertal vault is long and low, its size and shape are quite different than *H. erectus*. The Neandertal cranium is large, much larger than that of *H. erectus* or *H. sapiens*; presumed females have an average cranial capacity of 1,300 cc and presumed males an average of 1,600 cc. Research on Neandertal brains (as studied from endocasts) suggests they were fully modern in their organization and that the large size of the brain was a function of large body size and adaptation to the cold environments in which they evolved (Holloway, 1984).

In addition to these size differences, vault shape differs in important ways. The maximum cranial breadth in Neandertals tends to be in the middle of the cranium,

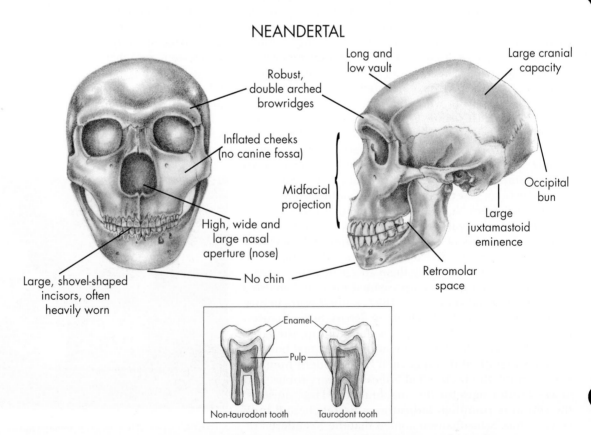

NEANDERTAL

- Long and low vault
- Large cranial capacity
- Robust, double arched browridges
- Inflated cheeks (no canine fossa)
- Midfacial projection
- High, wide and large nasal aperture (nose)
- No chin
- Large, shovel-shaped incisors, often heavily worn
- Occipital bun
- Large juxtamastoid eminence
- Retromolar space

Enamel — Pulp

Non-taurodont tooth — Taurodont tooth

FIGURE 12.14 The Neandertal skull and teeth. Neandertals have taurodont molars.

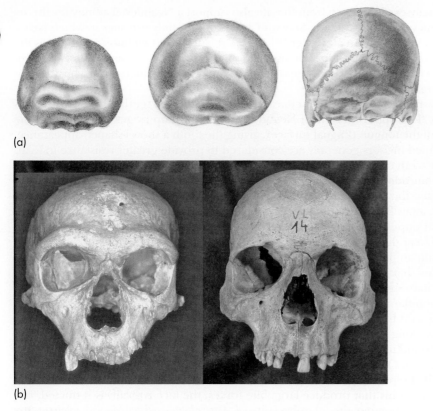

(a)

(b)

FIGURE 12.15 (a) From behind, Neandertal vaults (middle) are oval shaped compared to *H. erectus* (left) and *H. sapiens* (right) (b) The faces of Neandertal (left) and anatomically modern *H. sapiens* (right) display anatomical differences including a double-arched brow and absence of a canine fossa in Neandertals.

giving it an oval appearance when viewed from the rear. In contrast, in humans, the maximum cranial breadth is higher on the skull, and the side walls are parallel, whereas in *H. erectus* maximum breadth is low on the vault, and the side walls slope inward, forming a pentagon in rear view (Figure 12.15a). At the back of the Neandertal cranium, the occipital bone bulges posteriorly, forming the occipital bun. The mastoid process in Neandertals is smaller than in modern humans, but a ridge of bone just next to it, the **juxtamastoid eminence,** is larger than the mastoid process.

The face of the Neandertals also differs from those of *H. erectus* and modern humans. Among the most important of the derived characters of the Neandertals is their midfacial prognathism (Figure 12.15b). The middle part of the face, around the nose, projects strongly anteriorly, and the cheek region is placed far posteriorly, with an even grade between the two. It is almost as if someone has grabbed the Neandertal nose and pulled it away from the cheeks, forming a smooth transition from cheek to nose. Therefore, the cheeks of Neandertals are often described as "swept back." The face as a whole is also quite tall. Probably related to the anterior position of the midface (and upper dentition) is the presence on the rear of the mandible of a retromolar space between the third molar and the ascending ramus. Like earlier hominins, Neandertals show no development of a chin.

There are also important differences between the inner ear anatomy of Neandertals and that of modern humans and *H. erectus.* The semicircular canals of the inner ear assist in maintaining balance, but there is variation in their structure even between closely related species. Although modern humans and *H. erectus* do not differ in inner ear anatomy, work by Fred Spoor and his colleagues using three-dimensional imaging shows that Neandertals have a different and probably derived inner ear anatomy (Figure 12.16 on page 314; Spoor et al., 2003). The differences are so clear that they have been used to identify the infant temporal bone from Arcy-sur-Cure as a Neandertal, an important identification for this site that had otherwise nondiagnostic fossil remains (Hublin et al., 1996).

juxtamastoid eminence A ridge of bone next to the mastoid process; in Neandertals, it is larger than the mastoid process itself.

Detailed analyses of the teeth from the site also support a Neandertal affinity for the remains (Bailey & Hublin, 2006). Arcy-sur-Cure is one of only two sites in which Neandertals are associated with an Upper Paleolithic (blade-based) technology known as the Châtelperronian and may also show association with symbolic remains. These clear-cut differences in ear anatomy also support the idea that the Neandertals may be a species separate from modern humans.

Three prominent features characterize Neandertal teeth (Figure 12.14 on page 312): The upper incisors of Neandertals had built-up ridges of enamel on the side nearest the tongue (lingual surface), giving the tooth a shovel-shaped appearance. Shovel-shaped incisors generally are considered to provide greater resistance to wear. The molar teeth of Neandertals had expanded pulp cavities and fused roots, a feature known as **taurodontism.** Taurodont teeth can sustain more wear than nontaurodont teeth because they maintain a broader base for wear after the enamel of the crown has been worn away. Both taurodont molars and shovel-shaped incisors are found in modern human populations at various frequencies. The anterior teeth show an unusual amount of wear that is much greater than that on the molars and is greater than among modern human populations, even those who use their anterior teeth extensively. This may indicate that Neandertals used these as teeth a third hand to hold objects.

Many have speculated about why Neandertals had such prognathic faces and large noses. A popular idea is that the nose warmed cold air before it reached the respiratory system and brain. Among modern humans, however, cold-dwelling populations tend to have long and narrow noses to restrict cold airflow to the brain, whereas broad noses are found in more tropical climates and facilitate heat dissipation (Stringer and Gamble, 1993). Others argue that the prognathic midface (and the large nose associated with it) helps dissipate heavy biting on the anterior dentition. However, in animals and hominins that produce large bite forces, the face typically is retracted, not prognathic (remember the adaptive suite of *Australopithecus boisei* and *robustus*, for

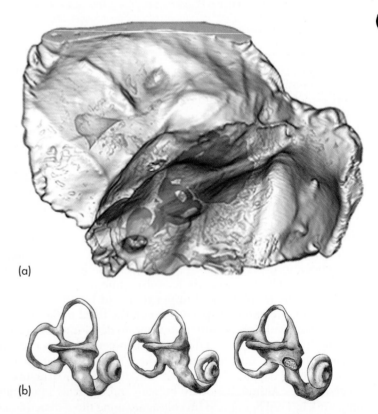

(a)

(b)

FIGURE 12.16 Neandertal inner ear anatomy is distinctive from modern humans. The inner ear is figured in blue in this temporal bone from Engis, images by Antoine Balzeau (a). The size and shape of the canals differ between the Neandertal ear (on the right) and the modern human ear on the left (b).

example). No convincing argument for an adaptive function for the large Neandertal face and nose has yet to be generally accepted, and it may be that Neandertal facial morphology results from a variety of phylogenetic trends or evolutionary forces. Erik Trinkaus (2003) points out that the large faces of Neandertals reflect continuation of a trend seen in archaic *H. sapiens*; thus, modern humans should be thought of as having small faces. Similarly, large nose size again reflects well-established evolutionary trends observed in a wide range of middle and late Pleistocene hominins (Franciscus, 1999, 2003). In particular, genetic isolation in glacial environments may have produced the Neandertal face via genetic drift from an already prognathic ancestor, such as the Sima de los Huesos specimens. Tim Weaver, Charles Roseman, and Chris Stringer have used new population genetic models to convincingly argue that the Neandertal face is likely the result of gene drift (Weaver et al., 2007).

The postcranial skeleton of the Neandertals was massive compared with that of modern humans, although Neandertals were on average shorter than late Pleistocene humans (Figure 12.17). Neandertal males are estimated to have been on average 169 cm (5 ft 6.5 in.) in height, with a weight of 65 kg (143 lb), whereas females were 160 cm (5 ft 3 in.) and 50 kg (110 lb) (Stringer and Gamble, 1993). The Neandertal chest was barrel-shaped, and the limbs, especially the forearm and shin, were short. These characteristics are consistent with a body designed to conserve heat in a cold climate (see Bergman's and Allen's rules in Chapter 6), and Neandertals have been described as having "hyper-polar" bodies (Holliday, 1995). The long bones and major joints were all larger and more robust than those found in modern humans, features that Neandertals may have shared with earlier hominins and that indicate a physically demanding lifestyle.

Neandertal and modern human postcranial skeletons differ in several other respects. One of the most striking differences appears in the anatomy of the pubic bone, which forms the front part of the pelvis. The upper, anterior part of the pelvis, formed by the superior pubic ramus, was longer and more gracile in Neandertals than in modern humans. This is in direct opposition to the pattern established by the rest of the skeleton. However, from the complete Neandertal pelvis discovered at Kebara, Israel, we know that the lengthened pubis does not result in a larger pelvic outlet, so it is not related to either increased birth efficiency or increased gestation time, as had been previously argued. Indeed recent CT reconstructions show that Neandertal neonates had similar brain sizes at birth as modern humans, but may have grown somewhat faster after birth (Ponce de Leon et al., 2008). The broader pelvis may simply have been the Neandertal way of establishing greater body breadth (and greater volume relative to surface area for heat retention).

In the late 1990s, the original Neandertal remains again came to the attention of the scientific world when it was announced that DNA from this specimen had been successfully extracted, amplified, and sequenced (see Innovations: Neandertal Genes on pages 316–317; Krings et al., 1997). DNA from the recently discovered Mezmaiskaya subadult and a number of other individuals has also been extracted and analyzed (Schmitz et al., 2002). Attempts to extract DNA from fossils (hominins or other animals) this old often are unsuccessful, but the cold climate the Neandertals lived in may have helped to preserve their DNA. Initially scientists had only small snippets of Neandertal mitochondrial DNA that is quite different from that of living humans. Recently two groups of scientists have isolated nuclear DNA as well (Noonan et al., 2006; Green et al., 2006). The entire Neandertal genome was published in 2010 (Green et al., 2010). The phylogenetic implications of these results are discussed in Chapter 13.

taurodontism Molar teeth that have expanded pulp cavities and fused roots.

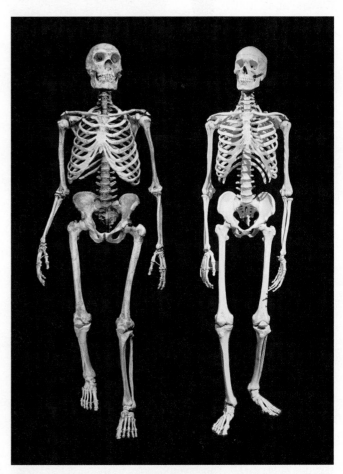

FIGURE 12.17 These articulated skeletons suggest that Neandertals (left) were much more heavily built than anatomically modern humans.

Neandertal Genes

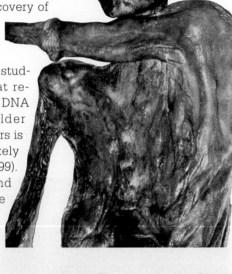

Ancient DNA (aDNA) recovered from fossils provides a direct window into the genetics of past populations. Unfortunately, only a small percentage of fossils actually preserve any DNA. Several factors influence whether DNA will be preserved. Age is a critical factor. Although in the early days of ancient DNA research (the late 1980s and early 1990s) many claims were made for the recovery of DNA from samples more than 1 million years old, subsequent studies indicate that recovering usable DNA from fossils older than 100,000 years is extremely unlikely (Wayne et al., 1999). Temperature and humidity are also critical to whether DNA will be preserved: Cold and dry is better than warm and wet. For example, late Pleistocene mammoths preserved in arctic permafrost and Östi the ~5,000–year-old "Tyrolean Iceman" discovered in the Alps preserve DNA quite well (Rollo et al., 2006). In terms of hominin fossils, this suggests those from northern Europe and northern Asia are the most likely to provide intact DNA, whereas hominins in the tropics such as portions of Africa and Southeast Asia are least likely.

Ancient DNA from several Neandertals and modern humans has been recovered and analyzed. Ancient samples from archaic *H. sapiens* specimens have not yet been obtained. The Neandertal samples include two from the Feldhofer Cave, Germany, the original site of the Neandertal's discovery (Krings et al., 1997; Schmitz et al., 2002), three from the Vindija Cave in Croatia (Krings et al., 2000; Serre et al., 2004), and one each from Mezmaiskaya Cave in the northern Caucasus (Ovchinnikov et al., 2000), the sites of Engis and Scladina in Belgium (Serre et al., 2004; Orlando et al., 2006), El Sidrón in Spain (Lalueza-Fox et al., 2005), Monte Lessini in Italy (Caramelli et al., 2006), Rochers de Villeneuve and La Chapelle-aux-Saints in France (Serre et al., 2004; Beauval et al., 2005), and Okladnikov in Siberia (Krause et al., 2007). These samples cover much of the Neandertal geographic and temporal range including some of the last surviving Neandertals (the Mezmaiskaya infant dating to

about 29,000 years ago) and some of the older Neandertals (the Scladina site is the oldest sampled with an age of about 100,000 years ago). The modern human samples include two from Mladec in Czechoslovakia, one each from Cro-Magnon, Abri Pataud, and La Madeleine in France (Serre et al., 2004), and two from Italy (Caramelli et al., 2003). More than twenty-five Neandertals and forty fossil humans were sampled to achieve these few results.

Most of the DNA extracted from Neandertals is ancient mitochondrial DNA, some of it from the hypervariable region 1. Remember that mtDNA is passed down only through the maternal lineage, and represents a fairly small part of the whole genome (see Chapter 2 for a review). The snippets of mtDNA recovered from Neandertals are all fairly similar to one another. They cluster together as a group to the exclusion of DNA from ancient *H. sapiens* and from living humans. Like living humans, Neandertals have relatively little diversity in their mtDNA. The amount of variation between Neandertals and ancient *H. sapiens* is greater than amongst living humans, but it is much less than the variation seen among chimpanzees and gorillas. This difference in diversity is probably related to a rapid population expansion in the human lineage before *H. sapiens* and Neandertals diverged.

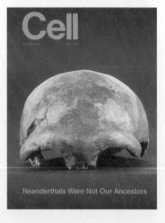

Neanderthals Were Not Our Ancestors

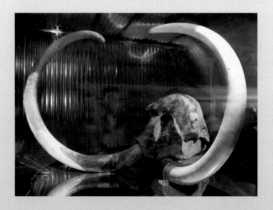

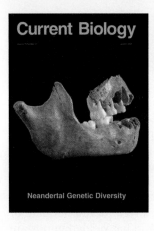

Current Biology

Neandertal Genetic Diversity

Recent studies of both mitochondrial and nuclear DNA have yielded some surprises. DNA analyses have extended the geographic range of Neandertals into Siberia at a site called Oklad- nikov. And nuclear DNA from Neandertals at El Sidrón in Spain has suggested that, like living humans, some Neandertals had pale skin and red hair (Lalueza-Fox, 2007). This suggests that Neandertals had evolved phenotypic adaptations to low UV radiation, including skin depigmentation, as modern human populations have. However, the adaptations are not identical. The mutation in the Neandertal DNA differs from that seen in modern humans and this means that the two groups evolved these adaptations separately, rather than having gained it from a common ancestor or by interbreeding.

The date for the most recent common ancestor (MRCA) of *H. sapiens* and Neandertals is between 365,000 and 853,000 years ago. Using mitochondrial DNA, an MRCA date for the western (Feldhofer and Vindija) and eastern (Mezmaiskaya) Neandertal samples has been estimated to be between 151,000 and 352,000 years ago.

Nuclear DNA has been sequenced as well (Green et al., 2006; Noonan et al., 2006). Originally, nuclear DNA came from just a single fossil from Vindija and was sequenced by two different research groups using two different techniques that yielded similar results (Noonan et al., 2006; Green et al., 2006). DNA was also isolated from cave bear fossils from the same site and compared to modern

carnivores to test the technique. Now a draft of the entire nuclear genome of Neandertals is available, having been spliced together from fragments of multiple individuals from Vindija with comparisons to smaller sequences from El Sidrón, Neander, and Mezmaiskaya (Green et al., 2010). This was no small job because the fossil bones also included DNA of fungi and bacteria from the soil in which the remains were buried, and aDNA is always highly degraded. The results are the product of the Neanderthal Genome Project, a joint collaboration between the Max Planck Institute for Evolutionary Anthropology and 454 Life Sciences. These data indicate a date for the split

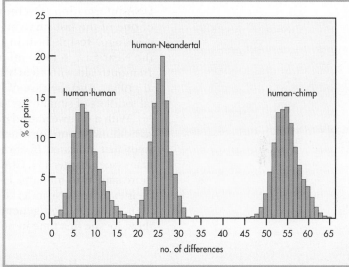

between Neandertal and *H. sapiens* of between 270,000 and 440,000 years, a range that is compatible with that produced by mtDNA. And they also suggest that there was a small genetic contribution from Neandertals into the modern human gene pool, perhaps around 1–4%. The researchers also found evidence of uniquely human genetic traits, the implications of which we discuss in Chapter 14.

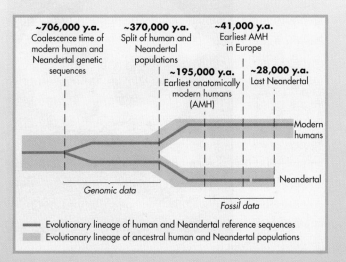

Growing up Neandertal

Neandertals are the only fossil group to be reasonably well represented by children's remains of nearly all ages, from newborn (or even fetal) to adult. In Europe, the earliest Neandertal to be discovered from Engis is 2- to 3-year-old, deciduous (baby) teeth found at Spy, and a 3- to 5-year-old was found at Devil's Quarry on Gibraltar. In France, at La Ferrassie, remains of six children ranging in age from not much older than newborn to about 12 years of age were found, and at La Quina an important cranium of an 8-year-old child was discovered. Of the thousands of bone fragments at Krapina in Croatia, many of the individuals were subadults, and in the northern Caucasus, northeast of the Black Sea, a partial skeleton of a Neandertal neonate or fetus has recently been recovered from Mezmaiskaya Cave and has yielded important DNA information (Ovchinnikov et al., 2000). This infant may have been a member of one of the last surviving Neandertal populations; the date for this site is 29,000 years ago. Teshik Tash in Uzbekistan yielded the skeleton of a 9-year-old child. In the Near East, several infant remains have been found at Amud Cave, including a 10-month-old who clearly bears Neandertal features in its cranial anatomy (Rak et al., 1994). And the cave of Dederiyeh in Syria has yielded the skeletons of 2 Neandertal toddlers of similar age (Figure 12.18; Akazawe & Muhesun, 2002).

With a relative abundance of children's remains, the Neandertals are the only fossil hominin group for which detailed studies on growth have been made. In the same study that indicated *H. erectus* had a faster dental developmental rate than modern humans (see Chapter 11), Chris Dean found Neandertals had a dental developmental rate more similar to humans. However, studies of growth of the mandible indicate that in their early years Neandertal children may have grown faster than modern human children, although their general growth rates are similar to ours. Neandertals thus seem to show, for the first time in hominin evolution, growth patterns similar to our own.

Health and Disease

The history of Neandertal research has been strongly influenced by the recognition and interpretation of pathological conditions in bone. Recall that the type specimen from the Neander Valley was at the center of an argument over whether it was a pathological human or a distinct species or subspecies. For many years the common perception of Neandertals as primitive, shuffling creatures came from reconstructions produced by Marcellin Boule from a Neandertal skeleton from La Chapelle, France. The "Old Man"

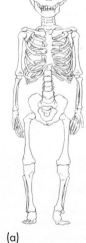
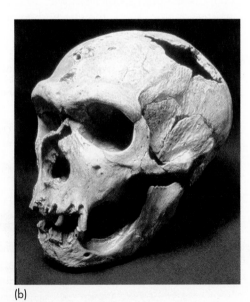

FIGURE 12.18
Neandertal development and aging. (a) Remains of a 17- to 19-month-old child from Dederiyeh. (b) The "Old Man" from La Chapelle shows extensive tooth loss.   (a)   (b)

of La Chapelle-aux-Saints dates to about 40,000 years ago and is clearly that of an older male, although in this context *old* means about 40 years of age. He suffered from numerous pathological conditions: a deformation in the pelvis, a crushed toe, severe arthritis in several of the vertebrae, and a broken rib sustained not long before death. He was missing many teeth, and the mandible and maxilla showed a significant amount of bone loss (Figure 12.18). In part, Boule's reconstruction of La Chapelle as having a stooped posture may have been misled by the numerous pathological conditions in the skeleton, but recent investigators who have examined the skeleton and Boule's work also believe that his interpretation of the skeleton was biased by his negative preconceptions about the "primitive" Neandertals (to be fair to Boule, the excavators of the Spy Neandertals also interpreted the skeletons as having a stooped posture). Nonetheless, Boule's appraisal formed the "scientific" basis for the negative image of Neandertals for decades. A new reconstruction at the American Museum of Natural History by Gary Sawyer and colleagues shows a more robust, upright Neandertal (Figure 12.17 on page 315).

Other Neandertal skeletons provide abundant evidence of traumatic injuries. Nearly all of the Shanidar individuals from Iraq, dated to about 40,000–50,000 years ago, show some type of pathological condition, most related to trauma (Trinkaus 1983). Shanidar 1, an older male 30–45 years old, had sustained a blow to the left side of his head, causing a break in the eye socket, and may have been blind in the left eye. The right side of his body had suffered even more extensive trauma: The lower right arm and hand were missing (the skeleton was otherwise intact and well preserved), probably because of an extensive injury that led to an atrophy of the upper right arm and shoulder; he also showed signs of injury in the right leg and foot. It is possible that this individual could have survived such injuries only with help from other Neandertals, although drawing such a conclusion based on pathological conditions alone is problematic (Dettwyler, 1991).

In fact, so many Neandertals exhibit healed fractures that their cause has been sought. Some scientists argue the fractures, especially the high incidence of head and neck fractures, indicate that Neandertals were routinely getting close to dangerous prey while hunting (Berger and Trinkaus, 1995). But the spears from Schoeningen suggest that Neandertals should have been able to hunt from a distance. Others scientists suggest that fracture rates may vary by geographic region according to the ruggedness of the terrain.

Neandertal Behavior

Reconstructing Neandertal lifeways is a difficult task. When we reconstruct past human behavior based on the archaeological record, we make inferences based on direct observation of living humans. We can be fairly certain that modern humans do not provide a particularly good model for Neandertal behavior, but we do not know how bad the fit is. Take something as fundamental to human behavior as language. It is not unreasonable to assume that the Neandertals possessed some fairly sophisticated form of spoken communication, but how did it compare to language in its ability to transmit ideas and information (see Chapter 14)? The Neandertals' large brains indicate that they were among the most cognitively sophisticated species that have ever lived, but what exactly did they do with these abilities?

Material Culture

Most Neandertal fossils have been found in association with Middle Paleolithic tools. In general, this tool industry builds on past tool cultures such as the Acheulean by using some similar tools, such as bifaces, adding prepared-core techniques, and a greater reliance on small flaked tools than in Acheulean industries. In addition, there is systematic variation in tool complexity in the Middle Paleolithic. Likewise, all early Neandertals and contemporaneous anatomically modern humans (such as those from Skhul and Qafzeh) are associated with Mousterian tools. This reminds us that there is no reason to expect that stone tool traditions will correlate with anatomical differences between hominins.

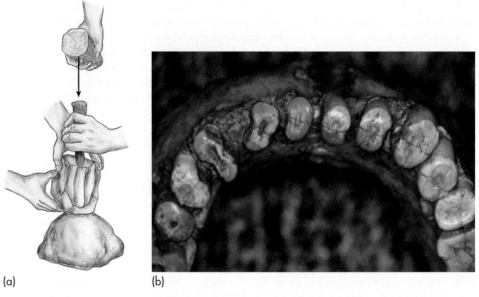

(a)   (b)

FIGURE 12.19   (a) Upper Paleolithic stone tools, include blade-based tools, as seen here being produced from a blade core. (b) Neandertals used their front teeth as tools. As a result, these teeth show heavy wear as seen here in the La Ferrassie Neandertal.

All later anatomically modern humans and a few later Neandertals are found with the **Upper Paleolithic (Later Stone Age),** which we discuss in more detail in Chapter 13 (Figure 12.19). The Saint-Césaire and Arcy-sur-Cure Neandertals from France are associated not with the Middle Paleolithic but rather with tools from an Upper Paleolithic industry, the **Châtelperronian** (Hublin et al., 1996). Upper Paleolithic industries are characterized by the development of blade-based technology. **Blades** are flakes that are twice as long as they are wide. In addition, Upper Paleolithic technologies use more refined flaking techniques and an increase in the variety of flaked tools. Saint-Césaire and Arcy-sur-Cure demonstrate that Neandertals were capable of producing Upper Paleolithic technology, regardless of whether it was a completely Neandertal invention or an adoption of a modern human production technique. At some archaeological sites without hominins, we find Châtelperronian and another Upper Paleolithic industry, the Aurignacian (which is associated with modern humans), interstratified through time in the site as if the groups were taking turns using the area. Given that most Neandertals produced Middle Paleolithic tools and only a few, late Neandertals produced Upper Paleolithic tools, it is possible that this technology may have been borrowed from anatomically modern groups.

Middle Paleolithic assemblages have few bone or antler tools. Although there have been no wood tool discoveries directly associated with Neandertal remains, the 130,000-year-old Lehringen wood spear from Germany suggests that Neandertals, like earlier archaic *H. sapiens*, must have made extensive use of wood. For example, many smaller Mousterian points probably were hafted to wooden shafts to form spears or lances.

The anterior dentition of the Neandertals may constitute the most unusual tool that we can recover from the archaeological record (Figure 12.19b). As mentioned earlier, the anterior teeth of Neandertals are large and heavily worn compared with the back teeth, indicating that they were used in a vise-like manner. Wear patterns on the teeth indicate that both animal and vegetable matter were held in the front teeth. Cut marks on the teeth indicate that Neandertals held objects with their front teeth while cutting what they held, perhaps hide or pieces of meat, with stone tools. It is possible to imagine—but difficult to prove—any number of tasks that the Neandertals might have accomplished using their front teeth. All we can say for certain is that most Neandertals regularly used their front teeth as tools. And new research on the archaic *H. sapiens* from Atapuerca Sima de los Huesos, Spain, show these hominins also had cutmarks on their teeth and probably used them like a vise (Lozano et al., 2008).

Coping with Cold

Neandertal bodies are typical of cold-adapted populations, and their archaeological sites also give indications of behavioral adaptations to cold. One way to cope with cold is through the use of fire. Charcoal deposits and ashy dump spots are commonly found in Middle Paleolithic sites, indicating that Neandertals used fire. True hearths are rare, but they have been identified in a 60,000-year-old Middle Paleolithic site in Portugal. It is also very likely that Neandertals used animal skins and hides to protect themselves from the cold. No tools that could be used as sewing implements, such as awls or bone needles, have been found in the Middle Paleolithic; if they did use hides, it is unlikely that they were sewn. In Molodova in the Ukraine, a Middle Paleolithic site has yielded a ring of mammoth bones, approximately 5 × 8 m (13 × 24 ft) in size, that encloses a dense concentration of artifacts, bones, and ash. Many scientists think that this site represents a living space of some kind, a wind-sheltering structure, or perhaps even a tent. It is assumed that the walls of the structure were constructed from animal hides. As yet, there is no evidence of more substantial Neandertal structures.

Another way to cope with cold is to avoid it, either by seasonally migrating over long distances or by moving as overall conditions get colder (or warmer) during all parts of the year. Middle Paleolithic archaeological deposits indicate that Neandertal sites served as temporary camping, hunting, or food processing locales. But the extent of their mobility seems to have been limited: Most of the raw materials for stone tools came from within 5 km (3 miles) of their source rock, with a maximum of 80 km (Stringer and Gamble, 1993). Thus, Neandertal mobility was not of a large enough scale to avoid seasonal cold altogether but probably reflected local movements necessary to exploit scarce resources within a small area. However, the distribution of Neandertal sites through time indicates that they did migrate in and out of areas over longer periods of time depending on whether glacial or interglacial conditions persisted. For example, across the eastern Russian plain, Neandertal sites are found far north only during interglacial periods and are located further south during glacial periods, as if the Neandertals were retreating in the face of the harsh glacial climate. And Neandertals never, even during interglacials, lived as far north as anatomically modern humans eventually would.

Similarly, Neandertals appeared to move south into the Near East during glacial times, and modern humans occupied the region during warmer interglacials. Five prominent cave sites located on Mount Carmel in Israel have been the focus of much attention over the years (excavations in this area began in the late 1920s) because they possess either Neandertal or anatomically modern fossils. Three of these sites have produced classic Neandertals: Tabūn (dating to about 110,000 years ago), Kebara (60,000 years ago), and Amud (35,000–40,000 years ago). And two, Skhūl and Jebel Qafzeh, have yielded anatomically modern human fossils dated to about 90,000–110,000 years ago. All these hominins, Neandertal and modern human, were found in association with Mousterian (Middle Paleolithic) stone tools, which are more typically found in association with Neandertals. If you accept Neandertals as a separate species, then it is likely that Neandertals and modern humans were alternatively using the region during varying climatic times: Neandertals during cold spells, modern humans during warmer spells.

Hunting, Subsistence, and Cannibalism

Stable isotope ratios of carbon and nitrogen indicate that Neandertals were heavily reliant on animal resources (Richards et al., 2000). They undoubtedly used all the hunting strategies known by archaic *H. sapiens* and earlier hominins. Different Neandertal sites indicate that they used a variety of subsistence strategies depending on local conditions and the game available in a given area. Although they may have scavenged meat opportunistically, there is little evidence that Neandertals engaged in scavenging on a broad scale (Marean and Assefa, 1999). In fact, a high percentage of the animal remains at Kebara, Israel, were from prime adults, indicating that these Neandertals were very capable hunters. A consistent distribution of burned bones

Upper Paleolithic (Later Stone Age) Stone tool industries that are characterized by the development of blade-based technology.

Châtelperronian An Upper Paleolithic tool industry that has been found in association with later Neandertals.

blades Flakes that are twice as long as they are wide.

FIGURE 12.20 The Krapina remains may provide evidence of cannibalism by some Neandertals.

indicates that they were cooked rather than accidentally burned after consumption (Speth and Tchernov, 1991). In general, Neandertals appear to have been competent distance hunters and in some cases large-game hunters.

There is also evidence of possible cannibalism among Neandertals. In human cultures, cannibalism is typically undertaken in a political or ritualistic context but cases of subsistence cannibalism are also known. Because there is little evidence of ritual behavior in Neandertals, cannibalism may be classified as a kind of specialized subsistence strategy. Early claims for Neandertal cannibalism came from Italy based on a cranium (known as Guattari 1) discovered in a cave at Monte Circeo near Rome in 1939 and dated to about 60,000 years ago. Early researchers claimed that it was likely that a large hole in the base of the cranium had been deliberately made to facilitate access to the brain during a cannibalistic rite, which was indicated by the supposed placement of the skull in a circle of stones. However, the base of the cranium is a weak part of the skull, often broken by natural forces; thus, the absence of the base of a cranium is not direct evidence of cannibalism. More substantial evidence of cannibalism can be found in the fragmentary remains from Krapina, Croatia, dated to about 130,000 years ago (Figure 12.20). Among the thousands of fragmentary hominin bones almost no intact long bones were present, a sign that the bones may have been split open for the marrow within. Furthermore, many of the bones showed signs of burning. The excavator, D. Gorjanovi'c-Kramberger, thought that the bias toward juveniles at the site was an indication of cannibalism. More recent research has found cut marks on some of the bones as well, although this is not in itself evidence of cannibalism (Russell, 1987).

The recently excavated Mousterian cave site of Moula-Guercy in France, dating to about 100,000 years ago, provides an even better case for Neandertal cannibalism (Defleur et al., 1999). Seventy-eight hominin bone fragments mixed in with several hundred animal bone fragments (mostly from red deer) were found. The Neandertal remains from Moula-Guercy display numerous cut marks. All crania and long bones have been broken, presumably to gain access to the brain and marrow. A key piece of evidence indicates that these remains were processed for access to meat rather than for some other purpose is that the deer and other animal remains from the site were treated in the same manner as the hominin remains. Because it is unlikely that the game species were being treated to some sort of mortuary processing that did not involve being eaten, Alban Defleur and his colleagues conclude that the Neandertals were also being eaten by other Neandertals. This seems like a reasonable conclusion because only Neandertals are known in this area at this time. However, recent genetic revelations about another non-Neandertal hominin group in Siberia, the Denisovans, whose ancestors left Africa in the middle Pleistocene urge caution in assuming that Neandertals were entirely alone until modern humans arrived (see Insights and Advances: The Denisovans).

Burials

The notion that some Neandertals may have buried their dead goes back to the discovery of the Spy skeletons in Belgium in the 1880s (Stringer et al., 1984). Unlike the earlier discoveries from Gibraltar and Neanderthal, the Spy Cave remains were carefully excavated. The two Spy adult skeletons were found complete and fully articulated, suggesting that they may have been intentionally buried in the cave. Since that time, numerous Neandertals have been found in caves; most excavators of these sites believed that they were deliberate burials. For example, evidence of Neandertal burials came from the site of La Ferrassie in southern France (excavated in the early 1900s), where several adults and subadults, forming a burial complex, were found at a single cave site. Many researchers believe that the assemblage of individuals at the site was not an accidental grouping but a deliberate burial. In 1938, the skeleton of a 9-year-old child found in the small cave of Teshik Tash in Uzbekistan was claimed to have been interred surrounded by six pairs of upright goat horns, reflecting some sort of ritualistic activity. Although there is no doubt that the goat horns were found near the boy, most researchers today are skeptical that they were distributed in a meaningful way. In the 1950s, the idea of Neandertal burial and compassionate Neandertals was further supported by the claim that the Shanidar 4 individual (an older individual) from the 40,000 to 50,000-year-old Iraqi site excavated by Ralph Solecki (1971) had been buried and covered in (or on a bed of) wildflowers. A large quantity of wildflower pollen had been found in association with this burial, but there is no certainty that they were put there deliberately by Neandertal mourners. The same pollen exists in the region today and could have been blown into the cave (Figure 12.21).

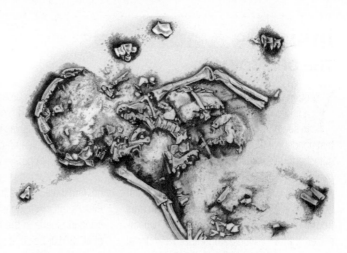

FIGURE 12.21   The Dederiyeh infant burial from Syria.

However, some investigators believe that it is possible to account for the deposition of articulated Neandertal skeletons in caves via natural forces (Gargett, 1989, 1999). One criticism, definitely valid in some cases, is that many Neandertal sites were excavated decades ago, before the development of modern excavation techniques or accurate record keeping. Without a clear rendering of the excavation context, it is difficult to assess the status of a claim of deliberate burial. Recent excavators of Neandertal sites, mindful of the need to provide evidence for burial rather than simply assume it, have gone to some effort to prove what was once considered the obvious. Recently excavated Neandertal infants from Amud (Hovers et al., 2000) and Mezmaiskaya Cave (Golovanova et al., 1999) are both claimed to be from deliberate burials, and the context of these discoveries strongly indicates that such small and delicate remains probably were preserved because they were shielded from damage by deliberate burial.

Neandertal burials represent a novel behavioral development of the Middle Paleolithic. Before that time we may have evidence of mortuary practices in the defleshing of the Bodo cranium and the possibly deliberate deposition of remains in the bone pit of Sima de los Huesos at Atapuerca. But there is no evidence of deliberate burial of archaic *H. sapiens* remains. On the other hand, Neandertal burials are significantly different from later Upper Paleolithic burials of anatomically modern *H. sapiens*. Neandertals have not been found to be interred with grave goods, objects placed with the corpse at the time of burials. On occasion, a stray animal bone or horn has been found in association with a Neandertal burial, but it is very difficult to demonstrate that they were placed there deliberately. Another difference between Neandertal and Upper Paleolithic burials is that the Neandertal burials always occur in cave sites, whereas burials at open-air sites are common, in the late Upper Paleolithic.

It is easy to assume that Neandertal burial indicates some kind of ritualistic belief or significance, but the context of Neandertal burials could be indicative of corpse disposal rather than ritualized internment (Stringer and Gamble, 1993). It is clear, however, that some Neandertals dedicated a significant amount of time and energy to the burial of the dead, selecting an appropriate site, placing the body in a certain position, and covering the body with a large stone. Furthermore, chimpanzees and other mammals can show attachments to the remains of deceased infants or individuals with whom they have had a long-term relationship, even though they ultimately abandon the body. Thus, even if it is impossible to know whether there was a ritual or symbolic content to the burial of the dead in Neandertals, it is reasonable to assume that it was both an emotional and a pragmatic decision when they chose to dispose of a corpse in this manner.

Ritual and Symbolic Behavior

If burials cannot be seen as evidence of ritualistic or symbolic behavior, then there is very little else in the Neandertal archaeological record to indicate such behaviors. A small number of incised bones have been recovered from

insights & advances

THE DENISOVANS

You might call the child Pinky, because just a finger bone was discovered from a cave in southern Siberia in 2008 (Figure A). Yet that nondescript finger bone yielded a complete mitochondrial DNA sequence that stunned the paleoanthropological community. The finger was found in a layer dating to between about 30 and 48,000 years ago, and the researchers from the Neanderthal Genome Project hypothesized that they would find either Neandertal or *Homo sapiens* DNA. The site of Okladnikov, also in Siberia, had recently yielded Neandertal DNA, so the team was hopeful that Pinky would prove to be a Neandertal as well. Surprisingly, Pinky's mtDNA differs by 385 bases from that of modern humans—more than Neandertals do. And it also differs from Neandertals. In fact, Pinky's mtDNA suggested a third hominin was living in Siberia in the late Pleistocene (Krause et al., 2010; Reich et al., 2010).

The cave, known as Denisova, is situated in the Altai mountains. Since the initial discovery, it has also yielded a very large, upper third molar, the anatomy of which is clearly neither Neandertal nor modern human (Figure B). And the mtDNA from the tooth matches the finger bone, suggesting the two shared a similar matriline. Initial comparisons of the finger mtDNA suggested that the occupants of Denisova cave were the descendants of a hominin who had left Africa around 500,000 years ago and was equally distant from Neandertals and modern humans (Figure C). Perhaps they could have been a relict group of archaic *H. sapiens* or a late dispersing *H. erectus*, neither of which we have DNA from. But more recently the complete mtDNA sequence and a nuclear DNA sequence have been analyzed, and these results now indicate that the Denisovans are more closely related to Neandertals, and that the last common ancestor of the two lived after their common ancestor with modern humans (Figure C). Other alternatives might include that the archaic sections of the DNA came into the Denisovan population via gene flow from a more archaic hominin (like *H. erectus* perhaps).

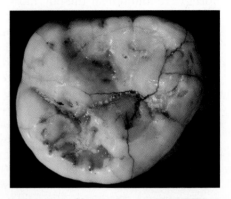

FIGURE B   A third molar from Denisova differs anatomically from Neandertals and modern humans and has similar DNA to the finger bone.

So far, the researchers have resisted naming a new species, preferring to call these new fossils Denisovans. Reasonably, they want to wait for additional nuclear and mtDNA from other known species of hominin as well as from the Denisovans themselves. Additionally, although the single molar is anatomically different than Neandertals, it would not be the best type specimen for a species. Thus, more anatomically informative skeletal parts would be welcome before naming a species. Whether a new species or not, the Denisovans, like Neandertals, seem to have shared at least some of their DNA with some modern human groups—in the case of Denisovans their DNA shows up in modern humans from Melanesia. And the Denisovans are a tantalizing clue that up until quite recently, we were not the only hominin on the planet.

(mm)
6

0
0   (mm)
                      10

FIGURE A   Dorsal view of a scan of the hand phalange of a child from Denisova that yielded mtDNA that differs from modern humans and Neandertals. We know that it is a child because of the unfused epiphysis (shown in blue).

Mousterian sites, but what these scratches might mean is beyond the scope of scientific inquiry. If Neandertals possessed something like human language, then obviously they were capable of symbolic behavior because language is reliant on symbolic representation. But there is no direct evidence of this in the archaeological record. The strongest evidence is that of personal adornment items, including pierced animal teeth from Arcy-sur-Cure in France. Other engraved or incised items include a plaque or incised plate of a mammoth tooth, from the site of Tata, and an incised flint from Quinetra in the Golan Heights (Marshack, 1996; White, 2001). All these occur late in Neandertal times, with the most secure—those from Arcy-sur-Cure and Quinetra—being 55,000 years old or younger. Even if we accept these finds as symbolic behavior by Neandertals, they are qualitatively different from the systematic evidence of such behavior, including extensive personal adornment, in Upper Paleolithic sites, as we shall see in Chapter 13.

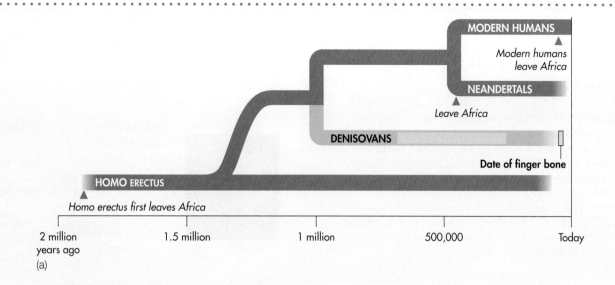

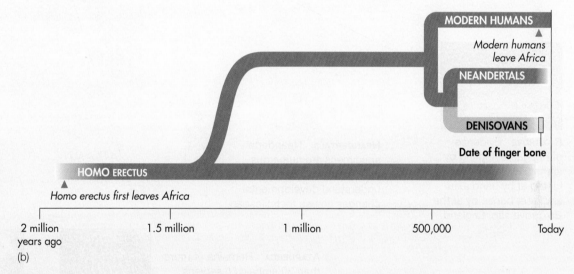

FIGURE C   (a) Initial mtDNA results suggested modern humans and Neandertals were equally distantly related to Denisovans. (b) A more complete genome links Denisovans to Neandertals.

Phylogenetic and Taxonomic Issues: An Overview

Our interpretations of taxonomic and phylogenetic relationships between late middle and late Pleistocene hominins depend largely on how we view the origins of anatomically modern *H. sapiens*. However, we can have a preliminary discussion based on the archaic *H. sapiens* and Neandertal fossil records.

The labels "archaic *H. sapiens*" and "Neandertal" are not taxonomically formal designations. We use informal labels because there is no consensus as to what the formal labels should be. Archaic *H. sapiens* include a widely distributed group of hominins who lived from about 150,000 to 800,000 years ago (Figure 12.22 on pages 326–327). Neandertal refers to a predominantly European and western Asian group

FIGURE 12.22

Hominin Evolution in the Mid to Late Pleistocene

Beginning about 600,000 years ago in Africa, hominins who were somewhat larger-brained than classic *H. erectus* but still cranially robust appeared in Africa, and then later in Europe and Asia. This group is usually referred to as archaic *Homo sapiens* (or by some as *H. heidelbergensis*). In Europe and western Asia, a distinct type of hominin, the Neandertals, appeared about 140,000 years ago. Their antecedents may be represented among the archaic *H. sapiens* specimens of Europe, dating up to 400,000 years ago.

ARCTIC OCEAN

ATLANTIC OCEAN

Neander Valley
Swanscombe
Boxgrove
Schöningen
Mauer
Steinheim
Atapuerca
Arago
Ambrona/Torralba
Salé

BOXGROVE Evidence of big game hunting by archaic *H. sapiens* is hinted at by hand axes and deer bones by at the Boxgrove site, England.

NEANDERTALS Neandertal specimens are numerous enough that we can begin to understand developmental changes across their lifespan.

ATLANTIC OCEAN

ATAPUERCA Remains of more than 30 archaic *H. sapiens* individuals have been found in the Sima de los Huesos at Sierra de Atapuerca, Spain.

STEINHEIM is a possible contemporary of Petralona.

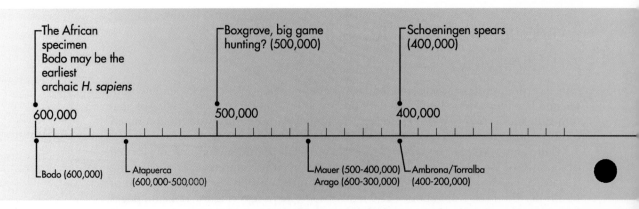

The African specimen Bodo may be the earliest archaic *H. sapiens*

Boxgrove, big game hunting? (500,000)

Schoeningen spears (400,000)

600,000   500,000   400,000

Bodo (600,000)

Atapuerca (600,000-500,000)

Mauer (500-400,000)
Arago (600-300,000)

Ambrona/Torralba (400-200,000)

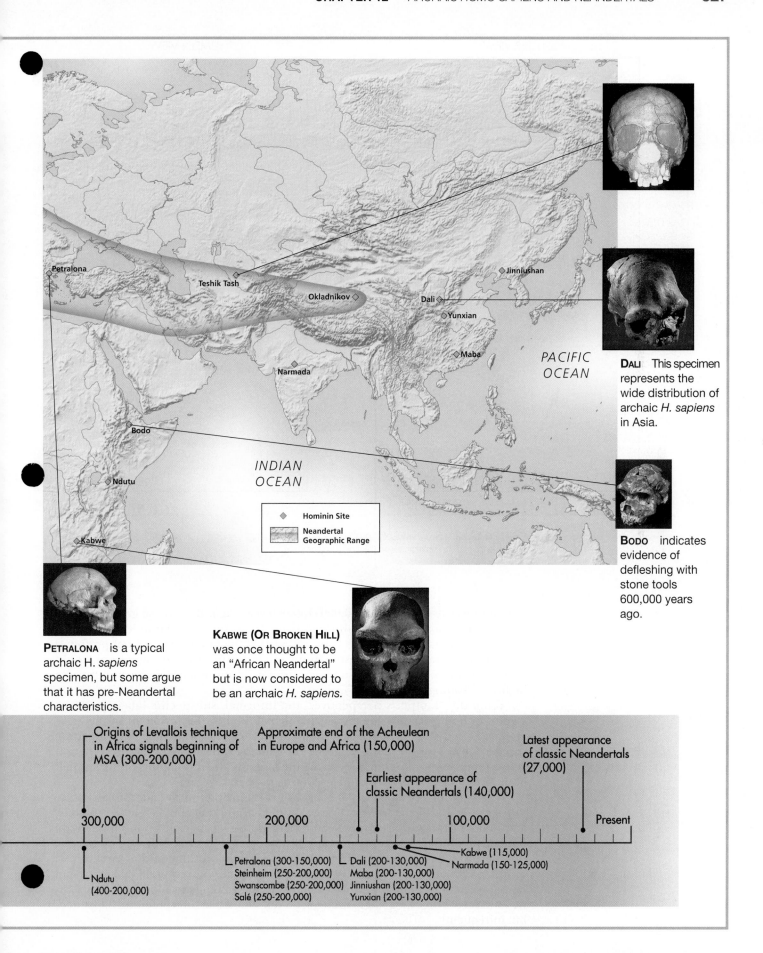

DALI This specimen represents the wide distribution of archaic *H. sapiens* in Asia.

BODO indicates evidence of defleshing with stone tools 600,000 years ago.

PETRALONA is a typical archaic H. *sapiens* specimen, but some argue that it has pre-Neandertal characteristics.

KABWE (OR BROKEN HILL) was once thought to be an "African Neandertal" but is now considered to be an archaic *H. sapiens.*

Hominin Site

Neandertal Geographic Range

Origins of Levallois technique in Africa signals beginning of MSA (300-200,000)

Approximate end of the Acheulean in Europe and Africa (150,000)

Latest appearance of classic Neandertals (27,000)

Earliest appearance of classic Neandertals (140,000)

300,000   200,000   100,000   Present

Ndutu (400-200,000)

Petralona (300-150,000)
Steinheim (250-200,000)
Swanscombe (250-200,000)
Salé (250-200,000)

Dali (200-130,000)
Maba (200-130,000)
Jinniushan (200-130,000)
Yunxian (200-130,000)

Kabwe (115,000)
Narmada (150-125,000)

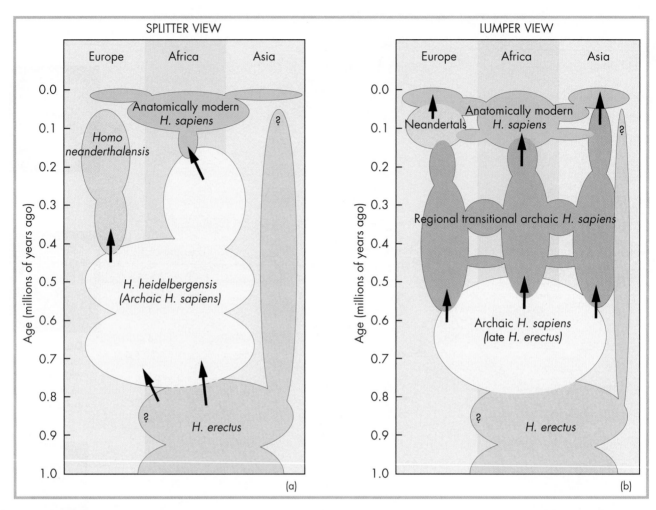

FIGURE 12.23   Two views of the phylogenetic relationship between Neandertals and modern *H. sapiens*. (a) The splitter view. (b) The lumper view.

of hominins who lived about 30,000–150,000 years ago. Both these groups possess features that clearly distinguish them from *H. erectus* and anatomically modern *H. sapiens*. Yet many researchers argue either that the differences are not profound enough to warrant species designations or that using such designations would arbitrarily impose separations on a continuous evolutionary lineage and thus be highly misleading (Figure 12.23).

From the "lumper's perspective," the informal, subspecific labels for these groups of hominins provide an acceptable solution to the problem. In this view, archaic *H. sapiens* and Neandertals were all part of one potentially interbreeding species. Obviously, there was regional variation within the species—and variation across time as well—but lumpers see all the larger-brained hominins of the last half of the Pleistocene as part of a single evolving species.

The "splitter's perspective" begins with recognizing the Neandertals as a separate species: *H. neanderthalensis*. Many splitters argue that the distinctive anatomy and limited distribution of the Neandertals indicate a specialized hominin taxon fundamentally different from anatomically modern *H. sapiens*. The species designation means that Neandertals and modern humans did not or could not interbreed or did so very infrequently; it suggests that Neandertals represent an extinct type of hominin that was ultimately replaced across its entire range by modern humans. As we have seen from the genetic evidence, it does look like interbreeding happened, but infrequently.

In the splitter's view, archaic *H. sapiens* also gets a species designation: *H. heidelbergensis*. *H. heidelbergensis* is considered a species distinct from *H. erectus*, based on the anatomical features we discussed earlier. In effect, *H. heidelbergensis* becomes the stem species for both Neandertals and anatomically modern *H. sapiens*. In Europe, *H. heidelbergensis* specimens such as Petralona and those from Sima de los Huesos are seen to be proto-Neandertals, extending the Neandertal lineage back hundreds of thousands of years. In Africa, *H. heidelbergensis* specimens such as Bodo and Kabwe are thought to be early representatives of a population from which anatomically modern *H. sapiens* evolved.

At the same time as Neandertals were living in Europe and western Asia, hominin evolutionary developments were also taking place in other parts of the world, most significantly the evolution of anatomically modern *H. sapiens*. In Chapter 13 we will more fully explore the evolutionary connections between our own species and these earlier forms. As we will see, the debate about the origins of modern humans involves not only paleontological and archaeological data but also genetic information derived from contemporary humans and a few fossil specimens.

Archaic *Homo sapiens* and Neandertals

The Muddle in the Middle—Archaic *H. sapiens*

Anatomical Characteristics

- Larger brain size Sus than *H. erectus* but without the characteric angular shape.
- More parallel-sided vault.
- The supraorbital torus is more double-arched than bar-like.
- The midface is large.
- Some European fossils have an incipient suprainiac fossa. **[pp 302–303]**

Time and Geography

- Middle Pleistocene—about 800,000 to about 200,000 years ago, depending upon which fossils are included.
- Some scholars include just the European pre-Neandertal lineages. Others include specimens from Africa and Asia. **[pp 303–306]**

Tools and Behavior

- Usually associated with Middle Stone Age and Early Stone Age tools.
- Bone tools are also known from these time periods.
- They may have hunted big game. **[pp 307–309]**

Evolutionary Relationships

- Sometimes also called *H. heidelbergensis*, these hominins may not form a good, cohesive species.
- They are likely to be ancestral to later hominins in their regions. In Europe, they seem to be ancestral to Neandertals. In Africa, they are likely ancestral to modern humans. **[p 304]**

Neandertal Bodies

Anatomical Characteristics

- The brain case is large, but long and low. From behind, the brain case is oval shaped, with the greatest breadth in the middle of the parietal. The mastoid processes are small and juxtamastoid eminences large. A suprainiac fossa and an occipital bun are present, but an occipital torus is lacking.
- The midface is prognathic, with a swept-back cheek region and large nasal aperture.

Browridges are large and double-arched. A retromolar fossa is present on the mandible. Neandertals have no chin.

- Postcranially, they are robust, heavily muscled, and stocky with "hyper-polar" adapted bodies (quite wide for height, short distal limb segments, barrel-shaped chests). **[pp 312–315]**

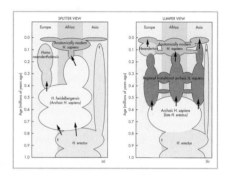

Time and Geography

- Earliest Neandertals appear in western Europe around 150,000 years ago.
- The last Neandertals exist somewhere around 30,000 years ago, overlapping for a few thousand years with *H. sapiens*.
- Many Neandertals lived around the Mediterranean, with some found as far east as Uzbekistan and Siberia and as far south as the Near East. **[pp 309–312]**

Cold Adaptation

- Neandertal bodies are cold-adapted, following both Bergmann's and Allen's rules.
- Archaeological hearths indicate that Neandertals routinely used fire.
- Animal skins and hides were probably also used for protective shelters and cloaks.
- Neandertals migrated seasonally, and during long-lasting glacial events, their range seems to extend further south and not so far north. **[pp 312–315]**

Growth, Health, and Diet

- Neandertal newborns had large brains similar to those of modern humans.
- Their teeth indicate that they grew similarly to modern humans, although some parts of their skeleton may have matured more quickly. **[pp 318–319]**

Phylogenetic Relationships and DNA

- Neandertals likely evolved from archaic *H. sapiens* (*H. heidelbergensis*), who preceded them in Europe.
- Neandertal DNA is relatively distinct from modern humans, suggesting that they did not contribute much to the recent human gene pool. **[pp 316–317; 325–329]**

Neandertal Minds

Tool Technologies

- Most Neandertals are found with Middle Paleolithic tool industries.
- A few later Neandertals are associated with an Upper Paleolithic industry, known as the Châtelperronian.
- They possessed at least thrusting spears and may have had projectile technology. **[pp 319–321]**

Symbolic Behavior

- Neandertals left relatively little evidence of symbolic behavior in the form of beads or artwork.
- They are likely to have buried their dead either for ritual or practical purposes. Few if any grave goods have been found with these burials. **[pp 322–324]**

Ranging, Diet, and Cannibalism

- Stable isotopic studies suggest Neandertals ate a great deal of animal resources (meat and marrow).
- Archaeological bone assemblages suggest Neandertals were probably hunters rather than scavengers.
- A few sites suggest that Neandertals practiced cannibalism, at least occasionally. **[pp 321–322]**

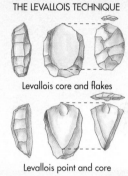

THE LEVALLOIS TECHNIQUE

Levallois core and flakes

Levallois point and core

Tools of the Middle and Upper Paleolithic

Middle Paleolithic (Middle Stone Age) Industries

- Characterized by prepared-core technologies, in which multiple steps are required to release a flake with specific characteristics (e.g., Levallois technique, disk cores etc.)
- They include both soft and hard hammer techniques and bone tools.
- Include more tool types than Early Stone Age industries.
- Appear in the middle Pleistocene and persist until about 30–40 ka.
- Found with archaic *H. sapiens*, the earliest *H. sapiens*, and Neandertals. **[p 320]**

Upper Paleolithic Industries

- Characterized by blades and and blade cores
- They include many more tool types and more regional specialization than the Middle Paleolithic.
- Bone tools and hard and soft hammer techniques.
- Beads and portable art often included in these industries.
- Found with *H. sapiens* and with some of the final Neandertals. **[p 320]**

Chapter 13 Preview

After reading this chapter, you should be able to:

- Identify the anatomical characteristics of modern humans compared to earlier hominins.

- Discuss how the upper paleolithic or later stone age differs from middle and early stone age tool technologies and describe the behavioral differences and role of symbolism in the Upper Paleolithic.

- Compare and contrast the two major models of modern human origins: replacement and multiregional, review the archaeological and molecular genetic evidence for modern human origins and how paleontology, archaeology, and genetics are interpreted.

- Discuss the settling of the New World and the Pacific Islands.

- Describe the physical influence on the skeleton of subsistence changes such as the origin of agriculture.

Source: Image top left, bottom left, bottom right.

The Emergence, Dispersal, and Bioarchaeology of *Homo sapiens*

13

Behind the building, a chaotic scree of cobbles, flakes, and deer antlers—the residue of years of experimental archaeology—were shaded by the branches of an old-growth redwood tree. A new crop of twenty-somethings in jeans, goggles, and leather gloves stood tentatively round the edges of the pile while their instructor demonstrated simple knapping techniques. She didn't flinch as the flakes parted from the underbelly of the cobble with each strike of her hammerstone. Her strikes were easy and confident—as theirs would grow to be over the semester. Some minutes later, the instructor presented the roughed out form of a hand axe to the class and invited them to try their hand.

The students moved in, each selecting a likely cobble of fine-grained basalt or chert. As they worked, fingers were pounded, and not a little blood was shed. Eventually, over days and weeks, they grew more agile and confident. As they worked they would gather in small groups, exchanging stories about their lives, their worries, their successes. They would go on weekend expeditions to gather stone from the beach or from the mountains. They became connoisseurs of form and angle—stones of just the right material, size, and shape were coveted.

By semester's end everyone could make choppers, flakes, and hand axes that resembled, at least vaguely, the Oldowan and Acheulean. Some students became specialists in more complex forms—one mastered the multistep process toward producing a Levallois core and flake, the heart of many Middle Paleolithic assemblages. Blades, beads, and microliths—the heart of the Upper Paleolithic—were more elusive still. They demanded talent and patience, and only one student mastered these.

Using a pile of soft greenish stone gathered on their last expedition, this student formed a series of oblong blanks from which would emerge several beads. She rounded one end of each blank, and then with another stone she began chipping flakes out of the center of the blank, working first on one side and then on the other. She kept chipping and listening to her classmates' stories. An hour later, the two indentations merged forming a hole that she slowly and carefully enlarged. Happy with its size, she spent the next hour polishing the bead to a lustrous finish, and then dropped it onto a growing pile of similar beads. She had spent many hours now fashioning just a few beads. Yet Upper Paleolithic sites yielded hundreds of such beads representing thousands of hours of work. Those beads showed signs of having been carefully sewn onto garments. She wondered if these Paleolithic sequins had signaled clan affiliations and trade networks critical in some way for survival. Because of the amount of time each bead took to craft, the student knew that the advantage that such symbols conferred must have been great enough to outweigh the time lost to other critical pursuits such as foraging or hunting. She didn't have to choose between making a bead and eating a meal, but for her Paleolithic counterparts she knew the benefit of the bead must have outweighed its cost in some important way.

333

Modern human origins are not simply a matter of anatomy but also of behavior. No matter how cognitively sophisticated our close cousins the Neandertals or archaic *Homo sapiens* were or how close the size of their brains was to our own, they did not attain the same level of technological achievement. The bead described in the vignette is not much of an artifact; it is not even a tool. But it is a clue about personal decoration and symbolism. Such evidence is abundant in the archaeological record of modern humans and all but absent from the records of Neandertals and archaic *H. sapiens*.

In this chapter, we review the three sources of evidence used to reconstruct the critical events surrounding the emergence of modern people. Paleontological and geological data chart the distribution in time and space of anatomically modern *H. sapiens*. Archaeological data shed light on the changes in behavior that allowed modern humans to exploit the natural world in a way that would ultimately make us the dominant species on the planet. Genetic data provide information on the web of biological relationships between us and our closest relatives. By synthesizing data from these interrelated realms, biological anthropologists attempt to address the fundamental question of our field: How did human beings evolve? We then look at examples from **bioarchaeology** of the ways modern people adapted to local environments.

The Emergence of Modern Humans

The emergence of modern humans can be seen anatomically in a combination of cranial features that distinguish us from archaic *H. sapiens* and Neandertals (Chapter 12). These features include a gracile skull and postcranial anatomy, limited development of brow ridges or other cranial superstructures, a rounded cranium with a high maximum cranial breadth, and parallel sides in rear view; a prominent mastoid process; a retracted face with a canine fossa, small teeth and jaws, and development of an obvious chin (Figure 13.1). However, large brain size does not set us apart from archaic *H. sapiens* and the Neandertals. Many middle and late Pleistocene hominin specimens possess cranial capacities that are easily within the modern human range (whose average is about 1,350 cc), and a number of them exceed the human mean by a substantial amount.

Despite the fact that there is no significant difference in absolute brain size, when we look at the archaeological record most often associated with modern humans—the Upper Paleolithic or Later Stone Age—we find evidence of substantial behavioral differences between our close relatives and us. Compared to the Lower and Middle Paleolithic, the Upper Paleolithic is characterized by the appearance of a wide range of diverse tool types, the use of novel materials to make tools, an accelerated pace of technological development, and, perhaps most important, the appearance of art and ornamentation, which are undeniable reflections of symbolic thinking. The rapid pace of change and the appearance of symbolic behavior are two of the hallmarks of the Upper Paleolithic revolution, which some scientists think occurred with the sudden appearance of anatomically modern humans (Klein and Edgar, 2002). Other scientists think that different aspects of Upper Paleolithic culture appear at different times during the later Middle Stone Age (MSA), thus indicating a more gradual evolution of behaviorally modern humans (McBrearty and Brooks, 2000).

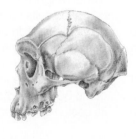
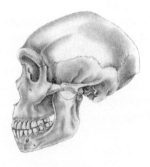
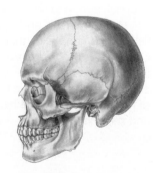

FIGURE 13.1 Variations on a theme: archaic *Homo sapiens*.

Archaic
Homo sapiens

Neandertal

Anatomically modern
Homo sapiens

Models of Modern Human Origins

Many scientists have attempted to assemble anatomical, behavioral, and genetic data into comprehensive models of the origins of modern humans. In the past two decades, two basic frameworks have been debated: the replacement and multiregional models. Both frameworks agree that there was an initial dispersal of *H. erectus* (or *H. ergaster*) from Africa into the rest of the Old World. However, they disagree as to what happened next.

Replacement and Multiregional Models

The **replacement models** suggest that modern humans had a localized origin—usually thought to be in Africa—and then dispersed into areas already occupied by *H. erectus* and its descendants. Replacement models thus require a second hominin dispersal from Africa. These models often are called "Out of Africa" models or "Out of Africa II," in recognition of the earlier *H. erectus* dispersal. As the word *replacement* implies, these models predict that anatomically modern humans did not interbreed substantially (or at all) with the indigenous hominins whom they ultimately replaced. One implication is that all geographic variation seen in modern humans today evolved recently, after the origin of anatomically modern humans.

Multiregional models propose that our origins cannot be pinned down to a single population or area. Instead, gene flow, via repeated population movements and intermixing, is thought to have been extensive among Old World hominin populations. Thus, the appearance of anatomically modern humans throughout the Old World resulted not from replacement of many populations by one, but from the transmission of alleles underlying the modern human phenotype between populations that were in genetic contact. Therefore, multiregional models do not suggest the later dispersal of a second hominin species from Africa. Note that the multiregional models do not call for separate and multiple origins for modern humans; rather, they suggest that modern humans originated in the context of gene flow between multiple regions.

Predictions of the Two Models

Replacement models predict that we should first see modern human fossils in Africa and then at least two anatomically distinct lineages of hominins in each region of the Old World: Neandertals and modern humans in Europe, *Homo heidelbergensis* (archaic *H. sapiens*) and modern humans in mainland Asia, and possibly relict populations of *H. erectus* and modern humans in Southeast Asia. Replacement further predicts that these lineages will overlap for at least a brief period of time in each region. Like the anatomy, the archaeological record would show abrupt changes in technology and behavior (as modern humans brought their technology with them to new areas), and the genetic record would indicate little overlap between the gene pools of the two lineages.

In contrast, multiregional models predict only a single evolving lineage that displays slightly different anatomical trends in each region. Across regions, we should see anatomical evidence of this evolution in the form of intermediate fossils with characteristics of the ancestors and the descendants. In addition, we should see regional anatomical characters continue from earlier to later populations. The archaeological record should show evidence of behavioral continuity, and the genetic evidence should show substantial ancient contributions to the modern gene pool, assuming there has not been a strong genetic bottleneck.

In the next section, we will see how these predictions fare against the empirical data in the fossil, archaeological, and genetic records.

Anatomy and Distribution of Early Humans

Early modern human fossils are rare (Figure 13.2 on page 336–337). Using archaeological evidence alone to assess the early appearance of modern humans is risky because, as we have seen before, it is unwise to assert that a given tool culture is the

bioarchaeology   The study of the biological component (usually osteology) of the archaeological record. Includes mortuary archaeology.

replacement models   Phylogenetic models that suggest that modern humans evolved in one location and then spread geographically, replacing other earlier hominid populations without any or with little admixture.

multiregional models   Phylogenetic models that suggest that modern humans evolved in the context of gene flow between Mid- to Late-Pleistocene hominid populations from different regions, so there is no single location where modern humans first evolved.

FIGURE 13.2

Modern Human Fossil Sites in the Old World

The oldest known fossil *Homo sapiens* are found in Africa. Fossil modern humans are found throughout the Old World starting after 50,000 years ago. In some parts of the Old World, such as the Near East and Europe, modern humans appear to have overlapped with other hominin species, such as Neandertals. But in other areas, such as Asia, they probably did not.

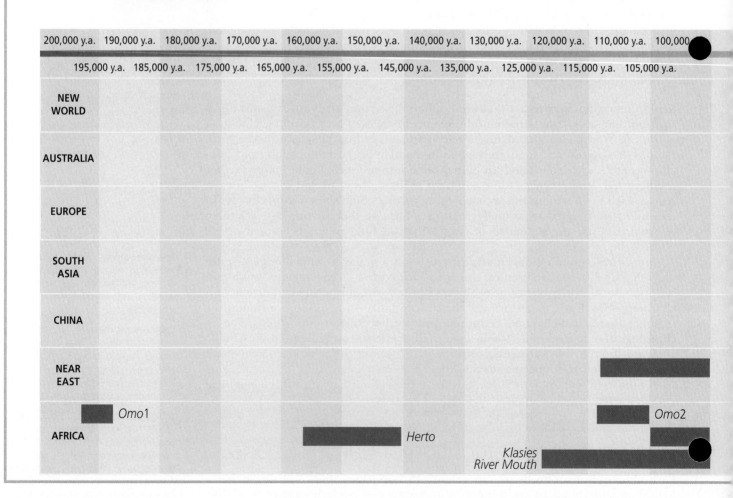

	200,000 y.a.	195,000 y.a.	190,000 y.a.	185,000 y.a.	180,000 y.a.	175,000 y.a.	170,000 y.a.	165,000 y.a.	160,000 y.a.	155,000 y.a.	150,000 y.a.	145,000 y.a.	140,000 y.a.	135,000 y.a.	130,000 y.a.	125,000 y.a.	120,000 y.a.	115,000 y.a.	110,000 y.a.	105,000 y.a.	100,000
NEW WORLD																					
AUSTRALIA																					
EUROPE																					
SOUTH ASIA																					
CHINA																					
NEAR EAST																			▬▬▬▬▬		
AFRICA	▬ *Omo1*								*Herto* ▬▬▬▬										*Omo2* ▬▬		

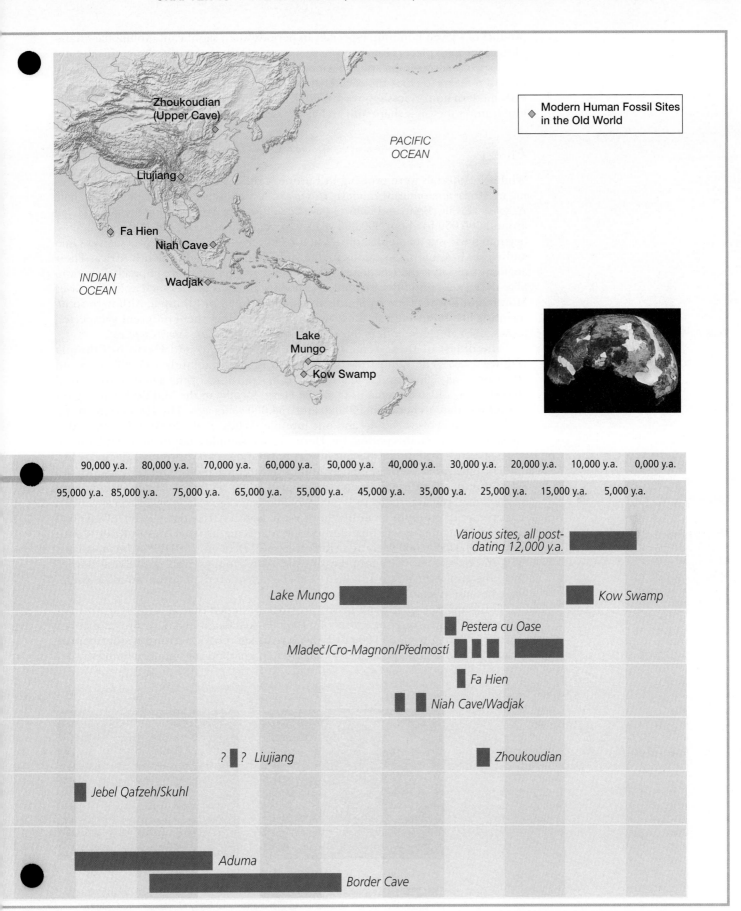

Modern Human Fossil Sites in the Old World

Zhoukoudian (Upper Cave)

Liujiang

Fa Hien

Niah Cave

Wadjak

Lake Mungo

Kow Swamp

PACIFIC OCEAN

INDIAN OCEAN

| 90,000 y.a. | 80,000 y.a. | 70,000 y.a. | 60,000 y.a. | 50,000 y.a. | 40,000 y.a. | 30,000 y.a. | 20,000 y.a. | 10,000 y.a. | 0,000 y.a. |

| 95,000 y.a. | 85,000 y.a. | 75,000 y.a. | 65,000 y.a. | 55,000 y.a. | 45,000 y.a. | 35,000 y.a. | 25,000 y.a. | 15,000 y.a. | 5,000 y.a. |

Various sites, all post-dating 12,000 y.a.

Lake Mungo

Kow Swamp

Pestera cu Oase

Mladeč/Cro-Magnon/Předmostí

Fa Hien

Niah Cave/Wadjak

? ? Liujiang

Zhoukoudian

Jebel Qafzeh/Skuhl

Aduma

Border Cave

product of a given hominin, especially in periods when significant evolutionary transformations took place. However, where we are certain that earlier hominins did not exist (such as in Australia and the Americas), we can use archaeological sites without human remains to chart the earliest appearance of modern humans. In many cases, early modern human fossils possess both derived features linking them to us and primitive features they may share with archaic *H. sapiens* or Neandertals (Pearson, 2000).

Africa

While Neandertals were evolving in Europe, a different kind of hominin was evolving in Africa: anatomically modern *H. sapiens*. As we discussed in Chapter 12, archaic *H. sapiens* fossils (Bodo and Kabwe) have been found in Africa during the period from around 600,000 to about 200,000 years ago. Starting at about 200,000 years ago we begin to see fossils that look more—but not entirely—modern from sites such as Omo and Herto in Ethiopia, Ngaloba in Tanzania, and Florisbad in South Africa. Their anatomy typically is intermediate in form, and their ages often are imprecisely known. Slightly later, we find fully anatomically modern humans at sites such as Klasies River Mouth and Border Cave in South Africa and Aduma in Ethiopia. Although some scientists like to distinguish these two groups by calling them different subspecies, most scholars include both in our species and subspecies, *H. sapiens sapiens*.

The oldest of these remains are those from Omo and Herto in Ethiopia (Figure 13.3). The Omo I partial skeleton is approximately 195,000 years old (Pearson et al., 2008) and remains from other portions of the site date to around 105,000 years old. The remains from the Herto locality in the Middle Awash region of Ethiopia date to between 160,000 and 154,000 years ago. The Herto remains include the crania of two adults and one juvenile (White et al., 2003). Like other African specimens from this period, the Herto crania "sample a population that is on the verge of anatomical modernity but not yet fully modern" (White et al., 2003, p. 745).

The later group, represented by Aduma in Ethiopia and Border Cave and Klasies River Mouth in South Africa, date to about 120,000–50,000 years ago. Aduma preserves cranial remains dated to 105,000–70,000 years ago (Haile-Selassie et al., 2004). A partial adult cranium from Border Cave in South Africa dates to 80,000–50,000 years ago. Fragmentary cranial and postcranial remains from Klasies River Mouth date to 120,000–90,000 years ago (Rightmire and Deacon, 1991). For the most part, early *H. sapiens sapiens* are found with typical MSA tool assemblages. But at Border Cave, the Howieson's Poort industry may be considered an advanced MSA assemblage because it features microliths.

This sequence of African fossils provides evidence that *H. sapiens sapiens* was well established throughout Africa by 100,000 years ago. Furthermore, a series of specimens dating from 200,000 to 100,000 years ago provide strong evidence of the African transformation of archaic *H. sapiens* into anatomically modern humans.

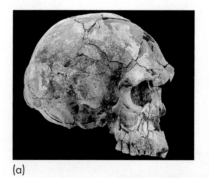

(a)   (b)

FIGURE 13.3 (a) Hominin remains from Herto, Ethiopia, are among the oldest anatomically modern humans yet discovered. (b) Early *H. sapiens* from Omo, Ethiopia date to 195,000 years ago.

Near East

The Near East is the only region outside Africa to have yielded reliable evidence of modern humans earlier than 60,000 years ago. As discussed in Chapter 12, anatomically modern *H. sapiens* dating to 110,000–90,000 years ago have been found at the sites of Skūhl and Qafzeh, located on Mt. Carmel in Israel. The Near East sits between Africa and Asia, so if modern humans (or modern human morphology) first evolved in Africa some time after 150,000 years ago, then the Skūhl and Qafzeh hominins (Figure 13.4) could be considered the first sign of an expansion out of Africa, which would only later (60,000–40,000 years ago) spread into Asia, Australia, and Europe. Neandertals are known to have occupied the Near East for tens of thousands of years, usually during glacial periods. Many scientists have interpreted the correlation of anatomically modern human specimens with warm (interglacial) periods and of later Neandertals with cold (glacial) periods as a sharing of this area by these two groups through time. Both Neandertals and early *H. sapiens sapiens* in the Near East are associated with MSA tool assemblages.

FIGURE 13.4 Anatomically modern humans from the Israeli cave sites of Skūhl and Qafzeh may be the earliest found outside Africa.

Europe

Scores of Neandertal remains have been recovered in Europe that date to 150,000–30,000 years ago. However, modern human skeletal remains do not appear in Europe until relatively late, perhaps 40,000 years ago. An Upper Paleolithic assemblage known as the Aurignacian, so far found only in association with *H. sapiens sapiens*, appeared in Europe about 40,000 years ago, but skeletal remains have been found only later from perhaps around 36,000 years ago. A mandible recently discovered in the Carpathian region of Romania, at the site of Peștera cu Oase ("cave with bones"), is the oldest modern human known from Europe, dating to 36,000–34,000 years ago (Trinkaus et al., 2003). Like other early modern human specimens, the Oase 1 mandible is robust and is argued to exhibit a mix of clearly derived features aligning it with anatomically modern *H. sapiens* (development of the chin) and primitive features (such as its robustness and anatomy of the mandibular foramen—a small hole in the lower jaw through which nerves and blood vessels pass) linking it to Neandertals (Figure 13.5).

The central European sites of Mladeč and Předmostí, both located in the Czech Republic, have yielded numerous specimens of anatomically modern *H. sapiens*, that also display characters that may align them with Neandertals (Smith, 1984; Frayer et al., 2006). These sites date to between 35,000 – 25,000 years ago, with the Předmostí site being somewhat younger than Mladeč. Several crania, probably representing males, show development of an occipital bun or hemi-bun. Though not as fully developed as the Neandertal occipital bun, this feature, in combination with the development of brow ridges, has been argued by some scholars to show a Neandertal ancestry in these early human remains.

In contrast, early Upper Paleolithic human postcranial skeletons appear to be tropically adapted, lacking the cold-adapted proportions we saw in Neandertal skeletons. They have narrower, more linear body proportions of the limbs and thorax, associated with humans living in tropical climates who easily dissipate heat (see Chapter 5). Some scholars interpret this to be evidence that modern humans migrated from tropical Africa to cold Europe more quickly than their skeleton could adapt to the climatic shift. If true, this would support a replacement model.

The best-known early anatomically modern humans from Europe come from the Cro-Magnon rock shelter located in the Dordogne region of France, which includes a number of Neandertal sites as well. Discovered in 1868, the Cro-Magnon remains include at least four adults and an infant that date to 27,000 years ago, or well after the appearance of modern humans in Europe (Gambier, 1989). Cro Magnon 1 or (The "Old Man" of Cro-Magnon) combines a very small face with a large and bulbous braincase, in striking anatomical contrast to Neandertals from the same region

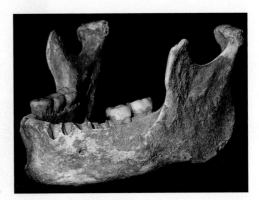

FIGURE 13.5 Oase 1 mandible, earliest modern human in Europe.

(Figure 13.6). Because of these anatomical differences, archaeologists developed an evolutionary scenario for western Europe in which the Middle Paleolithic Neandertals were replaced quickly by Upper Paleolithic modern humans, some time between 40,000 and 30,000 years ago. However, critics argue that Cro-Magnon 1 is not representative of other early modern humans in Europe (including those from central Europe and even some of the other Cro-Magnon individuals), who show a more mosaic pattern of archaic and modern features.

FIGURE 13.6 The "Old Man" of Cro-Magnon, from the Dordogne region of France.

Asia and Southeast Asia

In Asia there is a gap in the hominin fossil record between about 100,000 and 40,000 years ago. Archaic or premodern *H. sapiens* are known from a number of sites dating from between 250,000 and 100,000 years ago in China (Etler, 1996), but anatomically modern humans do not appear until perhaps as early as 65,000 years ago in China and possibly 40,000 years ago in Indonesia.

Dating is a problem for establishing the earliest human remains in Asia. In China, the site of Liujiang has been dated to at least 18,000 years ago, perhaps as old as 67,000 years, but there is some question as to the provenience of the human remains relative to the date (Shen et al., 2002). Well-accepted dates of 25,000 years ago have been obtained for the site of Hebei and for the Upper Cave at Zhoukoudian (approximately 42 km southwest of Beijing). Although clearly modern humans, the three Upper Cave skulls differ anatomically from one another and are not similar to skulls of recent East Asian peoples. Stringer and Andrews (1988) think that the Upper Cave skulls most closely resemble early modern humans from the European sites of Mladeč and Předmostí (Figure 13.7) which would mean that both European and Asian early modern human populations had a common origin (presumably Africa) and that there is little evidence of regional continuity.

The earliest *H. sapiens sapiens* in Southeast Asia are equally problematic. Specimens such as the "Deep Skull" from the Niah Cave complex in Borneo (Figure 13.8) and Wadjak from Java (one of the first specimens discovered by Eugene Dubois's team) have been assigned dates of about 40,000 years ago (Barker et al., 2006), but complex cave stratigraphy provenience issues make such dates provisional.

The possible evolutionary relationships of these Asian modern humans exemplify contrasting views of the origin of all modern humans: Some researchers argue that they represent the culmination of an unbroken evolutionary trajectory in China and Indonesia that began with variants of *H. erectus* in each area and that extends to contemporary East Asian populations (Wolpoff et al., 1994). Other researchers argue that the Upper Cave individuals do not resemble modern Asians in any meaningful way, nor do the early Indonesians represent modern Indonesians, and that

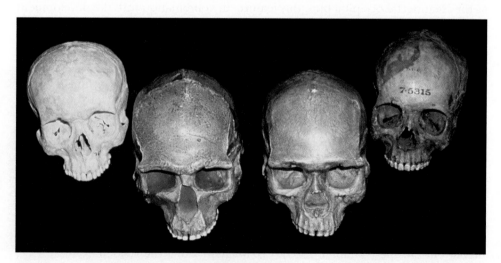

FIGURE 13.7 Fossil remains of anatomically modern humans from the Czech Republic and from China (center crania) are more robust than recent human crania but are otherwise anatomically identical. All four crania are *Homo sapiens sapiens*.

FIGURE 13.8   The Niah Cave complex in Borneo.

both may represent a migration into the region by individuals of an early, geographically undifferentiated modern human group. Filling the Asian fossil gap between 100,000 and 40,000 years ago will be essential in resolving some of these issues.

Australia

Although Australia is separated by water from the major Eurasian landmass, evidence suggests that modern humans were in Australia at least as early as if not earlier than they were in Europe. To get to Australia, modern humans almost certainly had to go through island Southeast Asia; so the ages of the earliest Australian occupation are also relevant to the peopling of Southeast Asia. During glacial maxima, when sea levels are lowest, Australia and New Guinea form a single land mass known as Sahul. Sahul is at all times separated by water from the landmass Sunda, which forms from some of the islands of Southeast Asia. Although all kinds of primates, including extinct hominins, occupy or occupied Sunda, only modern humans were able to disperse throughout Sahul. However, as we saw in Chapter 12 a stunning recent discovery from Flores, Indonesia, shows that at least one other hominin was able to make the jump from Sunda. Some scientists argue that the settlement of Australia, New Guinea, and other islands of Melanesia was a fundamental advance in the behavior of modern humans over that of earlier hominins (Noble and Davidson, 1996), in part because settlement of these islands could have been accomplished only by using a boat or raft of some kind.

The earliest human remains from Australia come from a site in the southeastern part of the continent known as Lake Mungo. Two incomplete skeletons from burials, along with other fragmentary remains and some cremations, have been found and recently dated to 40,000 years ago (Figure 13.9). Flake tools from Lake Mungo date to 50,000 years ago, which matches the earliest archaeological dates in Australia (Bowler et al., 2003). Mungo I, the buried remains of a young female, shows signs of having been cremated; the other burial, Mungo III, is an old male whose body was covered with red ochre. These are the earliest known examples of such mortuary practices. Both specimens are anatomically modern *H. sapiens*, and they both exhibit a gracile build.

Other Australian sites, such as Kow Swamp and Willandra Lakes, have yielded a number of reasonably complete crania that are substantially more robust than those of the Lake Mungo people. They are also substantially younger, dating to 13,000–9,500 years ago. The Kow Swamp and some Willandra individuals are interesting, however,

((•—[**Listen** to the **Podcast** "Humanlike 'Hobbit' Fossils Puzzle Scientists'" on **myanthrolab**

FIGURE 13.9   Partially cremated calvaria from Lake Mungo, Australia.

FIGURE 13.10 Evidence of regional continuity: (a) the anatomically modern Willandra Lakes Hominin 50 calvaria from Australia and (b) a later *Homo erectus* calvaria from Ngandong, Indonesia.

because their thick cranial bones and moderate development of brow ridges have been argued to demonstrate their close affinities with the latest *H. erectus* found at the site of Ngandong in Indonesia (Wolpoff et al., 1984; Hawks et al., 2000) (Figure 13.10).

Archaeology of Modern Human Origins

There is no doubt that the archaeological remains of later modern humans reflect cultural and individual behaviors that are substantially more complex than those indicated by the archaeological remains of earlier hominins or even the earliest *H. sapiens sapiens*. It is important to explore the archaeology of the earliest modern humans if we are to understand the behaviors that allowed them to become the dominant hominin species throughout the world by about 40,000 years ago.

Stone and Other Tools

We can look at the changes in tool cultures or industries associated with the emergence of anatomically modern *H. sapiens* as a tale of two continents: Europe and Africa. For many years, the European archaeological record, in conjunction with the rich trove of hominin remains recovered from European sites, stood as the basic model to explain the emergence of modern people. Over the past few decades, however, increasing research into the archaeology of Africa has provided a new context for understanding human origins.

The European Upper Paleolithic and the African Later Stone Age are distinguished from the MSA by a greater reliance on the standardized production of blades: long flakes that could be used as blanks to produce a variety of different flaked tools. A number of blades could be taken off a prepared stone core in a systematic manner (see Figure 12.8 on page 307). Refinements in tool flaking techniques also distinguish Upper Paleolithic and Later Stone Age tool industries from the MSA. For example, long, exquisitely flaked blades from the Solutrean industry of Europe demonstrate the extraordinary level of skill of Upper Paleolithic tool makers (Figure 13.11).

Microliths are another common feature of Upper Paleolithic and Later Stone Age tool industries, and appeared after 25,000 years ago in most regions. Microliths are small, flaked tools that probably were designed to be attached to wood or bone to make composite tools. Arrowheads are a kind of microlith and appear for the first time in North America around 13,000 to 10,000 years ago. The rate and kind of change in tool types and flaking techniques also increase from the MSA to the Upper Paleolithic and Later Stone Age.

Another striking feature of the Upper Paleolithic and Later Stone Age is the vastly greater use of tools made from bone, ivory, antler, and shell. These were ground, polished, and drilled to form objects such as harpoons, spear-throwers, awls, needles, and buttons. (Such materials were used but at a much cruder level and

FIGURE 13.11 Upper Paleolithic refinement in stone tool production, a Solutrean blade.

Randall White

CM

very rarely in earlier stone industries.) Upper Paleolithic Europeans also produced well-known examples of representational cave art and other artistic or ritual objects.

With one or two exceptions, the appearance of Upper Paleolithic tool industries in Europe coincided with the appearance of anatomically modern humans. In the nineteenth century, the shift from the Mousterian to the Upper Paleolithic was considered to represent a behavioral or cultural revolution that occurred when modern humans replaced Neandertals in Europe. For decades many scientists thought the European archaeological record reflected similar replacement events in other parts of the world. However, given the relatively late appearance of modern humans in Europe, it seems unlikely that Europe should be considered a model for the original appearance of modern humans.

Because anatomically modern humans first appeared in Africa more than 100,000 years ago, we should assess whether a cultural revolution in the African archaeological record accompanied the appearance of this new biological type. It was long thought that the Middle Paleolithic of Europe and MSA of Africa were roughly contemporaneous and reflected a similar level of technological development. However, many archaeological elements thought to be uniquely associated with the Upper Paleolithic and Later Stone Age actually made their first appearance in the MSA of Africa (McBrearty and Brooks, 2000). These innovations did not appear suddenly in a single locality but in different sites at different times. For example, blades are known from several sites, dating from 75,000 years ago to perhaps as early as 280,000 years ago in East Africa. Flake technologies based on the production of points rather than scrapers (a hallmark of the Mousterian in Europe) are also abundant in MSA sites, some dating to 235,000 years ago. More surprisingly, microliths (Figure 13.12),

microliths Small, flaked stone tools probably designed to be hafted to wood or bone; common feature of Upper Paleolithic and Later Stone Age tool industries.

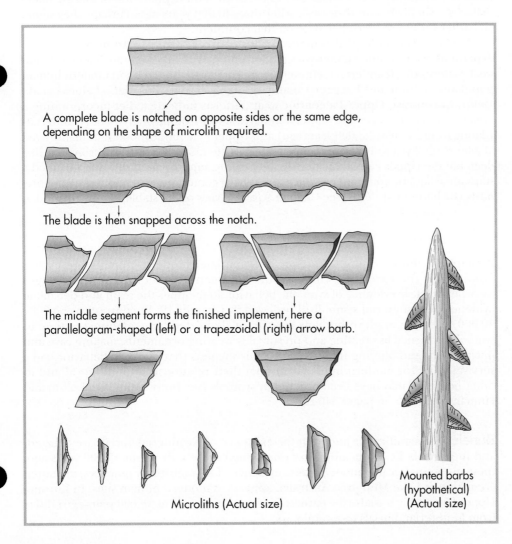

A complete blade is notched on opposite sides or the same edge, depending on the shape of microlith required.

The blade is then snapped across the notch.

The middle segment forms the finished implement, here a parallelogram-shaped (left) or a trapezoidal (right) arrow barb.

Microliths (Actual size)

Mounted barbs (hypothetical) (Actual size)

FIGURE 13.12 Microlith production. Although microliths are typically considered an Upper Paleolithic technology, their origins can be traced to the Middle Stone Age of Africa.

which are typically associated with the late Upper Paleolithic, were being made in the African MSA 65,000 years ago. Sally McBrearty and Alison Brooks (2000) suggest that the transition to the kind of cultural assemblage we associate with modern humans was more evolutionary than revolutionary. Thus, the European perspective which may indeed represent the rapid replacement of the Middle Paleolithic by the Upper Paleolithic there may not be representative of what happened in Africa, the region where modern humans first appeared. The pattern of change in the Australian archaeological record appears similarly gradual (Habgood and Franklin, 2008).

Subsistence

Much evidence supports the idea that modern humans exploited a wider variety of foodstuffs than those used by Neandertals or archaic *H. sapiens*. Ultimately, this ability to exploit natural resources for food led to the development of agriculture, starting about 12,000 years ago, which allowed a sustained increase in population growth. However, by expanding their subsistence base in other ways, early anatomically modern humans may have established a pattern of increased population growth relative to other hominins at the very origins of our species, long before the introduction of agriculture.

One example is the use of aquatic resources, such as fish and shellfish. Although there is earlier evidence of the limited use of marine resources, including use by some Neandertal populations, aquatic resources become a widespread and systematic part of human subsistence only in the Upper Paleolithic and Later Stone Age. However, a number of MSA coastal sites in Africa show exploitation of marine mammals, fish, shellfish, and tortoises earlier than 40,000 years ago. Perhaps they signal an earlier shift to modern behavior on that continent.

Besides archaeological remains, other sources of information point to the expansion of subsistence patterns in modern humans. Microwear analyses show that wear patterns on Neandertal teeth were more similar to those seen in modern human populations (Inuit and Fuegians) that have highly carnivorous diets (Lalueza et al., 1996). In contrast, Upper Paleolithic wear patterns indicate a diet incorporating a greater amount of vegetable matter. Similarly, stable isotope analyses of Neandertals (dating from 130,000–28,000 years ago) and Upper Paleolithic modern humans (aged 26,000–20,000 years) indicate that Neandertals ate mostly terrestrial herbivores, like deer, but the Upper Paleolithic people were eating a more varied diet that included a substantial aquatic component, which could have come from fish, mollusks, or shorebirds (Richards et al., 2001; see Chapter 9 for a review of the stable isotope methods).

Symbolism, Burial, and Art

Perhaps the most striking difference between later modern humans and earlier hominins is the extent to which modern human archaeological assemblages incorporate clear evidence of symbolic behavior. Remember the scant and debatable evidence of Neandertal symbolism reviewed in Chapter 12. In contrast, by 50,000–40,000 years ago modern humans apparently dedicated large amounts of time to symbolic acts such as creating and presumably wearing ornaments, making cave and portable art, and burying their dead. All this suggests that symbolic behavior had a survival value for modern humans and that their relationship to the world and to other hominins may have been ordered by symbols (see Innovations: Symbolism and Human Evolution on pages 346–347).

Burials The significance and even the existence of Neandertal burials are debated, and their symbolic implications are questioned as well. By about 40,000 years ago, these questions became moot because evidence of new mortuary practices, including cremation at Lake Mungo in Australia, appears at modern human sites. In Europe, Upper Paleolithic burials (the earliest of which date to about 28,000 years ago) differ from Mousterian burials in several ways.

Whether found in caves or open air sites, Upper Paleolithic burials are composed of burial pits. More important perhaps, a number of Upper Paleolithic burials contain an elaborate array of grave goods, and multiple, carefully arranged bodies (Figure 13.13). Upper Paleolithic European burials often are covered in beads and bear other indications that the dead were buried in decorated garments representing hundreds or thousands of hours of time in their preparation. (Stringer & Gamble, 1993). Obviously, not every Upper Paleolithic burial is an elaborate affair complete with an abundance of finely made grave goods. However, such burials are completely absent in the earlier archaeological records. Interestingly, evidence of deliberate burial of any kind in the later MSA is quite scanty, and Aurignacian burials are also scarce.

FIGURE 13.13 Anatomically modern humans left archaeological clues, including evidence of burials that indicated ritual and symbolic behavior were important parts of their culture.

Art and Ornamental Objects Unlike the equivocal engravings of Neandertals, the artistic expression of Upper Paleolithic humans is astounding. Cave art and *petroglyphs* (rock carvings) occur not only in Europe but also in Africa and Australia. Ornamental objects like statues, beads, and pendants are also prevalent in the Upper Paleolithic (see Innovations: Symbolism and Human Evolution on pages 346–347). These elaborate displays of human symbolic behavior occur late in the archaeological record of modern humans, usually 40,000 years ago or later, not with the earliest moderns. However, several examples of perforated shell, bone, and stone have been found at African MSA sites earlier in time, and perforated shell beads have recently been argued to be present at 73,000 years ago at Blombos Cave in South Africa (Henshilwood et al., 2004). If these prove on further inspection to be worked beads, they would represent the earliest known ornamentation and important support for a gradual accumulation of modern human behaviors.

The extensive evidence of artistic abilities of late Pleistocene modern humans, expressed in a wide range of media over a large number of populations, stands in stark contrast to the paucity of evidence for such activities in Neandertals and other hominins. Of course, this does not mean that earlier hominins were incapable of symbolic or artistic expression. Indeed, two examples of putative anthropomorphic carvings have been found in Acheulean deposits from Morocco and Israel dated to between about 400,000 and 250,000 years ago (Bednarik, 2003), which may give us a hint of the artistic abilities of archaic *H. sapiens*. Nonetheless, even though modern humans may not have been the only hominin capable of making art, it is clear that symbolic behavior took on a whole new significance with the evolution of our species.

Molecular Genetics and Human Origins

In looking at modern human origins, geneticists have used two types of data. The first considers living human genetic variation with the goal of identifying the **most recent common ancestor (MRCA)** of all people living today. The second set of data attempts to isolate DNA sequences from fossil hominins. These ancient DNA analyses then consider the difference between the ancient groups and the extent of relatedness between them.

In a phylogenetic tree, the MRCA is indicated by the deepest node from which all contemporary variants can be shown to have evolved. Because all living people are genetically related to each other, the deepest node in a phylogenetic tree corresponds to a basic biological reality: All the variation we observe today evolved from a common ancestor. After identifying the deepest node in a tree, researchers want to know the date of the node. Putting a date to the node representing the MRCA entails calibration and an accurate determination of rates of genetic change (that is, setting the molecular clock; see Chapter 9). We need to remember that the MRCA need not have been an anatomically modern human. Genetic data provide no insights into what the bodies carrying the genes looked like.

The molecular identification of the MRCA does not give us any idea about the physical or behavioral changes that led to the establishment of our species; the fossil

most recent common ancestor (MRCA)   In a phylogenetic tree, the MRCA is indicated by the deepest node from which all contemporary variants can be shown to have evolved.

INNOVATIONS

Symbolism and Human Evolution

Symbols are things that, by accepted practice, represent other things—like the red and white stripes and white stars of the flag of the United States represent the country itself. Symbols are powerful things because they convey often complex meaning to others, but understanding their meaning requires knowledge of the conventions and norms of the group using the symbol. So, for some groups the U.S. flag may imply positive American sentiments, such as baseball and apple pie, but for others it might have negative associations, such as imperialism or capitalism. While we can never know what the precise meanings were of the symbols used by our fossil ancestors, we can see when in human evolution symbolic behavior, possibly group identity, and perhaps extended kin networks started to be important for survival.

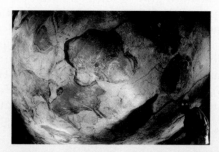

By the end of the Pleistocene, say 40 to 50,000 years ago, the archaeological record is replete with evidence of symbolic behavior. *Homo sapiens* were burying their dead with elaborate displays of grave goods, making art, and using personal ornaments. All of these activities took time, time that could otherwise have been used to gather food or hunt or on some other survival practice. Archaeologists are using new experimental methods and theory to understand the meaning of these practices.

Perhaps the most stunning evidence of symbolic behavior is the practice of cave painting. Many paintings are found deep in caves, often in nearly inaccessible places. Imagine being an early modern human, with no flashlight to light your way and no climbing gear to ease your passage, moving into the dark, damp chambers of a cave, with a small flame throwing shadows around you, barely lighting your way. What inspired you to voyage into this space? What were you seeking to convey?

The earliest cave art known in Europe appeared about 32,000 years ago at Chauvet, France, and is complex in its technique and representation. Rock art appeared in Africa about 26,000 years ago at Apollo 11 cave in Namibia, and somewhat earlier than that in Australia, at places such as Carpenter's Gap, which may be 40,000 years old. The rock art of Australia, which spans thousands of years, provides a particularly rich record of human artistic expression. The animals represented on cave walls in Chauvet were once interpreted as sympathetic magic to assist in hunting success. But when compared with animal remains at archaeological sites of the

Randall White

---

record has no direct information about whether any past species or populations had any descendants. At a fundamental level, the biological issue of modern human origins can be addressed only by combining both genetic and anatomical (paleontological) data.

Mitochondrial DNA

Mitochondrial DNA is transmitted maternally (only through the mother), has a relatively rapid rate of evolution, and does not undergo recombination (see Chapter 3). In the 1980s, researchers began using mtDNA to investigate modern human origins. In a pioneering study, Rebecca Cann and her colleagues (1987) constructed a phylogenetic tree based on sequence differences distributed throughout the human mtDNA genome: the mtDNA came from a large group of people representing several populations. The tree was quite complex, and there was much overlap between individuals from different populations. There was one exception: At the deepest node (representing the MRCA), on one side of the tree there was a cluster of mtDNA lineages found only in Africa. Although African mtDNA lineages were also found on the other side of the tree, the exclusive African cluster indicated that the MRCA lived in Africa. Cann and her colleagues

same period, these images suggest that people were mostly depicting animals they did not hunt. Perhaps the animals had some other symbolic or ritual importance for them.

Red ochre (iron oxide) and the color red were of great significance to modern humans. Evidence from one of the Lake Mungo burials in Australia indicates that the body may have been covered with red ochre. At the Qafzeh site, dating to about 92,000 years ago, seventy-one red ochre pieces, including some that were flaked or marked in some way, were associated with remains of anatomically modern humans, and several stone artifacts were stained with red ochre, although there was no evidence that the bodies themselves were covered in ochre (Hovers et al., 2003). Erella Hovers and her colleagues suggest that the form and distribution of the red ochre pieces indicate they were deliberately mined from a variety of local sources.

Portable art and ornaments are also prevalent in modern human archaeological sites. The most famous are the so-called Venus figurines that represent various female figures, often interpreted as fertility totems. However, other figurines also exist, including many zoomorphic (animal) statuettes. All are small enough to be carried around in a pocket, although we do not know if they were. Pendants made from ivory and even from animal teeth, often from animals that Upper Paleolithic

Randall White

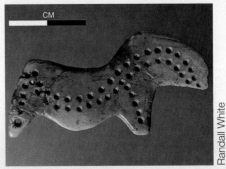

Randall White

people did not eat, such as fox, are also found. There are even examples of pendants made from human molars. And thousands of beads have been found at Upper Paleolithic sites. Some beads were found isolated or in batches, and others were found laying on bodies within burials suggesting the individuals were decorated before burial. Experimental work by Randall White suggests that most beads were attached to garments and took a few hours per bead to make. Thus, the Upper Paleolithic peoples invested a huge amount of time into making these grave items and personal ornaments, indicating that they had significant symbolic meaning and probably were in some way important for survival.

We must remember that symbols are not edible, and unlike stone tools, they do not even help you break open bones, cut meat off a carcass, or access a nut or fruit that you might eat. But symbols may help in survival in other ways. Perhaps they help to identify you as part of a particular group, one that lives over an extended range and with whom you might exchange food resources during difficult times. Or perhaps this group will recognize you as part of an extended group of "friends" not "foes" when they recognize your symbols, even if you do not know one another personally. We can't know for sure, but what is clear is that organizing the world in symbolic ways was of considerable importance to modern humans after about 40,000 years ago.

View "Cave of Lascaux" on myanthrolab

suggested a tentative date for the MRCA between 90,000 and 180,000 years ago (Figure 13.14 on page 348). Although an mtDNA phylogeny traces the lineages down to a single mtDNA source, it is important to remember that there was more than one female in the population at the time; we should not think of the mtDNA studies as identifying an African Eve.

Subsequently, Max Ingman and his colleagues (2000) confirmed that the three deepest branches of the tree were exclusively African, with the next deepest being a mixture of Africans and non-Africans (Figure 13.14 on page 348). Ingman and colleagues argued that such a pattern would arise if mtDNA lineages evolved initially for some time in Africa, followed by a migration out of Africa of a small number of individuals. This resulted in a population bottleneck, followed by a population expansion, with all later Eurasian mtDNA lineages derived from this initial small population that left Africa. Ingman and colleagues put the date of the MRCA for the whole tree at 171,500 (±50,000) years ago, somewhat earlier than that found in the Cann study. The date of the earliest clade that included African and non-African mtDNA was 52,000 (±27,500) years ago.

Much research on the modern human mtDNA has been conducted over the past 25 years. The effects of natural selection, population structure, and methods of

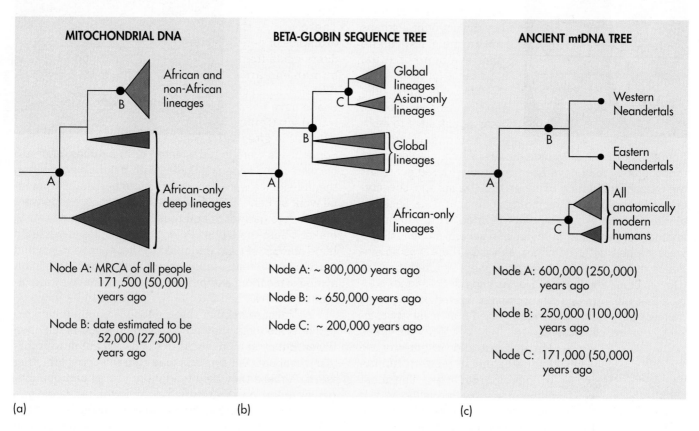

FIGURE 13.14   Three phylogenetic representations of modern human origins: (a) mtDNA, (b) beta globin gene, and (c) ancient mtDNA.

calibration on rates of mtDNA evolution have been studied in the hopes of getting a more precise estimate of the human MRCA date. Current estimates range from 108,000 to 203,000 years ago (see Endicott et al., 2009, for a review), which are fairly similar to the initial MRCA estimate reported by Cann et al. (1987).

The Y Chromosome

The Y chromosome is in some ways the male equivalent of mtDNA. Like mtDNA, it is transmitted across generations in only one sex, in this case males. Although parts of the Y chromosome undergo recombination, a large portion does not, and studies of this portion have been widely used in evolutionary research (Mitchell and Hammer, 1996; Stumpf and Goldstein, 2001; Jobling and Tyler-Smith, 2003). Phylogenetic analyses of the Y chromosome are based on both sequence and haplotype data. Haplotypes are combinations of mutations found together on a single chromosome; we can analyze them phylogenetically or calculate population frequencies for different haplotypes (see Chapter 5). There are at least eighteen major haplotype groups for the Y chromosome, which are themselves composed of dozens of different haplotypes. Haplotypes are useful for tracing population movements and demographic events that have occurred across human history, such as the spread of the Mongol Empire.

The Y chromosome data seem to generally support the mtDNA story (Underhill and Kivisild, 2007). Several estimates of a date for the Y chromosome MRCA have been suggested; most researchers accept an estimate of 100,000–180,000 years ago. Thus, the variation we observe in the Y chromosome and mtDNA of living humans appears to have evolved within similar timeframes. For both, the MRCA is dated with some confidence to less than 200,000 years ago. The Y chromosome and mtDNA data also both place the location of the MRCA in Africa. As was the case for the mtDNA, the deepest Y chromosome lineages are found exclusively in Africa, indicating evolution there first, followed by a population expansion into other parts of the world. Both kinds of genetic information provide evidence of founder effects in more isolated populations. Some differences between Y chromosome and mtDNA phylogenies can be found in Europe, where the mtDNA suggest a more unified population, but the Y chromosome indicates a split between Eastern and Western European populations. The Y chromosome also shows that there was a late Pleistocene migration out of Africa into Europe that is not represented in mtDNA data.

MRCAs for Nuclear Genes

Although the Y chromosome is part of the nuclear genome, it is a special case because such a large proportion of it is nonrecombining, and it has a small number of genes that are subject to natural selection. The remainder of the nuclear genome affords countless opportunities for reconstructing the evolutionary histories of human populations.

Large-scale compilations of protein allele data (see Chapter 6) are generally consistent with the evolutionary picture provided by mtDNA and the Y chromosome (Cavalli-Sforza et al., 1994; Cavalli-Sforza and Feldman, 2003), especially in locating the MRCA in Africa. In a phylogenetic tree derived from an analysis of allelic variation in 120 protein genes distributed in 1,915 populations, Luca Cavalli-Sforza and his colleagues show that the deepest node in the tree represents a split between African populations and all other populations.

In contrast to mtDNA and Y chromosome analyses, phylogenetic analyses of some nuclear genes (or portions of genes) and noncoding regions of chromosomes indicate MRCAs that are substantially older than 200,000 years. Rosalind Harding and her colleagues (1997) analyzed a 3,000–base pair region of the beta-globin gene (one of the chains of the hemoglobin protein). They calculated an MRCA for the gene as existing 800,000 years ago, with the oldest sequence coming from Africa (Figure 13.14b). This finding does not contradict the mtDNA and Y chromosome results because the variation in this gene could have arisen and evolved in Africa before a population expansion out of Africa less than 200,000 years ago. However, Harding and her colleagues also found Asia-specific beta-globin sequences that had MRCAs more than 200,000 years ago. This would indicate that Asian populations that existed before 200,000 years ago made unique genetic contributions to the contemporary human genome, a finding that is difficult to reconcile with the mtDNA and Y chromosome results, although one that may be consistent with the data from the Denisovan DNA (see Insights and Advances: The Denisovans in Chapter 12 on pages 324–325). Harding and her colleagues also found evidence of gene flow between Asian and African populations during the last several hundred thousand years. Results broadly similar to those for the beta-globin gene have been obtained in other studies of the nuclear genome (Zhao et al., 2000).

The mapping of the entire human genome has provided even more information from nuclear DNA that can be used by geneticists to chart population history. For example, individual human genomes contain large numbers of base pair substitutions, many of which occur in non-coding regions. Like any other kind of genetic variation, these *single nucleotide polymorphisms* (SNPs) can be used to construct phylogenetic trees. As might be expected, people from the same family or same population share more SNPs than those who are less closely related. This fact is sometimes used in forensic analyses (see Chapter 15). Brian McEvoy and colleagues (2011) looked at 242,000 SNPs found in 17 populations from throughout the world. Again, Africa was found to be the source for modern humans. However, their analysis also indicated that there have been multiple "Out of Africa" events in the last 50,000 years or so, and a major division between Europeans and East Asians at around 22,000 years ago.

Ancient DNA

Ancient DNA (aDNA) recovered from fossils can provide a direct window into the genetics of past populations. Ancient mtDNA has been isolated from more than a dozen Neandertals and fossil *H. sapiens*. Nuclear DNA has now been isolated as well (see Chapter 12, Innovations: Neandertal Genes on pages 316–317).

These studies agree that the Neandertal mtDNA samples all fall outside the range of variation that has been observed in modern humans (Figure 13.14c on page 348). And, Neandertal samples cluster together as a clade separate from living humans on a phylogenetic tree. Sequence variation in the Neandertal clade is approximately equivalent to that observed in living modern human groups. More important, ancient mtDNA from Neandertals falls outside the range of variation found in ancient DNA from fossil modern humans. And all fossil humans fail to show any Neandertal mtDNA or any intermediate sequences and are much closer to living human DNA, despite being closer in age to the Neandertal remains.

Researchers estimate from ancient mtDNA that the MRCA for modern humans and Neandertals lived between 365,000 and 853,000 years ago. The recently extracted nuclear DNA suggests a broadly similar picture. The inferred population split is between 270,000 and 440,000 years ago. Many researchers think that the Neandertal ancient DNA data strongly support the replacement model of modern human origins. However, some analysts (e.g., Nordborg, 1998; Relethford, 2001) argue that a small number of divergent mtDNA sequences from Neandertals do not rule out the possibility that they may have interbred with anatomically modern humans; it is not that difficult to construct mathematical population models that can account for the mtDNA data in the context of modern human–Neandertal admixture and the nuclear DNA suggest at least a small amount (1–4%) of Neandertal genetic contribution (see Chapter 12).

Interpreting Models of Human Origins

Let us now review how our three sets of data, paleontology, archaeology, and genetics, are interpreted with respect to the origin of modern humans.

Paleontology and Archaeology

As originally developed by Milford Wolpoff, Wu Xin Zhi, and Alan Thorne (1984), the Multiregional model proposed that *local regional anatomical continuity* provides strong evidence of the multiregional origins of modern humans (see also Wolpoff et al., 1994; Wolpoff and Caspari, 1997). *Local regional continuity* means we can trace a particular evolutionary trajectory through a suite of anatomical features shared by fossil specimens in a particular region: We can identify this regional anatomical pattern despite the fact that here has been a substantial amount of morphological evolution between *H. erectus* and anatomically modern *H. sapiens*. For example, widely dispersed populations of *H. erectus* exhibited regional anatomical variation (see Chapter 11), and that regional variation may have been retained in later hominin populations living in the same area.

In contrast to the Multiregional model, the Out of Africa model suggests that the earliest modern humans should look very different from the local populations they replaced and should exhibit regional continuity in only one source region, Africa (Bräuer, 1984; Stringer and Andrews, 1988). Fossil lineages from archaic *H. sapiens* at Bodo to Herto, Aduma, and Klasies River Mouth provide evidence of an African origin of *H. sapiens sapiens* that predates such a lineage elsewhere in the world. At the same time as anatomically modern humans appear in Africa, archaic *H. sapiens* populations in Europe seem to be evolving into classic Neandertals. From about 40,000 to 30,000 years ago, Neandertals and anatomically modern humans appear to overlap in time and space in Europe, although they are physically and culturally distinct. By about 30,000 years ago modern humans replaced Neandertals in Europe.

Multiregional model proponents argue that the occasional appearance of occipital buns in modern human crania, the appearance of a retro-molar gap in some early human fossils, and the general robustness of early European modern human fossils, especially those from central Europe, are all evidence of regional continuity (Smith, 1984). However, some of these transitional populations, such as Vindija and Mladeč, reveal no sign of genetic admixture in their ancient DNA (Vindija is entirely Neandertal-like, Mladeč entirely modern humanlike), does not support the multiregional position. However, nuclear DNA does suggest a small genetic contribution by Neandertals to modern humans generally (see Chapter 12).

Asia and Australia may provide the best evidence of multiregional evolution. In Asia multiregional proponents argue that regional characters seen in *H. erectus* in China and Indonesia are mirrored in modern humans in China and Australia. For example, the high vertical frontal lobe of Chinese *H. erectus* is considered continuous with that seen in Chinese modern humans. The sagittal keel, occipital torus, and supraorbital tori of Indonesian *H. erectus* are suggested to continue through, in lesser degrees, to modern human Australians. Likewise, multiregional proponents argue that the Ngandong hominins are thought to represent morphological and temporal intermediates between *H. erectus* and some modern Australians (Frayer et al., 1993). Alternatively, replacement proponents counter that Ngandong is morphologically *H. erectus* and potentially overlaps in time and space with modern humans of the region (Swisher et al., 1996). Replacement proponents also suggest that early modern human fossils from Asia more closely resemble modern humans from other regions of the world than they do earlier Asian *H. erectus* (Stringer and Andrews, 1988).

It is probably safe to say that within the paleoanthropological community, there is more support for some form of the replacement viewpoint than for the multiregional version of evolution. However, it is equally safe to say that the field is far from consensus on the issue and that many paleoanthropologists think that the fossil record provides at least some support in some regions for multiregional evolution.

Molecular Genetics

Genetic data from both living humans and fossil remains provide some clear support for a replacement model of human origins. Although the molecular data can say nothing about the anatomy of the MRCA, the picture presented by mtDNA and the Y chromosome is easy to reconcile with the paleontological replacement model, which places the origins of anatomically modern humans in Africa during roughly the same time period of the MRCA for these molecular phylogenies. The divergent mtDNA sequences of the Neandertals provide further support for a replacement event in Europe, especially in light of the fact that early modern humans in Europe have mtDNA that is well within the range of variation seen in contemporary humans. However, newer ancient nuclear DNA analyses as well as the ancient DNA from Denisova (see Chapter 12) point to some level of gene flow between archaic hominins and modern humans. This means that a strict replacement model without any interbreeding cannot be supported.

There is no simple answer to the question, Where did modern humans come from? (Table 13.1 on page 352). Genetic, paleontological, and archaeological data can be woven together to produce several different scenarios to explain our complex origins. Some of the controversy surrounding the issue derives from scientific success as new dating methods, new archaeological and fossil discoveries, and innovative genetic approaches have all provided an unprecedented amount of information devoted to a single evolutionary event. The evolution of modern humans may have been far more complicated than either of the original models proposed. However, the controversy over which particular model of human origins is correct should not blind us to the fact that we know far more about the biological and cultural evolution of our own species than ever before.

Bioarchaeology After the Origin of Modern Humans

Whichever model of modern human origins is correct, humans soon ventured into new areas, adapted to new selective pressures, and molded our environments both intentionally and unintentionally. To reveal this prehistory of human populations, bioarchaeologists study skeletal remains from archaeological sites in the Holocene

TABLE 13.1   Comparing Replacement and Multiregional Models of Human Origins

	Fact	Replacement Interpretation	Multiregional Interpretation
Paleontological Record, Middle Pleistocene	Between about 200,000 and 500,000 years ago, archaic *H. sapiens* lived in Africa, Europe, and Asia.	Archaic *H. sapiens* in Europe evolved into Neandertals.	Neandertals and modern humans are not separate evolutionary lineages. Neandertals are transitional to European modern humans.
	Fully modern humans and classic Neandertals appeared by 125,000 years ago.	African archaic populations evolved into anatomically modern *Homo sapiens*.	
Paleontological Record, Late Pleistocene	The anatomically modern human phenotype first appeared outside Africa 90,000–100,000 years ago in the Middle East.	Anatomically modern humans replaced preexisting hominins throughout the Old World without any or with little genetic mixing.	Anatomically modern humans arose from extensive gene flow between middle and late Pleistocene hominin populations throughout the Old World.
		Similarities between early anatomically modern humans from widely dispersed populations are best explained by evolution from a common source population in Africa.	Some fossils show transitional anatomy.
Recent DNA Studies	mtDNA and the Y chromosome phylogenies indicate greatest variability in Africa, suggesting that the most recent common ancestor (MRCA) of modern humans lived in Africa 150,000–200,000 years ago.	mtDNA and the Y chromosome support an African origin for modern humans and indicate a population expansion out of Africa starting about 100,000 years ago.	
	Nuclear gene sequences indicate MRCAs that significantly predate 200,000 years ago. Furthermore, deep lineages of these trees have been traced to variants that appear to have originated outside Africa.	Nuclear gene sequences reflect the age of the first dispersal (*H. erectus*) from Africa and do not preclude another dispersal by modern *H. sapiens* about 100,000 years ago. They are inconsistent with a complete replacement event.	Nuclear gene sequences indicate extensive gene flow between Old World populations over the last 500,000 years and perhaps longer. Diverse ancient Old World populations contributed to the modern human gene pool.
Ancient DNA	Ancient DNA from Neandertal and modern human fossils of the same age differ more from one another than does the DNA of living human groups.	Neandertals are a separate species that did not make a substantial genetic contribution to modern humans.	Differences between Neandertals and humans are less than those between chimp species and do not support a separate species for Neandertals.
	Differences between Neandertal and modern human DNA are not as great as those between chimp species.	Neandertals were replaced across their range 30,000–40,000 years ago.	
	Even some fossils considered transitional in anatomy do not have transitional DNA. But Neandertal nuclear DNA may indicate a 1–4% contribution to recent populations.	Neandertals were replaced across their range, but a small amount of interbreeding occurred. The majority of the gene pool is of African origin.	Any interbreeding implies a single species and continuity rather than replacement.

(in the last 10,000 years) and sometimes late Pleistocene. Because the form of the skeleton reflects both its function and its evolutionary history, bioarchaeologists can reconstruct the probable age and sex of an individual from his or her skeletal remains. They can observe the influence of certain kinds of diseases on the skeleton, and differentiate among marks on bone that happened just before, around the time of, and after an individual's death. Bioarchaeologists can then combine information from multiple individuals to assess the biological adaption and health of the population. It is especially interesting to consider the changes across important cultural transitions—such as the initial peopling of the New World or the Pacific, the transition from hunting and gathering to farming, or the impact of European contact on indigenous peoples in the new world and elsewhere. It also means using biological clues to better understand the biological impact of cultural practices, such as the influence of social stratification on diet and disease. Bioarchaeologists approach a diverse number of evolutionary questions in this interdisciplinary way.

Settlement of the New World and Pacific Islands

View the Map "Human Colonization of the New World and Pacific Islands" on myanthrolab

Using behavioral rather than physical adaptations and perhaps ordering their world symbolically, modern humans also had the ability to dominate environments that were already occupied by other hominins and to settle regions that earlier hominins could not. As we have seen, modern humans were the first to colonize Australia, perhaps 50,000 years ago. The last of these "hominin free" areas to be settled were high-latitude areas (by 30,000 years ago), the Americas (by 15,000 years ago), and the remote islands of the Pacific (by 3,500 years ago).

The Americas During ice ages, when sea levels are at their lowest, the Old and New Worlds are connected via the Bering land bridge, a broad swath of land (more than 2,000 km wide at its maximum) linking eastern Siberia with western Alaska (Figure 13.15). This bridge was open and ice free only periodically. Most recently it was closed between about 24,000 and 15,000 years ago (Goebel et al., 2007). Crossing the land bridge, even when it was ice free, was no walk in the park. The effort seems to have entailed a level of technological or subsistence development not reached by earlier hominins. Alternatively, we know that at least some modern human populations had watercraft by about 40,000 years ago, as demonstrated by the successful over-water

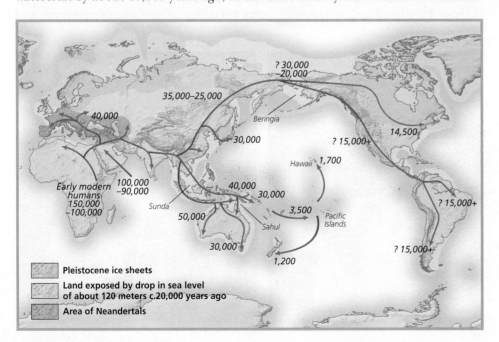

FIGURE 13.15   Routes for the human colonization of the New World and Pacific islands.

colonization of Australia. Thus, colonization of the New World via the coast of Siberia and Alaska or along the Pacific Rim may have been possible (Dixon, 2001).

By around 13,000 years ago, Paleo-Indian sites of the Clovis culture, which is distinguished by a characteristic finely flaked point, appeared all over North America. Additional Paleo-Indian sites appear not much later at sites in Central and South America. For many years the Clovis people were considered the first colonizers of the New World. However, scholars continue to argue over whether a pre-Clovis settlement existed, and new evidence suggests it may have (see Insights and Advances: Peopling of the New World).

Archeological sites aside, Paleo-Indian skeletal remains are rare. The earliest of them, such as Kennewick Man from Washington State (8,400 years old; see Figure 13.16a), the Browns Valley skull from Minnesota (8,700 years old), and the Warm Mineral Springs crania from Florida (perhaps 10,000 years old; see Figure 13.16b), exhibit features that differentiate them from recent Native American populations. These Paleo-Indian skulls show a great degree of variation and do not typically show a strong resemblance to contemporary Native American populations (Jantz & Owsley, 2001). The settlement history of the Americas is clearly complex and is being addressed by genetic, linguistic, archaeological, and paleontological researchers.

The Pacific Islands The last regions of the world to be colonized by humans are the Pacific Islands. Although people crossed the ocean between Sunda and Sahul about 50,000 years ago and inhabited islands such as New Britain off the east coast of Papua New Guinea as early as 28,000 years ago, most of the Pacific was not colonized until 3,500 years ago or later. Only the invention of long-distance voyaging technology allowed such crossings, which settlers undertook over vast areas of ocean (Irwin, 1992).

Genetic, archaeological, and linguistic data seem to indicate that the peopling of the Pacific started with populations somewhere in East Asia or the islands of Southeast Asia moving into New Guinea, fusing with peoples and cultures there, and then moving into Polynesia (Kirch, 2001). The earliest expansion of these peoples in the Pacific often is traced by their archeological sites, characterized by a pottery style called Lapita. The Lapita peoples appeared earliest in Near Oceania (the Bismarck Archipelago) around 3,500 years ago and from there spread to Fiji (around 3,000 years ago) and then further out to Tonga, Samoa, and Far Oceania. Presumably in outrigger canoes, they brought with them pigs, dogs, rats, agricultural crops, and enough food and water to survive their journey. Once on these remote islands, humans did what we do best. They modified the landscape, took advantage of new natural resources, and

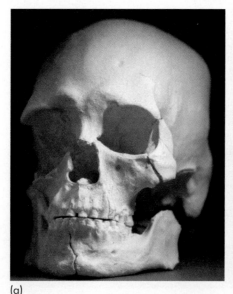
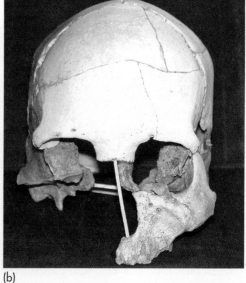

(a)   (b)

FIGURE 13.16   Some of the earliest skeletal remains of Paleo-Indians include (a) Kennewick and (b) Warm Mineral Springs.

insights & advances

PEOPLING OF THE NEW WORLD

When and how did people enter the New World? They could have come through an ice-free corridor in the middle of the Bering land bridge. Or, perhaps they travelled a coastal route. Was it a quick dispersal around 13,000 years ago, or a more leisurely one that started earlier? Did they carry the Clovis toolkit, or were they a pre-Clovis people? Recent genetic and archaeological evidence is providing new insights to these longstanding questions.

Nuclear, mitochondrial, and Y-chromosome DNA suggest that all Native Americans came from a common genetic source population in Asia (Goebel et al., 2007). The DNA of these groups suggests that Native Americans diverged from their Asian ancestors sometime between 15,000 and 25,000 years ago, and it has been inferred from these and other data that the colonization of the Americas began between 16,000 and 11,000 years ago. Although much of the Bering land bridge and coast were locked in glacial ice over parts of the late Pleistocene, the coastal corridor was probably ice free by about 15,000 years ago, and the interior corridor somewhat later—perhaps 14,000 or 13,000 years ago.

Clovis sites with their signature fluted lanceolate projectile points are well documented and well dated to about 13,000 years old (12,800–13,200 years ago; Waters and Stafford, 2007). These sites appear nearly simultaneously across North America, perhaps in a span of as little as 200 to 300 years, although the direction of this speedy dispersal is hard to determine. The assemblages are bifacial, Upper Paleolithic stone, bone, and antler tools that seem to signify a highly mobile hunter-gatherer population. As the best documented and dated sites, many scholars infer that the Clovis people were the first to enter the New World and that they dispersed quickly into new, unoccupied territories. Such a suggestion is not incompatible with the timing indicated by the genetic data, although some would argue that aspects of the genetic patterning suggest that the differences among Native Americans could not have arisen over such a quick dispersal time. But even if an earlier, perhaps slower dispersal had occurred, finding earlier sites has proved challenging. Pre-Clovis sites in the Americas are few, far between, and highly contentious.

However, new evidence of pre-Clovis assemblages has been surfacing. Monte Verde is a site in Chile that is widely accepted as indicating an old age (13,900–14,200 years ago) for a pre-Clovis industry. This site, with evidence of the use of coastal resources such as seaweed, would seem to support an early coastal migration (Dillehay et al., 2008). The Paisley 5 Mile Point Caves in Oregon yielded mtDNA from human coprolites that date to about 14,000 years ago, but few tools were found, making the relationship to Clovis or pre-Clovis industries difficult to establish (Gilbert et al., 2008). Recently, a pre-Clovis industry known as the Buttermilk Creek Complex has been discovered in the Friedkin Site along the Buttermilk Creek in Texas (Figure A; Waters et al., 2011). The site has a fairly long sequence that includes tool assemblages from youngest

FIGURE B   Pre-Clovis artifacts of the Buttermilk Creek Complex are small in size and use a different mode of production than Clovis artifacts.

to oldest that are typical of the Late Archaic, Early Archaic, Paleo-Indian, Folsom, Clovis, and Pre-Clovis. Most importantly for this discussion, the site includes both a younger (stratigraphically higher) Clovis component and below that an older pre-Clovis component. The site was dated using the Optically Stimulated Luminescence (OSL) technique described in Chapter 9. The thick pre-Clovis unit is dated to between 15,500 and 13,200 years ago, and the tool assemblage is reasonably large with more than 15,000 pieces, 56 of which are formal tools. The tools (Figure B) are mostly small in size, and they are made in a different way than is the Clovis material.

So recent evidence, including the presence of these and other pre-Clovis sites, has begun to suggest that it was a pre-Clovis people, perhaps taking initially a coastal and then an inland route, who first colonized the Americas. The quick spread of Clovis may not have been the initial peopling of the continent, but a secondary dispersal or the diffusion of a toolkit itself.

FIGURE A   The Friedkin Site in Texas yielded a long sequence of artifacts from the Late Archaic through the pre-Clovis (Buttermilk Creek Complex). The site is dated using the OSL method.

interacted with the environment in symbolic ways. The archaeological records of most islands reveal strong, not necessarily positive, human influences on these island ecosystems, including the extinction of land birds and evidence of deforestation.

These settlements mark the end of the initial colonization of the globe by humans. Although the rest of human history on Earth will be marked by both dispersal and migration, no longer is it into ecosystems never before occupied by humans.

Biological Changes at the Origins of Agriculture and Shifts to Sedentism

Comparisons of groups of skeletons of individuals with very different activity patterns offer insights into the influence of, for example, subsistence change on lifestyles. Activity patterns are often assessed through computed tomography studies of the postcrania that take advantage of the fact that systematic changes in activity influence the development of the human skeleton. The distribution of bone in cross-sections of the leg bones, for example, reflects the predominant direction of force through the limb.

Using this technique, bioarchaeologists have shown that as agriculture was adopted there were many skeletal consequences. For example, Native American hunter-gatherers occupied the coastal region of Georgia continuously for thousands of years before European contact (Ruff et al., 1984; Larsen and Ruff, 1994). Around 1150, these hunter-gatherers incorporated maize agriculture into their economy and became more sedentary. Comparisons of the strength of their femora (thigh bones) before and after the switch to sedentary agriculture show a decrease in bone strength in the agricultural population and a decrease in the presence of arthritis. The results suggest a decrease in overall activity level and a shift in the types of activities once agriculture was adopted. Interestingly, comparison of the leg strength of these agriculturalists with early contact period (1565–1680) groups of sedentary Native Americans living in missions in Georgia found the later groups were stronger. Scientists interpret this to mean that the Native Americans living in missions, although also sedentary, were working harder than their precontact forebears (Larsen and Ruff, 1994). It should be noted, however, that other agricultural populations became stronger—the difference in results relates to specific local conditions before and after the switch.

Agriculture and particularly cooking may have had an influence on cranial shape, jaw size, and dental crowding due to eating softer foods. Depending on the agricultural crop, the incidence of cavities increased. Reduced food toughness may have led to smaller jaws and many instances of malocclusion—perhaps one of the reasons so many of us need orthodontic work today! Agriculture also had the effect of allowing increases in population size and density, which often led to environmental degradation, increased disease loads, and interpersonal conflict. In fact, increases in population density even without agriculture will have these effects.

In the Channel Island's populations of prehistoric California (7200 B.C. to 1780 A.D.), increased exploitation of marine foods has been linked to increases in population size and density through time. Archaeological evidence of increasing quantities of fish and shellfish, and the tools for catching and processing these fish, has been found in Channel Island sites. These very local marine resources allowed Channel Islanders to lead more sedentary lives and allowed their populations to grow in size and density, even though they did not have agriculture. With these changes, their social organization became more complex. General health also declined; with increasing population density, more individuals show bone infections and stature decreases—both indicators of general stress (Lambert and Walker, 1991). Other indicators of general stress, such as linear defects in tooth enamel (dental hypoplasia), are often found with increasing population density (Figure 13.17). In Channel Islands populations, cranial fractures increased, indicating an increase in interpersonal violence perhaps due to stresses associated with increasing population size (Walker, 1989). Only the combination of these archaeological data with the biological profiles of hundreds of individuals allows the interpretations and understanding of these widespread changes in the Channel Island populations through time.

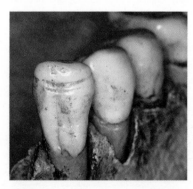

FIGURE 13.17 Linear defects in tooth enamel, as seen on this canine, are responses to high fevers, disease, or other insults during development.

Physical and Cultural Consequences of Colonization

The combination of archaeological and biological information can also be used to understand the complex interaction among cultural practices, health, and disease. Biological profiles and detailed analyses of health indicators in a group of skeletons of known time period, environmental context, and social status can help us understand the evolution of disease and the influence of culture change on the health of a population. These clues can be used to assess the results of European colonization on indigenous peoples in the Americas and elsewhere, such as remote Oceania.

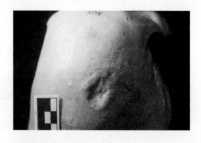

FIGURE 13.18   Radial lesions of the cranial vault are often present in syphilis.

For example, some infectious diseases, like syphilis and tuberculosis, may leave their mark on the skeleton (Figure 13.18). A particular distribution of bone abnormalities is often typical of a particular disease, although diseases are also sometimes difficult to tell apart. In the case of syphilis and tuberculosis, skeletal evidence forms the primary argument for whether these diseases are Old World introductions to the New World, or vice versa. DNA and bone evidence suggests that both diseases may have existed in the New World before Columbus and his men arrived, although the case is stronger for tuberculosis (Salo et al., 1994). In addition, the New World disease related to syphilis was probably a nonvenereal form, that is, a disease that is not sexually transmitted.

European contact also influenced cultural practices. For example, on Mangaia, the second largest and southernmost of the Cook Islands in the South Pacific, archaeological and bioarchaeological studies document changes in burial practices through time. Prior to European contact, which occurred on Mangaia in 1823 with the arrival of Christian missionaries, individuals were buried under house floors and in burial caves, but after contact, many individuals were buried in church cemeteries (Antón and Steadman, 2003). Using the biological profiles of the skeletal remains we see that, even though burial caves continued to be used after contact, the style of the burials changed. Before contact nearly equal numbers of adults and children were placed in burial caves and evidence of secondary burials, in which the skeleton had been rearranged, and of multiple burials, in which several individuals were buried simultaneously, was frequent (Figure 13.19). After European contact, few adults were found in burial caves and they were buried individually. In addition, secondary burials do not seem to have been present. These changes suggest that indigenous mortuary practices, and likely religion, were influenced by Christian missionaries. Individuals were no longer buried near or among the living, and the more unusual practices (from a Christian perspective), such as secondary processing of skeletal remains, were eliminated. Although burial caves are no longer used on Mangaia today, they remain places of reverence and connection to ancestors. Only through the combined perspective of both archaeological and biological data can we see when this transition began and how it emerged.

Primate evolution in the Cenozoic is the study of the history of adaptation in ourselves and our ancestors. That process of adaptation can be assessed for skeletal populations in the recent past, and in the next section we will learn how human biologists assess the ongoing adaptations in living humans.

(a)   (b)

FIGURE 13.19   Burial caves from Mangaia, Cook Islands, document the changing patterns of mortuary ritual. Secondary burials, seen here in detail (a) and from a distance (b) are rare after contact with Christian missionaries.

The Emergence and Dispersal of *Homo sapiens*

Models of Modern Human Origins

Replacement Scenarios

- Hypothesizes a single, probably African, origin of modern humans, with subsequent dispersal into the Old World and replacement of archaic hominins by *H. sapiens*.
- Indicate little or no gene flow between modern humans and earlier hominins in the various regions of the Old World.
- Predict anatomically distinct, temporally overlapping lineages of hominins in each region of the world.
- Predict possible disjunction in the archeological and genetic records. **[pp 335–337; 350–352]**

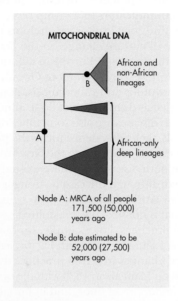

MITOCHONDRIAL DNA

African and non-African lineages

B

A

African-only deep lineages

Node A: MRCA of all people 171,500 (50,000) years ago

Node B: date estimated to be 52,000 (27,500) years ago

Multiregional Scenarios

- Hypothesize that the origin of modern humans is the result of the diffusion of the genetic underpinnings of the modern human phenotype among multiple archaic hominins from multiple regions via gene flow.
- Indicate significant regional input into the modern human gene pool.
- Predict single, evolving lineages with the presence of intermediate fossil forms in each region.
- Predict continuity of behavior (as inferred from the tool types).
- Predict genetic contribution from archaic to modern populations in a region and greater similarity between archaic hominins and modern *H. sapiens* in a region. **[pp 335–357; 350–352]**

Defining *Homo sapiens*

Anatomical Characteristics

- The face: presence of a chin, reduced facial size, reduced brow size, and presence of a canine fossa.
- The vault: large globular brain case with parallel sides and the greatest breadth high on the parietals, and a distinct mastoid process.
- The postcranium: relatively gracile compared to Neandertals or archaic *H. sapiens*. **[pp 335–342]**

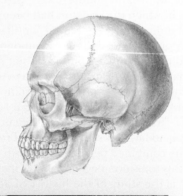

Time and Geography

- Earliest appear in Africa about 195,000 years ago.
- First outside Africa are in the Near East around 100,000 years ago.
- Dispersal into Island Southeast Asia and Australasia by 50,000 years ago. **[pp 335–342]**

Archaeology and Behavior

- Earliest AMH are found with Middle Stone Age technologies.
- Upper Paleolithic technologies are more typical of most AMH-associated finds.
- Symbolic behavior, as represented by personal ornaments, portable art, cave art, and burials, seems an increasingly important part of how *H. sapiens* organized the world, suggesting that symbolism had important survival value. **[pp 342–345]**

Phylogenetic Relationships and DNA

- Two models for the origins of modern humans have been proposed: replacement and multiregional models.
- Ancient DNA suggests that fossil *H. sapiens* of Europe are more similar to living humans than they are to fossil Neandertals from Europe of the same geologic age.
- The last common ancestor for all *H. sapiens* is reconstructed to be approximately 200,000 to 800,000 years ago based on various kinds of DNA comparisons. **[pp 345–350]**

Bioarcheology After the Origin of Modern Humans

Dispersal into the New World and Pacific

- These are the last of the initial dispersals by humans into "hominin-free" ecosystems.
- *H. sapiens* disperses into the New World by at least 13,000, the Pacific by 3500 years ago.
- These late dispersals are characterized by heavy direct and indirect human influences on the ecosystems into which they move.
- After these migrations, human migration involves one set of humans colonizing another. **[pp 353–356]**

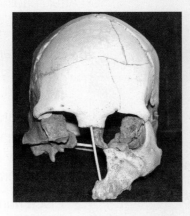

Physical and Behavioral Consequences of Colonization

- Colonization of one group of humans by another has both physical and cultural consequences.
- Colonization of the New World facilitated the spread of disease between the New and Old Worlds; skeletal evidence suggests tuberculosis originated in the New World.
- Colonization of the Pacific influenced traditional religious practices and changed, for example, how the dead were buried. **[p 357]**

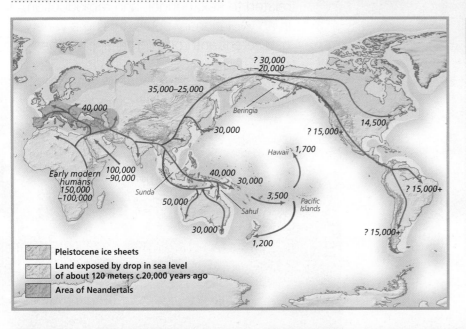

Pleistocene ice sheets

Land exposed by drop in sea level of about 120 meters c.20,000 years ago

Area of Neandertals

Physical Responses to Changes in Activity Level, Sedentism, Agriculture

- The skeleton responds to physical stresses, and behavior can be partially read through these responses.
- The shift from hunting and gathering to farming in some regions shows a decrease in leg strength, suggesting that agriculture was less physically demanding.
- The shift to sedentism, even without a shift to farming, increases population density, which is correlated with increasing evidence of nutritional stress (e.g., rates of infection, decreased stature, developmental defects), and often interpersonal violence. **[p 356]**

My AnthroLab CONNECTIONS

Watch. Listen. View. Explore. Read.

MyAnthroLab is designed just for you. Each chapter features a customized study plan to help you learn and review key concepts and terms. Dynamic visual activities, videos, and readings found in the multimedia library will enhance your learning experience.

Resources from this Chapter:

Listen on myanthrolab

▶ *Humanlike 'Hobbit' Fossils Puzzle Scientists*

View on myanthrolab

▶ *Human Colonization of the New World and Pacific Islands*
▶ *Cave of Lascaux*

Explore on myanthrolab In MySearchLab, enter the Anthropology database to find relevant and recent scholarly and popular press publications. For this chapter, enter the following keywords: Modern human origins, Bioarcheology, Paleopathology, Multiregionalism

Read on myanthrolab

▶ *Killing Lascaux* by Paul Bahn
▶ *New Women of the Ice Age* by Heather Pringle
▶ *Lithic Analysis: Chipped Stone Tools and Waste Flakes in Archaeology* by Robert L. Kelly

Chapter 14 Preview

After reading this chapter, you should be able to:

- Understand the implications of changes in brain size and organization in human evolution.

- Identify the nature and critical role of spoken language in human evolution and how language has had an impact on our brain, body, and behavior.

- Place human behavior, including that related to sex, gender, and reproduction, in an evolutionary context using a variety of different anthropological approaches.

Evolution of the Brain and Behavior

14

During the mid-1970s, new evolutionary and eco-logical approaches to understanding animal behavior were starting to be applied to human behavior. Increasing knowledge about the sophis-ticated social behavior of other primates further fueled the effort to place human behavior in a broader evolu-tionary and zoological context. These efforts were vigorously contested by academics and activists opposed to any bio-logical interpretation of contemporary human behavior.

In early 1978, the American Association for the Advancement of Science held a meeting in Washington, D.C., which attempted to bring together representatives from all sides in what came to be called "the sociobiology debate." Two of the most prominent scientists to attend the meeting were Edward Wilson, a proponent of the evolutionary study of human behavior (which was then called sociobiology), and Stephen Jay Gould, who cautioned that arguments about the biological basis of human behavior historically had been used to justify racist and sexist ideologies. Many of Wilson's critics accused him of arrogance for suggesting that evolu-tionary explanations of human behavior would come to dom-inate thinking in the traditional social sciences. In contrast, proponents of sociobiology felt that Wilson and other work-ers in the field were being unfairly accused of holding political and ideological views that they themselves found to be re-pugnant. Advocates on both sides of the debate were fueled by arrogance and righteousness, a volatile combination.

Sociologist of science Ullica Segerstråle attended this landmark meeting. She describes the extraordinary scene when Wilson faced some of his more enthusiastic critics:

"The two-day symposium featured about twenty speakers in all. As a member of the audience, I can say that for those who anticipated a public showdown, it was somewhat disappointing to sit through rather technical talks dealing with animal sociobiology . . . . But there was

anticipation in the air, particularly in the session where both Wilson and Gould were to speak. The ballroom was filled to capacity. Would Gould demolish sociobiology? Would Wilson stand up to Gould? By now, the audience wanted some action. The result exceeded anybody's expectation.

"What happens is a total surprise. The session has al-ready featured Gould, among others, and Wilson is one of the later speakers. Just as Wilson is about to begin, about ten people rush up on the speaker podium shouting 'Racist Wilson you can't hide, we charge you with genocide!' While some take over the microphone and denounce sociobiology, a couple of them rush up behind Wilson (who is sitting in his place) and pour a pitcher of ice-water over his head, shouting 'Wilson, you are all wet!' Then they quickly disappear again. Great commotion ensues but things calm down when the ses-sion organizer steps up to the microphone and apologizes to Wilson for the incident. The audience gives Wilson a standing ovation. Now Gould steps up to the microphone saying that this kind of activism is not the right way to fight sociobiology—here he has a Lenin quote handy, on 'radicalism, an infantile disorder of socialism.' For his valiant han-dling of the situation, Gould, too, gets a standing ovation. (The audience does not quite know how to react to any of this but applauding seems somehow right.) Wilson—still wet—gives his talk, in spite of the shock of the physical attack . . . . his calmly delivered talk is some-thing of an anticlimax" (Segerstråle, 2000).

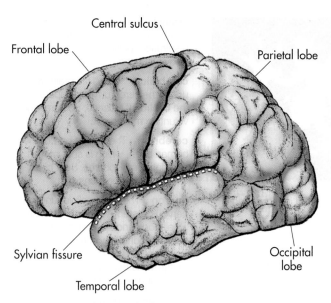

Central sulcus

Frontal lobe

Parietal lobe

Sylvian fissure

Occipital lobe

Temporal lobe

FIGURE 14.4 The major lobes of the cerebrum.

Different regions of the cerebrum have different functions. It is important to keep in mind that different regions work in concert to produce complex behaviors. The cerebral cortex is divided into two kinds of functional areas. **Primary cortex** is involved directly with either motor control or input from the senses. *Primary motor* regions are concentrated in the *frontal lobe*, the part of the cerebrum located just behind the eyes and forehead (Figure 14.4). *Primary sensory* regions are distributed throughout the cerebrum. Most of the human cerebral cortex is not primary cortex but rather **association cortex.** We can think of the association cortex as the regions where the processing of primary inputs or information occurs. It is generally believed that in mammals, as brain size increases, the proportion of the brain devoted to association rather than primary regions also increases. Some association areas receive inputs from only one primary area, and other regions receive inputs from multiple primary regions. Anything that we think of as a higher-level function, such as thought, decision-making, art, or music, originates in association cortices.

Issues in Hominin Brain Evolution

The complexity of the human brain suggests an evolutionary history that is equally complex. Given that brains themselves are not preserved in the fossil record, evolutionary investigations have focused in particular on issues related to brain size, the relative size of different parts of the brain, and those aspects of functional organization that can be reconstructed from fossil remains. It is important to note, however, that advances in brain imaging and molecular neurobiology are changing the way scientists look at brain evolution. The next few decades promise to be exciting ones in the field of hominin brain evolution.

Humans Have "Large" Brains

One of the defining features of the genus *Homo,* and especially of our own species, is large brain size (Allen, 2009). But what do we mean by "large"? In absolute terms, the human brain weighs in at about 1,300 g, and human cranial capacities usually are reported to be in the region of 1,300 to 1,400 cc. These are average figures, and there is much variation in brain size. However, for purposes of cross-species comparisons, the 1,350-cc estimate for the volume of the typical human brain is good enough.

Look at the cranial capacities of various primates listed in Table 14.1. As you can see, humans have the largest brains among primates. The second largest brains belong to the gorillas. Among the Old World monkeys, baboons appear to have relatively large brains. As discussed in Chapter 6, among the New World monkeys, spider monkeys have substantially larger brains than their close relatives, howler monkeys. To put these data in a broader zoological context, cattle have brains of about 486 cc and horses of about 609 cc—somewhat larger than that seen in a great ape (Figure 14.5). The bottle-nosed dolphin has a brain volume of about 1,118 cc, which is nearly human-sized (Hofman, 1988).

Many scientists find absolute brain size values to be of limited usefulness in understanding brain evolution or the relationship between brain size and behavior. After all, it comes as no surprise that bigger animals have bigger brains than smaller animals, but just because a big animal has a big brain does not mean that the animal is more intelligent. For many years, scientists have tried to determine ways to measure brain size relative to body size. Researchers such as Harry Jerison (1991) and Robert Martin (1983) have shown that the relationship between brain size and body size is somewhat more complicated than a simple linear relationship. By looking at large numbers of mammal species, they derived equations that allow us to calculate

primary cortex Regions of the cerebral cortex that are involved directly with motor control or sensory input.

association cortex Parts of the cerebral cortex where inputs from primary motor and sensory cortex are processed.

encephalization quotient (EQ) The ratio of the actual brain size of a species to its expected brain size based on a statistical regression of brain to body size based on a large number of species.

TABLE 14.1　Cranial Capacities, Body Weights, and EQs of Several Primate Species

Species	Cranial Capacity (cc)	Body Weight (kg)	EQ
APES			
Homo sapiens, male	1,424.5	71.9	4.32
Homo sapiens, female	1,285.2	57.2	4.64
Gorilla gorilla (gorilla), male	537.4	169.5	0.85
Gorilla gorilla (gorilla), female	441.4	71.5	1.34
Pan troglodytes (chimpanzee)	388.6	83.7	1.48
Pongo pygmaeus (orangutan), male	393.1	87.7	1.08
Pongo pygmaeus (orangutan), female	341.2	37.8	1.69
Hylobates lar (gibbon)	98.3	5.5	2.10
OLD WORLD MONKEYS			
Papio anubis (baboon), male	166.4	23.5	1.18
Papio anubis (baboon), female	141.4	11.9	1.69
Cercocebus albigena (gray-cheeked mangabey)	97.3	7.69	1.63
Colobus guerza (black and white colobus)	75.4	9.05	1.11
NEW WORLD MONKEYS			
Ateles geoffroyi (spider monkey)	126.4	6.00	2.55
Alouatta palliata (howler monkey)	62.8	6.55	1.18
Saimiri sciureus (squirrel monkey)	24.4	0.68	2.58

Note: Values from Kappelman (1996), using Martin's (1983) formula for EQ. New World monkey values calculated from Harvey et al. (1987). If male and female values are not shown, midpoint values between male and female averages are shown.

the expected brain size for a mammal of any size. The **encephalization quotient (EQ)** is a ratio of the actual brain size to the expected size. Thus mammals that have EQs greater than 1.00 have brains that are larger than expected for a mammal of their size; an EQ less than 1.00 means that it is smaller than expected.

Returning to Table 14.1, we see that humans have the largest brains not only in absolute but also in relative terms, as measured by the EQ. In general, anthropoid primates have EQs greater than 1.00, indicating that their brains are larger than would be expected for mammals of their size. So even though cattle and horses have brains that are ape-sized in absolute terms, their EQs are smaller than those of apes because of their larger body sizes. It is generally assumed that the larger brain size in anthropoid primates has evolved in conjunction with the evolution of complex social behavior and adaptation to the arboreal environment.

Can we say that mammals with higher EQs are in some sense "smarter" than those with lower EQs? Yes and no. Terrence Deacon (1997) points out that the encephalization quotient is derived from both brain size *and* body size and that there is a tendency to overlook the fact that animals face strong selection pressures that shape body size as well as brain size. Among dog breeds, for example, chihuahuas are more encephalized than German shepherds; artificial selection on chihuahuas has driven body size down at a faster rate than brain

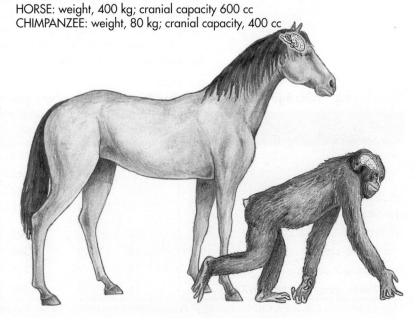

HORSE: weight, 400 kg; cranial capacity 600 cc
CHIMPANZEE: weight, 80 kg; cranial capacity, 400 cc

FIGURE 14.5　Chimpanzees and horses have brains that are similar in size.

FIGURE 14.6 Encephalization is a function of both brain size and body size.

size (Figure 14.6). But no one (except chihuahua fanciers) would argue that a chihuahua is smarter than a German shepherd. In anthropoids, small or even dwarfed species, such as the squirrel monkey in the New World or the talapoin monkey in the Old World, have high EQs. Again, rather than interpreting this as a sign of large brain size, we could also see it as an example of selection for small body size, which is probably more correct.

Brain Size and the Fossil Record

In previous chapters, you read that increasing brain size is a characteristic of genus *Homo*. A compilation of average cranial capacities of different hominin fossil taxa is presented in Table 14.2. (Please note that the *H. sapiens* values in Tables 14.1 on page 365 and 14.2 differ because they are based on different samples.) As you can see, the different groups can be sorted to some extent according to their cranial capacities and EQs.

Early Hominins and Robust *Australopithecus* Brain size increases from the early australopithecines (*A. afarensis* and *A. africanus*) to the "robust australopithecines," or *Paranthropus*. The early australopithecines have cranial capacities in the range of 400 to 500 cc, whereas the later *A. robustus* and *A. boisei* are in the 475 to 530 cc range. Are the robust australopithecines species more encephalized than the earlier australopithecines? Estimating body mass of fossilized individuals is very difficult and depends on how well sizes of available parts of the skeleton correlate to overall body size. EQs calculated for any individual fossil specimen therefore should be taken with a grain of salt. Henry McHenry (1992; see also Kappelman, 1996) estimates that *A. afarensis*, *A. africanus*, and *A. robustus* had male body sizes of 40 to 45 kg and female sizes of 30 to 32 kg; *A. boisei* was about 10% larger. These estimates indicate that these hominins were smaller than contemporary great apes; given that their cranial capacities were at least as large, we can conclude that gracile and robust australopithecines were indeed more encephalized than the great apes. In addition, the brain size increase seen in the robust forms relative to the earlier forms may reflect a further increase in encephalization. However, the reworking of the robust australopithecine skull in response to the biomechanical demands of hard object chewing could have increased cranial capacity without changing brain size. The relationship between cranial capacity and brain size varies somewhat across species, and the relatively small increase in cranial capacity we see in going from gracile to robust australopithecines may or may not have resulted in (or been the result of) more brain tissue (Allen, 2009).

TABLE 14.2 **Average Cranial Capacities for Fossil Hominins (adult specimens only)**

Taxon	Number of Specimens	Average Cranial Capacity (cc)	Range (cc)	Estimated EQ
A. afarensis	2	450	400–500	1.87
A. africanus	7	445	405–500	2.16
A. robustus and *A. boisei*	7	507	475–530	2.50
H. habilis	7	631	509–775	2.73–3.38
H. erectus	22	1,003	650–1,251	3.27
Archaic *H. sapiens*	18	1,330	1,100–1,586	3.52
H. neanderthalensis	19	1,445	1,200–1,750	4.04
Modern *H. sapiens* (older than 8,000 years)	11	1,490	1,290–1,600	5.27

Note: Estimated EQs are not derived using all the specimens included in the second column.
Sources: Aiello and Dean (1990), Kappelman (1996), and Holloway (1999).

Early *Homo* and *Homo erectus* Hominin fossils assigned to *Homo habilis* or early *Homo* have cranial capacities substantially larger on average (by 25–30%) than those seen in *Australopithecus* or the great apes (see Chapter 11). Although the smallest early *Homo* specimens (for example, KNM-ER 1813, which has a cranial capacity of 509 cc) and the largest gorillas may overlap in cranial size, the relatively small habiline body size, estimated by McHenry (1992) to be 52 kg for males and 32 kg for females, combined with the larger brain size, represents a clear increase in encephalization over earlier hominins. As you read earlier, the appearance of *H. habilis* roughly coincides with the appearance of stone tools in the archaeological record, providing evidence of at least one kind of cognitive evolution.

The average cranial capacity of fossils assigned to *H. erectus* shows an even more profound jump than *H. habilis* in both relative and absolute size compared with earlier hominin taxa. Although both brain and body size increased in *H. erectus*, brain size may have increased relatively more quickly leading to an increase in encephalization (Kappelman, 1996). As discussed in Chapter 12, *H. erectus* was widely distributed geographically and exhibited gradual change over its more than 1 million years in existence. On average, the earliest *H. erectus* specimens (such as KNM-ER 3883 and KNM-ER 3733) have smaller cranial capacities than do later specimens. Thus the range of cranial capacities seen in *H. erectus* specimens is quite large (from 650–1,250 cc), which is one reason that some investigators have justified splitting the taxon into two or more species.

Archaic *Homo sapiens*, Neandertals, and Modern *Homo sapiens* Cranial capacities in the modern range are found in both archaic *H. sapiens* and Neandertal specimens. Indeed, one of the apparent paradoxes of the later hominin fossil record is that Neandertal cranial capacities often exceed the average cranial capacity of modern humans (see Table 14.1 on page 365 and Table 14.2). Even the archaic *H. sapiens* mean is within the range of modern *H. sapiens*. The increase in average cranial capacity from *H. erectus* to the later *Homo* species is quite profound and undoubtedly exceeds any increase in body size. Thus the hominin trend for increasing brain size and encephalization continues—and even accelerates—through the appearance of archaic *H. sapiens* and Neandertals.

What about the apparent decline in brain size in modern humans compared with Neandertals and even with earlier modern humans? We should keep in mind that there may be some kind of sampling bias (for example, toward larger males); after all, we have only small numbers of fossils available to compare with large numbers of modern humans. More critically, John Kappelman (1996) points out that the larger body size of archaic *H. sapiens* and Neandertals, relative to modern humans, often is overlooked or underemphasized (see Chapter 12). Thus modern humans are more encephalized than Neandertals because their bodies are much smaller but their brains are almost as large as Neandertal brains (Figure 14.7).

Although Neandertal and modern human brains are similar in size, their overall shapes are quite different. Modern humans have brains that are much more globe-shaped than Neandertal archaic *Homo sapiens* brains (Lieberman et al., 2002; Bruner, 2004). This "globularization" may reflect in particular changes in the parietal lobes and the region around the border of the temporal and parietal lobes. Studies of endocasts of very young Neandertal and human children suggest that this difference in shape emerges very early, within the first year of life (Gunz et al., 2010). The globularization of the human brain thus appears to reflect a unique pattern of brain growth and development within primates, which may be distinct from changes in size.

((•[**Listen** to the **Podcast** "When Did We Become Mentally Modern?" on **myanthrolab**

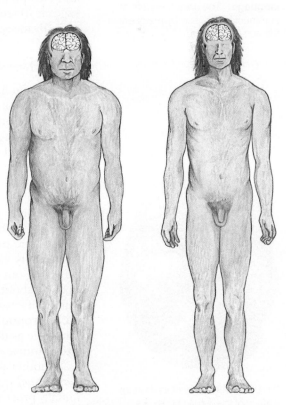

FIGURE 14.7 Although Neandertal brain sizes fall well within (or exceed) the modern human range, their EQ is lower than modern humans because they had larger bodies.

FIGURE 14.8 Cranial capacity has increased approximately fourfold over the past 3.5 million years of hominid evolution.

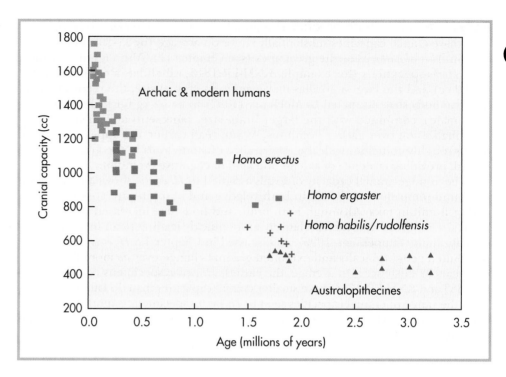

olfactory bulbs Knob-like structures located on the underside of the frontal lobes, that form the termination of olfactory nerves running from the nasal region to the brain.

language The unique system of communication used by members of the human species.

Brain size increase and increased encephalization have characterized hominin evolution over the past 3 to 4 million years (Figure 14.8). These trends have become more marked over the past 2 million years, as absolute brain size has nearly tripled. During the past 2 million years, increases in brain size have outpaced increases in body size, thus leading to increasingly encephalized hominins. Although brain size and encephalization are not everything, expanding brain size in the hominin lineage clearly reflects an adaptation, given how "expensive" brain tissue is (see Insights and Advances: The Ten-Percent Myth: Evolution and Energy).

Brain Reorganization

As the brain has expanded, its functional organization has also changed. Functional reorganization can occur in three ways. An anatomical region of the brain (linked to some function) can become larger or smaller compared with the rest of the brain. Functional regions of the brain can shift or change position, which may or may not be associated with regional expansion or contraction. Finally, new behaviors may lead to the evolution of new functional fields, which would supplant or enhance previously existing functional associations in those areas (as occurs with the development of a new complex behavior such as language; see below).

In the human brain, an example of size reorganization can be seen in the **olfactory bulbs,** which control our sense of smell; these are small, knob-like structures found on the bottom of the frontal lobes in each hemisphere (Figure 14.9). In humans, these measure only about 0.1 cc in volume (Stephan et al., 1981), reflecting our decreasing reliance on smell. In contrast, wolves have olfactory bulbs that are about 6 cc in volume, a sixty-fold advantage over the human-sized olfactory bulb. Olfactory reduction is characteristic of most haplorhine species (although more pronounced in humans); humans have olfactory bulbs that are about the same size as those found in strepsirhine species whose brains are only 1%–2% the size of human brains.

Another part of the human brain that has undergone reorganization is the *primary visual region*, the part of the brain where visual information from the eyes is initially processed. Although it is present in the *occipital lobes* (the rear portion of the cerebrum) in both humans and other primates, in humans the primary visual region is located in a sulcus on the inner surface of the lobe, whereas in primates the primary visual cortex encompasses most of the lobe's outer surface. Furthermore, the

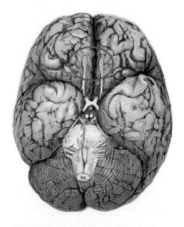

FIGURE 14.9 View of the bottom surface of the human brain. The olfactory bulbs are small structures located on the underside of the frontal lobes.

insights & advances
THE TEN-PERCENT MYTH: EVOLUTION AND ENERGY

We have all heard the myth that we humans use only 10 percent of our brains. Indeed, it is apparent that not only have many people heard it, but they believe it. The origins of this idea are vague, but it has been around for quite some time (Beyerstein, 1999). One of the first groups that latched onto and spread the myth was the early self-improvement ("positive thinking") industry. For example, a 1929 advertisement states that "scientists and psychologists tell us that we use only about TEN PERCENT of our brain power" and that by enrolling in the course being advertised, a person might tap some of that brain that is not being used. The advertisement uses the 10 percent figure as though it were common knowledge. Barry Beyerstein (1999) has tried to identify the "scientists and psychologists" who may have said something like this, but specific references to it in the literature are nonexistent. Whatever "scientists and psychologists" may have thought in 1900, there is plenty of evidence today from neurology and psychology indicating that the 10 percent figure is wholly untenable; it is basically neuro-nonsense.

One of the most compelling arguments against the 10 percent myth comes from the perspective of energy and evolution. The brain uses a lot of energy. In humans, it accounts for about 2 percent of the body mass but uses about 16 percent to 20 percent of the total energy and oxygen consumed by the body. It is an "expensive tissue" (Aiello and Wheeler, 1995). The brain cannot store significant energy reserves and is extremely vulnerable if the oxygen supply is cut off.

From an evolutionary standpoint, maintaining such an expensive organ only to use 10 percent of it does not make any sense. When you consider that there are other costs associated with large brain size, such as birth difficulties; (see Chapter 15), if we used only 10 percent of the brain, there would have been substantial fitness benefits in reducing the brain to a more efficient and less costly size. This did not happen, of course, as brain expansion has characterized evolution in genus *Homo.*

Leslie Aiello and Peter Wheeler point out that the brain is not the only expensive tissue in the body. The heart, kidney, liver, and gastrointestinal tract consume at least as much energy as the brain. Human bodies use energy at about the rate that would be expected for a mammal our size. Given that our brains are much larger than would be expected for a mammal our size, how do we maintain the expected energy consumption rate? Aiello and Wheeler argue that a trade-off with one of the other expensive tissues has occurred. Specifically, at the same time as the brain has increased in size in human evolution, it appears that the stomach and intestines have decreased in size. These size reductions presumably have been accompanied by a reduction in energy use. The smaller gastrointestinal tract also indicates a reliance on higher-quality, easier-to-digest foods (such as meat).

The complex relationship between behavior, brain size, diet, and gut size is one of the most fascinating problems in the study of human evolution. Although it is tempting to see brain size and gut size as engaged in a neat trade-off, the situation probably was a bit more complex than that. Nonetheless, Aiello and Wheeler make clear that we have to pay for what we have: a large, energy-hungry brain. And a brain that wastes 90 percent of its volume could never have evolved.

---

visual cortex is smaller than we would expect for a primate brain its size: It is only about 1.5 times larger than the visual cortex of a chimpanzee or gorilla, whereas the brain as a whole is about three times larger (Stephan et al., 1981). The reduction and shift of the visual region in primates presumably has allowed the expansion of the parietal association cortex, a region where sensory information from different sources is processed and synthesized. It may be possible to track some organizational changes in the brain by studying brain endocasts from fossil specimens (Figure 14.10), although this is an area of study that has prompted much debate over the years (Allen et al., 2006).

Language: Biology and Evolution

Much of what makes human behavior more complex and more sophisticated than the behavior of other animals depends on our possession of spoken **language.** Language is an adaptation. It is easy to imagine that a social group of hominins who possess language would have an advantage over a social group of hominins who did not. But language ability is as much an anatomical as a behavioral adaptation. As we will see, modern humans are shaped by natural selection—in the anatomy of their throats and respiratory system and in various aspects of the structure and function of their brains—to produce language.

FIGURE 14.10 Endocasts from South African australopithecines.

What is language? Language is the system of communication used by members of the human species. Although linguists differ on which features are most critical in defining language, they all tend to agree on certain critical aspects that make language a unique form of animal communication. Language is *spoken*, and we are anatomically specialized to produce language and to process language-oriented sounds. Language is *semantic*: The words we use when speaking have meanings that represent real-world objects, events, or actions. Language is *phonemic*. Words are made from small sound elements called phonemes; there is no biological limit to the number of words that can be formed from phonemes and there is no intrinsic association between a word and the object or concept it represents. Finally, language is *grammatical*. All languages have a grammar, an implicit set of rules that governs the way word classes are defined and used. Although there may be a limit on the number of words a person can know, there is no limit on the ways they may be grammatically linked together. Grammar allows *recursion*, the ability to string together clauses in a sentence, or to embed clauses one within another. Some cognitive scientists believe that recursion in language reflects the unique ability of the human mind to keep track of multiple ideas, objects, and processes all at the same time. As a child acquires its first language, he or she assimilates the grammatical rules of language subconsciously.

◉ Watch the **Animation** "Major Language Areas of the Brain" on **myanthrolab**

Language in the Brain

We can define a *language area* of the brain as any part of the brain that is activated during the production or comprehension of speech. The classical language regions are found around the left (in the vast majority of people) Sylvian fissure, or *perisylvian language area* (Figure 14.11). In the frontal lobe, there is *Broca's area*. As we saw earlier, a lesion in Broca's area causes a disruption in speech production (an *aphasia*), yet comprehension remains intact. At the posterior end of the Sylvian fissure, spanning the top of the temporal lobe and the bottom of the parietal lobe, is another language area that was identified by German physician Carl Wernicke in 1874. *Wernicke's area* lesions cause a person to have difficulties in speech comprehension. People with Wernicke's area aphasia produce fluent but nonsensical speech, substituting one word for another or producing incomprehensible strings of words. Wernicke predicted that because it is likely that his area and Broca's area are in communication, different lesions in the white matter joining the two should produce aphasias with different symptoms. These *conduction aphasias* have been observed; for example, a lesion in the projection from Wernicke's area to Broca's area causes someone to produce fluent, nonsensical speech while retaining comprehension (Damasio & Damasio, 1989). Wernicke's insights about conduction aphasias taught us to think about language as the product of interactive networks in the brain rather than of just one or two areas.

Language Lateralization When a function of the brain typically and consistently occurs in only one of the hemispheres, we say that function is *lateralized*. In 95% of people, the perisylvian language area is in the left hemisphere. Most people are also

FIGURE 14.11 The major language areas of the left hemisphere of the brain. The connection between Wernicke's and Broca's areas passes through the angular gyrus.

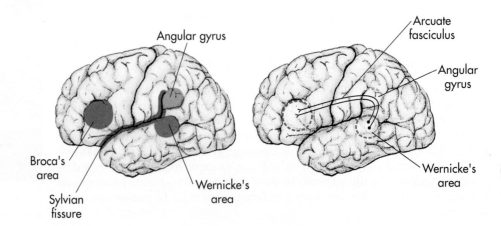

right-handed, and because motor control of one side of the body is housed in the opposite side of the brain, it is very likely that right-handedness and language ability evolved in tandem. The classical view that both language and right-handedness are associated with the left hemisphere has led to the notion of left hemisphere dominance over the right hemisphere (except in about half of the left-handers—who make up about 10% of the population—who have right hemisphere dominance).

Although it is easy to focus on the classical left perisylvian regions as the seat of language, keep in mind that lesions in other parts of the brain also disrupt normal speech. Lesions in the right hemisphere (of people with left hemisphere language dominance) disrupt the musical or *prosodic* elements of speech. Prosody is essential for speech to sound normal; otherwise, it would have the flat sound of computer-synthesized speech.

Language in the Throat

Although there is little evidence that evolving language capabilities has cost us anything in terms of brain function—just the opposite, in fact—it is quite clear that the rearrangement of the anatomy of our throats for language purposes has introduced new risks in everyday life that our ancestors did not have to worry about (Laitman, 1984; Lieberman, 1991). To offset these risks, there must have been a strong selective advantage for the development of language abilities over the course of hominin evolution.

The *supralaryngeal airway* is a more precise way to describe the parts of the throat and head that have undergone changes during hominin evolution (Figure 14.12). As the name suggests, it is that part of the airway that is above the *larynx*, or voice box. The larynx sits at the top of the *trachea* and has vocal folds (vocal cords), which can modulate the passage of air through the trachea to produce different sounds. The cavity above the larynx, at the back of the mouth, is known as the *pharynx*. The posterior part of the tongue, the epiglottis, and the soft palate form the boundaries of the pharynx.

When we compare the supralaryngeal airway of a human with that of a more typical mammal, such as a chimpanzee, we can see several differences that have profound functional implications (Figure 14.12). First, the larynx in humans is much lower than in other mammals. The new position of the larynx leads to an expansion of the pharynx. This expanded pharynx's anterior wall is formed uniquely in humans by a shortened and rounded tongue, is much more efficient for modifying the stream of air passing through the larynx to generate a greater variety of sounds, leading to fully articulate speech. These changes in anatomy have a profound cost; however, they greatly increase the risk of choking on food or liquid. There is too much distance between the human larynx and nasal cavity for a sealed connection to form between the two, as it does in the typical mammal. The epiglottis and soft palate are separated by the rear part of the tongue. Everything we swallow must pass over the incompletely sealed opening of the larynx, which greatly increases the risk of choking and suffocation. Interestingly, human babies less than 1 year old have a supralaryngeal anatomy that more closely resembles the mammalian norm. This allows them to drink, swallow, and

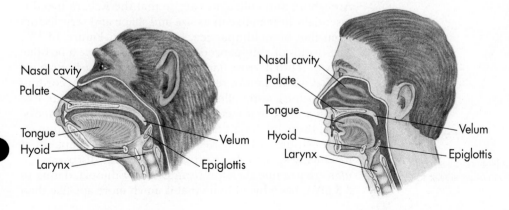

FIGURE 14.12 The supralaryngeal airway in a chimpanzee and a human. Note the relatively low position of the larynx in the human and how the back of the thickened and shortened tongue forms the front part of the pharynx.

Nasal cavity
Palate
Tongue
Hyoid
Larynx
Velum
Epiglottis

Nasal cavity
Palate
Tongue
Hyoid
Larynx
Velum
Epiglottis

hyoid bone A small "floating bone" in the front part of the throat that is held in place by muscles and ligaments.

breathe at the same time, which greatly enhances their suckling ability. During the second year, the larynx begins the shift to the adult position, which increases their risk of choking while increasing their ability to produce articulate speech. Darwin noted in *On the Origin of Species* that the position of the trachea in the human throat was an example of natural selection working with what history makes available to it.

Language Ability and the Fossil Record

The brain and supralaryngeal tract—anatomical structures that demonstrate most clearly our adaptations associated with the production of spoken language—are composed primarily of soft tissues that do not fossilize. However, we do have endocasts, which might preserve information about gross changes in the brain that might be associated with the development of language. In addition the supralaryngeal tract is connected by muscles and ligaments to bony structures at the base of the cranium and in the neck. It is possible some insights into the evolution of the soft tissues of the throat may be gained by examining these bony structures.

Endocasts and the Evolution of Brain Asymmetries Language in the brain is associated with a leftward lateralization of function. Is it possible that asymmetries in gross brain structure may be pronounced enough that they can be seen in endocasts, indicating the possible origins of spoken language in the fossil record?

For example, researchers have looked for evidence of asymmetry in Broca's area. The endocast of 1470 (*H. habilis*) has a well-preserved left inferior frontal region (the location of Broca's area). Anthropologists interested in hominin endocasts tend to agree that 1470 resembles humans more than pongids in the region corresponding to Broca's area (Holloway, 1976, 1999; Falk, 1983b; Tobias, 1987). A similar claim has been made for a more recently discovered Indonesian *H. erectus* specimen, Sambungmacan 3 (Broadfield et al., 2001). Although this specimen has protrusions in the inferior frontal lobe on both left and right hemispheres, the total size of the protrusion is larger in the left hemisphere, indicating the possible presence of a Broca's area in that hemisphere. These asymmetries may indicate the development of spoken language (or its precursors) in species ancestral to modern *Homo sapiens*.

Hyoid Bone According to some investigators, the bony remains—especially the base of the cranium—of fossil hominins yield real clues to the form and position of the supralaryngeal tract, offering insights into the vocal abilities of these earlier hominins (Laitman and Reidenburg, 1988). However, most of these claims are somewhat controversial and reflect the inherent difficulty of reconstructing complex soft tissue structures from fossil remains (Arensburg et al., 1990).

A potentially more direct source of evidence about the speech abilities of extinct hominins has come with the discovery of a Neandertal **hyoid bone** from Kebara Cave, Israel, dating to about 60,000 years ago (Arensburg et al., 1990). The hyoid is a small, free-floating bone (that is, it does not articulate with any other bones) that sits in the throat in front of the larynx and in close association (via muscles and ligaments) with the mandible, larynx, and other structures. Arensburg and colleagues argue that the Kebara hyoid is essentially human-like in its size and shape and very distinct from that of a chimpanzee, for example (Figure 14.13). The hyoids of chimpanzees and other apes have a box-like body with two narrow, flaring horns, whereas the human hyoid has a much more regular horseshoe shape. According to Arensburg and colleagues, its position was human-like within a neck that was similar in length to human necks. Thus, they conclude that the larynx was also in a human-like position and that Neandertals were fully capable of producing speech. In contrast, the recently discovered *A. afarensis* juvenile skeleton from Dikika, Ethiopia, dating to 3.3 MYA, has a hyoid bone that is much more ape-like than

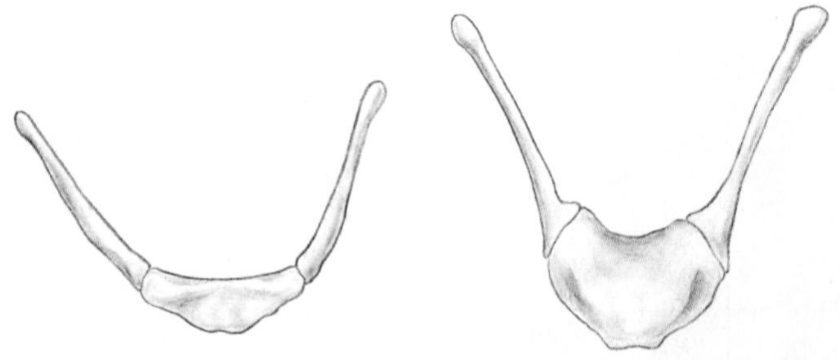

FIGURE 14.13 The hyoid bone from a Neandertal and a chimpanzee. The Neandertal hyoid is much more similar to those found in modern humans.

human-like (Alemseged et al., 2006). If hyoid shape is indeed a good indicator of spoken language ability, then it would seem it is a behavior that had not evolved in the earlier australopithecines.

Scenarios of Language Evolution

The absence of direct evidence concerning the evolution of language ability means that there are many theories or models for how it might have occurred (Hewes, 1999). For example, it has been suggested that language "piggy-backed" on throwing ability (improved hunting efficiency), which is another activity associated with hand-edness (Calvin, 1983); that it replaced grooming as a social facilitator in increasingly large groups (Dunbar, 1997); or that it critically enhanced the formation of exclusive reproductive relationships in the context of multimale/multifemale social groups (Deacon, 1997). Most of these suggestions are untestable, although it is possible to assess the plausibility of some of the claims based on contemporary data. It is safe to say that no single model or theory of language origins is accepted by the majority of anthropologists, psychologists, or linguists, and that we can expect many more models to be put forth in the coming years that will incorporate new insights into the nature of brain and language.

The Evolution of Human Behavior

Studying the evolution of the human brain and language serves as a foundation for developing a broader understanding of the evolution of human behavior in general. Human behavior is, of course, an enormous topic, and we can only touch on a few aspects of its evolution in this chapter. However, let us begin by considering the ways in which biological anthropologists analyze the evolution of human behavior.

The Evolution of Human Behavior: Four Approaches

Anthropologists and other scientists use varied approaches to study the evolution of human behavior, depending on their particular research interests and training (Figure 14.14). Four of the most common approaches are paleontological

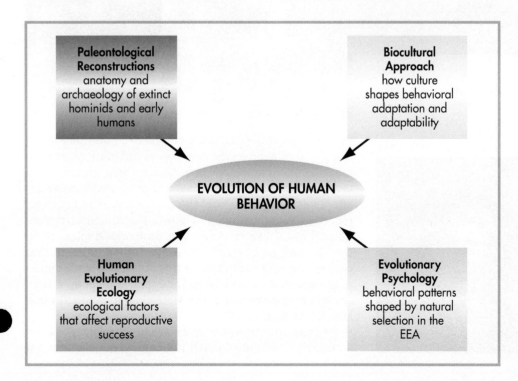

FIGURE 14.14 Four approaches to studying the evolution of human behavior.

INNOVATIONS
Music, the Brain, and Evolution

Music is a cross-cultural universal. If we survey the world's cultures, we will find that people engage in vocal behaviors that use standardized tones (notes) and rhythmic patterns; these elements form the basis of musical production. The notes and rhythms are not the same in all cultures, just as the phonemes employed in different languages are not all the same, but it is possible to recognize musical behavior as distinct from other kinds of behaviors (e.g., talking versus singing; walking versus dancing). In our culture, a sharp line can be drawn between musicians and nonmusicians, reflecting differences in formal or informal training or professional status. It is important to remember, however, that almost everyone can sing or dance at some level, even if there are great individual differences in competence (Peretz, 2006).

Over the past decade, neuroscientists, with their growing arsenal of imaging tools, have become increasingly interested in music and the brain. What evidence is

there for the biological basis of music? First, there is the existence of people who have great difficulty producing or recognizing music, even with extensive training; this is a condition known as *amusia*, or tone deafness, and it affects about 4 percent of the population. The congenital absence of this ability suggests that the more typical human brain has structures or networks dedicated to the recognition of tones. Imaging studies indicate that part of the right frontal lobe (the inferior frontal gyrus) is important for processing tone, and that people with amusia may have reduced neuronal connections in this area (Hyde et al., 2006).

At the other extreme, there are people who have *perfect pitch*, an ability to identify musical notes without a reference tone. Only a small proportion of all trained musicians have perfect pitch. Many famous musicians and composers had it (among them Mozart, Beethoven, and Jimi Hendrix), but many others did not. The existence of people with perfect pitch suggests an elaboration of the structures in the more typical brain dedicated to musical ability. Anatomical studies suggest that there are differences between musicians, those with and those without perfect pitch, in the regions of the temporal lobe associated with processing sound (Schlaug et al., 1995). In addition, Robert Zatorre has used functional brain imaging to show that when identifying tones, people with perfect pitch use their working memory differently than those without it (Zatorre, 2003).

Both amusia and perfect pitch likely reflect the individual differences in musical ability with which people are born; however, neuroscientists are also interested in looking at the effects of formal musical training on brain structure. Producing music requires integrating mental and physical operations—such as memory, reading, and complicated hand and arm movements—into the production of sound that must be simultaneously self-monitored by listening (Gaser & Schlaug, 2003). One area of the brain that appears to reflect intensive musical training is the anterior part of the corpus callosum. This part of the *corpus callosum* includes the connections between the motor regions of the frontal lobes of the two hemispheres. Gottfried Schlaug (2001) has found that this region is bigger in musicians who began musical training before the age of 7 years as compared to those who started training at a later age. He suggests that the development of the fibers of the corpus callosum reflects the plasticity of the brain during childhood, and

that greater connections between these two regions may be a result of the coordinated bimanual action required in keyboard and string playing.

What about the evolution of musical ability? We have seen that there is individual variation in musical ability that is both biologically and genetically based. Such variability is the possible raw material for selection to have acted on, if musical ability was a kind of adaptation. Some researchers, such as the cognitive scientist Steven Pinker, see music as the evolutionary equivalent of cheesecake—we like it, but it simply takes advantage of senses and abilities that are in place for other reasons. For example, spoken language also employs rhythm and tone, so it is possible that musical ability arises from those abilities without being specifically selected for. In terms of selection, many researchers have pointed out that vocal calling, as seen in gibbons, is usually the result of sexual selection (Geissman, 2000). Could singing be a product of sexual selection? It's possible, but if so, it would be competing with sexual selection that is operating in several other potential domains (e.g., body size and shape, provisioning ability, even language ability itself). It has also been suggested that the rhythmic qualities of music work to enhance group solidarity and it may have been selected for in that context.

There is still much to be learned about the biological basis and origins of music. People sing, dance, and chant for many reasons and in many contexts, ranging from the ridiculous to the sublime. Whatever the evolutionary history of music, it remains a quintessentially human activity.

evolutionary psychology
Approach to understanding the evolution of human behavior that emphasizes the selection of specific behavioral patterns in the context of the environment of evolutionary adaptedness.

environment of evolutionary adaptedness (EEA)   According to evolutionary psychologists, the critical period for understanding the selective forces that shape human behavior; exemplified by hunter-gatherer lifestyles of hominids before the advent of agriculture.

human evolutionary ecology
Approach to understanding the evolution of human behavior that attempts to explore ecological and demographic factors important in determining individual reproductive success and fitness in a cultural context.

bridewealth   Payment offered by a man to the parents of a woman he wants to marry.

reconstructions of behavior, biocultural approaches, evolutionary psychology, and human evolutionary (or behavioral) ecology. The examples covered in this chapter make use of the latter three approaches.

Paleontological Reconstructions of Behavior   In Chapters 10 to 13 we discussed several reconstructions of the behavior of earlier hominins. These reconstructions were based on the anatomy of extinct hominins and, when present, the archaeological remains with which they were associated. They were also based on correlations among behavior, anatomy, and ecology we have observed in nonhuman primate species and in contemporary humans, especially those living under traditional hunter–gatherer conditions. Any reconstruction of the behavior of our hominin ancestors is a synthesis of both paleontological and contemporary data.

Biocultural Approaches   It is clear that human cultural behavior has influenced human evolution. One aspect of human behavior that we have already discussed in detail—language—is a prime example. Other examples include the adoption of slash-and-burn agriculture, which had an indirect effect on the evolution of the sickle cell polymorphism, and the development of dairying in some populations, which was a direct selective factor in the evolution of lactose tolerance (Chapter 6). As we will see below, there are instances where human biology may influence patterns of behavior observed across different human cultures.

Evolutionary Psychology   The relatively new discipline of **evolutionary psychology** is characterized by an adherence to three main principles. First, human and animal behavior is not produced by minds that are general-purpose devices. Rather, the mind is composed of cognitive modules with an underlying neuroanatomical basis that express specific behaviors in specific situations. Language and visual processing are prime examples of this kind of modular processing, but evolutionary psychologists believe that almost any adaptive behavior (say, a fear response to a snake moving in the grass) could be considered in modular terms. Second, cognitive modules are complex design features of organisms. Because natural selection is the only way to evolve complex design features, evolutionary psychology focuses on understanding behaviors or cognitive modules as adaptations. Third, for most of our history, humans and hominins have lived in small groups as hunter-gatherers. Evolutionary psychologists believe that our evolved behavior may reflect or should be interpreted in terms of this hypothetical **environment of evolutionary adaptedness (EEA)** (Barkow et al., 1992; Tooby and Cosmides, 2000).

Human Evolutionary (or Behavioral) Ecology   In contrast to evolutionary psychology, which focuses more on psychological experiments and surveys of people living in developed countries, **human evolutionary ecology** focuses on the ecological factors that influence reproductive success in the few remaining hunter–gatherer populations. Among the groups studied most intensely have been the Yanomamö of Amazonia (Chagnon, 1988, 1997), the Aché of Paraguay (Hill & Hurtado, 1996), and the Hadza of Tanzania (Hawkes et al., 2001). Topics of interest to human evolutionary ecologists include the relationship between status and reproductive success, demographic effects of tribal warfare and aggression, and the underlying social impact of hunting and food sharing. Researchers use data on contemporary hunter–gatherer groups to refine models that purport to reconstruct the behavior of extinct hominins (Marlowe, 2005).

Traditional Lives in Evolutionary Ecological Perspective

Over the past four decades, human evolutionary ecologists have undertaken intensive study of traditional cultures to better understand the interplay between biological and cultural factors in human behavior and human behavioral evolution

(Figure 14.15). Studies of traditional hunter–gatherers and traditional agricultural cultures are important because their lifestyles reflect more closely the natural selection environments (the EEA) that shaped hominin evolution, until the advent of agriculture and large-scale societies starting about 10,000 years ago.

Wealth, Reproductive Success, and Survival

One of the basic tenets of human evolutionary ecology is that cultural success should be related to increased fitness (Irons, 1979). William Irons tested this hypothesis in a study of fertility and mortality among the tribal Turkmen of Iran. In this culture, wealth (in terms of money, jewelry, and consumable goods) is a primary measure of cultural success. Irons found that for men, fertility and survivorship were higher for the wealthier half of the population than for the poorer half (Figure 14.16); survivorship was significantly higher for the wealthier women, but there was no difference in fertility. He also found that reproductive success was more variable among men than among women (that is, the difference between the richer and poorer halves was more pronounced for men than for women), as predicted by sexual selection theory.

Monique Borgerhoff Mulder (1987, 1990) looked at the relationship between wealth and reproductive success in a different population, the Kipsigis of Kenya (Figure 14.17 on page 378). The Kipsigis are a pastoral people who moved into Kenya from northeastern Africa in the late eighteenth century. The wealth of a Kipsigis man is defined in terms of his land holdings, the number of animals he has, and his household possessions. Borgerhoff Mulder found that all these measures correlate strongly to amount of land owned, so she used that as her primary statistic of wealth.

The Kipsigis practice *polygyny*, which means that a man can have more than one wife at a time. When a man wants to marry a young woman, he approaches her parents with an offer of **bridewealth,** a payment that can equal up to a third of an average man's wealth. Borgerhoff Mulder looked at wealth and reproductive success among Kipsigis men in a series of different age groups and found a strong correlation between wealth and number of offspring. For example, in a group of forty-four men who were circumcised between 1922 and 1930 (circumcision marks coming of age), there was a very high correlation between number of offspring and acres of land

FIGURE 14.15 Evolutionary ecologists live and do research in contemporary cultures that maintain all or some aspects of their traditional lifeways, such as these tribespeople from New Guinea.

FIGURE 14.16 Male Turkmen in the wealthier half of the population had higher fertility rates than those in the poorer half.

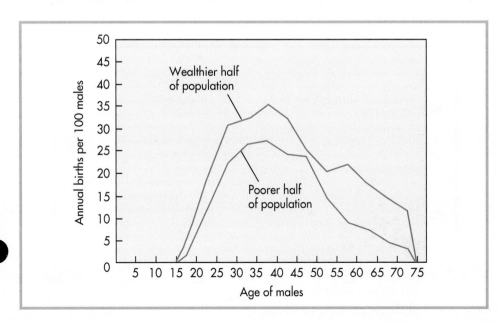

FIGURE 14.17   The Kipsigis of Kenya.

owned (Figure 14.18). Ownership of 30 acres correlated to having fifteen to twenty surviving offspring, whereas men with 90 acres had twenty-five to thirty offspring. In general, the fertility of the wives of richer and poorer men was approximately the same. Wealthier men have more children because they can have more wives, being able to afford more bridewealth payments. And although larger families may lead to increased wealth, Borgerhoff Mulder found no evidence that this was the causal direction: Wealthier men were able to afford large families, not the other way around.

The Turkmen and Kipsigis studies, and others done elsewhere, support the hypothesis that one measure of cultural success—wealth—correlates with reproductive success. However, this correlation does not generally hold for developed, urbanized, capitalist cultures, where higher socioeconomic status typically is not associated with a higher birth rate. This is an important example of the kind of fundamental biocultural change that can occur in a society when it transforms from an undeveloped to a developed economy.

Physiology and Ecology

Another method for quantifying the relationship between cultural and ecological factors in human behavior is to look at the way physiological measures vary across ecological contexts. For example, Peter Ellison (1990, 1994) developed a method of measuring levels of reproductive hormones in saliva as a noninvasive means to assess reproductive function in women living in diverse environments.

Progesterone is a steroid hormone produced by the corpus luteum and the placenta that prepares the uterus for pregnancy and helps maintain pregnancy once fertilization has occurred. Progesterone levels measured in saliva correlate with ovarian function. Ellison and his colleagues found that salivary progesterone levels are strongly correlated with age over the course of a woman's reproductive life (between about ages 15 and 50 years). Progesterone levels increase from a baseline level at the end of puberty, peaking between 25 and 30 years of age, and dropping off thereafter. Ellison suggests that ovarian function matures at approximately the same age as the pelvis becomes structurally mature (early to mid-20s).

Studies among two traditional agricultural groups, the Lese of Zaire and the Tamang of Nepal, and women from the Boston area, showed that the basic age-dependent curve of salivary progesterone production was the same in all three

FIGURE 14.18   The relationship between number of acres a Kipsigis man owns and the number of offspring he has during his lifetime.

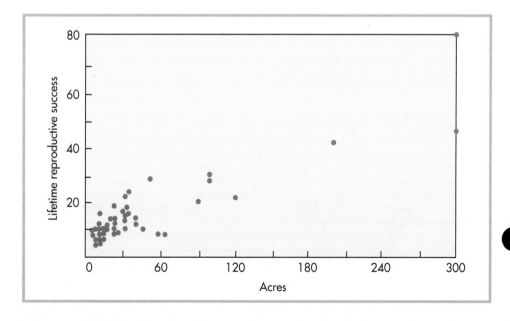

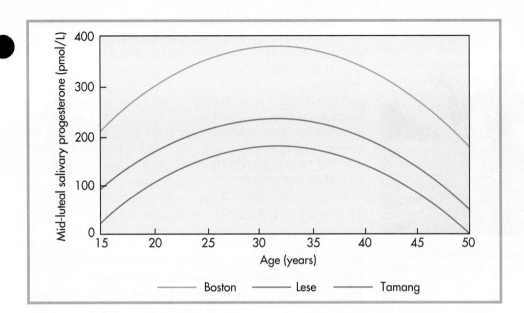

FIGURE 14.19 The age-dependent curve of salivary progesterone levels in three populations.

populations (Figure 14.19). Ellison believes that this pattern probably represents a fundamental feature of human reproductive physiology. This discovery refines our view of the female reproductive years as an evolved life-history stage (beginning at menarche and ending at menopause).

Although the shapes of the progesterone-versus-age curves were the same in Boston, Lese, and Tamang women, the amount of progesterone produced varied among the groups. Boston women, who presumably had the most nutritionally rich environment with few infectious diseases, had higher progesterone levels at every age than were found in the other two populations. Ellison suggests that chronic stress that delays growth and maturation, such as nutritional deficiencies, could lead to lower levels of ovarian function throughout the lifetime. Such a stress-response relationship could be adaptive because in a stressful environment it may be better to devote more effort and energy to body maintenance and survival rather than reproduction.

Another steroid hormone whose levels can be measured in saliva is **testosterone.** Testosterone is produced primarily in the testes and ovaries; it is known as the "male hormone" since the testes produce about 10 times as much as the ovaries, and testosterone is primarily responsible for the development of the primary male sexual characteristics in the fetus and the secondary characteristics at puberty. It has also been hypothesized that testosterone is an important modulator of behavior, especially in the context of male dominance and reproductive behavior. Much evidence for this hypothesis has been gathered from studies of numerous mammal species, but what is the situation in humans?

One way to test the hypothesis claiming that testosterone influences behaviors related to male–male competition and mate-seeking behavior is to compare testosterone levels in men who are in a committed relationship with those who are single. T. C. Burnham (2003) and his colleagues found that in a sample of 122 American business school students, men who were married or in a committed relationship had 21% lower salivary testosterone levels than those who were single. Peter Gray and his colleagues (2006) looked at testosterone levels in a group of men in Beijing, China, and they found that married non-fathers had slightly lower levels than unmarried men but the difference did not reach statistical significance; however, they did find that married fathers had significantly lower levels than either of the other two groups. In a study in East Africa, Martin Muller and his colleagues (2009) compared testosterone levels between non-fathers and fathers in Hadza foragers and in Datoga pastoralists. Hadza fathers are much more involved in paternal care than Datoga fathers, thus Muller and his colleagues predicted that in the Hadza, testosterone levels should be lower in fathers rather than non-fathers, while in the Datoga, there should be no difference. This is exactly what they found: The intensive childcare given by Hadza fathers appears to suppress testosterone production. Note that there was no overall difference in testosterone levels between the Hadza and Datoga men.

progesterone A steroid hormone produced by the corpus luteum and the placenta that prepares the uterus for pregnancy and helps maintain pregnancy once fertilization has occurred.

testosterone A steroid produced primarily in the testes and ovaries, and at a much higher level in men than in women. Responsible for the development of the male primary and secondary sexual characteristics. Strongly influences dominance and reproductive behavior.

FIGURE 14.20 The evolutionary significance of "Man the Hunter" (or in this instance "Man the Fisher") has been debated for decades.

These studies demonstrate that testosterone levels vary in human males according to their marital/parental status, and that these patterns can be observed in a variety of biological and cultural groups. They support the hypothesis that testosterone level is a modulator of, or reacts to, an individual male's reproductive situation. Burnham and colleagues (2003) point out that since testosterone may impair immune function and encourage risk-taking, lower levels of testosterone in married men may help explain the fact that married men generally are healthier and have lower mortality than unmarried men.

Hunting, Gathering, and the Sexual Division of Labor

Recent research on contemporary hunter–gatherer groups has revolutionized our knowledge of how people without agriculture acquire the food they eat and how hunting and gathering patterns in hominins may have evolved. It has become increasingly clear that earlier speculations (Lee & DeVore, 1968) were based on inadequate understanding of hunter–gatherer lifeways. The concept of "man the hunter, woman the gatherer" reflects a division of labor between the sexes in all human cultures, but it is all too easy to turn it into a simplistic, stereotypical picture of evolved, hardwired gender roles (Bird, 1999; Panter-Brick, 2002). Furthermore, observing sex differences in food acquisition practices is not the same as explaining why they exist.

In almost every traditional foraging culture, both men and women devote a substantial portion of their time and energy to the search for and acquisition of food. And in almost every culture, despite the fact that they live in the same environment, men and women exploit different aspects of that environment when acquiring food, leading to a pronounced sexual division of labor, although not necessarily along the simplistic division that "men hunt and women gather." For example, among the aboriginal peoples of Mer Island in the Coral Sea, both men and women forage for food on the coral reef. Men concentrate on using large spears to kill large fish swimming around the edges of the reef while women walk the dry part of the reef, collecting shellfish or catching small fish or octopus with small spears (Figure 14.20). Women almost always succeed in bringing home a reasonable amount of food, whereas the men have much more variable success (Bird, 1999). In the Hadza of Tanzania, men concentrate on large game hunting while women focus almost exclusively on foraging for berries, nuts, fruits, and roots (O'Connell et al., 1992; Hawkes et al., 1997).

There are several models for the origins of the sexual division of labor. The *cooperative provisioning model,* based on the study of monogamous birds, predicts that the sexual division of labor occurred as a result of the evolution of monogamous relationships, because it would allow the pair to more fully exploit the environment if they did not compete with each other for resources (see discussion of Lovejoy's model in Chapter 10). An alternative model, the *conflict model,* suggests that hominin males and females were already exploiting the environment in fundamentally different ways before males began contributing energy and resources to females and their young (Bird, 1999). The "sexual division of labor" is not really a division but reflects the fact that males and females have different problems to overcome (conflicts) in the course of mating, reproduction, and parenting.

It is nonsensical to ask whether hunting *or* gathering is more important. Neither provides more energy than the other on a regular basis. The productivity of hunting and gathering varies by season, environment, and a host of other factors (Kaplan et al., 2000). Women and men do vary in the *package size* of the food they focus on acquiring. Women concentrate on small foodstuffs that tend to be predictable, immobile, and obtainable while caring for infants and young children. Even though she almost always receives assistance from others, including female relatives and the father of her children, an individual woman is responsible primarily for feeding herself and her children.

Men concentrate on obtaining foods in large sizes that they cannot consume at once by themselves and that they redistribute to families or the larger social group. These foods almost always come in the form of dead animals, which may be obtained by hunting, trapping, fishing, or even scavenging. In some Melanesian societies, however, men compete to grow the largest yams, which, although they are too fibrous to eat, can be distributed and used for propagation of new plants (Weiner, 1988). Big yams aside, animals provide protein and fat in quantities not available from any other source, and animal food is almost always highly prized in human cultures. As Hilliard Kaplan and colleagues (2000, p. 174) state, "The primary activity for adult males is hunting to provide nutrients for others . . . . [Hunting] is a fundamental feature of the human life-history adaptation."

Sexual Selection and Human Behavior

((•─ **Listen** to the **Podcast** "For Cave Women, Farmers Had Extra Sex Appeal" on **myanthrolab**

The sexual division of labor sits firmly within the broader context of sexual selection. As we discussed in Chapter 5, sexual selection was Darwin's other great idea about mechanisms underlying evolutionary change in animals, including humans. The study of human sexual behavior has been revolutionized over the past 25 years by investigators who take sexual selection seriously in our species. The development of an evolutionary perspective has informed our views on human reproductive strategies, sex and gender differences in behavior, and cross-cultural patterns of attractiveness and mate selection (Symons, 1979; Fisher, 1992; Buss, 2003). For example, research on human mate selection and standards of attractiveness in different cultures indicate that women tend to value resource-providing ability in their partners, whereas men tend to value youth and appearance (indicators of reproductive potential) in their potential partners (Buss, 2003). These observations are consistent with predictions derived from mammalian evolutionary biology. Of course, these are statistical patterns generated from surveys of large numbers of individuals. Obviously, different cultures define sexual attractiveness differently, and there is much individual variation in sexual preferences. Nonetheless, according to many evolutionary researchers, the statistical patterns of sexual behavior that are observed across cultures are not easily explained by cultural convergence. Instead, they may reflect underlying behavioral trends that have been shaped by natural selection. For example, it has long been noted that the behavior of young males—more so than an other age/sex category—is frequently at odds with accepted cultural norms. Why should this be the case?

Risk-Taking Behavior

Sex difference in risk-taking behavior has long been recognized, and found in several different behavioral domains. When we look across human cultures, we find that as a group young adult males (ages 15–29) have the highest death rates from accidents or violence (Figure 14.21). For example, death rates in motor vehicle accidents for 20-year-old Americans are three to four times higher in men than women (Hill & Chow, 2002). Young males do not die from accidents more often because they are unlucky but because they are more likely to put themselves in risky situations (Figure 14.22 on page 382). Beyond accidents, young, single males take greater financial risks with their money compared to their female counterparts (Jianakoplos & Bernasek, 1998). In addition, laboratory studies (in which risk taking is assessed with a simulation) suggest that men respond to an acute stress by increasing risk-taking

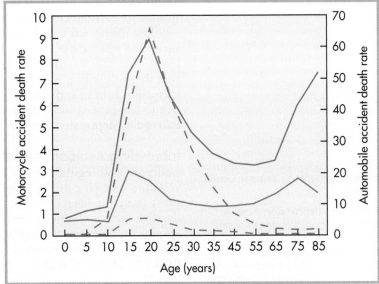

FIGURE 14.21 Risk of death from motorcycle accidents (dashed lines) and passenger car accidents (solid lines) per 100,000 U.S. population during 1980–1986 for males (green lines) and females (maroon lines).

FIGURE 14.22 Risk-taking behavior by young males.

behavior, while women become more risk-aversive. (Lighthall et al., 2009). Proclivity toward risk-taking behavior in males may reflect a significant sex difference in human behavior, which may have a long evolutionary history (Low, 2000).

Why should males engage in risk-taking behavior more than females? Bobbi Low (2000) argues that the reason goes back to general sex differences in mammalian biology. For a female mammal, the costs associated with risk-taking behavior are unlikely to outweigh the benefits. She is likely to be able to find mates and fulfill her reproductive potential throughout her lifetime, so she has no particular need to engage in risk-taking behavior to acquire mates. On the other hand, male mammals vary much more in reproductive success. A male mammal may engage in high-risk, potentially very costly (even life-threatening) activities because such behaviors could have a potentially high reproductive benefit. For example, aggressive behavior between male mammals over access to females is very common; it has clearly been selected for in the context of sexual access to mates. Females may also find risk-taking in males to be attractive because they may consider it a manifestation of ambition or "good genes" or a proxy for the ability to provide resources for the female and her offspring.

Elizabeth Hill and Krista Chow (2002) suggest that risky or binge drinking may also be understood in the context of sexual selection for risk-taking behavior. First, among college-age people, risky drinking is about 50% more common in men than women (48% versus 33%, although figures vary depending on criteria for defining a binge), and males are more likely to engage in driving after drinking. The peak age for alcohol abuse in males is 15 to 29 years. College men who were not married were twice as likely to engage in binge drinking as those who were married. These aspects of risky drinking in young men suggest to Hill and Chow that it is another manifestation of the evolved pattern of risk-taking behavior. They argue that risk-taking behaviors are not deviant but that we should recognize them as an evolved response to environmental instability. With specific reference to risky drinking at the individual level, Hill and Chow suggest that dealing with instability in the person's family or work life may be one avenue of therapy for the treatment for alcohol abuse.

Inbreeding Avoidance and Incest Taboos

Evolutionary factors may have played an important role in shaping not only mate choice preferences but also mate choice aversions. **Inbreeding** is defined as reproduction between close relatives. Close inbreeding has several major biological costs (Rudan & Campbell, 2004). A highly inbred population or species loses genetic variability over time. Reduced variability means that the population cannot respond quickly via natural selection to environmental change.

The likelihood that lethal or debilitating recessive alleles will be expressed is increased when close relatives interbreed. Because relatives share a high percentage of their alleles, there is a greater chance (compared to unrelated individuals) that they will both possess the same lethal recessives that may be passed on to their offspring. Inbred individuals suffer from greater mortality or loss of fitness relative to less-inbred individuals in the same species; this phenomenon is known as **inbreeding depression** (Mettler et al., 1988).

Inbreeding Avoidance and Incest Rules All human cultures have rules and traditions that regulate sexual contact and reproductive relationships. **Incest** is any violation of such rules by members of a kin group. Incest rules are sometimes explicit (stated in legal or customary form) and sometimes implicit (followed but not overtly stated or codified). Definitions of kin vary from culture to culture and do not always closely follow biological patterns of relatedness. For example, in American culture, sexual contact between stepparents and stepchildren, or between relatives linked by adoption, is generally regarded as being incestuous, although from a biological standpoint a pregnancy that resulted from such a mating would not constitute inbreeding.

Both cultural and biological scientists agree on the universality of cultural rules governing sexual relations between close kin—the *incest taboo*—but they differ on

inbreeding Mating between close relatives.

inbreeding depression Lesser fitness of offspring of closely related individuals compared with the fitness of the offspring of less closely related individuals, caused largely by the expression of lethal or debilitating recessive alleles.

incest A violation of cultural rules regulating mating behavior.

why it exists. For many years, Freudian ideas dominated cultural explanations of the incest taboo: Incest rules were necessary to prevent people from acting on their "natural" desire to commit incest. The evidence that people innately desire to commit incest is very slight, and the Freudian viewpoint, despite its historical popularity, has little cross-cultural, empirical support (Thornhill, 1991). Biological theories of inbreeding avoidance have focused on the fact that mechanisms that encourage outbreeding should be selected for; the cross-cultural universality of the incest taboo, which is essentially a mechanism for outbreeding, is taken to be evidence that such an adaptive mechanism may be present in the human species as a whole.

Brother–Sister Inbreeding and the Westermarck Hypothesis

Finnish anthropologist Edvard Westermarck (1891) long ago suggested, in what became known as the *Westermarck hypothesis,* that siblings raised together develop an aversion to seeing each other as reproductive partners when they are adults. In order for the aversion to develop, siblings must be in proximity to one another during a *critical period,* usually thought to encompass the first 5 years of life. The psychological mechanism governing this aversion may be an adaptation because it was probably selected for as a mechanism to promote outbreeding.

Evidence for the Westermarck hypothesis comes from a variety of sources, including some natural experiments. In the mid-twentieth century, the *kibbutz* movement in Israel led to the establishment of numerous small, independent communities dedicated to socialist and egalitarian principles. Similarly aged boys and girls were raised communally in "children's houses" in some of these kibbutzim (Shepher, 1983) (Figure 14.23). In his groundbreaking study, anthropologist Joseph Shepher found that of 2,769 marriages between children raised in kibbutzim, only 14 united couples had been reared in the same children's house. Shepher interpreted these results as strong evidence for the Westermarck hypothesis. The child-rearing arrangement in the kibbutz "fooled" biology (and the psychological mechanism leading to sexual aversion) by bringing unrelated children into close proximity with one another during the critical period. In usual circumstances, children raised in close proximity to one another are close relatives, and there should be strong selection pressures against them mating with one another. Thus kibbutz children raised in the same children's house saw each other as siblings and did not see their housemates as potential spouses.

Similar evidence supporting the Westermarck hypothesis has been obtained from the study of *sim-pua* marriages in Taiwan (Wolf, 1966, 1970). Sim-pua is a form of arranged marriage whereby a girl is adopted into a household at a young age and then later expected to marry a biological son of the same family when they are older. These marriages were found to have much higher rates of divorce and lower numbers of offspring than non–sim-pua marriages. Anthropologist Arthur Wolf, who conducted the research, suggests that these marriages often failed because of a sexual aversion that developed between the adopted sister and her brother/groom who were raised in close proximity during the critical period.

The Westermarck hypothesis is supported by evidence from these diverse natural experiments and is based on a strong theoretical foundation in the context of the biological costs of close inbreeding (although see Shor & Simchai, 2009 for a critique). It applies only to sibling inbreeding avoidance, of course. Clearly, different biological or cultural mechanisms would have to regulate intergenerational inbreeding avoidance.

We have traveled a great distance in this survey of the evolution of human behavior—from the neuron to the cultural rules governing the sexual behavior of close kin. The goal here has not been to provide a comprehensive rendering of how human behavior evolved, but to introduce some of the basic approaches to understanding this important topic. We will not really know the evolution of our species until we know how and why we behave the way we do. And we cannot understand human behavior fully until we understand the ecological and cultural contexts in which it evolved.

FIGURE 14.23 Children in a kibbutz.

Evolution of the Brain and Behavior

Evolution of the Human Brain

Issues of Complexity

- The increase in complexity of human behavior and cognition has been made possible by changes in the size and functional organization of the brain.

- Compared to other primates, human brains are larger in both absolute and relative size, although some brain structures are relatively smaller in humans.

- The fossil record provides a reasonably good record of changes in brain size over evolution, but only a small amount of information about changes in organization. **[pp 362–369]**

Language Is a Biological Adaptation

- Several areas of the brain play a specialized role in language production, and language function, like handedness, is highly lateralized in the brain.

- Changes in the anatomy of the throat in humans indicate that language ability compromises other functions, such as swallowing.

- Claims that hominin fossil remains can be used to reconstruct language ability have been made, but these claims should be regarded with caution.

- Many scenarios have been suggested for how and why language evolved. **[pp 369–373]**

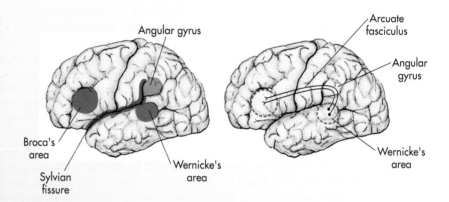

Evolution of Human Behavior

Approaches to Its Study

- The complexity of human behavior requires different perspectives to understand its evolution.

- Paleontological reconstructions, ecological studies of people living in traditional settings, modeling the interaction between biology and culture, and psychological approaches are all used to understand the evolution of behavior. **[pp 373–376]**

Paleontological Reconstructions
anatomy and archaeology of extinct hominids and early humans

Biocultural Approach
how culture shapes behavioral adaptation and adaptability

EVOLUTION OF HUMAN BEHAVIOR

Human Evolutionary Ecology
ecological factors that affect reproductive success

Evolutionary Psychology
behavioral patterns shaped by natural selection in the EEA

Traditional Lives in Evolutionary Perspective

- Human ecologists study traditional societies that may more reasonably reflect the conditions under which human behavior evolved rather than contemporary societies.
- Associations between economic success and increased fitness may have been important in human evolution.
- Links between physiology and behavior have been studied by looking at hormonal profiles in males and females. **[pp 376–381]**

Sexual Selection in Humans

- The sexual division of labor is found in almost all human cultures.
- Evolutionary models to explain its evolution focus variously on cooperation and competition between the sexes.
- Increased risk-taking behavior in males (especially younger ones) and females may have an evolutionary basis and myriad social implications.
- Studies of inbreeding avoidance suggest that human reproductive and sexual behavior are shaped by a range of biological and cultural factors. **[pp 381–383]**

My AnthroLab CONNECTIONS

Watch. Listen. View. Explore. Read.

MyAnthroLab is designed just for you. Each chapter features a customized study plan to help you learn and review key concepts and terms. Dynamic visual activities, videos, and readings found in the multimedia library will enhance your learning experience.

Resources from this Chapter:

Watch on myanthrolab

▶ *Major Language Areas of the Brain*

Listen on myanthrolab

▶ *When Did We Become Mentally Modern?*
▶ *For Cave Women, Farmers Had Extra Sex Appeal*

View on myanthrolab

▶ *3-D Brain Anatomy*

Explore on myanthrolab In MySearchLab, enter the Anthropology database to find relevant and recent scholarly and popular press publications. For this chapter, enter the following keywords: brain, language, sex, gender, behavior

Read on myanthrolab

▶ *A Telling Difference* by Stephen R. Anderson
▶ *Natural Variation in Human Fecundity* by Peter T. Ellison

Chapter 15 Preview

After reading this chapter, you should be able to:

- Explain how anthropologists make use of a biocultural perspective on health and diet.

- Apply the concept of an environmental mismatch between adaptive and contemporary environments towards an understanding of human health and disease.

- Explain how forensic anthropologists use the theory and method of biological anthropology to develop a biological profile from a skeleton.

- Discuss the various applications of forensic anthropology.

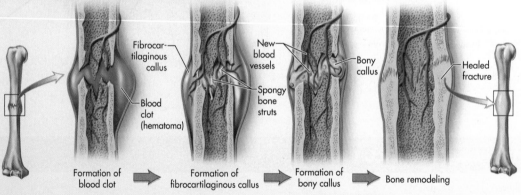

Fibrocar-
tilaginous
callus

New
blood
vessels

Bony
callus

Healed
fracture

Blood
clot
(hematoma)

Spongy
bone
struts

Formation of
blood clot → Formation of
fibrocartilaginous callus → Formation of
bony callus → Bone remodeling

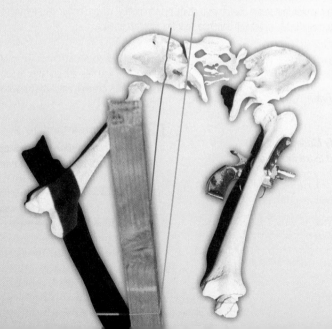

Biomedical and Forensic Anthropology

15

Lunchtime on a late summer day 20,000 years ago in the southwestern part of what is now France: A small group of boys have been playing since mid-morning, exploring the caves that are common in their region, looking for old stone tools that have been left behind by hunting parties. They are starting to get hungry. They do not head back to their village for food: The morning and evening meals will be provided by their parents and other adults in the tribe, but they are on their own between those two meals.

At this time of year, the boys do not mind foraging on their own. The summer has been rainy and warm, and a large variety of nuts, berries, and seeds are beginning to ripen. Because the summer growing season has been a good one, small game such as rabbits and squirrels are well fed and will make a good meal if the boys can manage to catch one. They spend an hour or two moving from site to site where food can be found, covering a couple of miles in the process. They see a rabbit and spend 20 minutes very quietly trying to sneak up on it before realizing that it is no longer in the area. Even without the rabbit, they are all happy with the amount of food they managed to find

during their midday forage. In mid-afternoon, they stop by a stream for a rest, and then one by one they fall asleep.

Lunchtime on a late summer day in the early twenty-first century, at a middle school in the United States: A large group of children line up in the cafeteria to get their lunch. They have spent the morning behind desks, doing their school work. They have had one short recess, but they will not have another during the afternoon. They have a physical education class only once a week because budget cutbacks have meant that their school can afford only one gym teacher for more than 1,200 students.

As the children pass through the cafeteria line, most of them ignore the fruit, vegetables, and whole-wheat breads. Instead, they choose foods high in fat, salt, and sugar: chicken nuggets, fries, and cake. The children do not drink the low-fat milk provided but instead favor sweet sodas and fruit-flavored drinks. After they sit down, the children have 15 minutes to finish their meals. Most of them would say that they really like the food the cafeteria gives them. When they are finished, they return to their classrooms for more instruction.

At first glance, children in developed countries in the early twenty-first century are much healthier than their counterparts who lived 20,000 years ago. They are bigger and more physically mature for their age, and unlike their Paleolithic ancestors, they can reasonably expect to live well into their 70s. They have been vaccinated against several potentially life-threatening viral illnesses, and they need not worry that a small cut, a minor broken bone, or a toothache will turn into a fatal bacterial infection. They are blissfully free of parasites.

On the other hand, a child from 20,000 years ago might have grown up more slowly than a contemporary child, but upon reaching adulthood he would have had a strong, lean body, with much more muscle than fat. He would not have spent a lifetime consuming more calories than he expended. If he were lucky enough to avoid infectious disease, injury, and famine, in his middle and old age he would have been less likely to suffer from

biomedical anthropology The subfield of biological anthropology concerned with issues of health and illness.

heart disease, high blood pressure, diabetes, and even some kinds of cancer than would an adult living today.

Health and illness are fundamental parts of the human experience. The individual experience of illness is produced by many factors. Illness is a product of our genes and culture, our environment and evolution, the economic and educational systems we live under, and the things we eat. When we compare how people live now to how they lived 20,000 years ago, it is apparent that it is difficult to define a healthful environment. Is it the quantity of life (years lived) or the quality that matters most? Are we healthier living as our ancestors did, even though we cannot re-create those past environments, or should we rejoice in the abundance and comfort that a steady food supply and modern technology provide us?

In this chapter, we will look at many aspects of human health from both biocultural and evolutionary perspectives, and we will see how what we can learn from the skeleton about life, health, and disease is used by forensic anthropologists in recent criminal cases. We will see how health relates to growth, development, and aging. We will consider infectious disease and the problems associated with evolving biological solutions to infectious agents that can also evolve. We look at the interaction between diet and disease and the enormous changes in our diet since the advent of modern agriculture. Finally, we will see how the skeleton retains clues about our lives and deaths that can be used to solve criminal cases.

Biomedical Anthropology and the Biocultural Perspective

Biomedical anthropology is the subfield of biological anthropology concerned with issues of health and illness. Biomedical anthropologists bring the traditional interests of biological anthropology—evolution, human variation, genetics—to the study of medically related phenomena. Like medicine, biomedical anthropology is a biological science, which relies on empiricism and hypothesis testing and, when possible, experimental research to further the understanding of human disease and illness. Biomedical anthropology is also like cultural medical anthropology in its comparative outlook, and its attempt to understand illness in the context of specific cultural environments.

A central concept of biomedical anthropology is adaptation. As we have discussed in previous chapters, an adaptation is a feature or behavior that serves over the long term to enhance fitness in an evolutionary sense. But we can also look at adaptation in the short term; this is known as *adaptability* (Chapter 6). A basic question biomedical anthropologists try to answer is: To what extent is adaptability itself an adaptation? For example, the life history stages that all people go through have been shaped by natural selection, but our biology must be flexible enough to cope with the different environmental challenges we will face over a lifetime.

In addition to an adaptation-based evolutionary approach, many biomedical anthropologists look at health from a biocultural perspective. The *biocultural approach* recognizes that when we are looking at something as complex as human illness, both biological and cultural variables offer important insights. The biocultural view recognizes that human behavior is shaped by both our evolutionary and our cultural histories and that, just as human biology does, our behavior influences the expression of disease at both the individual and population levels (Wiley 2004; Wiley and Allen, 2009).

An example of an illness that can be understood only in light of both biology and culture is *anorexia nervosa,* a kind of self-starvation in which a person fails to maintain a minimal normal body weight, is intensely afraid of gaining weight, and exhibits disturbances in the perception of his or her body shape or size (Figure 15.1) (American Psychiatric Association, 1994). The anorexic person fights weight gain by not eating, purging (vomiting) after eating, or exercising excessively. The prevalence rate for anorexia is about 0.5%–1.0% among teenaged and young women; about 90% of all sufferers are female. Anorexia is a serious illness with both long- and short-term increases in mortality. For example, at 6–12 years' follow-up, the mortality rate is 9.6 times the expected rate (Nielsen, 2001).

FIGURE 15.1 A teenaged girl with anorexia.

The thin ideal of female attractiveness often is thought to be a cultural stress leading to the development of anorexia. Studies conducted among teenage girls in Fiji have shown that the introduction of television (with Western programming) in 1995 lead to an increased concern with maintaining a thin body and increased rates of dieting and purging (Becker et al., 2007). Anorexia in some non-Western cultures takes a somewhat different form, however. Anorexia patients in Hong Kong do not have the "fat phobia" we associate with Western anorexia, but rather exhibit a generalized avoidance of eating (Katzman and Lee, 1997). This indicates that even though anorexia is not limited to Western cultures, the focus on fat (rather than a more generalized obsession with self-control) is shaped by the Western cultural concerns with obesity, thinness, and weight loss.

Most young women maintain their body weight without starving themselves, habitually purging, or even dieting. In a 1-year longitudinal study of the eating and dieting habits of 231 American adolescent girls, medical anthropologist Mimi Nichter and colleagues (1995) showed that most of the subjects maintained their weight by watching what they eat and trying to follow a healthful lifestyle rather than taking more extreme measures. Anthropological studies such as this are important because clinicians are not as interested in what the healthy population is doing, and they help to provide a biocultural context for the expression of disease.

Birth, Growth, and Aging

All animals go through the processes of birth, growth, and aging. Normal growth and development are not medical problems per se, but the process of growth is a sensitive overall indicator of health status (Tanner, 1990). Therefore, studies of growth and development in children provide useful insights into the nutritional or environmental health of populations.

Human Childbirth

Nothing should be more natural than giving birth. After all, the survival of the species depends on it. However, in industrialized societies birth usually occurs in hospitals. Of the more than 4 million births in the United States in 2000, more than 90% occurred in hospitals; in 2007, 31.8% of all American births were Cesarean deliveries (Martin et al., 2010). This rate is not extraordinary among developed countries: it is somewhat higher than those seen in Europe, but lower than rates in many parts of China and Latin America (Betrán et al., 2007). In 1900, only 5% of U.S. births occurred in a hospital (Wertz & Wertz, 1989). At that time, given the high risk of contracting an untreatable infection, hospitals were seen as potentially dangerous places to give birth.

Human females are not that much larger than chimpanzee females, yet they give birth to infants whose brains are nearly as large as the brain of an adult chimpanzee and whose heads are very large compared with the size of the mother's pelvis. The easiest evolutionary solution to this problem would be for women to have evolved larger pelves, but too large a pelvis would reduce bipedal efficiency. Wenda Trevathan (1999) points out that the shape as well as the size of the pelvis is a critical factor in the delivery of a child. Not only is there a tight fit between the size of the newborn's head and the mother's pelvis, but the baby's head and body must rotate or twist as they pass through the birth canal, which is a process that introduces other dangers (such as the umbilical cord wrapping around the baby's neck). In contrast to humans, birth is easy in the great apes. Their pelves are substantially larger relative to neonatal brain size, and the shape of their quadrupedal pelves allows a more direct passage of the newborn through the birth canal (Figure 15.2).

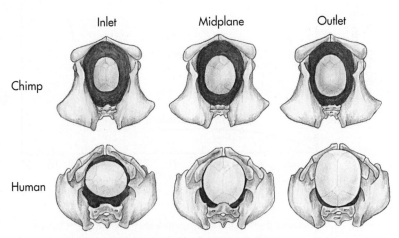

FIGURE 15.2 Compared to a chimpanzee, the human newborn has relatively little room to spare as it passes through the birth canal.

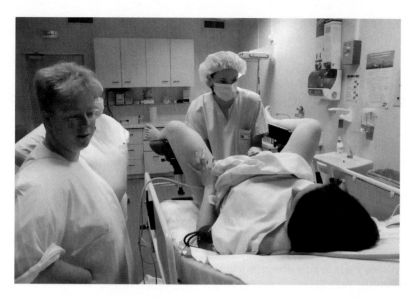

FIGURE 15.3   Women giving birth in traditional cultures usually receive help from other women, or midwives. Midwife-assisted births are also becoming increasingly common in hospital settings.

In traditional cultures, women usually give birth with assistance from a midwife (almost always a woman). Trevathan observes that although women vary across cultures in their reactions to the onset of labor, in almost all cases, the reaction is emotion-charged and results in the mother seeking assistance from others. She hypothesizes that this behavior is a biocultural adaptation. A human birth is much more likely to be successful if someone is present to assist the mother in delivery. Part of the assistance is in actually supporting the newborn through multiple contractions as it passes through the birth canal, but much recent research has shown that the emotional support of mothers provided by birth assistants is also of critical importance (Klaus & Kennell, 1997). Such emotional support often is lacking in contemporary hospital deliveries, although there has been some effort in recent years to remedy this situation (Figure 15.3). Recent research has shown that birth for large-brained Neandertal babies was just as difficult as for modern humans (Ponce de León et al., 2008). It is interesting to consider the possibility that Neandertal mothers may have also received support from kin and others during birth.

Patterns of Human Growth

The study of human growth and development is known as **auxology.** All animals go through stages of growth that are under some degree of genetic control. However, the processes of growth and development can be acutely sensitive to environmental conditions. Thus, patterns of growth that emerge under different environmental conditions can provide us with clear examples of *biological plasticity* (Mascie-Taylor and Bogin, 1995) (Chapter 6).

We chart growth and development using several different measures including height, weight, and head circumference. Cognitive skills, such as those governing the development of language, also appear in a typical sequence as the child matures. We can also assess age by looking at dentition or sexual reproductive capacity. Different parts of the body mature at different rates (Figure 15.4). For example, a nearly adult brain size is achieved very early, whereas physical and reproductive maturation all come later in childhood and adolescence.

Stages of Human Growth

In the 1960s, Adolph Schultz (1969) proposed a model of growth in primates that incorporated four stages shared by all primates. This model is presented in Figure 15.5. In general, as life span increases across primate species, each stage of growth increases in length as well.

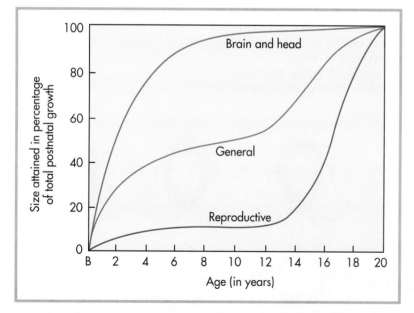

FIGURE 15.4   Different parts of the body mature at different rates. "General" refers to the body as a whole: the major organ systems (nonreproductive), musculature, and blood volume.

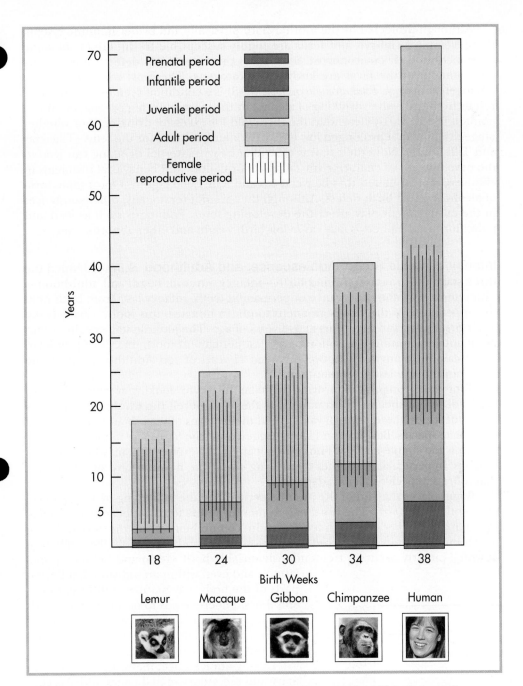

FIGURE 15.5 The four stages of life expressed in five different primates. Note that gestation length increases with increased life span, and the long postreproductive (female) life span seen in humans but not in other primates.

The Prenatal or Gestational Stage The first stage of growth is the prenatal or gestational stage. This begins with conception and ends with the birth of the newborn. As indicated in Figure 15.5, gestational length increases across primates with increasing life span but is not simply a function of larger body size. Gibbons have a 30-week gestation, compared with the approximately 25-week gestation of baboons, even though gibbons are much smaller. Growth during the prenatal period is extraordinarily rapid. In humans, during the *embryonic stage* (first 8 weeks after conception), the fertilized ovum (0.005 mg) increases in size 275,000 times. During the remainder of the pregnancy (the *fetal period*), growth continues at a rate of about 90 times the initial weight (the weight at the end of the embryonic stage) per week, to reach a normal birth weight of about 3,200 g.

auxology The scientific study of human growth and development.

teratogens Substances that cause birth defects or other abnormalities in the developing embryo or fetus during pregnancy.

Although protected by the mother both physically and by her immune system, the developing embryo and fetus are highly susceptible to the effects of some substances in their environment. Substances that cause birth defects or abnormal development of the fetus are known as **teratogens.** The most common human teratogen is alcohol. *Fetal alcohol syndrome* (FAS) is a condition seen in children that results from "excessive" drinking of alcohol by the mother during pregnancy. At this point, it is not exactly clear what the threshold for excessive drinking is or whether binge drinking or a prolonged low level of drinking is worse for the fetus (Thackray and Tifft, 2001). Nonetheless, it is clear that heavy maternal drinking can lead to the development of characteristic facial abnormalities and behavioral problems in children. It is estimated that between 0.5 and 5 in 1,000 children have some form of alcohol-related birth defect. Although they are not teratogens, other substances in the environment may affect the developing fetus. Pollutants such as lead and polychlorinated biphenyls may cause low birth weight and other abnormalities.

Infancy, Juvenile Stage, Adolescence, and Adulthood Schultz defined the three stages of growth following birth—infancy, juvenile stage, and adulthood—with reference to the appearance of permanent teeth. Infancy lasts from birth until the appearance of the first permanent tooth. In humans, this tooth usually is the lower first molar, and it appears at 5–6 years of age. The juvenile stage begins at this point and lasts until the eruption of the last permanent tooth, the third premolar, which can occur anywhere between 15 and 25 years of age. Adulthood follows the appearance of the last permanent tooth.

Tooth eruption patterns provide useful landmarks for looking at stages of growth across different species of primates, but they do not tell the whole story. Besides length of stages, there is much variation in the patterns of growth and development in primate species. Barry Bogin (1999) suggests that the four-stage model of primate growth is too simple and does not reflect patterns of growth that may be unique to humans. In particular, he argues that during *adolescence,* humans have a growth spurt that reflects a species-specific adaptation.

Bogin places the end of the juvenile period, and the beginning of adolescence, at the onset of *puberty.* The word *puberty* literally refers to the appearance of pubic hair, but as a marker of growth it refers more comprehensively to the period during which there is rapid growth and maturation of the body (Tanner, 1990). The age at which puberty occurs is tremendously variable both within and between populations, and even within an individual, different parts of the body may mature at different rates and times. Puberty tends to occur earlier in girls than boys. In industrialized societies, almost all children go through puberty between the ages of 10 and 14 years (Figure 15.6).

During adolescence, maturation of the primary and secondary sexual characteristics continues. In addition, there is an *adolescent growth spurt.* According to Bogin (1993, 1999), the expanding database on primate maturation patterns indicates that the adolescent growth spurt—and therefore adolescence—is most pronounced in humans. Why do we need adolescence? The length of the juvenile stage, most of which occurs after brain size has reached adult proportions, varies widely among mammal species. There is a cost to a prolonged juvenile stage because it delays the onset of full sexual maturity and the ability to reproduce. But the juvenile stage is also necessary as a training period during which younger animals can learn their adult roles and the social behaviors necessary to

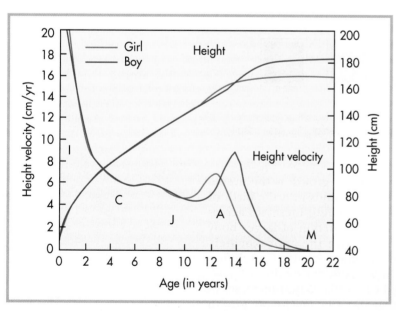

FIGURE 15.6   The adolescent growth spurt in humans is seen as a "bump" in the height curve and a "spike" in the height velocity curve.

survive and reproduce within their own species. The evolutionary costs of delaying maturation are offset by the benefits of social life. Among mammals, the juvenile stage is longest in highly social animals, such as wolves and primates. Humans are the ultimate social animal. Bogin argues that the complex social and cultural life of humans, mediated by language, requires an extended period of social learning and development: adolescence.

The Secular Trend in Growth

One of the most striking changes in patterns of growth identified by auxologists is the *secular trend in growth*. By using data collected as long ago as the eighteenth century, they demonstrated that in industrialized countries, children have been growing larger and maturing more rapidly with each passing decade, starting in the late nineteenth century in Europe and North America (Figure 15.7). The secular trend started in Japan after World War II, and it is just being initiated now in parts of the developing world. In Europe and North America, since 1900, children at 5 to 7 years of age averaged an increase in stature of 1 to 2 cm per decade (Tanner, 1990). In Japan between 1950 and 1970, the increase was 3 cm per decade in 7-year-olds and 5 cm per decade in 12-year-olds. A more recent secular trend in growth has been seen in South Korea, where surveys of children conducted between 1965 and 2005 show a continuing increase in both height and weight (Kim et al., 2008). Twenty-year-old Korean men were 5.3 cm taller and 12.8 kg heavier than their 1965 counterparts; women were 5.4 cm taller and 4.1 kg heavier. The onset of puberty was clearly earlier in the 2005 group, since the greatest differences from the 1965 group were seen in the 10–15-year-old age groups.

The secular trend in growth undoubtedly is a result of better nutrition (more calories and protein in the diet) and a reduction in the impact of diseases during infancy and childhood. We find evidence for this over the short term from *migration studies,* which have shown that changes in the environment (from a less healthful to a more healthful environment) can lead to the development of a secular trend in growth. Migration studies look at a cohort of the children of migrants born and raised in their new country and compare their growth with either their parents' growth (if the children have reached adulthood) or that of a cohort of children in the country from which they immigrated. Migration studies of Mayan refugees from

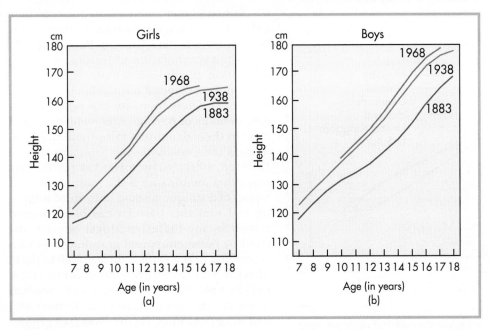

FIGURE 15.7   The secular trend in growth as measured in Swedish (a) girls and (b) boys between 1883 and 1968.

menarche The onset of a girl's first menstrual period.

menopause The postreproductive period in the lives of women, after the cessation of ovulation and menses.

senescence Age-related decline in physiological or behavioral function in adult organisms.

Guatemala to the United States show evidence of a secular trend in growth (Bogin, 1995). Mayan children raised in California and Florida were on average 5.5 cm taller and 4.7 kg heavier than their counterparts in Guatemala. Although the secular trend in growth appears to highlight a straightforward relationship between increased stature and industrialization, the stature each individual achieves is the result of the complex interaction of genetics, economic status, and nutrition.

Menarche and Menopause

Another hallmark of the secular trend in growth is a decrease in the age of **menarche**—a girl's first menstrual period—seen throughout the industrialized world. From the 1850s until the 1970s, the average age of menarche in European and North American populations dropped from around 16 to 17 years to 12 to 13 years (Figure 15.8) (Tanner, 1990; Coleman & Coleman, 2002). A comprehensive study of U.S. girls (sample size of 17,077) found that the age of menarche was 12.9 years for white girls and 12.2 years for black girls (Herman-Giddens et al., 1997). This does not reflect a substantial drop in age of menarche since the 1960s.

In cultures undergoing rapid modernization, changes in the age of menarche have been measured over short periods of time. Among the Bundi of highland Papua New Guinea, age of menarche dropped from 18.0 years in the mid-1960s to 15.8 years for urban Bundi girls in the mid-1980s (Worthman, 1999). Over the long term, the rate of decrease in age of menarche in most of the population was in the range 0.3 to 0.6 years per decade. For urban Bundi girls, the rate is 1.29 years per decade, which may be a measure of the rapid pace of modernization in their society.

Menarche marks the beginning of the reproductive life of women, whereas **menopause** marks its end. Menopause is the irreversible cessation of fertility that occurs in all women before the rest of the body shows other signs of advanced aging (Peccei, 2001a). Returning to Figure 15.5 on page 391, note that of all the primate species illustrated, only in humans does a significant part of the life span extend beyond the female reproductive years. In fact, as far as we know, humans are unique in having menopause (with the exception of a species of pilot whale). Menopause has occurred in the human species for as long as recorded history (it is mentioned in the Bible), and there is no reason to doubt that it has characterized older human females since the dawn of *Homo sapiens*. Although highly variable, menopause usually occurs around the age of 50 years.

At first glance, menopause looks to be a well-defined, programmed life–history stage. Why does it occur? Jocelyn Peccei (1995) suggests a combination of factors, including adaptation, physiological tradeoff, and an artifact of the extended human life span. Some adaptive models focus on the potential fitness benefits of having older women around to help their daughters raise their children, termed the *grandmothering hypothesis* (Hill & Hurtado, 1991). Kristen Hawkes (2003) proposes that menopause is the most prominent aspect of a unique human pattern of longevity and that this pattern has been shaped largely by the inclusive fitness benefits derived by postmenopausal grandmothers who contribute to the care of their grandchildren. There is some empirical support for this idea. For example, a study of Finnish and Canadian historical records indicates that women who had long postreproductive lives had greater lifetime reproductive success (Lahdenpera et al., 2004).

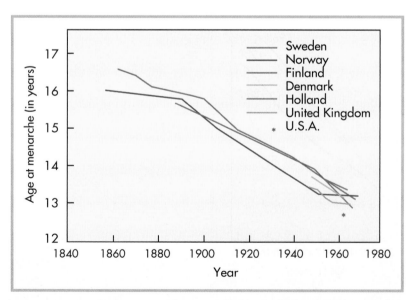

FIGURE 15.8 The declining age of menarche over the past 150 years has been measured in many European countries, and has also been observed more recently in developing countries.

Peccei suggests that an alternative to the grandmothering hypothesis may be more plausible: the mothering hypothesis. She argues that the postreproductive life span of women allows them to devote greater resources to the (slowly maturing) children they already have and that this factor alone could account for the evolution of menopause. This hypothesis is supported by population data from Costa Rica covering maternal lineages dating from the 1500s until the 1900s (Madrigal and Meléndez-Obando, 2008). These data showed that the longer a mother lived, the higher her fitness; however, there was a negative effect on her daughter's fitness. Thus there was support for the mothering hypothesis but not the grandmothering hypothesis. Clearly, more research needs to be done in this area. The relationship between maternal longevity and reproductive fitness is complex, and we will need data from many populations before there is a general perspective on that relationship in the human species as a whole.

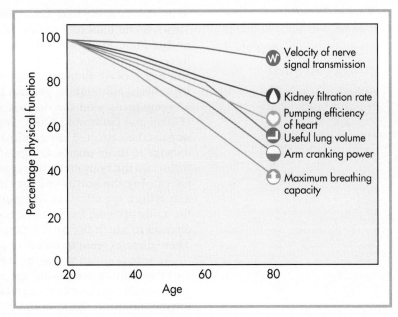

FIGURE 15.9 The effects of aging can be seen in the decline in function of many physiological systems.

Aging

Compared with almost all other animal species, humans live a long time, at least as measured by maximum life span potential (approximately 120 years). But the human body begins to age, or to undergo **senescence,** starting at a much younger age. Many bodily processes actually start to decline in function starting at age 20, although the decline becomes much steeper starting between the ages of 40 and 50 (Figure 15.9). The physical and mental changes associated with aging are numerous and well known, either directly or indirectly, to most of us (Schulz & Salthouse, 1999).

Why do we age? We can answer from both the physiological and the evolutionary standpoints (Figure 15.10). From a physiological perspective, several hypotheses

View "U.S. Department of Health and Human Services Administration on Aging" on **myanthrolab**

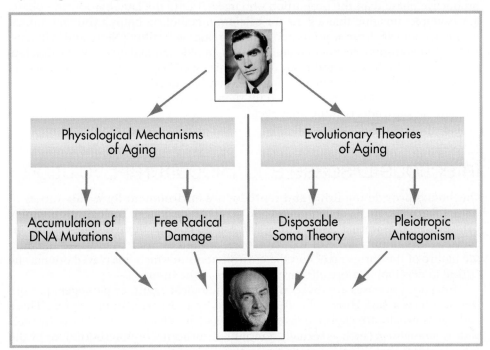

FIGURE 15.10 Physiological and evolutionary theories of aging.

or models of aging have been offered (Nesse & Williams, 1994; Schulz & Salthouse, 1999). Some have focused on DNA, with the idea that over the lifetime, the accumulated damage to DNA, in the form of mutations caused by radiation and other forces, leads to poor cell function and ultimately cell death. Higher levels of DNA repair enzymes are found in longer-lived species, so there may be some validity to this hypothesis, although in general the DNA molecule is quite stable. Another model of aging focuses on the damage that *free radicals* can do to the tissues of the body (Finkel and Holbrook, 2000). Free radicals are molecules that contain at least one unpaired electron. They can link to other molecules in tissues and thereby cause damage to those tissues. Oxygen-free radicals, which result from the process of oxidation (as the body converts oxygen into energy), are thought to be the main culprit for causing the bodily changes in aging. Antioxidants, such as vitamins C and E, may reduce the effects of free radicals, although it is not clear yet whether they slow the aging process. Further evidence for the free radical theory of aging comes from diseases in which the production of the body's own antioxidants is severely limited. These diseases seem to mimic or accelerate the aging process.

In wild populations, aging is not a major contributor to mortality: Most animals die of something besides old age, as humans did before the modern age. Thus, aging per se could not have been an adaptation in the past because it occurred so rarely in the natural world (Kirkwood, 2002). Two nonadaptive evolutionary models of aging are the *disposable soma hypothesis* (Kirkwood and Austad, 2000) and the *pleiotropic gene hypothesis* (Williams, 1957; Nesse and Williams, 1994). Both take the position that old organisms are not as evolutionarily important as young organisms. The disposable soma hypothesis posits that it is more efficient for an organism to devote resources to reproduction rather than maintenance of a body. After all, even a body in perfect shape can still be killed by an accident, predator, or disease. Therefore, organisms are better off devoting resources to getting their genes into the next generation rather than fighting the physiological tide of aging.

The pleiotropic gene hypothesis has a similar logic, although it comes at the problem from a different angle. As you recall (Chapter 4), *pleiotropy* refers to the fact that most genes have multiple phenotypic effects. For all organisms, the effects of natural selection are more pronounced based on the phenotypic effects of the genes during the earliest rather than later phases of reproductive life. The simple reason for this is that a much higher proportion of organisms live long enough to reach the early reproductive phase than the proportion who make it until the late reproductive phase. For example, imagine that a gene for calcium metabolism helps a younger animal heal more quickly from wounds and thus increase its fertility (Nesse and Williams, 1994). A pleiotropic effect of that same gene in an older animal might be the development of calcium deposits and heart disease; this "aged" effect has little influence on the lifetime fitness of the animal. Aging itself may be caused by the cumulative actions of pleiotropic genes that were selected for their phenotypic effects in younger bodies but have negative effects as the body ages.

Infectious Disease and Biocultural Evolution

Our bodies provide the living and reproductive environment for a wide variety of viruses, bacteria, single-celled eukaryotic parasites, and more biologically complex parasites, such as worms. As we evolve defenses to combat these disease-causing organisms, they in turn are evolving ways to get around our defenses. Understanding the nature of this "arms race" and the environments in which it is played out may be critical to developing more effective treatments in the future.

Infectious diseases are those in which a biological agent, or **pathogen,** parasitizes or infects a *host*. Human health is affected by a vast array of pathogens. These pathogens usually are classified taxonomically (such as bacteria or viruses), by their *mode of transmission* (such as sexually transmitted, airborne, or waterborne), or by the organ systems they affect (such as respiratory or brain infections, or "food poisoning" for the digestive tract). Pathogens vary tremendously in their survival strategies.

pathogen An organism and entity that can cause disease.

Some pathogens can survive only when they are in a host, whereas others can persist for long periods of time outside a host. Some pathogens live exclusively within a single host species, whereas others can infect multiple species or may even depend on different species at different points in their life cycle.

Human Behavior and the Spread of Infectious Disease

Human behavior is one of the critical factors in the spread of infectious disease. Actions we take every day influence our exposure to infectious agents and determine which of them may or may not be able to enter our bodies and cause an illness. Food preparation practices, sanitary habits, sex practices, whether one spends time in proximity to large numbers of adults or children—all these can influence a person's chances of contracting an infectious disease. Another critical factor that influences susceptibility to infectious disease is overall nutritional health and well-being. People weakened by food shortage, starvation, or another disease (such as cancer) are especially vulnerable to infectious illness (Figure 15.11). For example, rates of tuberculosis in Britain started to decline in the nineteenth century before the bacteria that caused it was identified or effective medical treatment was developed. This decline was almost certainly due to improvements in nutrition and hygiene (McKeown, 1979).

Just as individual habits play a prominent role in the spread of infectious disease, so can widespread cultural practices. Sharing a communion cup has been linked to the spread of bacterial infection, as has the sharing of a water source for ritual washing before prayer in poor Muslim countries (Mascie-Taylor, 1993). Cultural biases against homosexuality and the open discussion of sexuality gave shape to the entire AIDS epidemic, from its initial appearance in gay communities to delays by leaders in acknowledging the disease as a serious public health problem.

Agriculture Agricultural populations are not necessarily more vulnerable to infectious disease than hunter–gatherer populations. However, larger and denser agricultural populations are likely to play host to all the diseases that affect hunter–gatherer populations and others that can be maintained only in larger populations. This is the basis of the first epidemiological transition discussed earlier. For example, when a child is exposed to measles, his or her immune system takes about 2 weeks to develop effective antibodies to fight the disease. This means that in order to be maintained in a population, the measles virus needs to find a new host every 2 weeks; in other words, there must be a pool of twenty-six new children available over the course of a year to host the measles virus. This is possible in a large agricultural population but almost impossible in a much smaller hunter–gatherer population (Figure 15.12).

FIGURE 15.11 A child suffering from malaria, one of the most common and deadly infectious diseases.

FIGURE 15.12 Risks of infectious disease increase in (a) high-density agricultural populations compared to (b) low-density, dispersed hunter-gatherer populations.

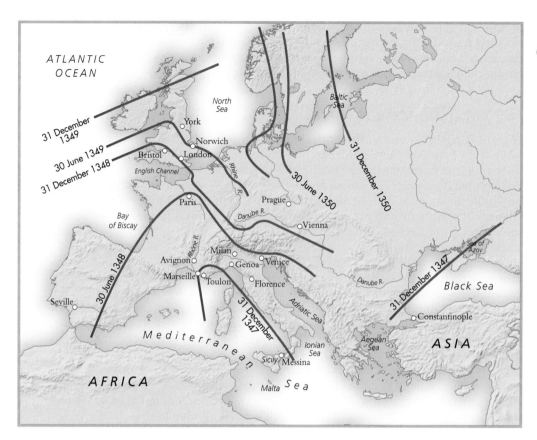

FIGURE 15.13   The Black Death spread over much of Europe in a three-year period in the middle of the fourteenth century.

Agricultural and nonagricultural populations also differ in that the former tend to be sedentary, whereas the latter tend to be nomadic. Large, sedentary agricultural populations therefore are more susceptible to bacterial and parasitic worm diseases that are transmitted by contact with human waste products. In addition, many diseases are carried by water, and agricultural populations are far more dependent on a limited number of water sources than nonagricultural populations. Finally, agricultural populations often have domestic animals and also play host to a variety of commensal animals, such as rats, all of which are potential carriers of diseases that may affect humans.

Specific agricultural practices may change the environment and encourage the spread of such infectious diseases as sickle cell and malaria. Slash-and-burn agriculture leads to more open forests and standing pools of stagnant water. Such pools are an ideal breeding ground for the mosquitoes that carry the protozoa that cause malaria.

Mobility and Migration   The human species is characterized by its mobility. One price of this mobility has been the transmission of infectious agents from one population to another, leading to uncontrolled outbreaks of disease in the populations that have never been exposed to the newly introduced diseases. These are referred to as *virgin soil epidemics.*

The Black Death in Europe (1348–1350) is one example of just such an outbreak (Figure 15.13). The "Black Death" was bubonic plague, a disease caused by the bacterium *Yersinia pestis.* The bacterium is transmitted by the rat flea, which lives on rats. When the fleas run out of rodent hosts, they move to other mammals, such as humans. The bacteria can quickly overwhelm the body, causing swollen lymph nodes (or *buboes,* hence the name) and in more severe cases lead to infection of the respiratory system and blood. It can kill very quickly. An outbreak of bubonic plague was recorded in China in the 1330s, and by the late 1340s it had reached Europe. In a single Italian city, Florence, a contemporary report placed the number dying between March and October 1348 at 96,000. By the end of the epidemic, one-third of Europeans (25–40 million) had been killed, and the economic and cultural life of Europe was forever changed.

Similar devastation awaited the native peoples of the New World after 1492 with the arrival of European explorers and colonists. Measles, smallpox, influenza, whooping cough, and sexually transmitted diseases exacted a huge toll on native populations throughout North and South America, the Island Pacific, and Australia. Some populations were completely wiped out, and others had such severe and rapid population depletion that their cultures were destroyed. In North America, for example, many communities of native peoples lost up to 90% of their population through the introduction of European diseases (Pritzker, 2000). Infectious diseases often reached native communities before the explorers or colonizers did, giving the impression that North America was an open and pristine land waiting to be filled.

⊙ Watch the **Animation** "Spread of the Black Death (or Plague)" on **myanthrolab**

Infectious Disease and the Evolutionary Arms Race

As a species, we fight infectious diseases in many ways. However, no matter what we do, parasites and pathogens continuously evolve to overcome our defenses. Over the last 50 years, it appeared that medical science was gaining the upper hand on infectious disease, at least in developed countries. However, despite real advances, infectious diseases such as the virus that causes AIDS and antibiotic-resistant bacteria remind us that this primeval struggle will continue.

The Immune System One of the most extraordinary biological systems that has ever evolved is the vertebrate immune system, the main line of defense in the fight against infectious disease. At its heart is the ability to distinguish self from nonself. The immune system identifies foreign substances, or **antigens,** in the body and synthesizes **antibodies,** which comprise a class of proteins known as **immunoglobulins,** which are specifically designed to bind to and destroy specific antigens (Figure 15.14).

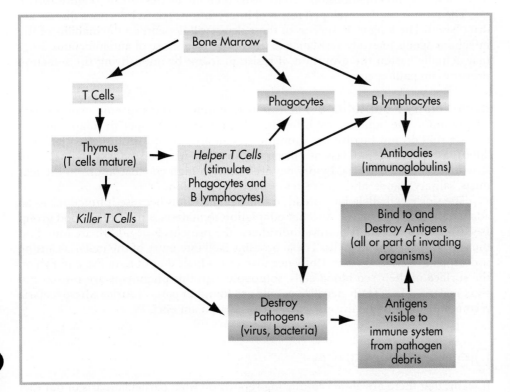

antigens Whole or part of an invading organism that prompts a response (such as production of antibodies) from the body's immune system.

antibodies Proteins (immunoglobulins) formed by the immune system that are specifically structured to bind to and neutralize invading antigens.

immunoglobulins Proteins produced by B lymphocytes that function as antibodies.

FIGURE 15.14 The immune system has several different components that work in concert.

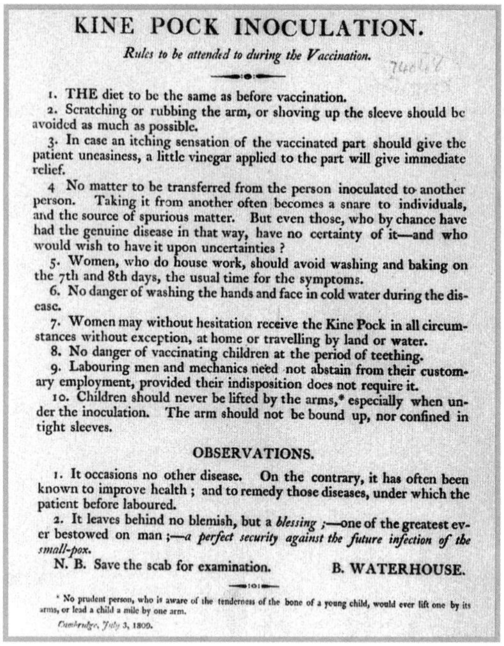

KINE POCK INOCULATION.

Rules to be attended to during the Vaccination.

1. THE diet to be the same as before vaccination.
2. Scratching or rubbing the arm, or shoving up the sleeve should be avoided as much as possible.
3. In case an itching sensation of the vaccinated part should give the patient uneasiness, a little vinegar applied to the part will give immediate relief.
4. No matter to be transferred from the person inoculated to another person. Taking it from another often becomes a snare to individuals, and the source of spurious matter. But even those, who by chance have had the genuine disease in that way, have no certainty of it—and who would wish to have it upon uncertainties ?
5. Women, who do house work, should avoid washing and baking on the 7th and 8th days, the usual time for the symptoms.
6. No danger of washing the hands and face in cold water during the disease.
7. Women may without hesitation receive the Kine Pock in all circumstances without exception, at home or travelling by land or water.
8. No danger of vaccinating children at the period of teething.
9. Labouring men and mechanics need not abstain from their customary employment, provided their indisposition does not require it.
10. Children should never be lifted by the arms,* especially when under the inoculation. The arm should not be bound up, nor confined in tight sleeves.

OBSERVATIONS.

1. It occasions no other disease. On the contrary, it has often been known to improve health ; and to remedy those diseases, under which the patient before laboured.
2. It leaves behind no blemish, but a *blessing* ;—one of the greatest ever bestowed on man ;—*a perfect security against the future infection of the small-pox.*

N. B. Save the scab for examination. B. WATERHOUSE.

* No prudent person, who is aware of the tenderness of the bone of a young child, would ever lift one by its arms, or lead a child a mile by one arm.

Cambridge, July 3, 1800.

FIGURE 15.15 Early instructions for administration of the smallpox vaccine. Note in the last lines that it was considered to be a "blessing."

The immune system is a complex mechanism that has evolved to deal with the countless number of potential antigens in the environment. An example of what happens when just one of the components of the immune system is not functioning occurs in AIDS. The *human immunodeficiency virus* (HIV) that causes AIDS attacks the helper T cells. As mentioned earlier, the helper T cells respond to antigens by inducing the B lymphocytes to produce antibodies, leading to the production of phagocytes; when their function is compromised, the function of the entire immune system is also compromised. This leaves a person with HIV infection vulnerable to a host of opportunistic infections, a condition that characterizes the development of full-blown AIDS.

Cultural and Behavioral Interventions Although the immune system does a remarkable job fighting infectious disease, it is obviously not always enough. Even before the basis of infectious diseases was understood, humans took steps to limit their transmission. Throughout the Old World, people with leprosy were shunned and forced to live apart from the bulk of the population. This isolation amounted to *quarantine,* in recognition of the contagious nature of their condition.

One of the most effective biocultural measures developed to fight infectious diseases is vaccination. The elimination of *smallpox* as a scourge of humanity is one of the great triumphs of widespread vaccination. Smallpox is a viral illness that originated in Africa some 12,000 years ago and subsequently spread throughout the Old World (Barquet & Domingo, 1997). It was a disfiguring illness, causing pustulant lesions on the skin, and it was often fatal. Smallpox killed millions of people upon its introduction to the New World; in the Old World, smallpox epidemics periodically decimated entire populations. In 180 CE, a smallpox epidemic killed between 3.5 and 7 million people in the Roman Empire, precipitating the first period of its decline. Crude vaccination practices against smallpox were developed hundreds of years ago, but these often carried a significant risk of developing the disease. During the twentieth century, modern vaccination methods worked to virtually eliminate this disease (Figure 15.15).

The most recently developed forms of intervention against infectious disease are drug based. The long-term success of these drugs will depend on the inability of the infectious agents to evolve resistance to their effects. Overuse of anti-infectious drugs may actually hasten the evolution of resistant forms by intensifying the selection pressures on pathogens.

Evolutionary Adaptations The immune system is the supreme evolutionary adaptation in the fight against infectious disease. However, specific adaptations to disease that do not involve the immune system are also quite common (Jackson, 2000). For example, a class of enzymes known as *lysozymes* attacks the cell wall structure of some bacteria. Lysozymes are found in high concentrations in the tear ducts, salivary glands, and other sites of bacterial invasion.

The sickle cell allele has spread in some populations because it functions as an adaptation against malaria. Another adaptation to malaria is the Duffy blood group (see Chapter 6). In Duffy-positive individuals, the proteins Fya and Fyb are found on the surface of red blood cells. These proteins facilitate entry of the malaria-causing protozoan *Plasmodium vivax.* Duffy-negative individuals do not have Fya and Fyb on the surface of their red blood cells, so people with this phenotype are resistant to vivax malaria. Many Duffy-negative people are found in parts of Africa where malaria is common; others, who live elsewhere, have African ancestry.

Diet and Disease

It seems that there are always conflicting reports on what particular parts of our diet are good or bad for us. Carbohydrates are good one year and bad the next. Fats go in and out of fashion. From a biocultural anthropological perspective, American attitudes toward diet and health at the turn of the twenty-first century provide a rich source of material for analysis. However, despite all the confusion about diet, we all have the same basic nutritional needs. We need energy (measured in calories or kilojoules) for body maintenance, growth, and metabolism. Carbohydrates, fat, and proteins are all sources of energy. We especially need protein for tissue growth and repair. In addition to energy, fat provides us with essential fatty acids important for building and supporting nerve tissue. We need vitamins, which are basically organic molecules that our bodies cannot synthesize but that we need in small quantities for a variety of metabolic processes. We also need a certain quantity of inorganic elements, such as iron and zinc. For example, with insufficient iron, the ability of red blood cells to transport oxygen is compromised, leading to anemia. Finally, we all need water to survive.

The Paleolithic Diet

For most of human history, people lived in small groups and subsisted on wild foods that they could collect by hunting or gathering. Obviously, diets varied in different areas: Sub-Saharan Africans were not eating the same thing as Native Americans on the northwest Pacific coast. Nonetheless, S. Boyd Eaton and Melvin Konner (Eaton & Konner, 1985; Eaton et al., 1999) argue that we can reconstruct an *average* Paleolithic diet from a wide range of information derived from paleoanthropology, epidemiology, and nutritional studies. A comparison of the average Paleolithic and contemporary diets is presented in Table 15.1 (Eaton et al., 1999).

TABLE 15.1 Comparison of Paleolithic and Contemporary Diets

Dietary Component	Paleolithic Diet	Contemporary Diet
Energy (calories)	High caloric intake and expenditure to support active lifestyle and large body size.	More sedentary lifestyle uses fewer calories, yet caloric consumption often exceeds expenditure.
Micronutrients (vitamins, antioxidants, folic acid, iron, zinc)	High consumption (65–70% of diet) of foods rich in micronutrients, such as fruits, roots, nuts, and other noncereals.	Low consumption of foods rich in micronutrients.
Electrolytes (sodium, calcium, and potassium, needed for a variety of physiological processes)	High consumption of potassium relative to sodium (10,500 mg/day vs. 770 mg/day). High blood pressure is rare in contemporary hunter–gatherers with high potassium/sodium ratios.	Low consumption of potassium relative to sodium (3,000 mg/day vs. 4,000 mg/day). High sodium intake from processed foods is associated with high blood pressure.
Carbohydrates	Provide about 45–50% of daily calories, mostly from vegetables and fruits, which are rich in amino acids, fatty acids, and micronutrients.	Provide about 45–50% of daily calories, mostly from processed cereal grains, sugars, and sweeteners, which are low in amino acids, fatty acids, and micronutrients.
Fat	Provides about 20–25% of daily calories, mostly from lean game animals, which have less fat and saturated fat than domestic animals, leading to lower serum cholesterol levels.	Provides about 40% of calories, mostly from meat and dairy products. Some contemporary diets, such as from Japan and the Mediterranean region, are low in total or saturated fat and are associated with lower heart disease rates.
Protein	High consumption, providing about 30% of daily calorie intake, mostly from wild game that is low in fat.	Recommended daily allowance about 12% of total calories. High-protein intake has been associated with higher heart disease rates, probably because contemporary high-protein diets also tend to be high in fat.
Fiber	50–100 g/day. High-fiber diets sometimes are considered risky because of loss of micronutrients, but this would be less of a worry in a Paleolithic diet rich in micronutrients.	20 g/day.

The contemporary diet is not simply a more abundant version of the hunter–gatherer diet. It differs fundamentally in both composition and quality. Compared with contemporary diets, the hunter–gatherer diet can be characterized as being high in micronutrients, protein, fiber, and potassium and low in fat and sodium. Total caloric and carbohydrate intake is about the same in both diets, but hunter–gatherers typically were more active than contemporary peoples and thus needed more calories, and their carbohydrates came from fruits and vegetables rather than processed cereals and refined sugars.

The comparison between hunter–gatherer and contemporary diets indicates that increasing numbers of people are living in nutritional environments for which their bodies are not necessarily well adapted. With few exceptions (such as the evolution of lactose tolerance) there has not been enough time, or strong enough selection pressures, for us to develop adaptations to this new nutritional environment. Indeed, because most of the negative health aspects of contemporary diets (obesity, diabetes, cancer) become critical only later in life, it is likely that health problems associated with the mismatch between our bodies and our nutritional environment will be with us for some time.

Agriculture and Nutritional Deficiency

Agriculture allowed the establishment of large population centers, which in turn led to the development of large-scale, stratified civilizations with role specialization. Agriculture also produced an essential paradox: From a nutritional standpoint, most agricultural people led lives that were inferior to the lives of hunter–gatherers. Agricultural peoples often suffered from *nutritional stress* as dependence on a few crops made their large populations vulnerable to both chronic nutritional shortages and occasional famines. The "success" of agricultural peoples relative to hunter–gatherers came about not because agriculturalists lived longer or better lives but because there were more of them.

With their dependence on a single staple cereal food, agricultural populations throughout the world have been plagued by diseases associated with specific nutritional deficiencies. As in the Illinois Valley, many populations of the New World were dependent on maize as a staple food crop. Dependence on maize is associated with the development of *pellagra*, a disease caused by a deficiency of the B vitamin *niacin* in the diet. Pellagra causes a distinctive rash, diarrhea, and mental disturbances, including dementia. Ground corn is low in niacin and in the amino acid tryptophan, which the body can use to synthesize niacin. Even into the twentieth century, poor sharecroppers in the southern United States and poor farmers in southern Europe, both groups that consumed large quantities of cornmeal in their diets, were commonly afflicted with pellagra. Some maize-dependent groups in Central and South America were not so strongly affected by pellagra because they processed the corn with an alkali (lye, lime, ash) that released niacin from the hull of the corn.

In Asia, rice has been the staple food crop for at least the last 6,000 years. In China, a disease we now call *beriberi* was first described in 2,697 BCE. Although it was not recognized at that time, beriberi is caused by a deficiency in vitamin B1 or *thiamine*. Beriberi is characterized by fatigue, drowsiness, and nausea, leading to a variety of more serious complications related to problems with the nervous system (especially tingling, burning, and numbness in the extremities) and ultimately heart failure. Rice is not lacking in vitamins; however, white rice, which has been polished and milled to remove the hull, has been stripped of most of its vitamin content, including thiamine.

Agriculture and Abundance: Thrifty and Nonthrifty Genotypes

The advent of agriculture ushered in a long era of nutritional deficiency for most people. However, the recent agricultural period, as exemplified in the developed nations of the early twenty-first century, is one of nutritional excess, especially in terms of the consumption of fat and carbohydrates of little nutritional value other than calories. The amount and variety of foods available to people in contemporary societies are unparalleled in human history.

In 1962, geneticist James Neel introduced the idea of a *thrifty genotype,* a genotype that is very efficient at storing food in the body in the form of fat, after observing that many non-Western populations that had recently adopted a Western or modern diet were much more likely than Western populations to have high rates of obesity, diabetes (especially Type 2 or non–insulin-dependent diabetes), and all the health problems associated with those conditions (see also Neel, 1982). Populations such as the Pima-Papago Indians in the southwest United States have diabetes rates of about 50%, and elevated rates of diabetes have been observed in Pacific Island-, Asian-, and African-derived populations with largely Western diets (Figure 15.16).

According to Neel, hunter–gatherers needed a thrifty genotype to adapt to their nonabundant nutritional environments; in contrast, the thrifty genotype had been selected against in the supposedly abundant European environment through the negative consequences of diabetes and obesity. The history of agriculture and nutritional availability in Europe makes the evolution of a *nonthrifty genotype* unlikely (Allen & Cheer, 1996); Europe was no more nutritionally favored than other agricultural or hunter–gatherer populations. However, the notion of a thrifty genotype retains validity. At its heart is the idea that we are adapted to a lifestyle and nutritional environment far different from those we find in contemporary populations.

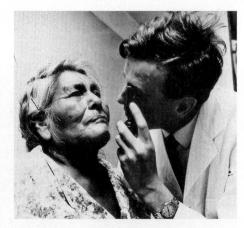

FIGURE 15.16   Pima Indian woman receiving an eye exam. Eye problems are a common result of diabetes.

We have seen how growth patterns, infectious disease exposure, nutritional status, and a host of other health-related issues are fundamentally changed by the adoption of new cultural practices and technologies. Conditions such as rickets and diabetes have been called diseases of civilization because they seem to be a direct result of the development of the industrialized urban landscape and food production. But this label is misleading. Rickets could also be called a disease of migration and maladaptation to a specific environment. Diabetes could be characterized as a disease of nutritional abundance, which was certainly *not* a characteristic of civilization for most of human history.

Biomedical anthropology is interested in understanding the patterns of human variation, adaptation, and evolution as they relate to health issues. This entails an investigation of the relationship between our biologies and the environments we live in. Understanding environmental transitions helps us understand not only the development of disease but also the mechanisms of adaptation that have evolved over thousands of years of evolution. Change is the norm in the modern world. In the future, we should expect human health to be affected by these changes. By their training and interests, biological anthropologists will be in an ideal position to make an important contribution to understanding the dynamic biocultural factors that influence human health and illness.

Forensic Anthropology, Life, Death, and the Skeleton

View "So You Want to Be a Forensic Anthropologist" on **myanthrolab**

The field of forensic anthropology has achieved recent popularity due in part to television shows such as *CSI* and *Bones.* But like most popularizations, the fantasy is more glamorous than the reality. Each state has medical examiners or coroners who are legally responsible for signing death certificates and determining the cause and manner of death of people not in the care of a doctor. They also have the authority to consult other experts in their investigations, including forensic anthropologists. A forensic anthropologist is often consulted in cases in which soft-tissue remains are absent or badly decomposed.

Forensic anthropologists work with clues about growth, health, disease and adaptation that are visible in each of our skeletons. These scientists are specialists

FIGURE 15.17 The first step in field recovery involves surveying the site, sometimes with special equipment.

in human osteology who use the theory and method of biological anthropology to answer questions about how recent humans lived and died. They study skeletal remains from crime scenes, war zones, and mass disasters within the very recent past to reveal the life history of the individual, to identify that individual, and to understand something about the context in which death occurred. They use osteological identification and archaeological field methods to retrieve remains and to develop a profile of the age, sex, and other biological attributes of an individual. Because the way the skeleton of a human or any other animal looks is dictated by its function in life and its evolutionary history, forensic anthropologists can reconstruct the probable age, sex, and ancestry of an individual from his or her skeletal remains. They can observe the influence of certain kinds of diseases on the skeleton, and they can assess some aspects of what happened to an individual just before, around the time of, and after his or her death. Unlike pathologists and medical examiners, forensic anthropologists bring an anthropological perspective and a hard-tissue focus to investigations of skeletal remains.

Field Recovery and Laboratory Processing

Forensic investigations rely on good contextual information. Things like body position, relationship to nearby items such as bullets or grave goods, and structures near the individual require precise and thorough documentation in the field. Without such documentation, we would not know if the bullet recovered at the scene was 10 feet from the individual, or within the victim's chest cavity. These associations are crucial for inferring the meaning of a burial and the circumstances surrounding the death of an individual. So to ensure full recovery and good contextual information, we rely on archaeological techniques to find, document, and remove remains from the site. When the site is identified it is cordoned off and surveyed for additional remains. Such surveys commonly include an individual or team of investigators walking a systematic path searching for remains, associated items, or evidence of burial (Figure 15.17).

In the field, any surface discoveries are mapped and photographed. A permanent **datum point** for the site is established that represents a fixed position from which everything is measured so that the precise "find spot" of each object can be relocated in the future. If the remains are buried, the anthropologist will excavate using archaeological techniques. The excavator begins by skimming off shallow layers of dirt using a hand trowel. Objects are revealed in place and their coordinates, including their depth, are recorded relative to the grid system (Figure 15.18), and photographs are taken. The dirt is sieved through fine mesh to ensure that even the smallest pieces of bone are recovered (Figure 15.19). Soil samples may be saved to assist in the identification of insects and plants. In the field, the anthropologist makes a preliminary determination of whether the remains are human or nonhuman (they could be those of a dog or deer, for instance) and, based on the bones, whether more than one individual is present. Once exposed and mapped, individual bones are tagged, bagged, and removed to the laboratory.

In the lab more detailed curation and examination can begin. A strict **chain of custody** is established to ensure that the remains cannot be tampered with, in case they should become evidence in a court of law. Detailed notes are taken to demonstrate that the remains in question are those from the scene, that they have not been contaminated or modified since their removal from the scene, and who has had access to them.

FIGURE 15.18 Bioarchaeologists and forensic anthropologists use archaeological excavation techniques to recover remains.

After the remains are cataloged, they are cleaned of any adhering soft tissue and dirt, and then laid out in anatomical position, the way they would have looked in the skeleton in life (Figure 15.20). An inventory is made of each bone present and its condition. Most adult humans have 206 bones, many of which are extremely small (see Appendix A). Because most bones develop as several bony centers that fuse together only later in life, fetuses and children contain many more bones than do adults. Often the scientist works with no more than a few bone fragments.

FIGURE 15.19   After excavation, recovered remains are screened to ensure that even tiny fragments are retrieved and saved.

The Biological Profile

Once the initial inventory has been completed, the scientist sets about evaluating the clues that the skeleton reveals about the life and death of the individual. The first step in this process is constructing the **biological profile** of the individual—including determining age, sex, height, and disease status.

Age at Death

As the human body develops, from fetus to old age, dramatic changes occur throughout the skeleton. Scientists use the more systematic of these changes to estimate the age at death of an individual. However, whenever scientists determine age, they always report it as a range (such as 35–45 years) rather than as a single definitive number. This range reflects the variation in growth and aging seen in individuals and across human populations and denotes the person's biological rather than chronological age (age in years). The goal is that the range also encompasses the person's actual age at the time of their death.

Because the skeleton grows rapidly during childhood, assessing the age of a subadult younger than about 18 years of age is easier and often more precise than estimating the age of an adult skeleton. Virtually all skeletal systems except the small

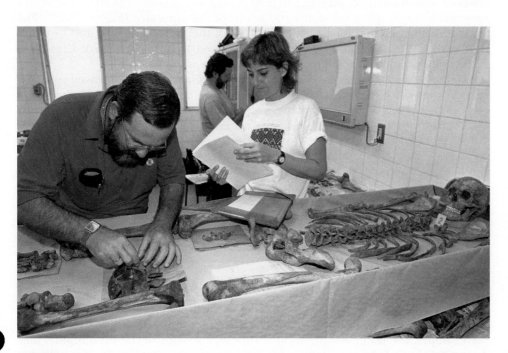

FIGURE 15.20   After skeletal remains are cleaned, they are laid out in anatomical position for inventory.

datum point   A permanent, fixed point relative to which the location of items of interest are recorded during archaeological mapping and excavation.

chain of custody   In forensic cases, the detailed notes that establish what was collected at the scene, the whereabouts of these remains, and the access to them after retrieval from the scene.

biological profile   The biological particulars of an individual as estimated from his or her skeletal remains. These particulars include estimates of sex, age at death, height, ancestry, and disease status.

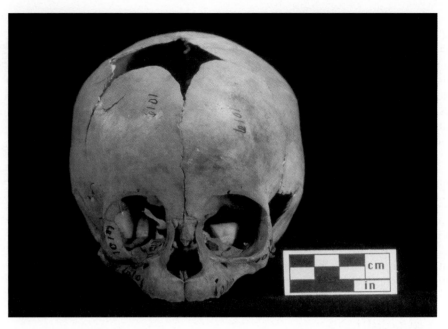

FIGURE 15.21   Bones change radically in size and shape from newborn to adult. This young infant's cranium has several "soft spots" where bone is lacking that allow later growth, and the face is very small compared to the braincase.

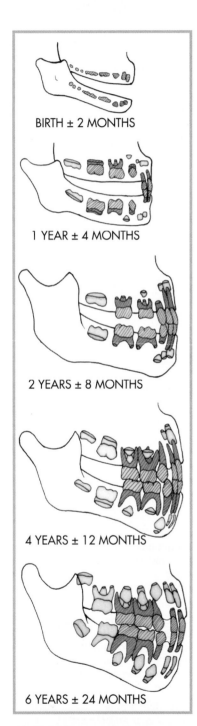

BIRTH ± 2 MONTHS

1 YEAR ± 4 MONTHS

2 YEARS ± 8 MONTHS

4 YEARS ± 12 MONTHS

6 YEARS ± 24 MONTHS

FIGURE 15.22   Tooth development and eruption are commonly used to assess age in the subadult skeleton. Deciduous (baby) teeth are indicated by hatching and shades of brown.

bones of the ear (the ear ossicles) change from newborn to adult. For example, in small children the degree of closure of the cranial bones (covering the fontanelles, or "soft spots" of the skull) changes with age, as does the development of the temporal bone, the size and shape of the wrist bones, and virtually every other bone (Figure 15.21). However, dental eruption and the growth of long bones are the most frequently used means of assessing subadult age.

Humans have two sets of teeth of different sizes that erupt at fairly predictable intervals. Which teeth are present can help distinguish between children of different ages and between older subadults and adults of the same size (Figure 15.22). For more precise ages, the relative development of the tooth roots can also be used. However, once most of the adult teeth have erupted, by about the age of 12 years in humans, the teeth are no longer as good a guide to predicting age.

In these older children, growth of the limb bones can also be used to assess age. The long bones of the arms and legs have characteristic bony growths at each end—the epiphyses—which are present as separate bones while the person is still growing rapidly (Figure 15.23). Most epiphyses are not present at birth—which helps to separate fetuses from newborns—but appear during infancy and childhood. The lengths and proportions of bones change in predictable ways as children grow and are especially good indicators for assessing fetal age (Sherwood et al., 2000). In older children, the epiphyses start to fuse to the shafts of the limb bones around the age of 10 in some bones, and fusion of most epiphyses is completed in the late teenage years. However, the process of fusion may occur as late as the early twenties in a few bones (such as the clavicle). Depending upon which bones and which parts of those bones are fused, a reasonably good estimate of subadult age can be made.

In adults, age is harder to determine because growth is essentially complete. Some of the last epiphyses to fuse, such as the clavicle and top of the ilium, can be used to estimate age in young adults in their early twenties. But estimating the age of the older adult skeleton relies mostly on degeneration of parts of the skeleton. For example, the pubic symphysis and auricular surface of the innominate, and the end of the fourth rib near the sternum all show predictable changes with age (Todd, 1920, 1921; McKern & Stewart, 1957; Iscan et al., 1984; Lovejoy et al., 1985). Examination of as many of these bones as possible helps to increase age accuracy

(Bedford et al., 1993). The pubic symphysis is a particularly useful indicator of adult age, and age standards have been developed separately for males and females (Gilbert & McKern, 1973; Katz & Suchey, 1986; Brooks & Suchey, 1990). The standards show how the symphysis develops from cleanly furrowed to more granular and degenerated over time (Figure 15.24). These changes tend to occur more quickly in females than in males due to the trauma the symphysis experiences during childbirth.

The degree of obliteration of cranial sutures (the junction of the different skull bones) can also give a relative sense of age—obliteration tends to occur in older individuals (Lovejoy & Meindl, 1985). The antero–lateral sutures of the skull are the best for these purposes. However, the correlation between degree of obliteration and age is not very close, and the age ranges that can be estimated are wide.

Sex

If certain parts of the skeleton are preserved, identifying biological sex is easier than estimating age at death, at least for adults. The two parts of the skeleton that most readily reveal sex are the pelvis and the skull, and sex characteristics are more prominent in an adult skeleton than in a child. Humans are moderately sexually dimorphic, with males being larger on average than females (see Table 10.2 on page 258). But their ranges of variation overlap so that size alone cannot separate male and female humans.

The best skeletal indicator of sex is the pelvis. Because of selective pressures for bipedality and childbirth, human females have evolved pelves that provide a

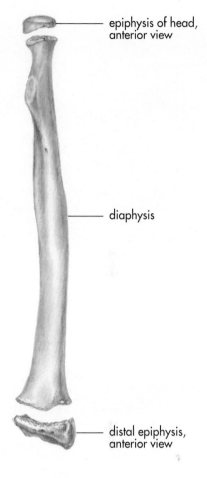

FIGURE 15.23 Long bones develop from several bony centers—one for the shaft and at least one for each end. The end caps are known as epiphyses.

epiphysis of head, anterior view

diaphysis

distal epiphysis, anterior view

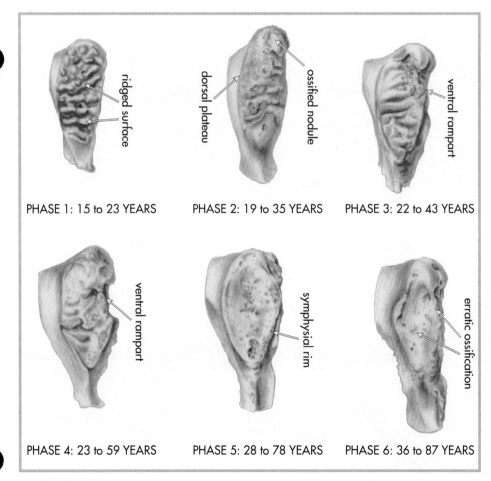

PHASE 1: 15 to 23 YEARS   PHASE 2: 19 to 35 YEARS   PHASE 3: 22 to 43 YEARS

ridged surface

dorsal plateau

ossified nodule

ventral rampart

PHASE 4: 23 to 59 YEARS   PHASE 5: 28 to 78 YEARS   PHASE 6: 36 to 87 YEARS

ventral rampart

symphysial rim

erratic ossification

FIGURE 15.24 The pubic symphysis of the pelvis is useful for estimating age in the adult skeleton.

relatively large birth canal (see Chapter 10). This affects the shape of the innominate and sacrum in females; the pubis is longer, the sacrum is broader and shorter, and the sciatic notch of the ilium is broader in females than in males (Figure 15.25). The method is highly accurate (Rogers & Saunders, 1993) because the pelvis reflects directly the different selective pressures that act on male versus female bipeds. Thus the pelvis is considered a primary indicator of the sex of the individual. And because the femur has to angle inward from this wider female pelvis to the knee (to keep the biped's foot under its center of gravity; see Chapter 10), the size and shape of the femur also differentiate males and females fairly well (Porter, 1995).

The skull is also a useful indicator of sex, at least in adults. Around puberty, circulating hormones lead to so-called secondary sex characters such as distribution of body and facial hair. During this time male and female skulls also diverge in shape. Male skulls are more robust on average than female skulls of the same population. However, these differences are relative and population dependent; some human populations are more gracile than others. The mastoid process of the temporal bone and the muscle markings of the occipital bone tend to be larger in males than in females, and the chin is squarer in males than in females (Figure 15.25). The brow-ridge is less robust and the orbital rim is sharper in females than in males, and the female frontal (forehead) is more vertical. These differences form a continuum and provide successful sex estimates in perhaps 80 to 85% of cases when the population is known.

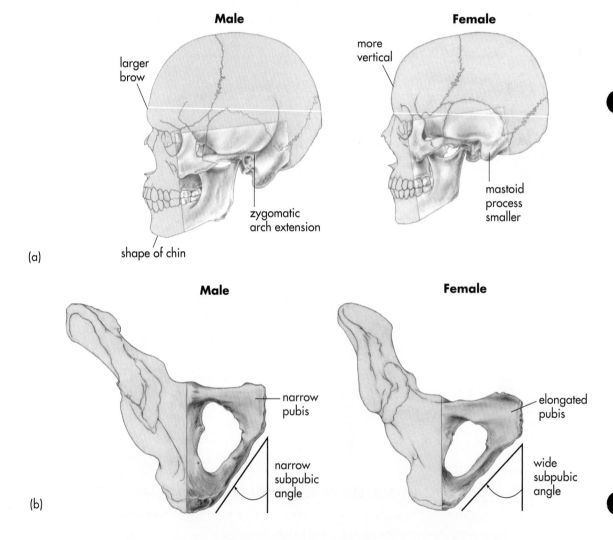

FIGURE 15.25   Comparison of (a) male and female skulls and (b) male and female pelves.

Ancestry

Knowing the ancestry of an individual skeleton is important for improving the accuracy of sex, age, and stature estimates. There is no biological reality to the idea of fixed biological races in humans (see Chapter 6), but we have learned that the geographic conditions in which our ancestors evolved influence the anatomy of their descendants. The term ancestry takes into account the place of geographic origin, which corresponds to biological realities in ways that the term race does not. Nonetheless, because of the way in which variation is distributed in humans (there is more variation within than between groups, and many variation clines run in directions independent of one another) assessing ancestry from the skeleton is less accurate than assessing age or sex, and the process is also highly dependent on the comparative groups used.

Forensic anthropologists base ancestry assessments on comparisons with skeletal populations of known ancestry. An isolated skull can be measured and compared using multivariate statistics with the University of Tennessee Forensic Data Bank of measurements from crania of known ancestry. This process provides a likely assignment of ancestry and a range of possible error. However, human variation is such that many people exist in every population whose skulls do not match well with most other skulls of similar geographic origin. Nonetheless, the ability to even partially assign ancestry can be useful in several forensic contexts. Missing person reports often provide an identification of ancestry, and although this is not based directly on the skeleton, a skeletal determination of ancestry may suggest a match that could be confirmed by other more time–consuming means such as dental record comparisons or DNA analysis (see Innovations: Ancestry and Identity Genetics on pages 410–411).

Height and Weight

Physical stature reflects the length of the bones that contribute to a person's height. Different body shapes have evolved in response to different climatic pressures (see the ecological rules described by Bergmann and Allen in Chapter 6). Thus, height and weight estimates will be more accurate if the population of the individual is known. These differences in proportions relate to differences in bone lengths; as a result, some populations will tend to have more of their stature explained by leg length, and some by torso length, for example.

The best estimates of stature from the skeleton are based on summing the heights of all the bones in the skeleton that contribute to overall height including the cranium, vertebral column, limb, and foot bones (Fully, 1956). This so-called Fully method is fairly accurate, but requires a complete skeleton, a rarity in archaeological or forensic contexts. Biological anthropologists have developed formulae, which vary by population, for estimating stature based on the length of a single or several long bones, so that the femur, tibia, or even humerus can be used to predict stature. These methods use the relationship between the limb bones and the height in skeletal remains of individuals of known stature to predict stature for an unknown individual (e.g., Trotter, 1970). For even more incomplete remains, there are formulae for estimating total length of a long bone from a fragment of that bone (e.g., Steele & McKern, 1969). The estimated length can then be used to estimate height—although the error margin increases with each estimate. Like age, stature is estimated as a range (for example, 5'10" to 6'0") that hopefully captures the person's true height at the time of death.

As you might expect, weight is more difficult to predict since it can vary quite a lot over an individual's life time. Nonetheless, formulae exist for predicting the approximate weight of an individual from his or her weight-bearing joints, such as the head of the femur. Using the entire skeleton, scientists can estimate body weight based on formulae that relate height and body breadth to weight in populations of a different build (Ruff, 2000). Some of these estimates also form the basis for inferring body size and weight in earlier hominins (see Chapters 11 and 12).

INNOVATIONS

Ancestry and Identity Genetics

Genetic studies have long been used for tracing the histories of populations (Chapters 6 and 13). As geneticists have discovered an increasing variety of markers that are associated with specific geographical regions and populations, the ability to trace individual genetic histories has increased greatly, and the ability to make direct matches to DNA from a crime scene has become an important forensic technique. In addition, the development of technologies allowing direct sequencing of DNA regions quickly and relatively inexpensively means that anyone can obtain a genetic profile in a matter of a few weeks.

There are two basic approaches to determining *personalized genetic histories* (PGHs) (Shriver and Kittles, 2004). The first one is the lineage-based approach. These are based on the maternally inherited mtDNA genomes and the paternally inherited Y chromosome DNA. The lineage-based approach has been very useful for population studies, and allows individuals to trace their ultimate maternal and paternal origins. For example, African American individuals can find out what part of Africa their founding American ancestors may have come from (http://www .african-ancestry.com). These are the same techniques that have been used to consider the dispersal and migration of ancient and recent peoples. For example, in a survey of more than 2,000 men from Asia using more than 32 genetic markers, Tatiana Zerjal and her colleagues (2003) found a Y chromosome lineage that exhibited an unusual pattern thought to represent the expansion of the Mongol Empire. They called this haplotype the star cluster (reflecting the emergence of these similar variants from a common source). The star cluster lineage is found in sixteen different populations, distributed across Asia from the Pacific Ocean to the Caspian Sea. The MRCA (most recent common ancestor) for this cluster was dated to about 1,000 years ago, and the distribution of populations in which the lineage is found corresponds roughly to the maximum extent of the Mongol Empire. The Empire reached its peak under Genghis Khan (c. 1162–1227) and Khan and his close male relatives are said to have fathered many children (thousands, according to some historical sources).

One additional population outside the Mongol Empire also has a high frequency of the star cluster: the Hazaras of Pakistan (and Afghanistan), many of whom through oral tradition consider themselves to be direct male-line descendants of Genghis Khan. The star cluster is absent from other Pakistani populations. The distribution of the star cluster could have resulted from the migration of a group of Mongols carrying the haplotype or may even reflect the Y chromosome carried specifically by Genghis Khan and his relatives.

From the perspective of determining an individual's PGH, however, the lineage-based approach is limited because it traces only the origins of a very small portion of an individual's genome and does not reflect the vast bulk of a person's genetic history. In contrast to the lineage-based approach, *autosomal marker-based tests* use information from throughout the genome. *Ancestry informative markers* (AIMs) are alleles on the autosomal chromosomes that show substantial variation among different populations. The more AIMs that are examined in an individual, the more complete the picture of that individual's *biogeographical ancestry* can

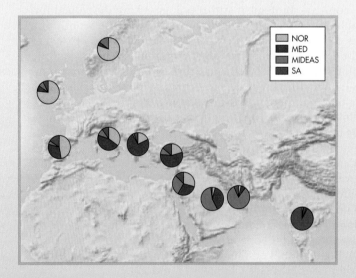

be obtained (Shriver and Kittles, 2004). Combining the information from all of these AIMs requires some major statistical analysis, which has to take into account the expression of each marker and its population associations. There will be some statistical noise in the system due to factors such as the overlapping population distribution of the markers and instances of convergent evolution. In addition, even when a hundred markers are used, the tests sample only a small portion of your genome that is the product of the combined efforts of thousands of ancestors. The biogeographical ancestry of a person, expressed in terms of percentage affiliations with different populations, is a statistical statement, not a direct rendering of a person's ancestry. And both AIMs and lineage-based tests are limited by the comparative samples that form the basis of our knowledge about the distribution of DNA markers. Thus, if you submit a cheek swab to several different companies with different comparative databases, you will get somewhat different ancestry results. Nonetheless, they provide us with an intriguing snapshot of the geographic origins of a person's ancestors.

Several commercial companies are now in the ancestry genetics business. We contacted one of these companies, DNAPrint Genomics (http://www.-AncestryByDNA.com), and obtained the biogeographical ancestry of two of the authors of this text, Craig Stanford (CS) and John S. Allen (JSA). The genetic testing product used is called Ancestry-ByDNA 2.5, which provides a breakdown of an individual's PGH in terms of affiliations with four major geographical groups: European, Native (aka Indigenous) American, Sub-Saharan African, and East Asian. It combines information derived from about 175 AIMs.

John Allen's results were: 46% European, 46% East Asian, 8% Native American, and 0% Sub-Saharan African. These results squared quite well with his known family history: His mother was Japanese and his father was an American of English and Scandinavian descent. The 8% Native American could have come from one or more ancestors on his father's side (some of whom arrived in the United States in the early colonial period). However, the 95% confidence intervals of the test indicate that for people of predominantly European ancestry, a threshold of 10% Native American needs to be reached before the result is statistically significant. For people of predominantly East Asian descent, the threshold is 12.5%. Therefore, in the absence of a family history of Native American ancestry, it is best to consider the 8% as statistical noise.

Craig Stanford's results were: 82% European, 14% Native American, 4% Sub-Saharan African, and 0% East Asian. The Native American result, which easily exceeds the statistical threshold, was a real surprise because CS has no family history of Native American ancestry. Following this result, his father was tested and was found to have 91% European and 9% Sub-Saharan African ancestry. Thus, all of CS's Native American ancestry was derived from his mother's side. Although she was not tested, it is reasonable to conclude that her Native American percentage would be greater than 25%—the equivalent of a grandparent, although this does not have to represent the contribution of a single individual. CS found this result to be somewhat ironic because earlier generations of women on his mother's side of the family had been proud members of the Daughters of the American Revolution, a lineage-based organization that was once (but is no longer) racially exclusionary. Stanford also requested a more detailed European ancestry genetic test (EuroDNA 1.0). Along with European ancestry, the tests showed 12% Middle Eastern ancestry. One of his paternal grandparents was from Italy, and the ancestry of southern Europeans often reflects population movements around the Mediterranean Sea, including Middle Eastern markers. In addition, there has been a long history of some gene flow from Sub-Saharan Africa into North Africa and the Middle East, which could explain his father's statistically significant Sub-Saharan African ancestry.

Ancestry genetics opens windows to the past, but in some cases, it raises more questions than answers about where you came from. This is not surprising because we know that the pattern of genetic variation across all humans is a complex one that does not partition well into regional or "racial" groups, that most of the genetic variation within humans exists within rather than between groups, and that different characteristics often follow cross-cutting clines. We can attest, however, that for anyone interested in their own biological ancestry, getting a personalized genetic history can be an exciting experience. Incidentally, humans are not the only species whose biological past can be explored: Genetic ancestry testing for dogs is also becoming available (http://www.whatsmydog.com) and paternity testing is available for both cats and dogs (http://www.catdna.org; http://www.akc.org/dna).

Premortem Injury and Disease

Injuries and sickness suffered during life are also an important part of the biological profile, and critical for understanding an individual's life and, perhaps, identity. Not all diseases or injuries leave marks on bone. However, we can distinguish the ones that do as having occurred while the person was alive because the bones show evidence of healing and remodeling (Figure 15.26[b]). Arthritis and infections of bone show up clearly in skeletal remains. Old healed injuries, such as broken limbs and even gunshot wounds that a person survived for several weeks, also leave their mark.

Premortem fractures can be key evidence of lifeways (Figure 15.26[a]). In forensic anthropology, multiple healed fractures—especially of the ribs and those typical of defensive wounds—can establish a series of episodes of violence, as is often the case in child abuse (Walker et al., 1997). Old injuries can also be matched to premortem Xrays taken when a victim sought medical attention, and thereby help to establish identity.

In addition to injury and disease, lifestyle may leave an indelible mark on the skeleton; an athlete who uses one side of the body for intense activity (such as a baseball pitcher or tennis player) will have a more robustly developed arm on that side—especially if he or she began the activity during childhood and continued through adulthood. Other repetitive activities also cause bone deposition to differ systematically between individuals. Injury, disease, and lifestyle all leave clues on the skeleton that tell the story of an individual's life. The skeleton may also be modified by events that occur well after or around the time of death. These changes can be critically important for understanding the context of death, but to be of use the scientist must be able to distinguish premortem bone changes from those that happened later in time.

Perimortem and Postmortem Trauma

For anthropologists, perimortem trauma is the physical evidence of activity that happened slightly before, during, or slightly after the time of death. We can differentiate it from premortem injury because in perimortem trauma no healing is evident. We can distinguish perimortem from postmortem trauma that happened well after death, because bones retain a large percentage of their organic component during the perimortem interval. As a result, they are more pliable and break differently than those that are well dried out after death; think of the difference between how a small branch that has just been plucked from a tree bends when you try to break it, whereas a long-dead, dried-out stick is brittle and snaps in two.

((•—[Listen to the **Podcast** "King Tut Felled by Injury and Malaria, Not Murder" on **myanthrolab**

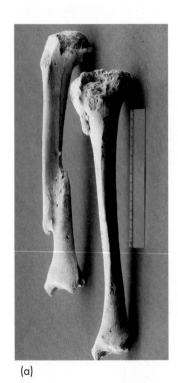

(a)

(b)

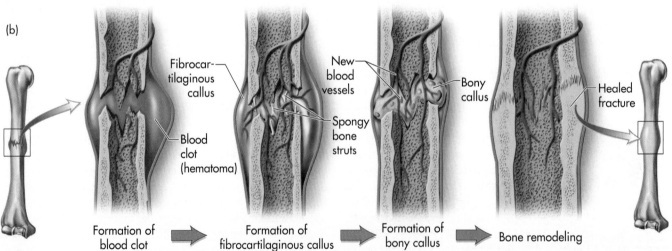

Fibrocartilaginous callus

Blood clot (hematoma)

New blood vessels

Spongy bone struts

Bony callus

Healed fracture

Formation of blood clot → Formation of fibrocartilaginous callus → Formation of bony callus → Bone remodeling

FIGURE 15.26 Healed bone fractures can provide clues about activities and fresh fractures can yield information about cause of death. (a) Note the fore-shortened tibia (left bone) due to a massive healed fracture, and the less severe fracture on one end (top) of the right bone. (b) The process of fracture healing starts with soft callus formation and proceeds to bone fusion.

Distinguishing perimortem trauma is one of the most routine tasks a forensic anthropologist undertakes. This type of evidence helps investigators understand what happened right around the time of death. This information also helps the medical examiner or coroner determine the cause and manner of death (whether homicide, suicide, or accident) and may help to establish intent in murder cases. For example, the presence of telltale fractures of the hyoid, a small bone in the neck, suggests strangulation. Perimortem trauma may also indicate a perpetrator's intent to hide or dispose of a body, implying that death was not accidental. Circular saws and reciprocating saws are often used to dismember bodies after a murder. These tools leave different marks on bone and sometimes leave traces of metal fragments embedded in bone. Experts can identify types of blades used and can indicate whether they are in the same class of tools as those owned by a suspect. Being able to show, based on anatomical knowledge, that a body was fleshed when dismembered rather than skeletonized has serious implications for inferring a crime or interpreting mortuary ritual in past societies.

Definitively postmortem events are not related to establishing cause and manner of death and are often of greater interest to bioarchaeologists than they are to forensic anthropologists. Analyses of postmortem events can be critical for establishing how bones arrived at a site: Were they deliberately placed in a burial cave, or did the individual unceremoniously fall through a chasm in the rock? Despite their greater importance for bioarchaeologists, postmortem events may rule out a crime if they suggest that marks on bone are made by natural causes, rather than knives, guns, or chainsaws, or if they show that the skeleton is of ancient rather than forensic interest. For instance, Willey and Leach (2003) cite a case in which forensic anthropologists sought to identify a human skull found in a suburban home. The skull was discolored in a variety of ways that most closely resembled the way in which skulls are sometimes treated when collected as trophies of war. As it turned out, the skull in question was a "souvenir" brought home from the Vietnam War by a man who had since moved away, leaving the skull in his garage.

Identification and Forensic Anthropology

Ideally, forensic anthropologists are trying to establish the identity of a victim. To do this they first develop the biological profile to narrow the field of focus of potential identities, and they define the time frame of the event. Once they have several possibilities, they can compare a number of different antemortem records to try to establish an identification. The most common are dental records, surgical implants, and the matching of antemortem and postmortem Xrays. But DNA can sometimes be used.

DNA analysis has given forensic scientists a powerful new tool for identifying victims and establishing the presence of an alleged perpetrator at a crime scene. However, there are also limitations to each of these uses. DNA testing can use tiny samples of hair, skin, blood, other body fluids, and even bone. However, the older the bone sample and the more hot and humid the environment in which it was buried, the less likely it is that DNA can be extracted from bone. Forensic scientists use a variety of tests, including DNA profiling (examining gene sequences that only kin would be likely to share), DNA typing (isolating particular segments of the genetic sequence for analysis), and DNA fingerprinting (the original DNA test, in which the same segments of DNA are lined up to examine the degree of similarity between samples from two people) (Nafte, 2000).

When skeletal material has been fragmented during a disaster (as in the World Trade Center crime scene in 2001), the identification process can be extraordinarily difficult; a biological profile may be impossible; and in such cases, forensic scientists may rely heavily on comparisons with DNA reference samples, typically obtained from relatives of the victims, to make positive identifications. To use DNA for identification, the scientist must have some knowledge of who the victim might have been to find living relatives to whom DNA can be matched, or to find personal items such as toothbrushes that might yield remnants of the victim's own DNA. Without such reference samples no identification can be made, although DNA may be able to narrow down the ancestry and identify the sex of the individual.

Besides DNA, other specific means for establishing a positive identification include obtaining antemortem medical or dental records, examining surgical implants or specific unique clothing or tattoos, or undertaking facial reconstruction (See Insights and Advances: If You Have DNA, Why Bother with Bones? on pages 416–417).

Time Since Death

One of the more difficult tasks for a forensic anthropologist is determining how long a victim has been dead. Anyone who has ever watched a police show knows that body temperature can be used to estimate time since death if the death is sufficiently recent. But over longer periods of time, other means are necessary. The research program in forensic anthropology at the University of Tennessee maintains an outdoor morgue in which bodies are left to decompose under a variety of controlled conditions so researchers can learn how natural processes affect the rate of decay (Bass & Jefferson, 2003). Many other such programs are now being developed. All the bodies used in the program are willed to the facility for this purpose, and once they are skeletonized the remains are curated in a research collection for other types of anthropological research including the development of comparative databases.

Decomposition is a continuum that includes a typical trajectory from cooling and rigidity, to bloating, skin slippage, liquefaction, deflation, and skeletonization. The rate at which decay proceeds is determined by aspects of the surrounding environment including burial depth, soil type, temperature, humidity, and so on. In general, bodies left on the surface of the ground decompose most quickly and those buried deeply in the ground most slowly. Surface remains decay more quickly because they are more likely to be interfered with by scavengers, such as rodents and carnivores, who destroy and scatter the remains. And insects also have greater access to surface remains, speeding up decomposition. The timing of insect life cycles is well known, and their preferences for certain types of tissues and extent of decay are also well studied. Forensic entomologists therefore are important members of any forensic team. Decomposition is quicker in the summer, averaging just a week or two for surface remains in the summer of the mid-Atlantic states. Although in very dry environments, such as deserts, bodies may mummify rather than skeletonize. The delay in wintertime decomposition is due almost entirely to lower temperatures and humidity, both of which reduce insect activity as well as the natural physiological rates of decay of the body itself. Corpses that are wrapped in impervious containers, like garbage bags, decompose more slowly than surface remains for many of the same reasons that buried bodies decompose more slowly. With all things being equal, single burials tend to decompose more quickly than do the more protected individuals in the middle of a mass grave—although individuals on the periphery decompose at rates similar to those of individual burials. Using all these clues and others, scientists work together to estimate time since death. This can help to narrow the focus of possible identifications and possible perpetrators by suggesting a time frame for the crime.

Antemortem Records, Facial Reconstruction, and Positive IDs

Your dentist keeps a chart of which teeth you have, which have been extracted, and which have been filled or crowned. All of your Xrays are also kept on file. These records can prove invaluable for making positive identifications because no two mouths are the same. However, comparing dental charts is time consuming, so the biological profile is used to limit the scope of possible identities. Forensic odontologists, specially trained dentists, work with forensic anthropologists to make identifications from dental records. Both dental Xrays and dental charts can be used for positive identifications (Adams, 2003). Exact matches of antemortem and postmortem dental Xrays can establish an identification in ways similar to antemortem medical Xrays (Stinson, 1975). But when Xrays are absent, comparing dental charts is an effective means of identification as well. A dental chart is made for the remains and this chart is compared, sometimes using the computerized program, OdontoSearch, with antemortem charts of missing individuals (Adams, 2003).

Medical Xrays taken before death can also be used for making identifications. An Xray of a person's head after an accident may reveal the frontal sinus, an air-filled space within the frontal bone just behind the brow area (Figure 15.27). The sinus is uniquely developed in each of us, so comparison of an Xray from a skull with an antemortem film of a known individual may lead to a positive identification. Healed wounds and infections that are caught on antemortem Xrays can also be compared to postmortem Xrays. If the healing is particularly idiosyncratic, this might lead to a positive identification or at least to a possible identification that could be confirmed by other tests.

Orthopedic implants and pins often resolve issues of identity. These implanted items often have either unique or batch serial numbers than can be traced back to an individual patient's medical records. And antemortem Xrays of a pin in place can also be compared to postmortem Xrays to lead to a positive identification. Sometimes, the biological profile doesn't match any possible identities, and so there are no antemortem records to establish a positive ID. In these cases, other more exploratory methods, such as facial reconstructions, may help the general public suggest a possible identity.

Facial reconstruction—the fleshing out of the skull to an approximation of what the individual looked like in life—is part art and part science. It is based on careful systematic studies of the relationship between skin thickness and bone features—and clay is used to layer on muscle, fat, and skin over a model of a victim's skull (Wilkinson, 2004). Digital technologies are also being developed to render three-dimensional virtual reconstructions. Eyes and ears are placed, although their color and shape can't be known for sure. The size of the nose is based on the height and breadth of the nasal aperture and the bony bridge. But some artistic license is required to estimate the shape of the end of the nose. Skin and hair color can't be known from the bone. For example, facial reconstructions of King Tut were commissioned by National Geographic magazine from two different artists. The two yielded similar facial reconstructions, much of which were dictated by the king's uniquely shaped head and slightly asymmetric jaw, but inferences about weight, skin and eye color varied. Once rendered, forensic facial reconstructions may be photographed and shown to the general public in the hopes that someone might recognize something about the individual. When possible identities are proposed, antemortem records can be checked—and perhaps an ID will be made.

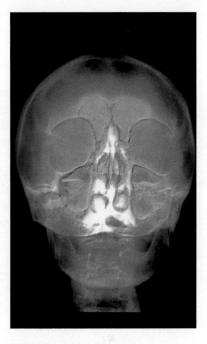

FIGURE 15.27 The frontal sinus, an air-filled space just behind the brow, is a unique size and shape in each of us and can be used to make a positive identification if antemortem Xrays are available.

Applications of Forensic Anthropology

Although forensic anthropologists most often work on cases of lone victims of homicide, suicide, or accidental death, they are also called to the scene of mass fatalities, to search for soldiers killed in combat, and to investigate human rights abuses that result in hidden or mass graves.

Mass Fatalities

In the days after the attack on the World Trade Center in New York on September 11, 2001, forensic anthropologists from around the country were called in to help identify the victims. The Oklahoma City bombing case seven years earlier had brought in a similar influx of anthropologists, as did the later devastation wrought by Hurricane Katrina. Forensic anthropologists play key roles in the attempt to identify victims of earthquakes, plane crashes, floods, and other natural and human-wrought disasters. The United States has regional emergency response teams called Disaster Mortuary Teams (DMORT) that include pathologists, forensic anthropologists, and forensic odontologists who are mobilized in response to national mass disasters such as the World Trade Center fire and collapse. Military forensic experts and sometimes DMORT respond when U.S. citizens or military are involved in mass fatalities abroad, such as the earthquake in Haiti for which DMORT was deployed to recover remains of American citizens.

Although we often think of mass disasters as involving hundreds or thousands of individual deaths, mass fatality incidents (MFIs) are defined as those in which the

insights & advances

IF YOU HAVE DNA, WHY BOTHER WITH BONES?

Each person has a unique DNA sequence, some of which can tell us the individual's sex or hint at their ancestry; other parts may tell us about hair and eye color. And in nearly every TV episode of *CSI* or *NCIS*, a DNA sequence is compared to a computer database and successfully identifies a perpetrator or a victim. The process apparently takes seconds to yield results. Since the 1980s when it was first used in court cases, DNA sequencing has revolutionized the forensic sciences. So if all this can be done with DNA from blood, semen, or saliva, why bother with bones and forensic anthropology at all?

In crime labs across the country, specific locations on nuclear DNA are used to establish a DNA profile. This profile is used to connect trace evidence such as blood, hair, skin, etc. from crime scenes to individuals; that is, to connect people to places and objects. Commonly, fifteen standardized locations on individual chromosomes are used to target known *short tandem repeats* (STRs) of nuclear DNA. STRs are short repeats of DNA sequences that come one right after the other. They do not code for anything in particular nor are they related to any particular external

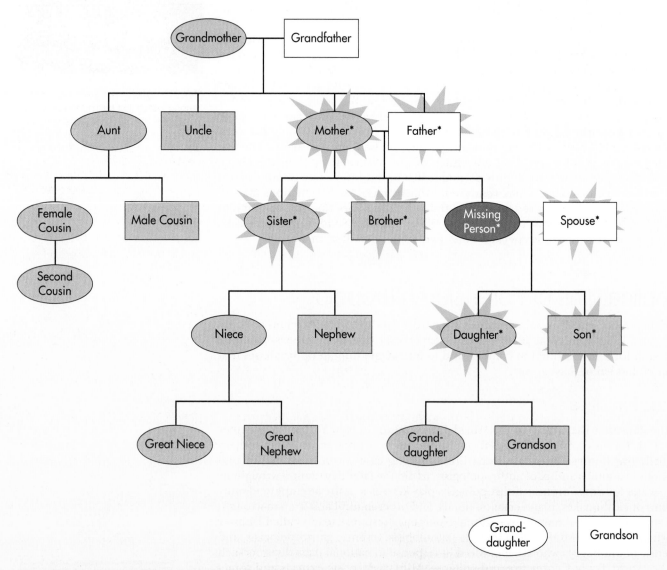

FIGURE A   For kinship analyses buccal swabs from close family are taken for comparison. In this chart males are indicated by squares and females by circles. Ideal samples are marked here in starbursts and include parents and offspring of the person to be matched. In the absence of these, maternal relatives (marked here in shaded boxes) may be sampled for mtDNA analyses.

feature like eye or hair color. That is, they have no known function. The number of repeats varies from individual to individual, and using the number of repeats at each of these 15 locations a DNA profile unique to that individual is developed. The chances of sampling the same profile in another individual is about 1 in a trillion, or more than the number of people alive on Earth today.

Say that you are called to a crime scene where there is a dead individual of unknown identity. The preferred sources for retrieving DNA are, in order of preference: nonclotted blood (DNA is present in the white blood cells only, because only they have nuclei), deep red (fresh) muscle, compact bone (say from the shaft of a long bone), any muscle, bone or tooth. Back in the lab, you attempt to extract DNA, which involves using the polymerase chain reaction to essentially make multiple copies of the DNA, and from these produce a DNA profile. If DNA is present, the length of each STR will be measured and translated into the number of repeats for that particular STR. Each STR will have two numbers associated with it, one each for the number of repeats on each locus of the individual's DNA (remember that each individual receives a strand from their mother and from their father).

But this DNA profile is useless for identifying the individual without something to compare it to. Ideally, an antemortem DNA sample is available from the victim—perhaps we have an idea of who they might be and we can search for medical samples taken before they died such as a Pap smear, a blood sample, a muscle biopsy, or a tooth saved by the tooth fairy. Other items, such as tooth brushes, are less desirable because we can't always be sure who they belonged to (or who used them). Any of these samples might yield a direct match. Making a direct match such as this, from a particular individual to a particular source, yields the kind of 1 in a trillion statistics mentioned above. Similarly, direct matches to individual DNA sequences that are in the Combined DNA Index System program (CODIS) and other databases can be powerful tools for linking individuals to trace evidence.

If no antemortem sample is available, a kinship analysis can be done by collecting DNA from the victim's direct relatives (Figure A). These are the kinds of analyses

FIGURE B A biological profile from the bony remains of an individual may be preferable to a DNA profile for a variety of reasons.

that were undertaken to confirm the recent death of Osama Bin Laden, for example. If both the biological mother and father are available, this is ideal. If not, the victim's children, full siblings, and maternal relatives are sought, and a lineage analysis using mtDNA and nuclear DNA may be undertaken. Sometimes there are surprises, such as finding out that parents or siblings are not as closely related as the family thought. Even in the best circumstances though, because of how human genetic variation is distributed across populations, kinship matches have lower statistic probabilities than do direct matches.

Under the best of circumstances, the process of extracting DNA profiles is time-consuming, expensive, and destructive. A single sample can take an entire day to process, and cases can involve hundreds of samples—in some instances, DNA may not work at all. In very hot and humid environments DNA degrades quickly, and even bones that appear perfect may retain no DNA. Or, destructive sampling may not be allowed, and families may be reluctant to provide reference samples. As we have seen, making a match requires having some idea of who the individual was in order to get antemortem or kinship samples. In all of these cases a biological

profile from the skeleton may be useful instead of, or in addition to, DNA extraction (Figure B). Biological profiles are relatively quick and cheap to complete, and they are nondestructive. They can also help to reduce the number of possible antemortem records that have to be considered, and positive identifications may be possible through comparisons to dental or medical records without ever having to resort to DNA. In many instances then, from individual crimes to airline crashes, the skeletal biological profile may be preferable. The DNA profile is a powerful tool for forensic scientists, but it's still not as fast or as easy as it seems on TV.

number of deaths overwhelms local resources—there is thus no minimum number and depending on the size of the municipality this might be fewer than 5 or 10 deaths. In such incidents, a main goal is to provide speedy and accurate disaster victim identification (DVI), which requires three big operational areas—search and recovery, morgue operations, and family assistance centers. Forensic anthropologists are critical participants in all three of these areas.

In 2005, DMORT was deployed to assist in DVI in the aftermath of Hurricane Katrina. Hurricane Katrina was a category 3 storm that devastated the Gulf Coast of the United States in August of 2005. Up to that time it was the most costly storm in U.S. history, and major damage was caused by the breaching of the levees that protected the city of New Orleans, which sits below sea level. More than 1800 deaths ensued, with flooding being the main cause of death and destruction. Because of widespread flooding, victim recovery was also delayed, requiring the assistance of forensic anthropologists in identifications. The identifications were made more difficult by the flooding which also destroyed or damaged much of the antemortem medical and dental records that are normally used in identification. DMORT teams were rotated in for two-week assignments, and forensic anthropologist were utilized in recovery, morgue operations, and family record collection.

War Dead

U.S. forensic anthropologists first became involved in the identification of those who died in war when the Central Identification Laboratory (CIL) in Hawaii (CILHI) was formed to aid in the identification of those missing in action during World War II. Since then the skeletal remains of U.S. soldiers and civilians from World War II, the Korean War, the Vietnam War, and other military actions have been recovered and identified by this group of anthropologists. The CIL, now part of the Joint Prisoner of War/Missing in Action Accounting Command (JPAC), sends teams around the world to identify and recover U.S. soldiers lost in the wars of the twentieth century. The remains are brought back to the CIL, thoroughly examined, and identified. In addition to standard forensic anthropological techniques, JPAC teams also extensively use forensic DNA techniques to reach a positive identification so that remains may be returned to the next of kin.

Not only does this group of forensic anthropologists help in identifying missing personnel, but they have also undertaken some of the most important systematic research used in forensic anthropology and bioarchaeology. For example, Dr. Mildred Trotter, an early director of the CIL, developed regression analyses for determining stature from long bone lengths based on the skeletal remains of soldiers who died in the Korean War. This large body of work remains a standard in forensic and bioarchaeological analyses today and would not have been possible without the detailed medical histories of these military personnel.

War Crimes and Genocide

Finally, forensic anthropologists may play a key role in uncovering mass graves and identifying bodies in them, and these scientists may be important witnesses in the investigation of war crimes. Whether in Cambodia, Rwanda, Argentina, Bosnia, or Iraq, when repressive regimes crack down on their citizens, they often attempt to intimidate the population through mass murder. The mass graves that are left contain the bodies of hundreds or even thousands of victims, whose loved ones spend lifetimes attempting to locate them and determine their fate. Forensic anthropologists help to identify the victims for the sake of surviving family members and may provide key evidence in reconstructing a mass crime scene in an effort to bring those responsible to justice. Forensic anthropologists in these areas work for both government and private groups such as Physicians for Human Rights, the International Commission for Missing Persons, and the United Nations (UN). Such teams often start work before the conflicts end; for example, U.S. forensic archaeologists and anthropologists are currently at work in Iraq.

One example of such work is the effort to exhume mass graves in the former Yugoslavia that began in 1996 under the auspices of the United Nations, and in particular the International Criminal Tribunal for the former Yugoslavia (ICTY), in partnership with Physicians for Human Rights. Some of these exhumations concentrated in eastern Croatia on a grave site known as Ovcara, which contained victims from a massacre in Vukovar. The Vukovar massacre occurred in November 1991. The forensic teams exhumed about 200 bodies from Ovcara, nearly all of them males (Figure 15.28). Mapping the grave site took more than a month. The remains were autopsied in Zagreb with the goals of constructing a biological profile that would help in identification and interpreting perimortem trauma to understand the cause of death. Many of the victims had multiple gunshot wounds and other forms of perimortem trauma. Biological profiles were com-

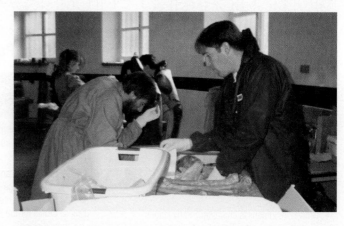

FIGURE 15.28 A team of forensic experts working on remains recovered from Ovcara in the former Yugoslavia.

pared with the medical and dental records of missing people (a task hampered by the destruction of hospitals and other medical facilities during the war) and lists of identifying characteristics (including tattoos) provided by family members of missing people. Through these comparisons, about half of the 200 were positively identified. This evidence has been used in the prosecution of war crimes by the UN-ICTY, including the case against the region's former leader, Slobodan Milošević.

Forensic anthropologists use the changes wrought in the human skeleton by natural selection and an individual's life experiences to read the clues of recent human history. They apply the same principles, theory, and method to recent humans that primate paleoanthropologists applied to understanding our 65-million-year-old fossil ancestors, all in a struggle to understand what makes us universally and uniquely human.

Epilogue

The place of humans in the natural world has been the major theme of this book. We have explored this topic from a wide variety of perspectives, including the fossil record, the behavior of living nonhuman primates, the lives of people in traditional societies, the workings of the brain, and the biology of modern people. However, our explorations of these diverse topics have been linked by a single common thread: evolutionary theory.

You've now completed a comprehensive look at your own evolutionary past, and at the place of humankind in the history of the world. As you have seen, the evidence of our past is present in us today. It's visible in our DNA, our hominin anatomy, our physiological adaptations, and even in aspects of our behavior. Many people live in denial or in ignorance of this evolutionary past. In contrast, we feel that embracing and understanding it is critical to being an enlightened citizen of the twenty-first century.

It is important to keep in mind, however, that to embrace an evolutionary perspective of humankind is not to deny the importance of culture in our lives. We have seen that culture may be the most fundamental of human traits. Many aspects of the biology of modern people are influenced in some way by culture, while at the same time our cultural nature is a direct outgrowth of our biology.

This book has been concerned with our evolutionary past, but the most pressing question for humankind in the early twenty-first century is whether our species will survive long enough to experience significant evolutionary change. Environmental degradation, overpopulation, warfare, and a host of other problems plague our species. It is safe to say that no species in Earth's history has contended with so many self-induced problems and survived. But of course, no other species has had the capability to solve problems and change its world for the better the way that we humans have.

Biomedical and Forensic Anthropology

Biomedical Anthropology and the Biocultural Perspective

Birth, Growth, and Aging

- Patterns of growth and development are a direct reflection of health status in a population, as evidenced by the secular trend in growth.
- Birth is a biocultural process in humans, in which the large head of newborns may have selected for the practice of midwifery or birth assistance.
- Growth in humans is characterized by stages that are seen in other primates, but which are each longer to accommodate the learning required of the large human brain.
- Adolescence and the adolescent growth spurt may be unique to humans.
- Menopause may be an aging-associated adaptation, although most evolutionary models of aging see it as a by-product of physiology. **[pp 388–396]**

Infectious Disease and Biocultural Evolution

- The spread and severity of infectious disease is influenced by a wide range of biological and cultural factors.
- The development of agriculture leading to the establishment of large, high-density populations fundamentally changed the infectious disease profile for the human species.
- Increases in human mobility and migration have facilitated the spread of infectious disease to immunologically vulnerable populations. **[pp 396–400]**

Diet and Disease

- There are fundamental differences between the contemporary diet and that of hunter-gatherers, (the "Paleolithic diet").
- Although they may support larger populations, agricultural diets are associated with specific and general nutritional deficiencies.
- The mismatch between the diet we evolved with and that which we currently have may be one cause of increases in diseases associated with lifestyle. **[pp 400–403]**

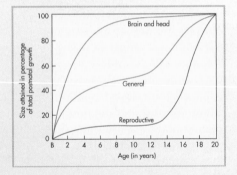

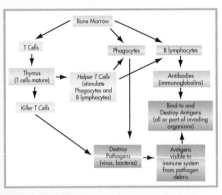

Forensic Anthropology

Forensic Anthropology, Scene Recovery, and Processing

- The human skeleton retains clues about an indvidual's life, death, and evolutionary adaptations.
- Forensic anthropologists use these clues and the theory and method of biological anthropology and related subjects in criminal cases.
- Archaeological techniques are used to survey a scene and excavate remains.
- Chain of custody is established, remains are inventoried, and a biological profile is prepared. **[pp 403–405]**

Biological Profiles

- Age at death can be estimated in children from dental eruption and bone development patterns and in adults from systematic degenerative changes to the pubic symphysis and other bones.

- Sex can be inferred in adults from primary sexual characteristics of the pelvis and secondary sexual characteristics of the skull and other bones.

- Ancestry is difficult to assess but may be inferred from cranial and postcranial features.

- Stature and weight are most usually estimated from the leg bones.

- Premortem trauma and disease may be evident as healed areas in the skeleton.

- Perimortem and postmortem trauma tells the forensic anthropologist about events that occurred around the time of death and well after death, respectively. **[pp 405–413]**

Forensic Identifications and Applications

- Forensic anthropologists provide information to the medical examiner or coroner that may assist in establishing a positive identification and cause and manner of death.

- DNA comparisons or matches with antemortem dental or medical records often provide the basis for identifications.

- In addition to individual criminal cases, forensic anthropologists also assist in victim identification in natural disasters, mass disasters, war crimes, and human rights violations. **[pp 413–419]**

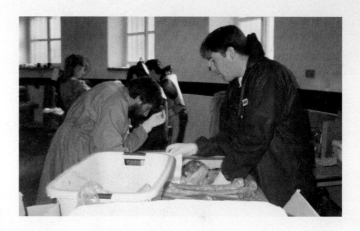

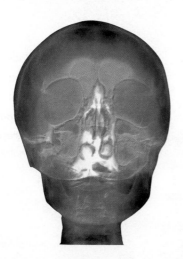

My AnthroLab CONNECTIONS

Watch. Listen. View. Explore. Read.

MyAnthroLab is designed just for you. Each chapter features a customized study plan to help you learn and review key concepts and terms. Dynamic visual activities, videos, and readings found in the multimedia library will enhance your learning experience.

Resources from this Chapter:

Watch on **myanthrolab**
- ▶ *Spread of the Black Death (or Plague)*

Listen on **myanthrolab**
- ▶ *King Tut Felled by Injury and Malaria, Not Murder*

View on **myanthrolab**
- ▶ *U.S. Department of Health and Human Services Administration on Aging*
- ▶ *So You Want to be a Forensic Anthropologist*

Explore on **myanthrolab** In MySearchLab, enter the Anthropology database to find relevant and recent scholarly and popular press publications. For this chapter, enter the following keywords: disease, diet, growth, birth

Read on **myanthrolab**
- ▶ *Evolution and the Origins of Disease* by Randolph M. Nesse and George C. Williams
- ▶ *Bare Bones Anthropology: The Bioarchaeology of Human Remains* by Clark Spencer Larsen
- ▶ *Dental Deductions: Why and How Anthropologists Study Teeth* by John R. Lukacs

Appendix A

Primate and Human Comparative Anatomy

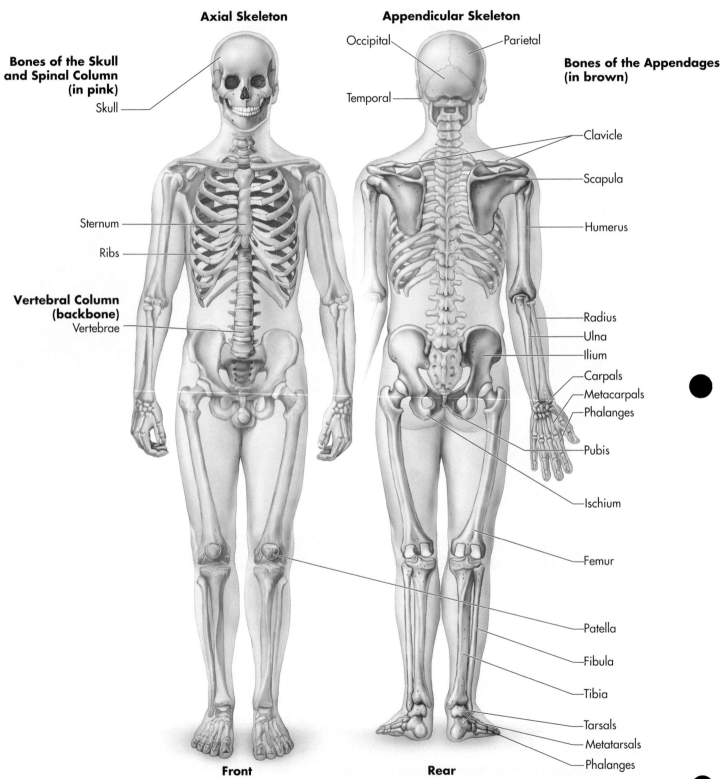

Axial Skeleton

Appendicular Skeleton

Bones of the Skull and Spinal Column (in pink)

Skull

Sternum

Ribs

Vertebral Column (backbone)

Vertebrae

Occipital

Parietal

Temporal

Bones of the Appendages (in brown)

Clavicle

Scapula

Humerus

Radius

Ulna

Ilium

Carpals

Metacarpals

Phalanges

Pubis

Ischium

Femur

Patella

Fibula

Tibia

Tarsals

Metatarsals

Phalanges

Front

Rear

FIGURE A.1 The axial (in pink) and appendicular (in brown) skeletons.

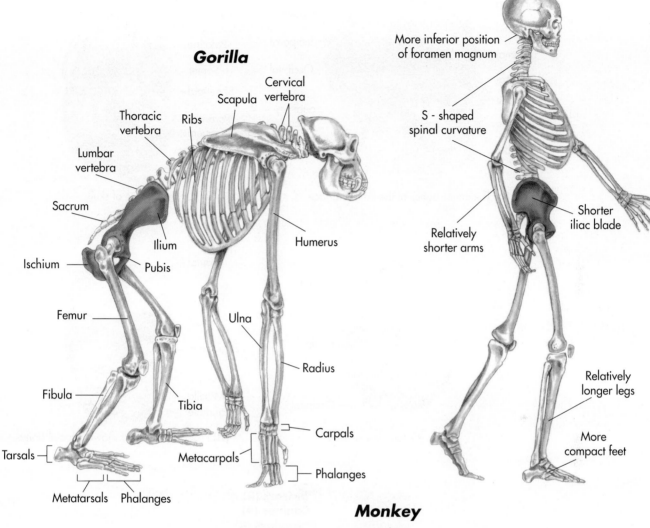

Homo

More inferior position of foramen magnum

S - shaped spinal curvature

Relatively shorter arms

Shorter iliac blade

Relatively longer legs

More compact feet

Gorilla

Cervical vertebra

Scapula

Thoracic vertebra

Ribs

Lumbar vertebra

Sacrum

Ilium

Ischium

Pubis

Femur

Humerus

Ulna

Radius

Fibula

Tibia

Carpals

Metacarpals

Phalanges

Tarsals

Metatarsals   Phalanges

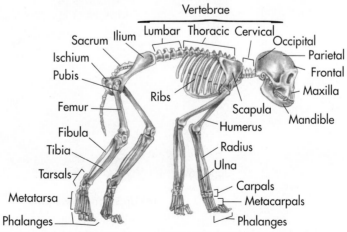

Monkey

Vertebrae

Sacrum   Ilium   Lumbar Thoracic Cervical   Occipital

Ischium   Parietal

Pubis   Frontal

Ribs   Maxilla

Femur   Scapula

Mandible

Fibula   Humerus

Tibia   Radius

Tarsals   Ulna

Metatarsa   Carpals

Metacarpals

Phalanges   Phalanges

FIGURE A.2 Comparisons of *Gorilla*, *Homo*, and *Proconsul* skeletons.

Human Skull

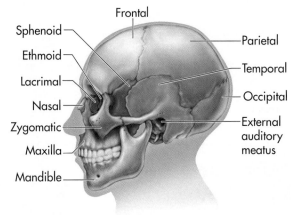

Sphenoid
Ethmoid
Lacrimal
Nasal
Zygomatic
Maxilla
Mandible
Frontal
Parietal
Temporal
Occipital
External auditory meatus

(a) The major bones of the skull and face

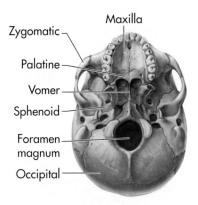

Zygomatic
Palatine
Vomer
Sphenoid
Foramen magnum
Occipital
Maxilla

(b) Lower surface of skull

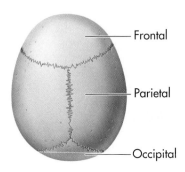

Frontal
Parietal
Occipital

(c) Top view of skull

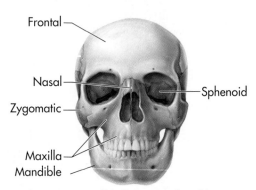

Frontal
Nasal
Zygomatic
Maxilla
Mandible
Sphenoid

(d) Front view of skull showing facial bones

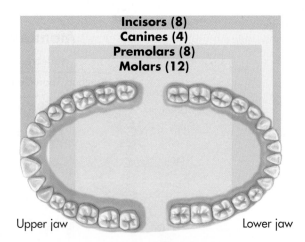

Incisors (8)
Canines (4)
Premolars (8)
Molars (12)

Upper jaw   Lower jaw

(e) Upper and lower jaws

FIGURE A.3   (a, b, c) The major bones of the skull and face, (d) facial bones and, (e) dentition.

The Vertebral Column

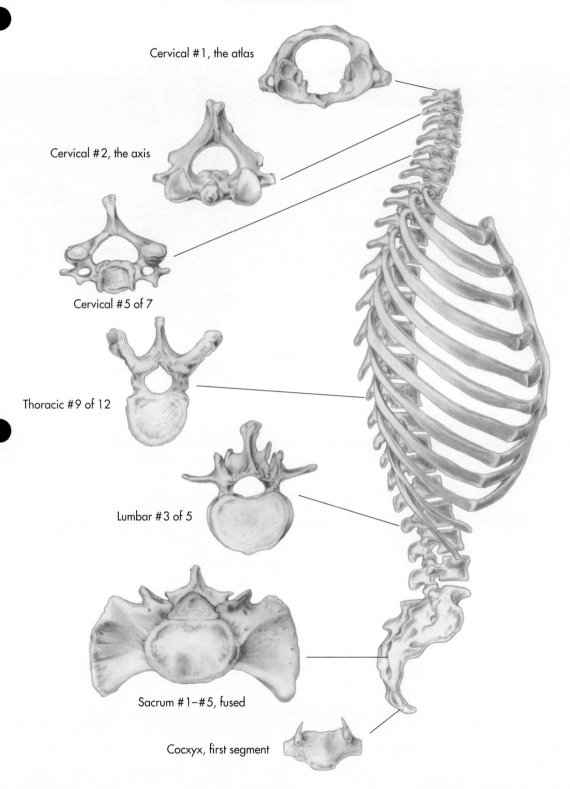

Cervical #1, the atlas

Cervical #2, the axis

Cervical #5 of 7

Thoracic #9 of 12

Lumbar #3 of 5

Sacrum #1–#5, fused

Cocxyx, first segment

FIGURE A.4   The vertebral column. The human vertebral column consists of 7 cervical, 12 thoracic, 5 lumbar, 5 fused sacral, and 4 or 5 diminutive coccygeal vertebrae.

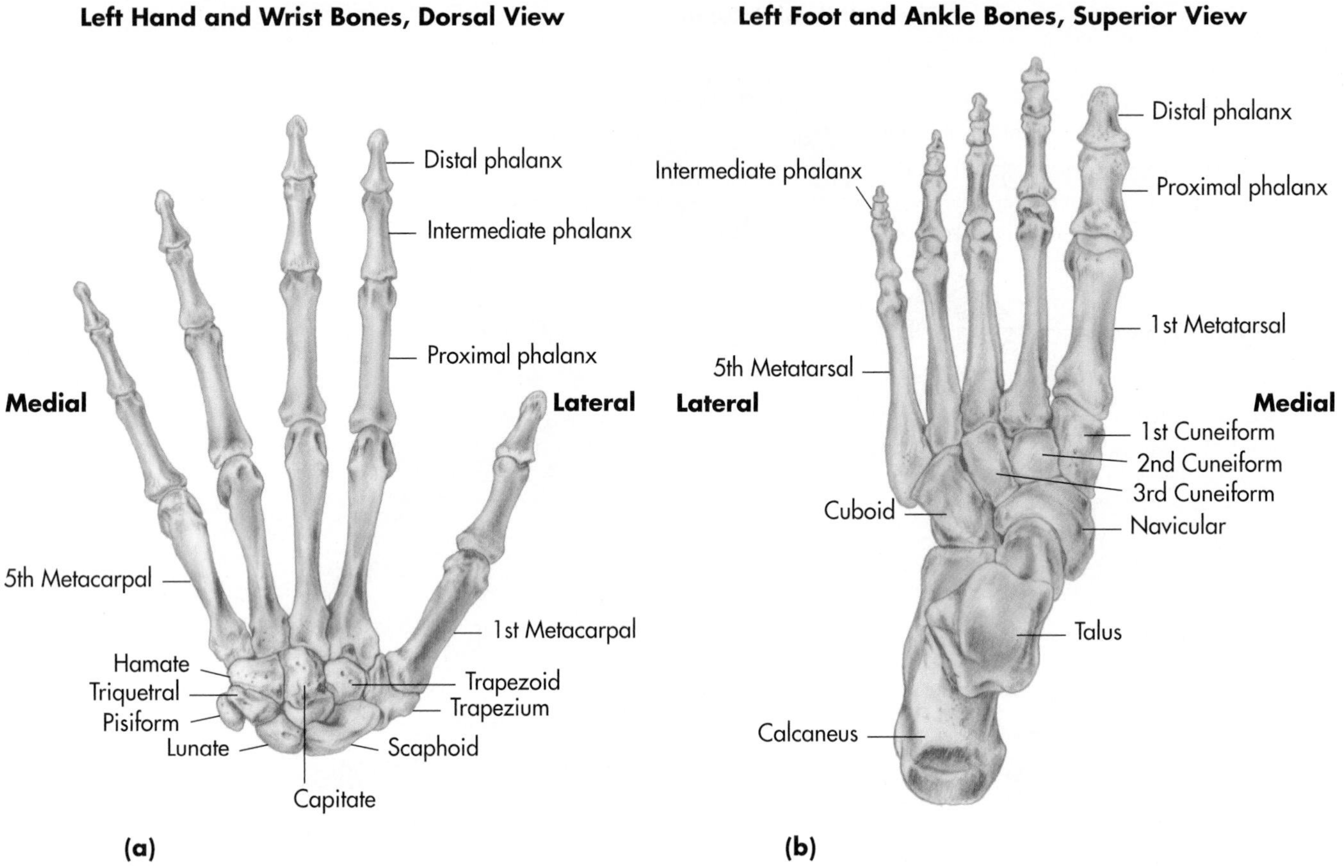

Left Hand and Wrist Bones, Dorsal View

Left Foot and Ankle Bones, Superior View

Distal phalanx

Intermediate phalanx

Proximal phalanx

Medial   **Lateral**

5th Metacarpal

Hamate
Triquetral
Pisiform
Lunate
Scaphoid
Capitate
1st Metacarpal
Trapezoid
Trapezium

(a)

Intermediate phalanx

Distal phalanx

Proximal phalanx

5th Metatarsal

1st Metatarsal

Lateral   **Medial**

Cuboid

1st Cuneiform
2nd Cuneiform
3rd Cuneiform
Navicular

Talus

Calcaneus

(b)

FIGURE A.5   (a) Left hand and wrist bones and (b) left foot and ankle bones.

The Hardy–Weinberg Equilibrium

In Chapter 5, we introduced the Hardy–Weinberg equilibrium in the context of our discussion of the forces of evolutionary change. Population genetics provides the mathematical underpinnings of evolutionary theory, and the Hardy–Weinberg equilibrium is at the heart of mathematical and quantitative approaches to understanding evolutionary change in diploid organisms. In this appendix, we will briefly go over a derivation of the Hardy–Weinberg equilibrium and show some applications of the equilibrium in evolutionary research.

Throughout the discussion, we will use the simplest case to illustrate our examples: a single gene (or locus) with two alleles, A and a. The frequency of A in the population is represented by p; the frequency of a is represented by q. By definition, $p + q = 1$.

Derivation of the Hardy–Weinberg Equilibrium

The Hardy–Weinberg equilibrium states that, given known allele frequencies p and q, we can represent the genotype frequencies by $AA = p^2$, $Aa = 2pq$, and $aa = q^2$. Furthermore, these allele frequencies remain constant from generation to generation if the following conditions are met:

- Large population size (or theoretically infinite population size), which minimizes the influence of genetic drift on allele frequencies
- Random mating (no inbreeding or assortative or disassortative mating)
- No mutation
- No gene flow
- No natural selection

Let us begin by considering a specific example, where the allele frequency of A is 0.6 ($p = 0.6$) and that of a is 0.4 ($q = 0.4$). To look at this another way, the probability that any given sperm or egg will carry A is 0.6, and the probability that it will carry a is 0.4. Thus under conditions of totally random mating, with no other evolutionary forces in effect (under equilibrium conditions), the probability of producing a zygote with a homozygous AA genotype is $(0.6)(0.6) = 0.36$. We can represent the probabilities of all the genotypes occurring in a modified Punnett square:

		Sperm	
		freq(A) = p = 0.6	freq(a) = q = 0.4
Eggs	freq(A)=p=0.6	freq(AA) = p^2 = (0.6)(0.6) = 0.36	freq(Aa) = pq = (0.6)(0.4) = 0.24
	freq(a)=q=0.4	freq(Aa) = pq = (0.6)(0.4) = 0.24	freq(aa) = q^2 = (0.4)(0.4) = 0.16

This gives us a population with genotype frequencies of 0.36 (for AA), 0.48 (for Aa), and 0.16 (for aa). What are the allele frequencies for this population? For A, it is $0.36 + (0.5)(0.48) = 0.36 + 0.24 = 0.6$, which is what the frequency of A was originally. The allele frequency of a is $0.16 + (0.5)(0.48) = 0.16 + 0.24 = 0.40$, which is the original frequency of a. This demonstrates that allele frequencies are maintained in equilibrium under conditions of random mating and in the absence of other evolutionary forces.

The general equation for the distribution of genotypes for a population in Hardy–Weinberg equilibrium is given by the equation

$$p^2 + 2pq + q^2 = 1$$

We can derive this equation directly from the modified Punnett square.

The constancy of allele frequencies over generations is shown by the following equations. Let p' equal the allele frequency of A in the first generation. From the preceding example we see that

$$p' = \text{(frequency of } AA\text{)} + (0.5)(\text{frequency of } Aa)$$

We want to count only half the alleles for A in the heterozygotes. Substituting the allele frequency values from the Hardy–Weinberg equation, we get

$$p' = p^2 + (0.5)(2pq)$$

Because $(0.5)(2pq) = pq$, we now have

$$p' = p^2 + pq$$

Which, factoring out p, is the same thing as

$$p' = p(p + q)$$

As you recall, $p + q = 1$; therefore,

$$p' = p$$

This demonstrates that allele frequencies remain constant in a population in Hardy–Weinberg equilibrium.

One of the main uses of the Hardy–Weinberg equation is to determine if a population is not in equilibrium. We do this by comparing observed allele frequencies with

427

observed genotype frequencies. If the observed genotype frequencies are significantly different from those expected based on the allele frequencies (which we usually check by using a chi-square statistical test), then we can say the population is not in equilibrium. This result indicates that one of the assumptions of the Hardy–Weinberg equilibrium is being violated and that an evolutionary force may be acting on the population or acted on the population in the past to produce the non-equilibrium distribution of alleles.

Another application of the Hardy–Weinberg equation is to estimate the frequency of heterozygotes in a population. As we discussed in Chapter 5, it is particularly useful for estimating the frequency in a population of carriers of recessive autosomal illnesses, such as Tay–Sachs disease or cystic fibrosis. The recessive allele frequency is simply

$$q = \sqrt{\text{frequency of autosomal recessive condition}}$$

And the dominant allele frequency is

$$p = 1 - q$$

Thus the frequency of heterozygous carriers = $2pq$.

Hardy–Weinberg and Natural Selection

The Hardy–Weinberg equilibrium can help us mathematically model the effects of any of the forces of evolution (mutation, genetic drift, gene flow, and natural selection). Let us consider how to use the Hardy–Weinberg equation to understand how natural selection may affect the distribution of allele frequencies in a population. In these equations, we assume that natural selection is the only force of evolution acting on the population.

In the simple case of one gene with two alleles, we have three possible genotypes that are subject to natural selection. To model the change in allele frequencies, we need to know not the absolute fitness of each genotype (which we could measure as its likelihood of survival), but rather each genotype's fitness relative to each other. Relative fitness usually is represented by the letter w; thus we have

$$w_{AA} = \text{relative fitness of } AA$$
$$w_{Aa} = \text{relative fitness of } Aa$$
$$w_{aa} = \text{relative fitness of } aa$$

Let's say that the homozygous genotype AA has the highest fitness; its relative fitness w_{AA} therefore would be equal to 1. The relative fitnesses of Aa and aa are lower, such that

$$w_{AA} = 1.0$$
$$w_{Aa} = 0.8$$
$$w_{aa} = 0.4$$

Let's also assume starting allele frequencies of $p = 0.7$ and $q = 0.3$.

If the population were in Hardy–Weinberg equilibrium, the expected genotype frequencies after one generation would be

$$p^2 = (0.7)(0.7) = 0.49 \text{ for } AA$$
$$2pq = 2(0.7)(0.3) = 0.42 \text{ for } Aa$$
$$q^2 = (0.3)(0.3) = 0.09 \text{ for } aa$$

However, natural selection is working on this population and affecting the survival of the different genotypes. So the genotype frequencies after selection are

$$w_{AA}p^2 = 1.0(0.7)(0.7) = 0.49 \text{ for } AA$$
$$w_{Aa}2pq = 0.8(2)(0.7)(0.3) = 0.336 \text{ for } Aa$$
$$w_{aa}q^2 = 0.4(0.3)(0.3) = 0.036 \text{ for } aa$$

The frequency of p after natural selection has acted on the population is

$$p' = [(0.49) + (0.5)(0.336)]/(0.49 + 0.336 + 0.036)$$
$$= 0.658/0.862$$
$$= 0.763$$

The frequency of q is

$$q' = 1 - p' = 1 - 0.763 = 0.237$$

So after only one generation of natural selection operating at these levels, there is a substantial change in allele frequencies, with A going from 0.7 to 0.763 and a decreasing from 0.3 to 0.237. Following this through five generations, the allele frequencies would be

Generation	1	2	3	4	5
P	0.763	0.813	0.852	0.883	0.907
q	0.237	0.187	0.148	0.117	0.093

In the case of a lethal autosomal recessive condition (such as Tay–Sachs disease), in which the relative fitness of the recessive homozygote is 0 and for the other two genotypes it is 1, we can represent the change in allele frequency of the recessive allele by a simple equation (which is derived from the Hardy–Weinberg equation):

$$q_g = q_0/(1 + gq_0)$$

where g is the number of generations passed, q_g is the frequency of a in generation g, and q_0 is the starting frequency of a. Consider a founding population in which the allele frequency of a lethal recessive is 0.20. Over ten generations, the frequency of this allele will decrease to

$$q_{10} = 0.2/[1 + (10)(0.2)]$$
$$= 0.2/3$$
$$= 0.067$$

Of course, a small founding population violates one of the conditions of the Hardy–Weinberg equilibrium (infinite population size), but we can ignore that for the sake of this example.

Metric–Imperial Conversions

METRIC UNIT	IMPERIAL EQUIVALENT
1 centimeter	0.39 inches
1 meter	3.28 feet
1 kilometer	0.62 miles
1 kilogram	2.20 pounds
454 grams	1 pound
1 gram	0.035 ounces
1 liter	1.06 quarts
400 cubic centimeters	24.4 cubic inches
1 square kilometer	0.39 square miles
1 square kilometer	247 acres
0 degrees Celsius	32 degrees Fahrenheit

Glossary

ABO blood type system Refers to the genetic system for one of the proteins found on the surface of red blood cells. Consists of one gene with three alleles: A, B, and O.

acclimatization Short-term changes in physiology that occur in an organism in response to changes in environmental conditions.

Acheulean Stone tool industry of the early and middle Pleistocene characterized by the presence of bifacial hand axes and cleavers. This industry is made by a number of *Homo* species, including *H. erectus* and early *H. sapiens.*

activity budget The pattern of waking, eating, moving, socializing, and sleeping that all nonhuman primates engage in each day.

adapoids Super family of mostly Eocene primates, probably ancestral to all strepsirhines.

adaptability The ability of an individual organism to make positive anatomical or physiological changes after short-or long-term exposure to stressful environmental conditions.

adaptation A trait that increases the reproductive success of an organism, produced by natural selection in the context of a particular environment.

adaptationism A premise that all aspects of an organism have been molded by natural selection to a form optimal for enhancing reproductive success.

adaptive radiation The diversification of one founding species into multiple species and niches.

alleles Alternative versions of a gene. Alleles are distinguished from one another by their different effects on the phenotypic expression of the same gene.

Allen's rule Stipulates that in warmer climates, the limbs of the body are longer relative to body size to dissipate body heat.

allopatric speciation Speciation occurring via geographic isolation.

amino acids Molecules that form the basic building blocks of protein.

anagenesis Evolution of a trait or a species into another over a period of time.

analogous Having similar traits due to similar use, not due to shared ancestry.

angular torus A thickened ridge of bone at the posterior angle of the parietal bone.

anthropoid Members of the primate suborder Anthropoidea that includes the monkeys, apes, and hominins.

anthropology The study of humankind in a cross-cultural context. Anthropology includes the subfields cultural anthropology, linguistic anthropology, archaeology, and biological anthropology.

anthropometry The measurement of different aspects of the body, such as stature or skin color.

antibodies Proteins (immunoglobulins) formed by the immune system that are specifically structured to bind to and neutralize invading antigens.

antigens Whole or part of an invading organism that prompts a response (such as production of antibodies) from the body's immune system.

arboreal hypothesis Hypothesis for the origin of primate adaptation that focuses on the value of grasping hands and stereoscopic vision for life in the trees.

archaeology The study of the material culture of past peoples.

argon–argon Radiometric technique modified from K–Ar that measures ^{40}K by proxy using ^{39}Ar. Allows measurement of smaller samples with less error.

association cortex Parts of the cerebral cortex where inputs from primary motor and sensory cortex are processed.

artifacts The objects, from tools to art, left by earlier generations of people.

autoimmune diseases Diseases caused by the immune system reacting against the normal, healthy tissues of the body.

autosomal dominant disease A disease that is caused by a dominant allele: Only one copy needs to be inherited from either parent for the disease to develop.

autosomal recessive disease A disease caused by a recessive allele; one copy of the allele must be inherited from each parent for the disease to develop.

autosomes Any of the chromosomes other than the sex chromosomes.

auxology The scientific study of human growth and development.

balanced polymorphism A stable polymorphism in a population in which natural selection prevents any of the alternative phenotypes (or underlying alleles) from becoming fixed or being lost.

base Variable component of the nucleotides that form the nucleic acids DNA and RNA. In DNA, the bases are adenine, guanine, thymine, and cytosine. In RNA, uracil replaces thymine.

Bergmann's rule Stipulates that body size is larger in colder climates to conserve body temperature.

biface A stone tool that has been flaked on two faces or opposing sides forming a cutting edge between the two flake scars.

binomial nomenclature Linnean naming system for all organisms, consisting of a genus and species label.

bioarchaeology The study of human remains in an archaeological context.

bioarchaeology The study of the biological component (usually osteology) of the archaeological record. Includes mortuary archaeology.

biocultural anthropology The study of the interaction between biology and culture, which plays a role in most human traits.

biogeography The distribution of animals and plants on the earth.

biological anthropology The study of humans as biological organisms, considered in an evolutionary framework; sometimes called physical anthropology.

biological profile The biological particulars of an individual as estimated from his or her skeletal remains. These particulars include estimates of sex, age at death, height, ancestry, and disease status.

biological species concept Defines species as interbreeding populations reproductively isolated from other such populations.

biomedical anthropology The subfield of biological anthropology concerned with issues of health and illness.

biostratigraphy Relative dating technique using comparison of fossils from different stratigraphic sequences to estimate which layers are older and which are younger.

blades Flakes that are twice as long as they are wide.

brachiation Mode of arm-hanging and arm-swinging that uses a rotating shoulder to suspend the body of an ape or hominin beneath a branch or to travel between branches.

brainstem The part of the brain that controls basal metabolic rates, respiration, pulse, and other basic body functions.

breccia Cement-like matrix of fossilized rock and bone. Many important South African early humans have been found in breccias.

bridewealth Payment offered by a man to the parents of a woman he wants to marry.

butchering site A place where there is archaeological evidence of the butchering of carcasses by hominins. The evidence usually consists of tool cut marks on fossilized animal bones or the presence of the stone tools themselves.

calibrated relative dating techniques Techniques that can be correlated to an absolute chronology.

calotte The skullcap, or the bones of the skull, excluding those that form the face and the base of the cranium.

calvaria The braincase; includes the bones of the calotte and those that form the base of the cranium but excludes the bones of the face.

canine fossa An indentation on the maxilla above the root of the canine, an anatomical feature usually associated with modern humans that may be present in some archaic *Homo* species in Europe.

captive study Primate behavior study conducted in a zoo, laboratory, or other enclosed setting.

Catarrhini Infraorder of the order Primates that includes the Old World monkeys, apes, and hominins.

catastrophism Theory that there have been multiple creations interspersed by great natural disasters such as Noah's flood.

centromere Condensed and constricted region of a chromosome. During mitosis and meiosis, location where sister chromatids attach to one another.

cerebellum The "little brain" tucked under the cerebrum and important in the control of balance, posture, and voluntary movement.

cerebral cortex The layer of gray matter that covers the surface of the cerebral hemispheres, divided into functional regions that correspond to local patterns of neuronal organization.

cerebrum The largest part of the human brain, which is split into left and right hemispheres. Seat of all "higher" brain functions.

cervical vertebrae   The seven neck vertebrae.

chain of custody   In forensic cases, the detailed notes that establish what was collected at the scene, the whereabouts of these remains, and the access to them after retrieval from the scene.

Châtelperronian   An Upper Paleolithic tool industry that has been found in association with later Neandertals.

chromatin   The diffuse form of DNA as it exists during the interphase of the cell cycle.

chromosome   Discrete structure composed of condensed DNA and supporting proteins.

chronometric dating techniques   Techniques that estimate the age of an object in absolute terms through the use of a natural clock such as radioactive decay or tree ring growth.

cladogenesis   Evolution through the branching of a species or a lineage.

cladogram   Branching diagram showing evolved relationships among members of a lineage.

cleaver   Type of Acheulean bifacial tool, usually oblong with a broad cutting edge on one end.

cline   The distribution of a trait or allele across geographical space.

coccyx   The fused tail vertebrae that are very small in humans and apes.

codominant   In a diploid organism, two different alleles of a gene that are both expressed in a heterozygous individual.

codon   A triplet of nucleotide bases in mRNA that specifies an amino acid or the initiation or termination of a polypeptide sequence.

compound temporonuchal crest   Bony crest at the back of the skull formed when an enlarged temporalis muscle approaches enlarged neck (nuchal) muscles; present in apes and *Au. afarensis*.

convergent (or parallel) evolution   Similar form or function brought about by natural selection under similar environments rather than shared ancestry.

core area   The part of a home range that is most intensively used.

core   The raw material source (a river cobble or a large flake) from which flakes are removed.

cosmogenic radionuclide dating   Radiometric dating technique that uses ratios of rare isotopes such as ^{26}A, ^{10}Be, and ^{3}He to estimate the time that sediments and the fossils in them have been buried.

CP$_3$ honing complex   Combination of canine and first premolar teeth that form a self-sharpening apparatus.

cranial crests   Bony ridges on the skull to which muscles attach.

creation science   A creationist attempt to refute the evidence of evolution.

crossing over   Exchange of genetic material between homologous chromosomes during the first prophase of meiosis; mechanism for genetic recombination.

culture   The sum total of learned traditions, values, and beliefs that groups of people (and a few species of highly intelligent animals) possess.

cultural anthropology   The study of human societies, especially in a cross-cultural context; the subdivision of anthropology that includes ethnology, archaeology, and linguistics.

cytoplasm   In a eukaryotic cell, the region within the cell membrane that surrounds the nucleus; it contains organelles, which carry out the essential functions of the cell, such as energy production, metabolism, and protein synthesis.

data   The scientific evidence produced by an experiment or by observation, from which scientific conclusions are made.

datum point   A permanent, fixed point relative to which the location of items of interest are recorded during archaeological mapping and excavation.

daughter isotope   (product) The isotope that is produced as the result of radioactive decay of the parent isotope.

deduction   A conclusion that follows logically from a set of observations.

deletion mutation   A change in the base sequence of a gene that results from the loss of one or more base pairs in the DNA.

deme   Local, interbreeding population that is defined in terms of its genetic composition (for example, allele frequencies).

dental apes   Early apes exhibiting Y-5 molar patterns but monkey-like post-cranial skeletons.

dental arcade   The parabolic arc that forms the upper or lower row of teeth.

deoxyribonucleic acid (DNA)   A double-stranded molecule that is the carrier of genetic information. Each strand is composed of a linear sequence of nucleotides; the two strands are held together by hydrogen bonds that form between complementary bases.

diastema   Gap between anterior teeth.

diploid number   Full complement of paired chromosomes in a somatic cell. In humans, the diploid number is 46 (23 pairs of different chromosomes).

directional selection   Natural selection that drives evolutionary change by selecting for greater or lesser frequency of a given trait in a population.

diurnal   Active during daylight hours.

dominance hierarchy   Ranking of individual primates in a group that reflects their ability to displace, intimidate, or defeat group mates in contests.

dominant   In a diploid organism, an allele that is expressed when present on only one of a pair of homologous chromosomes.

Duffy blood group   Red blood cell system useful for studying admixture between African- and European-derived populations.

Early Stone Age (or Lower Paleolithic)   The earliest stone tool industries including the Oldowan and Acheulean industries, called the ESA in Africa and the Lower Paleolithic outside Africa.

ecology   The study of the interrelationships of plants, animals, and the physical environment in which they live.

electron spin resonance (ESR)   Electron trap technique that measures the total amount of radioactivity accumulated by a specimen (such as tooth or bone) since burial.

electron trap techniques   Radiometric techniques that measure the accumulation of electrons in traps in the crystal lattice of a specimen.

encephalization quotient (EQ)   The ratio of the actual brain size of a species to its expected brain size based on a statistical regression of brain to body size based on a large number of species.

endocast   A replica (or cast) of the internal surface of the braincase that reflects the impressions made by the brain on the skull walls. Natural endocasts are formed by the filling of the braincase by sediments.

endoplasmic reticulum (ER)   An organelle in the cytoplasm consisting of a folded membrane.

environmentalism   The view that the environment has great powers to directly shape the anatomy of individual organisms.

environment of evolutionary adaptedness (EEA)   According to evolutionary psychologists, the critical period for understanding the selective forces that shape human behavior; exemplified by hunter-gatherer lifestyles of hominids before the advent of agriculture.

enzyme   A complex protein that is a catalyst for chemical processes in the body.

estrus   Hormonally influenced period of sexual receptivity in some female mammals that corresponds to the timing of ovulation.

ethnic group   A human group defined in terms of sociological, cultural, and linguistic traits.

ethnobiology   The study of how traditional cultures classify objects and organisms in the natural world.

ethnography   A cell that possesses a well-organized nucleus.

ethnology   The study of human societies, their traditions, rituals, beliefs, and the differences between societies in these traits.

eukaryotes   The practice of cultural anthropology. Ethnographers study the minute-to-minute workings of human societies, especially non-Western societies.

eutheria   Mammals that reproduce with a placenta and uterus.

evolution   A change in the frequency of a gene or a trait in a population over multiple generations.

evolutionary psychology   Approach to understanding the evolution of human behavior that emphasizes the selection of specific behavioral patterns in the context of the environment of evolutionary adaptedness.

experimentation   The testing of a hypothesis.

falsifiable   Able to be shown to be false.

female philopatry   Primate social system in which females remain and breed in the group of their birth, whereas males emigrate.

femoral condyles   The enlarged inferior end of the femur that forms the top of the knee joint.

field study   Primate behavior study conducted in the habitat in which the primate naturally occurs.

fission–fusion   Form of mating system seen in chimpanzees, bonobos, and a few other primates in which there are temporary subgroups but no stable, cohesive groups.

fission–fusion polygyny   Type of primate polygyny in which animals travel in foraging parties of varying sizes instead of a cohesive group.

fission track dating   Radiometric technique for dating noncrystalline materials using the decay of ^{238}Ur and counting the tracks that are produced by this fission. Estimates the age of sediments in which fossils are found.

fitness   Reproductive success.

flake   The stone fragment struck from a core, thought to have been the primary tools of the Oldowan.

folivores   Animals that eat a diet composed mainly of leaves, or foliage.

foramen magnum   Hole in the occipital bone through which the spinal cord connects to the brain.

forensic anthropology   The study of human remains applied to a legal context.

fossils   The preserved remnants of once-living things, often buried in the ground.

founder effect   A component of genetic drift theory, stating that new populations that become isolated from the parent population carry only the genetic variation of the founders.

frequency-dependent balanced polymorphism   Balanced polymorphism that is maintained because one (or more) of the alternative phenotypes has a selective advantage over the other phenotypes only when it is present in the population below a certain frequency.

frugivorous   An animal that eats a diet composed mainly of fruit.

galago   Live in many African forests; Also called Bushbabies.

gametes   The sex cells: sperm in males and eggs (or ova) in females.

gene flow   Movement of genes between populations.

gene   The fundamental unit of heredity. Consists of a sequence of DNA bases that carries the information for synthesizing a protein (or polypeptide) and occupies a specific chromosomal locus.

genetic bottleneck   Temporary dramatic reduction in size of a population or species.

genetic code   The system whereby the nucleotide triplets in DNA and RNA contain the information for synthesizing proteins from the twenty amino acids.

genetic drift   Random changes in gene frequency in a population.

genome   The sum total of all the genes carried by an individual.

genotype   The genetic makeup of an individual. Genotype can refer to the entire genetic complement or more narrowly to the alleles present at a specific locus on two homologous chromosomes.

geologic time scale (GTS)   The categories of time into which Earth's history is usually divided by geologists and paleontologists: eons, eras, periods, epochs.

geology   The study of the earth.

geomagnetic polarity time scale (GPTS)   Time scale composed of the sequence of paleomagnetic orientations of sediments through time.

gluteal muscles   Gluteus maximus, medius, and minimus, the muscles of walking, which have undergone radical realignment in habitual bipeds.

gradualism   Darwinian view of slow, incremental evolutionary change.

group selection   Notion largely discredited by the rise of Darwinian theory proposing that animals act for the good of their social group or of their species.

gyri (sing., gyrus)   Ridges on the surface of the brain that are formed by sulci.

half-life   The time it takes for half of the original amount of an unstable isotope of an element to decay into more stable forms.

hammerstone   A stone used for striking cores to produce flakes or bones to expose marrow.

hand axe   Type of Acheulean bifacial tool, usually teardrop-shaped, with a long cutting edge.

haploid number   The number of chromosomes found in a gamete, representing one from each pair found in a diploid somatic cell. In humans, the haploid number is 23.

haplorhine (Haplorhini)   Suborder of the order Primates that includes the anthropoids and the tarsier.

haplotypes   Combinations of alleles (or at the sequence level, mutations) that are found together in an individual.

hard-object feeding   Chewing tough, hard-to-break food items such as nuts or fibrous vegetation.

Hardy–Weinberg equilibrium   The theoretical distribution of alleles in a given population in the absence of evolution, expressed as a mathematical equation.

hemoglobin   Protein found in red blood cells that transports oxygen.

heritability   The proportion of total phenotypic variability observed for a given trait that can be ascribed to genetic factors.

heterozygous advantage   With reference to a particular genetic system, the situation in which heterozygotes have a selective advantage over homozygotes (for example, sickle cell disease); a mechanism for maintaining a balanced polymorphism.

heterozygous   Having two different alleles at the loci for a gene on a pair of homologous chromosomes (or autosomes).

home base   Archaeological term for an area to which early hominins may have brought tools and carcasses and around which their activities were centered.

home range   The spatial area used by a primate group.

hominin   A member of the primate family Hominidae, distinguished by bipedal posture and, in more recently evolved species, a large brain.

homologous chromosomes   Members of the same pair of chromosomes (or autosomes). Homologous chromosomes undergo crossing over during meiosis.

homology   Similarity of traits resulting from shared ancestry.

homozygous   Having the same allele at the loci for a gene on both members of a pair of homologous chromosomes (or autosomes).

hormone   A natural substance (often a protein) produced by specialized cells in one location of the body that influences the activity or physiology of cells in a different location.

human biology   Subfield of biological anthropology dealing with human growth and development, adaptation to environmental extremes, and human genetics.

human evolutionary ecology   Approach to understanding the evolution of human behavior that attempts to explore ecological and demographic factors important in determining individual reproductive success and fitness in a cultural context.

human leukocyte antigen (HLA) system   Class of blood group markers formed by proteins expressed on the surface of white blood cells (leukocytes).

hylobatid (Hylobatidae)   Member of the gibbon, or lesser ape, family.

hyoid bone   A small "floating bone" in the front part of the throat that is held in place by muscles and ligaments.

hypothesis   A preliminary explanation of a phenomenon. Hypothesis formation is the first step of the scientific method.

ilium   The blade of the innominate to which gluteal muscles attach.

immunoglobulins   Proteins produced by B lymphocytes that function as antibodies.

immutability (or fixity)   Stasis, lack of change.

inbreeding depression   Lesser fitness of offspring of closely related individuals compared with the fitness of the offspring of less closely related individuals, caused largely by the expression of lethal or debilitating recessive alleles.

inbreeding   Mating between close relatives.

incest   A violation of cultural rules regulating mating behavior.

inclusive fitness   Reproductive success of an organism plus the fitness of its close kin.

infanticide   The killing of infants, either by members of the infant's group or by a member of a rival group.

innominate bones (os coxae)   The pair of bones that compose the lateral parts of the pelvis; each innominate is made up of three bones that fuse during adolescence.

insertion mutation   A change in the base sequence of a gene that results from the addition of one or more base pairs in the DNA.

intelligent design   A creationist school of thought that proposes that natural selection cannot account for the diversity and complexity of form and function seen in nature.

ischium   Portion of the innominate bone that forms the bony underpinning of the rump.

isotopes   Variant forms of an element that differ based on their atomic weights and numbers of neutrons in the nucleus. Both stable and unstable (radioactive) isotopes exist in nature.

juxtamastoid eminence   A ridge of bone next to the mastoid process; in Neandertals, it is larger than the mastoid process itself.

karyotype   The complete chromosomal complement of an individual; usually based on a photograph of the chromosomes visualized under the microscope.

kin selection Principle that animals behave preferentially toward their genetic kin; formulated by William Hamilton.

k-selected Reproductive strategy in which fewer offspring are produced per female, interbirth intervals are long, and maternal investment is high.

lactose intolerant The inability to digest lactose, the sugar found in milk; most adult mammals (including humans) are lactose intolerant as adults.

language The unique system of communication used by members of the human species.

Levallois technique A Middle Paleolithic technique that made use of prepared cores to produce uniform levallois flakes.

linguistic anthropology The study of language, its origins, and use; also called anthropological linguistics.

linkage Genes that are found on the same chromosome are said to be linked. The closer together two genes are on a chromosome, the greater the linkage and the less likely they are to be separated during crossing over.

lithostratigraphy The study of geologic deposits and their formation, stratigraphic relationships, and relative time relationships based on their lithologic (rock) properties.

locus The location of a gene on a chromosome. The locus for a gene is identified by the number of the chromosome on which it is found and its position on the chromosome.

lumbar vertebrae The five vertebrae of the lower back.

macroevolution Large-scale evolutionary change over a long time period or evolution of major phenotypic changes over relatively short time periods.

male philopatry Primate social system in which males remain and breed in the group of their birth, whereas females emigrate.

mastoid process A protrusion from the temporal bone of the skull located behind the ear.

maternal–fetal incompatibility Occurs when the mother produces antibodies against an antigen (for example, a red blood cell surface protein) expressed in the fetus that she does not possess.

material culture The objects or artifacts of past human societies.

megadontia Enlarged teeth.

meiosis Cell division that occurs in the testes and ovaries that leads to the formation of sperm and ova (gametes).

melanin A dark pigment produced by the melanocytes of the epidermis, which is the most important component of skin color.

melanocytes Cells in the epidermis that produce melanin.

menarche The onset of a girl's first menstrual period.

Mendel's law of independent assortment Genes found on different chromosomes are sorted into sex cells independently of one another.

Mendel's law of segregation The two alleles of a gene found on each of a pair of chromosomes segregate independently of one another into sex cells.

menopause The postreproductive period in the lives of women, after the cessation of ovulation and menses.

messenger RNA (mRNA) Strand of RNA synthesized in the nucleus as a complement to a specific gene (transcription). It carries the information for the sequence of amino acids to make a specific protein into the cytoplasm, where at a ribosome it is read and a protein molecule synthesized (translation).

metatarsals Five foot bones that join the tarsals to the toes and form a portion of the longitudinal arch of the foot.

metatheria Mammals that reproduce without a placenta, including the marsupials.

metopic keel Longitudinal ridge or thickening of bone along the midline of the frontal bone.

microevolution The study of evolutionary phenomena that occur within a species.

microliths Small, flaked stone tools probably designed to be hafted to wood or bone; common feature of Upper Paleolithic and Later Stone Age tool industries.

Middle Paleolithic (Middle Stone Age) Stone tool industries that used prepared-core technologies.

midfacial prognathism The forward projection of the middle facial region, including the nose.

mitochondrial DNA (mtDNA) Small loop of DNA found in the mitochondria. It is clonally and maternally inherited.

mitochondria Organelles in the cytoplasm of the cell where energy production for the cell takes place. Contains its own DNA.

mitosis Somatic cell division in which a single cell divides to produce two identical daughter cells.

molecular clock A systematic accumulation of genetic change that can be used to estimate the time of divergence between two groups if relative rates are constant and a calibration point from the fossil record is available.

monogamy A mating bond; primates can be socially monogamous but still mate occasionally outside the pair bond.

most recent common ancestor (MRCA) In a phylogenetic tree, the MRCA is indicated by the deepest node from which all contemporary variants can be shown to have evolved.

Movius line The separation between areas of the Old World in which Acheulean technology occurs and those in which it does not; named by archaeologist Hallam Movius.

multiregional models Phylogenetic models that suggest that modern humans evolved in the context of gene flow between Mid- to Late-Pleistocene hominid populations from different regions, so there is no single location where modern humans first evolved.

muscles of mastication The chewing muscles: masseter, temporalis, medial and lateral pterygoids.

mutation An alteration in the DNA that may or may not alter the function of a cell. If it occurs in a gamete, it may be passed from one generation to the next.

myelin Fatty substance that sheaths neuronal axons, facilitating the transmission of electrical impulses along those axons.

natural selection Differential reproductive success over multiple generations.

neocortex The part of the brain that controls higher cognitive function; the cerebrum.

neuron The basic cellular unit of the nervous system. A neuron consists of a cell body and specialized processes called dendrites (which receive inputs from other neurons) and axons (outgrowths through which neurons send impulses to other neurons).

nocturnal Active at night.

nondisjunction error The failure of homologous chromosomes (chromatids) to separate properly during cell division. When it occurs during meiosis, it may lead to the formation of gametes that are missing a chromosome or have an extra copy of a chromosome.

nucleotide Molecular building block of nucleic acids DNA and RNA; consists of a phosphate, sugar, and base.

nucleus In eukaryotic cells, the part of the cell in which the genetic material is separated from the rest of the cell (cytoplasm) by a plasma membrane.

null hypothesis The starting assumption for scientific inquiry that one's research results occur by random chance. One's hypothesis must challenge this initial assumption.

observation The gathering of scientific information by watching a phenomenon.

occipital bun A backward- projecting bulge on the occipital part of the skull.

occipital torus A thickened horizontal ridge of bone on the occipital bone at the rear of the cranium.

Oldowan The tool industry characterized by simple, usually unifacial core and flake tools.

olfactory bulbs Knob-like structures located on the underside of the frontal lobes, that form the termination of olfactory nerves running from the nasal region to the brain.

omomyoids Super family of mostly Eocene primates, probably ancestral to all haplorhines.

ontogeny The life cycle of an organism from conception to death.

optically stimulated luminescence (OSL) Electron trap technique that uses light to measure the amount of radioactivity accumulated by crystals in sediments (such as sand grains) since burial.

osteodontokeratic culture A bone, tooth, and horn tool kit envisioned by Raymond Dart to be made by *Australopithecus*.

osteology The study of the skeleton.

paleoanthropology   The study of the fossil record of ancestral humans and their primate kin.

paleontology   The study of extinct organisms, based on their fossilized remains.

paleopathology   The study of diseases in ancestral human populations.

paleosol   Ancient soil.

paradigm   A conceptual framework useful for understanding a body of evidence.

parapatric speciation   Speciation occurring when two populations have continuous distributions and some phenotypes in that distribution are more favorable than others.

parent isotope   The original radioactive isotope in a sample.

particulate inheritance   The concept of heredity based on the transmission of genes (alleles) according to Mendelian principles.

pathogen   An organism and entity that can cause disease.

pedigree   A diagram used in the study of human genetics that shows the transmission of a genetic trait over generations of a family.

phalanges   Bones that form the fingers and toes.

phenotype   An observable or measurable feature of an organism. Phenotypes can be anatomical, biochemical, or behavioral.

phenylketonuria (PKU)   Autosomal recessive condition that leads to the accumulation of large quantities of the amino acid phenylalanine, causing mental retardation and other phenotypic abnormalities.

phylogeny   An evolutionary tree indicating relatedness and divergence of taxonomic groups.

physical anthropology   The study of humans as biological organisms, considered in an evolutionary framework.

platycnemic   A bone that is flattened from side to side.

platymeric   A bone that is flattened from front to back.

Platyrrhini   Infraorder of the order Primates that is synonymous with the New World monkeys, or ceboids.

pleiotropy   The phenomenon of a single gene having multiple phenotypic effects.

plesiadapiforms   Mammalian order or suborder of mammals that may be ancestral to later Primates, characterized by some but not all of the primate trends.

point mutation   A change in the base sequence of a gene that results from the change of a single base to a different base.

polyandrous mating system   Mating system in which one female mates with multiple males.

polyandry   Mating system in which one female mates with multiple males.

polygenic traits   Phenotypic traits that result from the combined action of more than one gene; most complex traits are polygenic.

polygyny   Mating system consisting of at least one male and more than one female.

polymerase chain reaction (PCR)   Method for amplifying DNA sequences using the Taq polymerase enzyme. Can potentially produce millions or billions of copies of a DNA segment starting from a very small number of target DNA.

polymorphic   Two or more distinct phenotypes (at the genetic or anatomical levels) that exist within a population.

polypeptide   A molecule made up of a chain of amino acids.

polytypic species   Species that consist of a number of separate breeding populations, each varying in some genetic trait.

pongid (Pongidae)   One of the four great apes species: gorilla, chimpanzee, bonobo, or orangutan.

population   An interbreeding group of organisms.

population genetics   The study of genetic variation within and between groups of organisms.

postorbital bar   A bony ring encircling the lateral side of the eye but not forming a complete cup around the eye globe.

postorbital constriction   The pinching-in of the cranium just behind the orbits where the temporalis muscle sits. Little constriction indicates a large brain and small muscle; great constriction indicates a large muscle, as in the robust groups of *Australopithecus (Paranthropus)*.

potassium–argon (K–Ar) dating   Radiometric technique using the decay of ^{40}K to ^{40}Ar in potassium-bearing rocks; estimates the age of sediments in which fossils are found.

prehensile tail   Grasping tail possessed by some species of the primate families Cebidae and Atelidae.

primary cortex   Regions of the cerebral cortex that are involved directly with motor control or sensory input.

primate   Member of the mammalian order Primates, including prosimians, monkeys, apes, and humans, defined by a suite of anatomical and behavioral traits.

primatology   The study of the nonhuman primates and their anatomy, genetics, behavior, and ecology.

progesterone   A steroid hormone produced by the corpus luteum and the placenta that prepares the uterus for pregnancy and helps maintain pregnancy once fertilization has occurred.

prognathic face   Projection of the face well in front of the braincase.

prokaryotes   Single-celled organisms, such as bacteria, in which the genetic material is not separated from the rest of the cell by a nucleus.

prosimian   Member of the primate suborder Prosimii that includes the lemurs, lorises, galagos, and tarsiers.

proteins   Complex molecules formed from chains of amino acids (polypeptide) or from a complex of polypeptides. They function as structural molecules, transport molecules, antibodies, enzymes, and hormones.

protein synthesis   The assembly of proteins from amino acids that occurs at ribosomes in the cytoplasm and is based on information carried by mRNA.

prototheria   Mammals that reproduce by egg-laying and then nurse young from nipples. The Australian platypus and echidna are the only living monotremes.

provenience   The origin or original source (as of a fossil).

pubis   Portion of the innominate that forms the anterior part of the birth canal.

punctuated equilibrium   Model of evolution characterized by rapid bursts of change, followed by long periods of stasis.

qualitative variation   Phenotypic variation that can be characterized as belonging to discrete, observable categories.

quantitative variation   Phenotypic variation that is characterized by the distribution of continuous variation (expressed using a numerical measure) within a population (for example, in a bell curve).

quarrying site   An archaeological site at which there is evidence that early hominins were obtaining the raw material to make stone tools.

race   In biological taxonomy, same thing as a subspecies; when applied to humans, sometimes incorporates both cultural and biological factors.

racism   A prejudicial belief that members of one ethnic group are superior in some way to those of another.

radiocarbon dating   Radiometric technique that uses the decay of ^{14}C in organic remains such as wood and bone to estimate the time since the death of the organism.

radiometric dating   Chronometric techniques that use radioactive decay of isotopes to estimate age.

recessive   In a diploid organism, refers to an allele that must be present in two copies (homozygous) in order to be expressed.

recombination   The rearrangement of genes on homologous chromosomes that occurs during crossing over in meiosis. Source of variation arising out of sexual reproduction; important for increasing rates of natural selection.

reductionism   Paradigm that an organism is the sum of many evolved parts and that organisms can best be understood through an adaptationist approach.

regulatory genes   Guide the expression of structural genes, without coding for a protein themselves.

relative dating techniques   Dating techniques that establish the age of a fossil only in comparison to other materials found above and below it.

relative rate test   A means of determining whether molecular evolution has been occurring at a constant rate in two lineages by comparing whether these lineages are equidistant from an outgroup.

replacement models   Phylogenetic models that suggest that modern humans evolved in one location and then spread geographically, replacing other earlier hominid populations without any or with little admixture.

reproductive isolating mechanisms (RIMs)   Any factor—behavioral, ecological, or anatomical—that prevents a male and female of two different species from hybridizing.

reproductive potential   The possible offspring output by one sex.

reproductive variance   A measure of variation from the mean of a population in the reproductive potential of one sex compared with the other.

rhesus (Rh) system   Blood type system that can cause hemolytic anemia of the newborn through maternal–fetal incompatibility if the mother is Rh-negative and the child is Rh-positive.

ribonucleic acid (RNA)   Single-stranded nucleic acid that performs critical functions during protein synthesis and comes in three forms: messenger RNA, transfer RNA, and ribosomal RNA.

ribosomes   Structures composed primarily of RNA that are found on the endoplasmic reticulum. They are the site of protein synthesis.

r-selected   Reproductive strategy in which females have many offspring, interbirth intervals are short, and maternal investment per offspring is low.

sacrum   The fused vertebrae that form the back of the pelvis.

sagittal crest   Bony crest running lengthwise down the center of the cranium on the parietal bones; for the attachment of the temporalis muscles.

sagittal keel   Longitudinal ridge or thickening of bone on the sagittal suture not associated with any muscle attachment.

scientific method   Standard scientific research procedure in which a hypothesis is stated, data are collected to test it, and the hypothesis is either supported or refuted.

semi-free-ranging environment   Primate behavior study conducted in a large area that is enclosed or isolated in some way so the population is captive.

senescence   Age-related decline in physiological or behavioral function in adult organisms.

sex chromosomes   In mammals, chromosomes X and Y, with XX producing females and XY producing males.

sexual dimorphism   Difference in size, shape, or color, between the sexes.

sexual receptivity   Willingness and ability of a female to mate, also defined as fertility.

sexual selection   Differential reproductive success within one sex of any species.

shovel-shaped incisors   Anterior teeth that, on their lingual (tongue) surface, are concave with two raised edges that make them look like tiny shovels.

sickle cell disease   An autosomal recessive disease caused by a point mutation in an allele that codes for one of the polypeptide chains of the hemoglobin protein.

sociality   Group living; a fundamental trait of haplorhine primates.

social system   The grouping pattern in which a primate species lives, including its size and composition evolved in response to natural and sexual selection pressures.

somatic cells   The cells of the body that are not sex cells.

speciation   Formation of one or more new species via reproductive isolation.

species   An interbreeding group of animals or plants that are reproductively isolated through anatomy, ecology, behavior, or geographic distribution from all other such groups.

stabilizing selection   Selection that maintains a certain phenotype by selecting against deviations from it.

stem cells   Undifferentiated cells found in the developing embryo that can be induced to differentiate into a wide variety of cell types or tissues. Also found in adults, although adult stem cells are not as totipotent as embryonic stem cells.

strata   Layers of rock.

stratigraphy   The study of the order of rock layers and the sequence of events they reflect.

strepsirhine (Strepsirhini)   Suborder of the order Primates that includes the prosimians, excluding the tarsier.

structural genes   Genes that contain the information to make a protein.

subspecies   Group of local populations that share part of the geographic range of a species, and can be differentiated from other subspecies based on one or more phenotypic traits.

sulci (sing., sulcus)   Grooves on the surface of the brain that divide the hemispheres into gyri.

supraorbital torus   Thickened ridge of bone above the eye orbits of the skull; a brow ridge.

systematics   Branch of biology that describes patterns of organismal variation.

taphonomy   The study of what happens to the remains of an animal from the time of death to the time of discovery.

tarsals   Foot bones that form the ankle and part of the arches of the foot.

taurodontism   Molar teeth that have expanded pulp cavities and fused roots.

taxon   A group of organisms assigned to a particular category.

taxonomy   The science of biological classification.

tephrostratigraphy   A form of lithostratigraphy in which the chemical fingerprint of a volcanic ash is used to correlate across regions.

teratogens   Substances that cause birth defects or other abnormalities in the developing embryo or fetus during pregnancy.

territory   The part of a home range that is defended against other members of the same species.

testosterone   A steroid produced primarily in the testes and ovaries, and at a much higher level in men than in women. Responsible for the development of the male primary and secondary sexual characteristics. Strongly influences dominance and reproductive behavior.

theory of inheritance of acquired characteristics   Discredited theory of evolutionary change proposing that changes that occur during the lifetime of an individual, through use or disuse, can be passed on to the next generation.

thermoluminescence (TL)   Electron trap technique that uses heat to measure the amount of radioactivity accumulated by a specimen, such as a stone tool, since its last heating.

thoracic vertebrae   The twelve vertebrae of the thorax that hold the ribs.

tool industry   A particular style or tradition of making stone tools.

transfer RNA (tRNA)   RNA molecules that bind to specific amino acids and transport them to ribosomes to be used during protein synthesis.

trinucleotide repeat diseases   A family of autosomal dominant diseases that is caused by the insertion of multiple copies of a three-base pair sequence (CAG) that codes for the amino acid glutamine. Typically, the more copies inserted into the gene, the more serious the disease.

type specimen   According to the laws of zoological nomenclature, the anatomical reference specimen for the species definition.

uniformitarianism   Theory that the same gradual geological process we observe today was operating in the past.

Upper Paleolithic (Later Stone Age)   Stone tool industries that are characterized by the development of blade-based technology.

uranium series (U-series) techniques   Radiometric techniques using the decay of uranium to estimate an age for calcium carbonates including flowstones, shells, and teeth.

vertebral column   The column of bones and cartilaginous disks that houses the spinal cord and provides structural support and flexibility to the body.

visual predation hypothesis   Hypothesis for the origin of primate adaptation that focuses on the value of grasping hands and stereoscopic vision for catching small prey.

X-linked disorders   Genetic conditions that result from mutations to genes on the X chromosome. They are almost always expressed in males, who have only one copy of the X chromosome; in females, the second X chromosome containing the normally functioning allele protects them from developing X-linked disorders.

zygomatic arch   The bony arch formed by the zygomatic (cheek) bone and the temporal bone of the skull.

zygote   A fertilized egg.

Bibliography

Abbate E, Albianelli A, Azzaroli A, et al. 1998. A one million year old *Homo* cranium from the Danakil (Afar) depression of Eritrea. *Nature* 393:458–460.

Adams BA. 2003. Establishing personal identification based on specific patterns of missing, filled, and unrestored teeth. *J. Forensic Science* 48:2–10.

Adcock GJ, Dennis ES, Easteal S, et al. 2001. Mitochondrial DNA sequences in ancient Australians: Implications for modern human origins. *Proceedings of the National Academy of Sciences* 98:537–542.

Aiello L. 2010. Five years of *Homo floresiensis*. *American Journal of Physical Anthropology* Vol. 142 Issue 2, 167–179.

Aiello L, Dean C. 1990. *An Introduction to Human Evolutionary Anatomy.* Academic Press, London.

Aiello LC, Key C. 2002. Energetic consequences of being a *Homo erectus* female. *American Journal of Human Biology* 14: 551–565.

Aiello LC, Wheeler P. 1995. The expensive-tissue hypothesis. *Current Anthropology* 36:199–221.

Akazawa T, Muhesun S. 2002. *Neandertal burials: Excavation at Dederiyeh Cave, Afrin, Syria.* International Research Center for Japanese Studies, Kyoto.

Alcock J. 2001. *The Triumph of Sociobiology.* Oxford University Press, New York.

Alemseged Z, Spoor F, Kimbel W, et al. 2006. A juvenile early hominin skeleton from Dikika, Ethiopia. *Nature* 443:296–301.

Allen JS. 1989. Franz Boas's physical anthropology: The critique of racial formalism revisited. *Current Anthropology* 30:79–84.

Allen JS. 1997. Are traditional societies schizophrenogenic? *Schizophrenia Bulletin* 23:357–364.

Allen JS. 2009. *The Lives of the Brain: Human Evolution and the Organ of Mind.* Belknap Press of Harvard University Press, Cambridge, MA.

Allen JS, Bruss J, Damasio H. 2006. Looking for the lunate sulcus: A magnetic resonance imaging study in modern humans. *The Anatomical Record Part A* 288A:867–876.

Allen JS, Cheer SM. 1996. The non-thrifty genotype. *Current Anthropology* 37:831–842.

Allen JS, Damasio H, Grabowski TJ. 2002. Normal neuroanatomical variation in the human brain: An MRI-volumetric study. *American Journal of Physical Anthropology* 118:341–358.

Allen JS, Damasio H, Grabowski TJ, et al. 2003. Sexual dimorphism and asymmetries in the gray-white composition of the human cerebrum. *NeuroImage* 18:880–899.

Allen JS, Sarich VM. 1988. Schizophrenia in an evolutionary perspective. *Perspectives in Biology and Medicine* 32:132–153.

Allison AC. 1954. Protection afforded by sickle-cell trait against malarial infection. *British Medical Journal* 1:290–294.

Almqvist EW, Bloch M, Brinkman R Craufurd D, Hayden MR. 1999. A worldwide assessment of the frequency of suicide, suicide attempts, or psychiatric hospitalization after predictive testing for Huntington disease. *American Journal of Human Genetics* 64:1293–1304.

Altmann J. 1980. *Baboon Mothers and Infants.* Harvard University Press, Cambridge, MA.

Alvarez LW, Alvarez W, Asaro F, Michel HV. 1980. Extraterrestrial cause for the Cretaceous–Tertiary extinction. *Science* 208:1095–1108.

Alvarez G, Ceballos FC, Quinteiro C. 2009. The role of inbreeding in the extinction of a European royal dynasty. *PLoS One* 4:e5174.

Alvarez W. 1997. *T. rex and the Crater of Doom.* Princeton University Press, Princeton, NJ.

Ambrose SH. 2001. Paleolithic technology and human evolution. *Science* 291:1748–1753.

American Psychiatric Association. 1994. *Diagnostic and Statistical Manual of Mental Disorders,* 4th ed. American Psychiatric Association, Washington, DC.

Anderson R. 1999. Human evolution, low back pain, and dual-level control. In *Evolutionary Medicine* (WR Trevathan, EO Smith, JJ McKenna, eds.), pp. 333–349. Oxford University Press, Oxford.

Andersson S. 1992. Female preference for long tails in lekking Jackson's widow-birds: Experimental evidence. *Animal Behavior* 43:379–388.

Andrews PJ. 1989. Palaeoecology of Laetoli. *Journal of Human Evolution* 18:173–181.

Antón SC. 1996. Tendon-associated bone features of the masticatory system in Neandertals. *Journal of Human Evolution* 31:391–408.

Antón SC. 2002. Evolutionary significance of cranial variation in Asian *Homo erectus*. *American Journal of Physical Anthropology* 118:301–323.

Antón SC. 2003. A natural history of *Homo erectus*. *Yearbook of Physical Anthropology* 46:126–170.

Antón SC, Leonard WR, Robertson M. 2002. An ecomorphological model of the initial hominid dispersal from Africa. *Journal of Human Evolution* 43:773–785.

Antón SC, Swisher CC III. 2001. Evolution and variation of cranial capacity in Asian *Homo erectus*. In *A Scientific Life: Papers in Honor of Professor Dr. Teuku Jacob* (E Indriati, SC Antón, J Kurtz, eds.), pp. 25–39. Bigraf Publishing, Yogyakarta, Indonesia.

Aoki K. 1986. A stochastic model of gene-culture coevolution suggested by the "cultural-historical hypothesis" for the evolution of adult lactose absorption in humans. *Proceedings of the National Academy of Sciences* 83:2929–2933.

Ardrey R. 1966. *The Territorial Imperative.* Atheneum, New York.

Arenas, E. 2010. Towards stem cell replacement therapies in Parkinson's disease. *Biochemical and Biophysical Research Communications* 396: 152–156.

Arensburg B, Schepartz LA, Tillier AM, et al. 1990. A reappraisal of the anatomical basis for speech in Middle Paleolithic hominids. *American Journal of Physical Anthropology* 83:137–146.

Armelagos G. 1997. Disease, Darwin, and medicine in the third epidemiological transition. *Evolutionary Anthropology* 5:212–220.

Arsuaga JL. 2002. *The Neanderthal's Necklace.* Four Walls Eight Windows, New York.

Arsuaga JL, Martines A, Garcia A, Lorenzo C. 1997. The Sima de los Huesos crania (Sierra de Atapuerca, Spain). A comparative study. *Journal of Human Evolution* 33:219–281.

Arsuaga JL, Martínez I, Lorenzo C, et al. 1999. The human cranial remains from Gran Dolina Lower Pleistocene site (Sierra de Atapuerca, Spain). *Journal of Human Evolution* 37:431–457.

Asfaw B, Gilbert WH, Beyene Y, et al. 2002. Remains of *Homo erectus* from Bouri, Middle Ethiopia. *Nature* 416:317–320.

Asfaw B, White TD, Lovejoy CO, et al. 1999. *Australopithecus garhi:* A new species of early hominid from Ethiopia. *Science* 284:629–635.

Atran S. 1998. Folk biology and the anthropology of science: Cognitive universals and cultural particulars. *Behavioral and Brain Sciences* 21:547–609.

Bajpai S, Kay RF, Williams BA, et al. 2008. The oldest Asian record of Anthropoidea. *Proceedings of the National Academy of Science* 105:11093–11098.

Bandyopadhyay AR, Chatterjee D, Chatterjee M, Ghosh JR. 2011. Maternal fetal interaction in the ABO system: A comparative analysis of healthy mother and couples with spontaneous abortion in a Bengalee population. *American Journal of Human Biology* 23:76–79.

Barkow JH, Cosmides L, Tooby J, eds. 1992. *The Adapted Mind: Evolutionary Psychology and the Generation of Culture.* Oxford University Press, New York.

Barquet N, Domingo P. 1997. Smallpox: The triumph over the most terrible ministers of death. *Annals of Internal Medicine* 127:635–642.

Bass WA, Jefferson J. 2003. *Death's Acre: Inside the body farm, the legendary forensic laboratory.* Putnam Adult, New York, NY.

Bateson W. 1900–1901. Problems of heredity as a subject for horticultural investigation. *Journal of the Royal Horticultural Society* 25:54–61.

Bateson W. 1902. *Mendel's Principles of Heredity: A Defence.* Cambridge University Press, Cambridge.

Beall CM. 2001. Adaptations to altitude: A current assessment. *Annual Review of Anthropology* 30:423–456.

Beall CM, Cavalleri GL, Deng L, et al. 2010. Natural selection of *EPAS1* (*HIF2a*) associated with low hemoglobin concentration in Tibetan highlanders. *Proceedings of the National Academy of Sciences* 107:11459–11464.

Beall CM, Decker MJ, Brittenham GM, et al. 2002. An Ethiopian pattern of human adaptation to high-altitude hypoxia. *Proceedings of the National Academy of Sciences* 99:17215–17218.

Beall CM, Steegman AT. 2000. Human adaptation to climate: Temperature, ultraviolet radiation, and altitude. In *Human Biology: An Evolutionary and Biocultural Perspective* (S Stinson, B Bogin, R Huss-Ashmore, D O'Rourke, eds.), pp. 163–224. Wiley-Liss, New York.

Beals KL, Smith CL, Dodd SM. 1984. Brain size, cranial morphology, climate, and time machines. *Current Anthropology* 25:301–330.

Beard CK, Qi T, Dawson MR, Wang B, Li C. 1994. A diverse new primate fauna from middle Eocene fissure fillings in southeastern China. *Nature* 368:604–609.

Bearder SK, Honess PE, Ambrose L. 1995. Species diversity among galagos with special reference to mate recognition. In *Creatures of the Dark: The Nocturnal Prosimians* (L Alterman, GA Doyle, MK Izard, eds.), pp. 1–22. Plenum, New York.

Beauval C, Maureille B, Lacrampe-Cuyaubere F, et al. 2005. A late Neandertal femur from Les Rochers-de-Villeneuve, France, *Proceedings of the National Academy of Sciences in the United States of America* 102:7085–7090.

Becker AE, Fay K, Gilman SE, Striegel-Moore R. 2007. Facets of acculturation and their diverse relations to body shape concern in Fiji. *International Journal of Eating Disorders* 40:42–50.

Bedford ME, Russell KF, Lovejoy CO, Meindl RS, Simpson SW, Stuart-Macadam PL. 1993. Test of the multifactorial aging method using skeletons with known ages-at-death from the grant collection. *American Journal of Physical Anthropology* 91:287–297.

Bednarik RG. 2003. A figurine from the African Acheulian. *Current Anthropology* 44:405–413.

Behe M. 1996. *Darwin's Black Box.* The Free Press, New York.

Behrensmeyer AK, Hill A, eds. 1980. *Fossils in the Making.* University of Chicago Press, Chicago.

Bellisari A. 2008. Evolutionary origins of obesity. *Obesity Reviews* 9:165–180.

Bellomo RV. 1994. Methods of determining early hominid behavioral activities associated with the controlled use of fire at FxJj 20 Main, Koobi Fora, Kenya. *Journal of Human Evolution* 27:173–195.

Benefit BR. 1999. *Victoriapithecus,* the key to Old World monkey and catarrhine origins. *Evolutionary Anthropology* 7:155–174.

Benefit BR, McCrossin ML. 1995. Miocene hominoids and hominid origins. *Annual Review of Anthropology* 24:237–256.

Benefit BR, McCrossin ML. 2002. The Victoriapithecidae, Cercopithecoidea. In *The Primate Fossil Record* (WC Hartwig, ed.), pp. 241–253. Cambridge University Press, Cambridge.

Benit P, Rey F, Blandin-Savoja F, et al. 1999. The mutant genotype is the main determinant of the metabolic phenotype in phenylalanine hydroxylase deficiency. *Molecular Genetics and Metabolism* 68:43–47.

Berger LR, de Ruiter DJ, Churchill SE, Schmid P, Carlson KJ, Dirks PHGM, Kibi JM. 2010. *Australopithecus sediba:* A new species of *Homo*-like Australopith from South Africa. *Science* 328:195–204.

Berger T, Trinkaus E. 1995. Patterns of trauma among the Neandertals. *Journal of Archaeological Science* 22:841–852.

Berlin B. 1992. *Ethnobiological Classification: Principles of Categorization of Plants and Animals in Traditional Societies.* Princeton University Press, Princeton, NJ.

Berlin B, Kay P. 1969. *Basic Color Terms: Their Universality and Evolution.* University of California Press, Berkeley.

Bermudez de Castro JM, Arsuaga JL, Carbonell E, et al. 1997. A hominid from the lower Pleistocene of Atapuerca, Spain: Possible ancestor to Neandertals and modern humans. *Science* 276:1392–1395.

Berry WBN. 1968. *Growth of a Prehistoric Time Scale Based on Organic Evolution.* WH Freeman, San Francisco.

Betrán AP, Merialdi M, Lauer JA, Bing-Shun W, Thomas J, Van Look P, Wagner M. 2007. Rates of caesarean section: Analysis of global, regional, and national estimates. *Paediatric and Perinatal Epidemiology* 21:98–113.

Betzig L, ed. 1997. *Human Nature: A Critical Reader.* Oxford University Press, New York.

Beyerstein BL. 1999. Whence cometh the myth that we only use 10% of our brains? In *Mind Myths* (S Della Sala, ed.), pp. 3–24. Wiley, New York.

Beynon AD, Dean M. 1988. Distinct dental development patterns in early fossil hominids. *Nature* 335:509–514.

Bickerton D. 1983. Pidgin and creole languages. *Scientific American* 249:116–122.

Bickerton D. 1990. *Language and Species.* University of Chicago Press, Chicago.

Bird R. 1999. Cooperation and conflict: The behavioral ecology of the sexual division of labor. *Evolutionary Anthropology* 8:65–75.

Bischoff JL, Williams RW, Rosenbauer RJ, et al. 2007. High-resolution U-series dates from the Sima de los Huesos hominids yields 600+66 kyrs: Implications for the evolution of the Neanderthal lineage. *Journal of Archaeological Science* 24:763–770.

Bix HP. 2000. *Hirohito and the Making of Modern Japan.* HarperCollins, New York.

Blixt S. 1975. Why didn't Gregor Mendel find linkage? *Nature* 256:206.

Bloch JI, Silcox MT. 2001. New basicrania of Paleocene–Eocene *Ignacius:* Re-evaluation of the Plesiadapiform–Dermopteran link. *American Journal of Physical Anthropology* 116:184–198.

Blum K, Cull JG, Braverman ER, Comings DE. 1996. Reward deficiency syndrome. *American Scientist* 84:132–145.

Blumenschine RJ. 1986. Carcass consumption sequences and the archaeological distinction of scavenging and hunting. *Journal of Human Evolution* 15:639–659.

Blumenschine RJ. 1987. Characteristics of an early hominid scavenging niche. *Current Anthropology* 28:383–407.

Boas F. 1912. Changes in the bodily form of descendants of immigrants. *American Anthropologist* 14:530–533.

Boas F. 1938 (1911). *The Mind of Primitive Man,* rev. ed. Macmillan, New York.

Boas F. 1940. *Race, Language, and Culture.* University of Chicago Press, Chicago.

Boesch C, Boesch H. 1989. Hunting behavior of wild chimpanzees in the Taï National Park. *American Journal of Physical Anthropology* 78:547–573.

Bogin B. 1993. Why must I be a teenager at all? *New Scientist* 137:34–38.

Bogin B. 1995. Plasticity in the growth of Mayan refugee children living in the United States. In *Human Variability and Plasticity* (CGN Mascie-Taylor, B Bogin, eds.), pp. 46–74. Cambridge University Press, Cambridge.

Bogin B. 1999. Evolutionary perspective on human growth. *Annual Review of Anthropology* 28:109–153.

Bookstein F, Schäfer K, Prossinger H, et al. 1999. Comparing frontal cranial profiles in archaic and modern *Homo* by morphometric analysis. *Anatomical Record (New Anat.)* 257:217–224.

Borgerhoff Mulder M. 1987. On cultural and reproductive success: Kipsigis evidence. *American Anthropologist* 89:617–634.

Borgerhoff Mulder M. 1990. Kipsigis women's preferences for wealthy men: Evidence for female choice in mammals. *Behavioral Ecology and Sociobiology* 27:255–264.

Bottini N, Meloni GF, Finocchi A, et al. 2001. Maternal-fetal interaction in the ABO system: A comparative analysis of healthy mothers and couples with recurrent spontaneous abortion suggests a protective effect of B incompatibility. *Human Biology* 73:167–174.

Bowler JM, Johnston H, Olley JM, et al. 2003. New ages for human occupation and climatic change at Lake Mungo, Australia. *Nature* 421:837–840.

Boyd R, Richerson P. 1988. *Culture and the Evolutionary Process.* University of Chicago Press, Chicago.

Boyd WC. 1950. *Genetics and the Races of Man.* Little, Brown, Boston.

Brace CL, Xinag-qing S, Zhen-biao Z. 1984. Prehistoric and modern tooth size in China. In *The Origins of Modern Humans: A World Survey of the Fossil Evidence* (F Smith, F Spencer, eds.), pp. 485–516. Alan R. Liss, New York.

Brain CK. 1981. *The Hunters or the Hunted? Introduction to African Cave Taphonomy.* University of Chicago Press, Chicago.

Branda RF, Eaton JW. 1978. Skin color and nutrient photolysis: An evolutionary hypothesis. *Science* 201:625–626.

Bräuer G. 1984. The "Afro-European *sapiens* hypothesis" and hominid evolution in East Asia during the Late Middle and Upper Pleistocene. *Courier Forschunginstitut Senckenberg* 69:145–165.

Breuer T, Ndoundou-Hockemba M, Fishlock V. 2005. First observations of tool use in wild gorillas. *PloS Biology* 3:e380.

Britten RJ. 2002. Divergence between samples of chimpanzee and human DNA sequences is 5%, counting indels. *Proceedings of the National Academy of Sciences* 99:13633–13635.

Broadfield DC, Holloway RL, Mowbray K, et al. 2001. Endocast of Sambungmacan 3: A new *Homo erectus* from Indonesia. *The Anatomical Record* 262:369–379.

Broca P. 1861. Remarks on the seat of the faculty of articulated language, following an observation of aphemia (loss of speech) [in French]. *Bulletin de la Société Anatomique* 6:330–357. English translation by CD Green available at psychclassics.yorku.ca/Broca/aphemie-e.htm.

Brockelman WY, Reichard U, Treesucon U, Raemakers JJ. 1998. Dispersal, pair formation, and social structure in gibbons (*Hylobates lar*). *Behavioral Ecology and Sociobiology* 42:329–339.

Bromage, TG. 1989. Ontogeny of the early hominid face. *Journal of Human Evolution* 18:751–773.

Brooks JL. 1984. *Just Before the Origin*. ToExcel Publishing, New York.

Brooks S, Suchey JM. 1990. Skeletal age determination based on the os pubis: A comparison of the Acsadi-Nemeskeri and Suchey-Brooks methods. *Human Evolution*, 5: 227–238.

Broom R. 1947. Discovery of a new skull of the South African ape-man, *Plesianthropus*. *Nature* 159:672.

Brown DE. 1991. *Human Universals*. McGraw-Hill, New York.

Brown FH. 1983. Correlation of Tulu Bor Tuff at Koobi Fora with the Sidi Hakoma Tuff at Hadar. *Nature* 306:210.

Brown FH. 1992. Methods of dating. In *The Cambridge Encyclopedia of Human Evolution* (S Jones, R Martin, D Pilbeam, eds.), pp. 179–186. Cambridge University Press, Cambridge.

Brown KH, Gilman R. 1986. Nutritional effects of intestinal helminths with special reference to ascariasis and strongyloidiasis. In *The Interaction of Parasitic Diseases and Nutrition* (C Chagas, GT Keusch, eds.), pp. 213–232. Pontifica Academia Scientarium, Vatican City.

Brown P, Sutikana T, Morwood MJ, et al. 2004. A new small-bodied hominid from the late Pleistocene of Flores, Indonesia. *Nature* 431:1055–1061.

Browne, Janet. 2002. *Charles Darwin: The Power of Place*. Alfred Knopf, New York.

Browner CH, Ortiz de Montellano BR, Rubel AJ. 1988. A methodology for cross-cultural ethnomedical research. *Current Anthropology* 29:681–702.

Brues AM. 1977. *People and Races*. Macmillan, New York.

Bruner E. 2004. Geometric morphometrics and paleoneurology: Brain shape evolution in the genus *Homo*. *Journal of Human Evolution* 47:279–303.

Brunet M, Beauvilain A, Coppens Y, et al. 1995. The first australopithecine 2,500 kilometres west of the Rift Valley (Chad). *Nature* 378:273–275.

Brunet M, Beauvilain A, Coppens Y, et al. 1996. *Australopithecus bahrelghazali*, une nouvelle espece d'hominide ancien de la region de Koro Toro (Tchad). *Comptes Rendus des Seances de l'Academie des Sciences* 322:907–913.

Brunet M, Guy F, Pilbeam D, et al. 2002. A new hominid from the upper Miocene of Chad, Central Africa. *Nature* 418:145–151.

Bshary R, Noë R. 1997. The formation of red colobus-diana monkey associations under predation pressure from chimpanzees. *Proceedings of the Royal Society of London* B 264:253–259.

Buckley GA. 1997. A new species of *Purgatorius* (Mammalia; Primatomorpha) from the Lower Paleocene Bear Formation, Crazy Mountains Basin, South-Central Montana. *Journal of Palaeontology* 71:149–155.

Bumpus HC. 1899. The elimination of the unfit as illustrated by the introduced sparrow, *Passer domesticus*. *Biol. Lectures, Marine Biological Laboratory, Woods Hole* 209–226.

Bunn HT, Ezzo JA. 1993. Hunting and scavenging by Plio-Pleistocene hominids: Nutritional constraints, archaeological patterns, and behavioural implications. *Journal of Archaeological Science* 20:365–398.

Burnham TC, Chapman JF, Gray PB, et al. 2003. Men in committed, romantic relationships have lower testosterone. *Hormones and Behavior* 44:119–122.

Buss DM. 2003. *The Evolution of Desire*. Basic Books, New York.

Byrne RW. 1995. *The Thinking Ape*. Oxford University Press, Oxford.

Byrne RW, Whiten A, eds. 1988a. *Machiavellian Intelligence: Social Expertise and the Evolution of Intellect in Monkeys, Apes, and Humans*. Clarendon, Oxford.

Byrne RW, Whiten A. 1988b. Towards the next generation in data quality: A new survey of primate tactical deception. *Behavioral and Brain Sciences* 11:267–273.

Calvin WH. 1982. Did throwing stones shape hominid brain evolution? *Ethology and Sociobiology* 3:115–124.

Calvin WH. 1983. *The Throwing Madonna*. McGraw-Hill, New York.

Calvin WH, Ojemann GA. 1994. *Conversations with Neil's Brain: The Neural Nature of Thought and Language*. Perseus Books, Reading, MA.

Campbell KHS, Alberio R, Choi L, et al. 2005. Cloning: Eight years after Dolly. *Reproduction in Domestic Animals* 40:256–268.

Cande SC, Kent DV. 1995. Revised calibration of the geomagnetic polarity timescale for the Late Cretaceous and Cenozoic. *Journal of Geophysical Research* 100:6093–6095.

Cann RL. 2001. Genetic clues to dispersal in human populations: Retracing the past from the present. *Science* 291:1742–1748.

Cann RL. 2002. Tangled genetic routes. *Nature* 416:32–33.

Cann RL, Stoneking M, Wilson AC. 1987. Mitochondrial DNA and human evolution. *Nature* 325:31–36.

Caramelli D, Lalueza-Fox C, Vernesi C, et al. 2003. Evidence for a genetic discontinuity between Neandertals and 24,000-year-old anatomically modern Europeans. *Proceedings of the National Academy of Sciences* 100:6593–6597.

Carbonell E, Bermudez de Castro J, Pares J, et al. 2008. The First Hominin of Europe. *Nature* 452, 465–469.

Cartmill M. 1974. Rethinking primate origins. *Science* 184:436–443.

Caspi A, Sugden K, Moffitt TE, et al. 2003. Influence of life stress on depression: Moderation by a polymorphism in the 5-HTT gene. *Science* 301:386–389.

Cavalli-Sforza LL, Bodmer WF. 1999 (1971). *The Genetics of Human Populations*. Dover, Mineola, NY.

Cavalli-Sforza LL, Feldman MS. 2003. The application of molecular genetic approaches to the study of human evolution. *Nature Genetics* (suppl.) 33:266–275.

Cavalli-Sforza LL, Menozzi P, Piazza A. 1994. *The History and Geography of Human Genes*. Princeton University Press, Princeton, NJ.

Cerling TE, Levin NE, Quade J, Wynn JG, Fox DL, Kingston JD, Klein RG, Brown FH. 2010. Comment on the Paleoenvironment of *Ardipithecus ramidus*. *Science* 328:1105.

Cerling TE, Mbaub E, Kireab F, et al. 2011. Diet of Paranthropus boisei in the early Pleistocene of East Africa, *PNAS* vol. 108 no. 23 9337–9341.

Chagnon NA. 1988. Life histories, blood revenge, and warfare in a tribal population. *Science* 239:985–992.

Chagnon NA. 1997. *Yanomamö: The Fierce People*. Holt, Rinehart, and Winston, New York.

Chaimanee Y, Suteethorn V, Jintasakul P, et al. 2004. A new orangutan relative from the Late Miocene of Thailand. *Nature* 427:439–441, doi:10.1038/nature02245.

Chakravarti A, Chakraborty R. 1978. Elevated frequency of Tay–Sachs disease among Ashkenazic Jews unlikely by drift alone. *American Journal of Human Genetics* 30:256–261.

Chargaff E. 1950. Chemical specificity of nucleic acids and mechanism for their enzymatic degradation. *Experientia* 6:201–209.

Charles-Dominique P. 1977. *Ecology and Behaviour of Nocturnal Prosimians*. Columbia University Press, New York.

Cheney DL, Seyfarth RM. 1991. *How Monkeys See the World*. University of Chicago Press, Chicago.

Chimpanzee Sequencing and Analysis Consortium. 2005. Initial sequence of the chimpanzee genome and comparison with the human genome. *Nature* 437:69–87.

Chomsky N. 1967. The formal nature of language (Appendix A). In *Biological Foundations of Language* (EH Lenneberg, ed.), pp. 397–442. Wiley, New York.

Clamp M, Fry B, Kamal M, Xie X, Cuff J, Lin MF, Kellis M, Lindblad-Toh K, Lander ES. 2008. Distinguishing protein-coding and noncoding genes in the human genome. *Proceedings of the National Academy of Sciences* 104:19428–19433.

Clark WEL. 1975. *The Fossil Evidence for Human Evolution*. University of Chicago Press, Chicago.

Clarke RJ. 1998. First ever discovery of a well-preserved skull and associated skeleton of *Australopithecus*. *South African Journal of Science* 94:460–464.

Clarke RJ, Tobias PV. 1995. Sterkfontein Member 2 foot bones of the oldest South African hominid. *Science* 269:521–524.

Coghlan A. 2003. A sad farewell for Dolly the sheep, the world's first cloned mammal. *New Scientist* 177:5.

Coleman L, Coleman J. 2002. The measurement of puberty: A review. *Journal of Adolescence* 25:535–550.

Collard M, Wood B. 2000. How reliable are human phylogenetic hypotheses? *Proceedings of the National Academy of Sciences.* 97:5003–5006.

Conroy GC. 1997. *Reconstructing Human Origins.* Norton, New York.

Conroy GC, Jolly CJ, Cramer D, Kalb JE. 1978. Newly discovered fossil hominid skull from the Afar depression, Ethiopia. *Nature* 275:67–70.

Cook D. 1979. Subsistence base and health in the lower Illinois Valley: Evidence from the human skeleton. *Medical Anthropology* 4:109–124.

Cook D, Buikstra JE. 1979. Health and differential survival in prehistoric populations: Prenatal dental defects. *American Journal of Physical Anthropology* 51:649–664.

Cooke GS, Hill AVS. 2001. Genetics of susceptibility to human infectious disease. *Nature Reviews: Genetics* 2:967–977.

Covert HH. 2002. The earliest fossil primates and the evolution of the prosimians: Introduction. In *The Primate Fossil Record* (WC Hartwig, ed.), pp. 13–20. Cambridge University Press, Cambridge.

Crews DE, Gerber L. 1994. Chronic degenerative diseases and aging. In *Biological Anthropology and Aging* (DE Crews, R Garruto, eds.), pp. 154–181. Oxford University Press, New York.

Crooks D. 1999. Child growth and nutritional status in a high-poverty community in eastern Kentucky. *American Journal of Physical Anthropology* 109:129–142.

Cuatrecasas PD, Lockwood H, Caldwell J. 1965. Lactase deficiency in the adult: A common occurrence. *Lancet* 1:14–18.

Curtin RA, Dolhinow P. 1978. Primate behavior in a changing world. *American Scientist* 66:468–475.

Dagosto M. 1993. Postcranial anatomy and locomotor behavior in Eocene primates. In *Postcranial Adaptation in Nonhuman Primates* (DL Gebo, ed.), pp. 567–593. Northern Illinois University Press, DeKalb.

Damasio A. 1994. *Descartes' Error.* Avon Books, New York.

Damasio H, Damasio AR. 1989. *Lesion Analysis in Neuropsychology.* Oxford University Press, New York.

Dart RA. 1925. *Australopithecus africanus:* The man-ape of South Africa. *Nature* 115:195–199.

Darwin C. 1839. *Journal of Researches into the Geology and Natural History of the Various Countries Visited by H.M.S. Beagle.* Colburn, London.

Darwin C. 1859. *On the Origin of Species by Means of Natural Selection; or, The Preservation of Favoured Races in the Struggle for Life.* John Murray, London.

Darwin C. 1871. *The Descent of Man and Selection in Relation to Sex.* J. Murray, London.

Dawkins R. 1976. *The Selfish Gene.* Oxford University Press, New York.

Deacon TW. 1990. Fallacies of progression in theories of brain-size evolution. *International Journal of Primatology* 11:193–236.

Deacon TW. 1997. *The Symbolic Species: The Co-Evolution of Language and the Brain.* Norton, New York.

Dean C. 2007. A radiographic and histological study of modern human lower first permanent molar root growth during the supraosseous eruptive phase. *Journal of Human Evolution,* 53:635–646.

De Bonis L, Koufos G. 1993. The face and mandible of *Ouranopithecus macedoniensis:* Description of new specimens and comparisons. *Journal of Human Evolution* 24:469–491.

Dedrick D. 1996. Color language universality and evolution: On the explanation for basic color terms. *Philosophical Psychology* 9:497–524.

Defleur A, White T, Valensi P, Slimak L, Crégut-Bonnoure E. 1999. Neanderthal cannibalism at Moula-Guercy, Ardèche, France. *Science* 286:128–131.

Dehaene S. 2003. Natural born readers. *New Scientist* 179:30–33.

Dehaene S, Dupoux E, Mehler J, et al. 1997. Anatomical variability in the cortical representation of first and second language. *NeuroReport* 8:3809–3815.

De Heinzelen J, Clark JD, White T, et al. 1999. Environment and behavior of 2.5 million-year-old Bouri hominids. *Science* 284:625–628.

Deino AL, Renne PR, Swisher CC. 1998. ^{40}Ar/^{39}Ar dating in paleoanthropology and archaeology. *Evolutionary Anthropology* 6:63–75.

Delgado RA, van Schaik CP. 2000. The behavioral ecology and conservation of the orangutan *(Pongo pygmaeus):* A tale of two islands. *Evolutionary Anthropology* 9:201–218.

Delson E. 1980. Fossil macaques, phyletic relationships and a scenario of deployment. In *The Macaques: Studies in Ecology, Behavior, and Evolution* (DG Lindburg, ed.), pp. 10–30. Van Nostrand Reinhold, New York.

d'Errico F, Blackwell LR, Berger LR. 2001. Bone tool use in termite foraging by early hominids and its impact on understanding early hominid behaviour. *South African Journal of Science* 97:71–75.

Dettwyler KA. 1991. Can paleopathology provide evidence for "compassion"? *American Journal of Physical Anthropology* 84:375–384.

de Waal FBM. 1982. *Chimpanzee Politics.* Johns Hopkins University Press, Baltimore.

de Waal FBM, Lanting F. 1997. *Bonobo: The Forgotten Ape.* University of California Press, Berkeley.

de Waal Malefijt A. 1968. *Homo monstrosus. Scientific American* 219:112–118.

Disotell TR. 1999. Human evolution: Origins of modern humans still look recent. *Current Biology* 9:R647–R650.

Dobzhansky T. 1973. Nothing in biology makes sense except in the light of evolution. *American Biology Teacher* 35:125–129.

Domb LG, Pagel M. 2001. Sexual swellings advertise female quality in wild baboons. *Nature* 410:204–206.

Dorval M, Bouchard K, Maunsell E, et al. 2008. Health behaviors and psychological distress in women intiating BRCA1/2 genetic testing: Comparison with control population.*Journal of Genetic Counseling* 17:314–326.

Dunbar RIM. 1983. *Reproductive Decisions: An Economic Analysis of Gelada Baboon Social Strategies.* Princeton University Press, Princeton, NJ.

Dunbar RIM. 1992. Neocortex size as a constraint on group size in primates. *Journal of Human Evolution* 20:469–493.

Dunbar RIM. 1993. Coevolution of neocortical size, group size, and language in humans. *Behavioral and Brain Sciences* 16:681–735.

Dunbar R. 1997. *Grooming, Gossip, and the Evolution of Language.* Harvard University Press, Cambridge, MA.

Eaton SB, Eaton SB III, Konner MJ. 1999. Paleolithic nutrition revisited. In *Evolutionary Medicine* (WR Trevathan, EO Smith, JJ McKenna, eds.), pp. 313–332. Oxford University Press, Oxford.

Eaton SB, Konner MJ. 1985. Paleolithic nutrition. A consideration of its nature and current implications. *New England Journal of Medicine* 312:283–289.

Ebenesersdóttir SS, Sigurösson A, Sánchez-Quinto F, Lalueza-Fox C, Stefánsson K, Helgason A. 2011. A new subclade of mtDNA haplogroup C1 in Icelanders: Evidence of pre-Columbian contact? *American Journal of Physical Anthropology* 144:92–99.

Elango N, Thomas J, Soojin Y, et al. 2006. Variable molecular clocks in hominoids, *PNAS,* January 2006.

Eldredge N, Gould SJ. 1972. Punctuated equilibrium: An alternative to phyletic gradualism. In *Models in Paleobiology* (TJM Shopf, ed.), pp. 82–115. Freeman, Cooper, and Co., San Francisco.

Ellison PT. 1990. Human ovarian function and reproductive ecology: New hypotheses. *American Anthropologist* 92:933–952.

Ellison PT. 1994. Advances in human reproductive ecology. *Annual Review in Anthropology* 23:255–275.

Endler J. 1983. Natural and sexual selection on color patterns in poeciliiad fishes. *Environmental Biology of Fishes* 9:173–190.

Endler J. 1986. *Natural Selection in the Wild.* Princeton University Press, Princeton, NJ.

Engels F. 1896. The part played by labor in the transition from ape to man.

Ennattah NS, Sahi T, Savilahti E, et al. 2002. Identification of a variant associated with adult-type hypolactasia. *Nature Genetics* 30:233–237.

Enoch MA, Goldman D. 1999. Genetics of alcoholism and substance abuse. *Psychiatric Clinics of North America* 22:289–299.

Etler DA. 1996. The fossil evidence for human evolution in Asia. *Annual Review of Anthropology* 25:275–301.

Evernden JF, Curtis GH. 1965. Potassium–argon dating of Late Cenozoic rocks in East Africa and Italy. *Current Anthropology* 6:643–651.

Eyre-Walker A, Keightley PD. 1999. High genomic deleterious mutation rates in hominids. *Nature* 397:344–347.

Fagan BM. 2001. *People of the Earth*, 10th ed. Prentice Hall, Upper Saddle River, NJ.

Fairbanks DJ, Rytting B. 2001. Mendelian controversies: A botanical and historical review. *American Journal of Botany* 88:737–752.

Fairburn HR, Young LE, Hendrich BD. 2002. Epigenetic reprogramming: How now, cloned cow? *Current Biology* 12:R68–R70.

Falk D. 1975. Comparative anatomy of the larynx in man and chimpanzee. *American Journal of Physical Anthropology* 43:123–132.

Falk D. 1980. A reanalysis of South African australopithecine natural endocasts. *American Journal of Physical Anthropology* 53:525–539.

Falk D. 1983a. Cerebral cortices of East African early hominids. *Science* 221:1072–1074.

Falk D. 1983b. The Taung endocast: A reply to Holloway. *American Journal of Physical Anthropology* 60:479–489.

Falk D. 1985a. Apples, oranges, and the lunate sulcus. *American Journal of Physical Anthropology* 67:313–315.

Falk D. 1985b. Hadar AL 162-28 endocast as evidence that brain enlargement preceded cortical reorganization in hominid evolution. *Nature* 313:45–47.

Falk D. 1989. Ape-like endocast of "ape-man" Taung. *American Journal of Physical Anthropology* 80:335–339.

Falk D. 1990. Brain evolution in *Homo:* The "radiator" theory. *Behavioral and Brain Sciences* 13:333–381.

Falk D. 1991. Reply to Dr. Holloway: Shifting positions on the lunate sulcus. *American Journal of Physical Anthropology* 84:89–91.

Falk D, Conroy G. 1983. The cranial venous sinus system in early hominids: Phylogenetic and functional implications for *Australopithecus afarensis*. *Nature* 306:779–781.

Falk D, Froese N, Sade DS, Dudek BC. 1999. Sex differences in brain/body relationships of rhesus monkeys and humans. *Journal of Human Evolution* 36:233–238.

Feathers JK. 1996. Luminescence dating and modern human origins. *Evolutionary Anthropology* 5:25–36.

Feibel CS. 1999. Tephrostratigraphy and geological context in paleoanthropology. *Evolutionary Anthropology* 8:87–100.

Feibel CS, Brown FH, McDougall I. 1989. Stratigraphic context of fossil hominids from the Omo Group deposits, northern Turkana Basin, Kenya and Ethiopia. *American Journal of Physical Anthropology* 78:595–622.

Feldman MW, Cavalli-Sforza LL. 1989. On the theory of evolution under genetic and cultural transmission with application to the lactose absorption problem. In *Mathematical Evolutionary Theory* (MW Feldman, ed.), pp. 145–173. Princeton University Press, Princeton, NJ.

Ferguson CA. 1964. Baby talk in six languages. *American Anthropologist* 66:103–114.

Fernald A. 1992. Human maternal vocalizations to infants as biologically relevant signals: An evolutionary perspective. In *The Adapted Mind* (JH Barkow, L Cosmides, J Tooby, eds.), pp. 391–428. Oxford University Press, New York.

Fernald A, Taeschner T, Dunn J, et al. 1989. A cross-language study of prosodic modifications in mothers' and fathers' speech to preverbal infants. *Journal of Child Language* 16:477–501.

Finkel T, Holbrook NJ. 2000. Oxidants, oxidative stress and the biology of aging. *Nature* 408:239–247.

Finlay BL, Darlington RB. 1995. Linked regularities in the development and evolution of mammalian brains. *Science* 268:1578–1584.

Fischbeck KH. 2001. Polyglutamine expansion neurodegenerative disease. *Brain Research Bulletin* 56:161–163.

Fisher H. 1992. *Anatomy of Love.* Fawcett Columbine, New York.

Fisher RA. 1958. *The Genetical Theory of Natural Selection*, 2nd ed. Dover Publications, New York.

Fleagle JG, Kay RF. 1987. The phyletic position of the Parapithecidae. *Journal of Human Evolution* 16:483–532.

Fleagle JG, Rosenberger AL, eds. 1990. The platyrrhine fossil record. *Journal of Human Evolution* 19:1–254.

Fleagle JG, Stern JT, Jungers WL, et al. 1981. Climbing: A biomechanical link with brachiation and with bipedalism. *Symposia of the Zoological Society of London* 48:359–375.

Fleagle JG, Tejedor MF. 2002. Early platyrrhines of southern South America. In *The Primate Fossil Record* (WC Hartwig, ed.), pp. 161–173. Cambridge University Press, Cambridge.

Foley RA, Lee PC. 1991. Ecology and energetics of encephalization in hominid evolution. *Philosophical Transactions of the Royal Society of London* B 334:223–232.

Fossey D. 1983. *Gorillas in the Mist.* Houghton Mifflin, Boston.

Franciscus RG. 1999. Neandertal nasal structures and upper respiratory tract "specialization." *Proceedings of the National Academy of Sciences* 96:1805–1809.

Franciscus RG. 2003. Internal nasal floor configuration in *Homo* with special reference to the evolution of Neandertal facial form. *Journal of Human Evolution* 44:701–729.

Frayer D, Wolpoff MH, Smith FM, et al. 1993. Theories of modern human origins: The paleontological test. *American Anthropologist* 95:14–50.

Frisancho AR, Baker PT. 1970. Altitude and growth: A study of the patterns of physical growth of a high altitude Peruvian Quechua population. *American Journal of Physical Anthropology* 32:279–292.

Froenicke, L. 2005. Origins of primate chromosomes—as delineated by Z00-FSH and alignments of human and mouse draft genome sequences. *Cytogenetic and Genome Research* 108:122–138.

Fully G. 1956. Une nouvelle methode de determination de la taille. *Ann. Med. Legale Criminol.* 35:266–273.

Furuichi T. 1987. Sexual swelling, receptivity, and grouping of wild pygmy chimpanzee females at Wamba, Zaïre. *Primates* 28:309–318.

Gabunia L, Antón SC, Lordkipanidze D, et al. 2001. Dmanisi and dispersal. *Evolutionary Anthropology* 10:158–170.

Gabunia L, Vekua A, Lordkipanidze D, et al. 2000. Earliest Pleistocene cranial remains from Dmanisi, Republic of Georgia: Taxonomy, geological setting, and age. *Science* 288:1019–1025.

Gagneux P, Wills C, Gerloff U, et al. 1996. Mitochondrial sequences show diverse evolutionary histories of African hominoids. *Proceedings of the National Academy of Sciences* 96:5077–5082.

Gajdusek DC, Gibbs CJ Jr, Alpers M. 1966. Experimental transmission of a kuru-like syndrome to chimpanzees. *Nature* 209:794–796.

Gajdusek DC, Zigas V. 1957. Degenerative disease of the central nervous system in New Guinea: The endemic occurrence of "kuru" in the native population. *New England Journal of Medicine* 257:974–978.

Galdikas BMF. 1985. Subadult male sociality and reproductive tactics among orangutans at Tanjung Putting. *American Journal of Primatology* 8:87–99.

Galdikas BMF, Wood JW. 1990. Birth spacing patterns in humans and apes. *American Journal of Physical Anthropology* 83:185–191.

Galik K, Senut B, Pickford M, et al. 2004. External and internal morphology of the BAR 1002'00 *Orrorin tugenensis* femur. *Nature* 305:1450–1453.

Gambier D. 1989. Fossil hominids from the early upper Paleolithic (Aurignacian) of France. In *The Human Revolution: Behavioral and Biological Perspectives on the Origins of Modern Humans* (P Mellars, C Stringer, eds.), pp. 194–211. Princeton University Press, Princeton, NJ.

Ganzhorn HU, Kappeler PM. 1993. *Lemur Social Systems and Their Ecological Basis.* Plenum, New York.

Garber PA. 1989. Role of spatial memory in primate foraging patterns: *Saguinus mystax* and *Saguinus fuscicollis*. *American Journal of Primatology* 19:203–216.

Gardner H. 1993. *Frames of Mind: The Theory of Multiple Intelligences*, 2nd ed. Basic Books, New York.

Gargett RH. 1989. Grave shortcomings: The evidence for Neandertal burial. *Current Anthropology* 30:157–190.

Gargett RH. 1999. Middle Paleolithic burial is not a dead issue: The view from Qafzeh, Saint-Césaire, Amud, and Dederiyeh. *Journal of Human Evolution* 37:27–90.

Gaser C, Schlaug G. 2003. Brain structures differ between musicians and non-musicians. *Journal of Neuroscience* 23:9240–9245.

Gazzaniga MS, Ivry RB, Mangun GR. 1998. *Cognitive Neuroscience: The Biology of the Mind.* Norton, New York.

Gebo DL. 1996. Climbing, brachiation, and terrestrial quadrupedalism: Historical precursors of hominid bipedalism. *American Journal of Physical Anthropology* 101:55–92.

Gebo DL, MacLatchy L, Kityo R, et al. 1997. A hominoid genus from the early Miocene of Uganda. *Science* 276:401–404.

Geissmann T. 2000. Gibbon song and human music from an evolutionary perspective. In *The Origins of Music* (N Wallin, B Merker, S Brown, eds.), pp. 103–123. The MIT Press, Cambridge, MA.

Gerber LM, Crews DE. 1999. Evolutionary perspectives on chronic degenerative diseases. In *Evolutionary Medicine* (WR Trevathan, EO Smith, JJ McKenna, eds.), pp. 443–469. Oxford University Press, Oxford.

Gibbard PL, Head MJ, Walker MJC, & The Subcommission on Quaternary Stratigraphy. 2010. Formal ratification of the quaternary system/period and the Pleistocene series/epoch with a base at 2.58 Ma. *Journal of Quaternary Sciences.* 25:96–102.

Gibbons A. 1991. Déjà vu all over again: Chimp-language wars. *Science* 251:1561–1562.

Giedd JN, Blumenthal J, Jeffries NO, et al. 1999. Brain development during adolescence: A longitudinal MRI study. *Nature Neuroscience* 2:861–863.

Gilbert BM, McKern TW. 1973. A method for aging the female *Os pubis.* *American Journal of Physical Anthropology* 38:31–38.

Gilbert WH, Asfaw B, eds. 2008 Homo erectus: Pleistocene evidence from the Middle Awash, Ethiopia. *University of California Press,* Berkeley, CA.

Gingerich PD. 1976. Cranial anatomy and evolution of early Tertiary Plesiadapidae (Mammalia, Primates). *Museum of Paleontology, University of Michigan, Papers on Paleontology* 15:1–140.

Gislén A, Dacke M, Kröger RHH, et al. 2003. Superior underwater vision in a human population of sea gypsies. *Current Biology* 13:833–836.

Glander KE, Wright PC, Seigler DS, Randrianasolo VB. 1989. Consumption of cyanogenic bamboo by a newly discovered species of bamboo lemur. *American Journal of Primatology* 19:119–124.

Gleason TM, Norconk MA. 2002. Predation risk and antipredator adaptation in white-faced sakis, *Pithecia pithecia.* In *Eat or Be Eaten: Predation Sensitive Foraging among Primates* (LE Miller, ed.), pp. 169–186. Cambridge University Press, Cambridge.

Godfrey LR, Jungers WL. 2002. Quaternary fossil lemurs. In *The Primate Fossil Record* (WC Hartwig, ed.), pp. 97–121. Cambridge University Press, Cambridge.

Godinot M, Dagosto M. 1983. The astragalus of *Necrolemur* (Primates, Microchoerinae). *Journal of Paleontology* 57:1321–1324.

Goldberg A, Wrangham RW. 1997. Genetic correlates of social behaviour in chimpanzees: Evidence from mitochondrial DNA. *Animal Behaviour* 54:559–570.

Goldberg E. 2001. *The Executive Brain: Frontal Lobes and the Civilized Mind.* Oxford University Press, New York.

Goldberg P, Weiner S, Bar-Yosef O, Xu Q, Liu J. 2001. Site formation processes of Zhoukoudian, China. *Journal of Human Evolution* 41:483–530.

Goldfarb LG. 2002. Kuru: The old epidemic in a new mirror. *Microbes and Infection* 4:875–882.

Golovanova LV, Hoffecker JF, Kharitonov VM, Romanova GP. 1999. Mezmaiskaya Cave: A Neanderthal occupation in the northern Caucasus. *Current Anthropology* 40:77–86.

Goodall J. 1963. Feeding behaviour of wild chimpanzees: A preliminary report. *Symposium of the Zoological Society of London* 10:39–48.

Goodall J. 1968. Behaviour of free-living chimpanzees of the Gombe Stream area. *Animal Behaviour Monographs* 1:163–311.

Goodall J. 1968. *In the Shadow of Man.* National Geographic Society, Washington, DC.

Goodall J. 1986. *The Chimpanzees of Gombe: Patterns of Behavior.* Harvard University Press, Cambridge, MA.

Goodman M. 1962. Immunochemistry of the primates and primate evolution. *Annals of the New York Academy of Sciences* 102:219–234.

Goodman M. 1963. Serological analysis of the systematics of recent hominoids. *Human Biology* 35:377–436.

Goodman M. 1999. The genomic record of humankind's evolutionary roots. *American Journal of Human Genetics* 64:31–39.

Goodman M, Porter CA, Czelusniak J, et al. 1998. Toward a phylogenetic classification of primates based on DNA evidence complemented by fossil evidence. *Molecular Phylogenetics and Evolution* 9:585–598.

Goodman SM, O'Connor S, Langrand O. 1993. A review of predation on lemurs: Implications for the evolution of social behavior in small, nocturnal primates. In *Lemur Social Systems and Their Ecological Basis* (PM Kappeler, JU Ganzhorn, eds.), pp. 51–66. Plenum, New York.

Gordon AD, Green DJ, and Richmond BG. 2008. Strong postcranial size dimorphism in *Australopithecus afarensis*: results from two new multivariate resampling methods for multivariate data sets with missing data. *American Journal of Physical Anthropology.* 135:311–328.

Gordon AD, Nevell L, Wood B. 2008. The *Homo floresiensis* cranium (LB1): Size, scaling, and early *Homo* affinities. *Proceedings of the National Academy of Science U.S.A.* 105:4650–4655.

Gossett TF. 1965. *Race: The History of an Idea in America.* Schocken Books, New York.

Gottesman II, Shields J. 1982. *Schizophrenia: The Epigenetic Puzzle.* Cambridge University Press, Cambridge.

Gould SJ, Lewontin RC. 1979. The spandrels of San Marco and the Panglossian paradigm. *Proceedings of the Royal Society of London* B 205:581–598.

Gradstein FM, Ogg JG, Smith AG. eds., 2004. *A Geologic Time Scale 2004.* Cambridge University Press, Cambridge.

Grant PR. 1986. *Ecology and Evolution of Darwin's Finches.* Princeton University Press, Princeton, NJ.

Gravlee CC, Bernard HR, Leonard WR. 2003. Heredity, environment, and cranial form: A reanalysis of Boas's immigrant data. *American Anthropologist* 105:125–138.

Gray PB, Yang C-FJ, Pope HG. 2006. Fathers have lower salivary testosterone levels than unmarried men and married non-fathers in Beijing, China. *Proceedings of the Royal Society of London* B 273:333–339.

Green RE, Krause J, Briggs AW, Maricic T, et al. 2010. A draft sequence of the Neandertal genome. *Science* 328:710–711.

Green RE, Krause J, Ptak SE, et al. 2006. Analysis of one million base pairs of Neanderthal DNA. *Nature* 444:330–336.

Groves C. 2001. *Primate Taxonomy.* Smithsonian Institution Press, Washington, DC.

Grün R, Huang PH, Huang W, et al. 1998. ESR and U-series analyses of teeth from the paleoanthropological site of Hexian, Anhui Province, China. *Journal of Human Evolution* 34:555–564.

Grün R, Huang PH, Wu X, et al. 1997. ESR analysis of teeth from the paleoanthropological site of Zhoukoudian, China. *Journal of Human Evolution* 32:83–91.

Grün R, Stringer CB. 1991. Electron spin resonance dating and the evolution of modern humans. *Archaeometry* 33:153–199.

Grün R, Stringer CB, Schwarcz HP. 1991. ESR dating of teeth from Garrod's Tabun Cave collection. *Journal of Human Evolution* 20:231–248.

Guglielmino CR, Desilvesteri A, Berres J. 2000. Probable ancestors of Hungarian ethnic groups: An admixture analysis. *Annals of Human Genetics* 64:145–159.

Gulati AP, Domchek SM. 2008. The clinical management of BRCA1 and BRCA2 mutation carriers. *Current Oncology Reports* 10:47–53.

Gunz P, Neubauer S, Maureille B, Hublin J-J. 2010. Brain development after birth differs between Neanderthals and modern humans. *Current Biology* 20:R921–R922.

Gursky S. 1994. Infant care in the spectral tarsier (*Tarsius spectrum*) Sulawesi, Indonesia. *International Journal of Primatology* 15:843–853.

Gursky S. 1995. Group size and composition in the spectral tarsier, *Tarsius spectrum:* Implications for social organization. *Tropical Biodiversity* 3:57–62.

Habgood P, Franklin N. 2008. The revolution that didn't arrive: A review of Pleistocene Sahul. *Journal of Human Evolution* 55:187–222.

Haile-Selassie Y, Asfaw B, White TD. 2004. Hominid cranial remains from upper Pleistocene deposits at Aduma, Middle Awash, Ethiopia. *American Journal of Physical Anthropology* 123:1–10.

Haile-Selassie Y, White T, Suwa G. 2004. Late Miocene teeth from Middle Awash Ethiopia and early hominid dental evolution. *Science* 303:1503–1505.

Haile-Selassie Y, Latime B, Alene M, Deino A, Gibert L, Melillo S, Saylor B, Scott G, Lovejoy CO. 2010. An early *Australopithecus afarensis* postcranium from Woranso-Mille, Ethiopia. *Proc Natl Acad Sci.* 107: 12121–12126.

Hajibabaei M, Singer GAC, Hebert PDN, Hickey DA. 2007. DNA barcoding: How it complements taxonomy, molecular phylogenetics and population genetics. *Trends in Genetics* 23:167–172.

Haller JS. 1970. The species problem: Nineteenth-century concepts of racial inferiority in the origin of man controversy. *American Anthropologist* 72:1321–1329.

Halverson MS, Bolnick DA. 2008. An ancient DNA test of a founder effect in Native American ABO blood group frequencies. *American Journal of Physical Anthropology* 137:342–347.

Hamilton WD. 1964. The genetical evolution of social behaviour, I and II. *Journal of Theoretical Biology* 7:1–52.

Hammer MF, Redd AJ, Wood ET, et al. 2000. Jewish and Middle Eastern non-Jewish populations share a common pool of Y-chromosome biallelic haplotypes. *Proceedings of the National Academy of Sciences* 97:6769–6774.

Hansson GC. 1988. Cystic fibrosis and chloride-secreting diarrhoea. *Nature* 333:711.

Harcourt AH. 1978. Strategies of emigration and transfer by primates, with particular reference to gorillas. *Zeitschrift für Tierpsychologie* 48:401–420.

Harding RM, Fullerton SM, Griffiths RC, et al. 1997. Archaic African and Asian lineages in the genetic ancestry of modern humans. *American Journal of Human Genetics* 60:772–789.

Hardy GH. 1908. Mendelian proportions in a mixed population. *Science* 28:49–50.

Harpending HC, Batzer MA, Gurven M, et al. 1998. Genetic traces of ancient demography. *Proceedings of the National Academy of Sciences* 95:1961–1967.

Harpending HC, Rogers A. 2000. Genetic perspectives on human origins and differentiation. *Annual Review in Genomics and Human Genetics* 1:361–385.

Harrison GA, Tanner JM, Pilbeam DR, Baker PT. 1988. *Human Biology*, 3rd ed. Oxford University Press, Oxford.

Harrison T, Gu Y. 1999. Taxonomy and phylogenetic relationships of early Miocene catarrhines from Sihong, China. *Journal of Human Evolution* 37:225–277.

Hartwig WC. 1994. Patterns, puzzles and perspectives on platyrrhine origins. In *Integrative Paths to the Past: Paleoanthropological Essays in Honor of F. Clark Howell* (RS Corruccini, RL Ciochon, eds.), pp. 69–94. Prentice Hall, Englewood Cliffs, NJ.

Harvey P, Martin RD, Clutton-Brock TH. 1987. Life histories in comparative perspective. In *Primate Societies* (BB Smuts, DL Cheney, RM Seyfarth, RW Wrangham, TT Struhsaker, eds.), pp. 181–196. University of Chicago Press, Chicago.

Hassold T, Hunt P. 2001. To err (meiotically) is human: The genesis of human aneuploidy. *Nature Reviews: Genetics* 3:280–291.

Hauser MD, Sulkowski GM. 2001. Can rhesus monkeys spontaneously subtract? *Cognition* 79:239–262.

Hausfater G. 1975. Dominance and reproduction in baboons (*Papio cynocephalus*). In *Contributions to Primatology*, vol. 7. Karger, Basel.

Hawkes K. 2003. Grandmothers and the evolution of human longevity. *American Journal of Human Biology* 15:380–400.

Hawkes K, O'Connell JF, Blurton Jones NG. 1997. Hadza women's time allocation, offspring production, and the evolution of long postmenopausal life spans. *Current Anthropology* 38:551–577.

Hawkes K, O'Connell JF, Blurton Jones NG. 2001. Hadza meat sharing. *Evolution and Human Behavior* 22:113–142.

Heider ER. 1972. Universals in color naming and memory. *Journal of Experimental Psychology* 93:10–20.

Henshilwood C, d'Errico F, Vanhaeren M, et al. 2004. Middle Stone Age shell beads from South Africa. *Science* 304:404.

Herman-Giddens ME, Slora E, Wasserman RC, et al. 1997. Secondary sexual characteristics and menses in young girls seen in office practice: A study from the Pediatric Research in Office Settings Network. *Pediatrics* 99:505–512.

Hershkovitz I, Kornreich L, Laron Z. 2007. Comparative skeletal features between *Homo floresiensis* and patients with primary growth hormone insensitivity (Laron syndrome). *American Journal Physical Anthropology* 134:198–208.

Hewes GW. 1999. A history of the study of language origins and the gestural primacy hypothesis. In *Handbook of Human Symbolic Evolution* (A Lock, CR Peters, eds.), pp. 571–595. Blackwell, Oxford.

Hey J. 2001. The mind of the species problem. *Trends in Ecology and Evolution* 16:326–329.

Hill EM, Chow K. 2002. Life-history theory and risky drinking. *Addiction* 97:401–413.

Hill EM, Ross L, Low B. 1997. The role of future unpredictability in human risk-taking. *Human Nature* 8:287–325.

Hill K, Hurtado AM. 1991. The evolution of premature reproductive senescence and menopause in human females: An evaluation of the "grandmother hypothesis." *Human Nature* 2:313–350.

Hill K, Hurtado AM. 1996. *Aché Life History: The Ecology and Demography of a Foraging People.* Aldine de Gruyter, New York.

Hill K, Kaplan H. 1993. On why male foragers hunt and share food. *Current Anthropology* 34:701–706.

Hirszfeld L, Hirszfeld H. 1919. Essai d'application des methods au problème des races. *Anthropologie* 29:505–537.

Hocket CF. 1960. The origin of speech. *Scientific American* 203:88–111.

Hodgen MT. 1964. *Early Anthropology in the Sixteenth and Seventeenth Centuries.* University of Pennsylvania Press, Philadelphia.

Hofman M. 1988. Size and shape of the cerebral cortex. II. The cortical volume. *Brain, Behavior and Evolution* 32:17–26.

Hohmann G, Fruth B. 1993. Field observations on meat sharing among bonobos (*Pan paniscus*). *Folia Primatologica* 60:225–229.

Holick MF, MacLaughlin JA, Doppelt SH. 1981. Regulation of cutaneous previtamin D3 photosynthesis in man: Skin pigment is not an essential regulator. *Science* 211:590–593.

Holliday TW. 1995. *Body size and proportions in the late Pleistocene western Old World and the origins of modern humans.* PhD dissertation, University of New Mexico, Albuquerque.

Holliday TW, Franciscus R. 2009. Body size and its consequences: Allometry and the lower limb length of Liang Bua 1 (*Homo floresiensis*). *Journal of Human Evolution* Vol. 57 Issue 3, 223–228.

Holloway RL. 1968. The evolution of the primate brain: Some aspects of quantitative relations. *Brain Research* 7:121–172.

Holloway RL. 1976. Paleoneurological evidence for language origins. *Annals of the New York Academy of Sciences* 280:330–348.

Holloway RL. 1980. Within-species brain–body weight variability: A reexamination of the Danish data and other primate species. *American Journal of Physical Anthropology* 53:109–121.

Holloway RL. 1981. Revisiting the South African Taung australopithecine endocast: The position of the lunate sulcus as determined by stereoplotting technique. *American Journal of Physical Anthropology* 56:43–58.

Holloway RL. 1984. The poor brain of *Homo sapiens neanderthalensis*: See what you please. In *Ancestors: The Hard Evidence* (E Delson, ed.), pp. 319–324. Alan R. Liss, New York.

Holloway RL. 1984. The Taung endocast and the lunate sulcus: A rejection of the hypothesis of its anterior position. *American Journal of Physical Anthropology* 64:285–287.

Holloway RL. 1991. On Falk's 1989 accusations regarding Holloway's study of the Taung endocast: A reply. *American Journal of Physical Anthropology* 84:87–88.

Holloway RL. 1999. Evolution of the human brain. In *Handbook of Human Symbolic Evolution* (A Lock, CR Peters, eds.), pp. 74–125. Blackwell, Oxford.

Holloway RL, de LaCoste-Lareymondie MC. 1982. Brain endocast asymmetry in pongids and hominids: Some preliminary findings on the paleontology of cerebral dominance. *American Journal of Physical Anthropology* 58:101–110.

Holloway RL, Kimbel WH. 1986. Endocast morphology of Hadar hominid AL 162-28. *Nature* 321:536–537.

Hollox EJ, Poulter M, Zvarik M, et al. 2001. Lactase haplotype diversity in the Old World. *American Journal of Human Genetics* 68:160–172.

Hooton EA. 1916. The relation of physical anthropology to medical science. *Medical Review of Reviews* April:260–264.

Hooton EA. 1946. *Up from the Ape*, rev. ed. Macmillan, New York.

Hovers E, Ilani S, Bar-Yosef O, Vandermeersch B. 2003. An early case of color symbolism: Ochre use by modern humans in Qafzeh Cave. *Current Anthropology* 44:491–522.

Hovers E, Kimbel WH, Rak Y. 2000. The Amud 7 skeleton: Still a burial. Response to Gargett. *Journal of Human Evolution* 39:253–260.

Howell FC. 1964. Pleistocene glacial ecology and the evolution of "classic Neandertal" man. *Southwestern Journal of Anthropology* 8:377–410.

Howell FC. 1966. Observations on the earlier phases of the European Lower Paleolithic. *American Anthropologist* 68:111–140.

Howell FC. 1994. A chronostratigraphic and taxonomic framework of the origins of modern humans. In *Origins of Anatomically Modern Humans* (MH Nitecki, DV Nitecki, eds.), pp. 253–319. Plenum, New York.

Howell WM, Calder PC, Grimble RF. 2002. Gene polymorphisms, inflammatory diseases and cancer. *Proceedings of the Nutritional Society* 61:447–456.

Howells WW. 1973. *Cranial Variation in Man*. Papers of the Peabody Museum, Cambridge, MA.

Hrdy SB. 1977. *The Langurs of Abu*. Harvard University Press, Cambridge, MA.

Hrdy SB, Whitten PL. 1987. Patterning of sexual activity. In *Primate Societies* (BB Smuts, DL Cheney, RM Seyfarth, RW Wrangham, TT Struhsaker, eds.), pp. 370–384. University of Chicago Press, Chicago.

Hublin JJ. 1985. Human fossils from the North African middle Pleistocene and the origin of *Homo sapiens*. In *Ancestors: The Hard Evidence* (E Delson, ed.), pp. 283–288. Alan R. Liss, New York.

Hublin JJ, Spoor F, Braun M, et al. 1996. A late Neanderthal associated with Upper Paleolithic artefacts. *Nature* 381:224–226.

Hunt KD. 1996. The postural feeding hypothesis: An ecological model for the evolution of bipedalism. *South African Journal of Science* 92:77–90.

Hurford JR. 1991. The evolution of the critical period for language acquisition. *Cognition* 40:159–201.

Huxley J, Kettlewell HBD. 1965. *Charles Darwin and His World*. Thames and Hudson London.

Huxley J, Mayr E, Osmond H, Hoffer A. 1964. Schizophrenia as a genetic morphism. *Nature* 204:220–221.

Hyde KL, Zatorre RJ, Griffiths TD, Lerch JP, Peretz I. 2006. Morphometry of the amusic brain: A two-site study. *Brain* 129:2562–2570.

Indriati E, ed. 2007. *Recent advances on Southeast Asian Paleoanthropology and Archaeology*. Yayasan Keluarga Hashim Djojohadikusomo, Jakarta, Indonesia.

Ingman M, Kaessmann H, Pääbo S, Gyllensten U. 2000. Mitochondrial genome variation and the origin of modern humans. *Nature* 408:708–713.

International Human Genome Consortium. 2001 A physical map of the human genome. *Nature* 409:934–941.

Irons W. 1979. Cultural and biological success. In *Evolutionary Biology and Human Social Behavior* (NA Chagnon, W Irons, eds.), pp. 257–272. Duxbury Press, North Scituate, MA.

Irwin G. 1992. *The Prehistoric Exploration and Colonisation of the Pacific*. Cambridge University Press, New York.

Isaac GL. 1978. The food-sharing behavior of proto-human hominids. *Scientific American* 238:90–108.

Isbell L, Young T. 1996. The evolution of bipedalism in hominids and reduced group size in chimpanzees: Alternative responses to decreasing resource availability. *Journal of Human Evolution* 30:389–397.

Iscan MY, Loth SR, Wright RK. 1984. Metamorphosis at the sternal rib end: a new method to estimate age at death in white males. *American Journal of Physical Anthropology* 65:147–156.

Ishida H, Pickford M. 1997. A new late Miocene hominoid from Kenya: *Samburupithecus kiptalami* gen et sp. nov. *Comptes Rendus de l'Academie des Sciences de Paris* 325:823–829.

Jablensky A, Sartorius N, Ernberg G, et al. 1992. Schizophrenia: Manifestations, incidence and course in different cultures: A World Health Organization Ten-Country Study. *Psychological Medicine* 20(suppl.):1–97.

Jablonski NG, Chaplin G. 1993. Origin of habitual terrestrial bipedalism in the ancestor of the Hominidae. *Journal of Human Evolution* 24:259–280.

Jablonski NG, Chaplin G. 2000. The evolution of human skin coloration. *Journal of Human Evolution* 39:57–106.

Jablonski NG, Chaplin G. 2002. Skin deep. *Scientific American* 287:74–81.

Jackendoff R. 1994. *Patterns in the Mind: Language and Human Nature*. Basic Books, New York.

Jackson FLC. 2000. Human adaptations to infectious disease. In *Human Biology: An Evolutionary and Biocultural Perspective* (S Stinson, B Bogin, R Huss-Ashmore, D O'Rourke, eds.), pp. 273–293. Wiley-Liss, New York.

Janson CH. 1985. Aggressive competition and individual food consumption in wild brown capuchin monkeys (*Cebus apella*). *Behavioral Ecology and Sociobiology* 18:125–138.

Jantz RL, Owsley DW. 2001. Variation among early North American crania. *American Journal of Physical Anthropology* 114:146–155.

Jeffreys AJ, Wilson V, Thein SL. 1985. Hypervariable "minisatellite" regions in human DNA. *Nature* 314:67–73.

Jensen-Seaman M, Kidd KK. 2001. Mitochondrial variation and biogeography of eastern gorillas. *Molecular Ecology* 10:2240–2247.

Jerison HJ. 1991. Brain size and the evolution of mind. In *59th James Arthur Lecture on the Evolution of the Human Brain, 1989*. Columbia University Press, New York.

Ji C-Y, Chen T-J. 2008. Secular changes in stature and body mass index for Chinese youth in sixteen major cities, 1950s–2005. *American Journal of Human Biology* 20:530–537.

Jianakoplos NM, Bernasek A. 1998. Are women more risk aversive? *Economic Inquiry* 36:620–630.

Jobling MA, Tyler-Smith C. 2003. The human Y chromosome: An evolutionary marker comes of age. *Nature Reviews Genetics* 4:598–612.

Johannsen W. 1911. The genotype conception of heredity. *American Naturalist* 45:129–159.

Johanson D, Edey M. 1981. *Lucy: The Beginnings of Humankind*. Simon & Schuster, New York.

Johanson DC, Lovejoy CO, Kimbel WH, et al. 1982. Morphology of the Pliocene partial hominid skeleton (A.L. 288-1) from the Hadar Formation, Ethiopia. *American Journal of Physical Anthropology* 57:403–452.

Johanson DC, Taieb M. 1976. Plio-Pleistocene hominid discoveries in Hadar, Ethiopia. *Nature* 260:293–297.

Johanson DC, White TD. 1979. A systematic assessment of early African hominids. *Science* 202:321–330.

Jolly CJ. 1970. The seed-eaters: A new model of hominid differentiation based on a baboon analogy. *Man* 5:1–26.

Jones FW. 1916. *Arboreal Man*. Edward Arnold, London.

Jordan P. 1999. *Neanderthal*. Sutton Publishing, Phoenix Mill, Gloucestershire.

Jöris O, Street M. 2008. At the end of the 14C time scale—the Middle to Upper Paleolithic record of western Eurasia *Journal of Human Evolution*, Volume 55, Issue 5, November 2008:782–802.

Kaessmann H, Heissig F, von Haeseler A, Pääbo S. 1999. DNA sequence variation in a non-coding region of low recombination on the human X chromosome. *Nature Genetics* 22:78–81.

Kandel ER, Schwartz JH, Jessell TM. 2000. *Principles of Neural Science*, 4th ed. McGraw-Hill, New York.

Kano T. 1992. *The Last Ape*. Stanford University Press, Stanford, CA.

Kaplan H, Hill K, Lancaster J, Hurtado AM. 2000. A theory of human life history evolution: Diet, intelligence, and longevity. *Evolutionary Anthropology* 9:156–185.

Kappelman J. 1996. The evolution of body mass and relative brain size in hominids. *Journal of Human Evolution* 30:243–276.

Karn MN, Penrose LS. 1951. Birth weight and gestation time in relation to maternal age, parity, and infant survival. *Annals of Eugenics* 16:147–161.

Katz D, Suchey JM. 1986. Age determination of the male Os pubis. *American Journal of Physical Anthropology* 69:427–435.

Katzman MA, Lee S. 1997. Beyond body image: The integration of feminist and transcultural theories in the understanding of self starvation. *International Journal of Eating Disorders* 22:385–394.

Kay P, Berlin B. 1997. Science imperialism: There are nontrivial constraints on color naming. *Behavioral and Brain Science* 20:196–201.

Kehrer-Sawatzki H, Cooper DN. 2007. Structural divergence between the human and chimpanzee genomes. *Human Genetics* 120:759–778.

Keith A. 1923. Man's posture: Its evolution and disorders. *British Medical Journal* 1:451–454, 499–502, 545–548, 587–590, 624–626, 669–672.

Keith A. 1940. Blumenbach's centenary. *Man* 40:82–85.

Kennedy KA, Sonakia A, Chiment J, Verma KK. 1991. Is the Narmada hominid an Indian *Homo erectus*? *American Journal of Physical Anthropology* 86:475–496.

Kessler RC, Berglund P, Demler O, et al. 2003. The epidemiology of major depressive disorder. *Journal of the American Medical Association* 289:3095–3105.

Kevles DJ. 1985. *In the Name of Eugenics.* Alfred A. Knopf, New York.

Kidd K. 1975. On the magnitude of selective forces maintaining schizophrenia in the population. In *Genetic Research in Psychiatry* (R Fieve, D Rosenthal, H Brill, eds.), pp. 135–145. Johns Hopkins University Press, Baltimore.

Kim J-Y, Oh I-H, Lee E-Y, Choi K-S, Choe B-K, Yoon T-Y, Lee C-G, Moon J-S, Shin S-H, Choi J-M. 2008. Anthropometric changes in children and adolescents from 1965 to 2005 in Korea. *American Journal of Physical Anthropology* 136:230–236.

Kimbel WH, Lockwood CA, Ward CV, et al. 2006. Was *Australopithecus anamensis* ancestral to *A. afarensis*? A case of anagenesis in the hominin fossil record. *Journal of Human Evolution* 51:134–152.

Kimbel WH, Rak Y, Johanson DC. 2004. *The Skull of* Australopithecus afarensis. Oxford University Press, New York.

King TE, Parkin EJ, Swinfield G, et al. 2007. Africans in Yorkshire? The deepest-rooting clade of the Y phylogeny within English genealogy. *European Journal of Human Genetics* 15:288–293.

Kirch PV. 2001. *On the Road of the Winds: An Archaeological History of the Pacific Islands before European Contact.* University of California Press, Berkeley.

Kirkpatrick M. 1982. Sexual selection and the evolution of female choice. *Evolution* 36:1–12.

Kirkwood TBL. 2002. Evolution theory and the mechanisms of aging. In *Brocklehursts' Textbook of Geriatric Medicine and Gerontology,* 6th ed. (R Tallis, HM Fillit, eds.), pp. 31–35. Churchill Livingstone, Edinburgh and New York.

Kirkwood TBL, Austad SN. 2000. Why do we age? *Nature* 408:233–238.

Klaus MH, Kennell JH. 1997. The doula: An essential ingredient of childbirth revisited. *Acta Paediatrica* 86:1034–1036.

Klein RG, Edgar B. 2002. *The Dawn of Human Culture.* Wiley, New York.

Klug WS, Cummings MR. 2003. *Concepts of Genetics.* Prentice Hall, Upper Saddle River, NJ.

Klug WS, Cummings MR, Spencer CA, Palladino MA. 2009. *Concepts of Genetics (9th edition).* Benjamin Cummings, Upper Saddle River, NJ.

Kochi Y, Suzuki A, Yamada R, Yamamoto K. 2010. Ethnogenetic heterogeneity of rheumatoid arthritis—implications for pathogenesis. *Nature Reviews Rheumatology* 6:290–295.

Koda Y, Tachida H, Liu Y, et al. 2001. Contrasting patterns of polymorphisms at the ABO-secretor gene (FUT2) and plasma (1,3)fucosyltransferase gene (FUT6) in human populations *Genetics,* 747–756.

Kornberg A. 1960. Biological synthesis of DNA. *Science* 131:1503–1508.

Kostianovsky M. 2000. Evolutionary origin of eukaryotic cells. *Ultrastructural Pathology* 24:59–66.

Krings M, Capelli C, Tschentscher F, et al. 2000. A view of Neandertal genetic diversity. *Nature Genetics* 26:144–146.

Krings M, Geisert H, Schmitz RW, et al. 1999. DNA sequence of the mitochondrial hypervariable region II from the Neandertal type specimen. *Proceedings of the National Academy of Sciences* 96:5581–5585.

Krings M, Stone A, Schmitz RW, et al. 1997. Neandertal DNA sequences and the origin of modern humans. *Cell* 90:19–30.

Lahdenpera M, Lummaa V, Helle S, et al. 2004. Fitness benefits of prolonged post-reproductive lifespan in women. *Nature* 428:178–181.

Laidlaw SA, Kopple JD. 1987. Newer concepts of the indispensable amino acids. *American Journal of Clinical Nutrition* 46:593–605.

Laitman J. 1984. The anatomy of human speech. *Natural History* 92:20–27.

Laitman JT, Heimbuch RC. 1982. The basicranium of Plio-Pleistocene hominids as an indicator of their upper respiratory systems. *American Journal of Physical Anthropology* 59:323–343.

Laitman JT, Reidenberg JS. 1988. Advances in understanding the relationship between skull base and larynx, with comments on the origins of speech. *Human Evolution* 3:101–111.

Lalueza C, Perez-Perez A, Turbon D. 1996. Dietary inferences through buccal microwear analysis of middle and upper Pleistocene human fossils. *American Journal of Physical Anthropology* 100:367–387.

Lalueza-Fox C, Caramelli D, Catalano G, et al. 2007. A Melanocortin 1 Receptor Allele Suggests Varying Pigmentation Among Neanderthals. *Science* Vol. 318 No. 5855, 1453–1455.

Lalueza-Fox C, Sampietro ML, Caramelli D, et al. 2005. Neandertal evolutionary genetics; mitochondrial DNA data from the Iberian Peninsula. *Molecular Biology and Evolution* 22:1077–1081.

Larick R, Ciochon RL, Zaim Y, et al. 2001. Early Pleistocene ^{40}Ar/^{39}Ar ages for Bapang Formation hominids, Central Java, Indonesia. *Proceedings of the National Academy of Science* 98:4866–4871.

Larsen CS, Matter RM, Gebo DL. 1998. *Human Origins: The Fossil Record,* 3rd ed. Waveland Press, Prospect Heights, IL.

Larson E. 1997. *Summer of the Gods: The Scopes Trial and America's Continuing Debate over Science and Religion.* Harvard University Press, Cambridge, MA.

Larson E. 2001. *Evolution's Workshop: God and Science on the Galapagos Islands.* Basic Books, New York.

Larson S, Jungers W, Morwood M, et al. 2007. Homo floresiensis and the evolution of the hominin shoulder. *Journal of Human Evolution* Vol. 53 Issue 6 718–731.

Larsen SG, Jungers WL, Tocheri MW, et al. 2009. Descriptions of the upper limb skeleton of *Homo floresiensis. Journal of Human Evolution,* 57: 555-570.

Latimer B, Ward C. 1993. The thoracic and lumbar vertebrae. In *The Nariokotome* Homo erectus *Skeleton* (A Walker, R Leakey, eds.), pp. 266–293. Harvard University Press, Cambridge, MA.

Leakey LSB. 1959. A new fossil skull from Olduvai. *Nature* 184:491–493.

Leakey LSB. 1962. A new lower Pliocene fossil primate from Kenya. *Annals of the Magazine of Natural History* 4:689–696.

Leakey MG, Feibel CS, McDougall I, Walker A. 1995. New four-million-year-old hominid species from Kanapoi and Allia Bay, Kenya. *Nature* 376:565–571.

Leakey MG, Spoor F, Brown FH, et al. 2001. New hominid genus from eastern Africa shows diverse middle Pliocene lineages. *Nature* 410:433–440.

Leakey MG, Spoor F, Brown FH, et al. 2003. A new hominid calvaria from Ileret (Kenya). *American Journal of Physical Anthropology* 36(suppl.):136.

Leakey R, Lewin R. 1978. *People of the Lake: Mankind and Its Beginnings.* Doubleday, New York.

LeBlanc S, Register K. 2003. *Constant Battles: The Myth of the Peaceful, Noble Savage.* St. Martin's Press, New York.

Ledoux J. 1996. *The Emotional Brain.* Touchstone, New York.

Lee RB, DeVore I, eds. 1968. *Man the Hunter.* Aldine, Chicago.

Lee-Thorp JA, van der Merwe NJ, Brain CK. 1994. Diet of *Australopithecus robustus* at Swartkrans from stable carbon isotope analysis. *Journal of Human Evolution* 27:361–372.

Le Gros Clark WE, Thomas DP. 1952. The Miocene lemuroids of East Africa. *Fossil Mammals of Africa* 5:1–20.

Leigh SR. 1992. Cranial capacity evolution in *Homo erectus* and early *Homo sapiens. American Journal of Physical Anthropology* 87:1–13.

LeMay M. 1985. Asymmetries of the brains and skulls of nonhuman primates. In *Cerebral Lateralization in Nonhuman Species* (SD Glick, ed.), pp. 233–245. Academic Press, Orlando, FL.

Leonard WR, Robertson ML. 1997. Rethinking the energetics of bipedality. *Current Anthropology* 38:304–309.

Li T, Etler DA. 1992. New middle Pleistocene hominid crania from Yunxian in China. *Nature* 357:484–487.

Lieberman P. 1984. *The Biology and Evolution of Language.* Harvard University Press, Cambridge, MA.

Lieberman P. 1991. *Uniquely Human: The Evolution of Speech, Thought, and Selfless Behavior.* Harvard University Press, Cambridge, MA.

Lieberman DE, McBratney BM, Krovitz G. 2002. The evolution and development of cranial form in *Homo sapiens. Proceedings of the National Academy of Sciences* 99:1134–1139.

Lifton RJ. 1986. *The Nazi Doctors.* Basic Books, New York.

Lighthall NR, Mather M, Gorlick MA. 2009. Acute stress increases sex differences in risk seeking in the Balloon Analogue Risk Task. *PLoS One* (4:e6002).

Lindee MS. 2000. Genetic disease since 1945. *Nature Reviews Genetics* 1:236–241.

Lindenbaum S. 2001. Kuru, prions, and human affairs: Thinking about epidemics. *Annual Review in Anthropology* 30:363–385.

Littlefield A, Lieberman L, Reynolds LT. 1982. Redefining race: The potential demise of a concept in physical anthropology. *Current Anthropology* 23:641–655.

Livingstone FB. 1958. Anthropological implications of sickle cell gene distribution in West Africa. *American Anthropologist* 60:533–562.

Ljung BO, Bergsten-Brucefors A, Lindgren G. 1974. The secular trend in physical growth in Sweden. *Annals of Human Biology* 1:245–256.

Loomis WF. 1967. Skin-pigment regulation of vitamin D biosynthesis in man. *Science* 157:501–506.

Lordkipanidze D, Jashashvili T, Vekua A, et al. 2007. Postcranial evidence from early *Homo* from Dmanisi, Georgia. *Nature* 449:305–310.

Lovejoy CO. 1978. A biomechanical review of the locomotor diversity of early hominids. In *Early Hominids of Africa* (CJ Jolly, ed.), pp. 403–429. St. Martin's, New York.

Lovejoy CO. 1988. The evolution of human walking. *Scientific American* 259:118–125.

Lovejoy CO, Meindl RS. 1985. Ectocranial suture closure: A revised method for the determination of skeletal age at death based on the lateral-anterior sutures. *American Journal of Physical Anthropology* Volume 68:57–66.

Lovejoy OW. 1981. The origin of man. *Science* 211:341–350.

Lovely EC, Kondrick LC. 2008. Teaching evolution: Challenging religious preconceptions. *Integrative and Comparative Biology* 48:164–174.

Low BS. 2000. *Why Sex Matters*. Princeton University Press, Princeton, NJ.

Lowe JJ, Walker MJC. 1997. *Reconstructing Quaternary Environments*, 2nd ed. Prentice Hall, Essex, England.

Lozano M, Bermúdez de Castro JM, Carbonell E, Arsuaga JL. 2008. Non-masticatory uses of anterior teeth of Sima de los Huesos individuals (Sierra de Atapuerca, Spain). *Journal of Human Evolution* 55:713–728.

Lozano M, Bermúdez de Castro JM, Martinón-Torres M, et al. 2004. Cut-marks on fossil human anterior teeth of the Sima de los Huesos site (Atapuerca, Spain). *Journal of Archaeological Science* 31:1127–1135.

Ludwig KR, Renne PR. 2000. Geochronology on the paleoanthropological time scale. *Evolutionary Anthropology* 9:101–110.

MacDorman MF, Minino AM, Strobino DM, Guyer B. 2002. Annual summary of vital statistics: 2001. *Pediatrics* 110:1037–1052.

Mackay-Sim AN, Silburn P. 2008. Stem cells and genetic disease. *Cell Proliferation* 41(Suppl. 1):85–93.

Mackintosh NJ. 1998. *IQ and Human Intelligence*. Oxford University Press, Oxford.

MacLatchy L, Gebo D, Kityo R, Pilbeam D. 2000. Postcranial functional morphology of *Morotopithecus bishopi*, with implications for the evolution of modern ape locomotion. *Journal of Human Evolution* 39:159–183.

Madrigal L, Meléndez-Obando M. 2008. Grandmothers' longevity negatively affects daughters' fertility. *American Journal of Physical Anthropology* 136:223–229.

Maggioncalda AN, Sapolsky RM, Czekala NM. 1999. Reproductive hormone profiles in captive male orangutans: Implications for understanding development arrest. *American Journal of Physical Anthropology* 109:19–32.

Malenky RK, Kuroda S, Vineberg EO, Wrangham RW. 1994. The significance of terrestrial herbaceous foods for bonobos, chimpanzees and gorillas. In *Chimpanzee Cultures* (RW Wrangham, WC McGrew, FB de Waal, PG Heltne, eds.), pp. 59–75. Harvard University Press, Cambridge, MA.

Mandryk C. 1992. Paleoecologist finds corridor ice-free but forbidding. *Mammoth Trumpet* March 1992.

Maples WR, Browning M. 1994. *Dead Men Do Tell Tales*. Broadway Books, New York.

Marcus G. 2004. *The Birth of the Mind*. Basic Books, New York.

Marean C. 1989. Sabertooth cats and their relevance for early hominid diet. *Journal of Human Evolution* 18:559–582.

Marean CW, Assefa Z. 1999. Zooarcheological evidence for the faunal exploitation behavior of Neandertals and early modern humans. *Evolutionary Anthropology* 8:22–37.

Marks J. 1992. Chromosomal evolution in primates. In *The Cambridge Encyclopedia of Human Evolution* (S Jones, R Martin, D Pilbeam, eds.), pp. 298–302. Cambridge University Press, Cambridge.

Marks J, Schmid CW, Sarich VM. 1988. DNA hybridization as a guide to phylogeny: Relations of the Hominoidea. *Journal of Human Evolution* 17:769–786.

Marlowe FW. 2005. Hunter-gatherers in human evolution. *Evolutionary Anthropology* 14:54–67.

Marshack A. 1996. A Middle Paleolithic symbolic composition from the Golan Heights: The earliest known depictive image. *Current Anthropology* 37:357–365.

Martin JA, Hamilton BE, Sutton PD, Ventura SJ, Mathews TJ, Kirmeyer S, Osterman MJ. 2010. Births: Final data for 2007. *National Vital Statistics Reports* 58:1–85.

Martin RD. 1983. Human brain evolution in an ecological context. In *52nd James Arthur Lecture on the Evolution of the Human Brain, 1982*. Columbia University Press, New York.

Martin RD, MacLarnon AM, Phillips JL, Dussubieux L, Williams PR, Dobyns WB. 2006. Comment on "The Brain of LB1, *Homo floresiensis*." *Science* 312:999.

Martin RH. 2008. Meiotic errors in human oogenesis and spermatogenesis. *Reproductive Biomedicine Online* 16:523–531.

Mascie-Taylor CGN. 1993. The biological anthropology of disease. In *The Anthropology of Disease* (CGN Mascie-Taylor, ed.), pp. 1–72. Oxford University Press, Oxford.

Mascie-Taylor CGN, Bogin B, eds. 1995. *Human Variability and Plasticity*. Cambridge University Press, Cambridge.

Matisoo-Smith E, Roberts RM, Allen JS, et al. 1998. Patterns of prehistoric mobility in Polynesia revealed by mitochondrial DNA from the Pacific rat. *Proceedings of the National Academy of Sciences* 95:15145–15150.

Mayr E. 1942. *Systematics and the Origin of Species*. Columbia University Press, New York.

Mayr E. 1963. *Animal Species and Evolution*. Harvard University Press, Cambridge, MA.

Mayr E. 1983. How to carry out the adaptationist program. *American Naturalist* 121:324–334.

Mazurek R. 1999. Back from the dead. *New Scientist* 164:40.

McBrearty S, Brooks AS. 2000. The revolution that wasn't: A new interpretation of the origin of modern human behavior. *Journal of Human Evolution* 39:453–563.

McBrearty S, Jablonski NG. 2005. First fossil chimpanzee. *Nature* 437:105–108, doi: 10.1038/nature04008.

McCollum MA. 2008. Nasomaxillary remodeling and facial form in robust *Australopithecus*: a reassessment. *Journal of Human Evolution*, Volume 54, Issue 1, January 2008, Pages 2–14.

McCown TD, Kennedy KAR, eds. 1971. *Climbing Man's Family Tree*. Prentice Hall, Englewood Cliffs, NJ.

McCracken RD. 1971. Lactase deficiency: An example of dietary evolution. *Current Anthropology* 12:479–517.

McCrossin ML, Benefit BR. 1993. Recently recovered *Kenyapithecus* mandible and its implications for great ape and human origins. *Proceedings of the National Academy of Sciences U.S.A.* 90:1962–1966.

McCrossin ML, Benefit BR, Gitau S, Blue KT. 1998. Fossil evidence for the origins of terrestriality among Old World higher primates. In *Primate Locomotion: Recent Advances* (EL Strasser, JG Fleagle, AL Rosenberger, HM McHenry, eds.), pp. 353–396. Plenum, New York.

McDermott F, Grün R, Stringer CB, Hawkesworth CJ. 1993. Mass-spectrometric U-series dates for Israeli Neanderthal/early modern hominid sites. *Nature* 363:252–255.

McDougall I. 1985. K–Ar and ^{40}Ar/^{39}Ar dating of the hominid-bearing Pliocene–Pleistocene sequence at Koobi Fora, Lake Turkana, northern Kenya. *Geological Society America Bulletin* 96:159–175.

McElroy A, Townsend PK. 1996. *Medical Anthropology in Ecological Perspective*, 3rd ed. Westview Press, Boulder, CO.

McFadden, et al. 1999. Ancient latitudinal gradients of C3/C4 grasses interpreted from stable isotopes of New World Pleistocene horse (Equus) teeth. *Global Ecology and Biogeography: A Journal of Macroecology* 8:137–149.

McGrew WC. 1992. *Chimpanzee Material Culture*. Cambridge University Press, Cambridge.

McHenry HM. 1991. Sexual dimorphism in *Australopithecus afarensis*. *Journal of Human Evolution* 20:21–32.

McHenry HM. 1992. Body size and proportions in early hominids. *American Journal of Physical Anthropology* 87:407–431.

McHenry HM. 1994. Behavioral ecological implications of early hominid body size. *Journal of Human Evolution* 27:77–87.

McHenry HM, Coffing K. 2000. *Australopithecus* to *Homo:* Transformations in body and mind. *Annual Review of Anthropology* 29:125–146.

McKern TW, Stewart TD. 1957. Skeletal age changes in young American male. The United States of America Army Quartermaster Research and Development Command, Technical Report EP-45, Natick, MA.

McKeown T. 1979. *The Role of Medicine: Dream, Mirage, or Nemesis?* Princeton University Press, Princeton.

McKusick VA, Eldridge R, Hostetler JA, Egeland JA. 1964. Dwarfism in the Amish. *Transactions of the Association of American Physicians, Philadelphia* 77:151–168.

McMurray CT. 2010. Mechanisms of trinucleotide repeat instability during human development. *Nature Reviews Genetics* 11:786–799.

McNeil WH. 1976. *Plagues and People.* Doubleday, New York.

McPherron S, Alemseged Z, Marean C, Wynn J, Reed D, Geraads D, Bobe D & Hamd Béarat H. 2010 Evidence for stone-tool-assisted consumption of animal tissues before 3.39 million years ago at Dikika, Ethiopia *Nature* 466:857–860.

Meehan JP. 1955. Individual and racial variations in vascular response to cold stimulus. *Military Medicine* 116:330–334.

Meier B, Albibnac R, Peyrieras A, et al. 1987. A new species of Hapalemur (Primates) from South East Madagascar. *Folia Primatologica* 48:211–215.

Meindl RS. 1987. Hypothesis: A selective advantage for cystic fibrosis heterozygotes. *American Journal of Physical Anthropology* 74:39–45.

Melnick D, Hoelzer GA. 1996. Genetic consequences of macaque social organization and behavior. In *Evolution and Ecology of Macaque Societies* (JE Fa, DG Lindburg, eds.), pp. 412–442. Cambridge University Press, Cambridge.

Mendel G. 1866. Versuche über Pflanzenhybriden [Experiments in plant hybridization]. *Verhandlungen des Naturforschenden Vereines in Brünn, Bd. IV für das Jahr 1865*, 3–47.

Menzel CR. 1991. Cognitive aspects of foraging in Japanese monkeys. *Animal Behaviour* 41:397–402.

Mettler LE, Gregg TG, Schaffer HE. 1988. *Population Genetics and Evolution.* Prentice Hall, Upper Saddle River, NJ.

Meyer D, Thomson G. 2001. How selection shapes variation of the human major histocompatibility complex: A review. *Annals of Human Genetics* 65:1–26.

Milton K. 1980. *The Foraging Strategy of Howler Monkeys: A Study in Primate Economics.* Columbia University Press, New York.

Milton K. 1981. Distribution patterns of tropical food plants as a stimulus to primate mental development. *American Anthropologist* 83:534–548.

Milton K. 1999. A hypothesis to explain the role of meat-eating in human evolution. *Evolutionary Anthropology* 8:11–21.

Minkoff H, Ecker J. 2008. Genetic testing and breach of patient confidentiality: Law, ethics, and pragmatics. *American Journal of Obstetrics and Gynecology* 198:498.e1–498.e4.

Mintz L. 1977. *Historical Geology: The Science of a Dynamic Earth.* Charles E. Merrill, Columbus, OH.

Mitani JC. 1985. Responses of gibbons (*Hylobates muelleri*) to self, neighbor and stranger song duets. *International Journal of Primatology* 6:193–200.

Mitani JC, Gros-Louis J, Manson JH. 1996. Number of males in primate groups: Comparative tests of competing hypotheses. *American Journal of Primatology* 38:315–332.

Mitchell RJ, Hammer MF. 1996. Human evolution and the Y chromosome. *Current Opinion in Genetics and Development* 6:737–742.

Mithen S. 1996. *The Prehistory of the Mind.* Thames and Hudson, London.

Mittermeier RA, Konstant WR, Rylands AB. 2002. Priorities for primate conservation in the first decade of the 21st century. XIXth Congress of International Primatological Society, Beijing, China (abstract).

Molnar S. 2002. *Human Variation,* 5th ed. Prentice Hall, Upper Saddle River, NJ.

Montagu A. 1974. *Man's Most Dangerous Myth: The Fallacy of Race,* 5th ed. Oxford University Press, London.

Moran EF. 2000. *Human Adaptability,* 2nd ed. Westview Press, Boulder, CO.

Morell V. 1995. *Ancestral Passions: The Leakey Family and the Quest for Humankind's Beginnings.* Simon & Schuster, New York.

Moorwood M, Brown P, Sutikna T, et al. 2005. Further evidence for small-bodied hominins from the Late Pleistocene of Flores, Indonesia. *Nature* 437, 1012–1017.

Morwood MJ, Jungers WL, Liang B, eds. 2009. *Journal of Human Evolution Special Issue: Research at Liang Bua, Flores, Indonesia.* Volume 57 number 5.

Moya-Sola S, Kohler M. 1996. The first *Dryopithecus* skeleton: Origins of great ape locomotion. *Nature* 379:156–159.

Muller MN, Marlowe FW, Bugumba R, Ellison PT. 2009. Testosterone and paternal care in East African foragers and pastoralists. *Proceedings of the Royal Society* B 276:347–354.

Mullis K. 1990. The unusual origins of the polymerase chain reaction. *Scientific American* April:56–65.

Murphy J. 1976. Psychiatric labeling in cross-cultural perspective. *Science* 191:1019–1028.

Murray FG. 1934. Pigmentation, sunlight, and nutritional disease. *American Anthropologist* 36:438–445.

Myrianthopoulos NC, Aronson SM. 1966. Population dynamics of Tay–Sachs disease. I. Reproductive fitness and selection. *American Journal of Human Genetics* 18:313–327.

Nafte M. 2000. *Flesh and Bone: An Introduction to Forensic Anthropology.* Carolina Academic Press, Durham, NC.

Neel JV. 1962. Diabetes mellitus: A thrifty genotype rendered detrimental by "progress"? *American Journal of Human Genetics* 14:353–362.

Neel JV. 1982. The thrifty genotype revisited. In *The Genetics of Diabetes Mellitus* (J Kobberling, R Tattersall, eds.), pp. 283–293. Academic Press, London.

Nesse RM. 1994. An evolutionary perspective on substance abuse. *Ethology and Sociobiology* 15:339–348.

Nesse RM. 2000. Is depression an adaptation? *Archives of General Psychiatry* 57:14–20.

Nesse RM, Berridge KC. 1997. Psychoactive drug use in evolutionary perspective. *Science* 278:63–66.

Nesse RM, Williams GC. 1994. *Why We Get Sick: The New Science of Darwinian Medicine.* Times Books, New York.

Newman RW, Munroe EH. 1955. The relation of climate and body size in U.S. males. *American Journal of Physical Anthropology* 13:1–17.

Newton PN. 1987. The variable social organization of Hanuman langurs (*Presbytis entellus*), infanticide, and the monopolization of females. *International Journal of Primatology* 9:59–77.

Nicholls, H. 2008. Let's make a mammoth. *Nature* 456:310–314.

Nichter M, Ritenbaugh C, Nichter M, Vuckovic N, Aickin M. 1995. Dieting and "watching" behaviors among adolescent females: Report of a multi-method study. *Journal of Adolescent Health* 17:153–162.

Nielsen S. 2001. Epidemiology and mortality of eating disorders. *Psychiatric Clinics of North America* 24:201–214.

Nimgaonkar VL, Ward SE, Agarde H, et al. 1997. Fertility in schizophrenia: Results from a contemporary US cohort. *Acta Psychiatrica Scandinavica* 95:364–369.

Nishida T. 1990. *The Chimpanzees of the Mahale Mountains.* University of Tokyo Press, Tokyo.

Noble W, Davidson I. 1996. *Human Evolution, Language and Mind.* Cambridge University Press, Cambridge.

Nolte J. 2002. *The Human Brain: An Introduction to Its Functional Anatomy,* 5th ed. Mosby, St. Louis.

Noonan JP, Coop G, Kudaravalli S, et al. 2006. Sequencing and analysis of Neanderthal genomic DNA. *Science* 314:1113–1118.

Nordborg M. 1998. On the probability of Neanderthal ancestry. *American Journal of Human Genetics* 63:1237–1240.

Nowak RM, Paradiso JL. 1983. *Walker's Mammals of the World,* 4th ed. John Hopkins University Press, Baltimore.

Nunn CL, van Schaik CP and Zinner D. 2001. Do exaggerated sexual swellings function in female mating competition in primates? A comparative test of the reliable indicator hypothesis. *Behavioral Ecology* 5:646–654.

Oakley K. 1963. Analytical methods of dating bones. In *Science in Archaeology* (D Brothwell, E Higgs, eds.). Basic Books, New York.

O'Connell JF, Hawkes K, Blurton Jones NG. 1992. Patterns in the distribution, site structure, and assemblage composition of Hadza kill-butchering sites. *Journal of Archaeological Science* 19:319–345.

Ogonuki N, Inoue K, Yamamoto Y, et al. 2002. Early death of mice cloned from somatic cells. *Nature Genetics* 30:253–254.

Omran AR. 1971. The epidemiologic transition: A theory of the epidemiology of population change. *Milbank Memorial Fund Quarterly* 49:509–538.

Online Mendelian Inheritance in Man. 2000. McKusick-Nathans Institute for Genetic Medicine, Johns Hopkins University, Baltimore, and National Center for Biotechnology Information, National Library of Medicine, Bethesda. http://www.ncbi.nlm.nih.gov/omim/.

Orlando L, Calvignac S, Schnebelen C, Douady CJ, Godfrey LR, Hänni C. 2008. DNA from extinct lemurs links archaeolemurids to extant indriids. *BMC Evolutionary Biology* 8:121.

Ovchinnikov IV, Götherström A, Romanova GP, et al. 2000. Molecular analysis of Neanderthal DNA from the northern Caucasus. *Nature* 404:490–493.

Panter-Brick C. 2002. Sexual division of labor: Energetic and evolutionary scenarios. *American Journal of Human Biology* 14:627–640.

Parfitt T, Egorova Y. 2005. Genetics, history, and identity: The case of the Bene Israel and the Lemba. *Culture, Medicine, and Psychiatry* 29:193–224.

Parish AR. 1996. Female relationships in bonobos (*Pan paniscus*). *Human Nature* 7:61–96.

Parra EJ, Marcini A, Akey J, et al. 1998. Estimating African American admixture proportions by use of population-specific alleles. *American Journal of Human Genetics* 63:1839–1851.

Partridge TC, Granger DE, Caffee MW, Clarke RJ. 2003. Lower Pliocene hominid remains from Sterkfontein. *Science* 300:607–612.

Paterson HEH. 1986. Environment and species. *South African Journal of Science* 82:62–65.

Paterson JD. 1996. Coming to America: Acclimation in macaque body structures and Bergmann's rule. *International Journal of Primatology* 17:585–611.

Pearson OM. 2000. Postcranial remains and the origin of modern humans. *Evolutionary Anthropology* 9:229–247.

Pearson OM, Fleagle JG, Grine FE, Royer DF. 2008. Further new hominin fossils from the Kibish Formation, southwestern Ethiopia. *Journal of Human Evolution* 55:444–447.

Peccei JS. 1995. The origin and evolution of menopause: The altriciality–lifespan hypothesis. *Ethology and Sociobiology* 16:425–449.

Peccei JS. 2001a. A critique of the grandmother hypothesis: Old and new. *American Journal of Human Biology* 13:434–452.

Peccei JS. 2001b. Menopause: Adaptation or epiphenomenon? *Evolutionary Anthropology* 10:43–57.

Peretz I. 2006. The nature of music from a biological perspective. *Cognition* 100:1–32.

Peschken CA, Esdaile JM. 1999. Rheumatic diseases in North America's indigenous peoples. *Seminars in Arthritis and Rheumatism* 28:368–391.

Petersen MB, Wang Q, Willems PJ. 2008. Sex-linked deafness. *Clinical Genetics* 73:14–23.

Petitto LA, Marentette PF. 1991. Babbling in the manual mode: Evidence for the ontogeny of language. *Science* 251:1493–1496.

Pickford M, Senut B. 2001. "Millennium Ancestor," a 6-million-year-old bipedal hominid from Kenya: Recent discoveries push back human origins by 1.5 million years. *South African Journal of Science* 97:2–22.

Pickford M, Senut B, Gommery D, Treil J. 2002. Bipedalism in *Orrorin tugenensis* revealed by its femora. *Concise Review Papers Paleoevolution* 1:191–203.

Pilbeam D. 1982. New hominoid skull material from the Miocene of Pakistan. *Nature* 295:232–234.

Piña-Aguilar RE, Lopez-Saucedo J, Sheffield R, Ruiz-Galaz LI, Barroso-Padilla JJ, Gutiérrez-Gutiérrez A. 2009. Revival of extinct species using nuclear transfer: Hope for the mammoth, true for the Pyrenean ibex, but is it time for "conservation cloning?" *Cloning and Stem Cells* 11:341–346.

Pinker S. 1994. *The Language Instinct.* HarperPerennial, New York.

Pinker S, Bloom P. 1990. Natural language and natural selection. *Behavioral and Brain Sciences* 13:707–784.

Polimeni J, Reiss JP. 2003. Evolutionary perspectives on schizophrenia. *Canadian Journal of Psychiatry* 48:34–39.

Ponce de Leon MS, Golovanova L, Doronichev, et al. 2008. Neanderthal brain size at birth provides insights into the evolution of human life history. *Proceedings of the National Academy of Sciences* 105: 13764–13768.

Pontzer H, Raichlen D, Sockol MD. 2009. The metabolic cost of walking in humans, chimpanzees, and early hominins. *Journal of Human Evolution* 56:43–54.

Porter AMW. 1995. Analyses of measurements taken from adult femurs of a British population. *International Journal of Osteoarchaeology* 5:305–323.

Potts R. 1984. Home bases and early hominids. *American Scientist* 72:338–347.

Potts R. 1988. *Early Hominid Activities at Olduvai.* Aldine, Chicago.

Potts R. 1996. *Humanity's Descent: The Consequences of Ecological Instability.* New York: William Morrow.

Pritzker BM. 2000. *A Native American Encyclopedia.* Oxford University Press, New York.

Pruetz JD, Bertolani, P. 2007. Savanna chimpanzees, *Pan troglodytes verus,* hunt with tools. *Current Biology* 17:412–417.

Pusey A, Williams J, Goodall J. 1997. The influence of dominance rank on the reproductive success of female chimpanzees. *Science* 277:828–831.

Radespiel U. 2006. Ecological diversity and seasonal adaptations of mouse lemurs (*Microcebus spp.*). In *Lemurs: Ecology and Adaptation* (L Gould, ML Sauther, eds.), pp. 211–234. Springer, New York.

Radinsky L. 1979. The fossil record of primate brain evolution. In *49th James Arthur Lecture on the Evolution of the Human Brain, 1979.* American Museum of Natural History, New York.

Rak Y, Kimbel WH, Hovers E. 1994. A Neandertal infant from Amud Cave, Israel. *Journal of Human Evolution* 26:313–324.

Rasmussen DT. 2002. The origin of primates. In *The Primate Fossil Record* (WC Hartwig, ed.), pp. 5–9. Cambridge University Press, Cambridge.

Ratjen F, Döring G. 2003. Cystic fibrosis. *Lancet* 361:681–689.

Reed KE. 1997. Early hominid evolution and ecological change through the African Plio-Pleistocene. *Journal of Human Evolution* 32:289–322.

Reed TE. 1969. Caucasian genes in American Negroes. *Science* 165:762–768.

Relethford JH. 2001. Absence of regional affinities of Neandertal DNA with living humans does not reject multiregional evolution. *American Journal of Physical Anthropology* 115:95–98.

Remis MJ. 1997. Ranging and grouping patterns of a western lowland gorilla group at Bai Hokou, Central African Republic. *American Journal of Primatology* 43:111–133.

Richard A. 1992. Aggressive competition between males, female-controlled polygyny and sexual monomorphism in a Malagasy primate, *Propithecus verreauxi. Journal of Human Evolution* 22:395–406.

Richards MP, Pettitt PB, Stiner MC, Trinkaus E. 2001. Stable isotope evidence for increasing dietary breadth in the European mid–Upper Paleolithic. *Proceedings of the National Academy of Sciences* 98:6528–6532.

Richards MP, Pettitt PB, Trinkaus E, et al. 2000. Neanderthal diet at Vindija and Neanderthal predation: The evidence from stable isotopes. *Proceedings of the National Academy of Sciences* 97:7663–7666.

Richmond BG, Strait DS. 2000. Evidence that humans evolved from a knuckle-walking ancestor. *Nature* 404:382–385.

Rightmire GP. 1990/1993. *The Evolution of Homo erectus, Comparative Anatomical Studies of an Extinct Human Species.* Cambridge University Press, New York.

Rightmire GP, Deacon HJ. 1991. Comparative studies of late Pleistocene human remains from Klasies River Mouth, South Africa. *Journal of Human Evolution* 20:131–156.

Ristau CA. 1999. Animal language and cognition projects. In *Handbook of Human Symbolic Evolution* (A Lock, CR Peters, eds.), pp. 644–685. Blackwell, Oxford.

Roberts DF. 1978. *Climate and Human Variability.* Cummings, Menlo Park, CA.

Roberts MB, Parfitt SA. 1999. A Middle Pleistocene Hominid Site at Eartham Quarry, Boxgrove, West Sussex. *English Heritage Archaeological Report 17.* English Heritage, London.

Roberts MB, Stringer CB, Parfitt SA. 1994. A hominid tibia from middle Pleistocene sediments at Boxgrove, U.K. *Nature* 369:311–313.

Robins AH. 1991. *Biological Perspectives on Human Pigmentation.* Cambridge University Press, Cambridge.

Roca AL, Georgiadis N, O'Brien SL. 2005. Cytonuclear genomic dissociation in African elephant species. *Nature Genetics* 37:96–100.

Rodman PS, McHenry HM. 1980. Bioenergetics and the origin of hominid bipedalism. *American Journal of Physical Anthropology* 52:103–106.

Rogers T, Saunders S. 1994. Accuracy of sex determination using morphological traits of the human pelvis. *Journal of Forensic Sciences* 39:1047–56.

Rose MD. 1984. Food acquisition and the evolution of positional behavior: The case of bipedalism. In *Food Acquisition and Processing in Primates* (DJ Chivers, BA Wood, A Bilsborough, eds.), pp. 509–524. Plenum, New York.

Rosenberg KR, Trevathan WR. 1996. Bipedalism and human birth: The obstetrical dilemma revisited. *Evolutionary Anthropology* 4:161–168.

Rosenberger AL. 2002. Platyrrhine paleontology and systematics: The paradigm shifts. In *The Primate Fossil Record* (WC Hartwig, ed.), pp. 151–159. Cambridge University Press, Cambridge.

Ross C, Williams B, Kay RF. 1998. Phylogenetic analysis of anthropoid relationships. *Journal of Human Evolution* 35:221–306.

Rowe JH. 1965. The Renaissance foundations of anthropology. *American Anthropologist* 67:1–20.

Rowell TE. 1988. Beyond the one-male group. *Behaviour* 104:189–201.

Rudan I, Campbell H. 2004. Five reasons why inbreeding may have considerable effect on post-reproductive human health. *Collegium Antropologicum* 28:943–950.

Ruff CB. 2000. Prediction of body mass from skeletal frame size in elite athletes. *American Journal of Physical Anthropology.* 113:507–517.

Russell MD. 1987. Bone breakage in the Krapina hominid collection. *American Journal of Physical Anthropology* 72:373–379.

Ruvolo M. 1997. Molecular phylogeny of the hominoids: Inferences from multiple independent DNA sequence data sets. *Molecular Biology and Evolution* 14:248–265.

Ryan MJ. 1990. Sexual selection, sensory systems, and sensory exploitation. *Oxford Surveys in Evolutionary Biology* 7:156–195.

Ryan T, Krovitz G. 2006. Trabecular bone ontogeny in the human proximal femur. *Journal of Human Evolution* 51:591–602.

Sabater-Pi J, Bermejo M, Ilera G, Vea JJ. 1993. Behavior of bonobos (*Pan paniscus*) following their capture of monkeys in Zaïre. *International Journal of Primatology* 14:797–804.

Sanders WJ, Bodenbender BE. 1994. Morphometric analysis of lumbar vertebra UMP 67-28: Implications for spinal function and phylogeny of the Miocene Moroto hominoid. *Journal of Human Evolution* 26:203–237.

Sarich VM, Wilson AC. 1967. Immunological time scale for hominid evolution. *Science* 158:1200–1203.

Sauther ML. 2002. Group size effects on predation sensitive foraging in wild ring-tailed lemurs (*Lemur catta*). In *Eat or Be Eaten: Predation Sensitive Foraging among Primates* (LE Miller, ed.), pp. 107–125. Cambridge University Press, Cambridge.

Sauther ML, Sussman RW, Gould L. 1999. The socioecology of the ring-tailed lemur: Thirty-five years of research. *Evolutionary Anthropology* 8:120–132.

Savage-Rumbaugh S, Lewin R. 1994. *Kanzi: The Ape at the Brink of the Human Mind.* Wiley, New York.

Savage-Rumbaugh S, Rumbaugh D. 1993. The emergence of language. In *Tools, Language, and Cognition in Human Evolution* (KR Gibson, T Ingold, eds.), pp. 86–108. Cambridge University Press, Cambridge.

Savage-Rumbaugh S, Shanker SG, Taylor TJ. 1998. *Apes, Language, and the Human Mind.* Oxford University Press, New York.

Schaaffhausen H. 1858. Zur Kentiss der ältesten Rassenschädel. *Archiv für Anatomie* 5:453–488.

Schell L. 1991. Pollution and human growth: Lead, noise, polychlorobiphenyl compounds and toxic wastes. In *Applications of Biological Anthropology to Human Affairs* (CGN Mascie-Taylor, GW Lasker, eds.), pp. 83–116. Cambridge University Press, Cambridge.

Schell L. 1995. Human biological adaptability with special emphasis on plasticity: History, development and problems for future research. In *Human Variability and Plasticity* (CGN Mascie-Taylor, B Bogin, eds.), pp. 213–237. Cambridge University Press, Cambridge.

Schell LM, Hills EA. 2002. Polluted environments as extreme environments. In *Human Growth from Conception to Maturity* (G Gilli, LM Schell, L Benso, eds.), pp. 249–261. Smith-Gordon, London.

Schick K, Toth N. 1993. *Making Silent Stones Speak: Human Evolution and the Dawn of Technology.* Simon & Schuster, New York.

Schick KD, Toth N, Garufi G, et al. 1999. Continuing investigations into the stone tool-making and tool-using capabilities of a Bonobo (*Pan paniscus*). *Journal of Archaeological Science* 26:821–832.

Schiller F. 1979. *Paul Broca: Founder of French Anthropology, Explorer of the Brain.* University of California Press, Berkeley.

Schlaug G. 2001. The brain of musicians. A model for functional and structural adaptation. *Annals of the New York Academy of Sciences* 930:281–299.

Schlaug G, Jäncke L, Huang Y, Staiger JF, Steinmetz H. 1995. Increased corpus callosum size in musicians. *Neuropsychologia* 33:1047–1055.

Schmitz RW, Serre D, Bonani G, et al. 2002. The Neandertal type site revisited: Interdisciplinary investigations of skeletal remains from the Neander Valley, Germany. *Proceedings of the National Academy of Sciences* 99:13342–13347.

Schoenemann PT. 1999. Syntax as an emergent characteristic of the evolution of semantic complexity. *Mind and Machines* 9:309–346.

Schoenemann PT, Budinger TF, Sarich VM, Wang WSY. 2000. Brain size does not predict general cognitive ability within families. *Proceedings of the National Academy of Sciences* 97:4932–4937.

Schoenemann T, Allen JS. 2006. Scaling of body and brain weight within modern and fossil hominids: Implications for the Flores specimen. *American Journal of Physical Anthropology* 129 S42:159–160.

Schoetensack O. 1908. *Der unterkiefer des* Homo heidelbergensis *aus den Sanden von Mauer bei Heidelberg.* W. Engelmann, Leipzig.

Schultz AH. 1969. *The Life of Primates.* Universe Books, New York.

Schulz R, Salthouse T. 1999. *Adult Development and Aging: Myths and Emerging Realities.* Prentice Hall, Upper Saddle River, NJ.

Schuman LM. 1953. Epidemiology of frostbite: Korea. In *Cold Injury: Korea 1951–52*, pp. 205–568. Army Medical Research Laboratory Report 113, Ft. Knox.

Scriver CR, Gregory DM, Sovetts D, et al. 1985. Normal plasma free amino acid values in adults: The influence of some common physiological variables. *Metabolism* 34:868–873.

Segerstråle U. 2000. *Defenders of the Truth: The Battle for Science in the Sociobiology Debate.* Oxford University Press, New York.

Seiffert ER, Simons EL, Attia Y. 2003. Fossil evidence for an ancient divergence of lorises and galagos. *Nature* 422:421–424.

Seiffert ER, Simons EL, Clyde WC, et al. 2005. Basal anthropoids from Egypt and the antiquity of Africa's higher primate radiation. *Science* 310:300–303.

Semendeferi K, Damasio H. 2000. The brain and its main anatomical subdivisions in living hominoids using magnetic resonance imaging. *Journal of Human Evolution* 38:317–332.

Semendeferi K, Damasio H, Franks R, Van Hoesen GW. 1997. The evolution of the frontal lobes: A volumetric analysis based on three-dimensional reconstructions of magnetic resonance scans of human and ape brains. *Journal of Human Evolution* 32:375–388.

Semendeferi K, Lu A, Schenker N, Damasio H. 2002. Humans and large apes share a large frontal cortex. *Nature Neuroscience* 5:272–276.

Serre D, Langaney A, Chech M, et al. 2004. No evidence of Neandertal mtDNA contribution to early modern humans. *PLoS Biology* 2:E57.

Seymour RM, Allan MJ, Pomiankowski A, Gustafsson K. 2004. Evolution of the human ABO polymorphism by two complementary selective pressures. *Proceedings of the Royal Society of London* B. 22:1065–1072 Vol. 22:1065–1072.

Shapiro B. 2008. Engineered polymerases amplify the potential of ancient DNA. *Trends in Biotechnology* 26:285–287.

Shapiro HL. 1939. *Migration and Environment.* Oxford University Press, Oxford.

Shell ER. 2002. *The Hungry Gene: The Science of Fat and the Future of Thin.* Atlantic Monthly Press, New York.

Shen G, Gao Z, Gao B, Granger DE. 2008. ^{26}Al/^{10}Be Age of Peking Man. *Nature Precedings* hdl: 10101/npre.2008.2275.1.

Shen G, Wang J. 2000. Chronological studies on Chinese middle–late Pleistocene hominid sites, actualities and prospects. *Acta Anthropologica Sinica* 19(suppl.):279–284.

Shen G, Wang W, Wang Q, et al. 2002. U-series dating of Liujiang hominid site in Guangxi, southern China. *Journal of Human Evolution* 43:817–829.

Shepher J. 1983. *Incest: A Biosocial View.* Academic Press, New York.

Sherman PW. 1977. Nepotism and the evolution of alarm calls. *Science* 197:1246–1253.

Shermer M. 2007. *Why Darwin Matters*. Holt, New York.

Sherwood RJ, Meindl RS, Robinson HB, May RL. 2000. Fetal age: Methods of estimation and effects of pathology. *American Journal of Physical Anthropology 113*:305–315.

Shipman P. 1981. *Life History of a Fossil*. Harvard University Press, Cambridge, MA.

Shipman P. 1986. Scavenging or hunting in early hominids. *American Anthropologist 88*:27–43.

Shipman P. 2001. *The Man Who Found the Missing Link*. Harvard University Press, Cambridge, MA.

Shipman P, Rose J. 1983. Evidence of butchery and hominid activities at Torralba and Ambrona. *Journal of Archaeological Science 10*:475–482.

Shipman P, Walker A. 1989. The costs of becoming a predator. *Journal of Human Evolution 18*:373–392.

Shipman P, Walker AC, Van Couvering JA, et al. 1981. The Fort Ternan hominoid site, Kenya: Geology, age, taphonomy and paleoecology. *Journal of Human Evolution 10*:49–72.

Shor E, Simchai D. 2009. Incest avoidance, the incest taboo, and social cohesion: Revisiting Westermarck and the case of the Israeli kibbutzim. *American Journal of Sociology 114*:1803–1842.

Shriver MD, Kittles RA. 2004. Genetic ancestry and the search for personalized genetic histories. *Nature Reviews Genetics 5*:611–618.

Sibley CG, Ahlquist JE. 1984. The phylogeny of the hominoid primates, as indicated by DNA–DNA hybridization. *Journal of Molecular Evolution 20*:2–15.

Sikes N. 1994. Early hominid habitat preferences in East Africa: Paleosol carbon isotopic evidence. *Journal of Human Evolution 27*:25–45.

Sillen A. 1988. Elemental and isotopic analyses of mammalian fauna from southern Africa and their implications for paleodietary research. *American Journal of Physical Anthropology 76*:49–60.

Simons EL. 1987. New faces of *Aegyptopithecus* from the Oligocene of Egypt. *Journal of Human Evolution 16*:273–290.

Simons EL. 1995. Egyptian Oligocene primates: A review. *Yearbook of Physical Anthropology 38*:199–238.

Simoons FJ. 1970. Primary adult lactose intolerance and the milking habit: A problem in biological and cultural interrelations. 2. A cultural historical hypothesis. *American Journal of Digestive Diseases 15*:695–710.

Simpson GG. 1961. *Principles of Animal Taxonomy*. Columbia University Press, New York.

Simpson SW, Quaide J, Levin NE, et al. 2008. A female *Homo erectus* pelvis from Gona, Ethiopia. *Science 322*:1089–1092.

Small MF. 1989. Female choice in nonhuman primates. *Yearbook of Physical Anthropology 32*:103–127.

Smith CI, Chamberlain AT, Riley MS, et al. 2003. The thermal history of human fossils and the likelihood of successful DNA amplification. *Journal of Human Evolution 45*:203–217.

Smith EO. 1999. Evolution, substance abuse, and addiction. In *Evolutionary Medicine* (WR Trevathan, EO Smith, JJ McKenna, eds.), pp. 375–406. Oxford University Press, New York.

Smith FH. 1984. Fossil hominids from the upper Pleistocene of central Europe and the origin of modern Europeans. In *The Origins of Modern Humans* (FH Smith, F Spencer, eds.), pp. 137–210. Alan R. Liss, New York.

Smith GE. 1913. The evolution of man. *Annual Report of the Board of Regents of the Smithsonian Institution 1912*:553–572.

Smith MT. 1998. Genetic adaptation. In *Human Adaptation* (GA Harrison, H Morphy, eds.), pp. 1–54. Berg, Oxford.

Smith RJ, Jungers WL. 1997. Body mass in comparative primatology. *Journal of Human Evolution*. 32, 523–559.

Smith SS. 1965 (1810). *An Essay on the Causes of the Variety of Complexion and Figure in the Human Species*. Belknap Press-Harvard University Press, Cambridge, MA.

Smuts BB. 1985. *Sex and Friendship in Baboons*. Aldine, New York.

Snow CC. 1982. Forensic anthropology. *Annual Review of Anthropology 11*:97–131.

Solecki R. 1971. *Shanidar: The First Flower People*. Knopf, New York.

Solter D. 2000. Mammalian cloning: Advances and limitations. *Nature Reviews: Genetics 1*:199–207.

Sommer V. 1994. Infanticide among the langurs of Jodhpur: Testing the sexual selection hypothesis with a long-term record. In *Infanticide and Parental Care* (S Parmigiani, F vom Saal, eds.), pp. 155–198. Harwood Academic Publishers, London.

Sorensen M, Leonard WR. 2001. Neandertal energetics and foraging efficiency. *Journal of Human Evolution 40*:483–495.

Sowell ER, Thompson PM, Holmes CJ, et al. 1999. *In vivo* evidence for post-adolescent brain maturation in frontal and striatal regions. *Nature Neuroscience 2*:859–861.

Sparks CS, Jantz RL. 2002. A reassessment of human cranial plasticity: Boas revisited. *Proceedings of the National Academy of Sciences 99*:14636–14639.

Speliotes EK, Willer CJ, Berndt SI, and (250+) others. 2010. Association analyses of 249,796 individuals reveal 18 new loci associated with body mass index. *Nature Genetics 42*:937–950.

Spencer F. 1990. *Piltdown: A Scientific Forgery*. Oxford University Press.

Spencer F, ed. 1997. *History of Physical Anthropology*. Garland, New York.

Speth JD, Tchernov E. 2001. Neandertal hunting and meat-processing in the Near East. In *Meat-Eating and Human Evolution* (CB Stanford, HT Bunn, eds.), pp. 52–72. Oxford University Press, New York.

Spoor F, Hublin JJ, Braun M, Zonneveld F. 2003. The bony labyrinth of Neanderthals. *Journal of Human Evolution 44*:141–165.

Spoor F, Leakey MG, Gathogo PN, et al. 2007. Implications of new early *Homo* fossils from Ileret, east of Lake Turkana, Kenya. *Nature 448*:688–691.

Spoor F, Leakey MG, Leakey LN. 2010. Hominin diversity in the Middle Pliocene of eastern Africa: The maxilla of KNM-WT 40000 *Philosophical Transactions of the Royal Society B*. 365:3377–3388. (doi:10.1098/rstb.2010.0042).

Spurdle AB, Jenkins T. 1996. The origins of the Lemba "Black Jews" of southern Africa: Evidence from p12F2 and other Y-chromosome markers. *American Journal of Human Genetics 59*:1126–1133.

Stanford CB. 1998a. *Chimpanzee and Red Colobus: The Ecology of Predator and Prey*. Harvard University Press, Cambridge, MA.

Stanford CB. 1998b. The social behavior of chimpanzees and bonobos: Empirical evidence and shifting assumptions. *Current Anthropology 39*:399–420.

Stanford CB. 1999. *The Hunting Apes*. Princeton University Press, Princeton, NJ.

Stanford CB. 2001. The subspecies concept in primatology: The case of mountain gorillas. *Primates 42*:309–318.

Stanford CB. 2002. Arboreal bipedalism in Bwindi chimpanzees. *American Journal of Physical Anthropology 119*:87–91.

Stanford CB. 2003. *Upright*. Houghton Mifflin, Boston.

Stanford CB. 2007. *Apes of the Impenetrable Forest*. Prentice Hall, Upper Saddle River, NJ.

Stanford CB, Nkurunungi JB. 2003. Sympatric ecology of chimpanzees and gorillas in Bwindi Impenetrable National Park, Uganda. Diet. *International Journal of Primatology 24*:901–918.

Stanton W. 1960. *The Leopard's Spots: Scientific Attitudes toward Race in America 1815–59*. University of Chicago Press, Chicago.

Steadman DW. 2003. *Hard Evidence: Case Studies in Forensic Anthropology*. Prentice Hall, Upper Saddle River, NJ.

Stedman HH, Kozyak BW, Nelson A, et al. 2004. Myosin gene mutation correlates with anatomical changes in the human lineage. *Nature 428*:415–418.

Steegman AT. 2003. Climate, racial category, and body proportions in the U.S. *American Journal of Physical Anthropology 36*(suppl.):199–200.

Steegman AT. 2007. Human cold adaptation: An unfinished agenda. *American Journal of Human Biology 19*:218–227.

Steele G, McKern TW. 1969. A method for assessment of maximum long bone length and living stature from fragmentary long bones. *American Journal of Physical Anthropology 31*:215–227.

Steno N. 1669. *De Solido intra Solidum Naturaliter Contento*. Dissertatio Prodromus, Florence.

Stephan H, Frahm H, Baron G. 1981. New and revised data on volumes of brain structures in insectivores and primates. *Folia Primatologica 35*:1–29.

Stern JT, Susman RL. 1983. The locomotor anatomy of *Australopithecus afarensis*. *American Journal of Physical Anthropology 60*:279–317.

Sternberg R. 1990. *Metaphors of Mind: Conceptions of the Nature of Intelligence.* Cambridge University Press, Cambridge.

Steudel KL. 1996. Limb morphology, bipedal gait, and the energetics of hominid locomotion. *American Journal of Physical Anthropology* 99:345–355.

Stewart C, Disotell TR. 1998. Primate evolution: in and out of Africa. *Current Biology* 8:R582–R588.

Stewart R, Pryzborski S. 2002. Non-neural adult stem cells: Tools for brain repair? *BioEssays* 24:708–713.

Stine GJ. 2003. *AIDS Update 2003.* Prentice Hall, Upper Saddle River, NJ.

Stinson PG. 1975. Radiology in forensic odontology. *Dental Radiography and Photography* 48:51–55.

Stocking GW. 1987. *Victorian Anthropology.* The Free Press, New York.

Stokes E, Raineya H, Iyengueta, F. 2008. *Survey of Raphia swamp forest, Republic of Congo, indicates high densities of Critically Endangered western lowland gorillas Gorilla,* Fauna & Flora International 2009.

Strier K. 2006. *Primate Behavioral Ecology,* 3rd ed. Allyn & Bacon, Boston.

Strier, K.B. (1994). Myth of the typical primate. Yearbook of Physical Anthropology 37: 233-271.

Stringer CB. 1994. Out of Africa: A personal history. In *Origins of Anatomically Modern Humans* (MH Nitecki, DV Nitecki, eds.), pp. 149–172. Plenum, New York.

Stringer CB, Andrews P. 1988. Genetic and fossil evidence for the origin of modern humans. *Science* 239:1263–1268.

Stringer CB, Gamble C. 1993. *In Search of the Neanderthals.* Thames and Hudson, New York.

Stringer CB, Grün R, Schwarcz HP, Goldberg P. 1989. ESR dates for the hominid burial site of Es Skhul in Israel. *Nature* 338:756–758.

Stringer CB, Hublin JJ, Vandermeersch B. 1984. The origin of anatomically modern humans in Western Europe. In *The Origins of Modern Humans* (FH Smith, F Spencer, eds.), pp. 51–136. Alan R. Liss, New York.

Stringer CB, Trinkaus E, Roberts MB, et al. 1998. The middle Pleistocene human tibia from Boxgrove. *Journal of Human Evolution* 34:509–547.

Stumpf MPH, Goldstein DB. 2001. Genealogical and evolutionary inference with the human Y chromosome. *Science* 291:1738–1742.

Sullivan RJ, Hagen EH. 2002. Psychotropic substance-seeking: Evolutionary pathology or adaptation? *Addiction* 97:389–400.

Surbeck M, Hohmann G. 2008. Primate hunting by bonobos at Lui Kotale, Salonga National Park. *Current Biology* 18:906–907.

Susman R, ed. 1984. *The Pygmy Chimpanzee.* Plenum, New York.

Sussman RL. 1991. Primate origins and the evolution of angiosperms. *American Journal of Primatology* 23:209–223.

Sussman RL. 1992. Male life history and intergroup mobility among ringtailed lemurs (*Lemur catta*). *International Journal of Primatology* 13:395–413.

Susman RL, Stern JT, Jungers WL. 1984. Arboreality and bipedality in the Hadar hominids. *Folia Primatologica* 43:113–156.

Suwa G, Asfaw B, Beyene Y, et al. 1997. The first skull of *Australopithecus boisei. Nature* 389:489–92.

Swisher CC, Curtis GH, Jacob T, et al. 1994. Age of the earliest known hominids in Java, Indonesia. *Science* 263:1118–1121.

Swisher CC III, Rink WJ, Antón SC, et al. 1996. Latest *Homo erectus,* in Java: Potential contemporaneity with *Homo sapiens* in Southeast Asia. *Science* 274:1870–1874.

Sy MS, Gambetti P, Wong BS. 2002. Human prion diseases. *Medical Clinics of North America* 86:551–571.

Symons D. 1979. *The Evolution of Human Sexuality.* Oxford University Press, New York.

Szalay FS. 1975. Where to draw the nonprimate–primate taxonomic boundary. *Folia Primatologia* 23:158–163.

Szalay FS. 1981. Phylogeny and the problems of adaptive significance: The case of the earliest primates. *Folia Primatologica* 34:1–45.

Szalay FS, Delson E. 1979. *Evolutionary History of the Primates.* Academic Press, New York.

Takahata N, Lee SH, Satta Y. 2001. Testing multiregionality of modern human origins. *Molecular Biology and Evolution* 18:172–183.

Tanner JM. 1990. *Fetus into Man* (2nd edition). Harvard University Press, Cambridge, MA.

Tanner NM, Zihlman AL. 1976. Women in evolution part 1: Innovation and selection in human origins. *Signs: Journal of Women, Culture, and Society* 1:585–608.

Tappen M. 2001. Deconstructing the Serengeti. In *Meat-Eating and Human Evolution* (CB Stanford, HT Bunn, ed.), pp. 13–32. Oxford University Press, New York.

Tattersall I. 1986. Species recognition in human paleontology. *Journal of Human Evolution* 15:165–175.

Taylor A. 2006. Feeding behavior, diet, and the functional consequences of jaw form in orangutans, with implications for the evolution of *Pongo. Journal of Human Evolution* 50:377–393.

Taylor RE. 2000. Fifty years of radiocarbon dating. *American Scientist* 88:60–67.

Templeton AR. 2002. Out of Africa again and again. *Nature* 416:45–51.

Terrace H. 1979. *Nim.* Knopf, New York.

Thackray HM, Tifft C. 2001. Fetal alcohol syndrome. *Pediatrics in Review* 22:47–55.

Thieme H. 1997. Lower palaeolithic hunting spears from Germany. *Nature* 385:807–810.

Thompson ME, Wrangham RW. 2008. Male mating interest varies with female fecundity in *Pan troglodytes schweinfurthii* of Kanyawara, Kibale National Park. *International Journal of Primatology* 29:885–905.

Thornhill NW. 1991. An evolutionary analysis of rules regulating human inbreeding and marriage. *Behavioral and Brain Sciences* 14:247–293.

Tibben A. 2007. Predictive testing for Huntington's disease. *Brain Research Bulletin* 72:165–171.

Tobias PV. 1967. The cranium and maxillary dentition of *Australopithecus* (Zinjanthropus) *boisei. Olduvai Gorge, Volume 2.* Cambridge University Press, New York.

Tobias PV. 1971. *The Brain in Hominid Evolution.* Columbia University Press, New York.

Tobias PV. 1987. The brain of *Homo habilis:* A new level of organization in cerebral evolution. *Journal of Human Evolution* 16:741–761.

Tocheri M, Orr CM, Larson SG, et al. 2007. The Primitive Wrist of *Homo floresiensis* and Its Implications for Hominin Evolution. *Science* 317:1743–1745.

Todd TW. 1920. Age changes in the pubic bone, 1. The male White pubis. *American Journal of Physical Anthropology* 3:285–334.

Tomasello M, Savage-Rumbaugh S, Kruger A. 1993. Imitative learning of actions on objects by children, chimpanzees and enculturated chimpanzees. *Child Development* 64:1688–1705.

Tooby J, Cosmides L. 2000. Toward mapping the evolved functional organization of mind and brain. In *The New Cognitive Neurosciences,* 2nd ed. (MS Gazzaniga, editor-in-chief), pp. 1167–1178. MIT Press, Cambridge, MA.

Toth N. 1985. Archaeological evidence for preferential right-handedness in the Lower and Middle Pleistocene, and its possible implications. *Journal of Human Evolution* 14:607–614.

Toth N, Schick K, Savage-Rumbaugh S. 1993. *Pan* the tool-maker: Investigations into the stone tool-making and tool using capabilities of a bonobo (*Pan paniscus*). *Journal of Archaeological Science* 20:81–91.

Trainor LJ, Austin CM, Desjardins RN. 2000. Is infant-directed speech prosody a result of the vocal expression of emotion? *Psychological Science* 11:188–195.

Trehub SE, Unyk AM, Trainor LJ. 1993. Maternal singing in cross-cultural perspective. *Infant Behavior and Development* 16:285–295.

Trevathan WR. 1987. *Human Birth: An Evolutionary Perspective.* Aldine de Gruyter, Hawthorne, NY.

Trevathan WR. 1999. Evolutionary obstetrics. In *Evolutionary Medicine* (WR Trevathan, EO Smith, JJ McKenna, eds.), pp. 183–207. Oxford University Press, Oxford.

Trevathan WR, Smith EO, McKenna JJ, eds. 1999. *Evolutionary Medicine.* Oxford University Press, Oxford.

Trinkaus E. 1983. *The Shanidar Neandertals.* Academic Press, New York.

Trinkaus E. 1995. Neanderthal mortality patterns. *Journal of Archaeological Science* 22:121–142.

Trinkaus E. 2003. Neandertal faces were not long; modern human faces are short. *Proceedings of the National Academy of Sciences* 100:8142–8145.

Trinkaus E, Moldovan O, Milota S, et al. 2003. An early modern human from the Petera cu Oase, Romania. *Proceedings of the National Academy of Sciences* 100:11231–11236.

Trinkaus E, Shipman P. 1992. *The Neandertals.* Vintage Press, New York.

Trotter M. 1970. Estimation of stature from intact long limb bones. In Personal Identification in Mass Disasters. (TD Stewart. ed.), pp. 71–83. National Museum Natural History, Washington:, DC.

Turner CG. 1989. Teeth and prehistory in Asia. *Scientific American* 260:88–91, 94–96.

Turner CG. 1990. Major features of Sundadonty and Sinodonty, including suggestions about East Asian microevolution, population history, and late Pleistocene relationships with Australian aboriginals. *American Journal of Physical Anthropology* 82:295–317.

Tutin CEG. 1996. Ranging and social structure of lowland gorillas in the Lopé Reserve, Gabon. In *Great Ape Societies* (WC McGrew, LF Marchant, T Nishida, eds.), pp. 58–70. Cambridge University Press, Cambridge.

Tuttle RH. 1981. Evolution of hominid bipedalism and prehensile capabilities. *Philosophical Transactions of the Royal Society of London* B 292:89–94.

Tyson E. 1972 (1699). Orang-outang sive Homo sylvestris: or the anatomy of a pygmie. In *Climbing Man's Family Tree* (TD Mc-Cown, KAR Kennedy, eds.), pp. 41–48. Prentice Hall, Englewood Cliffs, NJ.

Ulijaszek SJ, Lofink H. 2006. Obesity in biocultural perspective. *Annual Review in Anthropology* 35:337–360.

Van den Berghe PL. 1983. Human inbreeding avoidance: Culture in nature. *Behavioral and Brain Sciences* 6:91–123.

Vandermeersch B. 1985. The origin of the Neandertals. In *Ancestors: The Hard Evidence* (E Delson, ed.), pp. 306–309. Alan R. Liss, New York.

van Schaik CP. 2004. *Among Orangutans: Red Apes and the Rise of Human Culture.* Belnap Press, New York.

van Schaik CP, Hörstermann M. 1994. Predation risk and the number of adult males in a primate group: A comparative test. *Behavioral Ecology and Sociobiology* 35:261–272.

van Schaik CP, Kappeler P. 2004. *Sexual Selection in Primates.* Cambridge University Press, Cambridge.

van Schaik CP, Monk KR, Yarrow Robertson JM. 2001. Dramatic decline in orangutan numbers in the Leuser ecosystem, northern Sumatra. *Oryx* 35:14–25.

van Spronsen, FJ. 2010. Phenylketonuria: A 21st century perspective. *Nature Reviews Endocrinology* 6:509–514.

Van Valen L. 1976. Ecological species, multispecies, and oaks. *Taxon* 25:233–239.

Van Valen L, Mellin GW. 1967. Selection in natural populations.VII. New York babies (fetal life study). *Annals of Human Genetics* 31:109–127.

Vekua A, Lordkipanidze D, Rightmire GP, et al. 2002. A new skull of early *Homo* from Dmanisi, Georgia. *Science* 297:85–89.

Venter JC, Adams MD, Myers EW, et al. 2001. The sequence of the human genome. *Science* 291:1304–1351.

Vervaecke H, van Elsacker L, Möhle U, et al. 1999. Inter-menstrual intervals in captive bonobos (*Pan paniscus*). *Primates* 40:283–289.

Videan E, McGrew WC. 2001. Are bonobos (*Pan paniscus*) really more bipedal than chimpanzees (*Pan troglodytes*)? *American Journal of Primatology* 54:233–239.

Vollrath D, Nathans J, Davis RW. 1988. Tandem array of human visual pigment genes at Xq28. *Science* 240:1669–1672.

Volta U, Bellentani S, Bianchi G, et al. 2001. High prevalence of celiac disease in Italian general population. *Digestive Diseases and Sciences* 46:1500–1505.

Von Koenigswald GHR. 1952. *Gigantopithecus blacki* von Koenigswald, a giant fossil hominoid from the Pleistocene of southern China. *Anthropological Papers of the American Museum of Natural History* 43:291–326.

Walker A, Leakey R, eds. 1993a. *The Nariokotome* Homo erectus *Skeleton.* Harvard University Press, Cambridge, MA.

Walker AC, Leakey RE, Harris JM, Brown FH. 1986. 2.5-myr *Australopithecus boisei* from west of Lake Turkana, Kenya. *Nature* 322:517–522.

Walker A, Shipman P. 1996. *The Wisdom of the Bones.* Vintage Books, New York.

Walker AC, Teaford M. 1989. The hunt for *Proconsul. Scientific American* 260:76–82.

Walker A, Zimmerman MR, Leakey REF. 1982. A possible case of hypervitaminosis A in *Homo erectus. Nature* 296:248–250.

Walker PL, Cook DC, Lambert PM. 1997. Skeletal evidence for child abuse: a physical anthropological perspective. *Journal of Forensic Sciences* 42:196–207.

Walker R, Hill K, Kaplan H, McMillan G. 2002. Age-dependency in hunting ability among the Ache of eastern Paraguay. *Journal of Human Evolution* 42:639–657.

Walsh PD, Abernethy KA, Bermejo M, et al. 2003. Catastrophic ape decline in western equatorial Africa. *Nature* 422:611–614.

Walter RC, Aronson JL. 1982. Revisions of K/Ar ages for the Hadar hominid site, Ethiopia. *Nature* 296:122–127.

Ward CV. 1997. Functional anatomy and phylogenetic implications of the hominoid trunk and hindlimb. In *Function, Phylogeny and Fossils: Miocene Hominoid Evolution and Adaptation* (DR Begun, CV Ward, MD Rose, eds.), pp. 101–130. Plenum, New York.

Washburn SL. 1968. Speculation on the problem of man's coming to the ground. In *Changing Perspectives on Man* (B Rothblatt, ed.), pp. 191–206. University of Chicago Press, Chicago.

Watanabe H, Fujiyama A, Hattori M, et al. 2004. DNA sequence and comparative analysis of chimpanzee chromosome 22. *Nature* 429:382–388.

Watson JD, Crick FHC. 1953a. Genetical implications of the structure of deoxyribonucleic acid. *Nature* 171:964–967.

Watson JD, Crick FHC. 1953b. A structure for deoxyribonucleic acid. *Nature* 171:737–738.

Watts DP. 1989. Infanticide in mountain gorillas: New cases and a reconsideration of the evidence. *Ethology* 81:1–18.

Waugh J. 2007. DNA barcoding in animal species: Progress, potential, and pitfalls. *BioEssays* 29:188–197.

Wayne RK, Leonard JA, Cooper A. 1999. Full of sound and fury: The recent history of ancient DNA. *Annual Review in Ecology and Systematics* 30:457–477.

Weidenreich F. 1943. The skull of *Sinanthropus pekinensis:* A comparative study of a primitive hominid skull. *Palaeontologica Sinica* D10:1–485.

Weiner A. 1988. *The Trobrianders of Papua New Guinea.* Holt, Rinehart, and Winston, New York.

Weiner J. 1994. *The Beak of the Finch.* Vintage Books, New York.

Weiss KM. 2002. Goings on in Mendel's garden. *Evolutionary Anthropology* 11:40–44.

Wertz RC, Wertz DC. 1989. *Lying-In: A History of Childbirth in America.* Yale University Press, New Haven, CT.

Westermarck EA. 1891. *The History of Human Marriage.* Macmillan, New York.

Wheeler PE. 1991. The thermoregulatory advantages of hominid bipedalism in open equatorial environments: The contribution of increased convective heat loss and cutaneous evaporative cooling. *Journal of Human Evolution* 21:107–115.

White M. 2001. *Leonardo: The First Scientist.* Griffin, New York.

White R. 2001. Personal ornaments from Grotte du Renne at Arcy-sur-Cure. *Athena Review* 2:41–46.

White TD. 1986. Cut marks on the Bodo cranium: A case of prehistoric defleshing. *American Journal of Physical Anthropology* 69:503–509.

White TD, Ambrose SH, Suwa G, WoldeGabriel G. 2010. Response to Comment on the Paleoenvironment of *Ardipithecus ramidus. Science* 328:1105.

White TD, Asfaw B, DeGusta D, et al. 2003. Pleistocene *Homo sapiens* from Middle Awash, Ethiopia. *Nature* 423:742–747.

White TD, Harris JM. 1977. Suid evolution and correlation of African hominid localities. *Science* 198:13–21.

White TD, Moore RV, Suwa G. 1984. Hadar biostratigraphy. *Journal of Vertebrate Paleontology* 4:575–581.

White TD, Suwa G, Asfaw B. 1994. *Australopithecus ramidus*, a new species of early hominid from Aramis, Ethiopia. *Nature* 371:306–312.

Whiten A, Goodall J, McGrew WC, et al. 1999. Cultures in chimpanzees. *Nature* 399:682–685.

Wiens JJ. 2001. Widespread loss of sexually selected traits: How the peacock lost its spots. *Trends in Ecology and Evolution* 16:517–523.

Wiley A. 2011. *Re-Imagining Milk.* Routledge, New York.

Wiley A. 1992. Adaptation and the biocultural paradigm in medical anthropology: A critical review. *Medical Anthropology Quarterly* 6:216–236.

Wiley AS. 2004. *An Ecology of High-Altitude Infancy: A Biocultural Perspective.* Cambridge University Press, Cambridge.

Wiley AS, Allen JS. 2009. *Medical Anthropology: A Biocultural Perspective.* Oxford University Press, New York.

Willey P, Leach P. 2003. The skull on the lawn: trophies, taphonomy and forensic anthropology. In *Hard Evidence: Case Studies in Forensic Anthropology* (DW Steadman, ed.), pp. 176–188. Prentice Hall, Upper Saddle River, NJ.

Williams DR. 2003. The biomedical challenges of space flight. *Annual Review in Medicine* 54:245–256.

Williams GC. 1957. Pleiotropy, natural selection, and the evolution of senescence. *Evolution* 11:398–411.

Williams GC. 1966. *Adaptation and Natural Selection.* Princeton University Press, Princeton, NJ.

Williams RJ. 1956. *Biochemical Individuality.* University of Texas Press, Austin.

Wilson EO. 1975. *Sociobiology: The New Synthesis.* Harvard University Press, Cambridge, MA.

Wise RJ, Greene J, Buchel C, Scott SK. 1999. Brain regions involved in articulation. *Lancet* 353:1057–1061.

WoldeGabriel G, White TD, Suwa G, et al. 1994. Ecological and temporal placement of early Pliocene hominids at Aramis, Ethiopia. *Nature* 371:330–333.

Wolf AP. 1966. Childhood association, sexual attraction, and the incest taboo: A Chinese case. *American Anthropologist* 68:883–898.

Wolf AP. 1970. Childhood association and sexual attraction: A further test of the Westermarck hypothesis. *American Anthropologist* 72:503–515.

Wolff G, Wienker T, Sander H. 1993. On the genetics of mandibular prognathism: Analysis of large European noble families. *Journal of Medical Genetics* 30:12–16.

Wolpoff MH. 1999. *Paleoanthropology,* 2nd ed. McGraw-Hill, New York.

Wolpoff MH, Caspari R. 1997. *Race and Human Evolution.* Westview Press, Boulder, CO.

Wolpoff MH, Hawks J, Caspari R. 2000. Multiregional, not multiple origins. *American Journal of Physical Anthropology* 112:129–136.

Wolpoff MH, Senut B, Pickford M, Hawks J. 2002. Paleoanthropology: *Sahelanthropus* or *"Sahelpithecus"? Nature* 419:581–582.

Wolpoff MH, Thorne AG, Smith FH, et al. 1994. Multiregional evolution: A world-wide source for modern human populations. In *Origins of Anatomically Modern Humans* (MH Nitecki, DV Nitecki, eds.), pp. 175–199. Plenum, New York.

Wolpoff MH, Zhi WX, Thorne AG. 1984. Modern *Homo sapiens* origins: A general theory of hominid evolution involving the fossil evidence from east Asia. In *The Origins of Modern Humans* (FH Smith, F Spencer, eds.), pp. 411–484. Alan R. Liss, New York.

Wood B, Collard M. 1999. The changing face of genus *Homo. Evolutionary Anthropology* 8:195–207.

Wood B, Harrison T. 2011. The evolutionary context of the first hominins. *Nature* 470:347–352.

Worthman CM. 1999. Evolutionary perspectives on the onset of puberty. In *Evolutionary Medicine* (WR Trevathan, EO Smith, JJ McKenna, eds.), pp. 135–163. Oxford University Press, Oxford.

Wrangham RW, Jones JH, Laden G, et al. 1999. Cooking and human origins. *Current Anthropology* 40:567–594.

Wu R, Dong X. 1985. *Homo erectus* in China. In *Palaeoanthropology and Palaeolithic Archaeology in the People's Republic of China* (R Wu, JW Olsen, eds.), pp. 79–89. Academic Press, New York.

Wu X, Poirer FE. 1995. *Human Evolution in China: A Metric Description of the Fossils and a Review of the Sites.* Oxford University Press, New York.

Wynn TG. 1999. The evolution of tools and symbolic behaviour. In *Handbook of Human Symbolic Evolution* (A Lock, CR Peters, eds.), pp. 263–287. Blackwell, Oxford.

Wynne-Edwards VC. 1962. *Animal Dispersion in Relation to Social Behaviour.* Oliver & Boyd, Edinburgh.

Yarrow Robertson JM, van Schaik CP. 2001. Causal factors underlying the dramatic decline of the Sumatran orangutan. *Oryx* 35:26–38.

Yellen JE. 1991. Small mammals: Kung San utilization and the production of faunal assemblages. *Journal of Anthropological Research* 10:1–26.

Yokoyama Y, Falgueres C, Semah F, Jacob T, Grun R. 2008. Gamma-ray spectrometric dating of late *Homo erectus* skulls from Ngandong and Sambungmacan, Central Java, Indonesia. *Journal of Human Evolution* 55:274–277.

Yule GU. 1902. Mendel's laws and their probable relations to intra-racial heredity. *New Phytologist* 1:193–207, 222–238.

Zahavi A. 1975. Mate selection: A selection for a handicap. *Journal of Theoretical Biology* 53:205–214.

Zatorre RJ. 2003. Absolute pitch: A model for understanding the influence of genes and development on neural and cognitive function. *Nature Neuroscience* 6:692–695.

Zerjal T, Xue Y, Bertorelle G, et al. 2003. The genetic legacy of the Mongols. *American Journal of Human Genetics* 72:717–721.

Zhao Z, Jin L, Fu YX, et al. 2000. Worldwide DNA sequence variation in a 10-kilobase noncoding region on human chromosome 22. *Proceedings of the National Academy of Sciences* 97:11354–11358.

Zhu RX, Potts R, Xie F, et al. 2004. New evidence on the earliest human presence at high northern latitudes in northeast Asia. *Nature* 431:559–562.

Zubenko GS, Hughes HB, Maher BS, et al. 2002. Genetic linkage of region containing the CREB1 gene to depressive disorders in women from families with recurrent, early-onset, major depression. *American Journal of Medical Genetics* 114:980–987.

Photography; **256**, University College London / Cell & Developmental Biology; **256**, Kenneth Garrett Photography; **257**, University College London / Cell & Developmental Biology; **257**, University of Virginia School of Medicine; **257**, Dr. Timothy Ryan; **257**, Kenneth Garrett Photography; **259**, Fig. 10.21, David L. Brill Photography; **259**, Fig. 10.20b, National Museums of Kenya; **261**, Fig. 10.23, Kenneth Garrett Photography; **261**, Fig. 10.24, Susan C. Anton; **262**, Fig. 10.26, Lee Berger / University of Witswatersrand; **264**, Fig. 10.29, National Museums of Kenya; **264**, Figs. 10.31–10.31, Jeffrey K. McKee; **269**, Lee Berger / University of Witswatersrand; **269**, Jeffrey K. McKee.

Chapter 11: **270**, Kenneth Garrett Photography; **273**, Fig. 11.2, Kenneth Garrett Photography; **274**, Fig. 11.3, Susan C. Anton; **280**, Fig. 11.8, National Museums of Kenya; **282**, Fig. 11.10a, Javier Trueba / MADRID SCIENTIFIC FILMS; **282**, Fig. 11.10b, Susan C. Anton; **282**, Fig. 11.10c, David L. Brill Photography; **282**, Fig. 11.10d, Pat Shipman / Alan Walker / National Museums of Kenya; **282**, Fig. 11.10e, Kenneth Garrett Photography; **282**, Fig. 11.10f, Susan C. Anton; **283**, Figs. 11.10g–11.10h, Kenneth Garrett Photography; **283**, Figs. 11.10i–11.10j, Susan C. Anton; **284**, Fig. 11.11, Kenneth Garrett Photography; **284**, Fig. 11.12, National Museums of Kenya; **285**, Fig. 11.14, David L. Brill Photography; **285**, Fig. 11.15b, David Lordkipanidze; **285**, Fig. 11.13, Smithsonian National Museum of Natural History; **285**, Fig. 11.15a, Susan C. Anton; **286**, Kenneth Garrett Photography; **287**, Martin Harvey / Gallo Images / Corbis; **289**, Fig. 11.17a, Kenneth Garrett Photography; **289**, Fig. 11.17b, Susan C. Anton; **289**, Fig. 11.18a, Susan C. Anton; **289**, Fig. 11.18b, Kenneth Garrett Photography; **290**, Fig. 11.19, Carl Swisher; **291**, Fig. 11.20b, Javier Trueba / MADRID SCIENTIFIC FILMS; **291**, Fig. 11.20a, José María Bermúdez de Castro; **292**, Fig. A, Dr. Peter Brown; **293**, Fig. 11.21, Kenneth Garrett Photography; **295**, Fig. 11.23, Dr. Peter Ungar; **298**, David Lordkipanidze; **298**, Kenneth Garrett Photography; **298**, Susan C. Anton; **299**, Kenneth Garrett Photography.

Chapter 12: **300**, Kenneth Garrett Photography; **300**, Francisco Marquez / Bios / PhotoLibrary; **300**, Susan C. Anton; **301**, American Museum of Natural History; **304**, Fig. 12.3, Kenneth Garrett Photography; **304**, Fig. 12.4b, Kenneth Garrett Photography; **304**, Fig. 12.4a, Dr. Milford H. Wolpoff; **305**, Fig. 12.5, Javier Trueba / MADRID SCIENTIFIC FILMS; **306**, Fig. 12.6, American Museum of Natural History; **306**, Fig. 12.7, Kenneth Garrett Photography; **307**, Figs. 12.8b–12.8c, Christian Tryon; **308–309**, Figs. 12.9–12.10, Susan C. Anton; **310**, Fig. 12.11, National Geographic / National Geographic Magazine; **311**, Fig. 12.13, Kenneth Garrett Photography; **313**, Fig. 12.15b, Dr. Milford H. Wolpoff; **314**, Fig. 12.16, Antoine Balzeau; **315**, Fig. 12.17, American Museum of Natural History; **316**, Waltraud Grubitzsch / epa / Corbis Wire / Corbis; **316**, Elsevier Inc.; **316**, GERHARD HINTERLEITNER / AFP / Getty Images / Newscom; **316**, REUTERS / Issei Kato IK / KI / JV; **317**, Elsevier Ltd; **317**, Francisco Marquez / PhotoLibrary; **317**, Katy McDonnell / Digital Vision / Thinkstock; **318**, Fig. 12.18b, John Reader / Photo Researchers, Inc.; **320**, Fig. 12.19b, Susan C. Anton; **322**, Fig. 12.20, Kenneth Garrett Photography; **324**, Figs. A–B, Bence Viola, MPI Evolutionary Anthropology; **326**, Fig. 12.22a, Kenneth Garrett Photography; **326**, Fig. 12.22b, Susan C. Anton; **326**, Fig. 12.22d, Javier Trueba / MADRID SCIENTIFIC FILMS; **326**, Fig. 12.22e, Kenneth Garrett Photography; **327**, Fig. 12.22f, Dr. Milford H. Wolpoff; **327**, Fig. 12.22g, Kenneth Garrett Photography; **327**, Fig. 12.22h, Dr. Milford H. Wolpoff; **327**, Fig. 12.22i, American Museum of Natural History; **327**, Fig. 12.22j, Kenneth Garrett Photography; **330**, Dr. Milford H. Wolpoff; **330**, Kenneth Garrett Photography; **331**, National Geographic / National Geographic Magazine.

Chapter 13: **332**, Kenneth Garrett Photography; **332**, on page: From the Collections of The Center for the Study of the First Americans, Department of Anthropology, Texas A&M University. Copy and Reuse Restrictions Apply; **333**, ON PAGE CREDIT: Randall White; **336**, Fig. 13.2a, Erik Trinkaus; **336**, Fig. 13.2b, John Reader / Photo Researchers, Inc.; **336**, Fig. 13.2c, Kenneth Garrett Photography; **336**, Fig. 13.2d, David L. Brill Photography; **337**, Fig. 13.2e, Dr. Peter Brown; **338**, Fig. 13.3a, David L. Brill Photography; **338**, Fig. 13.3b, Dr. Osbjorn Pearson; **339**, Fig. 13.5, Erik Trinkaus; **339**, Fig. 13.4, Kenneth Garrett Photography; **340**, Fig. 13.7, The Natural History Museum, London; **340**, Fig. 13.6, John Reader / Photo Researchers, Inc.; **341**, Fig. 13.9, Dr. Peter Brown; **341**, Fig. 13.8, John Krigbaum; **342**, Figs. 13.10a-13.10b, Dr. Milford H. Wolpoff; **342**, Fig. 13.11, ON PAGE CREDIT: Randall White; **345**, Fig. 13.13, Tomsich / Photo Researchers, Inc.; **346**, Penny Tweedie / Corbis Art / Corbis; **346**, Kenneth Garrett Photography; **346**, ON PAGE CREDIT: Randall White; **347**, Kenneth Garrett Photography; **347**, ON PAGE CREDIT: Randall White; **354**, Fig. 13.16a, AP Photo / Elaine Thompson; **354**, Fig. 13.16b, Susan C. Anton; **355**, Fig. A, on page: From the Collections of The Center for the Study of the First Americans, Department of Anthropology, Texas A&M University. Copy and Reuse Restrictions Apply; **355**, Figs. A-B,

on page: From the Collections of The Center for the Study of the First Americans, Department of Anthropology, Texas A&M University. Copy and Reuse Restrictions Apply; **356**, Fig. 13.17, Susan C. Anton; **357**, Fig. 13.18, Susan C. Anton; **357**, Figs. 13.19a–13.19b, Susan C. Anton; **358**, Tomsich / Photo Researchers, Inc.; **359**, Susan C. Anton.

Chapter 14: **360**, Juniors Bildarchiv / Alamy; **360**, from H. Damasio, T. Grabowski, R. Frank, A.M. Galaburda & A.R. Damasio (1994) The Return of Phineas Gage: clues about the brain from a famous patient, Science, 264, 1102–1105. Dornsife Neuroscience Imaging Center and Brain and Creativity Institute, University of Southern California.; **360**, Christian Murdock / MCT / Newscom; **360**, Ben Mangor / SuperStock; **361**, 2002–2007 Nature Picture Library; **363**, Fig. 14.2, from H. Damasio, T. Grabowski, R. Frank, A.M. Galaburda & A.R. Damasio (1994) The Return of Phineas Gage: clues about the brain from a famous patient, Science, 264, 1102–1105. Dornsife Neuroscience Imaging Center and Brain and Creativity Institute, University of Southern California.; **366**, Fig. 14.6, Juniors Bildarchiv / Alamy; **368**, Fig. 14.9, Custom Medical Stock Photo / Alamy; **369**, Fig. 14.10, John Reader / Photo Researchers, Inc.; **374**, Pictorial Press Ltd / Alamy; **374**, Cha Young-Jin / epa / Corbis; **374**, Alfredo Dagli Orti / The Art Archive / Corbis; **374**, SuperStock; **374**, Ben Mangor / SuperStock; **375**, steve bly / Alamy; **375**, Toby WALES / Lebrecht Music & Arts Photo Library; **375**, 2002–2007 Nature Picture Library; **377**, Fig. 14.15, Jack Fields / Encyclopedia / Corbis; **378**, Fig. 14.17, Corbis; **380**, Fig. 14.20, Cary Wolinsky / Aurora Photos; **382**, Fig. 14.22, Christian Murdock / MCT / Newscom; **383**, Fig. 14.23, Ted Spiegel / Corbis; **384**, John Reader / Photo Researchers, Inc.; **385**, Jack Fields / Encyclopedia / Corbis; **385**, Christian Murdock / MCT / Newscom.

Chapter 15: **386**, Courtesy of Paul Sledzik; **386**, The Granger Collection, NYC; **387**, Alfred Pasieka / Photo Researchers, Inc.; **388**, Fig. 15.1, AP Photo / Barrett Stinson / The Grand Island Independent; **390**, Fig. 15.3, BSIP / Photo Researchers, Inc.; **395**, Fig. 15.10b, Rafael Roa / Corbis Entertainment / Corbis; **395**, Fig. 15.10a, Album / Newscom; **397**, Fig. 15.11, WHO / National Library of Medicine; **397**, Fig. 15.12a, Sheldan Collins / Corbis; **397**, Fig. 15.12b, Martin Harvey / Corbis; **400**, Fig. 15.15, National Library of Medicine; **403**, Fig. 15.16, National Library of Medicine; **404**, Fig. 15.17, Susan C. Anton; **404**, Fig. 15.18, Courtesy of Paul Sledzik; **405**, Fig. 15.19, Susan C. Anton; **405**, Fig. 15.20, AP Photo / David Mercado, POOL; **406**, Fig. 15.21, Susan C. Anton; **410**, The Granger Collection, NYC; **411**, Craig Stanford / Jane Goodall Research Center; **411**, John S. Allen; **411**, Susan C. Anton; **412**, Fig. 15.26a, National Museum of Health and Medicine; **415**, Fig. 15.27, Alfred Pasieka / Photo Researchers, Inc.; **417**, Fig. A, Craig Stanford / Jane Goodall Research Center; **419**, Fig. 15.28, J. Josh Snodgrass; **420**, AP Photo / Barrett Stinson / The Grand Island Independent; **420**, Susan C. Anton; **421**, J. Josh Snodgrass.

Text Credits: **2**, Browne, Janet. 2002. Charles Darwin: The Power of Place. Alfred Knopf, NY; **3**, Laidlaw SA, Kopple JD. 1987. Newer concepts of the indispensable amino acids. American Journal of Clinical Nutrition 46:593–605; **6**, Parra EJ, Marcini A, Akey J, et al. 1998. Estimating African American admixture proportions by use of population-specific alleles. American Journal of Human Genetics 63:1839–1851; Adapted from Mourant et al. 1976. The Distribution of Human Blood Groups (2nd Edition). Oxford University Press, London; Cavalli-Sforza LL, Menozzi P, Piazza A. 1994. The History and Geography of Human Genes. Princeton University Press, Princeton, NJ; **7**, Nowak RM, Paradiso JL. 1983. Walker's Mammals of the World, 4th ed. John Hopkins University Press, Baltimore; **8**, Fossey D. 1983. Gorillas in the Mist. Houghton Mifflin, Boston; **9**, Alvarez W. 1997. T. rex and the Crater of Doom. Princeton University Press, Princeton, NJ; **10**, Wolpoff MH. 1999. Paleoanthropology, 2nd ed. McGraw-Hill, New York; Wolpoff MH. 1999. Paleoanthropology, 2nd ed. McGraw-Hill, New York; **11**, Walker A, Shipman P. 1996. The Wisdom of the Bones. Vintage Books, New York; Gabunia L, Antón SC, Lordkipanidze D, et al. 2001. Dmanisi and dispersal. Evolutionary Anthropology 10:158–170; **14**, Segerstråle U. 2000. Defenders of the Truth: The Battle for Science in the Sociobiology Debate. Oxford University Press, New York; Lieberman, P. 1991 Uniquely Human: The Evolution of Speech, Thought and Selfless Behavior. Harvard University Press, Massachusetts; Hill EM, Chow K. 2002. Life-history theory and risky drinking. Addiction 97:401–413; **15**, Evolutionary Medicine and Health: New Perspectives. (W. Trevathan, N. Smith, J. McKenna eds.). Oxford University Press, Oxford; Ljung BO, Bergsten-Brucefors A, Lindgren G. 1974. The secular trend in physical growth in Sweden. Annals of Human Biology 1:245–256; Bogan B. 2001. The Growth of Humanity. Wiley, New Jersey; Tanner JM. 1990. Fetus into Man (2nd edition). Harvard University Press, Cambridge, MA; Eaton et al., 1999. Paleolithic nutrition revisited. In Evolutionary Medicine (WR Trevathan, EO Smith, & JJ McKenna, eds.), pp. 313–332. Oxford University Press, Oxford.

Index